Confederate Military History of Alabama

Alabama During the Civil War, 1861-1865

Joseph Wheeler

eBooksOnDisk.com

2003

ISBN 1-932157-17-4

Copyright © 2003 eBooksOnDisk.com

All rights reserved. No part of this book may be reproduced or transmitted in any way, form or by any means, electronic or transmitted, including photo-copying, recording or by any information or retrieval system, or posted on the Internet or World Wide Web without written permission from the Publisher.

eBooksOnDisk.com and Moseley Hall Publishing
4986 Hickory Shores Blvd
Gulf Breeze, Fl 32563
www.ebooksondisk.com

CONTENTS

INTRODUCTION v

ABOUT THE AUTHOR vii

CHAPTER I. 1
INTRODUCTORY—THE FIRST SPANISH OCCUPATION OF ALABAMA—BATTLES FOUGHT BY DE SOTO —SETTLEMENT AT MOBILE — FRENCH AND SPANISH WARS—ENGLISH CONTROL — INDIAN WARS —WAR OF 1812—SEMINOLE AND FLORIDA WARS—ALABAMIANS IN THE WAR WITH MEXICO.

CHAPTER II. 9
SECESSION AND ITS CAUSES—THE SLAVERY QUESTION — ALABAMA'S DECLARATION PRIOR TO THE NOMINATION OF LINCOLN—THE CHARLESTON CONVENTION—RESULT OF THE ELECTION—HOPE OF PEACEABLE SECESSION—EXPRESSIONS OF ADAMS AND WEBSTER—GREELEY OPPOSED TO COERCION.

CHAPTER III. 21
THE STATE CONVENTION—VARIANCE OF OPINION ON SECESSION—ADOPTION OF THE ORDINANCE OF SECESSION—ORGANIZATION OF MILITARY FORCES-CAMPAIGNS AND BATTLES IN ALABAMA—SOME OF ALABAMA'S DISTINGUISHED SOLDIERS.

CHAPTER IV. 33
THE ALABAMA INFANTRY REGIMENTS-BRIEF HISTORY OF EACH ORGANIZATION—THEIR SERVICE AS SHOWN BY THE OFFICIAL RECORDS.

CHAPTER V. 178
THE ALABAMA CAVALRY COMMANDS — REGIMENTS, BATTALIONS AND DETACHED COMPANIES — REFERENCES TO THEIR SERVICES IN THE OFFICIAL RECORDS.

CHAPTER VI. 224
BATTERIES COMPOSED OF ALABAMA TROOPS—THEIR ORGANIZATION AND OFFICERS—RECORDS FROM THE OFFICIAL REPORTS.

CHAPTER VII. 247
BATTLES IN WHICH ALABAMA TROOPS WERE ENGAGED.

INDEX 287

PREFACE

THIS work is the result of contributions by many Southern men to the literature of our country that treats of the eventful years in which occurred the momentous struggle called by Mr. A. H. Stephens "the war between the States." These contributions were made on a well-considered plan, to be wrought out by able writers of unquestionable Confederate record who were thoroughly united in general sentiment and whose generous labors upon separate topics would, when combined, constitute a library of Confederate military history and biography. According to the great principle in our government that One may result from and be composed of Many-the doctrine of E pluribus unum-it was considered that intelligent men from all parts of the South would so write upon the subjects committed to them as to produce a harmonious work which would truly portray the times and issues of the Confederacy and by illustration in various forms describe the soldiery which fought its battles. Upon this plan two volumes-the first and the last-comprise such subjects as the justification of the Southern States in seceding from the Union and the honorable conduct of the war by the Confederate States government; the history of the actions and concessions of the South in the formation of the Union and its policy in securing the existing magnificent territorial dominion of the United States; the civil history of the Confederate States, supplemented with sketches of the President, Vice-President, cabinet officers and other officials of the government; Confederate naval history; the morale of the armies; the South since the war, and a connected outline of events from the beginning of the struggle to its close.

The two volumes containing these general subjects are sustained by the other volumes of Confederate military history of the States of the South involved in the war. Each State being treated in separate history permits of details concerning its peculiar story, its own devotion, its heroes and its battlefields. The authors of the State histories, like those of the volumes of general topics, are men of unchallenged devotion to the Confederate cause and of recognized fitness to perform the task assigned them. It is just to say that this work has been done in hours taken from busy professional life, and it should be further commemorated that devotion to the South and its heroic memories has been their chief incentive.

CLEMENT A. EVANS, Editor. (1899)

GEN. JOSEPH WHEELER, of Alabama, who prepared for this work an account of the part taken by his State and her people in the great conflict of 1861-1865, is beloved by all the people of the South, as he has been since his days of gallant leadership as one of the great cavalry generals of the Confederacy. His laurels were won, and his rank of lieutenant-general attained, before he had reached the age of thirty years. The middle period of his life was given to the civil interests, the restoration of the prosperity, and the re-establishment of the political status of his people, whom he has continuously represented in the United States Congress. In the past year, and just after he had prepared the Alabama war history for this work, he renewed his reputation as major-general of United States volunteers, commanding the cavalry in the Santiago campaign of the war with Spain, and attracted to himself, in addition to the love of the South, the admiration and pride of fellow-citizenship of the people in all parts of the united nation.

CHAPTER I.
INTRODUCTORY—THE FIRST SPANISH OCCUPATION OF ALABAMA—BATTLES FOUGHT BY DE SOTO —SETTLEMENT AT MOBILE — FRENCH AND SPANISH WARS—ENGLISH CONTROL — INDIAN WARS —WAR OF 1812—SEMINOLE AND FLORIDA WARS—ALABAMIANS IN THE WAR WITH MEXICO.

IT was Easter Sunday, March 27, 1513. The Southern sun was shining brightly over the placid bay of St. Augustine. Blooming flowers in the rich profusion characteristic of that soil and climate delighted the eye with their beauty and filled the air with their fragrance. The natives gathering on the beach gazed out upon the waters with awe and wonder at the white-winged ships slowly but surely approaching their shores. It was the fleet of Spain, commanded by John Ponce de Leon, who had been one of the companions of Columbus in his second voyage. He came now furnished with a royal charter to explore and conquer.

This expedition and others, dispatched in rapid succession during the century following the first voyage of Columbus, resulted in confirming the dominion of Spain in all of South and Central America, Mexico, and much of what is now the southern portion of the United States. In 1535, a French expedition under Cartier sailed up the St. Lawrence and gave the name of New France to the territory along its shores. As early as 1497 the Cabots received patents from the English crown to set up the royal standard in any of the newly-discovered lands, but with the exception of the expedition under the ill-starred Lord Raleigh, the first attempt to plant an English colony in America was that at Jamestown in 1607. So the Saxon or English-speaking people were nearly a century behind the Latin race in their attempt to assert jurisdiction over, take possession of and occupy territory upon the new continent. But, with the exception of Napoleon's momentary control in Louisiana, the rule of France in this country was effectually terminated by the treaty of Paris on February 7, 1763; and the Spanish crown, which once exercised dominion over all explored parts of America, and claimed the right to all by virtue of discovery, is now left without sovereignty in the Western hemisphere.

In April, 1528, Pamfilo de Narvaez landed with 300 men on the shore of Tampa bay. He marched northward, believing that in the interior he would find a wealthy empire similar to those of Mexico and Peru. The greater number of this expedition perished, but Alvar Nunez and four companions made their way westward, passed through south Alabama, and finally reached the Spanish settlement of Mexico. These were the first white men who ever trod the soil of Alabama. In May, 1539, Hernando de Soto, with 1,000 chosen cavaliers, most of them from the best blood of Spain and Portugal, sailed into Tampa bay and disembarked at about the same spot where Narvaez landed eleven years before. Many months were spent in exploring eastern Florida, and then he turned northwardly into Georgia, at every turn confronted by a trackless wilderness and often surrounded by hostile tribes of Indians. In one of his earliest conflicts with natives he rescued Jean Ortiz, one of the Spanish followers of Narvaez, who for eleven years had been held as a prisoner by the Indians. The knowledge of the Indian customs and language acquired by Ortiz during captivity was of invaluable use to De Soto.

On July 2, 1540, the army passed from Georgia into Alabama at the site of the Indian village of Costa, which was situated near where the city of Rome, Ga., now stands. De Soto was received kindly by the Indian chieftain, but depredations committed by some of the soldiers precipitated a conflict, which, however, was quelled by the courage and presence of mind of De Soto, and the wrath of the natives appeased. The wily Spaniard then enticed the chief within his lines and held him as hostage until he was ransomed with provisions and slaves. On July 26th, De Soto approached the town of Coosa. The chieftain with 1,000 tall, sprightly and active warriors came out to meet him with the most friendly greetings, but, like the chieftain of Costa, he, too, was held as a prisoner and hostage to enable De Soto to extort ransom and to prevent any hostility on the part of the Indian warriors. De Soto then turned southward to Maubila, the principal city of the Maubilians, which was situated at what is now Choctaw Bluff, Clarke county. Tuskaloosa, the chieftain of that tribe, was a very handsome man about forty years old and of most extraordinary stature; he was entirely undemonstrative, but it soon became evident that he regarded the Spaniards with grave suspicion. Nevertheless, upon entering the city they were received with music, the most graceful dancing of beautiful Indian girls, and other outward signs of hospitality. The Spaniards soon found that they were in the midst of an armed force of Indians fully ten times their number. A dispute between a native and a Spanish officer was the beginning of a most terrible battle; De Soto succeeded in getting outside of the gates, and deployed his soldiers so as to meet the swarm of Indians that were sweeping down upon them, a large body of which were directing their attack upon the horses of the Spaniards. The Indians used missiles of all kinds. Bows and arrows were used with great skill, while in hand-to-hand conflict the savages fought with wooden cleavers and enormous clubs. After three hours of battle, the Spanish were reinforced by the arrival of their rear guard under Muscoso. Encouraged by this addition of fresh troops, the heavily-armored Spaniards, with their superior weapons, rushed upon their opponents, indiscriminately slaughtering them without regard to age or sex. The Spanish accounts tell us this battle lasted nine hours; that 11,000 Indians were slain, while the Spaniards lost 81 killed and nearly every Spanish warrior was wounded. The killed included Rodriguez, a noble Portuguese of high rank, and two nephews of De Soto—Diego De Soto and Don Carlos Enriquez. Many of the Spanish horses were killed and much of their provisions, clothing and stores of various description were destroyed. The desperate condition of the Spaniards in a hostile wilderness, many of them seriously wounded and with scanty supplies, was more than counterbalanced by the terror which their prodigies of valor had aroused in the savages.

This conflict, one of the most severe in the history of that character of warfare, was very near the site of Fort Mims, where, on August 30, 1813, 273 years afterward, the Creek warrior, Weatherford, with 1,000 savage followers, attacked, and during a five hours' conflict slaughtered 531 men, women and children, including white soldiers, friendly Indians and negroes.

The original plan of De Soto was to rejoin his ships in Pensacola bay, but fearing that many of his followers would refuse to remain with him for further exploration he turned toward the northwest, passing through the country that now forms the counties of Clarke, Marengo, Greene and Pickens. During the journey he had many conflicts with the Indians, encountering a large force on the Black Warrior with which he had a very serious engagement. He then turned into the Indian village of Chickasaw, near the site of the modern city of Columbus, Miss. De Soto and his followers had occupied five months in passing through what is now the State of Alabama. They were met on the eastern border with the most hospitable and kindly treatment, which they returned with treachery, cruelty, injustice and destruction, leaving ruin and desolation in their path. The story of these five months of bloodshed by De Soto furnishes the first authentic account of warfare within the boundaries of Alabama.

Although after this for a century and a half the foot of white man never pressed the soil of this territory, still the inhabitants did not enjoy it in peaceful possession. After the death of Montezuma and the conquest of Mexico by Cortez, the Muscogees, a powerful tribe of Indians from the northwestern part of that country, being unwilling to submit to the control of the Spaniards, sought new homes to the eastward, and we have vague accounts of the battles fought, by which they despoiled weaker and more peaceful tribes and occupied the territory, where they were found by French explorers toward the end of the seventeenth century.

In April, 1682, La Salle took possession of the mouth of the Mississippi river, and the French Canadians were active about this time in founding settlements along that river and upon the Gulf coast. In 1699 the Spaniards made a settlement at Pensacola and also laid claim to Mobile bay. Lords Bienville and Iberville founded the town of Natchez, and in 1702 they built Fort Louis (de la Louisiana) at the mouth of Dog river. The French found large numbers of human bones on Dauphin island and for many years it was called the Island of Massacre. Treaties of peace were made with the Muscogees and Alabama Indians, but these treaties did not secure to the settlers any long-continued freedom from strife; and the early occupancy by the French of South Alabama was constantly disturbed by conflicts with the Indians of greater or less severity. The hostility of the Indians to the French was intensified by the intrigues of the English.

In 1707, France and Spain having united against England, Lord Bienville, with 150 French Canadians, went to the relief of Pensacola; but the English and their Indian allies evacuated the place before the arrival of the French. In 1711 the site of Mobile was permanently settled and three years later Lord Bienville, having succeeded in making treaties with the Indians, sailed up the Alabama river, passed the present location of Montgomery and established Fort Toulouse, at the site of the present town of Wetumpka. Later, a settlement was made at Montgomery, and Fort Tombecbee was established at what is now called Jones' Bluff. Fort Toulouse contained four bastions, mounted with eight cannon, and was garrisoned by the French till 1763, except for a short period in 1722 when the troops mutinied, killed their commander and deserted the garrison.

In 1719, France was at war with Spain, and on May 14th Lord Bienville attacked Pensacola, captured the garrison and sent the captives to Havana. Later, during the summer, Matamora, the Spanish governor of Cuba, retook Pensacola. The Spaniards landed on Dauphin island and bombarded Fort Filippe, but were repulsed by Sevigny, whose command consisted of 260 soldiers and 200 Indians. The French fleet arrived, Pensacola was again retaken by the French and held by them until 1723, when it was restored to Spain by treaty. It was during this year that the seat of government was transferred from Mobile to New Orleans, which materially lessened the importance of the former city. Ten years later the French, under Bienville and D'Artaguette, returned and established themselves at Mobile. The control of the French over the Indians was now seriously disturbed by the intrigues of the English, who had established strong and permanent settlements in the Carolinas. They sought every opportunity to incite the natives against the French, and in 1736 the irritation and disturbances ripened into warlike outbreaks. The French and their allies, the Choctaws, marched against the Chickasaws, who had joined the English. The principal battle was fought at Ackia, May 26, 1736, in which the French were defeated. Bienville retreated to Mobile with most of his army, but D'Artaguette and a part of the troops were cut off, taken prisoners, cruelly held as hostages for quite a period, and finally they were all murdered. Sixteen years later, in 1753, the French and Choctaws, under De Vaudreuil, again attacked the Chickasaws, only to meet another disaster. The Chickasaws are described as the bravest and most warlike of all the Indian inhabitants of Alabama. They finally dwindled away before the advance of civilization, but were never conquered by armed forces.

The aggressive English finally, in 1765, established themselves in Alabama, an agreement being made by which the territory then included under the name of Illinois was extended as far south as 32° 28', about the latitude of Demopolis. The claim of the Spaniards to Florida was based upon their treaty with England of 1783, and for many years there was incessant border warfare between the Spaniards and their Indian allies on one side and the colonists (mostly from Georgia) and their native allies on the other. This subjected our early settlers to almost constant Indian incursions for booty and massacre.

During this period the French were carrying on trade near the site of the present cities of Tuscumbia and Florence, and, mainly due to their influence, the Creeks and Cherokees were active in their hostilities upon the American settlers.

The war for independence between the colonists and Great Britain, which lasted from 1775 to 1781, was confined to the lakes, the Atlantic coast and adjacent territory, and the country now known as Alabama can hardly be said to have been affected thereby. The colonial government having been firmly established, Col. James Robinson in 1787 marched from the Cumberland region into Alabama against the depredating Indians. They were subdued for a time, but again renewed hostilities, until finally quelled by a band of brave Americans under Captain Shannon.

In 1806, the arrest of Aaron Burr near Fort Stoddard by Captain (afterward Major-General) Gaines, U. S. Army, added a feature to the military history of the State. Burr's Southwestern enterprise had proven a failure. In Mississippi he had been arrested and released, but his expedition had become a menace to our government and Captain Gaines therefore arrested and sent him under guard to Richmond, where in August, 1807, he was tried and finally acquitted.

One of the ablest and most sagacious enemies of the earlier settlers of Alabama was the great Shawnee Indian chief, Tecumseh. He was commanding in appearance and exercised a powerful influence among many of the native tribes of America. Upon the breaking out of war between the United States and Great Britain in 1812, Tecumseh and his followers became allies of the British, and during the summer of 1812 he was of great service to them in their operations around Detroit and upon the lakes. In October the British dispatched him to the South to incite the Seminoles, Creeks, Chickasaws and other tribes against the United States. Frequent outrages were perpetrated by the savages, and all the frontier settlements were in constant danger of attack.

In July, 1813, a battle was fought between the Creeks and the troops under Col. James Kellar. In August Gen. F. L. Claiborne reached Mobile from Baton Rouge. He constructed a series of forts and adopted other measures to secure the safety of the people. On August 30th the massacre of Fort Mims, before mentioned, took place. This was followed by many other atrocities on the people of Alabama, and under orders from the general government, Gen. Andrew Jackson at the head of a large force marched to these scenes of warfare. His advance, under General Coffee at the head of 900 men, crossed the Coosa, and with a loss of 5 killed and 41 wounded defeated the Indians, 200 strong, at Tallashatchee, destroying their villages and disabling 84 savages.

On November 9th, Gen. Andrew Jackson, commanding 2,200 men, defeated 1,000 Indians, with a loss of 15 killed and 86 wounded, inflicting on them a loss of 290. On November 18th, Gen. James White, with 260 men, defeated 360 Indians at Hillabee; 62 Indians were killed and 256 were made prisoners. On November 29th, Gen. John Floyd with a force 950 strong successfully attacked a large body of Indians at Autossee; 200 of the savages were killed, his loss being 11 killed and 54 wounded.

December 23d, Gen. F. L. Claiborne with a loss of 1 killed and 6 wounded dispersed a body of Indians at Eccanachaca, killing 30 of their number. On January 22d General Jackson, commanding a force of 1,150 strong, defeated 900 Indians at Emuckfa, killing 189 of the savages. January 27th, the Creeks attacked General Floyd at Camp Defiance, losing 37 of their warriors and inflicting a loss of 20 killed and 125 wounded.

March 27th, General Jackson fought the battle of Horse Shoe Bend; his force was 2,400 and his loss 26 killed and 111 wounded. These victories and minor successes in other parts of the State by Major Blue, commanding regular troops, and Colonel Pearson, of the North Carolina militia, effectually ended the Indian disturbances in Alabama, the savages gladly entering into a treaty of peace. General Jackson was placed in command of the Southern army and proceeded to Mobile to protect the Gulf coast, which was now menaced by the British fleet. He strengthened Fort Bowyer, situated on a tongue of land about thirty miles from Mobile, defending it with 20 guns and 160 men under Major Lawrence. This fort was on the present site of Fort Morgan.

On September 12th the fort was attacked by a party of 712 British and Indians under Colonel Nichols, assisted by two sloops and two brigs. They were beaten off with the loss of 200 men and one of the ships. The British ships also made an attack on Mobile, but retired without doing any material damage. General Jackson then marched with 4,000 men to Pensacola, drove the British from Fort Barrancas, and then proceeded to New Orleans, where, on January 8th, he won his great victory over the British General Pakenham. A month later a fleet of 38 British war vessels and 5,000 soldiers captured Fort Bowyer, but as peace had been declared, they only held it a few weeks. The withdrawal of the British troops enabled the government to make very satisfactory treaties with the Indians.

On March 1, 1817, the present territorial limits of Alabama were defined by Congress, and on December 14, 1819, it became one of the States of the Union. In 1830 the Choctaws ceded their lands to the government. In 1832 the Creeks made their cession, as did the Cherokees in 1835. Many of the Indians were opposed to the sale of their lands and considerable friction followed, making it necessary to assemble a large body of troops to suppress indications of outbreaks by both Creeks and Cherokees, but finally, in 1838, their removal to the West was peaceably accomplished.

From this time until the war of 1861 Alabama enjoyed a condition of peace, but its people held themselves ready to assist their brethren in neighboring States. Several companies of Alabamians volunteered and fought in the Seminole and Florida wars and a still greater number gave their services to assist in Texan independence. Many of these perished, a considerable number being victims of the Goliad massacre, where 330 persons were murdered in the most atrocious manner. Milton Irish and Bennet Butler, from Huntsville, were among the few who escaped, and Captain Shackleford, of Courtland, was spared because he was a physician and the Mexicans needed his services to attend their wounded. When war was declared against Mexico, thousands upon thousands of patriotic citizens of this State tendered their services to the government, but only one regiment composed entirely of Alabamians could be accepted. It was organized at Mobile in June, 1846, and designated as the First Alabama volunteers. Its officers were as follows: Col. John R. Coffee, Lieut.-Col. Richard G. Earle, Maj. Goode Bryan, Adjt. Hugh M. Watson, Capts. Sydenham Moore, Andrew P. Pickens, Hugh Cunningham, E. T. Smith, Zach Thomason, William G. Coleman, R. M. Jones, William H. Ketchum, D. P. Baldwin and J. D. Shelley. The regiment proceeded to Mexico, first served under General Pillow and afterward under General Shields. In 1847 Colonel Seibels, of Montgomery, organized a battalion; it reached Vera Cruz too late to join Scott's column, but performed garrison duty at Orizaba until the termination of hostilities. Its captains were: John G. Burr, T. E. Irby, Tennent Lomax, Blanton McAlpine and Gibbs. The Thirteenth regiment of regulars included a large number of Alabamians. Jones M. Withers, of Mobile, who graduated at West Point in 1835, was its lieutenant-colonel, and Egbert I. Jones, Hugh L. Clay and Nicholas Davis were among its officers. A small battalion commanded by Col. Phillip H. Raiford, composed of the companies of Captains Curtis, Downman and Ligon and independent companies commanded by Captains Desha, Elmore, Platt and James McGee, also volunteered and served in the war with Mexico. Of these the only cavalry company was that of Captain McGee; all the others were infantry.

Many of the Alabamians who served in Mexico became quite distinguished in civil life and in the war of 1861-65. Jones M. Withers was distinguished as a major-general in the army under General Bragg. Hugh L. Clay served with great credit in the department of the adjutant-general and was tendered the appointment of brigadier-general. Egbert I. Jones became quite prominent as a lawyer, was made colonel of the Fourth Alabama in 1861, and was mortally wounded at the battle of Manassas, leaving a glorious record for courage and bravery. Nicholas Davis was a member of the Confederate Provisional Congress, and was appointed lieutenant-colonel of the Nineteenth infantry, which position he declined in order to accept the command of an Alabama battalion. Hon. Jeremiah Clemens, who served as colonel of the Ninth regulars, won great reputation as a member of the United States House of Representatives and also as United States senator. Early in the war he was appointed major-general of the Alabama State troops, but did not enter the regular Confederate service.

Maj. Goode Bryan became a distinguished Confederate general. Col. Sydenham Moore practiced law and was elected to the United States Congress. He took part in the war as colonel of the Eleventh Alabama infantry and died of wounds received at the battle of Seven Pines. William H. Forney served during the entire four years of the war, became a brigadier-general and made a fine reputation as an officer and a soldier. He afterward was Alabama State senator for two years and a prominent representative in the United States Congress for eighteen years. Richard Gordon Earle became a Confederate cavalry general and was killed in battle at Kingston, Ga.

After returning from Mexico, Colonel Coffee lived for fifty years a respected and highly-esteemed citizen, and acquired great wealth. Colonel Seibels, like Colonel Coffee, declined to accept public office, preferring to devote himself to private business, in which he was very successful. Tennent Lomax was a splendid specimen of manhood, both physically and intellectually. Though quite young while in Mexico, he was appointed military governor of Orizaba. After the Mexican war he engaged in journalism. In 1861 he successfully performed the delicate duty of taking possession of Forts Barrancas and McRee at Pensacola. In April, 1861, he was appointed colonel of the Third Alabama infantry; was highly esteemed as a soldier; was promoted to a brigadier-generalship, but before receiving his commission was killed while gallantly leading his regiment at the battle of Seven Pines. Lieuts. John L. May and William R. King were among the officers from Alabama who were killed in battle during the Mexican war.

CHAPTER II.

SECESSION AND ITS CAUSES—THE SLAVERY QUESTION — ALABAMA'S DECLARATION PRIOR TO THE NOMINATION OF LINCOLN—THE CHARLESTON CONVENTION—RESULT OF THE ELECTION—HOPE OF PEACEABLE SECESSION—EXPRESSIONS OF ADAMS AND WEBSTER—GREELEY OPPOSED TO COERCION.

THREE decades and a half of years, the life of a generation, have passed since the close of the military career of the actors in that long and sanguinary struggle, the war of the Confederacy. Few comparatively are left of the hosts who fought under Lee and Jackson, the Johnstons and Bragg. Still, many of those from Alabama are yet living and hold positions of trust and honor, continuing to serve the State for which they fought. To form any idea of the motives which then, actuated them and the causes which precipitated the war, we must cast aside our environments of to-day, and looking backward find a point where we can stand face to face with the issues that confronted the statesmen of 1860. The prosperity of the South depended very largely upon the labor which constituted a great part of its wealth, most of which had been imported from Africa in New England ships and sold by New Englanders to people of the South. The Constitution of the United States guaranteed that all the power of the government should be exercised to protect and secure the people in the use and enjoyment of this property, but for more than a third of a century this valued constitutional right had been assailed by a party in the North that had gradually gathered to itself strength and power, one encroachment and violation of law following another.

People throughout the South were confronted with this situation. The most of the Northern States had by solemn enactment nullified the Constitution and the laws of Congress, and emissaries from the North, arousing the negroes to arson, rapine and murder, were being dispatched to the Southern States. Their partial success in the John Brown raid had caused widespread terror and alarm. The prevailing sentiment on every side was that prompt action was essential to protect lives and property. As early as 1848 this aggression on the rights of the South had become such a menace that John C. Calhoun contended that we ought to "force the issue of the slavery question in the North;" and said, moreover, "We are now stronger, relatively, than we shall be hereafter politically and morally."

The Democratic party of Alabama assembled in convention at Montgomery, January 11, 1860, and with' scarcely a dissenting voice adopted resolutions in substance as follows: "That the principles recognized by the Supreme court in the Dred Scott case should be maintained by the South; that their delegates to the approaching national Democratic convention at

Charleston should present these resolutions for the adoption of that body; that they insist upon the adoption of the resolutions in substance, and that if they be not adopted, the delegates must withdraw."

The Alabama legislature, on February 24, 1860, adopted the following:

Whereas, Anti-slavery agitation persistently continued in the non-slaveholding States of this Union for more than a third of a century, marked at every stage of its progress by contempt for the obligations of law and the sanctity of compacts, evincing a deadly hostility to the rights and institutions of the Southern people, and a settled purpose to effect their overthrow even by the subversion of the Constitution, and at the hazard of violence and bloodshed; and, Whereas, a sectional party calling itself Republican, committed alike by its own acts and antecedents, and the public avowals and secret machinations of its leaders to the execution of these atrocious designs, has acquired the ascedency in nearly every Northern State, and hopes by success in the approaching presidential election to seize the government itself; and, Whereas, to permit such seizure by those whose unmistakable aim is to pervert its whole machinery to the destruction of a portion of its members would be an act of suicidal folly and madness, almost without a parallel in history; and, Whereas, the General Assembly of Alabama, representing a people loyally devoted to the Union of the Constitution, but scorning the Union which fanaticism would erect upon its ruins, deem it their solemn duty to provide in advance the means by which they may escape such peril and dishonor, and devise new securities for perpetuating the blessings of liberty to themselves and their posterity, therefore,

Be it resolved, That, upon the happening of the contingency contemplated in the foregoing preamble, namely, the election of a President advocating the principles and action of the party in the Northern States, calling itself the Republican party, it shall be the duty of the governor, and he is hereby required, forthwith, to issue his proclamation, calling upon the qualified voters of this State ... to elect delegates to a convention of the State, to consider, determine and do whatever in the opinion of said convention, the rights, interests, and honor of the State of Alabama requires to be done for their protection.

The national Democratic convention met at Charleston, April 23, 1860. On the 27th the committee on resolutions disagreed. The majority report accepted the Cincinnati platform with a clause added which explained the doctrine of non-intervention as laid down in the decision of the Supreme court which was delivered by Chief-Justice Taney in the Dred Scott case. This was satisfactory to the Southern delegates. The minority report reaffirmed the Cincinnati platform and then proceeded to assert that "differences of opinion exist in the Democratic party as to the nature and extent of the powers of a territorial legislature and as to the powers and duties of Congress, under the Constitution of the United States, over the institution of slavery in the Territories."

The objections of the Southern delegates to this vague expression in the minority report were explained by Mr. Yancey in a speech in opposition to its adoption. After reviewing the situation he said:

> Gentlemen of the convention, that venerable, that able, that revered jurist, the Honorable Chief Justice of the United" States, trembling upon the very verge of the grave, for years kept merely alive by the pure spirit of patriotic duty that burns within his breast—a spirit that will not permit him to succumb to the gnawings of disease and the weaknesses of mortality—which hold him, as it were, suspended between two worlds, with his spotless ermine around him, standing at the altar of Justice, has given to us the utterance of the Supreme court of the United States upon this very question. (Applause.)
> Let the murmur of the hustings be stilled—let the voices of individual citizens, no matter how great and respected in their appropriate spheres, be hushed, while the law, as expounded by the constituted authority of the country, emotionless, passionless and just, rolls with its silvery cadence over the entire realm, from the Atlantic to the Pacific, and from the ice-bound regions of the North to the glittering waters of the Gulf. (Loud cheering.)
> What says that decision? That decision tells you, gentlemen, that the territorial legislature has no power to interfere with the rights of the slave-owner in the territory while in a territorial condition. (Cheers.) That decision tells that this government is a Union of Sovereign States; which States are co-equal, and in trust for which co-equal States the government holds the territories. It tells you that the people of those co-equal States have a right to go into these territories, thus held in trust, with every species of property which is recognized as property by the State in which they live, or by the Constitution of the United States. The venerable magistrate—the court concurring with him—decided that it is the duty of this government to afford some government for the territories which shall be in accordance with this trust, with this delegated trust power held for the States and for the people of the States. That decision goes still further: It tells you that if Congress has seen fit, for its own convenience and somewhat in accordance with the sympathies and instincts and genius of our institutions, to accord a form of government to the people of the territories, it is to be administered precisely as Congress can administer it, and to be administered as a trust for the co-equal States of the Union, and the citizens of those States who choose to emigrate to those territories. That decision goes on to tell you this: That as Congress itself is bound to protect the property which is recognized as such of the citizens of any of the States—as Congress itself not only has on" power, but is expressly forbidden to exercise the power to deprive any owner of his property in the territories; therefore, says that venerable, that passionless representative of justice, who yet hovers on the confines of the grave, therefore, no government formed by that Congress can have any more power than the Congress that created it.

Mr. Yancey then went on to explain that Mr. Douglas and his followers insisted upon a construction which virtually nullified the Dred Scott decision. He said:

They put themselves directly in conflict with the venerable chief justice of the Supreme court of the United States, and with the recorded decision of the court itself.... Now then, who shall the Democracy recognize as authority on this point—a statesman, no matter how brilliant and able and powerful in intellect, in the very meridian of life, animated by an ardent and consuming ambition, struggling as no other man has ever done for the high and brilliant position of candidate for the presidency of the United States, at the hand of his great party—or that old and venerable jurist who, having filled his years with honor, leaves you his last great decision before stepping from the high place of earthly power into the grave to appear before his Maker, in whose presence deception is impossible and earthly position as dust in the balance? (Loud and continued cheering.)

Notwithstanding this eloquent appeal, the vote was taken and by a bare majority the minority report was substituted for the majority report. This was the signal for disruption. The Alabama delegation withdrew from the convention, followed by those of the other Gulf States. On May 19th a convention met at Baltimore under the name of the "Constitutional Union party" (its motto being, "The Constitution, the Union and the Enforcement of the Laws"). John Bell, of Tennessee, and Edward Everett, of Massachusetts, were nominated as its candidates for President and Vice-President.

On June 18th, the Douglas members of the Charleston convention met in Baltimore, and the supporters of the majority report who had withdrawn at Charleston assembled at Richmond, afterward adjourning to meet at Baltimore. They were not, however, admitted to that convention, as the Douglas members excluded them from participation in its proceedings, seating in their stead new delegates who came pledged to support Mr. Douglas, who was nominated by this convention. Upon the exclusion of the old delegates, Mr. Cushing, the president of the convention and five others of the Massachusetts delegates, together with delegates from Virginia, North Carolina, Tennessee, Kentucky, Maryland, California, Oregon and Arkansas, the only Democratic States, withdrew to join them. Having organized under the title of the "National State Rights Democracy" and adopted the now famous "majority report" from Charleston, John C. Breckinridge, of Kentucky, was nominated. Mr. Lincoln having been the choice of the Republican convention at Chicago in May, the campaign opened with four presidential candidates in the field.

The vote for President of the United States on November 6, 1860, was:
>   Abraham Lincoln............................ 1,866,352
>   Stephen A. Douglas......................... 1,375,157
>   John C. Breckinridge....................... 845,581
>   John Bell.. 589,581

The vote in the Southern slave States:
>   Abraham Lincoln............................ 26,430

Stephen A. Douglas............................	163,525
John C. Breckinridge........................	543,781
John Bell...	488,923

The vote in the Gulf States:

Abraham Lincoln.............................	
Stephen A. Douglas..........................	24,926
John C. Breckinridge.......................	168,400
John Bell...	94,444

The vote in Alabama:

Abraham Lincoln.............................	
Stephen A. Douglas...........................	13,651
John C. Breckinridge........................	48,831
John Bell...	27,825

When on that fateful 6th of November, 1860. it was decided by the election of Mr. Lincoln that Black Republican rule was to dominate the Union and crush the South under with its compromising cruelty. The North and the South both knew that the election of Lincoln meant the destruction of slavery, to be so accomplished as to bring financial ruin, if not entire annihilation; for Wendell Phillips had said: "This state of things is just what we have attempted to bring about. . . . The Republican party is a party of the North, pledged against the South."

Believing firmly in the sovereignty of the State, there was never an idea among the masses of the people of the South that secession would entail war. A few of the prominent leaders and profound thinkers foresaw the consequences, still peaceable secession was the thought uppermost. Coercion, "*vi et armis*,' was not dreamed of; and these ideas were not confined to the Southern people. The opinion had always prevailed throughout the Union that secession was a right vested in each separate State, and that an attempt to coerce a sovereign State would be unwarrantable and unconstitutional. John Quincy Adams but gave expression to this universal sentiment when in a speech delivered April 30, 1839, on the occasion of the celebration of the fiftieth anniversary of our government under the Constitution, he said:

But the indissoluble union between the several States of this confederated nation is, after all, not in the right but in the heart. If the day should ever come (may Heaven avert it) when the affections of the people of these States shall be alienated from each other; when the fraternal spirit shall give way to cold indifference, or collision of interest shall fester into hatred, the bands of political asseveration will not long hold together parties no longer attracted by the magnetism of conciliated interests and kindly sympathies; and far better will it be for the people of the disunited States to part in friendship from each other than to be held together by constraint. Then will be the time for reverting to the precedents which occurred at the formation and adoption of the Constitution to form again a more perfect Union by dissolving that which could no longer bind, and to leave the separated parts to be reunited by the law of political gravitation to the center.

It is a remarkable fact that in 1848 the distinguished son of this illustrious gentleman received 291,267 votes as candidate of the Free Soil party for the vice-presidency.

This principle of the right of secession had been always sanctioned by the people of Massachusetts. When it was proposed to annex Louisiana to the Federal Union, the legislature passed the following resolution: "That the annexation of Louisiana to the Union transcends the constitutional power of the government of the United States. . It formed a new confederacy, to which the States united by the former compact are not bound to adhere." In the year 1844 it was resolved by that legislature: ". . . That the project of the annexation of Texas, unless arrested on the threshold, may drive these States into a dissolution of the Union."

The opinion of the conservative element in the North, that this agitation was an invasion of the constitutional rights of the South, was expressed by that grand old constitutional lawyer, Daniel Webster. In a speech at Buffalo, delivered on May 22, 1851, he said:

> Then there . . . was the fugitive slave law. Let me say a word about that. Under the provisions of the Constitution, during Washington's administration in the year 1793, there was passed by general consent a law for the restoration of fugitive slaves. Hardly any one opposed it at that period; it was thought to be necessary in order to carry the Constitution into effect; the great men of New England and New York all concurred in it. It passed and answered all the purposes expected from it till about the year 1841 or 1842, when the State interfered to make enactments in opposition to it. ... Now, I undertake as a lawyer and on my professional character to say to you and to all, that the law of 1850 is decidedly more favorable to the fugitive than General Washington's law of 1793. . . . Such is the present law, and, much opposed and maligned as it is, it is more favorable to the fugitive slave than the law enacted during Washington's administration in 1793, which was sanctioned by the North as well as by the South. The present violent opposition has sprung up in modern times. From whom does this clamor come? Why, look at the proceedings of the anti-slavery conventions; look at their resolutions. Do you find among those persons who oppose this fugitive slave law any admission whatever that any law ought to be passed to carry into effect the solemn stipulations of the Constitution? Tell me any such case. Tell me if any resolution was adopted by the convention at Syracuse favorable to the carrying out of the Constitution. Not one. The fact is, gentlemen, they oppose the constitutional provision; they oppose the whole. Not a man of them admits that there ought to be any law on the subject. They deny altogether that the provisions of the Constitution ought to be carried into effect. Look at the proceedings of the anti-slavery conventions in Ohio, Massachusetts and at Syracuse in the State

of New York. What do they say? That so help them God no colored man shall be sent from the State of New York back to his master in Virginia. Do not they say that? And to the fulfillment of that they pledge their lives, their fortunes and their sacred honor. Their sacred honor! They pledge their sacred honor to violate the Constitution; they pledge their sacred honor to commit treason against the laws of their country.

Mr. Webster, in his speech at Capon Springs, also said:

> The leading sentiment in the toast from the chair is the Union of the States. What mind can comprehend the consequences of that .Union, past, present, and to come. The Union of these States is the all-absorbing topic of the day; on it all men write, speak think, and dilate, from the rising of the sun to the going down thereof. And yet, gentlemen, I fear its importance has been but insufficiently appreciated.
>
> [Again Mr. Webster says:] How absurd it is to suppose that when different parties enter into a compact for certain purposes, either can disregard any one provision, and expect, nevertheless, the other to observe the rest. I intend for one to regard and maintain and carry out to the fullest extent the Constitution of the United States, which I have sworn to support in all its parts and all its provisions. It is written in the Constitution, "No person held to service or labor in one State under the laws thereof, escaping into another, shall, in consequence of any law or regulation therein, be discharged from such service or labor, but shall be delivered up on claim of the party to whom such service or labor may be due."
>
> This is as much a part of the Constitution as any other, and as equally binding and obligatory as any other on all men, public or private. And who denies this? None but the abolitionists of the North. And pray what is it they will not deny? They have but the one idea; and it would seem that these fanatics at the North and the secessionists at the South are putting their heads together to devise means to defeat the good designs of honest, patriotic men. They act to the same end and the same object, and the Constitution has to take the fire from both sides.
>
> I have not hesitated to say, and I repeat, that if the Northern States refuse willfully and deliberately to carry into effect that part of the Constitution which respects the restoration of fugitive slaves, and Congress provide no remedy, the South would no longer be bound to observe the compact. A bargain cannot be broken on one side and still bind the other side. I say to you, gentlemen in Virginia, as I said on the shores of Lake Erie and in the city of Boston, as I may say again in that city or else-where in the North, that you of the South have as much right to receive your fugitive slaves as the North has to any of its rights and privileges of navigation and commerce. Mr. Webster also said: I am as ready to fight and to fall for the constitutional rights of Virginia as I am for those of Massachusetts.

Horace Greeley, the noted abolitionist, one of the foster-fathers, if not the parent of free-soilism, perhaps the most widely popular and best informed of the Northern journalists, who must be regarded as an able exponent of the sentiments of the people, was outspoken even to rashness in upholding the doctrine of the right of secession. Indeed his course would seem to prove that he did all in his power to hasten the Southern States into secession. We give extracts from the New York Tribune, Mr. Greeley's paper, beginning with the date when it was first known that Mr. Lincoln was certainly elected.

New York Tribune, November 9, 1860.—If the cotton States shall become satisfied that they can do better out of the Union than in it, we insist on letting them go in peace. The right to secede may be a revolutionary one, but it exists nevertheless. [And again in the same issue of his widely-circulated and influential paper, Mr. Greeley said:] We must ever resist the asserted right of any State to remain in the Union and nullify or defy the laws thereof. To withdraw from the Union is quite another matter; and whenever a considerable section of our Union shall deliberately resolve to go out, we shall resist all coercive measures designed to keep it in. We hope never to live in a republic whereof one section is pinned to the residue by bayonets. Let them have both sides of the question fully presented. Let them reflect, deliberate, then vote; and let the action of secession be the echo of an unmistakable popular fiat. A judgment thus rendered, a demand for separation thus backed, would either be acquiesced in without the effusion of blood, or those who rushed upon carnage to defy and defeat it would place themselves clearly in the wrong.

New York Tribune, November 16, 1860.—Still we say, in all earnestness and good faith, whenever a whole section of this republic, whether a half, a third, or only a fourth, shall truly desire and demand a separation from the residue, we shall earnestly favor such separation. If the fifteen slave States, or even the eight cotton States alone, shall quietly, decisively, say to the rest, "We prefer to be henceforth separated from you," we shall insist they be permitted to go in peace. War is a hideous necessity at best, and a civil conflict, a war of estranged and embittered fellow countrymen, is the most hideous of all wars. Whenever the people of the cotton States shall have definitely and decisively made up their minds to separate from the rest of us, we shall urge that the proper steps be taken to give full effect to their decision.

New York Tribune, November 19, 1860.—Now we believe and maintain that the Union is to be preserved only so long as it is beneficial and satisfactory to all parties concerned. We do not believe that any man, any neighborhood, town, county or even State may break up the Union in any transient gust of passion; we fully comprehend that secession is an extreme, an ultimate resort—not a constitutional but a revolutionary remedy. But we insist that this Union shall not be held together by force whenever it shall have ceased to cohere by the mutual attraction of its parts; and whenever the slave States or the cotton States only shall unitedly and coolly say to the rest, "We want to get out of the Union," we shall urge that their request be acceded to."

New York Tribune, November 24, 1860.—Some of the Washington correspondents telegraph that Mr. Buchanan is attempting to map out a middle course in which to steer his bark during the tempest which now howls about him. He is to condemn the asserted right of secession but to assert in the same breath that he is opposed to keeping a State in the Union by what he calls Federal coercion. Now we have no desire to prevent secession by coercion, but we hold this position to be utterly unsupported by law or reason.

New York Tribune, November 30,1860.—Are We Going to Fight?— But if the cotton States generally unite with her in seceding, we insist that they cannot be prevented, and that the attempt must not be made. Five millions of people, more than half of them of the dominant race of whom at least half a million are able and willing to shoulder muskets, can never be subdued while fighting around and over their own hearthstones. If they could be, they would no longer be equal members of the Union, but conquered dependencies. . . . We propose to wrest this potent engine from the disunionists by saying frankly to the slave States: "If you choose to leave the Union, leave it, but let us have no quarrel about it. If you think it a curse to you and an unfair advantage to us, repudiate it, and see if you are not mistaken. If you are better by yourselves, go and God speed you. For our part, we have done very well with you, and are quite willing to keep along with you, but if the association is irksome to you, we have too much self-respect to insist on its continuance. We have lived by our industry thus far and hope to do so still, even though you leave us." We repeat that only the sheen of Northern bayonets can bind the South wholly to the evils of secession, but that may do it.

Let us be patient, neither speaking daggers nor using them, standing to our principles but not to our arms, and all will yet be well.

New York Tribune, December 8, 1860.—. . . . We again avow our deliberate conviction that whenever six or eight contiguous States shall have formally seceded from the Union, and avowed the pretty unanimous and earnest resolve of their people to stay out, it will not be found practicable to coerce them into subjection; and we doubt that any Congress can be found to direct and provide for such coercion. One or two States may be coerced, but not the entire section, or quarter of a Union. If you do not believe this, wait and see.

New York Tribune, December 17, 1860.— .... But if ever seven or eight States sent agents to Washington to say, 'We want to get out of the Union,' we shall feel constrained by our devotion to human liberty to say, 'Let them go.' And we do not see how we could take the other side without coming in direct conflict with those rights of man which we hold paramount to all political arrangements, however convenient and advantageous.

New York Tribune, December 24, 1860.—Most certainly we believe that governments are made for the peoples, not peoples for the governments; that the latter derive their just power from the consent of the governed; and whenever a portion of this Union, large enough to form an independent self-subsisting nation, shall show that and say authentically to the residue, "We want to get away from you," I shall say, and we trust self-respect, if not regard for the principles of self-government, will constrain the residue of the American people to say, "Go."

New York Tribune, December 28, 1860.— . . . Nor is it treason for the State to hate the Union and seek its disruption. A State, a whole section, may come to regard the Union as a blight upon its prosperity, an obstacle to its progress, and be fully justified in seeking its dissolution. And in spite of the adverse clamor, we insist that if ever a third or even a fourth of these States shall have deliberately concluded that the Union is injurious to them, and that their vital interests require their separation from it, they will have a perfect right to seek separation; and should they do so with reasonable patience and due regard for the rights and interests of those they leave behind, we shall feel bound to urge and insist that their wishes be gratified—their demand conceded.

During the session of the South Carolina convention, Greeley, in his issue of December 17th, as if to afford arguments to strengthen the Southern people in their opposition and to encourage them to be prompt in their action, says: "If it (the Declaration of Independence) justifies these cession from the British empire of 3,000,000 of colonists in 1776, we do not see why it would not justify the secession of 5,000,000 of Southrons from the Federal Union in 1861. If we are mistaken on this point, why does not some one attempt to show wherein and why? For our own part, while we deny the right of slaveholders to hold slaves against the will of the latter, we cannot see how 20,000,000 of people can rightfully hold 10,000,000, or even 5,000,000 in a detested Union with them by military force."

In the same issue of Mr. Greeley's paper we read the following: "If seven or eight contiguous States shall present themselves authentically at Washington, saying: 'We hate the Federal Union; we have drawn from it; we give you the choice between acquiescing in our secession and arranging amicably all incidental questions on the one hand and attempting to subdue us on the other,' we could not stand up for coercion, for subjugation, for we do not think it would be just. We hold the right of self-government even when invoked in behalf of those who deny it to others. So much for the question of principle."

After the Confederate government had been organized and its whole machinery in active operation and it had taken its place among the nations, Mr. Greeley endorsed its action in no ambiguous words. He said: "We have repeatedly said, and we once more insist, that the great principle embodied by Jefferson in the Declaration of American Independence, that Governments derive their just powers from consent of the governed, is sound and just; and that if the slave States, the cotton States or the Gulf States only, choose to form an independent nation, they have a clear moral right to do so. Whenever it shall be clear that the great body of Southern people have become conclusively alienated from the Union, and anxious to escape from it, we will do our best to forward their views."

Nor was the New York Tribune alone, for the whole New York press and prominent journals and able editors of Republican papers all over the North coincided with these views. "Wayward sisters, go in peace," was the cry on every hand, echoed from the lips of the general of the army, with the refrain uttered by the eminent Republican leader, Salmon P. Chase: "The South is not worth fighting for; let them alone."

I give a few quotations from some of the other leading journals. Did space allow, these might be multiplied almost *ad infinitum*.

From the New York Herald, November 23, 1860.—The Disunion Question—A Conservative Reaction in the South.—We publish this morning a significant letter from Governor Letcher, of Virginia, on the subject of the present disunion excitement in the South, Southern constitutional rights, Northern State acts of nullification, and the position of Virginia in this crisis. . . . To this end would it not be well for the conservative Union men of the city of New York to make a demonstration—a Northern movement of conciliation, concession and harmony? Coercion in any event is out of the question. A Union held together by the bayonet would be nothing better than a military despotism. Conciliation and harmony, through mutual concessions, in a reconstruction of the fundamental law, between the North and South, will restore and perpetuate the Union contemplated by the fathers. So now that the conservative men of the South are moving, let the Union men of the North second their endeavors, and let New York, as in the matter of the compromises of 1850, lead the way.

The following is from the New York Times of December 3, 1860: By common consent, moreover, the most prominent and tangible point of offense seems to be the legislation growing out of the fugitive slave law. Several of the Northern States have passed personal-liberty bills with the alleged intent to prevent the return of fugitive slaves to their masters. From Union men in every quarter of the South come up the most earnest appeals to the Northern States to repeal these laws. Such an act, we are assured, would have a powerful effect in disarming the disunion clamor in nearly all the Southern States and in promoting the prospects of a peaceful adjustment of all pending differences.

The next day, December 4th, the New York Times published another article, in which it said: Mr. Weed has stated his opinion of the crisis thus: 1. There is imminent danger of a dissolution of the Union. 2. The danger originated in the ambition and cupidity of men who desire a Southern despotism and in the fanatic zeal of the Northern abolitionists who seek the emancipation of slaves regardless of consequences. 3. The danger can only be averted by such moderation and forbearance as will draw out, strengthen and combine the Union sentiment of the whole country. Each of these statements will command general assent. The only question likely to arise relates to the practical measures by which the 'moderation and forbearance' can be displayed.

After Mr. Lincoln was inaugurated, the Commercial, the leading Republican paper of Ohio, in March, 1861, said: "We are not in favor of blockading the Southern coast. We are not in favor of retaking by force the property of the United States now in possession of the seceders. We would recognize the existence of a government formed of all the slaveholding States and attempt to cultivate amicable relations with it."

I have shown that not only were the Southern people sustained in their actions leading to secession by the conservative element of the North, as voiced in their daily and Weekly papers, but they were given to understand that they had nothing to hope for from the party about to assume the views of the government. Judge Chase made a speech before the Peace congress in which he declared unequivocally that the power being theirs, they would assuredly use it. The assaults on the Constitution were to culminate in the overthrow, at least, of its guarantees to the Southern people. Here is what he said:

> The result of the national canvass, recently terminated in the election of Mr. Lincoln, has been spoken of by some as the effect of a sudden impulse or of some irregular excitement of the popular mind; and it has been somewhat confidently asserted that, upon reflection and consideration, the hastily formed opinions which brought about that election will be changed. ... I cannot take this view of the result of the presidential election. I believe, and the belief amounts to absolute conviction, that the election must be regarded as a triumph of principles cherished in the hearts of the people of the free States. . . . We have elected him (Mr. Lincoln). After many years of earnest advocacy and of severe trial we have achieved the triumph of that principle. By a fair and unquestioned majority we have secured that triumph. Do you think we, who represent this majority, will throw it away? Do you think the people will sustain us if we undertake to throw it away? I must speak to you plainly, gentlemen of the South. It is not in my heart to deceive you. I therefore tell you explicitly that if we of the North and West would consent to throw away all that has been gained in the recent triumph of our principles, the people would not sustain us, and so, the consent would avail you nothing.

When some of the Northern people, alarmed at the prospect, held meetings and passed resolutions urging concessions to be made, Mr. Lincoln said: "I will suffer death before I will consent or advise my friends to consent to any concession or compromise which looks like buying the privilege of taking possession of the government to which we have a constitutional right." And Horace Greeley used these words to prove to the Southern people that it was useless to expect concessions from the dominant party, and these so-called concessions were matters pending before Congress, all of which were simply efforts to uphold the Constitution. Mr. Lincoln did not attempt to deny that the concessions referred to were right, but gives his refusal to entertain them in these words: "Whatever I might think of the merits of the various propositions before Congress, I should regard any concession in the face of menace as the destruction of the government itself and a consent on all hands that our system shall be brought down to a level with the existing disorganized state of affairs in Mexico."

CHAPTER III.

THE STATE CONVENTION—VARIANCE OF OPINION ON SECESSION—ADOPTION OF THE ORDINANCE OF SECESSION—ORGANIZATION OF MILITARY FORCES-CAMPAIGNS AND BATTLES IN ALABAMA—SOME OF ALABAMA'S DISTINGUISHED SOLDIERS.

I HAVE made quite a wide digression and have devoted considerable space to the endeavor to reproduce the sentiments prevailing among the most intellectual and patriotic leaders of the Northern States of the Union on the subject of State rights up to the very outbreak of hostilities.

In obedience to the act of the legislature, on December 6th, Governor Moore issued the proclamation ordering an election to be held on December 24th. The convention met on January 7, 1861, in the hall of representatives at Montgomery. Of the 100 men composing this body, many afterward proved their devotion to their State on the battlefield and in legislative halls, and some of them now hold high posts of honor in the reconstructed Union. The Rev. Basil Manly, ex-president of the State university, opened the proceedings with a touching and eloquent prayer:

> Almighty Father, Maker of Heaven and Earth; King eternal, immortal, invisible; the only wise God! We adore Thee, for Thou art God, and besides Thee there is none else; our Fathers' God and our God! We thank Thee that Thou hast made us men, endowed with reason, conscience and speech; capable of knowing, loving and serving Thee! We thank Thee for Thy Son, the Lord Jesus Christ, our only Mediator and Redeemer! We thank Thee for Thy word of truth, our guide to eternal life. We thank Thee for civil government, ruling in Thy fear; and we especially thank Thee that Thou didst reserve this fair portion of the earth so long undiscovered, unpolluted with the wars and the crimes of the old world, that Thou mightest here establish a free government and a pure religion. We thank Thee that Thou hast allotted us our heritage here, and hast brought us upon it at such a time as this. We thank Thee for all the hallowed memories connected with the establishment of the independence of Colonies, and their sovereignty as States, and with the formation and maintenance of our government, which we had devoutly hoped might last, unperverted and incorruptible, as long as the sun and moon endure.
>
> Oh, our Father, we have striven as an integral part of this great Republic, faithfully to keep our solemn covenants in the Constitution of our country; and our conscience doth not accuse us of having failed to sustain our part in the civil compact. Lord of all the families of the earth, we appeal to Thee to protect us in the land Thou hast given us, the Institution Thou hast established, the rights Thou hast bestowed. And now, in our troubles, besetting us like great waters round about, we, Thy dependent children, humbly entreat Thy fatherly notice and care. Grant to Thy servants now assembled, as the

direct representatives of the people of this State, all needful grace and wisdom for their peculiar and great responsibilities at this momentous crisis. Give them a clear perception of their duties as the embodiment of the people; impart to them an enlightened, mature and sanctified judgment in forming every conclusion; a steady, Heaven-directed purpose and will in attaining every right end. Save them from the disturbing influences of error, of passion, prejudice and timidity; from divided and conflicting counsels; give them one mind, and one way and let that be the mind of Christ. If Thou seest them ready to go wrong, interpose Thy heavenly guidance and restraint. If slow and reluctant to execute what duty and safety require, quicken and urge them forward. Let patient inquiry and candor pervade every discussion; let calm, comprehensive and sober wisdom shape every measure and direct every vote; let all things be done in Thy fear and with a just regard to their whole duty toward God and toward man. Preserve them in health, in purity, in peace; and cause that their session may promote the maintenance of equal rights, of civil freedom and good government; may promote the welfare of man, and the glory of Thy name. We ask all through Jesus Christ our Lord: Amen.

The delegates differed widely in their views as to the manner of procedure. Some were elected upon a platform, hereinafter quoted, which averred that it was the first duty "to use all honorable exertions to secure our rights in the Union." These had every reason to believe that they represented the majority of the people of the State. Others were sent instructed to secede at once; and these were found to make a majority of barely one. The whole course of the convention furnished a grand and glorious example of the dignity, moderation and self-sacrifice befitting the lofty patriotism of men whose whole souls were loyally devoted to their beloved State. With perhaps one exception, there was no harsh criticism, no impugning the motives nor questioning the patriotism of those differing on subjects of vital importance.

While opposing the ordinance for the immediate withdrawal of Alabama from the Union, one of the most distinguished of Alabama's sons but voiced the sentiments of the minority when he said:

I will not at this time express any argument of opposition I may entertain toward the ordinance of secession. . . . . I meet here a positive, enlightened and unflinching majority. I have respect for them, and I despair of being able to move them. In times like these, when neighboring States are withdrawing, one by one, from the Union, I cannot get my consent to utter a phrase which might be calculated, in the slightest degree, to widen the breaches at home. My opposition to the ordinance of secession will be sufficiently indicated by my vote; that vote will be recorded in the book; that book will take up its march for posterity; and the day is not yet come that is to decide on which part of the page of that book will be written the glory or the shame of this day.

It is important 6to the State that you of the majority should be right, and that I should be wrong. However much personal gratification I might feel hereafter in finding that I was right on this great question and that you were wrong, that gratification would, indeed, be to me a poor consolation in the midst of a ruined and desolated country. Therefore, as the passage of the ordinance of secession is the act by which the destiny of Alabama is to be controlled, I trust that you are right and that I am wrong. I trust that God has inspired you with His wisdom, and that, under the influence of this ordinance, the State of Alabama may rise to the highest pinnacle of national grandeur.

To show, sir, that the declarations I now make are not forced by the exigencies of this hour, I read one of the resolutions from the platform upon which I was elected to this convention: "Resolved, That we hold it to be our duty, first, to use all honorable exertions to secure our rights in the Union, and if we should fail in this, we will maintain our rights out of the Union; for, as citizens of Alabama, we owe our allegiance first to the State; and we will support her in whatever course she may adopt."

Thus, Mr. President, you will observe that the course I now take is the result of the greatest deliberation, having been matured before I was a candidate for a seat in this convention; and there is a perfect understanding on this subject between me and my constituents. It but remains for me to add, that when your ordinance passes through the solemn forms of legislative deliberation, and receives the sanction of this body, I shall recognize it as the supreme law of the land; my scruples will fall to the ground; and that devotion, which I have heretofore, through the whole course of my public life, given to the Union of the States, shall be concentrated in my allegiance to the State of Alabama.

Another said: "I have opposed secession as long as opposition was of any avail. Now that the ordinance will pass, as a patriot, I feel bound to take the side of my native State in any contest which might grow out of it. I will vote against the ordinance."

On the 11th of January, the secession of Alabama from the Federal Union was accomplished. I give the full text of the act:

An Ordinance to dissolve the union between the State of Alabama and other States united under the compact styled "The Constitution of the United States of America."

Whereas, The election of Abraham Lincoln and Hannibal Hamlin to the offices of President and Vice-President of the United States of America, by a sectional party, avowedly hostile to the domestic institutions and to the peace and security of the people of the State of Alabama, preceded by many and dangerous infractions of the Constitution of the United States by many of the States and people of the Northern section, is a political wrong of so insulting and menacing a character as to justify the people of the State of Alabama in the adoption of prompt and decided measures for their future peace and security; therefore,

Be it declared and ordained by the people of the State of Alabama in convention assembled, That the State of Alabama now withdraws, and is hereby withdrawn from the Union known as "the United States of America," and henceforth ceases to be one of said United States, and is, and of right ought to be, a sovereign and independent State.

Be it further declared and ordained by the people of the State of Alabama in convention assembled, That all the powers over the territory of said State, and over the people thereof, heretofore delegated to the government of the United States of America, be, and they are hereby withdrawn from said government, and are hereby resumed and vested in the people of the State of Alabama.

Be it resolved by the people of Alabama in convention assembled, That the people of the States of Delaware, Maryland, Virginia, North Carolina, South Carolina, Florida, Georgia, Mississippi, Louisiana, Texas, Arkansas, Tennessee, Kentucky and Missouri be, and are hereby invited to meet the people of the State of Alabama by their delegates in convention on the 4th day of February, A. D. 1861, at the city of Montgomery in the State of Alabama, for the purpose of consulting with each other as to the most effectual mode of securing concerted and harmonious action in whatever measures may be deemed most desirable for our common peace and security.

And be it further resolved, That the president of this convention be, and is hereby instructed to transmit forthwith, a copy of the foregoing preamble, ordinance and resolution to the governors of the several States named in said resolutions.

Done by the people of the State of Alabama in convention assembled at Montgomery, on this, the 11th day of January, A. D. 1861.

During December and January, Governor Moore had taken possession of Forts Morgan and Gaines and the arsenal at Mount Vernon. The forts were strongly garrisoned; and when the ordinance of secession was passed, the State was full of volunteers, busily drilling and preparing for hostilities.

Col. Tennent Lomax commanded the Second regiment of Alabama militia, which had been organized soon after the John Brown raid, and his were the first troops of Alabama to take position in preparing for the great struggle. After two months this regiment was disbanded and Colonel Lomax was put in command of the Third Alabama.

By October 7, 1861, the State had furnished fully 27,000 men to the Confederate cause, many of them being mere boys, and most of them drawn from the very flower of the land. There were sixty Alabama regiments of infantry, thirteen of cavalry, six battalions and twenty batteries, besides many companies from Alabama consolidated with those from other States in Confederate regiments, five of these being cavalry. Many of the regiments were commanded by veterans of the Mexican war, and some were led by officers fresh from West Point. Before the close of 1863, nearly 9,000 of these soldiers had been killed or had died of wounds, camp diseases and exposure. Alabama, which was the cradle of the Confederacy, was also its grave; for on her soil was fought, at Fort Tyler, April 16, 1865, the last bloody conflict of the war.

Early in 1862, Tennessee being in the possession of the Federals, the northern counties of Alabama were harassed by continuous raids. In April, Huntsville was occupied by General Mitchel and Colonel Turchin. Indignities of all kinds were heaped upon the defenseless citizens, until General Mitchel was replaced by a more humane and generous commander in the person of

General Buell. The Federals were driven back for a time by Bragg's advance into Kentucky, but they soon returned. In the fall of 1862, a spirited fight, principally with artillery, took place at Little Bear creek, near Tuscumbia, between General Sweeny and General Roddey, and the invaders were driven back to Corinth. Later on, Roddey's troops handsomely engaged the Federals at Barton Station, and again drove them back. In April, 1863, Forrest and Roddey fought Dodge's column at 0 and repulsed him; but the Federal leader on his retreat destroyed everything within reach and left the beautiful valley a scene of utter desolation.

Leaving Roddey in possession of Brown's Ferry, Forrest started in pursuit of Streight, who was advancing on Rome. Then followed one of the most thrilling and brilliant campaigns of the war. The Federals were overtaken in the lower part of Morgan county, and after a desperate fight of three hours, were driven back into Blount county with a heavy loss of men and baggage. The pursuit was continued and the retreat of the Federals became a rout. They made several desperate stands but were unable to rally their demoralized columns. On, through Blount and Etowah counties, rushed pursuers and pursued, scarcely stopping for food or rest until on May 2d, they rested for the night near Turkeytown, Cherokee county. Forrest, who had only 500 men, by his skillful maneuvers so magnified the appearance of his forces as to secure the surrender of Streight's whole command, numbering 1,466, besides a detachment of 230-men on their way to destroy Rome.

In January, 1864, the condition in northern Alabama was such as to evoke an appeal to the war department by the congressional delegation of the State. It is here quoted in full:

> The undersigned, senators and representatives from the State of Alabama, respectfully invite the attention of the Honorable Secretary of War to the consideration of a few suggestions relative to the present condition of North Alabama, and the necessity of permanently holding the south side of the Tennessee river in that State.
>
> You are aware that the enemy now claim and hold all the country in said State north of said river; that river, running through the entire width of the State from east to west, is both deep and wide, difficult to be crossed by an enemy, and is now the dividing line between us and our foes. Brigadier-General Roddey, with his command, is guarding a portion of the south side of the river; but to enable him to do so more effectually, and to protect the country from the enemy at Corinth, Miss., and also to draw supplies for our army from Middle Tennessee, which he is expected to do, he will require a much larger force than he now has under his command. A glance at the map of the country will satisfy any one that if the raiding parties of the enemy be permitted to cross the river, there is no natural barrier to prevent him from sweeping as low down the country as the Alabama river, penetrating that region of the State in which are located the mining and manufacturing establishments now getting into successful operation, and which it is believed are and will continue to be of great benefit to our cause.

To protect our people against such calamity as would result from the incursions of the enemy, we deem it of the utmost importance that General Roddey's command be retained in its present locality, and that he be permitted to increase his force from the adjacent country and from the region within the line of the enemy, and that he have returned to his brigade five companies of Alabama troops now under the command of Major-General Forrest. These companies were all raised by General Roddey, mostly within the enemy's lines and who entered the service expecting to continue under his command. They are very anxious to be restored to General Roddey's brigade, and we understand that General Forrest would not object to such restoration. These five companies are commanded respectively by Captains Steele, Moore, Barr, Warren and Hansell. From these sources we think that General Roddey will strengthen his command sufficiently to protect our people against the raids of the enemy, coming either across the Tennessee river or from the direction of Corinth. We think he will also be enabled to draw supplies of bacon, beef, cattle, hogs, grain, and leather from Middle Tennessee, in larger quantities than heretofore, though he has already drawn much in that way. Besides this, his position is such that should opportunity offer he could fall upon the enemy's communication with Chattanooga and do him serious damage.

Again, should the enemy be permitted to take possession of the country south of the Tennessee river, he will not find it difficult to extend his line to the Warrior and perhaps to the Alabama river, without meeting with serious opposition, but would, on the contrary, receive great encouragement in the mountain region in our State, where there is unfortunately in some parts a disaffected population.

In view of what is above set forth, we hope the Honorable Secretary of War will permit the necessary increase of General Roddey's force. We believe that by so doing the interest of the whole country would be greatly advanced.

THOS. J. FOSTER,   JOHN P. RALLS,
R. JEMISON, JR.,   C. C. CLAY, JR.
W. R. SMITH,

The northern counties, being subjected to incessant raids, were the scenes of continuous bloodshed, and side by side were to be witnessed acts of the most wanton brutality and of unexampled heroism and daring. Churches, colleges and libraries, as well as private dwellings, were ransacked and destroyed. Guntersville, Marshall county, was shelled several times without warning and was finally burned.

In Claysville, on the night of March 8, 1864, Federals were quartered in three houses. Capt. H. F. Smith, of Jackson, with 65 men, crossed the river at Gunter's landing, cut off the pickets, and forced the surrender of 66 men with a large supply of stores and provisions.

In May, 1864, Colonel Patterson, of Morgan county, assisted by Stewart's battalion of 500 men, attacked the Federal stockade and garrison at Madison Station, took 80 prisoners and a large quantity of provisions, and conveyed them across the river in the face of the enemy. The garrison numbered 400; Patterson's loss was 7 killed and wounded.

In July, 1864, General Rousseau made a raid into the central part of the State and was gallantly opposed by the State reserves, composed principally of very young men.

Athens was occupied by a large force of Federals, and Limestone county was suffering under the odious rule of Colonel Turchin. September 23d, General Forrest arrived before Athens with 3,000 men and was joined by General Roddey's forces, about 1,500 strong. He captured the horses and cantonments of the enemy, driving the men into the fort; and, deploying his men so as to make them appear as at least 10,000, he demanded of Colonel Campbell an unconditional surrender. He secured the fortress with 1,400 prisoners and defeated a detachment which had come to their relief, destroyed the Federal posts in the vicinity, and on the 25th, took Sulphur Trestle, capturing 820 men, 350 horses, 2 pieces of artillery and 20 loaded wagons.

The city of Mobile was the most important in Alabama, and had been at the beginning of the conflict put in a state of defense. Three strong lines of works surrounded the city, and so well planned were the fortifications that it was one of the best fortified cities of the South, and was the last to fall into the hands of the enemy. Below the city the water approaches were protected by batteries Huger and Tracy; rows of piles obstructed the channel and torpedoes were placed in different parts of the bay. Seven miles from the city, a line of defenses known as Spanish Fort protected the bay shore and Forts Gaines and Morgan stood at the entrance of the bay, four miles apart, the former under the command of Colonel Anderson and the latter under General Page. The ram Tennessee and the gunboats Gaines, Morgan, Selma and others contributed to the defenses.

Early in 1864, Farragut arrived off Mobile bay. The campaign against Mobile was planned to consist of an attack by water to be supported by an attack by land forces under General Banks.

It was impossible on account of Federal reverses in the Red River campaign to carry out these arrangements immediately. General Canby was placed in command of the West Mississippi division in May, 1864, but was obliged to send a large portion of his force to the defense of Washington, and the attack on Mobile was postponed.

On August 2, 1864, Gen. Gordon Granger, United States, army, arrived off Santa Rosa island with 1,500 men, proceeded to Dauphin island, and landed in spite of the resistance made by the fort guns and the gunboats.

At 6 o'clock, August 5th, fourteen vessels, with the Tecumseh in the lead, steamed toward Fort Morgan. The Tecumseh struck a torpedo and sank, but her place was filled by Farragut's flagship, the Hartford. This was engaged by the Tennessee, and a most desperate conflict ensued, until the ram was disabled and obliged to strike her colors. The Selma was captured, but the Morgan and Gaines escaped. Fort Gaines, shelled by the monitors on one side, and Granger's forces on the other, was compelled to surrender. Then followed the siege of Fort Morgan. Fire within the fort compelled the garrison to sacrifice most of their ammunition, and the interior of the fort was a mass of smouldering ruins in which lay the bodies of many of its brave defenders, when it was surrendered by General Page, August 23, 1864.

The Federal fleet now had control of the bay; and had the enemy known the real weakness of the garrison of Mobile, the reduction of the city would have been a matter of days rather than of months. Early in January, 1865, the Federal army went into camp at Barrancas, near the mouth of Pensacola bay. Fort Gaines was strongly garrisoned by them, and reinforcements continued to pour in to the ranks of the invaders on Dauphin island and at Barrancas.

By March, Canby's army amounted to 45,000 men. General Maury had about 9,000 men. His headquarters were at Blakely, about three miles from Spanish Fort, and General Gibson was in command of the fort.

To divert attention from their movements against Mobile, concerted attacks were to be made on the interior cities by Steele's column from the south and Wilson's from north Alabama.

Maury's cavalry was kept busy skirmishing in the direction taken by Steele's column, thus weakening the forces at Mobile. The advance was commenced March 17th, and was contested inch by inch, and the defenders were assisted by the natural obstructions found in the swampy roads, rendered almost impassable by incessant rains. March 27th, the siege of Spanish Fort commenced. The garrison comprised troops from Louisiana, Arkansas, Georgia, Texas and North Carolina, and the Alabama reserves under General Thomas. The latter were afterward relieved by Holtzclaw's brigade. The siege was most stubbornly contested. Day by day the enemy drew nearer, and gradually succeeded in getting siege-guns within range of the forts, while the garrison were continually fighting and repairing the breaches made in the walls. General Gibson described their life as "fighting all day and digging all night." They found it impossible to procure the labor and implements needed, and their force was daily growing less. In spite of this they made several brilliant sorties and inflicted terrible damage on the enemy.

April 8th, after a siege of thirteen days, a general bombardment was commenced, the besiegers having advanced steadily in spite of the heroic resistance of the garrison, whose lines were becoming painfully thin. Finally, after 300 yards of the left line had been broken and 350 prisoners taken, it was decided to evacuate the fort. Lieutenants Clark and Holtzclaw, with desperate bravery, held the enemy in check while the garrison evacuated the fort. The first was killed, the second dangerously wounded.

Many of the soldiers marched through the mire to Fort Blakely and some to Mobile. The siege of Blakely was then progressing, and though the fort was defended with the most desperate valor, the brave garrison were finally compelled to yield after a hand-to-hand encounter with overwhelming numbers. General Maury, with about 4,500 men, retired to Meridian, and the Federals entered Mobile without further opposition.

While these operations were going on in south Alabama, General Wilson was on his famous raid from Gravelly Springs, Lauderdale county, to

Selma. He had three divisions, commanded, respectively, by Generals McCook, Long and Upton. These three divisions were sent by different routes, meeting at the ford of the Black Warrior. They destroyed much valuable property and were opposed at various points by Roddey's and Crossland's brigades under Gen. Dan Adams, and by Forrest's troops, but nowhere could troops be massed in sufficient force to repulse the invaders. Selma, the most important depot of the Southwest, containing an arsenal and foundry, was besieged and taken, and given over to plunder, under orders to destroy everything which could benefit the Confederate cause. General Wilson proceeded to Montgomery, which he occupied April 12th, and then resumed his march into Georgia.

Meanwhile General Croxton marched toward Tuscaloosa, and twenty miles above the city was attacked by Gen. W. H. Jackson's division. Evading this force by a feint, he proceeded to Northport; crossing the bridge over the Black Warrior, he surprised the guard, captured the artillery and took possession of the town, destroyed the foundries and factories, the university, public works and stores, and remained there until April 5th. He then proceeded toward Eutaw. His progress was checked by a serious encounter with Gen. Wirt Adams, and only the firmness of the Second Michigan cavalry saved Croxton from overwhelming defeat. He remained near Northport for a few days and proceeded eastward.

April 16th, General Lagrange, who had been sent to reinforce Croxton, reached the vicinity of West Point with 3,000 men. A defense called Fort Tyler, manned by about 104 youths and convalescents, had been erected on the edge of Chambers county and confronted the enemy, whose whole force was directed against it. It was commanded by General Tyler, who resolved to defend it to the bitter end. He was killed, his successor, Captain Gonzalez, was mortally wounded, and then the command devolved upon Captain Parhan, who displayed the same invincible courage; but at last the overwhelming numbers of the enemy enabled them to scale the walls and throng into the little fortress, which was captured, and the Confederate flag torn from its last stronghold in the South. This was the last conflict of the war east of the Mississippi, with the exception of one of the same date at Columbus, Ga. Croxton's forces moved on toward Newnan, Ga.; but on the 26th, while they were crossing the river, a white flag appeared on the opposite bank, where the news awaited them of the fall of Richmond, the surrender of Lee and the assassination of Lincoln.

Many citizens of Alabama not mentioned on the rolls of the State troops made their names illustrious by chivalrous and daring deeds. Among the noble young heroes who laid down their lives for the cause of the South were John Pelham, John Herbert Kelly and John Gregg.

Colonel Pelham was a native of Calhoun county, Alabama, and was in the graduating class at West Point when the war broke out. Late in April, 1861, he returned home and reported at once for duty at Montgomery. He was commissioned as first lieutenant of artillery in the Confederate army and ordered to take charge of the ordnance at Lynchburg, Va. He was assigned as drill-master to Albertus' battery at Winchester, and his skill and daring in the handling of the guns at once attracted the attention of his superiors. Gen. J. E. B. Stuart intrusted him with the organization of a battery of horse artillery which he raised in Alabama, Virginia and Maryland. The men from Alabama were commanded by Lieut. William McGregor, a gallant and skillful officer. Pelham fought with great distinction at Williamsburg, First Cold Harbor, Second Bull Run, Sharpsburg, Shepherdstown and Fredericksburg, everywhere eliciting the unstinted admiration and warmest commendation of his commanding officers. His splendid daring at Fredericksburg drew from General Lee, who, in his report, calls him "the gallant Pelham," there-mark: "It is glorious to see such courage in one so young." He rapidly passed through the different grades by promotion, and his commission as lieutenant-colonel was issued a few days before his death, which occurred at Kelly's Ford, March 17, 1863, while gallantly leading a wavering regiment, as he said, "Forward to victory and glory!" Pelham was a good scholar, a splendid horseman, and a magnificent athlete. He was very tall, of light but sinewy build, and so youthful looking that strangers gazed with astonishment upon the hero of almost fabulous renown. He was modest, courteous and refined, of unblemished character and undaunted courage; and his death was considered an irreparable loss to the army.

Gen. John Herbert Kelly, though two years younger, was a classmate and friend of Pelham, and like him left the academy within a short time of his graduation, and offered his services to the Confederacy. He was appointed second lieutenant and sent to Fort Morgan. He soon after went with General Hardee into Missouri, was commissioned major and placed in command of an Arkansas battalion; after the battle of Shiloh, where he fought bravely, he was made colonel of the Eighth Arkansas regiment. He fought gallantly at Perryville and at Murfreesboro, where he was wounded. At Chickamauga he commanded a brigade and won high commendation on account of his skill and valor. He took part in the Sequatchie raid, and after its termination was recommended by General Wheeler as one of four officers he was authorized to select for promotion to the rank of brigadier-general, He was killed while leading a charge at Franklin, Tenn., August 20, 1864, deeply regretted by his comrades, who loved and admired him for his many noble qualities.

Gen. John Gregg, although a native of Alabama, entered the service from Texas, his adopted State, as lieutenant-colonel of the Seventh Texas. He was captured at Fort Donelson, and when exchanged, was assigned to the command of a brigade and was soon after made brigadier-general, in which position he was conspicuous for his courage and ability as a leader. He was killed while leading Field's division in the desperate assault upon the Federal lines, near Richmond, October 7, 1864. Professor Tutwiler, the distinguished teacher of Alabama, said of him: " Of the many noble young men who perished in our cause, none gave greater promise of distinction and usefulness to his country than John Gregg."

Admiral Raphael Semmes was another citizen of Alabama who made for himself a brilliant and unique record. He was born in Maryland and was educated at the United States naval academy. He became a resident of Alabama in 1842, and during the war with Mexico was flag lieutenant of Commodore Conner's flagship. He was placed in command of the Somers, employed in blockading Vera Cruz. When Alabama seceded, he resigned his commission in the United States navy, was at once commissioned naval commander of the Confederate service, and was sent to New York to purchase stores of war. He cruised six months with a small vessel called the Sumter, capturing 17 merchant vessels, but was finally blockaded at Gibraltar, and being unable to get coal, returned on an English vessel. He was put in command of the Alabama, and began his famous second cruise, during which he is said to have captured 50 merchant vessels. He fought and sunk the Federal steamer Hatteras, taking her crew to Jamaica, where they were paroled. Having dropped anchor in the port of Cherbourg, France, he was blockaded by the Kearsarge, which he challenged and fought, the action terminating disastrously for the Alabama, which sank just after striking her colors. Semmes and 40 of the crew were rescued by an English gentleman and taken to England, where a number of British officers presented him with a sword to replace the one he had thrown into the sea. Returning to America, he reached Richmond in January, 1865, and was assigned to the command of the James river fleet, consisting of 3 ironclads and 5 wooden steamers, which guarded the water approach to the city. On the evacuation of Richmond, he blew up his vessels, organized his marines into a brigade and proceeded to join the Confederate forces at Greensboro. After the surrender of Johnston's army, he returned quietly to Mobile, but was seized by order of the United States navy, taken to Washington and imprisoned, but after four months was released by the President's proclamation. Col. Melancthon Smith entered the service of the State of Alabama as a captain of light artillery, July 1, 1861. His military education at West Point rendered him very efficient, and at the recommendation of his superior officers he was made major in August, 1862. Later on, he was promoted to colonel. He was chief of artillery in Hardee's, and afterward Cheatham's corps. He served in the battles of Belmont, Shiloh, Perryville, Chickamauga, Missionary Ridge, the battles of the Atlanta campaign and the subsequent campaign in north Alabama and middle Tennessee. After the war he settled in Mobile and engaged in journalism.

Appropriate in this connection is the following joint resolution of the Confederate States Congress, approved February 15, 1864:

Joint resolution of thanks to the soldiers from the State of Alabama who have re-enlisted for the war:

Whereas, In addition to the various brigades and regiments of veteran troops from the State of Alabama, to whom Congress has heretofore given evidence of grateful appreciation by a vote of thanks for re-enlisting for the war, other brigades and regiments are nobly coming to the rescue of their imperiled country by such re-enlistments, thus furnishing evidence that the citizen soldiery from that State have determined never to abandon the struggle in which we are engaged until our independence shall have been achieved: Therefore,

Resolved by the Congress of the Confederate States of America, That the thanks of Congress are due, and are hereby tendered, alike to the gallant soldiers from the State of Alabama, who, in the first instance, enlisted for the war, and for those who, notwithstanding the toils and hardships of many a weary march and perils of many hard fought battles, have voluntarily come forward and offered their labors and lives.

Resolved, That such noble examples of heroism and self-sacrifice will ever be remembered by a grateful country, and should stimulate all those who remain at home to redouble their exertions to provide not only for the comfort and efficiency of those patriotic warriors, but for their families and loved ones whom they have left behind.

CHAPTER IV.

THE ALABAMA INFANTRY REGIMENTS-BRIEF HISTORY OF EACH ORGANIZATION—THEIR SERVICE AS SHOWN BY THE OFFICIAL RECORDS.

THE First Alabama infantry was the first in Alabama to enlist for one year, the first to re-enlist, and has the distinction of having served, though several times reorganized, from the beginning to the end of the conflict. Enlisting in March, 1861, it assembled at Pensacola and immediately began the hardest of work— in preparing for defense. It was assigned to the batteries and soon earned the title, ''Bragg's best artillerists.'' Col. Henry D. Clayton served during the year 1861; at the end of one year the regiment reorganized under Col. Isaiah G. W. Steedman. It took part in the battle of Santa Rosa, and was in the bombardment of Pensacola, where it earned high renown. Ordered to Memphis, March, 1862, it saw constant service until at Island No. 10, where a large part of the regiment was captured; the remainder were in the battle of Corinth.

In September the Island No. 10 prisoners were exchanged and the regiment was ordered to Port Hudson, where most of them were again captured. The enlisted men, 610 strong, were exchanged, and under command of the officers who escaped capture, fought at New Hope and Kenesaw, where a brilliant record was made; Peach Tree creek, Atlanta, Franklin, Nashville, Averasboro, and Bentonville. The regiment was greatly distinguished, suffering many losses in these battles, including Major Knox, the commander, who fell while leading his troops in the battle of Franklin.

EXTRACTS FROM OFFICIAL WAR RECORDS.

Vol. VI—(460) Report of General Anderson of battle of Santa Rosa, October 8, 1861. (492) General Bragg's report of bombardment of Pensacola, November 22-23, 1861, says: "Col. H. D. Clayton, First regiment of Alabama volunteers, whose entire regiment served both days at the batteries, has received the just commendation of the general. This gallant regiment has toiled for nearly ten months in the construction and garnishment of the works they almost despaired of using. Having been the first on the ground, much the largest portion of the labor fell to their lot. When least expected, the opportunity has been offered to test their skill, and most nobly have they availed themselves of it." (784) General Bragg calls it "a well-instructed body of artillery." (819) In Gen. Sam Jones' brigade, Bragg's army, February 1, 1862. (838) General Jones, Pensacola, March 5, 1862, says: "First Alabama leaves for Memphis this evening."

Vol. VII—(915) Ordered to Fort Pillow under command of General Withers. Memorandum of General Beauregard, March 3, 1862.

Vol. VIII—(129) Colonel Steedman's First Alabama regiment rendered gallant and efficient service on the 17th of March, 1862.—Report of Gen. J. P. McCown. (161) Commended in report of Capt. E. W. Rucker, regarding Madrid Bend and Island No. 10. (174-175) Report of Col. I. G. W. Steedman, Island No. 10: "Lieutenants Owens and Sanford acted gallantly as men could act." Lieutenant Clark killed, 5 men wounded. (778) "I sent you the First Alabama regiment two days ago; they are Bragg's best artillerists."—Gen. Leonidas Polk, March 13th.

Vol. XV—(276-277) Report of Gen. Frank Gardner, Port Hudson, March 14, 1863: "Battery served by 4 companies of Colonel Steedman's regiment; the other companies posted as sharpshooters. Gallant conduct of men at batteries deserving of highest praise." (278) One officer wounded, Port Hudson, La., March 14, 1863. (841) Aggregate present for duty 312—report of Gen. Wm. N. R. Beall, Port Hudson, October 22, 1862. (1033) Heavy artillery, Colonel Steedman commanding, March 31, 1863. (1062) Heavy artillery, Lieut.-Col. M. B. Locke commanding.

Vol. XVII, Part 2—(600) Abstract from statement of troops at and about Grenada, Miss., June 14, 1862. Aggregate 169, commanded by General Villepigue. (661) Aggregate 193, with General Van Dorn at Vicksburg, July, 1862. (726) "Steedman's regiment at Port Hudson."—General Ruggles' letter to Van Dorn, October 11, 1862. (815) With General Pemberton in Mississippi, December, 1862.

No. 38—(613) In heavy artillery brigade, department of Mississippi, General Pemberton. (707) Same assignment, April 20, 1863, Col. I. G. W. Steedman.

No. 41—(36-37) Report of Lieut.-Col. M. B. Locke of operations near Port Hudson, May 17, 1863: "Capt. J. G. Stubbs, Company C, held the enemy in check until nearly surrounded." Captain Pruett and Lieutenant Cregnies mentioned. One man wounded. (143) Paroled at Port Hudson, July, 1863. (144) Lieut. Thomas Frank killed at siege of Port Hudson. (147) Killed 2, wounded 2. Casualties in General Beall's brigade up to June 1, 1863. (156) Killed 2, wounded 8. Report of Colonel Steedman, operations May 25th to July 7th, Port Hudson. (157) Report of Colonel Steedman, May 26th, mentions Lieutenant-Colonel Locke. (161) Report of Colonel Steedman, June 10th, mentions Capts. J. P. Whitfield and James D. Meadows, also Maj. Samuel L. Knox. (156-163) Reports of Colonel Steedman, June 29th, Major Knox commanding. (163) April 20th, Colonel Steedman says: "The fine discipline and buoyant spirits of the regiment were conspicuous during the entire siege. In their exposed position they were assaulted incessantly, almost every day and night, but never successfully." (166) Mentioned in Lieut.-Col. J. H. Wingfield's report. (531) Report of Gen. Wm. Dwight, U. S. A., before Port Hudson, says: "First Alabama is 500 strong."

No. 42—(18) Letter of Lieutenant-Colonel Locke, commanding, May 25, 1863. (104) Letter of Capt. J. P. Jones, Port Hudson, July 5th, states:" First Alabama 585 strong." (431) Letter of Gen. Dabney H. Maury, Mobile,

November 21st, speaks of expected arrival of First Alabama.

No. 56—(630) Ordered to Meridian, Miss., November 4, 1863.

No. 58—(563) Asked for by General Maury, January 15, 1864. (583) January 20, 1864, aggregate, 745. (703) General Maury asks General Polk, February 10th: "Please send me Colonel Steedman's regiment to serve as heavy artillery." (734) "I shall send you the First Alabama regiment, General."—Polk to Maury, February 13th. (769) "First Alabama has arrived."—Maury to Polk, February 19th.

No. 59—(861) Major Knox commanding, with troops in district of the Gulf, April 30, 1864.

No. 65—(425) Mentioned by General Ashboth, U. S. A., affair at Bayou Grand, August 7, 1864. Spoken of as First Alabama artillery, number 400.

No. 66—(89) General Ashboth, U. S. A., Barrancas, May 9, 1864, says: "First Alabama infantry is at Pollard."

No. 74—(646) In General Cantey's division, Second brigade, army of Mississippi, July 10, 1864. (653) Walthall's division, June 30th, Major Knox commanding. (660) Same assignment. (665) In Quarles' brigade, General Walthall's division, Stewart's corps, army of Tennessee, July 31st. (671) Assignment as above, August 31, 1864. (894) Gen. D. H. Reynolds, of Walthall's division, in front of Atlanta, July 19th, says: "Major Knox arrived with his regiment." (923) General Walthall, September 3d, says: "Major Knox in command of the First Alabama regiment, a fine officer and veteran regiment, reports that the enemy came within 30 yards of his lines at almost all points," battle of Kenesaw, June 27th.

No. 74—(930) Gen. William A. Quarles, writing July 1, 1864, of the same operations, says: "To the First Alabama is due the whole credit of the most brilliant affair it has ever been my fortune to witness. I respectfully and most earnestly recommend the promotion of Major Knox. He has exhibited his capacity for higher rank on the field where commissions are most worthily won." (932) August 6th, General Quarles says: "Colonel (Major) Knox, of the First Alabama, well known as one of the most promising officers in the army, was severely and dangerously wounded in the early part of the action. It is praise enough of him to say that up to the time of his fall he sustained his former reputation." (933) "And to Lieutenant Neal, acting assistant-surgeon, First Alabama, I am much indebted for the zeal and promptness of [his] conduct." (934) Major Knox in report of same operations says: "We captured 18 prisoners, one of them Captain Wakefield, of the Fifty-third Indiana. We lost 1 sergeant killed and 5 privates wounded." (937) Mentioned by Gen. D. H. Reynolds in his report of same.

No. 78—(855) September 20, 1864, same assignment,, regiment commanded by Maj. Samuel L. Knox; inspection report gives Acting Lieut-Col. Richard Williams.

Vol. XCIII—(666) Same assignment in army of Tennessee, Gen. S. D. Lee; Lieut. Charles M. McRae commanding regiment December 20, 1864.

(685) Maj. S. L. Knox wounded and captured at Franklin. (725) Colors of First Alabama among others lost, color-bearers either killed or captured at Franklin.—General Walthall's report of battle.

Vol. XCVIII—(1063) Shelley's brigade, Stewart's corps. Gen. Joseph E. Johnston, as constituted after April 9, 1865 (consolidated with Sixteenth, Thirty-third and Forty-fifth Alabama), under Col. Robert H. Abercrombie.

Vol. C—(735) Quarles' brigade with Seventeenth and Twenty-ninth, commanded by Capt. Benjamin H. Screws,, March 31, 1865. (773) Assignment as above.

THE SECOND ALABAMA INFANTRY.

The Second Alabama, under Col. Harry Maury, formed the garrison of Fort Morgan until the spring of 1862; besides serving as infantry it was thoroughly drilled as heavy" artillery and manned the guns of the fort. It also served at Fort Pillow, and at the end of a year's service it disbanded, the officers and men joining other organizations.

EXTRACTS FROM OFFICIAL WAR RECORDS.

Vol. VI—(819) Army of Mobile, Gen. J. M. Withers; department of Alabama and West Florida, General Bragg, February 1, 1862.

Vol. VII—(915) Ordered to proceed to Fort Pillow under the command of General Withers. Memorandum of General Beauregard, at Jackson, Tenn., March 3, 1863.

Vol. XI, Part 1—(267) E. J. Allen, U. S. A., March 29, 1862, said: "Second Alabama infantry, 1,050 men, was. 3 miles from Yorktown on the road to Hampton." (Error; probably Third.)

No. 66—(111) General Ashboth, U. S. A., at Barrancas, June 3, 1864, says: "At Pollard are only 5 companies of the Second Alabama infantry." (Error.)

THE THIRD ALABAMA INFANTRY.

Col. Jones M. Withers organized the Third Alabama at Montgomery in April, 1861, and it was immediately dispatched to Virginia.

Colonel Withers was very early promoted to the rank of brigadier-general, and Tennent Lomax succeeded him as colonel of the regiment. It won great honor in the battles of Seven Pines, Malvern Hill, Winchester, Cedar Hill, Fredericksburg, Gettysburg, The Wilderness, Spottsylvania, Second Cold Harbor, Early's advance on Washington, the battles around Richmond, Petersburg and Appomattox. Colonels Lomax and B. B. Johnson were among the killed at Seven Pines. The regiment lost 207 killed, wounded and missing at the bloody battle of Malvern Hill.

EXTRACTS FROM OFFICIAL WAR RECORDS.

Vol. IX—(59) Mentioned by General Huger, Norfolk,. Va., March 8, 1862. (431) General Huger, Suffolk, Va., February 13, 1862, says: "I have ordered 1,000 men, Third Alabama, to Suffolk."

Vol. XI, Part 1—(774) "The force opposed to us was the Third Alabama, 1,000 strong." Francis C. Barlow, New York volunteers, Fair Oaks Station, Va., June 2, 1862. (785) Col. Paul Frank, Fifty-second N. Y. infantry, says in report of battle of Fair Oaks: "Part of the right-wing of the Third Alabama had broken the right of the Eighty-first Pennsylvania." (786) "The colonel and several line officers of the Third Alabama were killed." (790) Mentioned by Col. John R. Brooke, Fifty-third Pennsylvania.

Vol. XI, Part 2—(484) Rodes' brigade, D. H. Hill's, division, Jackson's corps, Seven Days' battles. (505) 37 killed, 170 wounded, June 26 to July 1, 1862. (625-627) Mentioned in report of Gen. D. H. Hill. (630-632) Gen. R. E. Rodes' report. (633) Casualties, June 27th, 2 killed, 14 wounded; July 1st, 37 killed, 163 wounded. (634) Mentioned in Col. J. B. Gordon's report. (635) Casualties as above, Malvern Hill. (636) Mentioned by Col. J. B. Gordon. (975-976) Casualties as above.

Vol. XI, Part 3—(435) Gen. Benjamin Huger, April 10, 1862, says that it is one of the best regiments. (650) Lieut-Col. C. A. Battle in command, July 23, 1862.

Vol. XIX, Part 1—(808) Assigned as above. (1021) General Hill in his report of operations, July 23d-September 27th, indorses General Rodes' report of Maryland campaign where he said that with the Fifth and Sixth, "the Third, commanded by Colonel Battle, deserve special mention for admirable conduct during the whole fight." (1024) Same report, further mention. (1035-1038) General Rodes' report of the battles of Boonesboro and Sharpsburg commends the regiment and its leader, Colonel Battle.

Vol. XXI—(541) Rodes' brigade, Stonewall Jackson's corps (Lee's roster), July 3, 1862. (560) 1 killed, 2 wounded in the battle of Fredericksburg. (1073) Assignment as above, December 20, 1862.

No. 39—(792) Assignment as above. Capt. M. F. Bonham in command. Chancellorsville campaign, May, 1863. (807) 17 killed, 121 wounded, battle of Chancellorsville. (943) Mentioned in General Rodes' report of Chancellorsville campaign. (948) 15 killed, 128 wounded at Chancellorsville. (949) General Rodes in report says; "The Third Alabama regiment captured and have in their possession two stand of Federal artillery colors." (950-953) Several mentions in Colonel O'Neal's report; he says: "The Third Alabama, under the command of Capts. M. F. Bonham, John W. Chester and Watkins Phelan (and other regiments), though passing through a dense and tangled forest for a mile, all the regiments moved in a regular, unbroken line, the officers exhibiting the greatest coolness and daring, cheering on their men by both voice and example. Capt. Watkins Phelan was wounded in this charge. He, with Captain Bonham, who commanded the regiment, and Captain Chester, commanding the right wing of the Third

Alabama, acted most gallantly. Each regiment did its whole duty. I am also greatly indebted to Adjts. A. H. Pickett and Samuel H. Moore, of the Third and Twenty-sixth Alabama regiments, who acted as aides, for valuable services in fearlessly carrying and delivering orders." (954) Mentioned also in Col. J. M. Hall's report. (955-957) Report of Col. M. F. Bonham, commanding regiment. (959, 960, 961, 976) Mentioned in reports of Colonel Lightfoot, Sixth Alabama, of Colonel Pickens, Twelfth Alabama, and of Gen. A. H. Colquitt. (1052) Confederate roll of honor, battle of Chancellorsville, Third regiment of infantry of Alabama: Sergt. Walter Ransom, Company C; Sergt. George H. Ellison, Company E; Corp. H. H. Hardy, Company G; Private C. D. Rouse, Company H; Corp. W. H. Powers, Company K. Companies A, B, D, F and L declined voting.

No. 44—(287) Third Alabama, Col. C. A. Battle, O'Neal's brigade, Rodes' division, army of Northern Virginia, at the battle of Gettysburg, July 1-3, 1863. (332, 342) 12 killed, 79 wounded at battle of Gettysburg. (444) General Ewell's report of battle of Gettysburg: "Third Alabama by some mistake left with Daniel's brigade." (560) In the skirmish at Manassas Gap. (563) List of field and staff officers present with their commands at the battle of Gettysburg . . . Col. C. A. Battle, Lieut.-Col. C. Forsyth, who sprained his ankle on July 2d, and Maj. R. M. Sands. (576) Mentioned by Col. William A. Owens. (579, 580) Also mentioned in report of General Iverson. (587) Gen. S. D. Ramseur in his report says: "Colonel Battle, with the Third Alabama, rendered brilliant and invaluable service. Attaching his regiment to my command on his own responsibility, he came in at the right place, at the right time and in the right way." (592, 593) Mentioned in Colonel (General) O'Neal's report. (594) Report of Lieutenant-Colonel Forsyth. (594, 595) Report of Col. C. A. Battle, who says: "I received instructions to move with General Daniel. These instructions were followed until their longer observance became impracticable. I then sent an officer to General Daniel for orders, who on his return said that General Daniel had no orders for me; that I must act on my own responsibility. I at once moved upon the right of General Ramseur then advancing to the attack, and offered him my regiment. The offer was accepted, and my command acted under this gallant officer in a charge which drove the enemy from one of his strongholds and then rejoined Rodes' brigade. I am indebted to Lieutenant-Colonel Forsyth and Major Sands for valuable assistance."

No. 45—(922, 1059) Rodes' brigade, June and July, 1863.

No. 48—(399) In Battle's brigade, Lee's army, Col. Charles Forsyth commanding regiment, September 30, 1863. (412) Killed 1, wounded 1, Bristoe campaign. (617) 1 wounded, October 26 to November 8, 1863. (818) Assignment as above, October 31, 1863. (838) 5 wounded at engagement on Payne's Farm and operations, Mine Run. (888) Report of Col. Charles Forsyth on operations near Mine Run. Detachment of sharpshooters under Lieut. John T. Huggins of Company E. Columbus Dunn, Company A, slightly wounded;

Benjamin Woodell, Company K, severely wounded; W. T. Hall, Company B, slightly wounded.

No. 49—(683, 900) Assignment as above.

Vol. LX—(1149) Joint Resolution of thanks to the Alabama troops who have re-enlisted for the war: Whereas, The Alabama troops, composing the brigade commanded by Brig.-Gen. Cullen A. Battle, in the army of Northern Virginia, volunteered in the service of the Confederate States in the early part of the year 1861, upon the first call for troops for the defense of Virginia, have participated in every battle fought by that army from the battle of Seven Pines to that of Gettysburg, always winning, by their gallantry and devotion deserved praise and honor; and now, after enduring for nearly three years the hardships and dangers of active military service, have re-enlisted for the war; Therefore, Resolved by the Congress of the Confederate States of America, That the thanks of Congress are due, and are hereby cordially tendered, to the Alabama troops, who, by their renewing the offer of their services to the country for the war in advance of any legislative action, have shown a spirit undaunted, a heroic determination to battle ever until the independence of their country is established, and a consecration to the cause of liberty worthy of imitation by their comrades. Resolved, That the President be requested to communicate a copy of these resolutions to the commander and troops of said brigade, as an evidence of the grateful appreciation by Congress of their fortitude and heroism during the trials and dangers of past services and of their late acts of patriotism, confirming the faith and reassuring the hope of the patriot. Approved February 6, 1864.

No. 67—(1024) Same assignment early in May, 1864. (1084) Mentioned in General Battle's report, operations. May 8th.

No. 88—(1217) Same assignment as above, August 31st.

No. 89—(1194) Same assignment, Capt. Watkins Phelan in command, October 31st. (1246) Same assignment, Colonel Forsyth in command, November 30th. (1364),

Same assignment, Colonel Forsyth commanding brigade, December 31, 1864.

No. 90—(564) In Battle's brigade, Ramseur's division, Gen. J. A. Early. Battle of Cedar Creek, October 19, 1864. (1002) Army of the Valley district, August 20, 1864. (1013) With Second army corps, army of Northern Virginia, Gen. J. A. Early.

No. 95—(1270) Same assignment, Capt. Cornelius Robinson, Jr., in command, Appomattox campaign.

No. 96—(1172) Same assignment, January 31, 1865. (1181) Same assignment, commanded by Capt. Benjamin F. K. Melton. (1270) Same assignment, February 28, 1865.

THE FOURTH ALABAMA INFANTRY.

The Fourth Alabama regiment, commanded by Col, Egbert I. Jones, was organized at Dalton, Ga., May, 1861, and immediately proceeded to Virginia. It fought with great distinction at Manassas, Seven Pines, Cold Harbor, Second Manassas, Boonesboro, Sharpsburg, Gettysburg, Chickamauga, The Wilderness, Spottsylvania, battles around Richmond and Petersburg. When General Lee surrendered at Appomattox, the regiment numbered but 202 men.

Among the many officers who were killed in these battles were Col. Egbert I. Jones and Captain Lindsay, both of whom fell at Manassas; Capt. G. B. Martin at Seven Pines; William Lee at Malvern Hill; Lieut. C. C. Ferris at Second Manassas; Capt. J. Sullivan at Sharpsburg; Colonel McLemore at Boonesboro; Capt. J. Keith at Fredericksburg; Capt. W. W. Leftwich at Gettysburg; Major Coleman at Chickamauga; Captain Kidd at Chickamauga; Capt. Bayless C. Brown at The Wilderness; Capt. H. Armistead at Gaines' Mill; Capt. Alfred C. Price at Gaines' Mill, and Capt. A. Murray at Petersburg.

EXTRACTS FROM OFFICIAL WAR RECORDS.

Vol. I—(470) Referred to in letter from S. A. M. Wood, Pensacola, August 8, 1861, to L. P. Walker, secretary of war.

Vol. II—(470) Assigned to General Bee's brigade, Gen. Joseph E. Johnston's division, army of the Shenandoah, June 30, 1861. (473,474) Mentioned in General Johnston's report of the operations of the army of Shenandoah and Potomac, May 23d-July 22d. (487-495) Several mentions in General Beauregard's report of same operations. He says: "The Fourth Alabama also suffered severely from the deadly fire of the thousands of muskets which they so dauntlessly confronted under the immediate leadership of Bee himself. Its brave colonel (E. J. Jones) was dangerously wounded and many gallant officers fell, slain or hors de combat. . . It was now that General Johnston impressively and gallantly charged to the front with the colors of the Fourth Alabama by his side, all the field officers of the regiment having been previously disabled. The brave Bee was mortally wounded at the head of the Fourth Alabama." (569) In the list of troops engaged in the battle of Manassas, sent in by Col. Thomas Rhett. (570) 40 men killed and 157 wounded at Manassas. (836) Fourth Alabama sent to Stonewall Jackson, Richmond, May 12, 1861. [Letter of General Lee, May 12, 1861.] (861) At Harper's Ferry, May 21, 1861.

Vol. V—(648) Mentioned by Col. George D. Wills, First Massachusetts. (1030) In Potomac district, General Beauregard, Whiting's brigade, January, 1862.

Vol. IX—(379) General McClellan, U. S. A., informs General Burnside that troops are moving from Richmond to North Carolina, March 25, 1862.

Vol. XI, Part 1 — (994) Mentioned in General Smith's report of battle of Seven Pines. (1076) Capt. G. B. Mastin killed at battle of Seven Pines.

Vol. XI, Part 2—(483) In Whiting's division, Jackson's corps, brigade commanded by its colonel, E. M. Law. (503) 25 killed and 113 wounded in fights before Richmond, June 26-July 1, 1862. (563-567) Highly commended in Gen. W. H. C. Whiting's report of battle around Richmond. General Whiting says: "Lieut.-Col. O. K. McLemore, Fourth Alabama, received a painful wound early in action, the command devolving on Capt. L. H. Scruggs, who conducted the regiment through." Casualties: 22 killed, 108 wounded at Gaines' Mill, and 2 killed, 13 wounded at Malvern Hill. (985) Capts. H. Armistead killed June 27th, and Alfred C. Price died of wounds received June 27th.

Vol. XI, Part 3—(114) Mentioned in report of Gen. Geo. B. McClellan, near Yorktown, April 20, 1862. (483) In Whiting's brigade, Johnston's army, April 30th, 459 strong. (531,652) Same assignment. (654) Mentioned in letter of General Lee to President Davis, July 25, 1862.

Vol. XII, Part 2—(547) In General Whiting's brigade, Hood's division, Northern Virginia, during battles of August 28-September 1, 1862. (560) 18 killed, 45 wounded, Manassas Plains, August, 1862. (567) General Longstreet's report of operations commends "Col. E. M. Law at Manassas Plains on August 29th and 30th, Boonsboro, and at Sharpsburg on the 16th and 17th.... It is with no common feeling that I recount the loss at Manassas Plains of ... Lieut.-Col. O. K. McLemore, Fourth Alabama." (604-606) Mentioned in General Hood's report of operations, including Freeman's Ford, Groveton and Manassas. (623-625) Report of same operations by Col. E. M. Law commanding Whiting's brigade. Mentions Colonel McLemore and highly commends Private Smith, and gives 19 killed, 44 wounded. (816) Lieut D. C. Farris killed August 29th.

Vol. XVIII—(782) Mentioned in letter from General Whiting to Major-General Smith.

Vol. XIX, Part 1—(805, 811) Law's brigade, Hood's division, Lee's army, Maryland campaign. Medical Director Lafayette Guild, in his report of casualties, gives 7 killed, 37 wounded, in operations from August 16th to September 2d. (922-924) Report of General Hood, of Maryland campaign, gives Fourth Alabama in engagements of Freeman's Ford, Rappahannock River, August 22d; Plains of Manassas, August 29th and 30th; Boonsboro Gap, Md., September 14th, and Sharpsburg, September 16th and 17th. At Boonsboro fell mortally wounded Lieut-Col. O. K. McLemore, a most efficient, gallant and valuable officer. Capt. L. H. Scruggs received several wounds. Colonel Law was conspicuous, commanding brigade. (937, 938) Report of Colonel Law, commanding brigade, of battle of Sharpsburg, says: "The Fourth Alabama pushed into the wood in which the skirmish had taken place the evening previous and drove the enemy through and beyond it ...

Captain Scruggs commanding the Fourth Alabama received wounds while discharging his duty."

Vol. XIX, Part 2—(719) Inspection report of Gen. R. H. Chilton, November 14, 1862: "Fourth Alabama, Col. P. D. Bowles: Arms mixed, in tolerable order, 12 wanting; 50 men needing clothes and shoes; 2 barefooted; camp in tolerable order."

Vol. XXI—(540, 559) In Law's brigade, Hood's division, army of Northern Virginia, General Longstreet, December, 1862. Medical director reports 3 killed and 16 wounded, battle of Fredericksburg, December 11 to 15, 1862. (622, 623) Report of General Hood of same battle mentions the Fourth Alabama, and gives casualties, 5 killed and 18 wounded. (624) General Law's report of the same says: "It is with deep sorrow that I report the death of Private U. S. Smith of the Fourth Alabama regiment, an acting officer on my staff. Alabama never bore a braver son, and our country's cause has never received the sacrifice of a manlier spirit. He fell where the hour of danger always found him—at his post." He gives casualties 4 killed, 18 wounded. (1071) Assignment as above.

No. 44—(284, 330, 339) In Law's brigade, Hood's division, army of Northern Virginia, Lieut.-Col. L. H. Scruggs in command of regiment, July, 1862. Return of casualties at battle of Gettysburg, July 1, 2 and 3, 1863, 17 killed and 49 wounded. (362) Mentioned in report of Gen. James Longstreet, Gettysburg campaign. Says General Law was severely wounded. (391, 392) Report of Lieut.-Col. L. H. Scruggs, Gettysburg campaign, says: "Both officers and men behaved with great gallantry, and many brave and good soldiers fell. Total of casualties, 87." (418,419) Report of Gen. Henry L. Benning, Gettysburg campaign, speaks well of the Fourth and their assistance in foiling the plans of the enemy.

No. 45—(920, 1059) Assignment as above. Col. P. D. Bowles commanding regiment.

No. 49—(683) and No. 50—(231) Same assignment.

No. 51—(18, 395) Assigned as above, Chickamauga campaign. Mentioned in report of Col. R. C. Tyler.

No. 54—(223, 225, 227) General Law's brigade, Hood's division, Lieut.-Col. L, H. Scruggs in command of regiment. Mentioned in report of Gen. E. M. Law, Lookout valley, Novembers, 1863: "With the assistance of the Fourth Alabama, which had cleared its front of the enemy, the line was re-established, and the enemy driven from it." (229, 230) Gen. J. L. Sheffield, commanding Law's brigade at engagement near Lookout creek, speaks several times especially of the Fourth; he says that Lieutenant-Colonel Scruggs, commanding the Fourth, co-operating with the Forty-fourth under Colonel Perry, drove the enemy from and beyond the breastworks; he returned but was again driven back. Reports 1 killed. (452) Assignment as above. Colonel Bowles in command of regiment, November 30th.

No. 55 — (658) Detached with Longstreet's corps, November 4th, for operations in East Tennessee.

No. 56—(573) Lieutenant Manston informs Major Buford, October 21, 1863, that he has some men of the Fourth on duty who are of great service on account of their knowledge of the country. (615, 890) Refers to organization.

No. 58—(641) Assignment, January 31, 1864, as above.

No. 59 — (722) Law's brigade, Buckner's division, department East Tennessee, March 31, 1864.

No. 60—(339, 349, 350) Mentioned by General Merritt and A. A. Humphreys, U. S. A., Culpeper, Va., January, 1864.

No. 67—(1022, 1060) General Law's brigade, Field's division, Lee's army, May, 1864. Twenty-two killed and 62 wounded, May 4th to 6th.

No. 80—(763) Three killed, 6 wounded, June 13 to July 31, 1864, Richmond campaign.

No. 82—(592) Mentioned by John C. Babcock, U. S. A.

No. 87—(877) Seven killed and 29 wounded, August 1st to December 31st.

No. 88—(34, 36, 159, 1215) Mentioned by Gen. B. F. Butler, Gen. R. S. Foster and in "list of rebel forces on north side of James River."

No. 89—(1188) Assignment as above, October 31, 1864, Colonel Bowles in command. (1238) November 30th, Capt. A. D. McInnis in command. (1364) December 31st, Colonel Bowles in command.

No. 95—(1268) Law's brigade, Field's division, Appomattox campaign, Lieutenant-Colonel Scruggs in command of regiment. (1171) January 31,1865, Colonel Bowles in command. (1179) Inspection reports. (1269) February 28, 1865. Lieutenant-Colonel Scruggs in command.

THE FIFTH ALABAMA INFANTRY.

The Fifth Alabama regiment was organized at Montgomery, May 5, 1861. Its first duty was at Pensacola, Fla. In August it was ordered to report to the commanding officer of the army of Northern Virginia.

Its first colonel was the renowned Robert E. Rodes, who was promoted to brigadier-general, October 21, 1861, and to the rank of major-general, May 2, 1863. He was distinguished in all the battles of Northern Virginia and was wounded and disabled at Seven Pines, but recovered sufficiently to resume command of the brigade at the battles of Boonsboro and Sharpsburg. He was then placed in command of a division, which he led in its brilliant charge on Hooker's line at Chancellorsville, and it was for his gallantry in this battle that he received the commission of major-general.

He was greatly distinguished at Gettysburg, The Wilderness, Spottsylvania, the second battle of Cold Harbor, Castleman's Ferry, Kernstown and Winchester. In the latter battle, while triumphantly leading his division, he received a mortal wound, lamented by his commanders and the entire army of Northern Virginia, toward whose great victories he had largely contributed. Generals Lee and Stonewall Jackson spoke of him in terms of highest commendation, and at Gettysburg his gallantry and skillful conduct elicited from General Lee his admiration and special thanks.

The next commander of this regiment was Christopher C. Pegues, who, like General Rodes, also reached great distinction, and after winning the encomiums of his commander for his gallantry in many battles, was killed while leading his regiment in the bloody charge at Cold Harbor.

Allen T. Jones, Lafayette Hobson and Josephus M. Hall afterward succeeded in command of this regiment.

John T. Morgan, afterward a brigadier-general, was at one time its lieutenant-colonel, and Eugene Blackford its major. Its first severe engagement was at Seven Pines, May 31 and June 1, 1862, where it lost 27 killed and 128 wounded. It also earned a well-merited meed of honor at Gaines' Mill and Cold Harbor,. June 27th and 28th; Malvern Hill, July 1st to 5th; Second Manassas, August 30th; Boonsboro, September 15th; Sharpsburg, September 17, 1862; Chancellorsville, May 1 and 4, 1863; Gettysburg, July 1 to 3, 1863; the Wilderness, May 5, 6 and 7, 1864; Spottsylvania, May 8 to 18, 1864; Second Cold Harbor, June 1 to 12, 1864; advance upon Washington, July, 1864; battle of Winchester, July 24, 1864, and the terrible conflict in the trenches around Petersburg, September, 1864, to April, 1865.

Among the other officers who were killed in battle were Capt. G. W. Johnson at Cold Harbor, Capt. William T. Renfro at Chancellorsville, Capt. N. R. E. Ferguson at the Wilderness, Capt. George Reed near Winchester, Capt. J. N. Gilchrist at Second Cold Harbor, Lieut. L. D. Wiley at Seven Pines, Lieutenant Ramsey at Gaines' Mill, and Lieut. Albert J. Wilcox at Gettysburg.

EXTRACTS FROM OFFICIAL WAR RECORDS.

Vol. II—(309, 423, 433) Mention by Col. O. B. Wilcox (Union), by Col. D. S. Miles, U. S. A., Centreville, Va., by Colonel Marsh (Union) as near Fairfax Court House. (440-446) Mentioned in report of Gen. G. T. Beauregard, Manassas: "With its excellent officer, Colonel Rodes, it made a resolute protracted defense against heavy odds. On the morning of the 17th, when the enemy appeared before that position, they were checked and held at bay with some confessed loss in a skirmish in advance of the works in which Major Morgan and Captain Shelley, Fifth Alabama regiment volunteers, acted with intelligent gallantry, and the post was only abandoned under general, but specific, imperative orders, in conformity with a long-conceived, established plan of action and battle." (447) Beauregard's special orders regarding position of regiment, July 8, 1861. (459-461) Colonel Rodes' report of the affair of Fairfax Court House, Va., says: "Captain Shelley's company having been sent out skirmishing, on the morning of the 17th, they were returning to camp for provisions, having been sent off in such a hurry as to prevent their making preparations for breakfast, and had gotten within three-quarters of a mile of camp before the approach of the enemy was announced to them by one of my couriers coming in with a prisoner who had been taken by a sentinel (Private Wethered of Company H). The outpost and guard fell back, fighting not very severely, but killing several of the enemy. One of the guard (Kennedy of Company H) killed 2, having taken two deliberate musket-shots from the same spot at 4 of the Federalists, all of whom fired at him. Shelley's company having advanced again to sustain the guards, had a sharp skirmish with them. The result of the skirmish may be summed up thus: On our side 2 men wounded slightly, one in leg, the other in the ear; on the side of the enemy, 1 prisoner and at least 20 killed and wounded." (537) Mentioned in General Ewell's report. (944) General Beauregard assigns regiment to Second brigade, June 20th. (1000) Same assignment, July 25, 1861.

Vol. V—(737) Mentioned as being near mouth of Bull Run, by E. J. Allen (Allen Pinkerton), January 27, 1862. (825) Ewell's brigade, Beauregard's corps, August, 1861. (1029) Rodes' brigade, Beauregard's "Potomac District," January 14, 1862.

Vol. XI, Part 1—(621) Mentioned in report of Capt. Wm. Hexauer, of action at West Point landing, May 7, 1862. (971-976) Mentioned in report of Gen. R. E. Rodes of battle of Seven Pines or "Fair Oaks," several times. Calls special attention to gallantry and coolness, among others, of Col. C. C. Pegues and Maj. E. L. Hobson; also reports 29 killed and 181 wounded. (977, 978) Report of Col. C. C. Pegues, same battle, speaks very highly of conduct of Major Hobson and Lieut. R. Inge Smith, acting adjutant. He reports 229 killed and wounded. (1076) Lieut. L. D. Wiley among killed.

Vol. XI, Part 2—(484) Rodes' brigade, Hill's division, Jackson's corps; Seven Days' battles around Richmond. (405) Casualties, 43 killed and 131 wounded, June 26 to July 1, 1862. (621) Mentioned in report of Col. Bradley Johnson, Maryland line. (625) Report of Gen. D. H. Hill speaks very highly of this regiment and its officers. He says: "Col. C. C. Pegues, the noble Christian commander of the Fifth Alabama, fell mortally wounded in this charge." (630-633) General Rodes' report of battle of Gaines' Mill, June 27th, says: "Lieutenant Ramsey and a private of the Fifth Alabama killed; all the regiment and regimental officers acted handsomely, but the Fifth and Twenty-sixth were especially distinguished for their courage. No troops ever acted better. Col. C. C. Pegues was wounded desperately and has since died. Upon falling he called to the next officer in command, Maj. E. L. Hobson, and told him that the Fifth had always been in the advance, and it was his last wish that he would let no other pass it. Major Hobson gallantly carried out his wishes, and led the regiment constantly ahead of all others in the division except the Twenty-sixth Alabama, which, under its brave Colonel O'Neal, kept steady with it." Reports loss of brigade as 31 killed and 114 wounded in engagements from June 27th to July 1st (of these, 21 killed and 45 wounded belonged to the Fifth Alabama). (633-635) Col. J. B. Gordon's report of same operations makes several mentions of regiment, also of gallant conduct of Major Hobson; gives casualties 26 killed, 66 wounded, and says "these figures are correct." (638) Mentioned in report of Col. B. B. Gayle. (975) Casualties at Gaines' Mill, 21 killed, 45 wounded. (976) Casualties at Malvern Hill, 26 killed, 66 wounded.

Vol. XI, Part 3—(482,532) Rodes' brigade, Early's division, about April 30, 1862, 660 strong. (601) Mentioned in order of Col. J. B. Gordon, June 15, 1862. (650) Assignment as above, July, 1862, Col. J. M. Hall in command.

Vol. XIX, Part 1—(808) Rodes' brigade, Lee's army, Maryland campaign, regiment commanded by Major Hobson. (1018-1030) Mentioned in Gen. D. H. Hill's report of Maryland campaign. Names particularly Major Hobson and Lieut. J. M. Goff. (1035-1038) General Rodes' report, battles of Boonsboro and Sharpsburg, speaks in the highest terms of commendation. He says: "Under Major Hobson's gallant management, though flanked, wheeled against the flanking party and by desperate fighting silenced the enemy so far as to enable them to make their way to the peak before mentioned. The men generally did well, but Major Hobson of the Fifth Alabama deserves special mention for admirable conduct during the whole fight. Major Hobson and Lieut. J. M. Goff (the latter with a musket) bore distinguished parts in the fight."

Vol. XXI—(541-560) Rodes' brigade, Hill's division. Loss, 1 wounded; battle of Fredericksburg. (1073) Lieut.-Col. E. L. Hobson in command of regiment.

No. 39—(792) Rodes' brigade, Hill's division, Jackson's corps. (807) Report of medical director, battle of Chancellorsville, 24 killed and 130 wounded. (943-946) Gen. R. E. Rodes' report of same battle says: "The Fifth and Twenty-sixth Alabama, with some other regiments, carried the heights in magnificent style, planting their colors inside the works." Attention called to gallantry of Colonel Hall; Lieutenant-Colonel Hobson severely wounded; also mentions Gilliam James of Company D. (948) Casualties given at killed 24, wounded 133. Colonel Hall, Lieutenant-Colonel Hobson, Maj. Eugene Blackford "under fire." (949) Mentioned by General Rodes. (951-953) Colonel O'Neal, commanding Rodes' brigade, mentions Major Blackford; he also says: "Capt. W. T. Renfro, commanding right wing of the Fifth Alabama after Colonel Hobson had been wounded, brought in 225 prisoners. . . . Lieutenant-Colonel Hobson was wounded while gallantly rushing in front of his men. Captured in the midst of the enemy's guns and intrenchments and some time before any other troops reached that point, the loss of their flag is one of the highest evidences of the gallant and daring service rendered by the Fifth Alabama regiment in the action of that day." (953-955) Colonel Hall's (commanding brigade) report of battle commends Captain Renfro, who was severely wounded while gallantly leading the Fifth. "Justice demands that I should mention Lieut.-Col. J. S. Garvin, commanding the Twenty-sixth Alabama, and Capt. W. T. Renfro, commanding the Fifth Alabama, who were both severely, if not mortally, wounded while gallantly leading their regiments, and giving the highest evidence of that coolness and skill which should ever characterize a true soldier." (957,958) Report of Col. J. M. Hall (Fifth

Alabama), same battle, says: "Lieutenant-Colonel Hobson, whose daring courage led him always to the front, was severely wounded. Major Blackford being in command of the sharpshooters, the senior captain (W. T. Renfro) was placed in command of the regiment wing and the pursuit continued. Both officers and men acted well and vied with each other in doing their whole duty. I would, however, respectfully mention the gallant conduct of Capt. T. M. Riley, Company C; Adjt. C. J. Pegues, Sergt.-Maj. Alfred G. Ward; also Sergt. Adam Swicegood and Corp. A. M. Ballard, Company E, and Private James Arlington, Company D. All of these men acted with the most undaunted courage, coolness and skill." (958,959) Report of Capt. T. M. Riley: "Captain Renfro, while bravely leading the advance and calling on the men to follow, fell, mortally wounded. Being senior officer, I now assumed command of the regiment." (965,966) Mentioned in reports of Colonel Garvin and Lieut. M. J. Taylor. (1052,1053) Roll of honor of the Fifth regiment, battle of Chancellorsville: Capt. W. T. Renfro, Company B; Private John Summers, Company B; Private F. M. Burnett, Company C; Sergt. John H. Cowan, Company D; Private L. H. Thornton, Company E; Private W. P. Stokes, Company A; Corp. H. F. Martin, Company K; Private R. L. Franklin, Company H; Private H. J. Robertson, Company I; Corp. John O'Donohoe, Company F; Private N. S. Franklin, Company G.

No. 40—(456) Mentioned by Gen. H. W. Slocum, Chancellorsville.

No. 44—(287) O'Neal's brigade, Rodes' division; Colonel Hall in command of regiment. Gettysburg, July 1 to 4, 1863. (332, 336, 342) Returns of casualties after battle of Gettysburg give 21 killed, 109 wounded. Regimental report gives loss 209. (444) Mentioned by Gen. A. S. Pendleton. (545-561) General Rodes' report of Gettysburg campaign gives the part taken by regiment. Refers to Major Blackford in terms of high praise. (563) List of officers with their commands at battle of Gettysburg gives Colonel Hall, Major Blackford; list of officers killed or wounded, Lieut. A. J. Wilcox. (592-594) Mentioned in report of Col. E. A. O'Neal. (595-597) Report of Col. J. M. Hall says: "I would respectfully state that the general conduct of my command was all that I could desire. I would beg to mention the names of the following officers: Capt. T. M. Riley; Capts. E. B. Mosley and J. M. Gilchrist; Lieuts. Burton Goode and John A. Kirkland; E. P. Jones and J. F. Christian, Adjt. C. J. Pegues acted with conspicuous gallantry; Lieut. Albert J. Wilcox, a most gallant officer, was killed on the field." Entire loss Gettysburg, 21 killed, 121 wounded. (598) Report of Maj. Eugene Blackford says: "Though all acted so well, I would scarcely like to make a distinction, yet I must call your attention to the conduct of Sergt. Christopher Clark, commanding a company from the Fifth Alabama regiment. He handled his company with great skill and courage and would well fill a commission."

No. 45—(922, 1059) General Rodes' division, Second army corps, General Ewell, Colonel Hall in command of regiment.

No. 48—(399, 818, 838) Assignment as above, September and October, 1863. Thirty-one wounded in engagements at Payne's Farm and

Mine Run, November 26th to December 3d. (889, 890) Highly commended in report of Col. J. M. Hall

No. 49—(683, 900) Assignment as above, December 31, 1863.

No. 60—(1 149) Joint resolution of thanks from Congress to Battle's brigade, February 6, 1864. [See Extracts under Third regiment.]

No. 67—(1024) and No. 88—(1217) Assignment as above.

No. 89 — (1194) Battle's brigade, Lieutenant-Colonel Hobson in command; Rodes' (late) division; regiment commanded by Capt. Thomas M. Riley, October 31, 1864. (1246) Colonel Hall commanding regiment, November 30, 1864. (1364) Colonel Hobson commanding regiment, December 31, 1864.

No. 90—(564) Battle's brigade, Ramseur's division, Colonel Hobson leading brigade after General Battle was wounded, battle of Cedar Creek, Va., October 19, 1864. (1002, 1013) Battle's brigade, Rodes' division, army of the Valley district, Colonel Hall in command of regiment, August 31st.

No. 95—(1270) Battle's brigade, Grimes' (late Rodes') division, Second army corps; Colonel Hobson and Capt. T. M. Riley. Appomattox campaign.

No. 96—(670, 1172, 1181, 1270) Assignment as above. Captain Riley in command, January 31, 1865.

THE SIXTH ALABAMA INFANTRY.

The Sixth Alabama infantry was organized at Montgomery, May, 1861. Its first colonel was John J. Seibels, who had commanded a battalion in the Mexican war. Its first service was at Corinth. It was soon ordered to Virginia, and during the winter of 1862 was stationed far in front of the army, at Manassas Junction. Its first serious battle was at Seven Pines, May 31 to June 1, 1862, where the regiment was greatly distinguished, losing 102 officers and men killed and wounded, including Lieut.-Col. James J. Willingham, Maj. S. Perry Nesmith, and Capts. Thomas Bell, Matthew Fox, W. C. Hunt, Augustus S. Flournoy and John B. McCarty.

The Sixth served in nearly all the battles of the army of Northern Virginia, including Mechanicsville, June 26, 1862; Cold Harbor or Gaines' Mill, June 27th and 28th; Malvern Hill, July 1st to 5th; Boonsboro, September 15th; Sharpsburg, September 17th; Fredericksburg, December 13th; Chancellorsville, May 1-4, 1863; The Wilderness, May 5, 6 and 7, 1864; Spottsylvania, May 8th to 18th; Winchester, July 24th, and all the numerous battles and conflicts around Petersburg, September, 1864, to April, 1865.

Lieut. -Col. Augustus M. Gordon was killed at Chancellorsville; Adjt. J. Whitt Thomas at Spottsylvania; Adjt. Edgar Watson at Farmville. Capt. W. C. Hunt, wounded at Seven Pines, was killed while gallantly leading his men at Cedar Creek. Capts. Matt. Fox, Thos. H. Bell and Augustus S. Flournoy were killed at Seven Pines, and Capt. Thomas Lightfoot at

Winchester. Among the other distinguished officers of the regiment were Lieut.-Col. James M. Lightfoot, Lieut.-Col. B. H. Baker, Lieut.-Col. George W. Hooker, Maj. Walker H. Weems and Maj. Isaac F. Culver. But probably the most distinguished officer was John B. Gordon, who entered the regiment as a captain, passed rapidly through the grades of lieutenant-colonel and colonel, was appointed brigadier-general May 7, 1863, and major-general May 14, 1864. At the close of the war in 1865 he was in command of an army corps in Northern Virginia.

EXTRACTS FROM OFFICIAL WAR RECORDS.

Vol. II—(440, 469) With Ewell's brigade occupying position in vicinity of the Union Mills ford, August, 1861. Beauregard's report, engagements from July 16 to 21, 1861. (537) General Ewell in his report of Manassas mentions Seibels' Sixth Alabama. (944, 1000) Assignment as above, general orders No. 20, June 20th, and No. 169, July 35th.

Vol. V—(737) Mentioned in letter of E. J. Allen, January 27, 1862. (825) Assignment as above, August 31, 1861. (1029) In Rodes' brigade, General Beauregard's district, January 14, 1862.

Vol. XI, Part 1—(971-976) Gen. R. E. Rodes' report of battle of Fair Oaks or Seven Pines, May 31 to June 1, 1862, says: Wound in his arm so painful that he was compelled to turn over command of brigade to Colonel Gordon, of the Sixth Alabama. " The regiment," he says, "lost more than half its force." Ninety-one killed and 277 wounded. "Lieutenant-Colonel Willingham and Major Nesmith, of the Sixth Alabama, and Capt. C. C. Otey, of the heavy artillery, who had been conspicuous for their gallantry and efficiency, fell while pushing forward with their men into the thickest of the fight. Among the living whose gallantry and coolness entitle them to distinction, I beg to mention Col. J. B. Gordon." Also speaks of Captains Fox and Bell of the Sixth as distinguished. "The Sixth Alabama lost nearly 60 per cent, of its aggregate force. The right company was engaged at such close quarters with the enemy that its brave commander, Captain Bell, after having fallen mortally wounded, was able to use his revolver with effect upon the enemy. The loss of his company was 21 killed and 23 wounded, out of a total of 50." (979, 980) Report of Col. James B. Gordon, commanding brigade, battle of Seven Pines: "Captain Fox, no less brave than accomplished, was killed." Colonel Gordon praises his regiment in the most unqualified terms for their unswerving and dauntless heroism in the face of the enemy. . . . "In this charge my fearless and efficient field officers, Lieutenant-Colonel Willingham and Major Nesmith, fell, nobly doing their whole duty. To me their loss at this trying hour was great indeed—to the regiment it is almost irreparable. . . . Company A, under command of Capt. Thomas H. Bell, than whom a more gallant officer never gave his life for love of country. In a sheet of fire, and within a few rods of overwhelming numbers, this company stood until the last officer and non-commissioned officer, except one corporal and 44 men of the 56 carried into action had fallen. Yet when General Rodes gave the order for his regiment to fall back, the few survivors were loading and firing all undaunted amid their fallen comrades. In my judgment history does not record an instance of greater courage and more steadiness of nerve than was exhibited by this entire regiment. ... Of Captains Flournoy and McCarty, and each man that fell, I can say he died at his post."

Vol. XI, Part 2—(484) Rodes' brigade, Jackson's corps, engagements around Richmond. (507, 975, 976) Casualties, 3 killed and 13 wounded, June 27, 1862, and 8 killed and 39 wounded, July 1st. (625) Mentioned in report of Gen. D. H. Hill. (630-633) Report of Gen. R. E. Rodes, battle of Gaines' Mill: "I was compelled (from a wound) to turn over the command of brigade to Colonel Gordon of the Sixth Alabama. I desire to call especial attention to the conduct of the above-mentioned officer; it was distinguished for all a soldier can admire." (635, 637) Report of Col. J. B. Gordon, battle of Gaines' Mill.

Vol. XI, Part 3—(426, 445) Gen. A. J. Dickinson mentions the Sixth. (482) Johnston's army, 1,100 strong, April 30, 1862. (532) Rodes' brigade, Johnston's army, near Richmond, May 21st. (601) Mentioned in circular of Col. J. B. Gordon, June 15th. (650) Assignment as above, army of Northern Virginia, July 23d, Colonel Gordon in command of regiment.

Vol. XIX, Part 1—(272) Report of Gen. T. Seymour, U. S. A., battle South Mountain, September 14, 1862. (808) Assignment as above during the Maryland campaign. (950) Mentioned in report of Captain Durham, Twenty-third South Carolina, Boonsboro and Sharpsburg. (1023-1028) General Hill, in his report of operations from June 23d to September 17th says: " Colonel Gordon, the Christian hero, excelled his former deeds at Seven Pines in the battles around Richmond. Our language is not capable of expressing higher commendation. [Sharpsburg] Col. J. B. Gordon, the Chevalier Bayard of the army. Lieutenant-Colonel Lightfoot of the Sixth was wounded at Sharpsburg." General Hill also speaks in high terms of Lieut. P. H. Larey and Sergt. J. B. Hancock, of the Sixth. (1034-1038) Report of Gen. R. E. Rodes, battles of Boonsboro and Sharpsburg, says: " The men generally did well, but Colonel Gordon, Sixth Alabama, deserves special mention for admirable conduct during the whole fight." He gives great praise to this regiment throughout his report.

Vol. XXI—(541, 1073) Rodes' brigade, Second corps, General Jackson, army of Northern Virginia, December, 1862. (560) Report of medical director, 1 killed and 7 wounded, Fredericksburg.

No. 39—(792) Colonel Lightfoot in command of regiment, April, 1863. (807) Medical director reports 24 killed and 125 wounded at the battle of Chancellorsville. (943-939-940) Report of Gen. R. E. Rodes of battle of Chancellorsville: "The fighting on the center and left was of a most desperate character, and resulted in the loss of many valuable officers; among them and most to be regretted was Maj. A. M. Gordon, of the Sixth Alabama (May 3d), a young officer of great promise and purity of character." (948) Casualties reported. (949) General Rodes says that the regiment captured a battery flag at Chancellorsville. (951) Captured 105 prisoners, May 2d. (952, 954, 955) Mentioned in General O'Neal's report, and Colonel Hall's (commanding brigade). (959, 960) Lieutenant-Colonel Lightfoot's report says: "In a word, my officers and men all acted exceedingly gallantly; 22 killed and 135 wounded. Maj. A. M. Gordon killed at the head of his regiment; his vacancy cannot be filled in the regiment." (976, 986) Mentioned by Gen. H. Colquitt and Gen. Alfred Iverson. (1053) Roll of honor: Private Matthew Benton, Company A; Private W. H. Digby, Company C; Sergt. E. O. Baker, Company E; Private H. L. Jones, Company G; Private James W. Evans, Company I; Sergt. H. W. Hale, Company L; Sergt. J. C. Gamble, Company B; Private H. H. Moore, Company D; Corp. G. P. Jones, Company F; Sergt. D. Madigan, Company H; Private H. I. Price, Company K; Private D. W. Moorer, Company M.

No. 44—(287) Second corps, Gen. R. S. Ewell; regimental commanders, Colonel Lightfoot and Capt. M. L. Bowie, July, 1863. (322, 342) Casualties at Gettysburg, 18 killed and 113 wounded. (336) 2 wounded in skirmishes en route from Pennsylvania. (545-553) Mentioned in report of Gen. R. E. Rodes. (563) Colonel Lightfoot and Maj. J. F. Culver wounded, July 1st. (592, 693) Report of Col. E. A. O'Neal. (599-600) Report of Capt. M. L. Bowie, from June 2d to July 3d, says: "The conduct of the men of the regiment was highly commendable, entitling them to the confidence of their commanding officers, and reflecting credit upon the name and character of the Sixth Alabama regiment;" 350 carried into battle; loss 162.

No. 48—(399) Assignment as above, September 30, 1863. (412) 1 killed and 1 wounded in Bristoe campaign, October 10th to 21st. (818) Battle's brigade, Second army corps, Colonel Lightfoot in command of regiment, October 31st. (890-891) Report of Maj. Isaac F. Culver; operations along Mine Run, November 27th to December 3d.

No. (60—(1149) Joint resolution of thanks from Congress to Battle's brigade, February 6, 1864. [See Extracts under Third regiment.]

No. 67—(545, 553, 561, 567) Mentioned in reports of General Warren, Col. Wm. S. Tilton and Maj. Mason W. Burt, U. S. A. (1024) Assignment as above, May, 1864. (1083) Mentioned in report of Gen. C. A. Battle, operations May 8, 1864. (1093) Report of Gen. N. H. Harris, operations May 12th and 13th, says: "The adjutant of the Sixth Alabama, with a few noble men, joined me and did heroic service. I asked his name on the field but do not remember it. A braver or more daring officer I never saw, and, I regret to say, sealed his devotion with his life blood."

No. 89—(1194) Battle's brigade, army Valley district, October 31, 1864, Capt. R. M. Greene in command of regiment, (1 246) Assignment as above, Colonel Lightfoot in command, November 30th. (1364) Battle's brigade, Second army corps, Captain Greene in command, December 31, 1864.

No. 90—(564) Battle's brigade, Ramseur's division, at battle of Cedar Creek, October 19, 1864. (1002, 1013) Rodes' division, Early's army, August 31st.

No. 95—(1270) Assignment as above, Appomattox campaign, Maj. J. F. Culver commanding regiment.

No. 96—(889) Mentioned by Gen. G. K. Warren, March 8, 1865. (1172, 1181, 1270) Assignment as above.

THE SEVENTH ALABAMA INFANTRY.

The Seventh Alabama infantry regiment was organized at Pensacola, in June, 1861, its field officers being: Sterling A. M. Wood, colonel; John G. Coltart, lieutenant-colonel; Alfred A. Russell, afterward distinguished as colonel of the Fourth Alabama cavalry, major. The regiment was engaged at the bombardment of Pensacola, October 9, 1861, and immediately afterward was ordered to East Tennessee. It enlisted for one year, and its time expired a short period prior to the battle of Shiloh. Colonel Wood had been made brigadier-general; Coltart, its lieutenant-colonel, had become colonel of the Twenty-sixth regiment (afterward denominated the Fiftieth), and Russell, the major, became colonel of the Fourth Alabama cavalry.

Two of the companies of the Seventh, commanded by Jesse J. Cox and T. G. Jenkins, were cavalry. They retained their organization, fought at the battle of Shiloh and afterward formed part of the Fifty-third cavalry. The other officers and men, with rare exceptions, joined other commands, or raised and organized other troops, of which they were made officers.

EXTRACTS FROM OFFICIAL WAR RECORDS.

Vol. I—(469, 470) "Seventh regiment near Pensacola," August 8, 1861. Letter of Col. S. A. M. Wood.

Vol. IV—(247, 248) "Regiment under command of Lieutenant-Colonel Coltart." Letter of Colonel Wood, November 17, 1861, at Chattanooga.

Vol. VI—(460) Three companies of Seventh were assigned to the Second battalion, commanded by Col. J. Patton Anderson, Pensacola, October 23, 1861. (777, 779) Referred to by General Bragg as having been transferred to East Tennessee, December 10, 1861.

Vol. VII—(689) Letter of Colonel Wood, Chattanooga, November 21, 1861. (713) Mentioned by Col. D. Leadbetter. (751) Mentioned by Gen. W. H. Carroll, Knoxville, December 9th. (762) Gen. A. S. Johnston writes he has ordered the Seventh from Chattanooga to Bowling Green, December 13th. (852) In Third brigade, General Wood; First division, army of Kentucky, General Hardee; January 31, 1862. (904) Colonel Coltart in command of regiment, February 23d.

Vol. X—(383) In Wood's brigade, Third corps, army of the Mississippi, April 6-7, 1862.

Vol. XVI, Part 1—(960) Mentioned in Col. John T. Wilder's (Seventeenth Indiana infantry) report, siege of Munfordville, Ky., September 14-17, 1862.

THE EIGHTH ALABAMA INFANTRY.

The Eighth Alabama infantry regiment deserves special mention. It was the first Confederate regiment to be enlisted for the war. Its first service was at Yorktown. It fought in the battle of Williamsburg, May 5th, and at Fair Oaks, May 31 and June 1, 1862, in both of which engagements it took an important part and its losses were very severe. It was then transferred to the brigade of Gen. Cadmus M. Wilcox and was greatly distinguished at Mechanicsville, June 26th. Two days later it was prominent in the assault upon the enemy at Gaines' Mill and on June 30th was again in the midst of the conflict at Frayser's Farm. It was present, though not severely engaged, at Manassas and Harper's Ferry, and was in the thickest of the fight at Antietam, September 17th. It fought with its usual bravery at Gettysburg, July 2, 1863; the Wilderness, Mays, 6, and 7, 1864; Spottsylvania, May 8th to 18th; Salem Church, Cold Harbor, June 1 to 12, 1864. It formed a portion of the troops engaged at the Weldon railroad, June 22 and 23, 1864; was distinguished at the capture of the Crater, July 30th, and was also warmly engaged in the battle on the plank road below Petersburg.

Upon its organization, its colonel was John A. Winston, who was succeeded by Young L. Royston, and he by Hilary A. Herbert, who commanded in many hard-fought battles, being severely wounded at Sharpsburg and the Wilderness. Colonel Herbert has since achieved eminence at the bar of Alabama and in legislative halls, having served 16 years in the Congress of the United States, and as secretary of the navy under Cleveland's second administration. Other field officers were Lieutenant-Colonel Frazier, Thomas E. Irby, killed at the Wilderness, John P. Emrich, wounded at Petersburg and at Gaines' Mill, and Duke Nail, who was mortally wounded at the Wilderness.

This regiment was fortunate in that its roll of honor found in the War Records is more complete than that of any other of the Alabama troops; and in the extracts below are the names of those conspicuous for bravery and courage, many of whom are still living, though the roll of immortal heroes is a long one. Capts. L. F. Summers and P. Loughry, and Lieut. Joshua Kennedy were killed at Seven Pines; Capt. Thomas Phelan, Lieuts. C. M. Maynard, Lane, Augustus Jansen, at Gaines' Mill and Frayser's Farm, and Capt. R. A. McCrary at Chancellorsville. Lieut. John D. McLaughlin died of wounds received in the battles before Richmond.

EXTRACTS FROM THE OFFICIAL RECORDS.

Vol. IV—(668,669) In general orders, No. 89, Octobers, 1861, assigned to Fifth brigade, army of the Peninsula, Colonel Winston commanding post at Yorktown.

Vol. IX—(37) Assigned to Second division, Gen. Lafayette McLaws commanding; General Magruder's department, January 31, 1862.

Vol. XI, Part 1—(267) E. J. Allen, March 29, 1862, reports "Eighth Alabama, 1,000 strong." (586) Mentioned in Gen. George E. Pickett's report of battle of Williamsburg, Va., May 5, 1862. (588,589) Roger A. Pryor's report of battle of Williamsburg, says: "The gallant and lamented Col. Thomas E. Irby, with 4 companies of the Eighth Alabama, reported to me for duty." (822) Mentioned in Gen. Daniel E. Sickles' report of battle of Seven Pines. (987,988) Mentioned in Gen. C. M. Wilcox's report of same battle. (1076) Capts. Leonard F. Summers and P. Loughry, and Lieut. Joshua Kennedy killed at Seven Pines.

Vol. XI, Part 2—(486, 503, 508) Wilcox's brigade, Longstreet's division, Jackson's corps, engagements around Richmond. Loss, 51 killed and 181 wounded. (508) June 30th, 1 reported killed. (771-775) Mentioned in Gen. C. M. Wilcox's report of Gaines' Mill and Frayser's Farm. Capt. Thomas Phelan, Lieuts. C. M. Maynard, W. H. Lane and Augustus Jansen, killed. Captain Hannon, Lieuts. M. Hugh and McGrath, severely wounded. (775) General Wilcox's report of battle of June 29th. Lieutenant-Colonel Royston sustained a severe wound. Surgeon Royston commended. (776-779) General Wilcox's report of battle of June 30th. (980) 31 killed, 132 wounded (10 mortally), battle of Gaines' Mill; 16 killed, 57 wounded at Glendale. (985) Lieut. John D. McLaughlin died of wounds received June 30th. (993) Roll of honor, battle of Williamsburg: Private William H. Duke*, Company A; Private J. R. Philips, Company C; Corp. William H. Powell*, Company D; Private James Ganavan, Company I. No selections from other companies. Battle of Seven Pines: Sergt. Frank Williams*, Company A; Private W. A. Hall, Company B; Private J. B. Tallen, Company C; Corp. Eli Shortridge*, Company D; Private John H. Deaton, Company E; Private Geo. W. Lee, Company F; Private Charles Hippler, Jr. *, Company G; Private John Caney, Company I; Private J. D. Garrison*, Company K. Battle of Gaines' Mill: Corp. Samuel L. Cochran*, Company A; Private R. T. Bush, Company B; Private John G. Shields, Company C; Private W. E. Donoho*, Company D; Sergt. J. B. Milner, Company F; Third Sergt. C. F. Walker, Company G; Sergt. W. H. McGraw*, Company H; Private Hugh McKewn, Company I; Private John W. Griffin, Company K. Battle of Frayser's Farm: Sergt. Joseph Jackson*, Company A; Corp. H. M. Howard, Company B; Private Robert Geddes, Company C; Private J. P. Wheelan, Company D; Fourth Sergt. G. Schwartz, Company G; Private J. Smith, Company G; Private John Lynch, Company I.

* Killed in action.

Vol. XI, Part 3—(390) Mentioned in General Magruder's report. (482) Col. J. A. Winston, commanding Pryor's brigade, 800 strong. Gen. Joseph E. Johnston's army on the peninsula about April 30, 1862. (532) Assignment as above, May 21st. (649) Wilcox's brigade, Longstreet's division, army of Northern Virginia, July 23d.

Vol. XII, .Part 2—(547) Assignment as above, August, 1862. (815) Roll of honor, second battle of Manassas: Corp. R. Murphy, Company A; Private James Jennings, Company I.

Vol. XIX, Part 1—(804) In Wilcox's brigade, commanded by Col. Alfred Cumming, army of Northern Virginia, Maryland campaign. (812) 12 killed and 63 wounded, Maryland campaign. (1056) Roll of honor, battle of Sharpsburg, September 17th: Corp. Davis Tucker, Company A; Private John Curry, Company C; Sergt. T. S. Ryan, Company E; Fifth Sergt. James Castello*, Company G; Private J. Herbert*, Company H; Private O. M. Harris*, Company K; Sergt. G. T. L. Robinson, Company B; Sergt. C. F. Brown, Company D; Corp. J. R. Searcy, Company F; Private James Ryan, Company I.

Vol. XXI—(539, 610, 1070) In Wilcox's brigade, First corps, 1 wounded at the battle of Fredericksburg.

No. 39—(790) Assignment as above, Col. Y. L. Royston; Lieut.-Col. H. A. Herbert, Chancellorsville campaign. (806, 854) Report of casualties, 7 killed, 45 wounded, at battle of Chancellorsville. Capt. Robert A. McCrary among the killed. (858-860) Gen. Wilcox's report of the battle of Chancellorsville: "I cannot call to your notice all officers that are deserving of special praise, for the conduct of all was excellent. Colonel Royston, Eighth Alabama, and after his severe wound, Lieutenant-Colonel Herbert, were intelligent, energetic and gallant in commanding, directing, and leading their men." He also speaks of the lamented Captain McCrary. (1056) Roll of honor, battle of Chancellorsville, May 1-4, 1863: Private Allen Boiling, Company A; Private J. N. Howard, Company B; Sergt. Robert Gaddes, Company C; Sergt. P. H. Mays, Company D; Sergt. T. A. Kelly, Company F; Private Patrick Leary, Company I; Private James Reynolds (killed), Company K.

No. 44—(288) In Wilcox's brigade, Anderson's division, Third corps, army of Northern Virginia, at the battle of Gettysburg, July 1st to 3d. (332, 343) Casualties, 22 killed, 139 wounded. (620, 621) Mentioned in Gen. C. M. Wilcox's report. (775) Roll of honor, battle of Gettysburg: Sergts. Edmund Clark, Company A; Robert Gaddes, Company C; L. L. McCurdy, Company D; James R. Strickland, Company E; C. P. Ragsdale (color-bearer), Company F; Privates Z. Haynes, Company B; C. G. Bush, Company G; J. Sprowl, Company H; Michael Duff, Company I; Michael Kane, Company I.

No. 45—(1061) Assignment as above, July 31, 1863, Col. Y. L. Royston commanding.

* Killed in action.

No. 48—(400, 412, 819) Assignment as above; casualties, 1 killed, 6 wounded, October 10-21, 1863.

No. 49—(685, 900) Assignment as above to December, 1863.

No. 60—(1145) Commended by Gen. R. E. Lee in general orders, No. 14, February 3, 1864.

No. 67—(1025) In Perrin's brigade, Third corps, army of Northern Virginia, May, 1864.

No. 80—(754) Sergt. John H. Deaton, Company E, captured colors of two Michigan regiments at Petersburg, Va., July 30th. (810) Roll of honor, battles near Petersburg: Sergt. John H. Deaton, Company E.

No. 89—(1190) In Sanders' brigade, Mahone's division, General Lee's army, October 31, 1864, Maj. John P. Emrich in command of regiment. (1239, 1367) Assignment as above to December 31st.

No. 95—(1273) Forney's brigade, Mahone's division, Appomattox campaign.

No. 96—(1174, 1272) Same assignment, Col. J. L. Royston in command of regiment, January 31, 1865. Lieut.-Col. J. P. Emrich commanding regiment, February 28, 1865.

THE NINTH ALABAMA INFANTRY.

The Ninth Alabama infantry, organized at Richmond in May, 1861, enjoyed the distinction of having a joint resolution of thanks given it by the Confederate Congress in February, 1864. It was engaged in the siege of Yorktown, April 5 and May 2, 1862; at Williamsburg, May 5th, and at Seven Pines, May 31st and June 1st. This regiment won imperishable renown at Gaines' Mill and Frayser's Farm, was under fire at Second Manassas, and assisted at the capture of Harper's Ferry, September 12 to 15, 1862. It was also engaged at Chancellorsville and Salem, May 1-3, 1863, and suffered very heavy loss at Gettysburg. It was in the battle of the Wilderness, May 5-7, 1864, Cold Harbor, June 1st to 12th, and fought in the trenches at Petersburg for nearly 9 months. Among its field officers were Cadmus M. Wilcox, afterward a very distinguished major-general; E. A. O'Neal, afterward brigadier-general, and since that time governor of Alabama; Col. Samuel Henry, Col. J. Horace King, Lieut.-Col. Gaines C. Smith, Majs. H. J. Williams and J. M. Crowe. Among the officers killed were Capts. Thomas H. Hobbs and E. Y. Hill, at Gaines' Mill; Captain Gillis, at Williamsburg; W. C. Murphy at Salem; J. W. Wilson and John Y. Rayburn, at Sharpsburg.

EXTRACTS FROM OFFICIAL WAR RECORDS.

Vol. II—(480) Wilcox's brigade, army of the Potomac (Special orders, July 20, 1861).

Vol. V—(1029) Same assignment, Potomac district, General Beauregard commanding, January 14, 1862, at this time at Centreville, Va.

Vol. XI, Part 1—(569) Casualties, 10 killed, 45 wounded, near Williamsburg, May 5, 1862. (570, 571) Gen. J. E. B. Stuart reports: "Captain Farley, who was in the entire fight, speaks in the highest terms of the heroic courage and fighting tact of the Ninth Alabama." (577, 578) Mentioned in report of Gen. A. P. Hill: Colonel Williams, with one or two companies of the Ninth Alabama, captured a battery of 8 guns. (590-593) General Wilcox's report says: "Among those that call for special notice are Capts. Warren Smith, Gillis and King. The companies of the first two were the first to enter the captured battery. Captain Gillis, greatly distinguished for courage, displayed an example of coolness set to his men. He was mortally wounded. Captain Murphy of the Ninth, conspicuous for pertinacity and courage, was painfully wounded in the arm. He remained on the field and commanded his company until shot through the body and borne from the field." (594, 595) Col. Sam. Henry's report: "The charge was made with a zeal and determination that would have done honor to tried veterans—not a man faltering. ... In conclusion, you will permit me to assure you of the coolness and gallantry of both officers and men during the entire day." The regiment took during the day 70 prisoners. (596, 599, 822) Mentioned in reports of Col. J. J. Woodward, Col. L. Q. C. Lamar, Gen. D. E. Sickles, U. S. A. (986-988) Mentioned in report of General Wilcox, Seven Pines, May 31, 1862.

Vol. XI, Part 2—(486, 503) Wilcox's brigade, Longstreet's division, Magruder's corps. Medical director reports 66 killed, 109 wounded, June 26th to July 1, 1862. (770-77S) Report of General Wilcox, Gaines' Mill, June 37th: "Capt. E. Y. Hill killed, far in advance, in field. Capt. T. H. Hobbs dangerously wounded. . . . Lieutenant Wayland, quartermaster, severely wounded. The latter officer's duties did not require his presence in battle, but he served with his company with great coolness and courage. He served in like manner at Seven Pines." (777-779) General Wilcox's report of battle of Frayser's Farm, June 30th: "Captain King, commanding the Ninth Alabama, is deserving of especial praise for his coolness and bravery; he also received a severe wound in the leg. ... Of the medical corps, Surgeon H. A. Minor of the Ninth Alabama (and others), have given abundant evidence of their skill and untiring industry and zeal." (980) Casualties, 34 killed and 96 wounded, Gaines' Mill; 31 killed and 95 wounded at Glendale. (985) Capts. E. Y. Hill killed, and Thomas H. Hobbs died of wounds received, June 27th.

Vol. XI, Part 3—(481) In General Wilcox's brigade, Johnston's army, about April 30, 1862, 550 strong. (649) General Wilcox's brigade with Stonewall Jackson, July 23, 1862. Col. Samuel Henry commanding regiment.

Vol. XII, Part 2—(547) Assignment as above during battles of campaign in Northern Virginia, August 28th to September 1st.

Vol. XIX, Part 1—(804) Wilcox's brigade, Longstreet's corps, Maryland campaign. (812) Medical director reports 12 killed and 42 wounded, Maryland campaign.

Vol. XXI—(539, 1070) Same assignment, Col. Samuel Henry in command, December 20, 1862.

No. 39—(790) Same assignment, Chancellorsville campaign. Maj. J. H. J. Williams commanding regiment. (806, 854) Casualties at battle of Chancellorsville, 23 killed and 89 wounded. (858-861) Report of General Wilcox: "The Ninth Alabama in rear of this regiment sprang forward as one man, and with the rapidity of lightning restored the continuity of our line, breaking the lines of the enemy with its deadly fire and forcing him to give way, and following him so that he could not rally. . . . Capt. W. C. Murphy, Ninth Alabama, highly distinguished at the battle of Williamsburg, where he. received two severe wounds. He fell at Salem Church in the thickest of the fight and in advance of his men." He speaks highly of Maj. J. H. J. Williams, Capts. J. H. King and M. G. May, who were distinguished, having with their companies captured 13 officers and 236 men. He continues: "I cannot close this report without calling to your especial notice the conduct of one entire regiment of this brigade, the Ninth Alabama. . . . I also beg leave to commend to your favorable notice Private J. W. Brundridge of the Ninth Alabama."

No. 44—(30) Mentioned by Gen. Dan Tyler, U. S. A., Maryland Heights, June 25, 1863. (288) Wilcox's brigade, Anderson's division, Third corps, Gen. A. P. Hill, army of Northern Virginia, Gettysburg, July 1-3, 1863. (332, 343) Casualties at battle of Gettysburg, 3 killed, 55 wounded. (619-621) Report of General Wilcox: "Capt. G. C. Smith, severe wound through the body (entitled to promotion to lieutenant-colonel). Capt. J. H. King (entitled to promotion to colonel) had a finger shot off. Private Brundridge severely wounded." He gives special praise to Captain King and Captain May on second day.

No. 45—(1061} Assignment as above, July 31, 1863, Maj. J. H. J. Williams in command of regiment.

No. 48—(400, 819) Assignment as above, Col. J. H. King in command of regiment, October 31, 1863.

No. 49—(685, 900) Assignment as above, December, 1863.

No. 60—(1152) Mentioned by General Lee as having re-enlisted, February 10, 1864, Orange Court House. (1182) Joint resolution of thanks to the Ninth Alabama regiment: "Resolved by the Congress of the Confederate States of America, That Congress hails with delight the manifestations evinced by the brave and gallant officers and privates of the Ninth regiment, Alabama volunteers, who have stood under the fire of the enemy for nearly 3 years, never to yield to Northern oppression, and for this act of partiotism and exalted self-sacrifice, in re-enlisting for the war, the thanks of Congress and the country are eminently due them. That the example of those brave men who have endured the dangers and perils of the war since its commencement is a happy omen for the future, and should encourage Congress and the country to rest with an abiding hope and confidence in the success of our arms and the final triumph of liberty, under the lead of those brave and unconquerable spirits. Approved February 16, 1864."

No. 67—(966, 976, 1025) Perrin's brigade, Lee's army, May, 1864. Mentioned in reports of battles of the Wilderness.

No. 80—(754) General Mahone, July 30, 1864, reports battleflag captured. (810) Roll of honor, battles near Petersburg, Va., July 30th: Private John M. Critcher, Company K.

No. 88—(684) Mentioned by Capt. J. McEntee, U. S. A. (1175, 1183) Mentioned in correspondence of General Lee and secretary of war, August, 1864. (1217) Sanders' brigade, Third corps, army of Northern Virginia, August 31, 1864; Col. J. Horace King commanding regiment.

No. 89—(1190) Same assignment, October 31, 1864, Capt. Archer Hayes commanding regiment. (1239) Colonel King commanding regiment. (1367) Assignment as above, December 31st.

No. 95—(1273) Forney's brigade, Lee's army, February 28, 1865. Maj. James M. Crowe commanding regiment.

No. 96—(1174, 1272) Assignment as above, January 31, 1865, Col. Horace King commanding regiment.

THE TENTH ALABAMA INFANTRY.

The Tenth Alabama infantry was organized at Montgomery, in May, 1861. Throughout its whole career this regiment was singularly distinguished for its dash and courage, and the great losses that it sustained in every battle. It fought at Dranesville, December 20, 1861; at the siege of Yorktown, April 5 to May 3, 1862; Williamsburg, May 5th; Seven Pines, May 31st to June 1st; Gaines' Mill, June 27th and 28th; at Frayser's Farm, June 30th, and Second Manassas, August 30th. It was engaged in the capture of Harper's Ferry, September 12th to 15th; at Sharpsburg, September 17th; at Hazel River, August 22d. It lost very heavily at Fredericksburg, December 13th; as it did at Salem, May 3, 1863; at Gettysburg, July 1st to 3d, and at Cold Harbor, June 1 to 12, 1864. Among its distinguished officers were Col. John H. Forney, afterward a major-general, and William H. Forney, afterward a brigadier-general and for many years in the United States Congress, both of whom were severely wounded. Col. John J. Woodward, Capts. William Lee, Robert W. Cowen and James D. Cunningham were killed at Gaines' Mill; Col. James E. Shelley, Capts. George P. Brown and Henry D. Coleman at Petersburg, and Capt. Walter Cook at Salem; Capt. George Whaley at Sharpsburg, and Capt. Richard C. Reagan at Spottsylvania; Capt. Pickens W. Black, at Cold Harbor; Lieut.-Col. James B. Martin at Dranesville, and Lieut. M. J. T. Harper at Chancellorsville. Among the other field officers were Col. John H. Caldwell, Lieut.-Col. William T. Smith and Majs. James D. Truss, Lewis W. Johnston and Paul Bradford. Lieut.-Col. Arthur S. Cunningham, of the regular Confederate army, was in temporary command of the regiment in 1863.

EXTRACTS FROM OFFICIAL WAR RECORDS.

Vol. II—(974) Jefferson Davis in letter July 10, 1861, to Gen. Jos. E. Johnston, mentions Colonel Forney's regiment.

Vol. V—(475) General McCall (Union) says: "Tenth regiment, Forney, 900 strong at Dranesville." (480) Mentioned by General Ord (Union). (490-493) Gen. J. E. B. Stuart in his report of the battle of Dranesville, December 20, 1861, says: "The Tenth Alabama rushed with a shout, in a shower of bullets, under the gallant lead of Colonel Forney and Lieutenant-Colonel Martin, the latter falling in the charge. A part of this regiment took position along a fence from which the enemy felt the trueness of their aim at short range. The colonel was here severely wounded and the command devolved on Major Woodward. ... I cannot speak in too high terms of Colonel Forney, that gallant son of Alabama whose conspicuous bravery, leading his men in a galling fire, was the admiration of all; nor of his Lieutenant-Colonel Martin, who, with the battlecry of 'Forward!' on his lips, fell, bravely encouraging his men. Nor can I do more than simple justice to the officers and men of that regiment who seemed determined to follow their colonel wherever he would lead." (494) General Stuart reports 15 killed and 45 wounded at Dranesville. (1029) In Wilcox's brigade, Potomac district, General Beauregard commanding, January 14, 1862.

Vol. IX—(379) General McClellan informs General Burnside, April 16, 1862, that this regiment with others is going to North Carolina.

Vol. XI, Part 1—(589-593) Under Col. J. J. Woodward at Williamsburg, May 5, 1862. Highly commended by General Wilcox in his report. He says: "The Tenth Alabama pressed on vigorously. Its major, W. H. Forney, was stricken down with a painful wound while leading the regiment, displaying both coolness and skill." Colonel Woodward, Major Forney and Lieutenant Shelley specially noticed. (594,595) Highly commended in the report of Col. Sam Henry, Ninth Alabama. (596,597) Colonel Woodward's report of same battle. (986,987) Mentioned in General Wilcox's report of the battle of Seven Pines.

Vol. XI, Part 2—(425) Report of Col. James Kirk (Union) of battle of Frayser's Farm says: "Tenth Alabama was almost totally annihilated." (486) Wilcox's brigade, Longstreet's division, engagements around Richmond. (503) Medical director reports 38 killed, 198 wounded, in the fights before Richmond, June 26th to July 1, 1862. (771-775) General Wilcox's report of Gaines' Mill mentions "Colonel Woodward shot through the head while leading his regiment, closely and heroically confronting the enemy in his stronghold." After the fall of Colonel Woodward, the command devolved upon Maj. J. H. Caldwell; Capt. W. M. Lee mortally wounded. Lieut. J. E. Shelley, adjutant, severely wounded. (777-779) General Wilcox's report of Frayser's Farm says: "Major Caldwell wounded by a piece of shell striking him over the eye." Commends Surgeon Taylor. (985) Lieut. James D. Cunningham killed June 30th.

Vol. XI, Part 3—(114) Near Yorktown, Va., April 20, 1862. (481) In General Wilcox's brigade at Williamsburg, 550 strong. (533) Wilcox's brigade, Smith's division, Johnston's army, near Richmond, May 21st. (649) General Longstreet's division, July 23d.

Vol. XII, Part 2—(547) Assignment as above, August 28th to September 1st.

Vol. XIX, Part 1—(804) Assignment as above, Maryland campaign. (812) Medical director reports 10 killed and 53 wounded, Maryland campaign.

Vol. XXI—(539, 1070) First corps, army of Northern Virginia, Colonel Forney in command of regiment, December, 1862.

No. 39—(806) Medical director reports 12 killed and 61 wounded at battle of Chancellorsville, May 1-5, 1863. (854) Another return, 17 killed and 55 wounded. (856-860) Mentioned by General Wilcox in report of Chancellorsville campaign: "Lieut. L. J. T. Harper fell fighting with the heroism of a veteran soldier." Notices particularly Col. Wm. H. Forney.

No. 44—(288) Wilcox's brigade, Third corps, army of Northern Virginia, Gettysburg campaign. Commanders, Colonel Forney and Lieut.-Col. Jas. E. Shelley. (332, 343) Casualties, 13 killed, 91 wounded, at battle of Gettysburg, July 1st, 2d and 3d. (613) Referred to in report of General Anderson (Union). (617-621) General Wilcox's report, action July 2d: "In this affair, so creditable to the Tenth Alabama and its gallant colonel (Forney), this regiment lost 10 killed and 28 wounded." Among those acting with great gallantry, Lieutenant-Colonel Shelley is mentioned

No. 48—(400, 412, 819) Assignment as above. Casualties, 2 wounded, October 10 to 21, 1863.

No. 49—(685, 900) Assignment as above, to December 31, 1863.

No. 60— (1152) Mentioned by General Lee as having re-enlisted, February 10, 1864.

No. 67—(1025) Perrin's brigade, Third corps, Lee's army of Northern Virginia, May, 1864.

No. 88—(1217) Sanders' brigade, Lee's army, August 31, 1864.

No. 89—(1190) Sanders' brigade, Mahone's division, Capt. Wilson L. Brewster in command of regiment, October 31, 1864. (1239) General Forney commanding brigade, Capt. Caleb W. Brewton in command of regiment, November 30. (1367) Capt. John F. Smith in command of regiment, December 31st.

No. 95—(1273) Assignment as above, Maj. Lewis W. Johnson in command of regiment about April, 1865.

No. 96—(1 174) Colonel Forney in command of regiment, January 31, 1865. (1272) Forney's brigade, Lee's army, Lieut.-Col. Wm. F. Smith in command of regiment.

THE ELEVENTH ALABAMA INFANTRY.

The Eleventh Alabama infantry was organized at Lynchburg, Va., in 1861. It was distinguished at Seven Pines, May 31 to June 1, 1862, and at Frayser's Farm, June 30th, where it charged with bayonets across an open field. It was at Second Manassas, August 30, 1862; Harper's Ferry, Sharpsburg, Fredericksburg, and Salem, May 3, 1863; Gettysburg, July 1 to

3, 1863; The Wilderness, May 5 to 7, 1864; Spottsylvania, May 8th-18th; the Crater, July 30th; Burgess' Farm, October 27th; and in numerous battles around Petersburg, June, 1864, to the surrender at Appomattox. Among the killed in the battles of this regiment were the distinguished Col. Sydenham Moore, at Seven Pines; Lieut.-Col. Stephen H. Hale and Lieut. W. C. Faith, at Gaines' Mill; Capts. James H. McMath, Thomas H. Holcombe, Stephen E. Bell, W.C.Y. Parker, Wm. M. Bratton, and Lieuts. A. B. Cohen, T. J. Michie, and A. N. Steele, all at Frayser's Farm; Captains Cadell and Brazleton and Adjt. R. Y. Ashe at Petersburg; Captain James at Cold Harbor; and Captain Harris at the Crater. Among the other field officers were Cols. John C. C. Sanders and George E. Tayloe, Maj. Archibald Gracie, Jr., afterward brigadier-general, killed; and Majs. Richard T. Fletcher and George Fields.

EXTRACTS FROM OFFICIAL WAR RECORDS.

Vol. V.—(1029) Wilcox's brigade, Gen. G. W. Smith's division, Potomac district, General Beauregard commanding, January, 1862.

Vol. XI, Part 1—(407) Mentioned in report of General Magruder, Yorktown, April 5 to May 3, 1862. (580) Referred to in report of Col. M. D. Corse, Seven Pines. (591) Referred to in General Wilcox's report, Williamsburg. (941) Colonel Moore mentioned in General Longstreet's report of Seven Pines. (986-988) General Wilcox's report of battle of Seven Pines says: "The leading regiment, the Eleventh Alabama, Col. Sydenham Moore, of my brigade, was ordered to the front. . . . Colonel Moore with two companies dislodged the enemy, receiving two wounds, one of which proved mortal. . . . His loss is scarcely reparable. Lieut. Walter E. Winn, adjutant of the Eleventh Alabama, was much distinguished for his zeal and courage. . . . Lieut.-Col. S. F. Hale of the Eleventh Alabama, though commanding the Ninth Alabama, was conspicuous for the skill with which he managed his regiment. Captains Tayloe and Holcombe were wounded in the first day's fight, the former seriously."

Vol. XI, Part 2—(486, 503) In Wilcox's brigade, Longstreet's division, Seven Days' battles. Casualties, 76 killed and 240 wounded. (773-779) General Wilcox, in his report of Gaines' Mill and Frayser's Farm, mentions Lieut.-Col. S. F. Hale as seriously, perhaps mortally, wounded; Lieut. W. C. Faith, killed; speaks most highly of Assistant-Surgeon Saunders and Lieut. Walter E. Winn, and gives a most graphic account of the glorious part taken by the regiment on June 30th, referring to Capts. J. H. McMath, S. E. Bell, T. H. Holcombe, W. M. Bratton and Lieut. A. B. Cohen, commanding companies; Lieuts. A. N. Steele and Michie mortally wounded; Capts. J. C. C. Sanders and W. C. Y. Parker severely wounded, also Lieuts. J. H. Prince and R. H. Gordon. (980) Casualties, 27 killed, 130 wounded, battle of Gaines' Mill; 49 killed, 121 wounded, at Glendale. (985) Lieutenant Faith killed June 27th; Capts. Stephen A. Bell, Thomas H. Holcombe and James McMath, Lieuts. W. M. Bratton and A. B. Cohen killed June 30th.

Vol. XI, Part 3—(481, 532, 649) In Wilcox's brigade at Williamsburg, 656 strong. Same assignment to July 23, 1863.

Vol. XII, Part 2—(547) Same assignment, August 28 to September 1, 1862.

Vol. XIX, Part 1—(804, 812) Assignment as above, Maryland campaign. Casualties, 3 killed and 26 wounded.

Vol. XXI—(539, 559, 610) Assignment as above, battle of Fredericksburg. Casualties, 3 killed and 5 wounded. (612) Referred to in General Wilcox's report of the battle of Fredericksburg. (1070) Col. J. C. C. Sanders in command of regiment.

No. 39—(790) Wilcox's brigade, Anderson's division, First corps, army of Northern Virginia, Chancellorsville campaign. (806) Casualties, 15 killed and 76 wounded at Chancellorsville; Lieut. O. L. Strudwick killed. (858-861) General Wilcox's report of battle speaks highly of Colonel Sanders and favorably commends Private J. C. J. Ridgeway. Reports Federal flag taken by regiment.

No. 44—(288) At the battle of Gettysburg, regiment in Wilcox's brigade, Anderson's division, Third corps. Colonel Sanders and Lieut.-Col. Geo. E. Tayloe in command. (332, 343) Casualties, 6 killed and 69 wounded, Gettysburg. (617-621) General Wilcox's report of Gettysburg says Colonel Sanders and Major Fletcher were severely wounded, and 17 men. Private Ridgeway (one of his couriers) was killed. Commends Lieutenant-Colonel Tayloe.

No. 45—(1061) No. 48—(400) No. 49—(685, 900) Assignment as above to December, 1863.

No. 60—(1145) Noble example of re-enlistment for the war mentioned by General Lee, in general orders, No. 14, February 3, 1864.

No. 80—(754) James N. Keeton, Company G, captor of Federal flag, July 30, 1864, at Petersburg. (810) Roll of honor, general orders, No. 87, December 10th: Private James N. Keeton, Company G.

No. 88—(1217) Sanders' brigade, Mahone's division, Third corps, Lee's army, August 31, 1864. Lieut.-Col. Geo. E. Tayloe commanding regiment.

No. 89—(1190, 1239, 1367) Assignment as above to December 31, 1864.

No. 95—(1273) Forney's brigade, Mahone's division, Appomattox campaign. Capt Martin L. Stewart commanding regiment.

No. 96—(1174, 1272) Same assignment to February 28, 1865.

THE TWELFTH ALABAMA INFANTRY.

The Twelfth Alabama infantry was organized at Richmond, July, 1861, formed a part of General Ewell's brigade, and was afterward under General Rodes. It fought at Yorktown, April 5 to May 3, 1862; Williamsburg,

May 5th; Seven Pines, May 31st to June 1st, where it made a gallant assault upon the strong position held by Casey's division; was engaged in the fights before Richmond, June 26th to July 1st; was distinguished at Boonsboro, September 15th, and Sharpsburg, September 17th; fought gallantly at Fredericksburg, December 13, 1862; Chancellorsville, May 1st to 4th; Brandy Station, June 9th; and Gettysburg, July 1st to 3d, and formed part of the rear guard in retiring from that bloody field. It was also in the engagements at the Wilderness, May 5 to 7, 1864; Spottsylvania, May 8th to 18th; Winchester, July 24th, and in the various battles around Petersburg from June, 1864, to April, 1865.

Among the distinguished officers killed were: Col. Robert T. Jones, Capts. R. H. Keeling and C. A. Darwin at Seven Pines; Col. Bristow B. Gayle at Boonsboro; Capts. E. Tucker and D. H. Garrison at Sharpsburg; Henry W. Cox at Chancellorsville; Davis at Gettysburg; J. McCassells at the Wilderness; John Rogers at Spottsylvania, and A. Majors at Snicker's Gap, August 19, 1864. Among the other field officers of this regiment were: Col. Samuel B. Pickens, Lieut.-Col. Theodore O'Hara, John C. Goodgame, and Edward D. Tracy, afterward killed when brigadier-general; also Majs. Adolph Proskaner and John C. Brown.

EXTRACTS FROM OFFICIAL WAR RECORDS.

Vol. II—(1000) Assigned to Second brigade, Gen. R. S. Ewell, First corps, army of Potomac, special order 169, Manassas Junction, July 25, 1861.

Vol. V—(1029) In Rodes' brigade, Van Dorn's division, Potomac district, General Beauregard commanding, January, 1862.

Vol. XI—(971-976) General Rodes' report of battle of Seven Pines, May 31st to June 1st, speaks of Col. R. T. Jones of the Twelfth Alabama, killed, as the most accomplished officer in the brigade. For gallantry he notes Capt. E. Tucker, and gives casualties, 59 killed, 149 wounded. (979) Mentioned in report of Col. J. B. Gordon, Seven Pines. (981,982) Col. B. B. Gayle, lieutenant-colonel commanding at Seven Pines, says that the Twelfth regiment, while advancing, charged directly through the camp of the enemy. The number of men carried into the fight, as near as can be ascertained, 408; number killed, 69; number wounded, 156. Thus, more than half carried into battle were killed or wounded.

Vol. XI, Part 2—(484) Rodes' brigade, Hill's division, Jackson's corps, Seven Days' battles. (505, 975) Medical director reports 1 killed, 11 wounded at Gaines' Mill. (555, 570, 621, 625) Mentioned in reports of Stonewall Jackson, Gen. C. Winder, Gen. Bradley Johnson, Gen. D. H. Hill, Seven Days' battles. (630-633) Mentioned in report of Gen. R. E. Rodes. (634, 638,639) Mentioned in reports of Col. J. B. Gordon and Col. B. B. Gayle.

Vol. XI, Part 3—(482, 532, 601, 650) 550 strong, Peninsula campaign. Col. B. B. Gayle commanding regiment, July 23, 1862.

Vol. XIX, Part 1—(261, 302) Mentioned in Federal reports of battles of South Mountain and Antietam. (808) Same assignment, Maryland campaign. Col. B. B. Gayle and Lieut.-Col. S. B. Pickens with regiment. (1021-1030) Gen. D. H. Hill, in report of operations July 23 to September 17, 1862, calls Colonel Gayle a most gallant and accomplished officer. (1034-1038) Report of General Rodes, battles of Boonsboro and Sharpsburg. The Twelfth lost heavily. Lieut.-Col. B. B. Gayle was seen to fall, and Lieut-Col. Samuel B. Pickens was shot through the lungs; the former was left on the field supposed to be dead; Pickens was brought off.

Vol. XXI—(541, 1073) Rodes' brigade, Second corps, army of Northern Virginia, battle of Fredericksburg, December 13, 1862. Lieut.-Col. S. B. Pickens in command of regiment.

No. 39—(792, 807) Assignment as above, Chancellorsville campaign. Medical director reports 14 killed and 77 wounded. (944-946) General Rodes calls attention to gallant and meritorious conduct of Colonel Pickens at Chancellorsville. (948, 951, 954, 955, 959, 960) Mentioned in reports of Col. E. A. O'Neal, Col. J. M. Hall and Col. J. N. Lightfoot. (960-964) Report of Colonel Pickens gives 6 killed and 32 wounded, May 2d, and 7 killed and 55 wounded, May 3d. Total loss at Chancellorsville, 14 killed and 87 wounded. (986) Gen. Alfred Iverson in report of Chancellorsville says: "I then communicated with Col. S. B. Pickens, commanding Twelfth Alabama, whose gallantry on this occasion I cannot too highly commend, so completely and courageously did he lend himself to aid me preparing the line to resist an attack." (1053) Roll of honor, Chancellorsville: Capt. H. W. Cox, Company B, killed in action; Sergt. William Lawless, Company C; Privates Louis Dondero, Company A; R. W. May, Company B; J. E. Bailey, Company D; C. H. Hunter, Company E; P. W. Chappell, Company E; R. B. Mitchell, Company G; W. S. Brown, Company H; H. N. Wooten, Company I; Thomas H. Eady, Company K.

No. 44—(287) Assignment as above, Gettysburg. (332, 343) Reports of casualties. (545-553) Mentioned in report of General Rodes. (563) Officers in command at Gettysburg: Col. S. B. Pickens, Maj. A. Proskaner, Lieut.-Col. J. C. Goodgame in command of the Twenty-sixth Alabama. (593-3) Mentioned in report of E. A. O'Neal, colonel commanding brigade. (600,601) Colonel Pickens reports 12 killed and 71 wounded, Gettysburg.

No. 48—(399) Battle's brigade, Second army corps, Colonel Pickens commanding regiment, September 30, 1863. (412, 617) Return of casualties, 2 killed, October 10th to 21st, October 20th to November 8th, 1 wounded. (818, 838) Assignment as above, and medical director's report. (892) Report of Major Proskaner of operations on November 27th and 28th, 2 wounded. Mentioned in Lieutenant-Colonel Garvin's report.

No. 49—(683, 900) Assignment as above to December, 1863.

No. 60—Joint resolution of thanks from Congress to Battle's brigade, February 6, 1864. [See Extracts under Third regiment.]

No. 67—(1024) Assignment as above, May, 1864. (1083) Mentioned in report of Gen. C. A. Battle, May 8, 1864.

No. 68—(715) Mentioned by Gen. G. K. Warren (Union), May 13, 1864.

No. 88—(1217) Assignment as above, August 31, 1864.

No. 89—(1194) Battle's brigade, Lee's army, October 31, 1864, Lieut.-Col. John C. Goodgame in command of regiment. (1246, 1364) Assignment as above, Colonel .

No. 90—(564) Battle's brigade, with Gen. J. A. Early, Cedar Creek, October 19, 1864. Capt. P. D. Ross commanding regiment. (1002, 1013) Assignment as above.

No. 95—(336) Mentioned in report of Capt. J. F. Carter (Third Maryland, U. S.) of operations, March 25, 1865. (1270) Battle's brigade, in Lee's army.

No. 96—(1172, 1181, 1270) Assignment as above to February 28, 1865.

No. 97—(263) Mentioned in report of Gen. J. G. Parke (U. S.), March 29, 1865.

THE THIRTEENTH ALABAMA INFANTRY.

The Thirteenth Alabama infantry was organized at Montgomery, July, 1861. It was warmly engaged at Seven Pines, May 31 to June 1, 1862, and in the battles around Richmond, June 26 to July 1, 1862. It also participated in the Maryland campaign and was engaged in the battles of Boonsboro, September 15th, and Sharpsburg, September 17th, and was present at Fredericksburg December 13th, but owing to its position was not engaged. It was particularly distinguished in the assault upon Hooker at Chancellorsville, May 1 to 4, 1863, and was superb in its charge at Gettysburg, where it planted its colors on the crest of the ridge, suffering frightfully in killed and wounded. It also took part in the battles of the Wilderness, and in the numerous engagements around Petersburg, June, 1864, to the surrender at Appomattox in April, 1865.

Among its killed were: Capt. John D. Clarke, at Mechanicsville, June 26, 1862; Adjt. John W. Rentz, at Sharpsburg; Maj. John T. Smith, at Chancellorsville; Adjt. L. P. Broughton, at the Wilderness; Capt. R. M. Cook, at Second Cold Harbor; Lieut. David R. Staggers, near Bristoe Station. Among the other field officers were: Birkett D. Fry, afterward distinguished as a brigadier-general; Col. James Aiken, Lieut.-Cols. Julius C. Mitchell, Samuel B. Marks, Reginald H. Dawson, William H. Betts and Maj. John D. Smith.

EXTRACTS FROM OFFICIAL WAR RECORDS.

Vol. II—(1000) Mentioned as belonging to General Ewell's brigade. (Evidently an error; Twelfth was meant.)

Vol. IV—(668) Under general orders, No. 89, Yorktown, October 3, 1861, assigned with Eighth Alabama to Fifth brigade under Colonel Winston. (669) Assigned to Yorktown, Colonel Winston commanding post.

Vol. IX—(37) First division, Gen. G. J. Rains, department of the Peninsula, January 31, 1862.

Vol. XI, Part 2—(485) With Colquitt's brigade, Hill's division, Stonewall Jackson's corps, during engagements around Richmond, June 26 to July 1, 1862. (505) Medical director reports 14 killed and 70 wounded in Seven Days' battles. His report gives assignment to Semmes' brigade, McLaws' division. (625) Referred to as in Colquitt's brigade in report of Gen. D. H. Hill. (976) Return of casualties, 4 killed and 40 wounded at Gaines' Mill; 10 killed and 47 wounded at Malvern Hill.

Vol. XI, Part 3—(482) 474 strong "within the post at Yorktown." (533) Rains' brigade, Fourth division, May 21, 1862. (650) Colquitt's brigade, Stonewall Jackson's army, July 23, 1862. Col. B. D. Fry in command of regiment.

Vol. XIX, Part 1—(809) Assignment as above during Maryland campaign. (1020, 1027) Report of D. H. Hill, Maryland campaign:" Colonel Fry, who had been wounded at Seven Pines, was once more wounded severely at Sharpsburg, while nobly doing his duty." Also mentions W. D. Tingle. (1054) Colonel Fry mentioned in Col. Colquitt's report.

Vol. XXI—(541, 1073) Colquitt's brigade, Second corps, at battle of Fredericksburg. (1 099) Transferred from Colquitt's brigade to Archer's brigade, January 19, 1863.

No. 39—(791) Archer's brigade, McLaws' division, Second corps, army of Northern Virginia, Chancellorsville campaign. (807) Medical director reports 13 killed, 127 wounded at Chancellorsville. (926) Return of casualties at 15 killed, 107 wounded. Among the killed were Maj. John T. Smith and Lieut. John J. Pendergrass. (927) Colonel Fry says: "I am gratified to be able to report that my commissioned officers, without exception, displayed zeal and courage; none more than the gallant Maj. John T. Smith, whose death is deeply lamented by the regiment."

No. 44—(289) Archer's brigade, Heth's division, Third corps, at the battle of Gettysburg, July 1-3, 1863. (333, 337, 344) Medical director's report gives 6 killed and 36 wounded; 3 wounded enroute from Pennsylvania. (647, 648) Referred to in report of Colonel Shepard, Gettysburg" campaign.

No. 48—(400) Assignment as above, September 30, 1863. (413) Medical director reports 2 killed and 4 wounded, October 10th to 21st. (434) Lieut. David R. Staggers killed near Bristoe Station, October 14th. (819) Assignment as above, October 31st.

No. 49—(685, 901) Assignment as above to December 31, 1863.

No. 67—(1025) Assignment as above, May, 1864, Rapidan to the James.

No. 88—(1218) Assignment as above. Lieut.-Col. James Aiken commanding regiment. (1273, 1274) Inspection report gives regiment in Fry's brigade, September 23, 1864. (1309) Archer's and Walker's brigades, commanded by General Archer, Heth's division, September 30th.

No. 89—(1189, 1240) Archer's brigade (consolidated under command of Col. R. M. Mayo), Lee's army, October and November, 1864.

No. 95—(1273) Forney's brigade, Mahone's division, Third army corps, Appomattox campaign, April, 1865, Capt. Samuel Sellers in command of regiment.

No. 96—(1025) Regiment transferred from Archer's brigade, Heth's division, Third corps, to Sanders' brigade, Mahone's division, same corps. Special order No. 8, January 9, 1865. (1174) Col. James Aiken in command of regiment. (1272) Forney's brigade, February 28th.

No. 97—(1279) Forney's brigade at Hancock's, April 2, 1865.

THE FOURTEENTH ALABAMA INFANTRY.

The Fourteenth Alabama infantry was organized at Auburn, 1861; remained in camp at Huntsville till October, when it was ordered to Virginia. It fought with distinction at Williamsburg, May 5, 1862; Seven Pines, May 31st to June 1st, and Mechanicsville, June 26th; made desperate charges at Frayser's Farm, June 30th, and Malvern Hill, July 1st, its losses of killed and wounded being very heavy. It served with distinction at Sharpsburg, September 17th; Salem, May 3, 1863, and Gettysburg, July 1st to 3d; the Wilderness May 5 to 7, 1864; Spottsylvania, May 8th to 18th, and in the many fights around Petersburg from June, 1864, to Appomattox, in April, 1865.

Among its distinguished killed in battle were: Capt. John Bell, killed at Mechanicsville; Lieut.-Col. David W. Baine, Capt. James S. Williamson, Lieuts. James E. Mayes, Nat M. Smith and C. H. Snead, at Frayser's Farm; Capt. J. Y. Wallace, at Matapony, August 6, 1862; Maj. Owen K. McLemore, at South Mountain, September 14, 1862; Maj. R. A. McCord, Lieuts. H. M. Cox and M. L. Bankston, at Chancellorsville; Capts. C. H. Lambeth and E. Folk, at Petersburg.

Among the other field officers were: Col. Thomas J. Judge, afterward on the supreme bench of Alabama, and Cols. Lucius Pinckard and Alfred C. Wood; Lieut.-Col. James A. Brown, and Majs. George W. Taylor and Mickleberry P. Terrell.

EXTRACTS FROM OFFICIAL WAR RECORDS.

Vol. IV—(416) Commanded by Col. Thomas J. Judge; brigaded with other Alabama regiments under Gen. L. P. Walker, September, 1861.

Vol. V—(938) Assigned to the Potomac district, special orders, No. 206, November 5, 1861. (954) Left Richmond November 14th for Fredericksburg and Manassas. (1012) Mentioned by Gen. S. D. French in report from Evansport, December 30th. (1013) Mentioned in General Holmes' letter from Brooks' Station, December 31st. (1018) Spoken of again by same, January 2, 1862. (1020) Ordered by secretary of war, January 5, 1862, to Richmond, "to regain their strength after going through the usual camp diseases." (1035) F. H. Holmes writes: "The regiment has suffered greatly from measles."

Vol. IX—(379) Mentioned by General McClellan.

Vol. XI, Part 1—(309) Mentioned in Gen. Winfield S. Hancock's report of reconnoissance toward Yorktown, April 7, 1862. (404) Mentioned in Gen. John B. Magruder's report of the siege of Yorktown. (583) Mentioned in Col. M. Jenkins' report of the battle of Williamsburg.

Vol. XI, Part 2—(486) In Pryor's brigade, Longstreet's division, Magruder's corps, engagements around Richmond. (503, 980) Casualties, 70 killed and 253 wounded in the fights before Richmond, June 26 to July 1, 1862. (781) Gen. Roger A. Pryor, writing of his brigade at Frayser's Farm: "The Fourteenth Alabama bore the brunt of the struggle and was nearly annihilated." (985) Lieut.-Col. D. W. Baine, Capt. James S. Williamson, Lieuts. James E. Mayes, Nat M. Smith and C. H. Snead killed June 30th; Capt John T. Bell, killed June 27th; Lieuts. J. T. Greenwood and D. V. Hines died of wounds received June

Vol. XI, Part 3 — (114, 340, 393, 404) Mentioned by Gen. G. B. McClellan, Gen. M. C. Meigs and Gen. W. H. Taylor. (482) 700 strong, Johnston's army in the peninsula, about April 30, 1862. (532, 649) In Pryor's brigade, Longstreet's division, Johnston's army near Richmond, May 21 to July 23, 1862.

Vol. XII, Part 2 — (547) Pryor's brigade, Wilcox's division, army of Northern Virginia, during the battles of August 2 8 to September 1, 1862. (561) Medical director reports 3 killed and 44 wounded at Manassas Plains, August 30th. (601) Mentioned in Gen. Roger A. Pryor's report of same battle.

Vol. XIX, Part 1— (804, 812) In Pryor's brigade, Anderson's division, Maryland campaign. Losses, 2 killed and 43 wounded.

Vol. XIX, Part 2 — (712) Ordered to be assigned to an Alabama brigade, November 10, 1862.

Vol. XXI — (539, 1070) Transferred November 10, 1862, to Wilcox's brigade, Anderson's division, First corps, army of Northern Virginia; Lieut.-Col. L. Pinckard in command of regiment December 20th.

No. 39 — (790, 806) Assignment as above, Chancellorsville campaign. Casualties, 7 killed and 116 wounded at battle of Chancellorsville, May 1st to 4th. (853) Referred to in letter of Gen. Thomas S. Mills, May 18, 1863. (854) Casualties given as 10 killed and 107 wounded at Chancellorsville. Among the killed are Lieuts. H. M. Cox and M. L. Bankston. (858) Gen. C. M. Wilcox's report of same battle says: "Lieuts. Bankston and Cox fell fighting with the heroism of veteran soldiers, against greatly superior forces of the enemy. Colonel Pinckard was severely wounded."

No. 44 — (288) Wilcox's brigade, Anderson's division, army of Northern Virginia, battle of Gettysburg, July 1-3, 1863. (332, 343) Medical director reports 7 killed and 41 wounded, Gettysburg, (620) Mentioned in General Wilcox's report.

No. 48 — (400, 819) In Sanders' brigade, Anderson's division, Third corps, General Lee's army, Col. L. Pinckard commanding regiment.

No. 49 — (685, 900) Assignment as above, to December 31, 1863.

No. 60—(1173) Re-enlisted for the war, as announced by Gen. R. E. Lee, February 15, 1864.

No. 67—(1025) In Perrin's brigade, Anderson's division, May, 1864.

No. 88—(1217) Assignment as above, August 31, 1864.

No. 89—(1190, 1239, 1367)Assignment as above, October 31, 1864, Capt. John. A. Terrill in command. November 30, 1864, Capt. Simon G. Perry in command.

No. 95—(1273) General Forney's brigade, Mahone's division, Third corps, Lee's army, April, 1865.

THE FIFTEENTH ALABAMA INFANTRY.

The Fifteenth Alabama infantry was organized at Fort Mitchell in 1861; served in Virginia in the brigade commanded by Gen. Isaac R. Trimble; was in Stonewall Jackson's army and fought with distinction at Front Royal, May 23, 1862; Winchester, May 25th; Cross Keys, June 8th; Gaines' Mill or Cold Harbor, June 27th and 28th; Malvern Hill, July 1st, and Hazel River, August 22d. It fought and lost heavily at Second Manassas, August 30th, and was in the battles of Chantilly, September 1st; Sharpsburg, September 17th; Fredericksburg, December 13th; Suffolk, May, 1863; Gettysburg, July 1 to 3, 1863. Ordered to join Bragg's army, the regiment fought at Chickamauga September 19th and 20th; Brown's Ferry, October 27th; Wauhatchie, October 27th; Knoxville, November 17th to December 4th; Bean's Station, December 14th. Returning to Virginia this regiment upheld its reputation and won further distinction, as shown by its long roll of honor at Fort Harrison. It was engaged at the Wilderness, May 5-7, 1864; Spottsylvania, May 8th to 18th; Hanover Court House, May 30th; and Second Cold Harbor, June 1st to 12th. It was also engaged before Petersburg and Richmond. At Deep Bottom, August 14th to 18th, one-third of that portion of the regiment engaged were killed. Among its killed in battle were Capt. R. H. Hill and Lieut. W. B. Mills, at Cross Keys; Captain Weams (mortally wounded), at Gaines' Mill; Capt. P. V. Guerry and Lieut. A. McIntosh, at Cold Harbor; Capts. J. H. Allison and H. C. Brainard, at Gettysburg, and Capt. John C. Gates died of wounds received in the same battle; Capt. Frank Park was killed at Knoxville, Captain Glover at Petersburg, and Capt. B. A. Hill at Fussell's Mill.

Among the other field officers were: Cols. John F. Treutlen, Alexander Lowther, William C. Oates (who was distinguished throughout the war and has since served many years as a member of Congress and also as governor of Alabama); Col. James Cantey, afterward brigadier-general; Lieut.-Col. Isaac B. Feagin and Maj. John W. L. Daniel.

EXTRACTS FROM THE OFFICIAL WAR RECORDS.

Vol. IV—(425) Gen. F. K. Zollicoffer, September 24, 1861, says: "There is at Knoxville the Fifteenth Alabama, numbering 900 men, of which only 300 are fit for duty."

Vol. V—(1030) In Trimble's brigade, Kirby Smith's division, Potomac district, January 14, 1862.

Vol. XI, Part 1—(415) Mentioned in Gen. L. McLaws' report of engagement, Dam No. 1 (Lee's Mill), April 16, 1862.

Vol. XI, Part 2—(484) In Ewell's division during the engagements around Richmond, Virginia. (506, 608) Casualties, 35 killed and 117 wounded, June 26 to July 1, 1862. (605) Mentioned in General Ewell's report Seven Days' battles. (614-616) Mention of regiment in Gen. I. R. Trimble's report of the battles around Richmond. Captain Guerry shot while cheering on his men. (857, 864) Mentioned by Gen. Maxcy Gregg and Col. D. Barnes. (985) Capt. P. V. Guerry, Lieut. A. McIntosh killed, June 27th.

Vol. XI, Part 3—(648) Trimble's brigade, Ewell's division, army of Northern Virginia, July 23, 1862.

Vol. XII, Part 1—(20) Mentioned by General Fremont. (713) Mentioned in Gen. T. J. Jackson's report of the battle of Cross Keys. (717) Casualties, 9 killed and 37 wounded, battle of Cross Keys and engagement at Port Republic. (779, 781, 784) Mentioned in General Ewell's report, at Cross Keys, June 8th: "The regiment made a gallant resistance, enabling me to take position at leisure." Capt. R. H. Hill and Lieut. W. B. Mills, killed; Lieuts. Brainard and A. A. McIntosh, wounded, and Lieut. W. T. Berry, missing. (794) Mentioned in General Trimble's report of the battle of Winchester, May 25th. (795-799) General Trimble's report of the battle of Cross Keys, June 8th: "To Colonel Cantey for his skillful retreat from picket, and prompt flank maneuver, I think special praise is due."

Vol. XII, Part 2—(180) Medical director's report. (184. 227) Mentioned in reports of Gen. T. J. Jackson and General Ewell of the battle of Cedar Run, August 9, 1862, (235, 236) General Trimble's report of Cedar Run shows that the regiment, under the command of Major Lowther, took a prominent part in that fight. Casualties, 1 killed and 7 wounded. (550, 562) In Trimble's brigade, Ewell's division, army of Northern Virginia, battles of Second Manassas. Casualties, 21 killed, 91 wounded, Manassas Plains, August, 1862. (708) Mentioned by General Early. (717) 4 wounded, battle of Ox Hill, September 1, 1862. (719) Mentioned in General Trimble's report of the battle of Hazel River, August 22, 1862. (716, 717, 810, 812, 813) 4 killed, 15 wounded, on the Rappahannock, August 220. to 24th; 15 killed, 38 wounded, at Manassas, August 28th; 9 wounded August 29th; 6 killed, 22 wounded, August 30th; 4 wounded, at Chantilly, September 1st.

Vol. XII, Part 3—(964) Assignment as above, near Gordonsville, Va., July 31, 1862.

Vol. XIX, Part 1—(806) Trimble's brigade, Ewell's division, Jackson's corps, Maryland campaign, Capt. I. B. Feagin commanding regiment. (813) Medical director reports 9 killed and 75 wounded, Maryland campaign. (973-975) Mentioned in General Early's report of operations, September 3-17, 1862. He reports 8 killed and 63 wounded at the battle of Sharpsburg, September 17th, and Captain Feagin seriously wounded at Boteler's Ford, September 19, 1862. (977) Col. James A. Walker, in his report of the battle of Sharpsburg, says: "Captain Feagin, commanding the Fifteenth Alabama regiment, behaved with a gallantry consistent with his high reputation for courage and that of the regiment he commanded."

Vol. XXI—(543, 561) Assignment as above, at battle of Fredericksburg. Loss, 1 killed and 34 wounded. (672) Mentioned in General Hoke's report of the battle of Fredericksburg, December 13th. (1072) Col. James Cantey commanding regiment. (1099) Transferred from Trimble's brigade, Ewell's division, Jackson's corps, to Law's brigade, Hood's division, Longstreet's corps, January 19, 1863.

No. 43—(625) Mentioned by Col. J. L. Chamberlain (Union), in his report of the battle of Gettysburg.

No. 44—(284) In Jackson's corps at battle of Gettysburg, July 1-3, 1863. (330, 339) Losses, 17 killed and 66 wounded, at the battle of Gettysburg. (362) Mentioned by General Longstreet. (392, 393) Colonel Gates' report: "Lieutenant-Colonel Feagin, a most excellent and gallant officer, received a severe wound, which caused him to lose his leg. Private A. Kennedy of Company .B, and William Trimmer of Company G, were killed; and Private G. E. Spencer, Company D, severely wounded. Loss was 17 killed and 54 wounded and brought off of field, and 90 missing; 8 officers were killed. (418, 419) Mentioned in Gen. Henry L. Benning's report.

No. 51—(18) In Law's brigade, Hood's division, army of Tennessee, General Bragg commanding, September 19-20, 1863. (303) Mentioned in Gen. T. C. Hindman's report, Chickamauga campaign. (332) Gen. Z. C. Deas' report: "Regiment behaved with great gallantry." (334) Mentioned in Col. S. K. McSpaddin's report.

No. 54—(223) Assignment as above, autumn of 1863. (225-228) General Law's report: "Col. W. C. Gates, the gallant and efficient commander of the Fifteenth Alabama, was wounded September 27, 1863, Lookout Valley." Also other mention of regiment. (229, 230) Mentioned in Col. J. L. Sheffield's report, 5 wounded. (452) Assignment as above, November 30th.

No. 55—(658) Same assignment, army of Tennessee, General Bragg commanding, November 20, 1863.

No. 56—(615, 890) Same assignment, to December 31, 1863.

No. 58—(641) Assignment as above, January 31, 1864.

No. 59—(722) In Law's brigade, Buckner's division, under General Longstreet, March 31, 1864.

No. 67—(1022) In Law's brigade, Field's division, First army corps, army of Northern Virginia, early in May, 1864. (1060) Partial return of casualties, 21 killed and 63 wounded in operations, April 14 to May 6, 1864.

No. 80—(763) Casualties, 3 killed and 8 wounded, Richmond campaign, June 13th to July 31st. (812) Roll of honor, Fort Harrison, September 30, 1864: M. L. Harper (killed), Company B; W. H. Cooper, Company C; R. S. Jones, Company D; B. J. Martin, Company E; A. Jackson, Company F; D. C. Cannon, Company G; J. T. Rushing, Company I; C. J. Fauk, Company K; T. R. Collins, Company L. (Company F declined making a selection.) Darbytown Road, October 7, 1864: A. E. Averett, Company A; Sergt. W. W. Johnson, Company D; Sergt. J. K. Edwards, Company E; H. V. Glenn, Company F; H. F. Satcher, Company G; Sergt. G. B. Barnett, Company I; W. F. Hill, Company K; J. F. Bean, Company L. Other companies declined making a selection. October 13, 1864: W. H. Quattlebaum, Company D; A. Powell, Company E; John Jackson, Company F; E. Grice, Company K; Lee Lloyd, Company L. Other companies declined making a selection.

No. 87—(877) Partial return of casualties, 10 killed and 92 wounded, August 1st to December 31st, Richmond campaign.

No. 88—(159, 1215) Assignment as above, Colonel Lowther in command of regiment, August 31, 1864.

No. 89—(1188, 1238, 1364) Assignment as above to December 31, 1864. November 30, 1864, Capt. F. Key Shaaff in command of regiment

No. 95—(1268, 1277) In Perry's brigade, paroled at Appomattox, April 9, 1865.

THE SIXTEENTH ALABAMA INFANTRY.

The Sixteenth Alabama infantry was organized at Courtland, August, 1861. It was assigned to General Zollicoffer's brigade, and its first battle was at Fishing Creek or Mill Spring, Ky., January 19 and 20, 1862. It was at Shiloh, April 6th and 7th; Triune, December 27th; Murfreesboro, December 31 to January 2, 1863; in the retreat from Tullahoma to Chattanooga, June 23d to July 4th; Chickamauga, September 19th and 20th; Missionary Ridge, November 23d to 25th; Ringgold, November 27th; in all the great battles under Johnston and Hood during the eventful campaign in 1864, and was particularly distinguished at Jonesboro, August 31st and September 1st, where it met with very severe loss. It participated in the fights at Buzzard Roost, Tunnel Hill and Rocky Face Ridge, February 25 to 27, 1864; around Dalton, May 8th to 12th; Resaca, May 13th to 26th; Adairsville, May 17th; Cassville, May 19th to 22d; Pickett's Mill, May 27th; Kenesaw Mountain, June 9th to 30th; Peachtree Creek, July 20th; Atlanta, July 22d, where it carried the enemy's works by assault and captured two stands of colors. It was also prominent in the battle of Franklin, November 30th, and of Nashville, December 15th and 16th.

Among the distinguished killed were its very gallant colonels, Fred A. Ashford and Brice Wilson at Franklin, Maj. J. H. McGaughey at Chickamauga, Capt. Robert M. Gregor at Nashville, Lieut. Wm. A. Patton at Shiloh, Lieuts. David E. Bentley, R. W. Garland, Lewis E. Jackson, Robt. W. Roebuck and Benj. H. Russell at Murfreesboro. Col. William B. Wood, who afterward became eminent on the bench as circuit judge, was the first colonel. He was succeeded by Cols. Alexander H. Helvenston and Frederick A. Ashford. Its lieutenant-colonels were John H. McGaughey, Joseph J. May and John W. Harris.

EXTRACTS FROM THE OFFICIAL WAR RECORDS.
Vol. IV—(237) Col. W. B. Wood commandant at Knoxville. (244, 246) Letter of General Zollicoffer, Knoxville, November 17, 1861, says he has started battalion of this regiment, with others, on the way to Jamestown, Tenn., and Monticello, Ky. (247) Ordered by Col. S. A. M. Wood back to Knoxville, November, 1861. (387) "Colonel Wood has been ordered from Tuscumbia to Russellville, Tenn.," August 31st. (409) Aggregate present, 867, Knoxville, September 15th. (412) Left at Knoxville with 300 men, able for duty, to guard the magazine. (520) Cumberland Gap, November 5, 1861, General Zollicoffer mentions battalion of the Sixteenth Alabama, in command of Lieutenant-Colonel Harris.

Vol. VII—(80) Report of Gen. George H. Thomas (Union), Logan's Cross Roads, says: "Lieut. Allen Morse and 5 officers of the medical staff, 81 non-commissioned officers and privates, taken prisoners." (82) Order of march, by General Crittenden, January 18, 1862, "Sixteenth Alabama, Colonel Wood, in reserve." (105-110) Report of Gen. G. B. Crittenden of battle of Mill Spring, January 19 and 20, 1862, mentions regiment several times. He says: "The Sixteenth Alabama, which was the reserve corps of my division, commanded by Colonel Wood, did, at this critical juncture, most eminent service." Also reports 9 killed and 5 wounded. (111-113) W. H. Carroll's report of same engagement: "Colonel Wood brought his men forward with the steadiness of veterans, and formed them in battle array with the coolness and precision of a holiday parade." (115, 116) Mentioned in report of Maj. Horace Rice. Wood's regiment numbered 330 men. (687) 325 present for duty, November 20th, at Wartburg, Tenn. (704) Mentioned by Gen. W. H. Carroll, Knoxville, November 26th. (751) Numbering about 800 men; report Gen. W. H. Carroll, Knoxville, December 9th. (753, 773, 814) Referred to by General Zollicoffer at Beech Grove, Ky. Present for duty, 378. (904) Brigade under General Wood, Second division of Central army, Murfreesboro, Tenn., February 23, 1862.

Vol. X, Part 1—(383) In S. A. M. Wood's brigade, Third corps, army of the Mississippi, April 6-7, 1862. (568) General Hardee reports this regiment helping in capture of 6 guns at Shiloh. (590-596) Mentioned in General Wood's report of the battle of Shiloh: "Major Helvenston had his horse killed, and was severely wounded by same ball." Six batteries captured; Lieut. Wm. Patton, behaving with great gallantry, was killed. Lieutenant-Colonel Harris, though laboring under severe illness, conducted his regiment throughout both days. (597,598) Col. John W. Harris reports that his men fought gallantly and bravely. "I was greatly assisted by Major Helvenston on the right, and I am indebted to him for many noble acts of daring and intrepidity, always at his post and at all times cheering on the soldiers. While gallantly charging a battery at the head of the column, he received a wound in the thigh. Captain Ashford, Company B, also acted nobly. At one time, when our force had been driven back, one piece of a battery was left by the gunners and drivers, the lead horse having been shot. Captain Ashford went to the piece, under the enemy's fire, cut the traces of the dead horse, ordered two men near by to assist him, and drove it away—preventing its capture by the enemy. Lieut. Wm. A. Patton, while at his post encouraging his men, fell, facing the foe." (603) Mentioned by Major Hardcastle, Shiloh. (605) Mentioned in report of Twenty-seventh Tennessee infantry. (788) Assignment as above, June 30, 1862.

Vol. XVI, Part 1—(1132) Mentioned in Colonel White's report of the battle of Perryville, October 8, 1862.

Vol. XVII, Part 2—(633) In Wood's brigade, General Bragg commanding army of the Mississippi, June 30, 1862.

Vol. XX, Part 1—(660) Same assignment, battle of Murfreesboro. (679) Return of casualties, 24 killed, 142 wounded. Lieuts. David E. Bentley, R. W. Garland, Lewis E. Jackson, Robert W. Roebuck and Benj. H. Russell, killed. (845-851) Mentioned several times in Gen. P. R. Cleburne's report. "The following officers and men of the Sixteenth Alabama distinguished themselves on the field: Col. W. B. Wood and Adjt. B. A. Wilson (wounded), Capt. William Hodges, Company F; Lieut. C. Davis, Company B; Lieut.-Col. G. W. W. Jones, Company G; Lieut. G. Pride, Company A; C. F. Carson, Company C, who remained fighting after he was wounded; Lieut. D. O. Warren, Company F; Lieut. Thomas Salter, Company D, who was wounded, but returned to the field the moment his wounds were dressed; Sergt.-Maj. Robert H. Cherry and Private Harvey G. Sargeant, Company H; Privates William Boyce and James Peeden, Company C; Sergeant Bowen, Company H; Sergt. H. W. Rutland, Company A; Private Peter White, Company F; Robert Williams, Company B; and H. D. Smith, Company A, the latter wounded in both legs." (896-900) Mentioned in Gen. S. A. M. Wood's reports. "Col. W. B. Wood was always in the lead." (900-903) Col. W. B. Wood, in his report, speaks of those mentioned above by General Cleburne; also highly commends Lieutenant-Colonel Helvenston, Major McGaughey, Adjt. A. B. Wilson, Lieuts. D. W. Alexander, W. S. Humphries and J. N. Watson; praises the efficient services of Capt. T. A. Kimball, chaplain, acting in the infirmary corps, and of Surgeon F. S. McMahon and Assistant-Surgeon Wm. M. Mayes. (906) Mentioned in Col. R. Charlton's report.

Vol. XXIII, Part 2—(246) Gen. G. M. Dodge (Union) gives force at 400, April 17, 1863. (942, 959) Assignment as above, July 31st, Maj. J. H. McGaughey in command. August 10, 1863, Col. A. H. Helvenston in command.

No. 51—(12) Assignment as above, Chickamauga campaign. (159-162) Mentioned in General Wood's report of the battle of Chickamauga, September 19-20, 1863; speaks of death from wounds of Major McGaughey. (163-165) Capt. F. A. Ashford, in his report, says: "Both officers and men discharged their duties gallantly. I may be permitted to allude particularly to the noble bearing and fearlessness in discharge of duty of First Lieut. Isaac C. Madding, Company B; Second Lieut. Robert H. Cherry, Company I; First Lieut. G. W. W. Jones, Company G; Second Lieut. John D. Oglesby, Company F, and our gallant commander, Maj. J. H. McGaughey." Gives loss at 25 killed and 218 wounded. (165, 166, 168) Mentioned in General Adams' reports and Col. E. B. Breedlove's report. (533) Roll of honor, battle of Chickamauga: Privates George W. Tims, Company A, killed in action; William A. Watts, Company B, killed in action; William Hill, Company C; Thomas Garner (killed), Company D; Joshua Lewis, Company E; John McMicken (killed), Company F.

No. 55 — (660) In Lowrey's brigade, Breckinridge's corps, army of Tennessee, Chattanooga-Ringgold campaign. (754-756, 768) Mentioned in reports of Gen. P. R. Cleburne and Gen. M. P. Lowrey. (769, 770) Report of Maj. F. A. Ashford, commanding, of the battle of November 27, 1863.

No. 56—(618, 804, 823, 885) Assignment as above, to December 31, 1863.

No. 58—(588) Assignment as above, January 20, 1864; Capt. Barton Dickson in command.

No. 59—(867) Assignment as above, April 30, 1864; Lieutenant-Colonel Ashford in command.

No. 74—(639, 647, 655, 662, 669) Assignment as above, to August 31, 1864. (731, 732) Gen. M. P. Lowrey's report of the engagement of July 22d says: "Regiment captured two Yankee flags." (733) Casualties, 5 killed and 56 wounded, July 22d.

No. 78—(852) Assignment as above. Gen. John B. Hood commanding army, September 20, 1864.

No. 93—(667) Assignment as above. Sixteenth, Thirty-third and Forty-fifth Alabama under Lieut.-Col. R. H. Abercrombie, Hood's army, December 10, 1864. (685) Col. F. A. Ashford killed in battle of Franklin, November 30th.

No. 98—(1063) First Alabama (consolidated Sixteenth, Thirty-third and Forty-fifth), Col. Robert H. Abercrombie, April 9, 1865, Shelley's brigade, Stewart's corps, Johnston's army.

No. 100—(736) In Lowrey's brigade, under Capt. J. J. Higgins, March 31, 1865. (773) Assigned to Shelley's brigade, near Smithfield, N. C., April 9, 1865.

No. 104—(1134) Mentioned by Gen. P. D. Roddey, March 20, 1865.

THE SEVENTEENTH ALABAMA INFANTRY.

The Seventeenth Alabama infantry was organized at Montgomery, August, 1861. Serving first at Pensacola, it was present at the bombardment of that place October 9, 1861. The Seventeenth was distinguished in the battle of Shiloh, taking a prominent part in the capture of Prentiss' division; served at Mobile from the autumn of 1862 to March, 1864; then joined the army of Tennessee, and, under the command of Gen. E. A. O'Neal, afterward governor of Alabama, fought during Sherman's campaign from Dalton to Lovejoy's Station. It was engaged in the battles of Resaca, May 9th, May 13th to 15th; Cassville, May 19th to 226.; Kenesaw Mountain, July 9th to 30th. At Peach Tree Creek its commander, Major Burnett, was severely wounded, and Captain Ragland was killed at Atlanta. The regiment was engaged in the battle of Atlanta, July 22d; at Jonesboro, August 31st to September 1st; and Lovejoy's Station, September 2d to 6th.

The Seventeenth regiment lost heavily at Franklin, November 30th, and at Nashville, December 13th to 16th. Its field officers were Col. Thomas H. Watts, who became attorney-general of the Confederate States; Col. Virgil S. Murphy; Col. J. T. Jones, temporarily assigned; Lieut.-Cols. Edward P. Holcombe, Robert C. Farris, and John Ryan, temporarily assigned, and Maj. Thomas J. Burnett.

EXTRACTS FROM THE OFFICIAL WAR RECORDS.

Vol. IV—(416) Hon. J. R. Benjamin, acting secretary of war, Richmond, Va., September 19, 1861, mentions the "Seventeenth Alabama regiment, commanded by Col. Thomas H. Watts, having been brigaded under Gen. L. P. Walker."

Vol. VI—(768) General Bragg, near Pensacola, November 17, 1861, says: "Colonel Watts' Alabama regiment, for the war, arrived yesterday, 900 strong." (819) Army of Pensacola, Gen. Sam Jones commanding, February 1, 1862.

Vol. X, Part 1—(383) In Jackson's brigade, Second corps, army of the Mississippi, battle of Shiloh. (553-556) Jackson's report, April 6th and 7th, speaks of the Seventeenth Alabama, Lieut.-Col. Robert C. Farris, and of two stands of colors captured by it. (789) Assignment as above, Third corps, June 3, 1862.

Vol. XV—(850) Army of Mobile, Gen. J. E. Slaughter commanding; district of the Gulf, October 31, 1862, Gen. John H. Forney in command. (1068) Assignment as above. General Buckner in command of department of the Gulf, "for April, 1863," at Bay Shore, near Mobile. Col. V. S. Murphy commanding detachment manning Apalachee battery.

Vol. XVI, Part 2—(733) General Bragg, Tupelo, Miss., July 23, 1862, detaches regiment, to form part of garrison of the defenses of Mobile.

No. 42—(39) Assignment as above, department of the Gulf, General Maury, Mobile, June 8, 1863. (120) General Maury, July 23, 1863, says: "Four companies were guarding bridges on Mobile & Ohio railroad. They are artillerists." (131) Cantey's brigade, with General Maury, August 1, 1863. (156) Seventeenth and Twenty-ninth are drilling as artillery, August 10, 1863. (157, 275, 402, 511, 561) Assignment as above, to December 31, 1863. (431) General Maury calls it a fine, large regiment, November 21, 1863.

No. 58—(582) Assignment as above, January 20, 1864.

No. 59—(872) Cantey's brigade, Johnston's army, April 30, 1864.

No. 74—(644) Assignment as above. (646) Cantey's division, with army of Mississippi, Gen. Leonidas Polk in command, June 10th. (653, 660, 665, 671) Cantey's brigade, Johnston's army, Maj. Thomas J. Burnett commanding regiment, June 30th. Thomas A. McCane commanding regiment, July 31st. (941-943) Mentioned in reports of Col. E. A. O'Neal in front of Atlanta, July 31, and August 22, 1864, Maj. T. J. Burnett in command. Captain Ragland killed, "a gallant and meritorious officer." Highly commends Capt. J. F. Tate.

No. 78—(855) Cantey's brigade, Hood's army, September 20, 1864. Capt. William W. McMillan commanding regiment.

No. 93—(666) Cantey's brigade, Hood's army, December 10, 1864. Capt. John Boiling, Jr., commanding regiment.

No. 98 — (1063) Shelley's brigade, Johnston's army, April 9, 1865. Col. Edward P. Holcombe in command of regiment.

No. 100—(735, 773) In Quarles' brigade, consolidated with First and Twenty-ninth Alabama, under Capt. Benj. H. Screws, March 31, 1865.

THE EIGHTEENTH ALABAMA INFANTRY.

The Eighteenth Alabama regiment was organized at Auburn, September, 1861. Its first duty was at Mobile. At the battle of Shiloh it engaged in the severe fighting which resulted in the capture of Prentiss' division, and was ordered by General Wheeler to carry the prisoners to Corinth. It returned to Mobile, where it remained till 1863. It was prominent in the battle of Chickamauga, September 19th and 20th, losing nearly two-thirds of its number, killed and wounded; participated in all the subsequent battles of the army of Tennessee and was distinguished in the Dalton and Atlanta campaign; engaged in the battles in front of Dalton, May 7th to 12th; Resaca, May 14th and 15th; Cassville, May 18th; New Hope Church, May 25th, and Pickett's Mill, May 27th. The regiment was also in battle at Peachtree Creek, July 20th; Atlanta, July 22d; Jonesboro, August 31st and September 1st; Lovejoy's

Station, September 2d to 6th; Franklin, Tenn., November 30th, and Nashville, December 15th and 16th. The Eighteenth was then ordered to Mobile and participated in the defense of Spanish Fort, March 26 to April 8, 1865.

Among the officers killed were: Lieut.-Col. Richard F. Inge, Captains Justice, Stringer, Hammond, and Mickle, and Lieutenants Fielder, McAdory and Kidd, all of whom met death at Chickamauga.

Its commanding officers were: Colonel Inge, whose name heads the roll of honor of the killed and wounded at Chickamauga, given below; Col. Edwin C. Bullock, one of the leading citizens of Alabama, died in November, 1861; Col. Eli S. Shorter, distinguished at Shiloh; Col. James T. Holtzclaw, who was wounded at Shiloh and afterward became distinguished as a brigadier-general, and Col. James Strawbridge, who was temporarily assigned; Lieut.-Col. Peter F. Hunley, and Majs. Sheppard Ruffin, William M. Moxley; also Bryan M. Thomas, who was temporarily assigned and was afterward a prominent brigadier-general.

EXTRACTS FROM OFFICIAL WAR RECORDS.

Vol. IV—(416) Commanded by Col. E. C. Bullock, September 19, 1861. Vol. VI—(772) Aggregate present, 858, December 2, 1861. (795) Mentioned by secretary of war, January 5, 1862. (806) General Bragg, January 14, 1862, says it was organized, and field officers appointed by President. (819) Brigaded under General Withers, in department of Alabama and West Florida, General Bragg in command, February 1, 1862. (836) Ordered to Corinth, Miss.,. February 26, 1862.

Vol. X, Part 1—(383) J. K. Jackson's brigade, Second corps, army of the Mississippi, General Bragg, April 6-7, 1862; Colonel Shorter commanding regiment. (533) Marched Prentiss' captured division to Corinth (General Withers' report). (553-555) Referred to in Gen. J. K. Jackson's report. (557) Colonel Shorter's report, Shiloh, gives 20 killed, 80 wounded. Lieut.-Col. Holtzclaw dangerously wounded while gallantly discharging his duty. (789) Assignment as above, June 30th.

Vol. XV—(850) Army of Mobile, Slaughter commanding; district of the Gulf, commanded by General Forney, October 31, 1862. (1069) Cumming's brigade, department of the Gulf, General Buckner commanding, April, 1863; Col. J. T. Holtzclaw commanding regiment.

Vol. XVI, Part 2—(733) Detached from Hardee's command at Tupelo and made part of garrison of the defenses of Mobile.

Vol. XXIII, Part 2—(943, 960) Clayton's brigade, Hill's corps, Bragg's army, July 31, 1863; Lieut-Col. R. F. Inge commanding regiment.

No. 42—(130) Correspondence relating to regiment— General Maury, August 1, 1863.

No. 51—(16) Assignment as above, battle of Chickamauga, September 19-20, 1863. Field officers: Colonel Holtzclaw, Lieutenant-Colonel Inge, Maj. P. F. Hunley. (367) Casualties, 36 killed, 250 wounded, September 18th to 20th. (369) Roll of honor, Chickamauga: Sergt. T. J. Durritt, Company

E; Private J. Jones, Company F; Corp. and Color-bearer J. B. Moore, Company G; Private T. F. Hughston, Company K. (400-404) Mentioned in report of General Clayton. Aggregate strength on 19th, 527; on 20th, 306. (405,406) Major Hunley's report says: "The regiment went into the fight with aggregate 527, and the total loss of the battle was 297. Colonel Holtzclaw was thrown from his horse and badly hurt. S. K. Fielder, first lieutenant, Company H, was mortally wounded while gallantly cheering on his men. Pollard and Harper, first and second lieutenants, Company A, were wounded, the first mortally, the last severely. Captain Wilkerson was wounded in the heel. Captain Mickle was severely wounded while leading his company (I) in the charge. Captain Stone of Company K, wounded in the neck. Lieutenant Johnston, Company I, wounded in the right forearm. Lieutenant Riser, Company K, knocked down twice during the charge, with grapeshot, but remained with the regiment until next day. Captain Justice (than whom there was not a more gallant officer in the service) and Lieutenant McAdory were killed outright. Lieut.-Col. R. F. Inge was mortally wounded while gallantly leading the right of the regiment. Captains Stringer, Company B, and Hammond, Company D, were mortally wounded. Officers and men all behaved well, and it hardly seems just to make any distinction when all tried to do their duty, but I cannot refrain from mentioning Captain Ruffin and Lieut. J. B. Darby of Company H, Captain Mickle, Company I, Lieutenant Stewart, Company E, and Lieutenant Riser, Company K, who were especially distinguished for their good conduct during the battle." (408, 411) Mentioned by Colonel Woodruff and Col. A. R. Lankford. (533) Roll of honor, Chickamauga: Lieut.-Col. R. P. Inge;* Capts. J. H. Justice,* Company A; Orville A. Stringer,* Company B; J. H. Hammond,* Company D; First Lieuts. A. J. Kidd,* Company D; S. K. Fielder,* Company H; Private J. M. Carpenter, Company A; Corp. J. W. Williams, Company B; Privates J. P. Young,* Company G; Hiram L. White, Company H (since dead); Corp. C. Roden,* Company I; Private David Stewart, Company K; Sergts. R. A. Micars,* Company C; R. A. Lambert, Company D; Privates W. Howard,* Company E; M. Smith, Company F; J. H. Gwin,* Company H; Sergt. J. F. Williamson, Company H; Corp. C. W. O'Hara, Company I;. Private W. A. McCarty,* Company K.

No. 55—(661) In Clayton's brigade, Bragg's army, November 20, 1863; Maj. Shep. Ruffin commanding regiment. (745) Casualties, 4 killed, 48 wounded, Chattanooga-Ringgold campaign.

No. 56—(618, 805) Assignment as above, to December 10, 1863. (824) Aggregate regimental strength, 827, December 14th. (887) Assignment as above, December 31, 1863, Colonel Holtzclaw commanding regiment.

No. 57—(479) Casualties, 7 wounded, at Rocky Face Mountain, February 24-25, 1864.

* Killed in action.

No. 74—(641, 649, 657, 664, 672) Holtzclaw's brigade, Johnston's army, from July 10, 1864, to August 31, 1864, Lieut.-Col. P. F. Hunley commanding regiment. (818) Mentioned in report of Gen. A. P. Stewart. Operations May 7 to 27, 1864. (832, 833) Mentioned in report of Gen. H. D. Clayton, for May 7th to 27th, "Captain Darby, of the Eighteenth, a gallant and zealous officer." (834) Casualties, 2 killed, 4 wounded. (836) Report of Colonel Hunley, 14 killed and 97 wounded. (841-844) Report of Colonel Bushrod Jones makes special mention of gallantry of Lieutenant Stewart. (862) Mentioned in report of Maj. J. E. Austin, Atlanta campaign.

No. 78—(854) Assignment as above, September 20, 1864.

No. 79—(897) Organization of Clayton's division, Lee's corps, army of Tennessee; aggregate of regiment, 765, November 7, 1864.

No. 93—(665) Assignment as above, December 10, 1864.

No. 103—(938) Holtzclaw's brigade left Meridian for Mobile, January 26, 1865. (1046) In Holtzclaw's brigade, district of the Gulf, March 10, 1865; Capt. A. C. Greene in command of regiment.

No. 104—(226) Mentioned by A. M. Jackson (Union), March 22 1865.

THE NINETEENTH ALABAMA INFANTRY.

The Nineteenth Alabama infantry was organized at Huntsville, August, 1861; served at Mobile and Pensacola until February, 1862, when it joined the army at Corinth; made a brilliant record at the battle of Shiloh, where it lost 219 killed and wounded; was in the Kentucky campaign and prominent at Murfreesboro, December 31st to January 2d; was engaged in the fighting incident to the retreat of the army from Tullahoma to Chattanooga, June 27 to July 4, 1863; added increased luster to its reputation at Chickamauga, September 19th and 20th, and was warmly engaged at Missionary Ridge, November 23d to 25th. The Nineteenth was in the Georgia campaign from May until September, 1864, taking part with great credit in the numerous battles of that heated campaign, including the fighting around Dalton, May 7th to May 9th; Resaca, May 13th to 15th; Cassville, May 19th to 22d; Kenesaw, June 9th. to 30th; Peachtree Creek, July 20th; the great battle on the Decatur road, July 22d; Ezra Chapel, July 28th; Jonesboro, August 31st and September 1st, and Lovejoy's Station, September 2d to 6th. The regiment went with General Hood into Tennessee, and fought with gallantry at Franklin, November 30th; at Nashville, December 13th to 16th, and also at Bentonville, N. C., March 19 to 21, 1865.

Among the killed were: Capts. William R. McKenzie, May 29th, at Corinth; R. J. Healey, at Murfreesboro; H. L. Houston, at Atlanta; Capt. Nathan J. Venable, at Marietta; Capt. Ed. Thornton, at Jonesboro; Lieut. Joseph B. High, at Chickamauga.

Its field officers were: Cols. Joseph Wheeler and Samuel K. McSpadden; Lieut.-Cols. Edward D. Tracy, afterward brigadier-general and killed near Port Gibson, May 1, 1863, George R. Kimbrough and Nick Davis. Its majors were James H. Savage and Solomon Palmer.

EXTRACTS FROM OFFICIAL WAR RECORDS.

Vol. IV—(416) Commanded by Col. Joseph Wheeler; assigned to Brig.-Gen. L. P. Walker, September 19, 1861.

Vol. VI—(772) Aggregate present, 940, December 2, 1861. (819) Army of Mobile, General Withers commanding; department of Alabama and West Florida, commanded by General Bragg, February 1, 1862.

Vol. X, Part 1—(383) In Jackson's brigade, army of the Mississippi, battle of Shiloh. (5 34,535) Mentioned in Gen. Jones M. Withers' report. Regiment covered rear guard. (552. 553) Mentioned by Gen. James R. Chalmers and Gen. John K. Jackson. (556) Stand of colors captured by Wheeler. (558-560) Colonel Wheeler's report. He particularly mentions Lieut.-Col. E. D. Tracy, Maj. S. K. McSpadden, Adjt. Clifton Walker, Lieuts. Solomon Palmer, R. H. Hagood, J. N. Barry, J. E. Nabbers, D. C. Hodo, W. H. Anderson, B. L. Porter, and Sergt.-Maj. P. L. Griffitts. (561-563) Mentioned by Col. John C. Moore. (788) In Gardner's brigade, June 30, 1862. (839) Wheeler's report, Farmington, May 10, 1862. (853) Wheeler's report, Bridge Creek, May 28th and 29th: "Capt. W. R. D. McKenzie, a most gallant and efficient officer, received a mortal wound." Particularly mentions Captain Hollinsworth and others.

Vol. XVI, Part 2—(764) In Gardner's brigade, Withers' division, army of the Mississippi, under Maj.-Gen. L. Polk, August 18 and 20, 1862.

Vol. XVII, Part 2—(633) Assignment as above, June 30, 1862.

Vol. XX, Part 1—(658) Deas' brigade, Withers' division, army of Tennessee, Stone's River campaign. (677) 8 killed, 143 wounded, Murfreesboro; Capt. Robert J. Healey killed.

Vol. XX, Part 2—(418, 431) Same assignment, November, 1862.

Vol. XXIII, Part 2—(735, 942, 958) In Deas' brigade, Withers' division, Polk's army corps, April to August, 1863, Col. S. K. McSpadden commanding regiment.

No. 51—(15) Assignment as above, September 19-20, 1863, battle of Chickamauga. (333-335) Report of Colonel McSpadden says: "While I cannot specify the many acts of gallantry and daring exhibited by the different officers and men under my command, there was one instance of valor and daring so extraordinary as to demand my attention. On the second charge in the evening, when the troops on my right began to waver, Capt. Hugh L. Houston, Company B, sprang to his colors, and, rushing with them to within 30 steps of the enemy's cannon, gallantly waved them and urged the men to follow their country's banner." Loss, 34 killed and 158 wounded. Lieut. Joseph B. High, Company H, a good man, a consistent Christian, fell while gallantly leading his company.

No. 56—(617, 805, 825, 886) Aggregate present and absent, 734, December 14, 1863. In Deas' brigade, Hindman's division, army of Tennessee,

Gen. Joseph E. Johnston commanding, December 31, 1863. Lieut.-Col. George R. Kimbrough.

No. 58—(589) Maj. Sol. Palmer commanding regiment, January 20, 1864.

No. 74—(346, 640, 648, 656) Assignment as above. Lieut.-Col. George R. Kimbrough in command of regiment, June 30, 1864. (663) In Johnston's brigade, Anderson's division, Lee's corps, army of Tennessee, July 31st. Lieut.-Col. Harry T. Toulmin in command of regiment. (776, 777) Report of Lieutenant-Colonel Toulmin, commanding brigade, of the engagement of the 28th of July, near Atlanta.

No. 78—(853) Assignment as above, September 20, 1864. Lieut.-Col. George R. Kimbrough commanding.

No. 93—(664) Assignment as above, December 10, 1864.

No. 98—(1065) In Pettus' brigade, Stevenson's division, Lee's corps, General Johnston commanding; Lieut.-Col. E. S. Gulley commanding regiment.

No. 100—(734) In Deas' brigade, army of Tennessee, March 31, 1865, Maj. Sol. Palmer in command of regiment.

THE TWENTIETH ALABAMA INFANTRY.

This regiment was organized in Montgomery, September 16, 1861. Its first service was at Mobile. It was in the campaign in Kentucky, under Gen. Kirby Smith; then was sent to Mississippi; fought with great gallantry and sustained severe loss at Port Gibson, May 1, 1863, and Champion's Hill, or Baker's Creek, May 16th; was distinguished for bravery in the siege of Vicksburg, and surrendered with that fortress. After being exchanged the regiment joined Bragg and fought with great gallantry at Missionary Ridge, and, during the campaign of 1864, took part in nearly all the battles from Dalton to Atlanta. It suffered severely at Rocky Face, May 5-9, 1864; Kenesaw, June 27th, and Jonesboro, August 31st and September 1st; but with unabated courage fought at Nashville, December 15 and 16, 1864; at Kinston, N. C., March 4, 1865, and at Bentonville, March 19th to 21st.

Its field officers were Cols. Isham W. Garrott, who was promoted brigadier-general and killed at Vicksburg, June 17, 1863; Robert T. Jones, who was transferred to the Twelfth Alabama and killed at the battle of Seven Pines; Edmund W. Pettus, who was promoted brigadier-general and afterward became United States senator; Charles D. Anderson and James M. Dedman. Its lieutenant-colonels were Mitchell T. Porter, and John W. Davis, who was wounded at Rocky Face and at Marietta. Its majors were Alfred S. Pickering, killed at Port Gibson, and John G. Harris. Capt. Jack Ayres, a gallant officer of the regiment, was killed at Jonesboro.

EXTRACTS FROM OFFICIAL WAR RECORDS.

Vol. VI—(772) Aggregate present, 836, December 2, 1861, district of Alabama, Gen. J. M. Withers commanding. (819) Army of Mobile, General Withers; department of Alabama and Florida, General Bragg; Mobile, February 1, 1862. (894) Bragg dispatches war department that regiment is on way to Knoxville, February 18, 1862.

Vol. XVI, Part 2—(715) In Barton's brigade, department of East Tennessee, Gen. Kirby Smith commanding, June, 1862, Col. Isham W. Garrott commanding regiment. (719) In Reynolds' brigade, department of East Tennessee, July 3d. (984) In Tracy's brigade, Second division, troops under Gen. Kirby Smith, October, 1862.

Vol. XVII, Part 2—(825) General Tracy gives regiment 630 strong, January 3, 1863.

No. 36—(678-682) Col. I. W. Garrott's report of the battle of Port Gibson, Miss., May 1, 1863, speaks of the fearless and chivalrous Lieut.-Col. E. W. Pettus; also of Capt. J. McKee Gould and Lieut. J. W. Parish, Capts. R. H. Pratt, B. D. Massingale and J. N. Dedman; Maj. A. S. Pickering fell mortally wounded while nobly discharging his duty; Sergt. Earle here fell while fearlessly carrying the colors. Loss, 18 killed, 112 wounded. Sergt. Powers highly commended; also Colonel Smith.

No. 37—(95) Mentioned in Gen. Carter L. Stevenson's, report of the battle of Champion's Hill, Miss., May 16, 1863. (101-103) Mentioned in Gen. Stephen D. Lee's report of same. (326) In S. D. Lee's brigade, army of Vicksburg, Lieut.-Gen. John C. Pemberton commanding, Col. E. P. Pettus commanding regiment, siege of Vicksburg, May 18 to July 4, 1863. (329) Col. Isham W. Garrott killed, June 17, 1863. (345) General Stevenson in his report of siege speaks most highly of Lieutenant-Colonel Pettus and Colonel Garrott. (350-352) Mentioned by Gen. S. D. Lee: "The officers who attracted my attention were Col. Isham W. Garrott, of Twentieth Alabama, the pure patriot and gallant soldier who was killed on June 17th while in the fearless discharge of his duties, respected and loved by all who knew him; a more attentive and vigilant officer was not in our service. Col. E. W. Pettus, Twentieth Alabama, won the admiration of every one by his daring on May 22d, and by his uniform good conduct during the remainder of the siege." (353) Mentioned in Capt. A. C. Roberts' report of siege. (357,358) In report of Col. T. N. Waul, of assault May 22d, says: "Lieutenant-Colonel Pettus, thoroughly acquainted with the locality and its approaches, came, musket in hand, and most gallantly offered to guide and lead the party into the fort. Three of Colonel Shelley's regiment also volunteered; with promptness and alacrity they moved to the assault, retook the fort, drove the enemy through the breach they entered, tore down the stand of colors still floating over the parapet, and sent it to the colonel commanding the legion, who immediately transmitted it with a note to General Lee."

No. 38—(612, 703) In Tracy's brigade, Stevenson's division, department of Mississippi and Eastern Louisiana; Gen. John C. Pemberton commanding. (1059) In Lee's brigade, Stevenson's division, army of Vicksburg, Demopolis, Ala., August 29th.

No. 55—(662) In Pettus' brigade, Stevenson's division, army of Tennessee, General Bragg commanding, November 20, 1863; Capt. John W. Davis commanding regiment. (724) Return of casualties: 9 killed, 39 wounded, Missionary Ridge. (725) General Cheatham in special orders thanks the officers and men of his command. He says: "It was Pettus' brigade (of his division) which first checked an enemy, flushed with victory on Lookout mountain, and held him at bay until ordered to retire." (731-732) Mentioned in Gen. E. W. Pettus' report of the battle of Missionary Ridge: "The Twentieth Alabama behaved gallantly."

No. 56—(804, 823, 884) In Pettus' brigade, Stevenson's division, army of Tennessee, December, 1863. Total present, 526; Lieut.-Col. M. T. Porter commanding regiment.

No. 59—(869) Assignment as above, April 30, 1864; Col. J. M. Dedman commanding regiment.

No. 74—(641, 649, 656, 663, 672) Assignment as above, April to August, 1864. Capt. I. W. Davidson commanding regiment, July, 1864.

No. 78—(853) Assignment as above, September 20, 1864.

No. 93—(665, 1224) Assignment as above, to December, 1864. (694) Gen. C. L. Stevenson's report of campaign in Tennessee, September 29 to December 17, 1864. Regiment highly commended.

No. 94—(799, 801) Aggregate present, 334, January 19, 1865. Pettus' brigade, Lieut.-Col. John W. Davis commanding regiment.

No. 98—(1065) Assignment as above. Forces commanded by Gen. Joseph E. Johnston, April 9, 1865; Lieut.-Col. James K. Elliott commanding.

No. 100—(733) Assignment as above, March 31, 1865, Lieut.-Col. John W. Davis commanding.

THE TWENTY-FIRST ALABAMA INFANTRY.

This regiment was organized in Mobile in October, 1861, and served that winter at Mobile. In March, 1862, it proceeded to Corinth and was distinguished in the battle of Shiloh, April 6th and 7th, being complimented in general orders. It also fought at Farmington, May 3d, after which the regiment was ordered back to Mobile. Two of its companies withstood a bombardment of two weeks from 5 gunboats and 6 mortar boats in their attempt to force an entrance to Grant's pass, August, 1864. They held out heroically until, overwhelmed by the immense resources of the enemy, they blew up the fort and evacuated it. The six companies stationed at Fort Gaines held out until August 8, 1864, when they were compelled to surrender. The rest of the regiment formed part of the garrison at Spanish Fort and engaged in its defense, March 26 to April 8, 1865. Lieutenant Dixon, a gallant Kentuckian of this regiment, and several of his command, volunteered to man a submarine torpedo boat in Charleston harbor. They went to sea the night of February 17, 1864, and blew up the Housatonic, of the Federal blockading squadron, but the brave crew all perished by the explosion which destroyed the Federal vessel.

Its colonels were James Crawford and Chas. D. Anderson. Its lieutenant-colonels were Andrew J. Ingersol, Stewart W. Cayce, Charles S. Stewart and James M. Williams. Its majors were Frederick K. Stewart, Franklin J. McCoy and Charles G. Johnston.

EXTRACTS FROM OFFICIAL WAR RECORDS.

Vol. VI—(756) General Bragg reports that Colonel Crawford's regiment has consented to change tenure of service and is mustered in for 12 months. (819) Brigaded under General Withers, army of Mobile, department of Alabama and West Florida, February 1, 1862.

Vol. VII—(915) Memoranda of Gen. G. T. Beauregard, Jackson, Tenn., March 3, 1862, says: "Regiment to go to Fort Pillow."

Vol. X, Part 1—(383) In Gladden's brigade, army of Mississippi, at battle of Shiloh, April 6-7, 1862. (534) Mentioned in Gen. Jones M. Withers' report. (538) Col. Z. C. Deas' report mentions Lieut.-Col. S. W. Cayce in command. (540, 541) Cayce's report thanks and praises Major Stewart and Capt. John F. Jewett. Mentions particularly Lieutenants Parker, Rogers, Williams, and Savage, and Captains Chamberlain and Stewart. Maj. F. Stewart resigned. (556-563) Mentioned in Col. John C. Moore's reports. (789) In Gen. J. K. Jackson's brigade, army of the Mississippi, General Bragg commanding, June 30, 1862.

XV—(850) First battalion at Choctaw and Owen, bluffs, Col. C. D. Anderson commanding. Second battalion at Forts Morgan and Gaines, Col. W. L. Powell commanding. District of the Gulf, Gen. J. H. Forney commanding, October 31, 1862.

Vol. XVII, Part 2—(633, 659) In Gen. J. K. Jackson's brigade, army of the Mississippi, June 30, 1862. By command of General Bragg, Twenty-first Alabama detached from the army of the Mississippi, and assigned to duty as part of garrison of Mobile, July 26th.

No. 42—(39, 131, 157, 275) Department of the Gulf, Cantey's and Powell's brigades, Gen. Dabney H. Maury commanding, June to September, 1863. (402) Third brigade, department of the Gulf, General Maury commanding, November, 1863. (511, 562) Third brigade, Gen. Edward Higgins, Mobile, commanding, to January 20, 1864.

No. 59—(861) In Page's brigade, General Maury's army, April 30, 1864.

No. 77—(428) General Maury, August 12, 1864, mentions the regiment as part of garrison of Fort Gaines. (441, 442) Col. James M. Williams' report of the evacuation and destruction of Fort Powell, on the night of August 5th.

No. 78—(678, 703, 752) In Page's brigade, General Maury's army, June to August, 1864.

No. 79—(876) Detachment under Capt. B. Frank Dade, in Taylor's command, November 1, 1864.

No. 84—(142) Colonel Myers (Union) says: "Eight companies, 50 men each, 400 strong, are at Fort Gaines, July 12, 1864." He says, July 10th, that they are guarding salt-works at Bonsecours bay.

No. 94—(633) Detachment of regiment in Taylor's, command, department of Alabama, Mississippi, and East Louisiana, December 1, 1864.

No. 103—(1046) In Thomas' brigade, district of the Gulf, March 10, 1865. Lieut.-Col. James M. Williams in command of regiment.

No, 104—(226, 1158, 1163) Mentioned by A. M. Jackson, H. L. D. Lewis and Gen. R. L. Gibson. (1184) General Gibson asks for the regiment to be sent to him at Blakely, April 1, 1865.

THE TWENTY-SECOND ALABAMA INFANTRY.

This regiment was organized at Montgomery, November, 1861, and armed by private enterprise. It first served in Mobile; from there it was ordered to Corinth and reached Tennessee in time for the battle of Shiloh, where it suffered severe loss. It fought at Munfordville, September 14 to 16, 1862; at Perryville, October 8th, and at Murfreesboro, December 31 to January 2, 1863. It took a very brilliant part in the impetuous assault on Rosecrans' army at Chickamauga, September 20th, and suffered severely, losing almost two-thirds of its forces, the killed including five color-bearers. It served in the campaign in Georgia, losing heavily in the battles around Atlanta, July, 1864, and at Jonesboro, August 31st and September 1st. It was also distinguished at Franklin, November 30th; at Nashville, December 15th and 16th; at Kinston, N. C., March 14, 1865, and at Bentonville, March 19th to 21st. In April it was consolidated with the Twenty-fifth, Thirty-ninth and Fiftieth, under Colonel Toulmin.

Col. John C. Marrast died in the service, after having made a glorious record. Capt. Abner C. Gaines was killed, and Maj. R. B. Armistead mortally wounded, at Shiloh. Lieuts. J. N. Smith and J. H. Wall fell at Murfreesboro, Lieut.-Col. John Weedon, Capt. James Deas Nott and Lieuts. Waller Mordecai and Renfroe were killed at Chickamauga; Col. Benj. R. Hart, Capt. Thomas M. Brindley, Lieuts. Leary and Stackpoole at Atlanta, and Capt. Ben. B. Little was killed at Jonesboro. The other field officers were Col. Zach C. Deas, afterward a noted brigadier-general; Col. Harry T. Toulmin, now U. S. district judge; Lieut.-Cols. Napoleon D. Rouse and Herbert E. Armistead; Majs. Thomas McPrince, Robert D. Armistead and Robert Donnell.

EXTRACTS FROM OFFICIAL WAR RECORDS.

Vol. VI—(764) General Bragg, in letter of November 5, 1861, near Pensacola, writes: "Colonel Deas' regiment (Twenty-second Alabama), armed by private enterprise, ordered to report to General Withers at Mobile." (772) Aggregate present, 709 for duty, with General Withers, district of Alabama, December 2d. (819) With General Bragg, February 1, 1862, in department of Alabama and West Florida, in army of Mobile, commanded by General Withers. (836) Ordered to Corinth by General Bragg, February 26, 1862.

Vol. X, Part 1—(13, 383) In General Gladden's brigade, army of Mississippi, battle of Shiloh, April 6-7, 1862. (538,539) Report of Col. Z. C. Deas says: "The indomitable courage and perseverance of the officers and men of this brigade; the willingness and gallantry with which they marched to the attack when called upon, after having endured almost superhuman fatigue in the desperate and long-continued struggles of Sunday and Monday, are deserving of the highest encomiums. Where so many acted nobly, it might appear invidious to particularize, but impartiality compels me to record as first in the fight the First Louisiana infantry and Twenty-second Alabama. I wish here to call the attention of my superiors to such field officers as especially distinguished themselves in my immediate vicinity for their coolness and gallant bearing under the hottest fire, Lieut.-Col. John Marrast, Adjutant Travis and Sergeant Nott." (540) Strength of regiment after the battle of April 6th was only 123. Col. J. Q. Loomis in his report of same battle, speaks in high terms of praise of Colonel Deas. (541) Col. Z. C. Deas' report says: "Maj. R. B. Armistead was mortally wounded in the first engagement, but he fell where every brave soldier should be found to fall, in the front rank, doing his whole duty and urging his men on to victory. In him his country has lost a most intelligent and gallant officer." (542,543) Report of Col. J. C. Marrast: "Captain Gaines, Company C, was killed, gallantly leading his company." On Monday morning, April 7th, the regiment was 143 strong. The following officers and privates are mentioned for being particularly conspicuous for soldierly bearing and bravery during the two days' action: Company A—Capt. John C. Weedon, Lieut. J. M. Whitney, Corps. Alexander Inman (killed), S. V. Cain (wounded), W. D. Sumner (wounded), Privates J. L. Penley, J. J. Faught. Company B—Capt. J. D. Nott, Privates Bartlett Anderson (wounded), H. C. McMillan. Company C— Capt. A. L. Gaines (killed), Private Frank Allen. Company H—Private William West. Company I—Capt. A. P. Love (wounded), First Sergt. S. J. Skinner. Company E—Capt. J. R. Northcott, Sergt. R. J. Moore (wounded), Corp. James M. Tedder (wounded). Company K—Capt. B. R. Hart, Lieut. R. L. Myrick (wounded), Privates. Aaron Coffey, Monroe Brown. Company D—Capt. E. H. Armistead, Capt. R. J. Hill (wounded), Adjt. E. F. Travis (wounded), Sergt.-Maj. Nott,Quartermaster-Sergt. C. I. Michailoffsky. (788) Gardner's brigade, Bragg's army, June 30th. (839) Mentioned in report of Gen. Joseph Wheeler; skirmish near Farmington, May 10th. (853) Mentioned in report of Col. Jos. Wheeler, operations May 28th and 29th.

Vol. XVI, Part 2—(764) Gardner's brigade with Gen. Leonidas Polk, August 18 and 20, 1862.

Vol. XVII, Part 2—(633) Gardner's brigade, Bragg's army, June 30, 1862.

Vol. XX, Part 1—(658) Withers' division, army of Tennessee, Stone's River campaign. (677) Casualties, 11 killed and 83 wounded. Among the killed, Lieuts. J. N. Smith and J. H. Wall. (973) Roll of honor, battle of Murfreesboro, December 31 to January 2, 1863: Sergt. W. D. Sumner, Company A; Private William Sellers, Company B; Corp. J. L. Husbands, Company C; Sergt. B. T. Nelson, Company D; Sergt. P. A. Minton, Company E; Corp. N. B. Walker, Company F; Private J. R. Black, Company G; Corp. W. R. Larry, Company H; Private J. J. McVey, Company I; Private J. N. Eilands, Company K.

Vol. XXIII, Part 2—(735) Twenty-second and Twenty-fifth Alabama commanded by Lieut.-Col. Geo. D. Johnston, Deas' brigade, Polk's army corps, April 1, 1863. (942) Col. John C. Marrast in command, July 31st. (958). Lieut.-Col. John Weedon in command, August 10, 1863.

No. 51—(15) Deas' brigade, Bragg's army, September 19 and 20, 1863. (335-337) Capt Harry Toulmin's report of the battle of Chickamauga: Went into action with 371 men; 44 killed and 161 wounded; total loss, 203. "Capt. J. D. Nott and Lieut. Waller Mordecai, of Company B, fell mortally wounded. No truer patriots ever lived; no better, braver soldiers ever died. Sergeant Leary, bravely bearing the colors, fell severely wounded. The colors were then seized by Lieutenant Leonard, and borne by him until wounded. They then fell into the hands of Lieutenant Renfroe, Company K, who gallantly carried them to the front and planted them almost within the enemy's line. We lost many brave spirits, none of whom deserve more honorable mention than Lieutenant Renfroe, who fell pierced through the head, with colors in his hand. Here, too, fell our brave, our true, our loved commander, Col. John Weedon. Having led with distinguished coolness and bravery his command to within 20 paces of the enemy's line, he fell to rise no more. He fell beneath the honored folds of that cherished flag, under which he had so gallantly led his brave men. Private Bushnell, bearing the colors, rushed fearlessly to the front and in advance of the line, where he was literally riddled with bullets. Where all did so well, both officers and men, it would be hard to discriminate, but I cannot fail to mention the coolness and gallantry of Adjt. W. G. Smith, and to express my appreciation of services rendered by him during the battle; nor can I close without the honorable mention of Lieutenant Michailoffsky, of Company B, whose conduct was so worthy the cause in which he fought, and whose gallantry was so conspicuous on every part of the field. I am proud to be able to state that the command displayed such conduct on the battlefield of Chickamauga as will entitle it to another star in the crown of glory it has already won."

No. 56—(617, 805, 886) Assignment as above, October to December, 1863. (825) Total present, 272, December 14th. Lieut.-Col. Benj. R. Hart commanding.

No. 74—(640, 648, 656) Assignment as above, April to July, 1864. (663) Johnston's brigade, July 31, 1864, Capt. Isaac M. Whitney in command of regiment. (776,777) Report of Col. Harry Toulmin (commanding brigade) of operations, July 28, 1864, Atlanta campaign, says: "We mourn the loss of many brave spirits who have given tip their lives in defense of their country's cause. Prominent among these was Col. B. R. Hart, of the Twenty-second Alabama regiment. It was in the first charge on the enemy's main line of works that he lost his life while gallantly leading on his men and cheering them to victory." (777,778) Report of Capt. I. M. Whitney, for July 28th, 5 killed and 35 wounded. "Lieutenant Leary, gallantly bearing the colors, fell with the folds covering his body. Lieutenant Stackpoole fell at the head of his company."

No. 93—(664) Deas' brigade, Hood's army, December to, 1864. Regiment commanded by Capt. W. H. Henry. (684) Maj. E. H. Armistead wounded at Franklin, November 30, 1864.

No. 98—(1064) Brantley's brigade, Lee's corps, Johnston's army. After April 9, 1865, consolidated with the Twenty-fifth, Thirty-ninth and Fiftieth Alabama, under Col. Harry T. Toulmin.

No. 100—(734) Deas' brigade, army near Smithfield, N. C., commanded by Gen. Joseph E. Johnston, March 31, 1865. Regiment commanded by Capt. Isaac M. Whitney.

THE TWENTY-THIRD ALABAMA INFANTRY.

This regiment was armed by private enterprise and organized at Montgomery in November, 1861; first served at Mobile and then in the Kentucky campaign. It took a prominent part at Port Gibson, May 1, 1863, and lost heavily; was at Baker's Creek, May 16th; at Big Black, May 17th; and served in the trenches during the siege of Vicksburg, May 18th to July 4th. It joined the army of Tennessee in October, 1864, and fought at Lookout Mountain and Missionary Ridge, November 23d to 25th; was with Johnston in his campaign in Georgia in 1864, and suffered very heavily at Jonesboro; was with Hood in Tennessee, and did splendid service in covering the retreat of Hood's army from Nashville. The regiment last won distinction at Bentonville, March 19-21, 1865. Capt. John Stevens was killed at Port Gibson, Col. Franklin K. Beck at Resaca, Maj. A. C. Roberts at New Hope, Capt. F. Butterfield at Atlanta, and Captain Rutherford at Jonesboro. Other field officers were Col. Joseph B. Bibb and Majs. Felix Tait, Francis McMurray, John J. Longmire, G. W. Mathieson and James T. Hester.

EXTRACTS FROM OFFICIAL WAR RECORDS.

Vol. VI—(764,765) General Bragg, writing from Pensacola, Novembers, 1861, says: "Colonel Beck's regiment, already armed by private enterprise, is ordered to report to General Withers at Mobile." (772, 819) Aggregate present, 674, December 2d. District of Mobile, commanded by Gen. J. M. Withers. (894) Sent to Knoxville by General Bragg, February 18, 1862.

Vol. XVI, Part 2—(715, 719) Taylor's brigade, department of East Tennessee, Gen. Kirby Smith, June and July, 1862. (984) In Tracy's brigade, same army, October, 1862.

Vol. XVII, Part 1—(684) Mentioned in Gen. S. D. Lee's report of battle at Chickasaw bayou, near Vicksburg, December 28-29, 1862. (688,689) Col. W. T. Withers' report of same.

Vol. XVII, Part 2—(825) Two companies mentioned in field report of General Tracy's command, January 3d, at Chickasaw bluffs.

No. 36—(664) Mentioned with commendation in Gen. J. S. Bowen's report of the battle of Port Gibson, Miss., May 1, 1863. (673,674) Gen. M. E. Green's report of same battle: "All fought well and did their duty. All stood at their posts until ordered to leave." (678-682) Mentioned, I. W. Garrott's report of same battle.

No. 37—(95-97) Mentioned in Gen. C. L. Stevenson's report, battle of Champion's Hill, Miss., May 16, 1863. (101-103) Gen. S. D. Lee's report: "The enemy was handsomely repulsed by the Twenty-third Alabama regiment, Forty-sixth and Thirtieth, all under the gallant Col. F. K. Beck, having moved forward under a heavy fire and driven back a battery of the enemy. These three regiments behaved with distinguished gallantry." (326) In Lee's brigade,, army of Vicksburg, General Pemberton commanding, July 4, 1863. (343) Mentioned by General Stevenson in his report of siege of Vicksburg. (350-352) Gen. S. D. Lee says: "Regiment fought gallantly at the siege of Vicksburg; Colonel Beck was particularly brave and vigilant." (352,353) Capt. A. C. Roberts' report of engagement at Big Black river, May 17th. (354) Mentioned in report of Maj. G. W. Mathieson of same engagement. Colonel Beck had his leg badly broken by kick from horse. Lieut. M. A. Cobb, an efficient and gallant officer, wounded in head. Seventeen were killed, 15 wounded; two of the latter died subsequently.

No. 55—(129) Mentioned by Gen. Gordon Granger at Orchard Knob, November 27, 1863. (662) In Pettus' brigade, Breckinridge's corps, army of Tennessee, General Bragg commanding; Lieut.-Col. J. B. Bibb commanding regiment, November 20, 1863. (724-726) Return of casualties, 2 killed and 16 wounded in the battles of Lookout Mountain and Missionary Ridge, November 24th and 25th.

No. 56—(804, 823, 884) Pettus' brigade, Stevenson's division, army of Tennessee. Total present, 374, December 14, 1863.

No. 57—(482) General Pettus reports 7 wounded, 1 mortally, at Rocky Face, February 25, 1864.

Nos. 58, 59, 74, 78—Assignment as above, January to September, 1864.

No. 93—(665, 1224) Assignment as above, December 10, 1864, under General Hood.

No. 94—(799, 801) Aggregate present 202, January 19, 1865.

No. 98—(1065) Assignment as above, after April 9th. Maj. Jas. T. Hester in command of regiment. (1098, 1099) General Pettus' report of Bentonville, March 19th, highly commends Col. J. B. Bibb for vigilance and activity.

No. 100—(733) Pettus' brigade, Lee's corps, army of Tennessee. Hardee's army corps, near Smithfield, N. C., March 31, 1865. Maj. James T. Hester commanding regiment.

THE TWENTY-FOURTH ALABAMA INFANTRY.

This regiment was organized at Mobile in August, 1861. In April it was ordered to Corinth, and was under fire at Farmington, May 9th, and Blackland, June 4, 1862. It was in the Kentucky campaign, but did not become engaged; lost heavily at Murfreesboro, and was distinguished at Chickamauga, where it lost over 30 per cent. of its number, and at Missionary Ridge. It was with General Johnston in the campaign of 1864, and fought in most of the battles from Dalton to Jonesboro. It was at Columbia, Tenn., November 29th; at Franklin, November 30th, and at Nashville, December 15th and 16th.

Capt. W. B. Smith and Lieutenant Cooper were killed at Murfreesboro, Capt. Wm. J. O'Brien at Chickamauga, and Capt. John B. Hazard, mortally wounded at Missionary Ridge, was taken prisoner and died at Johnson's Island.

Its commanders were Cols. William A. Buck and Newton N. Davis, Lieut.-Cols. Benjamin F. Sawyer, Wm. B. Dennett, Geo. A. Jennison and Wm. M. LeBaron, Maj. Junius J. Pierce. Capts. S. H. Oliver and Thos. J. Kimbell were at times in command of regiment.

EXTRACTS FROM OFFICIAL WAR RECORDS.

Vol. VI—(756) General Bragg, Mobile, October 25, 1861, says that "Colonel Buck's regiment has changed its time and tenure of service and is mustered in for twelve months." (819) Assigned to army of Mobile, General Withers commanding, department of Alabama and West Florida, Gen. Braxton Bragg, February 1, 1862. (875,876) Aggregate present, 680, under orders from Fort Morgan to Corinth; report of Gen. Sam Jones, April 15th.

Vol. X, Part 1—(789) Gen. J. K. Jackson's brigade, General Bragg's army, June 30, 1862.

Vol. XX, Part 1—(659) Anderson's brigade, Polk's corps, army of Tennessee, December, 1862. (678) Return of casualties, 20 killed, 95 wounded, at battle of Murfreesboro; Capt. William D. Smith killed. (696,697) Captains of Twenty-fourth, Twenty-eighth and Thirty-fourth Alabama join in statement that these troops made the first, the second and the third charge at Murfreesboro. (758) General Withers' report of same battle says: "Private M. G. Hudson of the Twenty-fourth Alabama, long engaged in the assistant adjutant-general's office, rendered service on the field evidencing his fitness and capacity for a more responsible position. (973) Roll of honor, battle of Murfreesboro: Capts. W. D. Smith (killed), Company A; W. P. Fowler, F; John B. Hazard, I; W. J. O'Brien, B. Lieuts. J. A. Hall, Company K; A. B. Nelson, D; R. T. B. Parham, H; A. Young, A. Sergt. Maj. William Mink. Sergt. J. M. J. Tally, Company K; John Ives, A; Samuel S. Wiley, D. Privates Martin Duggan, Company B; Melbourn Deloach, C; Joseph Hall, E; Samuel M. Roberts (killed), F; A. W. Scott, G; James R. Green, H; N. Lankford (killed), I; A. Posey, K.

Vol. XX, Part 2—(403) November 14, 1862, regiment transferred from General Jackson's to General Duncan's brigade, Withers' division. (432) Fourth brigade, Colonel Manigault, army of Tennessee, November, 1862. Lieut.-Col. W. B. Dennett commanding regiment.

Vol. XXIII, Part 2—(735) Assignment as above, April 1, 1863. (942, 959) Manigault's brigade, Withers' division, Polk's army corps, Col. N. N. Davis commanding regiment, August, 1863.

No. 51—(15) Manigault's brigade, Bragg's army, battle of Chickamauga, September, 1863. (342-344) Mentioned in General Manigault's report: "The Twenty-fourth Alabama lost one of its most efficient officers, Captain O'Brien, a gentleman of accomplished mind, and a brave and gallant officer. Captain Chamberlain and Lieutenant Cooper of same regiment were severely wounded and their valuable services will be for a long period lost to their country. Distinguished for their conduct were: Captains Hazard, Oliver, McCracken, Fowler and Hall; Lieutenants Higley, Chapman, Parham, Dunlap, Young, Enholm, Wood, Hanley, Northrup and Short; Adjutant Jennison and Sergeant-Major Mink. Color-Sergeant Moody behaved with great gallantry." (345-347) Col. N. N. Davis' report of same battle mentions the above names, also that of Lieutenant Nettles. Speaks highly of the officers and gives those of the men who behaved with great gallantry during the entire day: Sergeant. Neil and Private Crevillan, Company A; Sergeants Wylie (killed) and Moody, Company D; Sergeant Bumpers and Private Hall, Company E; Corporal Sweat and Private Boswell, Company F; Privates J. M. Ragland and C. P. Hurtel, Company G; Corporal Tatum and Private Smith, Company H; Sergeant New and Private Walters, Company I; Sergeant Tally, Privates Wilson, Carter, Scott, Love, Eubank and Fulmer, in fact, all of this company (K). J. B. Hall, a youth of 17 years of age, joined his brother's company (Company K) as an hide pendent volunteer and fell mortally wounded while gallantly fighting the enemy some distance in advance of the regiment. The regiment went into action with an aggregate of 381, and lost, killed 22, wounded 91, missing 3. (349) Mentioned in report of Colonel Reid, Twenty-eighth Alabama. (534)

Roll of honor: Privates Andrew Crevillari, Company A; Peter Cusac, B; G. C. Wells, C; Sergt. George Moody (color-bearer), D; Privates Thomas Hamilton, F; William Ginnery, H; William W. Meadow, I. (Companies E, G, and K declined selecting.)

No. 55—(659) Assignment as above, November 20, 1863.

No. 56—(617, 805, 825, 886) Assignment as above, December, 1863, Col. N. N. Davis commanding. Total present, 278, December 14th.

No. 58—(589)) Assignment as above, January 20, 1864, Lieut.-Col. Ben F. Sawyer commanding.

No.-59—(623) Orders given by General Forrest ordered revoked, March 14, 1864. (869) Assignment as above, April 30th.

No. 74—(640, 649, 656, 663, 671) Assignment as above, to August 31, 1864. (781) General Manigault in report of battle, July 28, 1864, speaks of "Twenty-fourth Alabama, Capt. S. H. Oliver;" says: "Lieut. Geo. A. Jennison, acting assistant adjutant-general, severely wounded, was conspicuous for courage and energy." (783, 784) Captain Starke H. Oliver's report of Twenty-fourth Alabama, same day, says: "Col. N. N. Davis had been appointed division officer of the day." Loss was 2 killed, 14 wounded. Lieut. Andrew Young, of Company A, was wounded while leading to the charge. Lieutenant Barbour, of Company F, was wounded while leading his men and fell into the hands of the enemy. (787) Mentioned in report of Captain Horne for July 22d and 28th.

No. 93—(664) Assignment as above, December 10, 1864, Capt. Thomas J. Kimbell in command of regiment.

No. 98—(1064) Consolidated with Twenty-eighth and Thirty-fourth, under Col. John C. Carter.

No. 100—(734) Assignment as above, March 31, 1865, Lieut. L. A. Lavender in command of regiment.

THE TWENTY-FIFTH ALABAMA INFANTRY.

This regiment, made up of Loomis' and McClellan's battalions, was organized at Mobile, December, 1861. It was engaged at Shiloh, April 6th and 7th, at Farmington, May 9th, and at Bridge creek, May 28th and 29th. Although with General Bragg in Kentucky, it did not take part in any serious action. At Murfreesboro, December 31st to January 2, 1863, it was distinguished and suffered severe losses in both officers and men. It was at Chickamauga, September 19th to 20th, and at Missionary Ridge, November 23 to 25, 1863; fought with Johnston in the Georgia campaign in 1864, and was particularly noted for its brilliant record at New Hope, May 25th to June 4th, especially in the battle of the 25th. In Hood's first sortie from Atlanta, July 22d, and the second sortie at Ezra Chapel, July 28th, the regiment lost half its force. It was engaged in the battles at Columbia, November 29th; at Franklin, November 30th, and at Nashville, December 15th to 16th. Fought at Kinston, March 14th, and Bentonville, N. C., March 19 and 21, 1865. It was consolidated about April 9th with the Twenty-second, Thirty-ninth and Fiftieth Alabama under Colonel Toulmin, and was surrendered at Greensboro, N. C.

Among its killed and wounded were Captain Harper, who fell at Shiloh; Capts. Archibald A. Patterson and D. P. Costello, and Lieuts. W. C. Gibson and H. B. Schofield, who were killed at Murfreesboro.

Its commanders were Cols. John Q. Loomis and George D. Johnston, afterward brigadier-general, and Lieut.-Col. William B. McClellan. Maj. Daniel E. Huger, at one time in command, was killed at Chickamauga while serving as assistant inspector-general on General Manigault's staff.

EXTRACTS FROM OFFICIAL WAR RECORDS.

Vol. VI—(772) First Alabama battalion of infantry, Col. John Q. Loomis. Aggregate present, 367, district of Alabama, Gen. Jones M. Withers commanding, December 2, 1861. (819) In army of Mobile, General Withers commanding, February 1, 1862.

Vol. X, Part 1—(383) Gladden's brigade, Withers' division, army of Mississippi, battle of Shiloh. (538, 539) Mentioned by Colonel Deas, of the Twenty-second Alabama, commanding brigade. He calls attention to Maj. George D. Johnston and Adjutant Stout. (539, 540, 544) Report of Col. J. Q. Loomis of same battle. On account of sickness, he had but 305 men. The regiment did its duty. Maj. George D. Johnston and Adjutant Stout are worthy of all praise. Specially mentions Capt. Pierre Costello and Lieuts. P. H. Smith and Thomas G. Slaughter. Sergeant Schofield captured two flags, and Private Vann was the first at a battery, and took the color-bearer's horse. (788) Gardner's brigade, Bragg's army, June 30, 1862. (853-858) Col. Joseph Wheeler's report of operations, May 28th and 29th, gives 1 killed, 1 wounded. Lieut. -Col. G. D. Johnston commanding regiment.

Vol. X, Part 2—(764) Assignment as above, August, 1862.

Vol. XX, Part 1—(658) Deas' brigade, Withers' division, Polk's corps, army of Tennessee, battle of Murfreesboro. (677) Return of casualties, 16 killed, 89 wounded. Lieuts. W. C. Gibson, A. A. Patterson and H. B. Schofield, killed. (754-758) Mentioned in General Withers' report; thanks Capt. D. E. Huger, assistant adjutant-general, for service. (973) Roll of honor, battle of Murfreesboro: Sergt. Isaac N. Rhoades, Company A; Privates Warren A. Jackson, B; Samuel Ellison, C; James A. Mote, D; Sergts. J. F. Coker (killed), Company F; Patrick H. Smith, G; Privates Marion F. Hazlewood, Company H; Charles W. Roper (killed), I; J. B. Peacock (killed), K.

Vol. XXIII, Part 2—(735) Deas' brigade, Withers' division, Polk's army, April 1, 1863, Twenty-second and Twenty-fifth Alabama under Lieut.-Col. G. D. Johnston. (942, 958) Assignment as above, to August 10, 1863.

No. 51—(15) Assignment as above. (337, 338) Colonel Johnston's report of battle of Chickamauga, September 19th and 20th, says the regiment bore itself to his satisfaction. It carried into the engagement, aggregate, 330. Lost, killed 15, wounded 95.

No. 56 — (617, 805, 825, 886) Assignment as above, October to December, 1863.

No. 59—(869) Assignment as above, April 30, 1864.

No. 74—(640, 648) Assignment as above, to June 30, 1864. (663) Johnston's brigade, Lee's corps, army of Tennessee, July 31, 1864. Capt. Napoleon B. Rouse in command of regiment. (671) Deas' brigade, army of Tennessee, August 31, 1864. (778-779) Captain Rouse's report of operations, July 22d and 28th. On the 22d it carried into the fight 273 men; killed, wounded and missing, 113, including two color-bearers. On the 28th it carried into the fight 173 men; killed, wounded and missing, 23, including two color-bearers.

No. 78—(853), No. 93—(664) Assignment as above, to December 10, 1864.

No. 98—(1064) Brantly's brigade, Lee's corps, Johnston's army. After April 9, 1865, consolidated with Twenty-second, Thirty-ninth and Fiftieth, under Colonel Toulmin.

THE TWENTY-SIXTH ALABAMA INFANTRY.

The Twenty-sixth Alabama infantry was organized at Tuscumbia in December, 1861. Its companies were recruited from the counties of Fayette, Marion, Walker, Winston, and the upper portions of Tuscaloosa county.

While yet in camp of instruction at Tuscumbia, two of its companies, under the command of Maj. John S. Garvin, were ordered to Fort Donelson, where they were captured; but, being released, rejoined their command in the spring, the regiment having in the meantime been transferred to the army of Northern Virginia and attached to Rodes' brigade of immortal memory, and served under Stonewall Jackson and R. E. Lee.

Many of the officers had already seen service in the Fifth Alabama, Colonel Rodes, and they were glad to be associated with their old command.

From the siege of Yorktown, April 5 to May 3, 1862, in which it took part, until the close of the war, the regiment was always in the battle front and won imperishable renown. It fought in the battles around Richmond. The regiment was led in the battle at Williamsburg, May 5th, by Gen. Joseph E. Johnston. It was distinguished at Seven Pines, May 31st and June 1st. It fought at Mechanicsville, June 26th; Gaines' Mill, June 27th and 28th; Frayser's Farm, June 30th; Malvern Hill, July 1st. In these engagements nearly half the regiment were killed or wounded. It was in the van of the army when it moved over the Potomac, and fought at Boonsboro, September 15th, and at Sharpsburg, September 17th. At Fredericksburg, December 13th, it displayed its accustomed valor, and led by Lieutenant-Colonel Garvin, its gallant Colonel O'Neal being in command of the brigade, it shared the honor with the Fifth Alabama of being the first to charge and win the enemy's works at Chancellorsville, capturing three batteries. Forced to fall back, it lost its colors, but returning, drove the enemy back and recovered them. The praise of the Twenty-sixth was on every tongue and every report teemed with commendation of its valor. It was at Gettysburg, July 1 to 3, 1863; Kelly's Ford, August 1st; and Mine Run, November 26th to 28th.

In the spring of 1864, the regiment was ordered on special duty to Dalton, Ga., and afterward assigned to General Johnston's command. It took part in the Atlanta campaign, always preserving its reputation and winning fresh laurels with every battle. The regiment was in Tennessee with Hood and was badly crippled at Nashville, only a small remnant being left to surrender at Greensboro, N. C.

Its colonels were William R. Smith, who resigned his commission to take a seat in the Confederate Congress; Edward A. O'Neal, afterward brigadier-general and twice elected governor of Alabama, a gallant officer who was wounded at Seven Pines, Boonsboro and Chancellorsville.

The lieutenant-colonels were John S. Garvin, William H. Hunt and William C. Reeder; the majors, R. D. Redden and David F. Bryan. Lieutenant-Colonel Garvin was wounded at Chancellorsville and Franklin. Capt. Sidney B. Smith was wounded seven times. Capt. Thos. Taylor and Lieut. R. K. Wood were killed at Chancellorsville; Lieuts. John Fowler and W. L. Branyon were killed at Gettysburg.

EXTRACTS FROM OFFICIAL WAR RECORDS.

Vol. VII—(137) Alabama battalion, Major Garvin, a detachment of the Twenty-sixth regiment, mentioned among the troops at Fort Henry, February 12, 1862, by General Tilghman. (148-150) Mentioned in Colonel Heiman's report of fall of Fort Henry and surrender of Fort Donelson. (358-364) Report of Gen. Bushrod Johnson of capture of Fort Donelson, mentions two companies of Twenty-sixth Alabama in Colonel Drake's brigade, among the troops surrendered February 16th.

Vol. XI, Part 2—(484) In Rodes brigade. Hill's division, Stonewall Jackson's corps, during the engagements around Richmond. (505) Medical director reports 18 killed and 109 wounded, June 26 to July 1, 1862. (625) General Hill's report of battle of Gaines' Mill, June 27th, says that the Fifth and Twenty-sixth captured a battery in their front. He also quotes from General Rodes' report. (630-633) General Rodes' report of same battle says: "The Fifth and Twenty-sixth Alabama were especially distinguished for their great courage; no troops ever acted better;" also says: "The Fifth and Twenty-sixth always in the lead, under its brave Colonel O'Neal." Gives in list of casualties, 4 killed, 28 wounded, at Gaines' Mill; 13 killed, 73 wounded, at Malvern Hill. (634, 635) General Gordon's report of battle of Malvern Hill calls especial attention to the conduct of Col. E. A. O'Neal; gives casualties, 10 killed, 76 wounded. (638) Mentioned in Col. B. B. Gayle's report of Gaines' Mill.

Vol. XI, Part 3 —(393) The Twenty-sixth Alabama, Colonel Smith, ordered to report to General Magruder at Yorktown, March 24, 1862. (404)

Magruder informed that Twenty-sixth Alabama, unarmed, will join him at Yorktown and be armed by him. (427) General Wilcox informed that the Twenty-sixth Alabama, Colonel O'Neal, will be sent to reinforce Yorktown, April 7th. (482) Two hundred and eighty-three strong within post at Yorktown, April 30th. (533) In Rains' brigade, Johnston's command, May 21st. (650) In Rodes' brigade, Stonewall Jackson's command, July 23d.

Vol. XIX, Part 1—(808) In Rodes' brigade, Jackson's corps, army of Northern Virginia, September, 1862. (1018-1030) General Hill's report of Maryland campaign makes several mentions, and says that Colonel O'Neal, who was wounded at Seven Pines, was again wounded at South Mountain and Sharpsburg, and Major Redden, wounded at South Mountain; says that these officers are especially deserving of mention. (1033-1039) General Rodes' report of battles of Boonsboro and Sharpsburg refers several times to regiment.

Vol. XXI—(541) Assignment as above, July, 1862. (560) Medical director reports 4 wounded, battle of Fredericksburg. (1073) Assignment as above, December 20th.

No. 39—(792) Assignment as above, May, 1863. Commanders, Col. E. A. O'Neal, Lieut.-Col. John S. Garvin and Lieut. M. J. Taylor. (807) Medical director reports 13 killed, 85 wounded, battle of Chancellorsville, May 4, 1863. (939-950) In General Rodes' report he praises the regiment in high terms: "In this charge the gallant Lieut.-Col. John S. Garvin fell desperately wounded, inside the works." Casualty returns, 12 killed, 77 wounded. Capt. Thomas Taylor and Lieut. R. K. Wood killed. (950-953) Col. Edward A. O'Neal's report of operations of Rodes' brigade from April 29th to May 6th. (954,955) Col. J. M. Hall's report of battle of Chancellorsville says: "Justice demands that I should mention Lieut.-Col. John S. Garvin, commanding the Twenty-sixth Alabama, who was severely, if not mortally, wounded while gallantly leading his regiment, and giving the highest evidence of that coolness and skill which should ever characterize the true soldier." (958, 959, 961) Mentioned in Capt. T. M. Riley's and Samuel B. Pickens' reports. (964,965) Col. John S. Garvin's report notices the bravery and gallantry of Maj. D. F. Bryan and the bravery of Lieuts. John Fowler and Willis Keenum; also the gallantry of Mr. G. M. Reek, a guest, who entered the ranks as private and did good service. (965,966) Report of Lieut. M. J. Taylor (commanding regiment after the lieutenant-colonel and major were wounded) says: "It is hard to say who acted the most noble part Some among the bravest fell at the redoubts." (1053) Roll of honor, battle of Chancellorsville: First Lieut. E. S. Stuckey, Company B; Privates L. Walters, A; Jos. H. Bounds, B; Sergt. J. H. Lockwill, C; Privates J. C. Pennington, D; Joseph Munsel, E; James H. Dowdle, F; Corp. Jesse Parsons, G; Private D. H. Spraddle, H; Sergt. B. Butler, I; Private B. F. Smith, K.

No. 44—(287) O'Neal's brigade, Rodes' division, army of Northern Virginia, July, 1863. Lieut.-Col. John C. Goodgame commanding brigade. (332, 342) Medical director reports 5 killed, 41 wounded, battle of Gettysburg,

July 1st, 26. and 3d. Regimental reports give total loss 130. (545-553) Mentioned several times in General Rodes' report (563) Lieuts. John Fowler and W. L. Branyon killed at Gettysburg. (592,593) Col. E. A. O'Neal says: "On July 23d, about 3 o'clock, the Fifth, Sixth and a part of the Twenty-sixth Alabama regiments, with the corps of sharpshooters, under Major Blackford, assisted in repelling three separate and distinct charges of the enemy." (601,602) Col. John C. Goodgame says: "I was detailed to take command of the Twenty-sixth Alabama regiment on June 26th at Chambersburg, Pa." Gives loss, 7 killed, 58 wounded.

No. 48—(399, 818) Battle's brigade, Rodes' division, Second army corps, Lee's army, September and October,

1863. (412) The Bristoe, Va., campaign; casualties, 3 wounded. (891) Mentioned by Maj. A. Proskaner in his report of battle at Mine Run, November 26th and 27th. (892,893) Col. J. S. Garvin's report of same.

No. 58—(629) Letter from General Polk to Colonel Jack, January 28, 1864, says that "O'Neal's Alabama regiment is to go to Montgomery." (726) Special order, No. 36—Colonel Swanson's regiment will form part of Battle's brigade to relieve Colonel O'Neal's regiment of same brigade.

No. 60—(1133,1134) Reply to General Lee, January 31, 1864, to Hon. Thomas J. Foster and others, who ask that the Twenty-sixth be transferred to that State: "This regiment has done most excellent service and is worthy of any compliment the State can bestow upon it. I do not see how the good of the service can be promoted by detaching this regiment and breaking up a veteran brigade which has just set the glorious example in this army of reenlisting for the war. ... If Colonel O'Neal desires duty in some other army, I will interpose no objection. ... I have a just appreciation of his gallantry and worth. . . . General Rodes' whole division acted at Chancellorsville with distinguished gallantry." (1149) Joint resolution of thanks from Congress to Battle's brigade, February 6, 1864. [See Extracts under Third regiment] (1176) General Winder, February 15, 1864, orders Colonel O'Neal's regiment to furnish guards to convey prisoners to Camp Sumter, Ga.

No. 66 — (484, 487) General Cooper, May 14, 1864, orders Twenty-sixth Alabama, then at Andersonville, to be sent to Dalton. (496) Twenty-sixth Alabama has left Andersonville for Montgomery, May 22d, before order to go to Richmond arrived.

No. 67—(1024) Reported as belonging to Battle's brigade, Rodes' division, army of Northern Virginia, May, 1864.

No. 68—(1101) Twenty-sixth Alabama, Colonel O'Neal, ordered to proceed immediately to Richmond, May 15, 1864.

No. 74—(646, 653, 665, 671) In Cantey's brigade, army of Mississippi, June to August, 1864. (940) Colonel O'Neal (commanding brigade), reporting battle of June 27th, says: "The enemy attempted to charge our line of skirmishers commanded by Capt. Sid. B. Smith, but did not succeed in approaching more than from 30 to 100 yards and were handsomely driven back. In this affair we had none killed and but 8 wounded. Captain Smith, his officers and men behaved with great gallantry and firmly held their line." (941,942) Colonel O'Neal's report of engagement at Peachtree Creek, July 20th, gives loss 279 killed, wounded and missing. (942, 943) Colonel O'Neal's report of engagement, July 28th, says: "I cannot close this report without acknowledging my obligations to Capt. Sid. B. Smith, acting on my staff." List of casualties, which was large, not found.

No. 75—(704, 728, 762) Col. E. A. O'Neal ordered to report with his regiment to General Johnston.

No. 93—(666) In Cantey's brigade, General Shelley commanding, Walthall's division, army of Tennessee, Gen. J. B. Hood commanding, December 10, 1864.

No. 100—(773) General order, No. 13, April 9, 1865, leaves regiment in Shelley's brigade, near Smithfield, N. C.

No. 104—(1134) Gen. P. D. Roddey, March 20, 1865, says he had requested transfer of regiment to his command.

THE TWENTY-SEVENTH ALABAMA INFANTRY.

The Twenty-seventh Alabama regiment was organized at Fort Heiman, in Tennessee, in the winter of 1861. It was sent to Fort Henry, then to Fort Donelson, where it was captured, though many of the command, being sick in the hospital, escaped the surrender and joined a Mississippi regiment. The captured men were exchanged in September, 1862, and were at Port Hudson during the winter. The regiment fought bravely at Baker's Creek, May 16, 1863, in the Jackson trenches, and in the retreat across Pearl river; passed the winter of 1863 at Canton. In the spring of 1864, when recruiting at Tuscumbia, it crossed the river and captured a Federal camp, with all the horses, arms and men. Beginning with Dalton it fought through the Georgia campaign with the army of Tennessee; at Peachtree Creek made a glorious record for dauntless courage; John E. Abernathy there captured the colors of a New Jersey regiment. It fought with heroism at Franklin, and again at Nashville.

The regiment in the summer of 1864 was consolidated with the remnants of the Thirty-fifth and Forty-ninth (after April 9, 1865; also the Fifty-fifth and Fifty-seventh, under Col. Ed. McAlexander), and was surrendered at Greensboro, N. C. Col. A. A. Hughes was captured at Fort Donelson; afterward died in the service. Colonel Ives was wounded at the battle of Franklin. Capt. W. A. Isbell, and Lieut. T. S. Taylor were killed at Baker's Creek. Capt. William Wood was killed at Perryville. Commanders: Cols. A. A. Hughes, James Jackson, and, after consolidation, S. S. Ives, Lieut.-Col. Edward McAlexander, Maj. R. G. Wright. Colonel Jackson was for a time in command of Loring's division.

EXTRACTS FROM OFFICIAL WAR RECORDS.

Vol. VII—(137-138) Mentioned several times in General Tilghman's report of bombardment of Fort Henry, February 6, 1862. (148-150) Mentioned by Colonel Heiman, commanding brigade. (279) Mentioned in General Pillow's report of the battle of the trenches, February 10th. (358-365) Report of Gen. Bushrod R. Johnson makes several mentions. (367-369) Report of R. B. Ryan, aide. (868) Assigned in general orders, No. 1, Fort Donelson, February 9, 1862.

Vol. XV—(934) General orders, No. 5, Port Hudson, La., January 7, 1863, assigns regiment to General Beall's brigade. (1033) Buford's brigade, department of Mississippi and East Louisiana, Gen. Franklin Gardner, March 31, 1863; Col. James Jackson commanding regiment. (1037) Ordered to proceed without delay to Jackson, Miss., to report to General Pemberton, April 6, 1863.

Vol. XVII, Part 2—(737) Ordered to report for duty at Meridian by Gen. Sterling Price, army of the West, October 26, 1862.

No. 37—(82-87) Report of General Buford of operations around Edwards depot (Baker's creek), May 16, 1863; Captain Isbell, Company G, and Lieut. T. S. Taylor, Company I, killed.

No. 38—(613) In Beall's brigade, district of Louisiana. (746) General orders, April 15, 1863, assigning regiment to General Buford's brigade. (782) Ordered to Clinton, Miss., April 24th. (786) Order regarding regiment, April 25th. (793) Order to Colonel Jackson from General Pemberton, April 27th. (805) With General Tilghman at Big Black bridge, April 30th. (937, 1040) Buford's brigade, Loring's division, army of Mississippi, July 30, 1863.

Nos. 53 and 56—Assignment as above, Gen. Jos. E. Johnston commanding army.

No. 57—(333) Assignment as above, Polk's army, February 20, 1864. (626-662) Colonel Jackson's report of engagement at Moulton, March 21st, "1 killed, 1 wounded badly, several slightly." (662) Mentioned in report of Col. S. S. Ives of skirmish near Florence, April 12, 1864.

No. 58—(583) Assignment as above, June 20, 1864. (816) Detached from Buford's brigade, to proceed to Selma and report to General Withers, February 29, 1864.

No. 59—(114, 389, 429, 441) Mentioned by General Dodge (Union), at Moulton, April, 1864, "Johnson's, Jackson's and Nash's regiments are from 5,000 to 7,000 strong." (623) Mentioned by General Polk, Demopolis, March 14th. (669) Engaged at Moulton, March 21st. (726) Colonel Jackson ordered by General Polk to fall back, March 31st. (735, 750, 752) Mention of regiment. (783) Letter of Lieut.-Col. J. W. Estissays: "Colonels Jackson and Ives, with too men each, crossed the Tennessee river on night of 12th of March, surrounded a camp of 48 Yankee cavalry; killed 4, captured 42—a whole company and officers—65 good horses, saddles and arms of company, losing 1 man killed, none wounded." (806-807) Letter from Colonel Jackson, dated Mount Hope, April 21st.

No. 74—(645, 652) Scott's brigade, army of Mississippi, June, 1864, Lieut.-Col. Ed. McAlexander commanding regiment. (659) Twenty-seventh, Thirty-fifth, Forty-ninth, consolidated, commanded by Col. S. S. Ives, Scott's brigade, army of Mississippi, June 30th. (664, 670) Scott's brigade, Stewart's corps, August, 1864. (877) General Loring's report of battle of Peachtree Creek, July 20th, says: "The regiment captured the colors of the Thirty-third New Jersey regiment and twice captured a four-gun battery. This brilliant charge of my gallant division was made so rapidly and with such intrepidity, that, up to this time, we had sustained but comparatively a small loss. . . . The enemy fled in confusion from his works. Our steady aim produced great slaughter in the ranks." (895) General Scott's report of same battle gives 2 killed, 31 wounded. Expresses admiration of the dauntless courage exhibited by men and officers. (896) Colonel Ives' report of same battle says the colors were captured by John E. Abernathy.

No. 78—(569) Col. George B. Hodge, Selma, Ala., May 2d, says: "On April 20, 1864, regiment (consolidated) on detached service." (854) Assignment as above, September 20, 1864.

No. 93—(666) Scott's brigade, Colonel Snodgrass commanding, Lieut.-Col. John D. Weedon in command of regiment, Hood's army, December 10, 1864. (684) Col. S. S. Ives, commanding Twenty-seventh, Thirty-fifth and Forty-ninth (consolidated), wounded at battle of Franklin, Tenn., November 30, 1864.

No. 98—(1063) Consolidated with Thirty-fifth, Forty-ninth, Fifty-fifth and Fifty-seventh Alabama, under Col. Edward McAlexander; after April 9th, in Shelley's brigade, Stewart's corps, Johnston's army.

No. 100—(735) Scott's brigade, commanded by Capt. John A. Dixon; consolidated regiment commanded by Capt. W. B. Beeson, Johnston's army, near Smithfield, N. C, March 31, 1865.

THE TWENTY-EIGHTH ALABAMA INFANTRY.

The Twenty-eighth Alabama was organized at Shelby Springs in March, 1862, to serve for three years. It was assigned to the army of Mississippi, brigaded under General Trapier, shortly afterward receiving Colonel Manigault for its brigade commander.

At Corinth, prostrated by the usual camp diseases, its ranks were perceptibly thinned by sickness and death. The regiment went into Kentucky with General Bragg, and at Munfordville, September 16, 1862, was greatly praised for the alacrity of its obedience and the calm, cool, heroic courage of its officers and men. At Murfreesboro, December 31st to January 2d, it led, with the Twenty-fourth and Thirty-fourth, three separate charges of the brigade, losing heavily. At Chickamauga, September 19-20, 1863, its conduct was superb, as described in the official reports.

At the battle of Lookout Mountain, November 24th, the regiment found itself in a tight place, nearly surrounded by the enemy, but it succeeded by desperate fighting in extricating itself with a loss of 172 killed, wounded and captured. At Missionary Ridge, November 25th, it was again engaged. During the winter of 1863-64, while wintering at Dalton, the regiment reenlisted and afterward took part in the Dalton-Atlanta campaign, and the Tennessee campaign. At Ezra Chapel, July 28, 1864, the second sortie from Atlanta, the regiment fought with its usual valor. At Franklin, November 30th, it was again engaged, and at Nashville, losing heavily. The remnant of the regiment, with those left of the Twenty-fourth and Thirty-fourth, after having fought together throughout their service, were consolidated under Col. J. C. Carter, Lieut.-Col. Starke H. Oliver and Maj. P. G. Wood, and were surrendered at Greensboro, N. C., with Gen. S. D. Lee's corps.

Capt. W. M. Hawkins was killed, and Capt. G. W. Hewitt wounded, at Murfreesboro; the latter was again wounded at Chickamauga, as was also Capt. James H. Graham. Capt. F. A. Musgrove was wounded at Murfreesboro. Lieutenant Jordan was killed after performing prodigies of valor at Chickamauga, Capt. W. R. McAdory at Missionary Ridge, Capt. William A. McLeod at Atlanta, Capt. H. G. Loller at Resaca, and Capt. John F. Wilson at Franklin. Capt. John H. Turpin was wounded and captured at Murfreesboro.

Its commanders were Col. J. W. Frazer, a West Point graduate, who first served as lieutenant-colonel of the Eighth Alabama; resigning his colonelcy of the Twenty-eighth, he was made a brigadier-general and was captured at Cumberland Gap; Col. J. C. Reid, Lieut. -Cols. T. W. W. Davis, transferred to the navy, and W. L. Butler, who was wounded and captured at Nashville; Colonel Carter, Lieutenant-Colonel Oliver and Major Wood, after the consolidation with the other regiments.

EXTRACTS FROM OFFICIAL WAR RECORDS.

Vol. X, Part 1—(789) Fourth brigade, Col. A. M. Manigault commanding, reserve corps, General Withers, army of the Mississippi, June 30, 1862.

Vol. X, Part 2—(461, 549) Assignment as above. General Trapier commanding brigade, April 28, 1862.

Vol. XVI, Part 1—(899) General Wheeler's report of operations, October 19, 1862, says: "It was the only occasion where any infantry engaged the enemy after the battle of Perryville." (983) Col. John W. Frazer, commanding the regiment, says in his report of the siege of Munfordville, Ky., September 16: "It gratifies the commanding officer to be able to say that the men and officers were calm, cool and cheerful during the entire day and obeyed every command with great alacrity and promptness." (988) Mentioned in report of Col. A. J. Lythgoe of same operations.

Vol. XVI, Part 2—(764) Manigault's brigade, Withers' division, army of the Mississippi; Lieut. -Col. John C. Reid commanding regiment, August, 1862.

Vol. XX, Part 1—(659) Anderson's brigade, Withers' division, army of Tennessee, Stone's River campaign. (678) Return of casualties, battle of Murfreesboro, December 31, 1862, 17 killed, 88 wounded. (696) Twenty-eighth, with the Twenty-fourth and the Thirty-fourth, led the first and second charges in battle of Murfreesboro. (697) Col. A. M. Manigault, commanding Fourth brigade, says: "The Alabama regiments partook in all attacks, as my report will show, and I again take this opportunity of bearing testimony to the heroic courage and fortitude displayed by them on that bloody field (Murfreesboro). The general conduct of all the regiments on that occasion was such that I can draw no distinction between them." (973) Roll of honor: Private Topley Murphey, Company B; Sergts. Elias Wood, Company G; W. B. Curry, Company K; Wm. E. Short, Company L. Other companies made no selections.

Vol. XX, Part 2—(419, 432) Assignment as above, November. 1862.

Vol. XXIII, Part 2—(735, 942, 959) Twenty-eighth in Polk's army corps, April to August, 1863. July 31st, Maj. W. L. Butler commanding regiment.

No. 51—(15) Assignment as above, September 19-20, 1863- (340, 344) General Manigault's report of battle of Chickamauga. Major Butler in command of skirmishers from all the regiments. "Twenty-eighth and Thirty-fourth moved steadily forward, also receiving a heavy fire, and drove the enemy from the works in front. . . . They fell back with an unbroken front. However, Colonel Reid moved his regiment forward, recovering the battery. Lieutenant Jordan conducted himself in a conspicuous manner, and, I regret to say, was killed. Captains Hopkins and Ford, Lieutenant Graham and Acting Adjutant Wood, were distinguished for their gallant conduct. Captain Reese and Sergeant Craig were efficient." He calls especial attention to the conduct and bearing of Col. J. C. Reid and Maj. W. L. Butler. (347, 351) Colonel Reid's report of battle of Chickamauga. One gun belonging to Waters' battery was left because of an accident. Lieutenant Graham, Captains Hopkins and Ford volunteered, made the attempt and brought out the piece. "The regiment was under heavy fire from the enemy in its front and on its left flank. At this critical moment, when humanity itself almost prompted a retreat, Gen. Bushrod Johnson's brigade moved upon the right of our brigade, and with the troops on our right, at sunset, we made one last desperate assault and drove them, routed, demoralized, from the field. The colonel commanding takes pride and gratification in returning his thanks both to the officers and men of his command for the promptness and alacrity with which they obeyed all his commands. Men never fought more gallantly than did my command. I cannot find words adequate to express the weight of obligation I am under to them for their heroic conduct." He also desires to return his thanks to the medical department for the zeal and faithfulness with which they labored to relieve the pain and distress of the wounded. He expresses his thanks to the ordnance for the promptness with which they discharged their duty; also to Capt. Carlos

Reese and Sergt. William Craig, of the commissary department. "The memory of Lieut. C. S. Jordan and his brave comrades who fell on the field nobly battling for the rights of freemen shall ever be cherished with the kindest remembrance by their commander. Men who sacrifice life and all they hold dear on earth in such a cause can never be forgotten, and deserve to live forever." (351-354) Report of Maj. John N. Slaughter. (534) Roll of honor, battle of Chickamauga: Privates George Aubrey, Company A; J. R. Gaither, B; First Sergt. W. H. Logan, C; Privates C. D. Goolsby, D; R. F. Sumner, E; Corp. David Knox, F; First Sergt. W. J. Wilson, G; Privates Hosea Vines, H; L. P. Wright, I; Sergt. James R. Smith, K; Private Jacob Smith, L.

No. 55—(659)Assignment as above, November 20, 1863.

No. 56—(617) Assignment as above, October 31, 1863. (805) Manigault's brigade, Breckinridge's corps, army of Tennessee, December 10th. (825,886) Total present, 276, in December.

No. 58—(589) Manigault's brigade, Hindman's division, army of Tennessee, commanded by Gen. J. E. Johnston, January 20, 1864. Regiment commanded by Capt. Hugh G. Lollar.

No. 74—(640, 649, 656, 663, 671) Manigault's brigade, Hindman's division, Hood's corps, Lieut.-Col. William L. Butler commanding regiment, April to August, 1864.

(781) Mentioned in General Manigault's report of engagement at Ezra Chapel, July 28th. (783, 785) Return of casualties, 4 killed, 24 wounded. (785-787) Mentioned in Major Slaughter's and Capt. E. W. Home's reports.

No. 93—(664) Manigault's brigade, Johnston's division, Lee's corps, army of Tennessee, General Hood, December 10, 1864.

No. 98—(1864) Consolidated with Twenty-fourth and Thirty-fourth, under Col. John C. Carter, about April, 1865.

No. 103—(939) Furlough for 10 days, approved by General Beauregard, January 28, 1865.

THE TWENTY-NINTH ALABAMA INFANTRY.

The Fourth Alabama battalion was organized during the fall of 1861, at Montgomery. In February, 1862, two companies were added and the organization became known as the Twenty-ninth Alabama. It was drilled in artillery practice; remained at Pensacola until the evacuation; was between Pollard and Pensacola and at Mobile for about a year, in Cantey's brigade, which was transferred to the army of Tennessee in the spring of 1864, and took part in the battle of Resaca, May 13th, where it fought brilliantly. At New Hope it lost heavily, and at Peachtree Creek it met with fearful slaughter. At Atlanta, July 28th, again its loss was terrible. It went with Hood to Tennessee, and was at Franklin and Nashville; in both battles its loss was great. Later it was transferred to the Carolinas, fought at Kinston and

Bentonville, and with less than 100 men surrendered at Greensboro. Capts. Berry G. Brown, John M. Hanna, Ulee W. Mills and J. C. Hailey were killed at Atlanta; Capts. E. Orear and John Allen at Franklin; Capt. Berry G. Brown at Nashville; Capts. William H. Musgrove, B. F. Sapps, Hugh Latham and J. B. Lowell died in the service. The field officers were: Col. J. R. F. Tattnall, transferred to the navy, and Col. John F. Conoly, Lieut.-Col. Benjamin Morris, and Maj. B. Turner, wounded at Atlanta.

EXTRACTS FROM OFFICIAL WAR RECORDS.

Vol. VI—(662) Col. Thomas M. Jones (acting brigadier-general) in his report of the evacuation of Pensacola, May 9, 1862, commends the conduct of Lieut.-Col. J. F. Conoly. The regiment, with some other companies, guarded railroad. (665) Order, May 9th, to Lieutenant-Colonel Conoly regarding destruction of public, and preservation of private property in Pensacola, and reply of Conoly. (844) Order, March 7th, to Lieutenant-Colonel Conoly regarding destruction of public property in Pensacola. (848-849) Orders concerning Lieutenant-Colonel Conoly's command. (858) Lieutenant-Colonel Conoly with his command at Pensacola, March 16th.

Vol. XV—(850) Connected with detachment of observation, General Forney's troops in district of the Gulf, October 31, 1862. Brigade commanded by Col. J. R. F. Tattnall. (1068) Eastern division, Gen. James Cantey. Conoly in command of regiment.

No. 42—(39, 131, 157, 275, 402, 511, 561) Assignment as above, June to December, 1863, under General Maury. (156) Regiment is drilling as artillery, August 10, 1863. (431) General Maury proposes to send the Twenty-ninth, a "fine, large regiment," to General Bragg, November 21st.

No. 53—(5) Mentioned as busy at Pollard, October, 1863, by General Hurlbut (Union).

No. 58—(582) Assignment still as above, January 20, 1864.

No. 59—(866, 872) With Cantey's brigade, joined army of Tennessee from department of Gulf, and encamped at Rome, Ga., April, 1864.

No. 74—(644, 646, 653, 660, 665, 671) Cantey's brigade, Loring's division, army of Mississippi, with General Johnston. Maj. Henry B. Turner commanding regiment, June, 1864. Capt. Samuel Abernathy in command of regiment, August. (941-942) Col. E. A. O'Neal, in report of the battle of Peachtree Creek, July 20th, refers several times to the regiment and says: "Each regimental commander bore himself gallantly, and I regret to state that Major Turner was severely wounded." (942-943) Col. E. A. O'Neal's report of the engagement, July 28th, speaks of Capt. J. A. Foster in command, and mourns the death of Captain Hanna, a valiant and meritorious officer.

No. 78, No. 93—Assignment as above, to December 10, 1864.

No. 98—(1063) With army in North Carolina. After April 9, 1865, the Twenty-ninth was commanded by Maj. Henry B. Turner, in Lowrey's brigade, Stewart's corps.

No. 100—(735) Consolidated with First and Seventeenth, Capt. Benj. H. Screws, Quarles' brigade, Walthall's division, Stewart's corps. (773) General Johnston, near Smithfield, N. C., announces change in assignments, Twenty-ninth to be in Shelley's brigade.

THE THIRTIETH ALABAMA INFANTRY

The Thirtieth was organized at Talladega in April, 1862, and reported for service at Chattanooga. It was later brigaded under General Tracy with the Twentieth, Twenty-third, Thirty-first and Forty-sixth Alabama regiments. It took part in the fights at Tazewell and Cumberland Gap, and went into Kentucky; then being sent to Mississippi, fought at Port Gibson, May 1, 1863, with severe loss, making a brilliant record there and at Baker's Creek; it was captured when Vicksburg fell, after having suffered untold hardships. When paroled, it recruited and joined the army near Chattanooga. It fought at Rocky Face and at Resaca, and was in the van of the army in the Tennessee campaign of the fall and winter of 1864. At New Hope, May, 1864; Atlanta, July 226., and Jonesboro, the regiment lost heavily; but it suffered still more severely at Nashville, whence it formed the rear guard in returning to Duck river. The regiment was transferred to the Carolinas, fought at Kinston and Bentonville, March 19, 1865, surrendering at last at Greensboro, with about 100 men. This regiment was noted for the number of its field officers killed.

Its field officers were Col. Charles M. Shelley, who was made brigadier-general and who afterward served in the United States House of Representatives; Col. James K. Elliott, wounded at Bentonville; Lieut.-Cols. Paul Bradford, who resigned; A. J. Smith, who was killed at Vicksburg; John C. Francis, killed at Rocky Face; Thomas Patterson, killed at Atlanta, and William H. Burr; Maj. William Patterson, who was wounded at Baker's Creek and resigned. Capt. Henry Oden was killed at Vicksburg, Captain Peacock at Bentonville, Capt. David Anderson at Baker's Creek, Capt. William S. McGhee at Atlanta, and Capt. Jack Derrill near Atlanta.

EXTRACTS FROM OFFICIAL WAR RECORDS.

Vol. XVI, Part 2—(715) Second brigade, General Stevenson's division, department of East Tennessee, Gen. Kirby Smith, June 30, 1862. (719, 984) Barton's brigade, department East Tennessee, July to October.

Vol. XVII—(825) Field report, near Vicksburg, Tracy's brigade of Smith's division, January 3, 1863, shows regiment 400 strong.

No. 36—(678-682) Colonel Garrott in his report of battle of Port Gibson, May 1, 1863, commends the regiment in the highest terms: "Commanded by the cool, brave and gallant Colonel Shelley and the five left companies of the Twentieth regiment under the immediate command of the fearless and chivalrous Lieut.-Col. E W. Pettus, had obstinately resisted every effort of the enemy to dislodge them. . . . All officers and men did their whole duty. It seemed to be impossible for men to behave better; but certain positions gave some better opportunities for distinction than others. This was particularly the case with the Thirtieth Alabama regiment." He thanks Sergt.-Maj. W. K. McConnell for his services.

No. 37—(95) Mentioned by Gen. C. L. Stevenson, report of battle of Baker's Creek, May 16, 1863. (101-103) Report of Gen. S. D. Lee, of same battle, says: "Regiment behaved with distinguished gallantry against heavy odds." Particularly mentions Colonel Shelley and Maj. T. H. Patterson, and Capt. David M. Anderson, who was killed. Adjutant Houston and Sergt.-Maj. W. K. McConnell particularly noticed. (326) Gen. S. D. Lee's brigade, army of Vicksburg, July 4, 1863, Capt. John C. Francis commanding regiment. (350) General Lee in his report of siege of Vicksburg, commends the regiment for its gallantry and vigilance. Particularly mentions Colonel Shelley, Lieut.-Col. J. B. Smith and Capt. John C. Francis. (354) Mentioned by Maj. G. W. Mathieson. (357-358) Mentioned in report of Col. T. N. Waul. [See Extracts, Twentieth Alabama.]

No. 38—(612, 703) Tracy's brigade, Stevenson's division, department of Mississippi and Eastern Louisiana, General Pemberton, January to April, 1863. (1059) Lee's brigade, army of Vicksburg, August 29, 1863.

No. 55—(662) Pettus' brigade, Stevenson's division, army of Tennessee, General Bragg, November 12, 1863. (724) Return of casualties, November 24th and 25th, 4 killed, 17 wounded. (725-727) Mentioned in report of Gen. J. C. Brown, commanding Stevenson's division, of battles of Lookout Mountain and Missionary Ridge.

No. 56—(804, 823, 884) Assignment as above, December, 1863, Hardee's army corps. Total present, 506. Maj. J. C. Francis commanding regiment.

No. 57—(482-483) Gen. E.W. Pettus, February 25, 1864, reports one man wounded.

No. 74—(641-672) Assignment as above, to August 31, 1864.

No. 93—(665) Assignment as above, December 10, 1864. Lieut.-Col. James K. Elliott commanding regiment. (694-697) Mentioned by General Stevenson in his report of campaign in Tennessee, September 29th to December 17th.

No. 94—(799, 801) Aggregate present, January, 1865, 275. Stevenson's division, Lee's corps, commanded by Gen. E. W. Pettus, January 20th.

No. 100—(733) Pettus' brigade, Colonel Bibb commanding, army of Tennessee. Capt. S. C. Kelly commanding regiment, March 31, 1865.

THE THIRTY-FIRST ALABAMA INFANTRY.

This regiment was organized at Talladega, April, 1862, and reported at Chattanooga; proceeded with the army at Knoxville, took part in the fight at Cumberland Gap, June 18, 1862, and at Tazewell, August 6th. It was in Kentucky, but not in the midst of the fighting. In Mississippi it fought well and suffered heavy loss at Port Gibson. It suffered all the privations of the long siege of Vicksburg and was surrendered with that place, having lost severely; when exchanged, was assigned to the army of Tennessee and brigaded under General Pettus; took a prominent part in the Dalton-Atlanta campaign. It went with Hood into Tennessee, suffering severely at Columbia and Nashville, and was in the rear guard of the army on its return. Sent into the Carolinas, it fought brilliantly at Bentonville with considerable loss, and finally surrendered at Greensboro, with but a small remnant of the over-full regiment that started out.

Capt. W. L. Hughes was wounded at Jonesboro; I. J. Nix wounded and captured at Baker's Creek and again wounded at Jonesboro. Lieutenant Bagley (commanding company) was killed at Bentonville; Capt. W. J. Rhodes wounded at Kinston and Bentonville; Lieut. W. H. Boggess killed at Vicksburg; Capt. S. L. Arrington died in service. The field officers were Col. Daniel R. Hundley, wounded and captured at Port Gibson and again captured at , Ga.; Lieut.-Col. Thomas M. Arrington and Maj. G. W. Mathieson.

EXTRACTS FROM OFFICIAL WAR RECORDS.

Vol. X, Part 2—(573) Col. D. R. Hundley, unattached, May 31, 1862. Department of East Tennessee, Gen. Kirby Smith, headquarters Knoxville. (581) To be sent toward Chattanooga, under certain circumstances, June 3d.

Vol. XVI, P'art 2—(697) Hundley's regiment especially asked for by Adjutant-General Belton, Knoxville, June 22, 1862. (716, 719, 984) Barton's brigade, with Gen. E. Kirby Smith, to October, 1862.

Vol. XVII, Part 1—(695) Colonel Thomas, in his report of battle at Chickasaw bayou, December 27, 1862, says: "Regiment behaved well."

Vol. XVII, Part 2—(825) Eight companies only arrived at Chickasaw bluffs, January 3, 1863, 260 strong; Smith's division commanded by General Tracy.

No. 36—(586) Mentioned in report of James Keigwin (Union), battle of Thompson's Hill, May 1, 1863. (678, 682) Mentioned in Col. Isham W. Garrott's report of battle of Port Gibson, May 1st. Col. D. R. Hundley, having ventured too far in front of his line in search of a better position nearer to the enemy, was severely wounded, and the command devolved upon Lieut.-Col. T. M. Arrington.

No. 37—(95) Mentioned in report of Gen. C. L. Stevenson, battle of Champion's Hill, May 16, 1863. (101, 103) Mentioned by Gen. S. D. Lee. Sergt.-Maj. W. W. Garrard particularly noticed. (326) Gen. S. D. Lee's brigade, army of Vicksburg, Gen. J. C. Pemberton, July 4, 1863. Lieutenant-Colonel Arrington commanding regiment. (350, 352) General Lee's report, siege of Vicksburg: "The Thirty-first Alabama attracted my attention by their good conduct. Lieutenant Arrington in command of a battery was gallant and vigilant." (353) Mentioned in report of Col. A. C. Roberds, siege of Vicksburg.

(354) Report of Maj. G. W. Mathieson, commanding regiment, gives loss, 21 killed and 3 7 wounded, and says: "The officers and men in the command submitted to the hardships and privations of the siege with great endurance and patience."

No. 38—(612) Tracy's brigade, Stevenson's division, to April, 1863. (1059) Lee's brigade, Stevenson's division, August 29, 1863.

No. 55—(662) Pettus' brigade, Stevenson's division, Breckinridge's corps, army of Tennessee, General Bragg, Missionary Ridge. (724) Casualties, November 24th and 25th, 2 killed, 16 wounded. (731, 732) Mentioned in report of General Pettus.

No. 56—(804, 823, 884) Pettus' brigade, Hardee's corps, army of Tennessee, December, 1863. Total present, 452.

No. 57—(482) Casualties in demonstration at Dalton, February 25, 1864, 3 wounded.

No. 59—(869) Assignment as above, April 30, 1864.

No. 73—(69) Mentioned in Col. E. A. Carmen's (Union) report of the battle of Resaca, May 15, 1864.

No. 74—(641-672) Assignment as above, Hood's corps, during Atlanta campaign. Capt. J. J. Nix commanding regiment, June 30th. Maj. Geo. W. Mathieson commanding regiment, July 10th.

No. 93—(665, 1224) Assignment as above, Lee's corps, December 10, 1864.

No. 94—(799, 801) Total present, 180, January 19, 1865. Lieut.-Col. Thos. M. Arrington commanding regiment.

No. 100—(733) Pettus' brigade, commanded by Col. Jos. E. Bibb, Lee's corps, army of Tennessee; regiment commanded by Maj. Geo. W. Mathieson, March 31, 1865.

No. 104—(1134) General Roddey asks for the parts of these regiments that are at home, March 20, 1865.

THE THIRTY-SECOND ALABAMA INFANTRY.

The rendezvous of the regiment was at Mobile, where it was organized in April, 1862. In July it was sent into Tennessee, and received its baptism of fire at Bridgeport, where it crossed the river. It was this regiment that captured Stevenson, Tenn. It was in middle Tennessee under General Forrest, and was overpowered and lost a number of prisoners at Lavergne, October, 1862. The regiment met severe loss at Murfreesboro and its roll of honor is a long one. It was sent to the relief of Vicksburg, and did valiant work in the trenches at Jackson, where, in repulsing an attack of the enemy without loss, it slaughtered 260. It rejoined the army of Tennessee and at Chickamauga suffered severely. During the winter of 1863-64, the regiment was transferred from Adams' to Clayton's brigade and consolidated with the Fifty-eighth under Col. Bush. Jones, and took part in the Atlanta campaign;

was with Hood in Tennessee, taking part at Franklin twice, at Columbia and Nashville. Transferred to the district of the Gulf under General Maury, it suffered serious losses during the siege of Spanish Fort and was finally surrendered at Meridian. Capt. G. W. Cox was severely wounded at Missionary Ridge, and Lieuts. J. J. Keith and Hiram Slay were killed at Murfreesboro.

The field officers were Col. Alexander McKinstry, Lieut.-Col. Harry Maury, captured at Lavergne, wounded at Murfreesboro and Jackson, afterward transferred to the command of the Fifteenth Confederate. After consolidation, Col. Bush. Jones was in command; he was promoted and succeeded by Maj. Harry Thornton, and later by Maj. John C. Kimbell. Majs. Thomas P. Ashe and Thomas S. Easton were also among its officers.

EXTRACTS FROM OFFICIAL WAR RECORDS.

Vol. XVI, Part 1—(889-891) Report of Gen. S. B. Maxey of attack at Bridgeport and Battle Creek, August 27, 1862: "I ordered the Twenty-third Alabama infantry, Colonel McKinstry, to cross the river. They crossed and formed in line of battle near the crest of the hill. The enemy's cavalry dashed forward at full speed and were permitted to come within 50 yards of the infantry before a gun was fired, when a galling fire was poured into them and they retreated. ... A company of the Thirty-second Alabama, armed with the Enfield rifle, commanded by Lieut. A. Sellers, was placed in the center, in ambush, and as the enemy came up the hill, in very close range, this company arose and delivered its deadly fire simultaneously with the wings, and they (the enemy) broke and fled in perfect confusion. ... The Thirty-second Alabama did nobly, fighting like veterans under their able colonel (McKinstry), seconded by Lieutenant-Colonel Maury, distinguished for gallantry and coolness on the field. Our loss was trifling." (952) Lieutenant-Colonel Maury informs General Jones that after a few hours' fighting, the enemy was driven from Stevenson and place occupied by our troops, August 31st.

Vol. XVI, Part 2—(762) August 17, 1862, to be left at Chattanooga, in Maxey's brigade, under Maj.-Gen. Sam Jones. (764) Gen. J. K. Jackson's brigade, army of the Mississippi, General Polk, August 18-20, 1862. (857) Gen. Sam Jones leaves Colonel McKinstry in command at Chattanooga, September 20, 1862. (862) Lieut.-Col. H. Maury ordered to take part at Tullahoma, September 21st. (864) Guards of Thirty-second to be relieved by Colonel Russell's cavalry, September 21st. (886, 890) Instructions to Colonel McKinstry. (907) Lieutenant-Colonel Maury ordered by General Jones to move regiment to Murfreesboro, October 4th. (918) Mentioned by General Jones. (929) Ordered to report to General Forrest, October 9th. (931) General Jones inquires regarding Lieutenant-Colonel Maury and regiment. (938) Lieutenant-Colonel Maury and 35 men reported captured at Lavergne, October. (981) Regiment assigned to Second brigade, Col. J. B. Palmer, army of Middle Tennessee, October 28, 1862, General Breckinridge.

Vol. XX, Part 1—(659) Daniel W. Adams' division, Hardee's corps, army of Tennessee, December and January, 1863. (678) Return of casualties, battle of Murfreesboro, December 31st, 21 killed, 84 wounded. Lieuts. J. J. Keith and Hiram Slay killed; 2 killed January 2d. (793, 794) Mentioned in report of same battle by General Adams: "Lieut.-Col. H. Maury was wounded in the side with a minie-ball while leading his men, with his colors in his hand, and deserves praise for his gallant conduct. Lieut. J. L. Chandler deserves great praise for his courage and coolness under the trying circumstances in which he was placed." (795-799) Reports of Col. Randall L. Gibson. Regiment held in reserve January 2d. Several times mentioned. Aggregate present, January 8th, 261. (800) Report of Lieut.-Col. Henry Maury: "Adjt. John L. Chandler acted with conspicuous gallantry. Officers and men all did their duty." (802) Mentioned in Maj. J. E. Austin's report. (973) Roll of honor, battle of Murfreesboro: Private James Clemens,* Company A; Corp. Vincent H. Joiner, B; Private Edmund Davis, C; Corp. John C. Oliver,* D; Private Reuben Dumas, E; Private Nathaniel F. Wheeler,* F; Corp. James H. Dove, G; Private Alfred C. Hulls, H; Sergt. Geo. W. Vansandt, I; Corp. Elijah P. Gabel,* K.

Vol. XX, Part 2—(419, 431) Second brigade, Col. J. B. Palmer, Breckinridge's division, Polk's corps, army of Tennessee, General Bragg, November, 1862. (456) Adams' brigade, Hardee's corps, near Eagleville, Tenn., December, 1862, (459) December 21st, assigned to duty with Preston's brigade until Adams' brigade joins division.

No. 37—(654) Casualties before Jackson, Miss., 1 wounded. (655, 656) Report of General Adams, engagement of July 12, 1863, gives great praise to regiment. Lieutenant-Colonel Maury was wounded. Capt. John C. Kimbell's report.

No. 51—(13) Adams' brigade, Breckinridge's division, Hill's corps, army of Tennessee, General Bragg, Chickamauga campaign. (197) Mentioned in report of General Breckinridge. (216-219) Mentioned in report of General Gibson of battle of Chickamauga; strength, 145. (219, 220) Maj. John C. Kimbell's report of September 20th, 2 wounded. (227) Mentioned in report of J. E. Austin.

No. 53—(661, 745) Clayton's brigade, army of Tennessee. Casualties, battle of Missionary Ridge, November 23 to 25, 1863, 8 killed and 34 wounded.

No. 56—(618, 686) October 31, 1863, regiment commanded by Capt. John W. Bell. Transferred to Clayton's brigade, Stewart's division, November 12th. (805, 824) Thirty-second and Fifty-eighth commanded by Col. Bush. Jones, December 10th. Total present (consolidated), 325.

No. 57—(479) Casualties at Rocky Face mountain, February 24 and 25, 1864, 3 killed, 31 wounded.

*Killed in action.

No. 74—(641, 649) Assignment as above. (657, 664, 672) Holtzclaw's brigade, Clayton's division, July to August, 1864. (832-834) Report of Gen. H. D. Clayton of engagements from May 7 to May 27, 1864 (Atlanta campaign), speaks of "their unexceptional conduct" at Resaca. "The Thirty-second and Fifty-eighth pushed up to within a few paces of the enemy's works without hesitation, though they knew what was before them, and the fate they would certainly encounter." List of casualties for the consolidated regiments gives 3 killed and 36 wounded. (841, 844) Report of Col. Bushrod Jones of operations May 7th to 28th: "Lieut. John H. Jones was unhurt in the fight, but was captured while endeavoring to have our wounded brought off the field. . . . Lieut. J. G. Goldthwait was wounded in wrist and Capt. G. W. Cox had his left thigh broken. My command behaved with rare and exemplary gallantry." May 15th, strength 345; killed 15, wounded 54; May 25th, strength, 225; killed 3, wounded 36; total, 18 killed, 90 wounded.

No. 78—(854) Assignment as above, Hood's army, September 20, 1864. Maj. Harry I. Thornton, of Fifty-eighth Alabama, in command of consolidated regiment.

No. 79—(879) Total present, 240, November 7, 1864.

No. 93—(665) Assignment as above, December 10, 1864.

No. 103—(1046) Holtzclaw's brigade, district of the Gulf, General Maury, March 10, 1865.

No. 104—(1131) Consolidated regiment, under Major Kimbell, directed to hold command in readiness to skirmish with enemy and, if hard pressed, to fall back in Spanish Fort, March 20, 1865. (1132) Near Hollywood, March 20, 1865.

THE THIRTY-THIRD ALABAMA INFANTRY.

The Thirty-third, organized at Pensacola, in April, 1862, was sent to Corinth soon after the battle of Shiloh. It took part in the Kentucky campaign at the capture of Munfordville, September 17th, and suffered heavy loss at Perryville, October 8th. It was greatly distinguished at Murfreesboro, December 31, 1862, to January 2, 1863. The brilliant record of the regiment was again established at Chickamauga, September 19th and 20th, where it lost 133 men. The Eighteenth battalion, Major Gibson, had been attached to the regiment and amalgamated with it, so that henceforth their history is identical, and in this battle perished the gallant leader of the battalion. The roll of honor of the organization is a long and creditable one. The regiment was at Lookout Mountain, November 24th, Missionary Ridge, November 25th, and Ringgold, November 27th. Worn, weary, many of the men barefooted, the regiment never lost its spirit, but fought on to the end with the same undaunted bravery. It wintered in Dalton and took part in all the battles and skirmishes from there to Chattanooga, always in the front. Its gallant Colonel Adams was killed at Atlanta, July 22, 1864. With Hood in

Tennessee, the regiment lost heavily, its strength of 285 men being reduced to less than 80. The regiment was transferred to North Carolina and surrendered at Smithfield.

Adjutant Stalworth died at Tupelo; Adjt. A. M. Moore and Capt. William S. Sims were killed at Chickamauga; Capt. William E. Dodson at Kenesaw; Capt. J. D. McKee at Perryville; Capts. John C. Norman and W. E. Cooper in a railroad accident.

Among the field officers were Col. Samuel Adams, killed at Atlanta, and Col. Robert Crittenden; Lieut.-Cols. Daniel H. Horn, and James H. Dunklin, who was wounded at Chickamauga.

EXTRACTS FROM OFFICIAL WAR RECORDS.

Vol. X, Part 1—(788) Hawthorn's brigade, Hardee's corps, army of the Mississippi, General Bragg, June "30, 1862.

Vol. XX, Part 1—(660, 680) Wood's brigade, Cleburne's division, army of Tennessee, at battle of Murfreesboro, 14 killed and 86 wounded. (851) Report of General Cleburne of operations December 26 to January 3, 1863: Col. Samuel Adams, Capts. W. E. Dodson and Thomas Seay, severely wounded; Sergt.-Maj. Mizell mortally wounded, Corp. Isaac R. Smith, Company C; Sergeant Stewart, Company H; Private Boyd, Company I; Foster, Company E, and Riley, Company D, specially mentioned. (896-900) Mentioned by Gen. S. A. M. Wood, in report of same battle, who speaks very highly of Col. Samuel Adams. (903, 906) Colonel Adams, in his report of Murfreesboro, says: "For nine days my men were continually marching in line of battle, or actually engaged in fighting; very frequently slept in the rain without tents, and during the whole time not a word of complaint was heard. The men acted very bravely in battle, many of them when the regiment was moving forward utterly regardless of their safety, and were at all times far in advance of the line. In these engagements Capt. W. E. Dodson, commanding Company C, and Capt. Thomas Seay, commanding Company K, acted with much coolness and bravery, being in all forward movements in advance of the regiment, cheering their men forward. Near the close of December 31, 1862, Captain Seay fell, severely wounded. Sergeant-Major Mizell, at his own request, carried a gun into action on 31st, and took position near the colors; he fell, mortally wounded, in the first charge, in advance of the regiment, cheering the men forward. Corp. Isaac R. Smith, Company C, Sergeant Stewart, Company H, Private Boyd, Company I, Private Foster, Company E, Private Riley, Company D, each acted with much coolness and bravery during the engagements."

Vol. XXIII, Part 1—(590) On picket near Wartrace, June 25, 1863, Gen. St. John R. Liddell's report.

Vol. XXIII, Part 2—(942, 959) Wood's brigade, Cleburne's division, Hill's corps, Bragg's army. August 10, 1863, Lieut.-Col. R. F. Crittenden commanding regiment.

No. 51—(12) Assignment as above, September 19-20, 1863, together with Eighteenth (Gibson's) battalion. (159-163) Mentioned in Gen. S. A. M. Wood's report of battle of Chickamauga. (165-167) Report of Col. Samuel Adams, Thirty-third regiment, commanding also Gibson's (Eighteenth) battalion, of battle of Chickamauga gives 16 killed and 133 wounded. "Officers and men acted very gallantly." Mentions particularly Captain Dodson, Company C, and Captain Hammett, Company D, as most distinguished for coolness and bravery. "Adjt. A. M. Moore was killed on the 19th, and Maj. J. H. Gibson, Gibson's battalion, was mortally wounded on the 20th. Both of these were brave and efficient officers, and in their death the country has sustained much loss." (167-169, 175) Mentioned in Col. E. B. Breedlove's and Lieutenant Goldthwaite's reports. (534) Roll of honor, battle of Chickamauga: Capt. W. E. Dodson, Company C; Capt. B. F. Hammett, D; Private W. R. Mock, A; Private J. D. Pevey, C; Sergt. C. L. Sessions,* D; Private P. H. L. Lewis,* E; Third Sergt. Richard R. Bush,* G; Corp. Alexander R. Bell, H; Private W. E. Hatten, I; Private William Harris, K. Roll of honor of Gibson's battalion: First Lieut. L. S. Mathews, Company B; Corp. R. A. Jones, A; Private Silas P. Button, B; Private George Ridley, C.

No. 55—(660) Lowrey's brigade, Bragg's army of Tennessee, November 20, 1863. (755, 769) Mentioned in Generals Cleburne's and Lowrey's reports of battle of Ringgold Gap, November 27, 1863. (770, 771) Report of Col. Samuel Adams, loss 2 killed, 9 wounded. Had several men engaged in fight who had marched from Missionary Ridge entirely barefooted.

No. 56—(618, 823, 885) Assignment as above. Total present, 536, December 14, 1863.

No. 74—Assignment as above, during Atlanta campaign. (725) Mentioned in General Cleburne's report of operations, May 27, 1864. (731-735) Mentioned in General Lowrey's report of the engagements from July 20th to September 1st, gives 7 killed and 38 wounded: "It was about 9:30 o'clock of this day (July 21st) that the gallant Col. Samuel Adams, Thirty-third Alabama regiment, was instantly killed by a Yankee sharpshooter. This true patriot and Christian hero—a perfect specimen of a soldier and gentleman—who had distinguished himself on many well-fought fields, fell at his post, leaving his gallant regiment to feel as orphans, and many other friends and comrades in arms to mourn an irreparable loss." Lieut.-Col. Robert F. Crittenden then took command.

No. 93—(667) Assignment as above, December 10, 1864. Sixteenth, Thirty-third and Forty-fifth Alabama under Colonel Abercrombie.

No 98—(1063) First Alabama (consolidated Sixteenth, Thirty-third and Forty-fifth), Col. Robert H. Abercrombie, April 9, 1865; Shelley's brigade, Stewart's corps, Johnston's army.

No. 100—(773) Transferred from Lowrey's to Shelley's brigade, near Smithfield, N. C., April 9, 1865.

*Killed in action.

THE THIRTY-FOURTH ALABAMA INFANTRY.

The Thirty-fourth Alabama infantry was organized at Loachapoka, April 15, 1862, went to Tupelo to join General Bragg's army, and was attached to Manigault's brigade, which assignment, with the Twenty-fourth and Twenty-eighth, it retained throughout the war, being at the end consolidated with these regiments. It proceeded with the army into Kentucky, but being on the reserve did little fighting. Its first battle experience—and it was a bitter one—was at Murfreesboro, December 31, 1862. The regiment went in early spring to East Tennessee; was at Chickamauga, September 19 and 20, 1863; at Missionary Ridge, November 25th, many of the command were made prisoners. In the winter of 1863-64 it recruited at Dalton, and next was in all the severe engagements from thereto Atlanta where, July 20th to 28th, its losses were heavy. It did not take part in the worst of the fight at Franklin, November 30th, but at Nashville, December 15th and 16th, it was almost annihilated. Going into the Carolinas it fought at Kinston, March 14, 1865, and at Bentonville, March 19th. Consolidated with the Twenty-fourth and Twenty-eighth, it was surrendered at High Point, not more than 100 men being left of the regiment that started out on that bright spring morning,, three years before, with overflowing ranks.

Lieut.-Col. John N. Slaughter and Capt. John Burch were wounded at Atlanta; Capts. R. G. Welch Chickamauga, W. G. Oliver at Jonesboro, W. H. Hoistein, J. Maury Smith and Jno. R. Colquitt at Atlanta. Capt. J. B. Bickerstaff was killed at Murfreesboro.

Field officers: Col. Julius C. B. Mitchell, Lieut.-Cols. James W. Echols, J. C. Carter; Majs. John N. Slaughter and Henry McCoy.

EXTRACTS FROM OFFICIAL WAR RECORDS.

Vol. X, Part 1—(789) Manigault's brigade, Withers' division, army of the Mississippi, June 30, 1862. Headquarters at Tupelo, Miss.

Vol. XX, Part 1—(659) Manigault's brigade, Withers' division, army of Tennessee, battle of Murfreesboro. (678) Casualties, December 31st to January 2d, 11 killed, 77 wounded. (696, 697) Statement of field officers of the Thirty-fourth, Twenty-eighth and Twenty-fourth Alabama, and endorsement of their bravery by General Manigault. (973) Roll of honor, battle of Murfreesboro: Corp. S. J. Numney, Company A; Privates J. R. Browning, C; C. P. Greer, D; James Shehorn, E; S. W. Reynolds, P; J. G. Whaley, G; T. N. Cloud, H; B. R. Covington, L; J. G. Metts, K.

Vol. XXIII, Part 2—(735-959) Assignment as above, April 1, 1863, with Twenty-eighth Alabama under Col. J. C. Reid. Maj. J. N. Slaughter commanding regiment, July; Colonel Mitchell in command, August.

No. 51—(15) In Manigault's brigade, left wing, General Longstreet, at battle of Chickamauga, September 19 and 20, 1863. Maj. John N. Slaughter commanding regiment. (341-344) Warmly commended by General Manigault, who highly compliments Major Slaughter. (348-350) Colonel Reid speaks of great service rendered by Lieutenant Mitchell and 30 of his men. (351-354) Major Slaughter says: " I feel it incumbent upon me to notice some special instances of gallantry. I would mention the names of Captain Burch, First Lieutenant Mitchell, Second Lieutenants Lambert, Oliver, Crockett and Bickerstaff; among the non-commissioned officers and privates, Sergeant Carlton, Company A, who was killed; Color-Corporal Ferguson, Company C; Color-Corporal Wellington, Company D, who was wounded while bearing the colors; Privates Adams, Company B, wounded; Riddle, Company B; Bone, Company F; Salmon, Company G, who was killed while leading in a charge on a battery. I was ably assisted by Acting Assistant Adjutant Cobb and Captain Carter" (534) Roll of honor, battle of Chickamauga: Sergts. J. L. Carlton, Company A; A. C. Ferguson, Company C; Privates W. M. Johnson, Company E; G. W. Smith, G; W. A. Houston, H; S. H. Pitts, I; Sergt. W. H. Long, Company K. Companies B and F declined making selection.

No. 55—(659) Assignment as above, at Missionary Ridge.

No. 56—(617, 886) Assignment as above to December, 1863, Colonel Mitchell in command of regiment, December 10th. Total present, 388 men, December 14th. Regiment commanded by Capt. R. G. Welch.

No. 58—(589) January 20, 1864, Capt. J. C. Carter commanding regiment.

No. 74—(640, 671) Manigault's brigade, Lee's corps, army of Tennessee, Hood, July 31, 1864. Capt. Henry J. Rix commanding regiment. August 31, 1864, Maj. J. N. Slaughter commanding. (781) Mentioned in General Manigault's report, battle at Ezra Church, July 28th. (783) Casualties, 14 killed and 46 wounded at Ezra church. (785-787) Maj. John N. Slaughter, in his report of the operations of July 28, 1864, speaks with great admiration and highest appreciation of the conduct of his regiment. He says: "We labored under great difficulties. The regiment was nearly without water, not having time to fill their canteens before going into action. They had marched two or three miles without resting. In this, as in most other engagements, the regiment has suffered from rapid movements, just before going under fire." Major Slaughter commends very highly Captains Welch and Rix, Lieutenants Bickerstaff and Craig, Sergeant Wright, Company A, and pays a beautiful tribute to Sergeant-Major Tinsley, who fell near the enemy's works. He says that it will probably not be his lot to again command this regiment, which "has conducted itself so well on all occasions and under all emergencies, that it has only to be known that it was engaged to know that it has done well," but he hopes their next commander may find them as faithful and gallant as he has.

No. 93—(664) Assignment as above, December 10, 1864, Lieut.-Col. John C. Carter commanding regiment.

No. 98—(1064) Consolidated with Twenty-fourth and Twenty-eighth, under Col. John C. Carter, about April 9, 1865.

THE THIRTY-FIFTH ALABAMA INFANTRY.

The Thirty-fifth regiment was organized at La Grange in April, 1862; ordered to Corinth, it was brigaded under General Breckinridge, and went to Louisiana under his command. It took part in the engagement at Baton Rouge, August 5th, where the regiment lost heavily and displayed the superb character of its officers and men. At Port Hudson it was highly complimented by General Breckinridge. At Corinth, October 3d, its losses again were heavy and General Van Dorn praised its work. It fought in Loring's division at Baker's Creek, and, after the siege of Jackson, was ordered to Tennessee, but was sent back to Mississippi early in 1864. It took part in the fighting in Georgia and the battles around Atlanta. Under Hood at Decatur it lost heavily, and at Franklin, November 30th, lost a large proportion of its force. At Nashville, December 15th and 16th, its loss was comparatively small. It went into the Carolinas and was surrendered with the remnants of the Twenty-seventh and Forty-ninth, with which it had been consolidated the previous summer, under its gallant commander, Col. A. E. Ashford. Capt. Thaddeus Felton was killed at Corinth; Capt. Samuel D. Stewart killed and Capt. J. B. Patten wounded at Franklin. Capt. John Hanna died in the service.

The field officers were Col. James W. Robertson; Edwin Goodwin, who died in the service; Samuel S. Ives, wounded at Franklin, and A. E. Ashford. Majs. William Hunt and John S. Dickson, killed at Franklin.

EXTRACTS FROM OFFICIAL WAR RECORDS.
Vol. XV—(18) Gen. Earl Van Dorn, in report of the defense of Vicksburg and other operations, June 27 to September 9, 1862, gives the Thirty-fifth, Colonel Robertson, brigaded under General Preston, as among his forces. (77) Mentioned by General Breckinridge in his report of engagement at Baton Rouge, August 5th, and in the storming and occupation of Port Hudson. He says that Colonel Thompson, commanding brigade, being severely wounded, the command devolved on Colonel Robertson, whose conduct fully justified the confidence of his troops. Lieutenant-Colonel Goodwin was on duty with sharpshooters. Both these officers afterward named for gallant conduct. (90-93) Mentioned in Gen. Daniel Ruggles' report of engagement at Baton Rouge, August 5, 1862. Casualties, 4 killed, 21 wounded. (93, 95, 96, 97) Colonel Robertson's report of same engagement, as brigade commander, commends the regiment highly and particularly Lieutenant-Colonel Goodwin. The officers commanding companies were conspicuous for coolness and courage. Lieutenant-Colonel Goodwin calls attention to the zeal and daring of the men, both officers and privates. (99) Colonel Crossland, Seventh Kentucky, says that the Thirty-fifth Alabama opened and kept up a hot fire, which broke the enemy's line. (1033) Rust's brigade, department of Mississippi and East Louisiana, General Gardner, March 31, 1863. (1125) Report of surgeon of First brigade, J. W. Thompson,

says that regiment, on arriving at Vicksburg, was 375 strong. Number for duty, August 11, 1862, 150; on account of sickness, asks that command be removed to a point further north.

Vol. XVII, Part 1—(375) Rust's brigade, district of the Mississippi, army of the West, General Van Dorn, October, 1862. (407-409) Mentioned in General Rust's report of operations near Corinth, October 2, 3 and 4, 1862. He says: "The conduct of the Thirty-fifth Alabama, commanded by Captain Ashford, though deprived by illness of their accomplished Colonel Robertson, could not have been improved by the presence of any officer."

No. 36—(544) General Loring, reporting from Enterprise, Miss., April 25, 1863, says: "Enemy demanded the town. They were represented 1,500 strong. Colonel Goodwin, with the Thirty-fifth Alabama, defied them."

No. 37—(77) General Loring's report of battle of Baker's Creek mentions the good service of the regiment. "The gallant Goodwin, Thirty-fifth Alabama, distinguished himself in the charge on the enemy's center." (82-87) General Buford's report says that Lieut. George C. Hubbard, acting as first lieutenant of Company F, Thirty-fifth Alabama, was killed. He was on a visit to the regiment and assigned temporarily to duty at the request of the captain. He calls special attention to Colonel Goodwin. (87, 88) Colonel Goodwin's report.

No. 38—(746) Transferred to Buford's brigade, with Twenty-seventh, Fifty-fourth and Snodgrass' (Fifty-fifth) Alabama regiments, by general order, No. 64, dated Jackson, Miss., April 15, 1863. (770) General Buford, April 20th, says: "Thirty-fifth Alabama left Chattanooga this morning." (937, 1040) Buford's brigade, Loring's division, army of Mississippi, May to July, 1863.

No. 57—(333) Assignment as above, February 20, 1864, General Polk in command. Col. Samuel S. Ives commanding regiment. (626) Colonel Johnson (cavalry) reports from near Moulton, March 24th, that regiment is near there recruiting and has determined to fall back to Smithville. Asks that it be detained there and mounted. (662, 663) Colonel Ives reports that April 12th, at night, his regiment, with detachments from the Twenty-seventh Alabama, crossed the river, surprised a camp, killing 3, and capturing 3 commissioned officers, 38 non-commissioned officers and privates, 1 negro butler and a considerable number of horses, mules, arms, equipments, etc., sustaining no loss whatsoever.

No. 58—Colonel Ives reports a skirmish near Mount Hope on March 24, 1864; put the enemy to flight and drove them to Decatur. Regiment at Moulton, about 250 strong, but first-rate troops. Lieut.-Col. John Estes' report, April 5th, says, "Regiment is near Mount Hope."

No. 74—(645, etseq.) Scott's brigade, Loring's division, General Polk's corps, Johnston's army in Georgia, after June 10, 1864. (For other extracts, see those in connection with the Twenty-seventh Alabama, brigade organization remaining the same.)

No. 98—(1063) Consolidated with Twenty-seventh, Forty-ninth, Fifty-fifth and Fifty-seventh Alabama, under Col. Edward McAlexander, after April 9th, in Shelley's brigade, Stewart's corps, Johnston's army.

THE THIRTY-SIXTH ALABAMA INFANTRY.

Thirty-sixth Alabama, organized at Mt. Vernon arsenal, May 12, 1862, was first engaged in constructing defenses at Oven and Choctaw bluffs, then remained at Mobile until April, 1863, when it was sent to Tullahoma and brigaded under General Clayton with the Eighteenth, Thirty-second, Fifty-eighth and Thirty-eighth Alabama. This brigade, with General Holtzclaw as commander after the promotion of General Clayton, was identical throughout the war. The regiment took part in the battle of Chickamauga, where it began its glorious battle record; the number of its wounded in every engagement shows the spirit which inspired its leaders. It wintered at Dalton; fought at Crow Valley, Rocky Face, May 9, 1864; Resaca, May 15th; New Hope, May 35th, fighting constantly from Dalton to Atlanta, and lost 300 men. At Jonesboro, August 31st and September 1st, it lost very heavily. It was with Hood in Tennessee and fought gallantly at Nashville, December 15th and 16th. Transferred with the brigade to General Maury it was stationed at Spanish Fort, where perhaps its greatest hardships were experienced and it lost 110 of its men, wounded and captured. The survivors were surrendered at Meridian. Capt. James A. Wemyss was wounded at Atlanta; John C. Adams, D. W. Kelly and James W. A. Wright at Missionary Ridge; John M. Walker was killed, and Washington Lott wounded at Resaca; John G. Cleveland killed at Chickamauga; William L. Higgins wounded at Jonesboro. Other names are given in the "Extracts" below.

The field officers were: Cols. Robert H. Smith, Lewis T. Woodruff (wounded at New Hope), and Thomas H. Herndon, who was severely wounded at Chickamauga and again at Atlanta, and whose conduct throughout the war was unsurpassed (he was the last man to leave the trenches at Spanish Fort); and Maj. Chas. S. Henegan.

EXTRACTS FROM OFFICIAL WAR RECORDS.
Vol. XV—(850) Slaughter's brigade, army of Mobile, Gen. J. H. Forney, October 31, 1862. (1069) Cumming's brigade, Western division, army of Mobile, General Buckner, April, 1863.

Vol. XXIII, Part 2—(943, 960) In Clayton's brigade, Stewart's division, Hill's corps, Bragg's army, Colonel Woodruff, Lieutenant-Colonel Herndon, summer of 1863.

No. 42—(130) General Maury, Mobile, August 1, 1863, asks that regiment detached and sent to General Bragg in April be returned.

No. 51—(16) In Clayton's brigade, Stewart's division, Buckner's corps, Bragg's army, September 19-20, 1863. (367) Casualties, 16 killed and

133 wounded at the battle of Chickamauga. (369) Color-bearer J. W. Tillinghast distinguished in the battle. (384) Mentioned in General Bate's report. (389) Thrilling account of action in battle of Chickamauga, given by Col. Bush Jones. (400-404) General Clayton mentions regiment and gives force on September 19th, 28 officers, 429 men, 401 guns; on September 20th, 22 officers, 338 men and 316 guns. (405) Mentioned in Maj. P. F. Hundley's report. (407,408) Colonel Woodruff's report gives among the wounded on the 19th, the names of Lieutenant-Colonel Herndon, Capt. J. G. Cleveland, Lieuts. A. H. Hutchinson, J. C. Knox and T. H. Shelton. Speaks of Lieutenants Gladden, Meek, Smith and Walker; also of Captain Derby, Lieutenants Bell, Bullen, Thompson, Banks, Walker, Cleveland and Wiggins. Lieuts. J. A. Cleveland and S. Bell were killed on the 20th, and Lieuts. W. H. P. Gordon, D. M. Prewitt, E. B. Lott and J. Banks were wounded. Commending every officer, he specially names Capt. A. J. Derby and Adjt. T. A. Hatch. "J. W. Tillinghast, of Company B, carried the colors both days, and always to the front; he is a cool, brave man and deserves special mention."

No. 55—(661, 745) Assignment as above. Casualties, 9 killed, 18 wounded, Lookout Mountain and Missionary Ridge, November 24 and 25, 1863.

No. 56—Assignment as above, October to December, 1863; total present, 353, December 14th.

No. 57 — (479) Casualties at Rocky Face Mountain, February 24 and 25, 1864, 11 wounded.

No. 74—(641, et seq.) In Clayton's (Holtzclaw's) brigade, Stewart's division, Hood's corps, Atlanta campaign. (831-834) Mentioned in Gen. H. D. Clayton's report of the several engagements from the 7th of May to the 25th, 1864 (including Rocky Face mountain, Resaca and New Hope church), highly commends regiment and says: "I feel I ought to particularly mention Lieut. John R. Hall, Lieut. J. M. Walker, and Lieut. J. T. Jackson, of the Thirty-sixth Alabama regiment." Casualties, 14 killed, 70 wounded. (836-838) Report of Capt. James A. Wemyss, in command of regiment: "Rocky Face mountain, May 10th, 1 killed, 5 wounded; Resaca, May 15th, 14 killed, 70 wounded; New Hope church, May 25th, Col. L. T. Woodruff was seriously wounded, 8 killed and 27 wounded.. Aggregate casualties, 133." (864) Mentioned by Col. J. C. Lewis.

No. 79—(897) Total present, 303, November 7, 1864.

No. 93—(665) December 10, 1864, Capt. Nathan M. Carpenter commanding regiment, Nashville campaign.

No. 103—(1046) In Holtzclaw's brigade, district of the Gulf, March 10, 1865.

THE THIRTY-SEVENTH ALABAMA INFANTRY.

The Thirty-seventh was organized at Auburn in the spring of 1862; sent to Columbus, Miss., from there to Tupelo. With Price at Iuka, September

19-20, 1862, it began its long roll of battles, and was highly commended by Brigadier-General Martin and by General Price. Both its colonel, J. F. Dowdell, and its lieutenant-colonel, A. A. Greene, were wounded in this fight, besides forty-three of the men. The regiment went into battle with 304 men, so that its loss was heavy. General Little, in whose division it was, was killed at Iuka. In the battle of Corinth, October 3-5, 1862, it lost heavily and its brigade commander, General Martin, was killed. Brigaded under General Moore, the winter of 1862-63 was spent in Mississippi. It took part at Chickasaw Bayou, was sent to Sunflower river, but returned before the close of the spring; was in the battles of Port Gibson, May 1, 1863, and Baker's Creek, May 16th, where it lost heavily. From that time till July 4th it formed part of the garrison at Vicksburg, and was captured with that place, where it had suffered greatly from losses and privations.

For awhile, after being exchanged, the regiment was in parole camp at Demopolis. Later it was transferred to the army of Tennessee, and took part in the battles of Lookout Mountain, November 24th; Missionary Ridge, November 25th. After wintering at Dalton, brigaded under Gen. Alpheus Baker, the regiment was ever in the van of the army in the battles of the Georgia campaign, at Rocky Face mountain, May 9th and 10th; Resaca, May 14th and 15th; and New Hope church, May 25th, where it lost heavily, officers and men. In the battles around Atlanta its casualties were great.

The regiment was sent for in the winter to do garrison duty at Spanish Fort, but early in the spring it was returned to the army of Tennessee, and again was in battle at Bentonville. Consolidated with the Forty-second and Fifty-fourth Alabama, commanded by Col. John A. Winter, it surrendered in North Carolina. This regiment was remarkable for the large number of its officers killed and wounded.

Capt. Marion C. J. Searcy was wounded at Corinth and killed at Missionary Ridge. Capt. W. W. Meadows was killed, and Capts. Moses B. Greene, John O. Davis and S. M. Robertson were wounded, at Corinth; Capt. J. C. Kendrick was wounded at Corinth and at Atlanta; Capt. J. J. Padgett was wounded; Capt. Joel G. Greene, at Atlanta; Capt. C. Pennington, at Resaca; Capt. J. M. Leach was killed at New Hope; Capt. C. E. Evans was wounded at Resaca and Atlanta; Capt. James H. Johnson wounded at Atlanta.

Its field officers were Col. James F. Dowdell, captured at Vicksburg; Lieut.-Col. A. A. Greene, wounded at Iuka and at Missionary Ridge, and killed at Atlanta; Lieut. -Col. W. F. Slaton, wounded at Corinth and captured at Lookout Mountain; and Majs. John P. W. Amorine and Joel C. Kendrick.

EXTRACTS FROM OFFICIAL WAR RECORDS.

Vol. XVII, Part 1—(123) Report of Gen. Sterling Price, of battle of Iuka, speaks of regiment as being in Martin's brigade. Says Col. James F. Dowdell and Lieut.-Col. A. A. Greene were wounded, the latter severely.

(132-133) General Martin's report of same engagement speaks in high commendation of the cool gallantry and daring of Col. James F. Dowdell; also of Lieutenant-Colonel Greene, who was severely wounded, and Major Slaton, who acted bravely and nobly. He gives casualties, 12 killed, 43 wounded. Acting Asst. Adjt.-Gen. J. W. McDonald gives the strength of regiment going into this battle as 304. (382) Five killed, 35 wounded, at the battle of Corinth, October 3-5, 1862. (386) Hebert's division, October 20, 1862. (688) Mentioned in Colonel Withers' report of operations, January 2, 1863.

No. 37—(327) In Moore's brigade, Forney's division, July 4, 1863, army of Vicksburg. (369) Casualties, 16 killed, 38 wounded, during the siege of Vicksburg, May 7th to July 4th. (381-382) Mentioned in Gen. John C. Moore's report.

No. 55—(658, 691, 704) In Moore's brigade, Cheatham's division, Hardee's corps, army of Tennessee. Casualties at Lookout Mountain, November 24th, and Missionary Ridge, November 25, 1863, 4 killed, 12 wounded. Mentioned in General Moore's report.

No. 56—(803, 822) Assignment as above, December, 1863. Lieut.-Col. Alex. A. Greene in command of regiment. Total present, 407.

No. 57—(481) Mentioned by Col. John H. Higley, February 25, 1864, in report of demonstration on Dalton.

No. 74—(649, et seq.) In Baker's brigade, Stewart's (later Clayton's) division, Hood's corps, army of Tennessee, General Johnston, Atlanta campaign. (818) Mentioned in Gen. Alex. P. Stewart's report of operations, May 7 to 27, 1864. "During the 27th the Thirty-seventh Alabama, Lieutenant-Colonel Greene, suffered severely from the fire of a battery, and, with the Fifty-fourth Alabama, who reinforced it, is especially entitled to mention for the fortitude with which they endured the ordeal. (819) Report of Gen. Henry D. Clayton of battle of Atlanta, July 22, 1864, deplores the loss of Lieutenant-Colonel Greene. (845-847) Gen. Alpheus Baker's report of Rocky Face, Resaca and New Hope church, speaks in the highest terms of the heroic fortitude of the Thirty-seventh. On the 27th the regiment lost 50 men killed and wounded, one of the latter being their brave and skillful commander, Lieutenant-Colonel Greene. (847-849) Report of Lieutenant-Colonel Greene gives a graphic description of the action of the regiment. He gives losses: Resaca, 4 killed, 3 wounded; New Hope church, 9 killed, 53 wounded. Total loss, 15 killed, 86 wounded, 8 missing. "The conduct of all my officers and almost all my men has been admirable in battle, and on the weary march, since the 7th of May."

No. 78—(803, 854) Transferred to Mobile with Baker's brigade, in August, 1864. Brigade consisted of Thirty-seventh, Fortieth, Forty-second and Fifty-fourth Alabama. (862) General Hood, September 22, 1864, asks that Baker's brigade be returned to him.

No. 93—(1232) Baker's brigade, Liddell's division, district of the Gulf, General Maury; department of Mississippi, Alabama and East Louisiana, Gen. Richard Taylor; November, 1864, with the Fortieth and Forty-second, under Col. John H. Higley.

No. 98—(1064) Brantly's brigade, Lee's corps, Johnston's army, consolidated with Forty-second and Fifty-fourth, under Col. John A. Minter, after April 9, 1865.

No. 100—(687) Two hundred and four prisoners taken by brigade, March 19, 1865. (698, 734) Baker's brigade, Clayton's division, Lee's corps, army of Tennessee, March, 1865; Capt. T. B. Richards.

No. 103—(940) Special order, No. 28, General Maury, Mobile, January 28, 1865: "Brig.-Gen. A. Baker will proceed with his brigade to Augusta, Ga., via Montgomery, Ala."

THE THIRTY-EIGHTH ALABAMA INFANTRY.

The Thirty-eighth regiment was organized at Mobile in May, 1862, and remained there until February, 1863. Its first brigade commander was General Slaughter; then General Cumming. Transferred to Bragg's army, it was under General Clayton until his promotion; then under General Holtzclaw from July, 1864, until its surrender at Meridian. At Hoover's Gap, June 24, 1863, it went into its first real battle, coming out almost unscathed; but at Chickamauga, September 19th and 20th, its loss was very great. At Missionary Ridge, November 25th, a large number, after fierce fighting, were captured.

The winter of 1863-64 was passed at Dalton, and with the spring of 1864 came the regiment's hardest work, in the Atlanta campaign. At Rocky Face mountain, May 7th to 10th; at Resaca, May 14th and 15th; New Hope church, May 25th, and at Atlanta, July 20th to 28th, its losses were severe, both in killed and wounded, and by capture. In Holtzclaw's brigade, it went with Hood into Tennessee and protected the rear of the army in the retreat. Transferred with the brigade to Mobile, it was in the defense of Spanish Fort, where it suffered its greatest privations. It held its original organization until the end, and surrendered its remnant of 80 men at Meridian. Adjt. Alfred R. Murray was wounded; Capts. W. R. Welsh, John B. Perkins and Charles E. Bussey were killed at Chickamauga; Capts. W. H. Wright, wounded and captured; John A. Jackson, captured at Missionary Ridge. Captain Jackson died in prison. Capt. Ben Lane Posey was captured at Chickamauga, and wounded at Kenesaw.

The field officers were Cols. Charles T. Ketchum, and A. R. Lankford, captured at Resaca; and Majs. O. S. Jewett, killed at Chickamauga, and W. J. Hearin, captured at Missionary Ridge.

EXTRACTS FROM OFFICIAL WAR RECORDS.

Vol. XV—(850) Army of Mobile, Gen. J. E. Slaughter; district of the Gulf, General Forney, October 31, 1862. (1069) Second brigade, General Cumming, Western division, department of the Gulf, General Buckner commanding.

Vol. XVII, Part 2—(310) Federal report: "Thirty-eighth Alabama regiment was sent to Mobile, by Pemberton, on October 21, 1862."

Vol. XXIII, Part 2—(943, 960) In Clayton's brigade, Stewart's division, General Bragg, July and August, 1863.

No. 42—(130) General Maury, August 1, 1863, says: "Regiment had been detached from garrison of Mobile and sent to General Bragg."

No. 51—(16) Assignment as above, at battle of Chickamauga. (367) Return of casualties, September 18 to 20, 1863, 37 killed, 143 wounded. (369) List of those who distinguished themselves in battle of Chickamauga: Sergt-Maj. J. R. Larkin; Sergt. J. W. George, Company H; Private J. P. Seabrook, Company I; Private Calloway Johnson, Company E. (389, 400-403) Mentioned in reports of Col. Bush Jones and Gen. Henry D. Clayton. (404) Carried into battle, on the 19th, 461 guns, 29 officers; on the 20th, 314 guns, 17 officers; report of Colonel Ketchum, commanding brigade. (409-411) Col. A. R. Lankford's report says: "The non-commissioned officers and men of my command exhibited the courage and gallantry which characterize all Southern soldiers, particularly Alabamians. He also commends the coolness and bravery of Color-bearer Joel Bell, Company E, who carried the colors of the regiment ahead of all others. (534) Roll of honor, battle of Chickamauga: Private T. C. Ezell,* Company A; Corp. James M. Moore, Company B; Corp. J. E. Platt, Company C; Private A. McAlpin,* Company C; Sergt. W. W. Buford,* Company D; Corp. Joel W. Bell, Company E; Private A. D. Sims, Company F; Sergt. W. W. Holly,* Company G; Private Patrick Dayton,* Company H; Sergt. G. F. Williamson,* Company I; Private Francis H. Wilson,* Company K; Sergt. John L. Mayse, Company K.

No. 56—(887) Total present, 272, December 14, 1863. In Clayton's brigade, Stewart's division, Breckinridge's corps, army of Tennessee, Johnston commanding, December 31, 1863.

No. 57—(479) Return of casualties at Rocky Face Mountain (February 24 and 25, 1864), 2 killed and 18 wounded.

No. 74—(641, et seq.) Assignment as above, Hood's corps, Atlanta campaign. June 30, 1864, Capt. Daniel Lee commanding regiment; Holtzclaw commanding brigade (Clayton's division), July 10th; Capt. Ben Lane Posey commanding regiment, August 31st. (832, 834) General Clayton's report (including Rocky Face mountain, Resaca and New Hope church) says: "After having two color-bearers killed, Colonel Lankford was last seen with his colors in his hand." He particularly mentions Joseph Plant, who was killed, and Lieut. L. F. Irwin, who was severely wounded. Report of casualties gives 2 killed, 15 wounded. (836-838) Mentioned in Colonel Wemyss' report. (838-840) Report of Capt. George W. Welch, in command of regiment: Loss at

* Killed in action.

Rocky Face, May 8th, 2 killed, 15 wounded; at Resaca, May 15th, 7 killed, 53 wounded. Colonel Lankford was captured at New Hope church the 25th; 27th, loss was 3 killed, 20 wounded.

No. 79—(897) Total present, 236, November 7, 1864; Maj. H. I. Thornton commanding regiment.

No. 93—(665, 704) In Holtzclaw's brigade, Clayton's division, December 10, 1864; Capt. Charles E. Bussey commanding regiment.

No. 103—(1046) Holtzclaw's brigade, district of the Gulf, General Maury, March 10, 1865; Capt. Charles E. Bussey commanding regiment.

THE THIRTY-NINTH ALABAMA INFANTRY.

The Thirty-ninth Alabama was organized in May, 1862, and went immediately to Mississippi, where it was brigaded under Gen. Frank Gardner with the Nineteenth, Twenty-second, Twenty-fifth and Twenty-sixth (Fiftieth) regiments. It went into Kentucky, but being generally in the reserve, its first battle of consequence was after its return, at Murfreesboro, December 31st, where it made a fine record. The regiment behaved gallantly at Chickamauga, September 19 and 20, 1863, losing nearly 27 per cent of its force. At Missionary Ridge, November 25th, it fought again with less loss. The regiment wintered at Dalton, and fought under Hood through the Dalton-Atlanta campaign. At Atlanta, July 20th to 22d, it suffered great loss, and Colonel Clifton was severely wounded. At Jonesboro, August 31st and September 1st, it was again in the sharpest of the fighting. At Nashville, December 15th and 16th, a large number were captured. The regiment went with Johnston into the Carolinas, fought its last fight at Bentonville, and was surrendered at Yadkin river bridge. Maj. J. D. Smith was killed at Jonesboro, Captain Roberts in North Carolina, Capt. Willis Banks near Atlanta, Capts. T. Q. Stanford and Joseph C. Clayton at Murfreesboro, and Capt. C. H. Matthews at Peachtree Creek.

The field officers were Henry D. Clayton, who was severely wounded at Murfreesboro and at Atlanta, promoted to brigadier, and afterward major-general, and displayed great skill and heroism to the end; Col. Whitfield Clark, Lieut.-Cols. James Flewellen, Lemuel Hargroves and W. C. Clifton.

EXTRACTS FROM OFFICIAL WAR RECORDS.

Vol. X, Part 1—(788) First brigade, Gen. Frank Gardner, reserve corps, General Withers, army of the Mississippi, General Bragg, June 30, 1862.

Vol. XVI, Part 2—(764) In Gardner's brigade, army of the Mississippi, General Polk commanding, August 18 to 20, 1862.

Vol. XX, Part 1—(658) In Deas' brigade, Withers' division, Polk's corps, army of Tennessee, at Murfreesboro. (677) Casualties, December 31, 1862, to January 2, 1863, 3 killed, 92 wounded. (754) Mentioned in Gen.

Jones M. Withers' report. (973) Roll of honor, battle of Murfreesboro: Adjt. J. M. Macon; Second Lieut. E. Q. Thornton, Company K; Second Lieut. E. O. Petty, Company B; Sergt. C. K. Hall, Company H; Sergt. W. J. White, Company H; Sergt. E. Priest, Company K; Private W. C. Menefee, Company A; Sergt. A. J. Talbot, Company A; Private Samuel M. Martin, Company B; Private John Dansby, Company C; Private Evander Burkett, Company D; Private Frank Jones, Company E; Sergts. John H. Poyner and T. F. Espy, Company G; Sergt. Abner Flowers, Company I; Sergt. James Wilson, Company K.

Vol. XXIII, Part 2—(735, 942, 958) In Deas' brigade, Withers' division (Twenty-sixth and Thirty-ninth under Colonel Clayton), April to August, 1863; July 31st, Col. Whitfield Clark in command.

No. 51—(15) In Deas' brigade, Hindman's division, at Chickamauga. (338) Col. Whitfield Clark's report of the battle gives 14 killed, 82 wounded. Regiment went into fight with 310 muskets. (339) Mentioned in Col. J. G. Coltart's report.

No. 56—In Deas' brigade, Hindman's division, Cheatham's army corps, to December, 1863. Total present, 337; Lieut.-Col. William C. Clifton commanding regiment, December 14, 1863.

No. 74—(640, et seq.) Assignment as above, Hood's corps, Atlanta campaign. August 31, 1864, Maj. Drewry H. Smith commanding regiment. (779,780) Report of Capt. A. J. Miller (commanding regiment), operations July 22d and 28th (Atlanta): "Lieutenant-Colonel Clifton was severely wounded. Capt. T. J. Brannon, who has since been sick, was in command."

No. 93—(664) Assignment as above, Johnson's division, Lee's corps, December 10, 1864.

THE FORTIETH ALABAMA INFANTRY.

The Fortieth Alabama was organized at Mobile in May, 1862. It went to Vicksburg by way of Columbus, Miss., and was brigaded with the Thirty-seventh and Forty-second under General Moore; was in Featherstone's command in the Steele's bayou expedition, March 16 to 22, 1863; was transferred to Bragg's army, and appears to have served in detachment as sharpshooters for the greater part of the time of its service. At Vicksburg it suffered severely, and a large portion was captured. Being paroled, it joined its command in Tennessee in time to take part in the battle of Chickamauga, September 19th and 20th, where it lost heavily, next fighting at Lookout Mountain, November 24th, and at Missionary Ridge, November 25th. Gen. Alpheus Baker became its brigadier, and it wintered at Dalton. It took a prominent part in the Atlanta campaign; at Rocky Face, May 9 and 10, 1864; Resaca, May 14th and 15th, and at New Hope church, May 25th, making gallant charges and earning a fine record, both collectively and individually, as will be seen in the extracts below. In midsummer, 1864, the brigade was transferred to Mobile, and, under General Maury, took part in the defense of Mobile; but Hood, who knew well the gallantry of these troops, clamored for their return, and in January, 1865, they were sent back to the army of Tennessee; and after skirmishing and fighting, last of all at Bentonville, March 18th, the regiment, consolidated with the Nineteenth and Forty-sixth, was surrendered at Yadkin river bridge.

Adjt. C. H. Ellerbee and Capt. James A. Latham were killed at Bentonville, Capt. Ed. Marsh at Dalton, Sergt. Preston S. Gilder, standard-bearer, at Resaca.

The field officers were Cols. A. A. Coleman and John H. Higley, Lieut.-Cols. Thomas Stone (who died in the service) and Ezekiel Gully, and Maj. E. D. Willett.

EXTRACTS FROM OFFICIAL WAR RECORDS.

Vol. XV.—(850) Army of Mobile, General Slaughter, district of the Gulf, General Forney, October 31, 1862.

Vol. XVII, Part 1—(666) General Pemberton in his report of operations, December 21, 1862, to January 2, 1863, says: "On 25th, the Fortieth Alabama regiment, Col. A. A. Coleman, was ordered from Columbus to Vicksburg."

Vol. XVII, Part 2—(797, 799) Colonel Coleman's regiment ordered to Columbus. (819) Captain Marsh's company, E, at Jackson, serving as provost guard. (825) In Vicksburg, 332 effectives, in Major-General Smith's command, January 3, 1863.

No. 36—(458-461) General Featherstone's report of engagements on Rolling Fork and Deer creek, March 19th to 29th, in which regiment is mentioned several times. (467, 510) Mentioned in Col. S. W. Ferguson's report of engagement of March 22d, the Steele's bayou expedition.

No. 37—(327, 369) In Moore's brigade, Forney's division, army of Vicksburg. Casualties in siege, 18 killed, 39 wounded. (381) Mentioned in J. C. Moore's report of siege, May 17 to July 4, 1863.

No. 38—(612, 705) Assignments. (762) Col. S. W. Ferguson, Rolling Fork, April 18, 1863, says: "I arrived here last night with the Fortieth Alabama." (957) Called "Alabama battalion sharpshooters," in Walker's division at and near Yazoo City, June 7th. (1041) Eastern Louisiana, Ector's brigade, Walker's division, July 30th; "Alabama battalion" under Maj. T. O. Stone.

No. 51—(14) "Stone's Alabama battalion sharpshooters," in Ector's brigade, September 19 and 20, 1863, army of Tennessee, General Bragg.

No. 55—(658) Moore's brigade, Hardee's corps, November 20, 1863, army of Tennessee, General Bragg. (691) Casualties, November 24 and 25, 1863, 4 killed, 20 wounded. (704) Mentioned in Gen. J. C. Moore's report of engagements on Lookout Mountain and Missionary Ridge.

No. 56—(726) Stone's sharpshooters, Ector's brigade, French's division, November 20, 1863. In department of Mississippi and East

Louisiana, General Johnston. (803) Moore's brigade, Cheatham's division, December 10,1863. In army of Tennessee, General Hardee. (822) December 14, 1863, 429 total present. (884) Assignment as above, December 31st.

No. 57—(480, 481) Report of Col. John H. Higley, commanding brigade, operations February 23 to 27, 1864.

No. 58—(583) On December 16, 1863, General Johnston was directed to turn over the immediate command of army of the Mississippi to General Polk. This department was officially called "The department of Alabama, Mississippi and East Louisiana." (584) "Stone's sharpshooters," Ector's brigade, January 20, 1864, in General Polk's army. (The sharpshooters under Lieutenant-Colonel Stone were evidently a detachment of the Fortieth.) (587) Moore's brigade, Hardee's corps, January 20, 1864, army of Tennessee, General Johnston; Lieutenant-Colonel Stone in command of regiment.

No. 59—(870) Baker's brigade, Stewart's division, April 30, 1864, Hood's corps, army of Tennessee; Capt. Elbert D. Willett commanding regiment.

No. 74—(641, et seq.) Assignment as above, April to August, 1864; August 31st, Col. John H. Higley commanding regiment. (844-847) Gen. Alpheus Baker's report: May 10th, Capt. E. Marsh, a valued officer, was killed; May 15th, standard-bearer (Sergt. Preston L. Gilder) acted with the highest gallantry and fell in front of his comrades, pierced by the bullets of the foe. He speaks also of Colonel Higley. (849, 850) Colonel Higley's report of Rocky Face mountain, May 10th: Captain Marsh and 2 privates killed; Lieut. J. C. Moore and 4 privates wounded. May 15th, Sergt. P. S. Gilder was killed several paces in front of his command; colors were left on field. Adjutant Ellerbee, Lieutenant Knighton and Lieutenant Peteet returned to field and secured colors under a heavy fire. Loss, 5 killed, 34 wounded; May 25th, loss 3 killed, 9 wounded. "I commenced the campaign May 7th with 416 effective men; at present (May 31st) I number 326 effective men. Total, 17 killed, 60 wounded, 3 missing." Conduct of officers and men commended highly.

No. 75—(481) Mentioned in General Sherman's communication, dated Big Shanty, Ga., June 15, 1864. (For other extracts, see those in connection with the Thirty-seventh Alabama, brigade organization remaining the same.)

No. 100—(734) Same assignment, March 31, 1865, army near Smithfield; Capt. Thomas M. Bronson commanding regiment.

THE FORTY-FIRST ALABAMA INFANTRY.

The Forty-first regiment, 1,250 strong, was organized in May, 1862; was ordered from Tuscaloosa to Chattanooga; was in Middle Tennessee for some months, doing guard duty principally; was sent to Kentucky in September, brigaded under General Hanson, being the only Alabama troops in his Kentucky brigade. Under its gallant and brave Colonel Stansel, who shared its vicissitudes from the beginning until the close, it fought valiantly at Murfreesboro, December 31st to January 2d, where two of its finest lieutenants were killed, as was its brigade commander, General Hanson. Gen. Marcus Wright and Colonel Hunt, successively, commanded the Kentucky brigade, but in May, 1863, it was assigned to General Helm, and moved to Tullahoma in Breckinridge's army. The regiment was engaged in the operations for the relief of Vicksburg, and in the trenches at Jackson through the long, weary summer of 1863. Rejoining the army of Tennessee, the regiment immortalized itself at Chickamauga, September 19 and 20, 1863. Of the 325 men who went into battle, 147 were killed and wounded, several of them officers. Again it lost its brigade commander, General Helm being killed in this battle. In November, we find the regiment brigaded with the Forty-third Alabama and the First, Second, Third and Fourth battalions, Hilliard's legion (afterward known as the Fifty-ninth and Sixtieth Alabama), and Stallworth's sharpshooters, under the command of General Gracie, which organization remained identical until the surrender; took part, with considerable loss, in the campaign of East Tennessee. In April, 1864, the brigade was sent to Virginia; was at Drewry's Bluff, May 12th to 16th, and at Dutch Gap. Took part in the siege of Petersburg, March 25th to April 2d, where Maj. L. D. Hudgins was killed, and the loss was very severe; suffered greatly at Hatcher's Run; at White Oak road it lost its brave and gallant Lieutenant-Colonel Trimmier. The regiment was bravely fighting at Appomattox, and had repulsed the enemy, when the flag of truce ended the fight, and, at the same time, the long war. Of 1,454 names on the rolls since its enrollment, there were 870 in this last fight, led by Stansel, and under the command of General Gordon. Capt. Robert H. McCord died in the service; Capt. B. A. Hudgins was wounded, and Lieuts. J. T. Hardaway and N. B. Lenderman were killed, at Murfreesboro. Capt. L. M. Clements was wounded, and Lieut. A. Hawkins and Sergt.-Maj. Ira Tarrant were killed, at Chickamauga; Capt H. M. Bell was wounded at Hatcher's Run.

The field officers were Cols. Henry Talbird and M. L. Stansel, wounded at Murfreesboro, and since distinguished in the political history of Alabama and at the bar; Lieut.-Cols. J. T. Murfee and T. G. Trimmier, who laid down his life at White Oak road; and Majs. Jesse G. Nash and L. D. Hudgins, the latter killed at Petersburg.

EXTRACTS FROM OFFICIAL WAR RECORDS.

Vol. XVI, Part 2—(717) Forty-first regiment at Tuscaloosa, 1,250 strong; ordered to Chattanooga, July 2, 1862. (762, 781, 789) Guarding bridge over Hiawassee, by order of General Bragg, August. Colonel Howard authorized to call on commander for assistance to enforce orders. (800) Three companies relieved from duty at Hiawassee and ordered to join regiment, September 7th. (835) Ordered to Kentucky, September 16th.

Vol. XX, Part 1—(659, 679) In Hanson's brigade, Hardee's corps, army of Tennessee, Stone's river campaign. Casualties at battle of Murfreesboro, 16 killed, 94 wounded. Lieutenants Hardaway and N. B. Lenderman killed. (782-788) Mentioned in report of General Breckinridge. (825-829) Mentioned in report of Colonel Trabue. "Lieutenant-Colonel Stansel commanded; regiment lost two of its best officers. Casualties, 18 killed, 89 wounded. Aggregate present, 521, January 8, 1863; aggregate present and absent, 938; aggregate last return, 1,055." (829, 830) Lieutenant-Colonel Stansel's report says: "During this time two of our best lieutenants, James T. Hardaway and N. B. Lenderman, were killed, and a number of men wounded: still, however, we held our position against the most terrific assaults the enemy could bring to bear against it—a point called by General Bragg, himself, the key of the battlefield. On Friday evening, January 2d, this regiment, together with the Second, Fourth and Sixth Kentucky regiments, was ordered to the right of our position, and proceeded down Stone's river to a point about one mile north of Wayne's hill, to make an attack upon a large body of the enemy enforced there. In this attack, from which ensued a most terrific battle, my officers and men demeaned themselves most gallantly, driving the enemy before them, across the river, entirely from the position they held, pushing forward until they came within the raking fire of the powerful batteries of the enemy, planted on the opposite bank of the river, and supported by almost their entire army. ... So gallant was the conduct of my officers and men in this, the hardest struggle of the battle, that it would seem invidious to discriminate between them. Casualties, 18 killed, 90 wounded." (832, 835, 836, 837) Mentioned in reports.

Vol. XX, Part 2—In Hanson's brigade, Breckinridge's division, November and December, 1863,

Vol. XXIII, Part 2—(620) Gen. Marcus Wright commanding brigade, Breckinridge's division, January 29, 1863. (625) February 3, 1863, brigade ordered to report to Colonel Hunt at Manchester. (703) Colonel Hunt, Manchester, April 22d, assumes command of brigade. (847) In Helm's brigade, Breckinridge's division, May 21st. (849) Moved to Tullahoma by command of General Hardee.

No. 37—(654) Before Jackson, Miss., July, 1863, 1 killed.

No. 38—(912) General Helm ordered to move direct to Tullahoma, May 23, 1863.

No. 51—(13) Assignment as above, at battle of Chickamauga. (197-201) Mentioned in General Breckinridge's report. (203) Mentioned in report of Colonel Lewis, commanding brigade: "The blood of her sons attests Alabama's chivalry and manhood." (206) Effective total, 401, previous to engagement at Chickamauga. (207, 208) Report of Colonel Stansel: "At about 5 p. m. (Sunday, the 20th) we were, with our brigade, constituting the center battalion in the final charge upon the fortifications occupied by the enemy, when they were completely routed and driven back for miles, resulting in a great victory to our arms. In this battle many of the officers and men demeaned themselves with marked gallantry, a fact which is amply corroborated by our large list of killed and wounded, and to them the highest commendation is due. The names of Major Nash, Captain Eddins and Adjutant Leland, and the officers in command of companies, deserve special mention. First Lieut. A. Hawkins, of Company D, fell, bravely leading his men on the works of the enemy, and Sergt.-Maj. Ira Tarrant fell, nobly discharging the duties of his position. The cool and fearless conduct of Color-Sergt. Clark Richey deserves honorable mention for the manner in which he bore the regimental colors through the shock of battle. The regiment went into battle with 325 men, and our casualties were 27 killed and 120 wounded."

No. 54—(452) In Gracie's brigade, Buckner's division, Longstreet's corps, November 30, 1863; Lieut.-Col. T. G. Trimmier commanding regiment. (534) Mentioned by Gen. Bushrod Johnson in report of operations from November 22 to December 21, 1863. Bean's Station, (December 14th), Lieutenant-Colonel Trimmier in command of regiment.

No. 56—(618, 628, 891) Transferred from Lewis' brigade to Gracie's brigade, November 3, 1863.

No. 68—(207) In Gracie's brigade, Ransom's division, General Beauregard's forces on the Richmond and Petersburg lines, May, 1864.

No. 69—(862) In Gracie's brigade, department of Richmond, Gen. Robert Ransom, May, 1864; near Drewry's bluff.

No. 80—(775, 779) Mentioned by Gen. B. R. Johnson.

No. 87—(909) Mentioned by Gen. B. R. Johnson, Petersburg, Va., November 6, 1864: "Three companies moved out and took the enemy's picket line in front of Gracie's salient, capturing 31 prisoners without firing a gun or losing a man."

No. 88, No. 89—Various returns, 1864, in Gracie's brigade, Longstreet's corps, Lee's army.

No. 95—(1287, 1288) Mentioned in report of Gen. Bushrod R. Johnson; operations from March 28 to April 9, 1865. March 30th, brigade commanded by Colonel Stansel at White Oak road. (1300) Brigade mentioned in Gen. Fitzhugh Lee's report as being at Hatcher's Run, March 31, 1865.

THE FORTY-SECOND ALABAMA INFANTRY.

The Forty-second Alabama, organized at Columbus, Miss., in May, 1862, was principally a reorganization of other regiments whose one year's service was completed. Lieutenant-Colonel Lanier, Maj. W. C. Fergus and Capt. George W. Foster were all from the Second Alabama, so that the regiment was immediately effective for the hard work before it. In September it was with the Thirty-seventh Alabama and Seventh Mississippi regiments in Maury's division of the army of the West. The next month it went into the siege of Corinth with 700 men, losing, killed and wounded, 348; of these, 11 were officers. The winter of 1862-63 was spent in Mississippi and the brigade was reorganized. It formed part of the garrison at Vicksburg, where it lost heavily and was captured. From the parole camp at Demopolis, it went to join the army of Tennessee, and served in the battle of Lookout Mountain, November 24, 1863, and at Missionary Ridge, November 25th, where it fought with its usual gallantry. Wintering around Dalton, it took part in the defense of that place, February 28, 1864, and in the campaign from there to Atlanta. March 19th, Gen. Alpheus Baker took command of the brigade, which now consisted of the Thirty-seventh, Fortieth, Forty-second and Fifty-fourth Alabama. It fought at Resaca, May 14th and 15th; at New Hope church, May 25th; at Atlanta, July 25th to 28th. The losses on the 28th were very heavy. It was sent to Spanish Fort in August, where it formed a part of the garrison until January, when it was returned to the army of Tennessee. Its subsequent history is identical with that of the rest of the brigade. After April 1st, it was consolidated with the Thirty-seventh and Fifty-fourth, Capt. William D. McNeill, lieutenant-colonel, and surrendered with the army of Tennessee. Capts. George W. Foster and Allen B. Knox were killed, and Capt. John W. Haley mortally wounded, at Corinth. Capt. Robert Best died in the service. Capt. Robert K. Wills was killed at Atlanta, and Lieut. Capers W. Bodie at Vicksburg.

The field officers were Col. John W. Portis, who was wounded at Corinth; Col. T. C. Lanier, wounded at Corinth and at New Hope, and Maj. W. C. Fergus. Capt. W. D. McNeill was made lieutenant-colonel after consolidation.

EXTRACTS FROM OFFICIAL WAR RECORDS.

Vol. XVII, Part 1—(375) Moore's brigade, Maury's division, army of Tennessee, General Van Dorn, October, 1862. (383) Casualties, battle of Corinth, October 3d to 5th, 11 officers wounded. (397-400) Report of Gen. John C. Moore of engagements at Corinth and at Hatchie bridge, October 5th, mentions Forty-second Alabama, Col. John W. Portis, belonging to brigade. Regiment "subjected to heavy fire on the 3d, though their loss in killed and wounded was but 8 or 10, including 1 officer. Corp. J. A. Goring, color-bearer of the Forty-second, deserves particular notice. Though shot down once, he gallantly bore the flag through the fight on the 4th."

No. 37—(327) Moore's brigade, army of Vicksburg, General Pemberton. (329) Lieut. Capers W. Bodie killed during the siege of Vicksburg. (362) Mentioned by General Forney, May 24, 1863. (369) Casualties, 8 killed and 19 wounded, May 17 to July 4, 1863, siege of Vicksburg. (381-383) Highly commended in General Moore's report of siege. (383) Lieut.-Col. Thomas C. Lanier coincides with other regimental leaders that the men are not able to make a successful evacuation. (385) Mentioned in Col. Ashbel Smith's report as "a gallant regiment."

No. 38—(721) Mentioned by Col. C. A. Fuller, April 7, 1863: "At Yazoo City a Columbiad is manned by 2 officers and 20 men of the Forty-second Alabama, who have had considerable experience at Fort Morgan." (1060) In Moore's brigade, Forney's division, parole camp, August 29, 1863.

No. 55—(266) Mentioned in report of taking of Missionary Ridge, by Colonel Nodine (Union), November 27, 1863. (691) Return of casualties at Lookout Mountain and Missionary Ridge, November 24th and 25th, 2 killed, 7 wounded. (704-706) Report of General Moore of same battles; Lieutenant-Colonel Lanier commanding regiment.

No. 56—(803, 822, 884) Moore's brigade, Cheatham's division, army of Tennessee; Lieut.-Col. Thomas C. Lanier commanding regiment. Total present, 311, December 14, 1863.

No. 57—(481) Mentioned in Colonel Higley's report of operations, February 23 to 27, 1864, at Dalton.

No. 74—(664) Assignment as above, July, 1864; Capt. W. B. Kendrick commanding regiment. (672) Assignment as above, August, 1864; Capt. William D. McNeill. (851,852) Report of Capt. W. D. McNeill of operations, May 7 to 13, 1864, says: "Sergeant Richey saved the colors of a Georgia regiment. We went into battle with 300 on the 15th (Resaca); 5 officers and 32 men wounded, 2 killed. Rev. J. P. McMillan, a missionary for the brigade, was killed. T. C. Mitchell and Capt. G. H. Gray were severely wounded. Total loss of regiment, 59."

No. 98—(1064) Consolidated with the Thirty-seventh and Fifty-fourth Alabama, after April 9, 1865. (For other extracts, see those in connection with the Thirty-seventh Alabama, brigade organization remaining the same.)

No. 100—(734) Same assignment, March 31, 1865; Capt. William D. McNeill commanding regiment.

THE FORTY-THIRD ALABAMA INFANTRY.

The Forty-third was organized at Mobile in May, 1862, and went without delay directly to Chattanooga, where it was brigaded under General Leadbetter. Its colonel, Archibald Gracie, Jr., soon displayed his ability and was afforded opportunity to early earn his promotion. First, as its colonel, and throughout the war from the fall of 1863 as its brigadier, he was never separated from the command. The regiment went into Kentucky with Kirby Smith, and returned, but did very little fighting. It spent the winter of 1862-63 at Cumberland gap. At the battle of Chickamauga (September 19th and 20th), it fought most valiantly, and its loss was very heavy. Colonel Jolly was seriously, and for a long time supposed to be mortally, wounded; both General Preston and General Gracie were enthusiastic in their commendation of the men and officers of this regiment, and the War Records preserve the names of many of the gallant soldiers.

It took part in the investment of Knoxville, November 17th to December 4th; was at Bean's Station, December 14, 1863, and wintered in East Tennessee.

About this time the brigade was reorganized, and comprised henceforward the Forty-first, Forty-third, Fifty-ninth (a consolidation of Milliard's Second and Fourth battalions), Sixtieth (a consolidation of Milliard's First and Third battalions), and the Twenty-third (Stallworth's) battalion of sharpshooters. In May the brigade was sent to Virginia to General Beauregard, to oppose the Federal attempts on the outposts of Richmond. It was hotly engaged at Drewry's bluff, May 12th to 16th; was almost continually in the trenches at Petersburg from June, 1865, till the end; and was fighting gallantly at Appomattox when the flag of truce called the halt which was eternal. It surrendered about 50 men.

Adjt. John R. Shelton was killed near Richmond; Adjt. John L. Stephens was wounded, and Capt. O. W. Pritchett killed, at Drewry's bluff; Capts. James A. Gordon, killed at Chickamauga; O. H. Prince, P. Gordon and Lieut. William H. Watkins, at Chattanooga; Capts. T. M. Hughes and J. A. Sylvester, at Petersburg.

The field officers were Cols. Archibald Gracie, Jr., and Y. M. Moody; Lieut.-Col. John J. Jolly, severely wounded at Chickamauga, and Majs. R. D. Hart, Y. M. Barber and William J. Mims.

EXTRACTS FROM OFFICIAL WAR RECORDS.

Vol. XVI, Part 2—(719) First brigade, General Leadbetter, Heth's division. (750) Department of East Tennessee, July 3, 1862. Colonel Gracie sent from Clinton with two regiments to clean out a force of the enemy at Huntsville, Tenn., August 10th. (985) Gracie's brigade, Heth's division, troops under command of Gen. E. Kirby Smith, October; Col. Y. M. Moody commanding regiment.

Vol. XX, Part 2—Assignment as above, to December, 1862, Cumberland Gap.

Vol. XXII, Part 2—(127) General Gilmore (Union) says, March 9, 1863, that there are 600 men under Colonel Gracie at Cumberland Gap. (644, 711, 792) Assignment as above, April 25th; Col. J. J. Jolly commanding regiment. (805-947) At Bean's Station, April 30th. To move to Morristown, May 7th. Ordered to march from Cumberland Gap and fall back, if necessary, on Knoxville, June 17th; Col. Y. M. Moody commanding regiment, July 31st. Regiment ordered to remain at Knoxville until relieved, August 3d.

No. 51—(418) General Preston's report of battle of Chickamauga, September 19th and 20th, specially notices Col. Y. M. Moody. (420-422) General Gracie's report of same battle speaks in high terms of commendation of Colonel Moody and of Lieut.-Col. J. J. Jolly, who, though seriously wounded in thigh, remained on field until obliged to be carried off. Also mentions some of the noble dead. (422-424) Colonel Moody's report says: "Almost in the beginning of the engagement (20th) Lieutenant-Colonel Jolly and six company commanders were killed, or so severely wounded as to be compelled to quit the field. Captain Gordon, Company C, was killed, and

Captain Prince, Company A, mortally wounded. They were among the best officers of the regiment, and fell encouraging their men and gallantly cheering them forward. Colonel Moody highly commends Acting Adjt. Lieut. John R. Shelton of Company C, and asks for his promotion to the captaincy of his company, made vacant by the death of Captain Gordon. I would mention the following enlisted men: Private W. C. Harris, Sergt. T. Cocke, Sergt. John B. Lanford, almost the foremost in regiment, with unflinching gallantry. There are vacancies in the second lieutenancies, and I apply for their promotion, Privates Peppenhorst, McCoy, Satterwhite, Sergeant Maxey, Sergeant Bruce and Private J. T. Elliott. Sergeant Stephenson and Private Hill also deserve notice, having done all that could be expected of the very best soldiers. My loss was, officers killed, 3; wounded, 7. Men killed, 13; wounded, 76." (534) Roll of honor, battle of Chickamauga: Private William R. Ethridge (killed), Company A; Private John A. Meness, Company B; Sergt. W. C. Johnson, Company D; Sergt. Newton Bruce, Company E; Sergt. E. N. Maxey, Company F; Private David Scott, Company G; Private Daniel F. Tubb, Company H; Private John Barnes, Company I; Private William W. Scales, Company K. Company C declined to make selection.

No. 54—(452) Gracie's brigade, Buckner's division, Longstreet's corps, November 30, 1863. (534-537) Mentioned in Gen. Bushrod Johnson's report of operations, including affair at Bean's Station, December 14th.

No. 68—(207) Gracie's brigade, Ransom's division, Mays, 1864; forces on Richmond and Petersburg lines; General Beauregard.

No. 69—(862) Gracie's brigade, department of Richmond, May 31, 1864, Gen. Robert Ransom, Jr.; regiment commanded by Capt. William W. Harder.

No. 88—(1166) Assignment as above, August, 1864; Lieut.-Col. John J. Jolly commanding regiment. (1227) Gracie's brigade, Johnson's division, September 1, 1864, department of North Carolina and Southern Virginia, commanded by General Beauregard. (1311) Gracie's brigade, September, Gen. Bushrod Johnson's command.

No. 95—(268) Mentioned by Gen. J. Chamberlain (Union) as being an attacking party near Hatcher's Run, March 25, 1865. (1274) Moody's brigade, Anderson's corps, Lee's army, April, 1865; Maj. Wm. J. Mims in command.

THE FORTY-FOURTH ALABAMA INFANTRY.

The Forty-fourth regiment was organized at Selma in May, 1862. The 1st of July found it in Richmond, brigaded with one Mississippi and two North Carolina regiments under Gen. A. R. Wright. In 1862, the Fourth Alabama was added, and in January, 1864, upon reorganization, the North Carolina commands were replaced by the Fifteenth, Forty-seventh and Forty-eighth Alabama, under General Law, who remained in command until January,

1865, when Colonel Perry was made the brigade commander. Camp diseases played havoc with the regiment, and with greatly thinned ranks it went into its first battle at Second Bull Run, August 30, 1862, and lost two of its captains, T. C. Daniel and William T. King. It took part at Harper's Ferry, September 15th; Sharpsburg, September 17th, where it suffered severely, losing nearly two-thirds of its effective force; Fredericksburg, December 13th, and Suffolk, December 28th; and, transferred to Law's brigade, it wintered on the Rappahannock. In the Suffolk, Va., campaign, companies A and B were captured at Hill's Point, April 18, 1864. At the battle of Gettysburg the regiment captured the first guns taken by the Confederates. It was sent with Longstreet's corps to the army of the West in time to take a prominent part in the battle of Chickamauga, September 19th and 20th, where again its loss was heavy. It fought at Lookout creek, October 28th, and at Knoxville, November 17th; again at Dandridge, January 16 and 17, 1864. The regiment was sent back to Virginia in time for the battle of the Wilderness, May 5th and 6th; and was at Spottsylvania, May 7th to 12th, where its casualties were great; also at Hanover Junction, Second Cold Harbor, June 1st to 12th; and Bermuda Hundreds, June 2d to 10th. It was in the trenches around Petersburg until the final scene at Appomattox. Capts. T. C. Daniel and William T. King were killed at Second Bull Run; Capts. D. A. Bozeman and John H. Neilson, at Spottsylvania; Capt. Joab Goodson died in the service, as did Capt. Patrick P. Riddle; Capts. John M. Teague and William T. Dunklin were killed at Gettysburg; Capt. John D. Adrian was wounded at the Wilderness and killed at Chaffin's Bluff; Capts. Wm. N. Greene and Joseph T. Johnston were wounded at Chickamauga.

The field officers were Cols. Charles A. Derby, killed at Sharpsburg; William F. Perry, who was made a brigadier, and John A. Jones; Lieut.-Col. George W. Gary, wounded near Richmond, and Maj. A. W. Denman.

EXTRACTS FROM OFFICIAL WAR RECORDS.

Vol. XI, Part 2—(487) Wright's brigade, Huger's division, June 25th to July 1, 1862. (789) General Huger's report of same engagement, as supporting battery at junction of New Road and Charles City road, June 28th.

Vol. XI, Part 3—(651) Wright's brigade, Anderson's division, July 23, 1862; Col. James Kent commanding regiment.

Vol. XII, Part 2—(546) September 1, 1862, "Right wing of army of Northern Virginia, or Longstreet's corps." (561) Medical director reports 5 killed and 22 wounded at Manassas Plains, August 30, 1862. (816) Capts. T. C. Daniel and William T. King killed.

Vol. XVIII—(336) Two companies, A and B, supporting Captain Stribling's battery at Hill's Point, Nansemond river, captured April 19, 1863.

Vol. XIX, Part 1—(812) Medical director reports 4 killed and 65 wounded, Maryland campaign.

Vol. XXI—(540) Transferred from Wright's to Law's brigade, Hood's division, November 26, 1862. (559) One killed, battle of Fredericksburg, December 13, 1862. (1071) Col. C. A. Derby commanding regiment. (1099) Law's brigade reorganized by detaching North Carolina regiments and replacing them with Alabama regiments, so that the brigade comprised the Fourth, Fifteenth, Forty-fourth, Forty-seventh and Forty-eighth, January, 1863.

No. 44—(284) Col. William F. Perry commanding regiment, Gettysburg campaign. (330, 339) Casualties, 24 killed and 64 wounded at battle of Gettysburg. (393,394) Colonel Perry's report: "General Law informed me that he expected my men to take a battery. Such was their extreme exhaustion, having marched without interruption twenty-four miles to reach the battlefield, and advanced at a double-quick step fully a mile to engage the enemy, that I hesitated for an instant to order them immediately forward. . . . However, I rushed forward, shouting to them to advance. It was with the greatest difficulty that I could make myself heard or understood above the din of battle. The order was, however, extended along the line, and was promptly obeyed. The men sprang forward, over the rocks, swept the position and took possession of the heights, capturing 40 or 50 prisoners around the battery and among the cliffs. . The conflict continued to rage with great fury until dark. Again and again the enemy with great force attempted to dislodge us from our position and retake the battery, in each case with signal failure and great loss. Lieut.-Col. John A. Jones, Maj. Geo. W. Gary and Lieut. W. P. Becker, acting adjutant, behaved with great coolness and courage. I abstain from mentioning by name others who deserve special commendation, because the list would be so long as to confer little distinction on any single individual, and because injustice might be done to others whose good conduct escaped my observation. The regiment lost 24 killed and 66 wounded."

No. 54—(223) Law's brigade, Hood's division, Longstreet's corps, at Chickamauga and Chattanooga. (227) General Law's report of operations of his brigade from October 8th to 28th, on duty beyond Lookout mountain. (229-231) Mentioned in Colonel Sheffield's report, engagement near Lookout creek, on night of October 28th.

No. 58—(641) Assignment as above, January 31, 1864; Col. Perry commanding brigade.

No. 59—(722) Law's brigade, Buckner's division, department of East Tennessee, March 31, 1864. (803) Brigade ordered to Charlotteville, Va., April 22d.

No. 67—(1022) Law's brigade, Field's division, Longstreet's corps, Lee's army, May, 1864. (1060) Casualties, 27 killed and 112 wounded in battle of the Wilderness, May 4th to 6th.

No. 80—(763) Return of casualties, June 13th to July 31, 1864, 5 killed and 15 wounded during siege of Petersburg.

No. 87—(877) Casualties, August 1st to December 31st, 12 killed and 29 wounded.

No. 88—(159) Law's brigade, Colonel Perry commanding. Mentioned as being on the north side of the James river, August, 1864.

No. 89—(1238) Assignment as above, November 30, 1864; Lieut.-Col. John A. Jones commanding regiment.

No. 95—(1268) In Perry's (late Law's) brigade, Lee's army, Field's division, Longstreet's corps, Appomattox campaign. (1277) Lieut.-Col. John A. Jones commanding regiment. Perry's brigade paroled at Appomattox, April 9, 1865.

THE FORTY-FIFTH ALABAMA INFANTRY.

The Forty-fifth regiment was organized at Auburn in May, 1862, and was sent immediately to Mississippi. At Tupelo it suffered very much from diseases incident to camp life, losing a number of its men. It was at first brigaded under Col. A. Reichard, the other regiments of the brigade being from Louisiana. This organization was of short duration. In Walthall's brigade, commanded by Gen. Patton Anderson, the regiment went into Kentucky, charged a battery at Perryville, October 8th, and met with severe loss. At Murfreesboro, December 31, 1862, to January 2, 1863, the casualties were numerous. Brigaded under General Wood early in 1863, the regiment remained with the army at Tullahoma until midsummer. General Lowrey was in command of this brigade at Chickamauga, September 19th and 20th, where the loss of the regiment was very heavy. It fought again at Missionary Ridge, November 15th, and at Ringgold gap, November 27, 1863. The next year found the regiment in the thick of the fights in the Dalton-Atlanta campaign; at Resaca, May 14 and 15, 1864; New Hope church, May 25th, and at Decatur and Atlanta, July 20th to 26th. On July 226. was perhaps the most terrific experience, for the fight was hand to hand. The color-bearers of the contending forces flaunted their flags into each other's faces. The regiment color-bearer was killed, and Colonel Lampley and Major Freeman wounded and captured. Again the regiment fought, at Jonesboro, August 31st and September 1st. It opened the battle at Franklin, November 30th, where it suffered fearfully, by a fight at Spring Hill on the evening before. It was in the battle at Nashville, December 15th and 16th. Consolidated with the Sixteenth and Thirty-third Alabama, under Colonel Abercrombie, transferred from Lowrey's to Shelley's brigade, it proceeded to North Carolina. At the time of the surrender, the remnant of the regiment had been consolidated with remnants of the First, Sixteenth, Seventeenth, Twenty-ninth and Thirty-third, still under Colonel Abercrombie, in Stewart's corps of Johnston's army.

Captains Perry and Torbert were wounded at Chickamauga, Clements at Murfreesboro, Jackson at Atlanta; Captains Gaffney killed at Perryville, John R. Carson at Franklin, Thomas Smith at Atlanta. Captain Lampley was promoted and became colonel; Capts. Geo. C. Freeman and James Jackson were also promoted.

The field officers were Cols. W. A. Goodwin, James C. Gilchrist, E. B. Breedlove, wounded at Murfreesboro, all of whom resigned; Harris D.

Lampley, killed at Atlanta, and R. H. Abercrombie, wounded at Franklin; Lieut.-Col. James Jackson and Maj. George C. Freeman, wounded at Atlanta.

EXTRACTS FROM OFFICIAL WAR RECORDS.

Vol. X, Part 1—(787) Reichard's brigade, Second corps, June 30, 1862; Bragg's army of Mississippi.

Vol. XX, Part 1—(659) Walthall's brigade (Gen. Patton Anderson), Withers' division, Polk's corps, army of Tennessee. (677) Casualties, Murfreesboro, December 31, 1862, 13 killed, 71 wounded. (695, 762-767) Mentioned in General Anderson's letter and report. (899) Mentioned in Gen. S. A. M. Wood's report.

Vol. XX, Part 2—(420) Powell's brigade, Anderson's division, Hardee's corps, November 22, 1862. (448) Transferred to Polk's corps, December 12th.

Vol. XXIII, Part 2—(942) Wood's brigade (Colonel Lowrey), Hill's corps, July 31, 1863; Col. E. B. Breedlove commanding regiment.

No. 51—(159-162) Mentioned in Gen. S. A. M. Wood's report of battle of Chickamauga, September 19 and 20, 1863, and in Capt. F. A. Ashford's report. (167-169) Report of Col. E. B. Breedlove, 22 killed, 95 wounded; officers and men behaved gallantly. (169-171, 174) Mentioned in reports of Col. M. P. Lowrey and Lieut. R. W. Goldthwaite.

No. 55—(755) Mentioned in Gen. P. R. Cleburne's report, battle at Ringgold gap. (758) Thanks of Congress to General Cleburne and troops under his command at Ringgold gap, November 27, 1863. (769-771) Mentioned in reports of General Lowrey, Col. Sam Adams, Lieut.-Col. H. D. Lampley; 1 killed, 8 wounded.

No. 56—(618, 823) Assignment as above, to December, 1863; Lieut.-Col. H. D. Lampley commanding regiment, December 14, 1863; total present, 366.

No. 74—(583) Mentioned in Gen. G. A. Smith's (Union) report of engagement of July 22, 1864. (595) Col. William Hall's (Union) report of same engagement mentions death of color-bearer. (606) Mentioned in Col. W. W. Belknap's (Union) report of action of July 22, 1864, in which he says: The enemy fought bravely and obstinately, and many of them were shot down, fighting at the muzzles of our guns." Again, he says: "Our loss was heavy" (viz: 131 out of 380 in line). (639-669) Assignments as above. (662) Lieut.-Col. Robert H. Abercrombie commanding regiment, July 31st. (731-733) Mentioned in Gen. M. P. Lowrey's report of engagement of July 22, 1864, in which he says the gallant Colonel Lampley was wounded and captured, leading the charge, and Maj. George C. Freeman twice wounded, and captured. The loss of this regiment was 27 killed, 72 wounded.

No. 93—(667) Assignment as above, December 10, 1864; Sixteenth, Thirty-third and Forty-fifth, under Lieutenant-Colonel Abercrombie. (685) Battle of Franklin, Tenn., November 30, 1864; Lieutenant-Colonel Abercrombie wounded.

No. 100—(773) Transferred from Lowrey's to Shelley's brigade, April 9, 1865, with Sixteenth, Twenty-sixth, Twenty-ninth and Thirty-third Alabama; general orders, No. 13, General Johnston.

THE FORTY-SIXTH ALABAMA INFANTRY.

The Forty-sixth regiment was organized at Loachapoka in May, 1862, and went immediately to East Tennessee, where it was brigaded under General Leadbetter, but in July transferred to General Taylor's command. At Tazewell it met with several casualties. Went into Kentucky in Stevenson's division, but took no part in any fight of consequence. Returning to Tennessee, the regiment was assigned with the Twentieth, Twenty-third, Thirtieth and Thirty-first Alabama, to General Tracy's brigade. Sent with the division to Mississippi, the regiment suffered greatly at Port Gibson (May 1st), where General Tracy was killed. At Baker's Creek, May 16, 1863, after a terrible fight and many casualties, one-half the command, with the field officers, were captured. The balance took part in the siege of Vicksburg, May 11th to July 4th, and after considerable loss were captured, with the fort. Exchanged, the regiment was in the parole camp at Demopolis, and was reorganized under General Lee; and under Pettus, as brigadier, it joined the army of Tennessee. It fought at Missionary Ridge, November 25th, and Ringgold, November 27th. The winter was passed at Dalton, and the regiment, with varying casualties and successes, fought through the campaign from Dalton to Atlanta, and back again to Tennessee. Its brilliant record at Columbia was never eclipsed, and it there suffered severely. At Nashville, December 15th and 16th, it was again engaged. In the retreat from Tennessee it was the rear-guard of the army and was highly complimented by General Hood.

Moving over to the Carolinas, it fought at Kinston, March 15 and 16, 1865, and at Bentonville, March 19th. It was consolidated with the Twenty-third, with Col. J. B. Bibb, Lieutenant-Colonel Kyle and Maj. J. T. Hester as field officers, and surrendered under the command of Captain Brewer, April 26th, at Salisbury.

Adjt. Thomas Riggs and Capts. McCaskill and James W. Powell were killed at Baker's Creek, Lieutenant McFarland at Jonesboro, and Capt. John F. Spinks during the retreat from Nashville. Capt. Leonidas Stephens died in the service. Capt. George E. Brewer, senior captain, was in command during the greater part of the existence of the regiment.

The field officers were Col. Mike L. Woods, Lieut.-Col. O. Kyle and Maj. James M. Handley, all of whom were captured at Baker's creek.

EXTRACTS FROM OFFICIAL WAR RECORDS.

Vol. XVI, Part 2—(716) Leadbetter's brigade, post of Chattanooga, department of East Tennessee, Gen. Kirby Smith, June 30, 1862; Col. M. L.

Wood commanding regiment. (719) Taylor's brigade, department of East Tennessee, July 3, 1862. (984) Tracy's brigade, October, 1862.

Vol. XVII, Part 2—(825) Field report of Second brigade, First division, commanded by Gen. E. D. Tracy, gives Twentieth, Twenty-third, Thirtieth, Thirty-first and Forty-sixth Alabama regiments; station, Chickasaw Bluffs, near Vicksburg, January 3, 1863. Forty-sixth had not yet reported there.

No. 36—(680-682) Mentioned in Col. I. W. Garrott's report of the battle of Port Gibson, Miss., May 1, 1863.

No. 37—(51) Mentioned by General McGinnis (Union), battle of Baker's Creek, Miss., May 16th. (101-103) Gen. S. D. Lee's report of same particularly mentions Major Handley. (326) S. D. Lee's brigade, army of Vicksburg, July 4, 1863; Capt. George E. Brewer commanding regiment. (329) Lieuts. J. K. P. Cotton and J. T. House killed during the siege. (350) Mentioned in Gen. S. D. Lee's report of the siege. (354,355) Capt. George E. Brewer (commanding regiment), in his report of the siege of Vicksburg, says: "Lieutenant-Colonel Pettus, who commanded at the time (May 22d), greatly distinguished himself by his gallantry." Casualties, 15 killed, 45 wounded.

No. 38—(1059) Lee's brigade, army of Vicksburg, Demopolis, Ala., August 29, 1863.

No. 55—(662) Pettus' brigade (reassigned November 12, 1863), Stevenson's division, Breckinridge's corps, army of Tennessee, General Bragg. (724) November 24 and 25, 1863, 5 wounded. (731) Mentioned in report of General Pettus, Lookout Mountain, November 24th.

No. 56—(804) Assignment as above, December, 1863;. Captain Brewer commanding regiment.

No. 57—(482) General Pettus reports 5 wounded at Dalton, Ga., February 25, 1864.

No. 58—(587) January 20, 1864, Capt. James R. Cross commanding.

No. 59—(869) Assignment as above, April 30, 1864; Capt. James R. Cross commanding.

No. 74—Assignment as above, April to August, 1864.

No. 78—(853) Assignment as above, September 20, 1864; Capt. James W. Powell commanding.

No. 93—Assignment as above, in Nashville campaign.

No. 94—(799) Pettus' brigade, January 19, 1865. Total present, 174.

No. 98—(1088) General Hill's report, operations May 7th to 21st, says: "Skirmish line placed under charge of Captain Brewer, corps officer of the day."

No. 100—(733) Assignment as in November, March 31, 1865; Capt. George E. Brewer commanding regiment; Col. Jos. B. Bibb commanding brigade, General Pettus' division.

THE FORTY-SEVENTH ALABAMA INFANTRY.

The Forty-seventh regiment was organized at Loachapoka, May 22, 1862. Later, in June, the regiment arrived in Virginia and was brigaded, under General Taliaferro, with the Forty-eighth Alabama and several Virginia regiments. It was in Stonewall Jackson's "own division." The regiment received its "baptism of fire" at Cedar Run, August 9th, where Captain Menefee was killed, and nearly one-half of the effective force of the regiment wounded more or less severely, 12 being killed outright. At Second Bull Run, August 30th, the regiment again suffered severely. It fought at Chantilly, September 1st; at Harper's Ferry, September 12th to 15th, and at the battle of Sharpsburg it did not lose its record for hard fighting and heavy loss. It was at Fredericksburg, December 13th, and wintered on the Rappahannock. In January, 1863, the Forty-seventh and Forty-eighth were transferred to Law's brigade, Hood's division, Longstreet's corps, with the Fourth, Fifteenth and Forty-fourth Alabama. The early part of the spring, the regiment, under Longstreet, was operating around Richmond and Suffolk. July found it in the thickest of the fight at Gettysburg, where 4 officers out of 21 were killed, and the casualties embraced one-third of its effective force. Transferred with Longstreet's corps to the army of Tennessee, it took a prominent part at the battle of Chickamauga, September 20th, and at Knoxville, November 17th to December 4th. In early spring, Longstreet's corps was sent back to the army of Northern Virginia in time for the battle of the Wilderness, May 5 and 6, 1864; and at Spottsylvania, May 7th to 12th, with a return, as usual, of severe losses. General Perry was made brigadier, with the same organization as above, Captain Clower commanding regiment when it was paroled at Appomattox. Capts. A. C. Menefee was killed at Cedar Run, Jos. Johnson at Gettysburg, and Jas. H. Sanford at the Wilderness; Lieut. George W. Gammell was killed at Sharpsburg, and William Grimmett at Second Bull Run.

The field officers were Cols. James M. Oliver, James W. Jackson and Michael J. Bulger; Lieut.-Col. L. R. Terrell, killed on the Darbytown road, and Majs. John G. Johnson and J. M. Campbell, the latter killed near Richmond.

EXTRACTS FROM OFFICIAL WAR RECORDS.

Vol. XI, Part 3—(648) Taliaferro's brigade, army of Northern Virginia, July 23, 1862, Stonewall Jackson's "own division."

Vol. XII, Part 2—(206,207) Report of Col. A. G. Taliaferro, commanding brigade, battle of Cedar Run, August, 1862, gives 12 killed, 85 wounded. (207-209) Lieut.-Col. J. W. Jackson states that it was the first battle that any of this regiment had ever been in, and that they acted well. One captain and 11 men were killed, and 90 wounded, some of them slightly. He says that Captain Menefee conducted himself with great gallantry, and that in his death the regiment has sustained a great loss. (210) Mentioned in Maj. J. Stover's report. (212) Mentioned in Maj. H. C. Wood's report.

Vol. XII, Part 2—(561) Medical director reports 7 killed, 25 wounded, Manassas Plains, August 30, 1862. (816) Lieut. William Grimmett, killed August 30th.

Vol. XIX, Part 1—(1009) Return of casualties, battle of Sharpsburg, September 17, 1862, 10 killed, 35 wounded; Lieut. George W. Gammell killed.

Vol. XXI—(543) Assignment as above, December 10, 1862; Taliaferro commanding division, Colonel Warren, brigade, and Capt. James M. Campbell, regiment. (686) Mentioned in Col. E. T. H. Warren's report of battle of Fredericksburg. (1099) Special order, General Lee, January 19, 1863, transfers regiment from Taliaferro's brigade, Jackson's old division, to Law's brigade, Hood's division, Longstreet's corps.

No. 44—(284) Law's brigade, consisting of the Fourth, Fifteenth, Forty-fourth, Forty-seventh and Forty-eighth Alabama regiments, in battle of Gettysburg; Hood's division, First army corps. Colonel Jackson, Lieutenant-Colonel Bulger and Maj. J. M. Campbell, successively, in command of regiment. (330) Medical director reports 10 killed, 30 wounded, in same battle. (392, 393) Mentioned in Col. William C. Gates' report. (395) Report of Maj. J. M. Campbell: "Lieut.-Col. M. J. Bulger fought most nobly. Out of 21 officers, 4 were killed; all the 21 acted well. About one-third of the whole number were killed and wounded." Footnote: "Lieutenant-Colonel Bulger was not killed. On July 16, 1863, he became colonel, vice James W. Jackson, resigned."

No. 51—(18) Law's brigade, commanded by Colonel Sheffield; Hood's division, commanded by General Law; Longstreet's corps from army of Northern Virginia, in army of Tennessee, General Bragg, September 19 and 20, 1863.

No. 54—(229, 230) Commended in Col. J. L. Sheffield's report of engagement near Lookout creek, October 28, 1863; no casualties in regiment.

No. 55—(658) Detached with Longstreet's corps for operations in East Tennessee, November 4th.

No. 59—(722) Law's brigade, Buckner's division, March 31, 1864, department of East Tennessee; Col. M. J. Bulger commanding regiment.

No. 67—(1060) Return of casualties (no date) gives 33 killed, 61 wounded; General Law wounded, June 3, 1863.

No. 80—(763) Casualties, June 13 to July 31, 1864, 6 killed, 9 wounded.

No. 87—(877) Casualties, August 1st to December 31st, 7 killed, 27 wounded.

No. 88—(159) Reported as being on north side of James river. Colonel Bulger commanding regiment; Law's brigade, commanded by Colonel Bowles, of the Fourth.

No. 89—Field's division, November 30, 1864, commanded by Capt. Henry C. Lindsey.

No. 95—(1268) Perry's (late Law's) brigade, Field's division, Longstreet's corps, April, 1865; Capt. Eli D. Clower commanding regiment. (1277) Perry's brigade paroled at Appomattox.

THE FORTY-EIGHTH ALABAMA INFANTRY.

The Forty-eighth Alabama was organized in May, 1862, at Auburn, and went into the war with overflowing ranks. Sent to Virginia, it was first brigaded under General Taliaferro, in Stonewall Jackson's division, with the Forty-seventh, from which it was never separated. The three Virginia regiments which were in the brigade were afterward exchanged for the Fourth, Fifteenth and Forty-fourth Alabama, in January, 1863—the brigade commanded by General Law—and the organization remained intact until the closing scene. The first battle of the regiment was at Cedar Run, August 9, 1862, where it lost heavily. The story of the Forty-eighth is that of the Forty-seventh.

Scarcely had the din of the fearful fight at Gettysburg passed away, when it was sent with Longstreet's corps to General Bragg, to take part in the terrible conflict at Chickamauga, September 20th; was at Lookout Valley and Knoxville, wintering in Tennessee. Still with Longstreet, the regiment returned to the scene of its earliest encounters and fought unremittingly at the Wilderness, May 5 and 6, 1864; Spottsylvania, May 7th to 12th; Hanover Junction, Second Cold Harbor, Bermuda Hundred, Petersburg, Fussell's Mill, Fort Harrison, Darbytown road, Williamsburg road, and Farmville, and surrendered at Appomattox, in Perry's brigade, with the other Alabama regiments with whom it had served so long.

Adjt. H. S. Figures was killed at the Wilderness; Capt. Reuben Ellis was wounded, and Capt. D. R. King killed, at Cedar Run; Capts. J. N. DeArman, killed at Petersburg, T. J. Eubanks at Lookout Valley, Isham B. Small at White Plains, R. C. Golightly at Sharpsburg, and Moses Lee at Second Bull Run. Capt. Samuel A. Cox died in the service.

Field officers: Cols. James L. Sheffield, wounded at Cedar Run, and William C. Oates, severely wounded at Fussell's Mill, who became distinguished as a statesman in the United States Congress after the war, and was later governor of Alabama; Lieut.-Cols. A. A. Hughes, Jesse G. Aldridge and William M. Hardwick; and Majs. Enoch Aldridge, wounded at Cedar Run, and J. W. Wigginton.

EXTRACTS FROM OFFICIAL WAR RECORDS.
Vol. XI, Part 3—(648) Taliaferro's brigade, July 23, 1862, Stonewall Jackson's division, army of Northern Virginia.
Vol. XII, Part 2—(179) Medical director reports 12 killed, 61 wounded, battle of Cedar Run, August 9, 1862. (206, 207) Report of Colonel Taliaferro, Twenty-third Virginia, commanding brigade, 15 killed, 58

wounded. (209) Col. A. A. Hughes, in his report, says: "The officers and men of my command behaved gallantly." (210) Mentioned by Major Stover, commanding Tenth Virginia, in his report. (212) Mentioned with commendation in Maj. H. C. Wood's report. (561) Medical director reports 50 wounded at Second Manassas, August 30th. (816) Capt. Moses Lee killed, August 30th.

Vol. XVIII—(338) Mentioned by Col. J. K. Conoly, siege of Suffolk, Va.

Vol. XIX, Part 1—(808) In Taliaferro's brigade, army of Northern Virginia, during Maryland campaign. Col. J. L. Sheffield commanding brigade, after Colonels Warren and Jackson. (1008) Col. J. W. Jackson and Colonel Sheffield commanding brigade. (1009) Casualties, 10 killed, 33 wounded, at the battle of Sharpsburg, September 17, 1862. Capt. R. C. Golightly killed.

Vol. XXI—(543) December 10, 1862, Capt. C. B. St. John commanding regiment. (562) Five wounded at battle of Fredericksburg, December 13, 1862. (686) Mentioned by Col. E. T. H. Warren, commanding brigade, in his report of same battle. (1099) Special orders, No. 19, General Lee, January 19, 1863, transferred Forty-eighth, Forty-seventh and Fifteenth Alabama from Taliaferro's brigade, Jackson's old division, Jackson's corps, to Law's brigade, Hood's division, Longstreet's corps.

No. 44—(284) Law's brigade (commanded by General Law and Colonel Sheffield), Hood's division, Longstreet's corps, July, 1863. (330) Medical director reports 8 killed, 67 wounded, at battle of Gettysburg, July 1 to 4, 1863. (395, 396) Colonel Sheffield's report of the battle of Gettysburg says: "Lieuts. F. M. Burk and R. L. Ewing, and Captains Eubanks and Edwards are especially noticed for their gallantry. Lieut.-Col. W. M. Hardwick and Maj. C. B. St. John were efficient until wounded." (411) Major Bane, of Fourth Texas, refers to "the gallant Colonel Sheffield, of the Forty-eighth Alabama."

No. 51—(18) Assignment as above, September 19 and 20, 1863, Bragg's army; Lieut.-Col. William M. Hardwick commanding regiment.

No. 54—(228-231) Colonel Sheffield's report of the engagement near Lookout Creek, October 28th. Captain Eubanks mortally wounded, and 3 privates. Thanks Lieut Joseph B. Hardwick and Sergeant-Major Robbins. (452) November 30, 1863, with troops in East Tennessee, commanded by General Longstreet.

No. 67—(1022) Assignment as above, May, 1864, in Field's division, Lee's army of Northern Virginia. (1060) Partial return of casualties, 11 killed, 30 wounded, May 4, 1864.

No. 80—(763) Casualties, June 13 to July 31, 1864, 1 killed, 4 wounded.

No. 87—(877) Partial return of casualties, August 1 to December 31, 1864, 8 killed, 20 wounded.

No. 88—(159) Law's brigade, Colonel Perry commanding, on north side of the James river, August, 1864.

No. 89—(1238) November 30, 1864, Col. Wm. F. Perry in command of brigade; Maj. John W. Wigginton commanding regiment.

No. 95—(1277) Perry's brigade paroled at Appomattox, April 9, 1865.

THE FORTY-NINTH ALABAMA INFANTRY.

The Forty-ninth regiment was organized at Nashville early in the year 1862, and brigaded in April, under Colonel Trabue, in Breckinridge's division. It was first known as Hale's Thirty-first, and some confusion has arisen in the documents of the War Records between the Forty-ninth and Hundley's Thirty-first regiment, but great pains have been taken in collecting the extracts below. The first battle of this regiment was Shiloh, April 6 and 7, 1862, when it was commanded by Lieutenant-Colonel Gilbreath and fought nobly, losing quite a large number. It was warmly praised by Colonel Trabue. It formed part of the defense of Vicksburg during 1862, when Lieut. W. H. Boggess was killed, and again at Baton Rouge, August 15th, where it lost severely It followed Van Dorn to Corinth, and there again met heavy loss in the attack on that place. The winter of 1862-63 was. spent in the vicinity of Port Hudson. For a short time General Beall commanded the brigade, then General Buford. At the long siege of Port Hudson, the regiment lost a large number of its men; the balance were captured. The regiment, when exchanged, was reorganized at Cahaba, and assigned to General Scott's brigade with the Twenty-seventh, Thirty-fifth, Fifty-fifth and Fifty-seventh Alabama. Sent to Johnston's army, the brigade, then in Loring's division, wintered at Dalton, taking part in the Dalton-Atlanta campaign, continually fighting and skirmishing, but with comparatively small loss until it came to Atlanta, where many were sacrificed on the altar of patriotism. The regiment, reduced to a paltry number, was merged into the Twenty-seventh, in July, 1864, by consolidation with the Twenty-seventh and Thirty-fifth Alabama, which had also been reduced to mere squads, and was commanded by Col. S. S. Ives, of the Thirty-fifth, with Lieut.-Col. John D. Weedon, of the Forty-ninth. The regiment was on detached service at Selma. With Hood, it fought in the battle of Franklin, November 30th, where Colonel Ives was wounded; again at Nashville, December 15th and 16th, where many were killed and many captured. Ordered to North Carolina, commanded by Capt. W. B. Beason, it surrendered with Johnston's army near Smithfield, March 31, 1865.

The captains killed were John R. Gardner, at Shiloh, and John D. Rivers and F. A. Payne, at Port Hudson. Capt. W. S. Bruce was captured at Port Hudson, and died in prison; Capt. G. C. Leadbetter died in service. The field officers were Cols. I. D. Hale and Jeptha Edwards; Lieut.-Cols. M.

Gilbreath, W. N. Crump, John D. Weedon; and Majs. B. Johnston and Thomas A. Street.

EXTRACTS FROM OFFICIAL WAR RECORDS.

Vol. VII—(905) Hale's battalion, in Breckinridge's brigade, Johnston's army, Murfreesboro, February 23, 1862.

Vol. X, Part 1—(384) First brigade, Col. R. P. Trabue, reserve corps, Gen. J. C. Breckinridge, April 6 and 7, 1862. (614-621) Mentioned in report of Col. Robert Trabue, Shiloh, April 6 and 7, 1862. Lieutenant-Colonel Gilbreath, commanding Thirty-first (Forty-ninth) Alabama, and the regiment, commended. "The regiment acted with praiseworthy gallantry in this action." Loss at Shiloh, 79.

Vol. X, Part 2—(550) First brigade, General Hawes, reserve corps, General Breckinridge, Beauregard's army of the Mississippi, Corinth, May, 1862.

Vol. XV—(18) Thirty-first Alabama volunteers, Colonel Edwards, mentioned in report of Gen. Earl Van Dorn, of defense of Vicksburg. (78) Mentioned in report of Gen. J. C. Breckinridge, engagement of Baton Rouge and occupation of Port Hudson, July 27 to August 4, 1862. (82) Two killed and 9 wounded; Lieut. W. H. Boggess killed, Vicksburg, July 15th. (84, 85) Mentioned in report of Col. J. Edwards, commanding, engagement at Baton Rouge, August 5, 1862. Lieutenant Childress, of Company K, was mortally wounded, and Lieutenant Hays, of Company G, and Sergeant Loughlin, of Company B, severely wounded while gallantly fighting. (273) Edwards' consolidated (Forty-ninth), Buford's brigade, March 15, 1863, at Port Hudson, La. (278) Casualties, 1 wounded during the bombardment of Port Hudson, La. (934) General orders, No. 5, Port Hudson, January 7, 1863, General Gardner assigns consolidated regiment, consisting of Twenty-seventh, Thirty-first, and Sixth Alabama battalion, to Beall's brigade. (1033) Buford's brigade, March 31, 1863, department of Mississippi and East Louisiana, General Gardner commanding; Col. Jeptha Edwards in command of regiment. (1037) Assigned to Beall's brigade, by command of General Gardner, Port Hudson; April 6th.

Vol. XVII, Part 1—(375) Rust's brigade, army of the West, Van Dorn commanding, at battle of Corinth, August 30 to October 12, 1862. (407-409) Mentioned in General Rust's report.

No. 38—(613) Beall's brigade, January 31, 1863, district of Louisiana, Pemberton. (707) Buford's brigade, April, 1863, Stevenson's division; Col. Jeptha Edwards commanding regiment.

No. 41—(143) Paroled at Port Hudson, July, 1863; Maj. T. A. Street with regiment. (147) Casualties up to June 1st, 3 killed, 18 wounded, in siege of Port Hudson. (150) Report of casualties of Beall's brigade. (551) Forty-ninth Alabama, 500 strong, at Port Hudson, La., as reported by (Union) General Dwight.

No. 58—(586) Forty-ninth Alabama and three companies of partisans and exchanged prisoners at military post, Cahaba, January 20, 1864.

No. 74—(645) Army of Mississippi, General Polk; Lieut.-Col. John Weedon commanding regiment. (652) Scott's brigade, army of Mississippi, General Loring; Capt. W. B. Beeson commanding regiment. (659) July 10,1864, Scott's brigade, army of Mississippi, consolidated with Twenty-seventh and Thirty-fifth Alabama, under Col. Samuel Ives; Lieut.-Col. John D. Weedon.

No. 75—(724) Ordered by secretary of war, May 16th, to proceed to Dalton and report to General Johnston. (For other extracts, see those in connection with the Twenty-seventh Alabama, brigade organization remaining the same.)

THE FIFTIETH ALABAMA INFANTRY.

The Fiftieth Alabama regiment was organized at Corinth in 1862, from two battalions recently enlisted. Placed in Gladden's brigade it fought at Shiloh, April 6 and 7, 1862, with a loss of 123 killed and wounded, out of 700 men engaged. It was called at first the Twenty-sixth, but as there was already a regiment by that name, it was, after July, 1863, known as the Fiftieth. It was in the battle of Bridge Creek, May 28, 1862, with a loss of 2 killed. In June, 1862, the regiment was placed in General Gardner's brigade, with the Nineteenth, Twenty-second and Thirty-ninth; moved into Kentucky and lost about 20 men in a fight with General Sills' division. Transferred to Deas' brigade, it fought with conspicuous gallantry at Murfreesboro, winning the commendation of its division commander, General Withers, and losing 80 men in killed and wounded. It spent the remainder of the winter at Tullahoma; was for a time consolidated with the Thirty-ninth, under command of Col. H. D. Clayton, and in July it was numbered the Fiftieth, and was alternately commanded by Col. J. G. Coltart and Lieut.-Col. N. N. Clements. At Chickamauga it lost 100 men, out of 500 engaged, and it also lost heavily at Missionary Ridge. It wintered at Dalton, and did arduous duty on the retreat to Atlanta, being engaged nearly every day, and losing heavily in the bloody battles around Atlanta during the last week of July, 1864.

The regiment moved into Tennessee with Hood, and was badly mutilated at Franklin. It then proceeded to the Carolinas and distinguished itself at Kinston, where a line of skirmishers, 40 strong, under Capt. E. B. Vaughan, captured a stand of colors and 300 men of the Fifteenth Connecticut. After April 9th it was consolidated with the Twenty-second, Twenty-fifth and Thirty-ninth, under Col. Harry T. Toulmin, and it was surrendered at Greensboro, N. C.

Col. John G. Coltart, who first led the regiment, was wounded at Shiloh and Atlanta. He was frequently in command of a brigade, and about the time of the surrender was in command of Hill's division. Lieut.-Col. N.

N. Clements was promoted from the line, and was frequently in command of the regiment. Capt. J. C. Hutto was promoted to major. Major Gwin was wounded at Shiloh. Adjt. John C. Bruckner and Capt. George Arnold were killed at Atlanta.

The "Limestone Rebels," who were mustered into service at Huntsville, September 17, 1861, formed Company E of this regiment, Capt. Jim Malone, Lieuts. Dr. N. D. Richardson, William Richardson and John B. McClelland, and Orderly-SergL George W. McKinney.

EXTRACTS FROM OFFICIAL WAR RECORDS.

Vol. X, Part 1—(383) Gladden's brigade, Withers' division, at Shiloh. (538) Mentioned in Col. Z. C. Deas' report of battle of Shiloh, April 6 and 7, 1862. (544-547) Lieut.-Col. William D. Chadick says: "The Twenty-sixth was hotly engaged, contributing a full share to the driving back of the enemy. When the charge was made upon the lines and into the camp of the enemy, the Twenty-sixth was among the first to penetrate them." Colonel Chadick commends the officers and men, and states that Col. John Coltart and Maj. John S. Garvin were wounded. (551) General Chalmers' report speaks of the forward movement of the Twenty-sixth regiment upon the enemy. (788) Gardner's brigade, June 30, 1862; reserve corps, General Withers. (853) Col. Joseph Wheeler's report states the Twenty-sixth was in his command in the battle of Bridge Creek, May 28, 1862; reports 2 killed.

Vol. XX, Part 1—(658) Deas' brigade, Withers' division, January, 1863, army of Tennessee. (677) Return of casualties, battle of Murfreesboro, January 2d, 4 killed and 76 wounded. (754) Commended in General Withers' report of same battle for gallantry. (973) Roll of honor, battle of Murfreesboro: Private B. A. Thomason, Company A; Sergt. J. E. Gilbert, Company B; Private L. P. Roberts, Company C; Private Reedy Ward, Company D; Sergt. F. E. Mitchell, Company E; Private J. T. McLain, Company G; Private J. H. Cotrel, Company H; Private John A. Usleton, Company I.

Vol. XX, Part 2—(431) November 29, 1862, Col. N. N. Clements commanding regiment.

Vol. XXIII, Part 2—(735) Deas' brigade, Twenty-sixth and Thirty-ninth, Col. H. D. Clayton commanding; April 1, 1863, Polk's corps, Bragg's army. (942) Under Lieut-Col. N. N. Clements, July 31, 1863. Henceforward called Fiftieth. (958) Col. J. G. Coltart.

No. 51—(15) Deas' brigade, left wing, General Longstreet, army of Tennessee, at Chickamauga. (318) Mentioned in report of Gen. Patton Anderson, September 19 and 20, 1863. (338, 339) Colonel Coltart's report gives loss 16 killed and 81 wounded. "The officers and men behaved with great gallantry, and I am proud to say there was less straggling than I have ever known. I have the honor to mention the names of the following non-commissioned officers and privates who have been reported to me as deserving much credit for their good conduct, viz: Sergt. L. Coker, Company F; Private J. B. Stewart, Company G; Private W. L. Bridges, Company G; Private P. M.

Light, Company G; Private M. Roberts, Company G; Private W. N. Pitts, Company H; Sergt. J. M. Pitts, Company I; Private E. H. Stinnet, Company B; Private Rudy Ward, Company D.

No. 56—(617-886) Total present, December 14, 1863, 289.

No. 58—(589) January 20, 1864, Lieut.-Col. N. N. Clements commanding regiment.

No. 74—(640, et seq.) Assignments as above, Hood's corps; June 30, 1864, Capt. G. W. Arnold commanding regiment; July 31st, Capt. Archibald D. Ray commanding regiment; (776) Lieut.-Col. Harry Toulmin, commanding brigade, in report of operations July 28, 1864, says: "The Fiftieth Alabama regiment made a gallant charge, planting their colors on the enemy's works. Lieut. J. T. Bruckner (Acting A. A.-G.) fell while nobly doing his duty." (780,781) Capt. A. D. Ray, commanding Fiftieth Alabama, says of same battle: "Immediately after commencing the advance, Colonel Coltart was wounded, but remained with us until we charged the enemy in their breastworks, the officers and men acting most gallantly. During the time, General Johnston was wounded and Colonel Coltart was in command of the brigade, and Captain Arnold in command of the regiment. During the second advance, Captain Arnold was severely wounded. During the engagement the officers and men under my observation acted gallantly and did their duty. Six killed and 33 wounded."

No. 75—(673) General Hindman asks for the Fiftieth, Dalton, Ga., May 7, 1864.

No. 78—(853) September 20, 1864, Col. John G. Coltart in command.

No. 98—(1064) Lee's corps moving to Georgia, January 20, 1865. Consolidated, after April 9th, with Twenty-second, Twenty-fifth and Thirty-ninth Alabama, under Col. Harry T. Toulmin, in Brantly's brigade.

No. 100—(734) Deas' brigade, March 31, 1865, Hill's division, Lee's corps; Capt. John E. Gilbert commanding regiment. Army near Smithfield, N. C., commanded by General Johnston.

THE FIFTY-FOURTH ALABAMA INFANTRY.

The Fifty-fourth Alabama infantry was made up of troops from Tennessee and Alabama, and four companies from Alabama, first in the regiment of Col. L. M. Walker, of Tennessee. Most of these commands had been captured at Island No. 10, after having served a year or more. The regiment was organized at Jackson, Miss., in October, 1862; was brigaded under General Tilghman, later under Buford; fought at Fort Pemberton and at Baker's Creek, and escaped with small loss. At Vicksburg, only a detachment under Lieutenant Abney was with General Pemberton, the rest of the regiment having gone with General Loring to take part in the defense of Jackson. From February until April, 1864, the regiment was temporarily detached from

Buford's command and sent to Montgomery for provost duty, when it was sent to the army of Tennessee, and in the brigade of General Baker, its former colonel, it took part in the Dalton-Atlanta campaign, losing very heavily at Resaca and at Atlanta, July 20 to 26, 1864. Among many killed was Lieut. Garrett Young. The brigade was with General Maury, in Mobile, for the next six months, when it was transferred to North Carolina. Its last engagement was at Bentonville, March 19th to 21st, and here, though there were but a few over 300 men, the regiment captured 200 and more of the enemy. It was consolidated with the Twenty-fifth, Thirty-ninth and Fiftieth Alabama regiments, under Col. Harry T. Toulmin, only a short time before the surrender at Smithfield. Adjt. Horace M. Smith died in service.

Its field officers were Cols. Alpheus Baker, who was promoted to brigadier, and, after the war, became distinguished as a lawyer, and John A. Minter; and Lieut. -Col. Thaddeus H. Shackelford.

EXTRACTS FROM OFFICIAL WAR RECORDS.

Fifty-fourth regiment Alabama infantry, formerly Fourth Confederate infantry, when first organized was called Fiftieth, but changed afterward to Fifty-fourth, formed from six companies, First Alabama, Mississippi and Tennessee infantry, and four companies, L. M. Walker's Fortieth Tennessee infantry. No. 36—(553) Gen. L. Tilghman, Canton, Tenn., April 24, 1863, reports that he has started regiment and section of artillery to Carthage.

No. 37—(82) General Buford's report of operations at Edwards' Depot, Miss., May 16, 1863. (328) General Pemberton's army at Vicksburg, July 4, 1863, includes a detachment tinder Lieut. Joel P. Abney.

No. 38—(613) In Tilghman's brigade, January 31, 1863, department of Mississippi, General Pemberton. (705) Tilghman's brigade, Loring's command, April, 1863. (746) Assigned to Buford's brigade, April 1 15th. (783) General Pemberton orders General Tilghman, at Canton, to call in regiment.

No. 53—(515) Buford's brigade, Loring's division, August 20, 1863, department of Mississippi, General Johnston.

No. 57— (333) Assignment as above, February 20, 1864; General Polk in command of army.

No. 58—(816) Temporarily detached from Buford's brigade, February 29, 1864, and ordered by General Polk to proceed to Selma to report to General Withers.

No. 59—(602) March 9, 1864, regiment ordered to Montgomery, Ala. (816) Relieved from duty at Montgomery, April 28, 1864, to report to General Johnston for assignment to Baker's brigade.

No. 74—(649, et seq.) Baker's brigade, Johnston's army of Tennessee; Lieut. -Col. John A. Minter commanding regiment, Atlanta campaign. (818) See Thirty-seventh regiment. (845) General Baker's report of operations, including battles of Rocky Face, Resaca and New Hope Church,

May 7 to June 2, 1864, says: "We have to mourn the loss, in this sanguinary conflict, of many brave men, among whom was First Lieut. Garrett L. Young, commanding Company C, Fifty-fourth Alabama, who fell within a short distance of the enemy's intrenchments, gallantly leading his command. Nor can I forbear to allude to the heroic death of the Rev. J. P McMullen, a missionary to this brigade, an aged Presbyterian clergyman of spotless and exalted character, who, having been to our soldiers the preceptor and example of all that is admirable in the Christian, won upon this bloody field the crowning honor with which the martyr patriot alone is worthy to be wreathed." (852-854) Report of Col. J. A. Minter, May 15th, 5 killed and 20 wounded; May 24th, 1 wounded; May 25th, 3 killed and 18 wounded; May 30th, 4 killed and 10 wounded. "In the fatiguing marches and the different engagements, the men have borne up with cheerful fortitude, like men who are determined to defend their rights and their country. In every engagement, Private Joseph Powell, of Company H, and Private James H. Flevin, of Company C, highly distinguished themselves for their daring, bravery and coolness. With much regret I have to report Joseph Powell wounded and captured while reconnoitering the enemy's position, on the evening of the 31st, and James Flevin severely wounded in the shoulder, in the same engagement."

No. 78—(854) Transferred to Mobile with Baker's brigade, subsequent to August, 1864.

No. 79—(875) Baker's brigade, November 1, 1864, Liddell's division, district of the Gulf, General Maury.

No. 98—(1064) Twenty-second Alabama (consolidated with Twenty-fifth, Thirty-ninth and Fiftieth), under command of Col. Harry T. Toulmin, after April 9, 1865.

No. 100—(734) March 31, 1865, in Baker's brigade, Johnston's army.

THE FIFTY-FIFTH ALABAMA INFANTRY.

The Fifty-fifth Alabama was made up of Snodgrass' and Norwood's battalions. Snodgrass' (Fourth) battalion was in Breckinridge's reserve brigade in February, 1862, and was employed for some time near Pensacola, under command of Lieutenant-Colonel Conoley. In Trabue's brigade it lost 30 men at the battle of Shiloh, April 6 and 7, 1862, where it fought under Maj. J. M. Clifton, and was highly commended in official reports. It was engaged in the defense of Vicksburg in 1862, where Maj. G. L. Alexander was killed, and at the battle of Baton Rouge, August 5, 1862, where it fought bravely and suffered severely. It fought in Rust's brigade near Corinth, in October, 1862, and was highly commended by its brigade commander. In March, 1863, at Port Hudson, it was consolidated with Norwood's battalion and formed the Fifty-fifth regiment, about 900 strong, under Col. John Snodgrass, in Buford's brigade.

The regiment fought at Baker's Creek with great loss; also at Jackson and subsequent engagements in Mississippi. Transferred to Scott's brigade, it served continuously in the army of Mississippi, until, as part of Stewart's corps, it joined the army of Tennessee in the spring of 1864, and took part in the continuous fighting of the Dalton-Atlanta campaign. At Peachtree Creek it was fearfully mutilated, losing more than half its number. It also lost heavily in Hood's winter campaign, suffering severely at Franklin and Nashville. Proceeding to North Carolina, it was consolidated after April 9, 1865, with the Twenty-seventh, Thirty-fifth, Forty-ninth and Fifty-seventh, under Colonel McAlexander, and was surrendered" at Greensboro with Johnston's army. Col. John Snodgrass led the regiment with untiring bravery throughout the war. At Peachtree Creek, which proved so disastrous to the regiment, many officers were lost. Maj. J. H. Jones, Adjt. J. C. Howell, Capts. J. W. Evans and Arthur B. Carter were killed, and Lieut.-Col. John W. Norwood, Capts. J. H. Cowan, J. M. Thompson and Peter Nunnally were wounded there. Capt. D. C. Daniel was wounded at Resaca and Atlanta.

EXTRACTS FROM OFFICIAL WAR RECORDS.

Fourth Battalion Infantry (also called Sixteenth), Lieut.-Col. John Snodgrass, merged into Fifty-fifth regiment.

Vol. VI—(838) March 4, 1862, near Pensacola, Fla. (848) Lieutenant-Colonel Conoley commanding; ordered to destroy buildings, etc., if attacked by overpowering force. (853) Mentioned in letter of Gen. Sam Jones.

Vol. VII—(905) February 23, 1862. In Breckinridge's reserve brigade, Murfreesboro, Tenn.

Vol. X, Part 1—(384) In Trabue's brigade, Breckinridge's reserve corps, April 6 and 7, 1862, Shiloh. (614, 615) Mentioned as under Maj. J. M. Clifton, in Colonel Trabue's report. (617, 618) Commended in Trabue's report. (620) Major Clifton commended by Trabue. (621) Battalion (called Clifton's) lost 30 men at Shiloh.

Vol. XV—(18) Mentioned in Gen. Earl Van Dorn's report, defense of Vicksburg; Lieutenant-Colonel Snodgrass commanding. (78) Mentioned in General Breckinridge's report of operations near Baton Rouge, August 5, 1862. (82) Three killed, 22 wounded, Vicksburg; Maj. G. L. Alexander killed. (85, 86) Colonel Snodgrass' report of Baton Rouge, August 5, 1862, says: "I take pleasure in calling your attention to the gallant and enthusiastic conduct of Privates John Thompson, Company F, and J. M. Byrd, Company G, who boldly moved in advance of the command and discharged their arms with due caution and alacrity. They were the first to open fire and the last to quit the field, and I am happy, while reporting the especially worthy conduct of these two privates, to not have a single instance of cowardice or wavering to report, the whole command having advanced and stood under fire, from which older troops and greater numbers had retired." One officer and 10 men wounded.

Vol. XVII, Part 1—(375) In Rust's brigade, with General Van Dorn, battle of Corinth. (407-409) Commended in General Rust's report of operations near Corinth, October 2, 3 and 4, 1862; skirmishers under Major Gibson.

Vol. XVII, Part 2—(786) Mentioned in General Lovell's report, Decembers, 1862; ordered south of the Yalabusha river. Smallpox in ranks.

No. 38—(613) January 31, 1863, in Rust's brigade, with General Pemberton. (707) April, 1863 (called Sixteenth battalion), in Buford's brigade, with General Pemberton.

Sixth Battalion, Alabama Infantry. Vol. XV—(934) January 7, 1863, consolidated with Twenty-seventh and Thirty-first Alabama, and commanded by Colonel Simonton, Port Hudson, La. (1033) March 31st, in Buford's brigade, with Gen. Frank Gardner's battalion; commanded by Lieutenant-Colonel Snodgrass.

No. 38—(613) January 31, 1863, in Beall's brigade, with General Pemberton. (707) April, in Buford's brigade, united with Fourth battalion, under Colonel Snodgrass.

Fifty-fifth Alabama Infantry, made up of the Sixth (Norwood's) and the Sixteenth, sometimes called Fourth, (Snodgrass') battalions. Vol. XV—(273) Snodgrass' consolidated (Fifty-fifth), in Buford's brigade, March 15, 1863, Port Hudson. (1037) General Buford, with Twenty-seventh and Fifty-fifth, ordered April 6, 1863, to report to General Pemberton at Jackson, Miss.

No. 37—(82) General Buford's report of operations, Edwards Depot, May 16, 1863.

No. 38—(746) Assigned to Buford's brigade, April 15, 1863. (824) Ordered to guard bridge near Edwards Depot, May 3d.

No. 53—(515) Buford's brigade, August 20, 1863, Loring's division, General Johnston's army.

No. 74—(645, etseq.) Scott's brigade, Loring's division, Polk's corps, Atlanta campaign. (895) General Scott's report of fight of Peachtree Creek, July 20, 1864, gives 29 killed and 63 wounded. (897) Colonel Snodgrass' report of same battle: "After the order to charge was given, my regiment moved forward under a terrible enfilading fire of grape, canister and minie, as well as a galling direct fire, until they had passed considerably the first line of the enemy's works. My regiment was considerably scattered, but none left the field."

No. 78—(854) September 20, 1864, General Hood in command of army; Maj. James B. Dickey commanding regiment;.

No. 93—(666) Same assignment, Nashville campaign.

No. 98—(1063) Twenty-seventh Alabama (consolidated with Thirty-fifth, Forty-ninth, Fifty-fifth and Fifty-seventh Alabama), under Col. Edward McAlexander, after April 9, 1865.

THE FIFTY-SEVENTH ALABAMA INFANTRY.

The Fifty-seventh regiment was organized at Troy, March, 1863, as part of Clanton's brigade; was temporarily attached to Slaughter's brigade, and in September was again with General Clanton. It was on duty at Mobile and Pollard until January, 1864. Moved to Demopolis, it was attached to Scott's brigade, and joined the army of Tennessee in time to share in the perils and hardships of the Dalton-Atlanta campaign; was in numerous battles and skirmishes, but did not suffer greatly until Peachtree Creek, when the regiment was severely cut up, losing almost half its number. It then moved into Tennessee and lost heavily; at the battles of Franklin and Nashville; was transferred to North Carolina, and fought at Bentonville with severe loss. It was consolidated with the Twenty-seventh, Thirty-fifth, Forty-ninth and Fifty-fifth regiments, under the command of Colonel McAlexander, and surrendered with Johnston's army at the close of the war.

Col. J. P. W. Amerine, its first colonel, was succeeded by Col. C. J. L. Cunningham, who led the regiment for the greater part of the war, after December, 1863; he was wounded at Franklin. Lieut.-Col. W. C. Bethune, Capt. A. L. Mulligan, Maj. J. H. Wiley and Capt. R. H. Lane were at different times in command. Lieut.-Col. Bethune and Captain Faison were wounded at Peachtree Creek; Major Arnold and Capt. Bailey M. Talbot were killed there.

EXTRACTS FROM OFFICIAL WAR RECORDS.

Fifty-seventh Alabama infantry, Col. J. P. W. Amerine, (also called Fifty-fourth). No. 42—(39) Temporarily attached to Slaughter's brigade, department of the Gulf, June 8, 1863; called "a new regiment from Clanton's brigade." (131) August 1st, Colonel Amerine commanding regiment and brigade. (156, 157) August 10, 1863, stationed at Pollard. (239, 240) September 19th, at Pollard, Ala., in General Clanton's brigade. (275, 402, 511, 561) Assignment as above, to December. (334) October 18th, spoken of by General Maury as being very large, and excellent in its appointments and drill. (550) December 26th, report of Maj. C. J. L. Cunningham, of Fifty-seventh regiment. (556) Highly commended by General Clanton, May 9, 1864.

No. 59—(604, 659, 862) March, 1864, under Col. C. J. L. Cunningham, in Scott's brigade, Polk's army. April 30th, Lieut.-Col. W. C. Bethune commanding.

No. 74—(645, et seq.) Assignment as above, Atlanta campaign; Colonel Cunningham. (664) July 31, 1864, Capt. Aug. L. Milligan commanding regiment, in Scott's brigade, Hood's army. (670) August 31st, Colonel Cunningham commanding regiment. (895) Report of General Scott, battle of July 20th, 13 killed and 98 wounded. (897) Report of Capt. A. L. Milligan, Fifty-seventh regiment: "The long list of casualties in this regiment, in the engagement of the 20th instant, will be sufficient evidence of its deep devotion to the cause of Southern liberty and independence. The regiment, commanded by Colonel Bethune, went into action 330 strong. It lost in killed, wounded and missing, 157, including 2 field officers and 1 staff officer, and 15 line officers."

No. 78—(589) Highly commended by General Clanton. (854) September 20, 1864, under Maj. J. Horatio Wiley, in Scott's brigade, Hood's army.

No. 93—(666) Same assignment, Nashville campaign.

No. 98—(1063) April 9, 1865, consolidated with Twenty-seventh, Thirty-fifth, Forty-ninth and Fifty-fifth, under Col. Ed. McAlexander, Shelley's brigade, Stewart's corps.

No. 100—(735) Under Capt. Reuben H. Lane, Scott's brigade, Johnston's army.

THE FIFTY-EIGHTH ALABAMA INFANTRY.

The Fifty-eighth regiment was formed from the Ninth battalion. This battalion was organized at New Bern, November, 1861, and proceeded to Corinth in the spring; was engaged at Shiloh, Farmington and in a number of skirmishes with slight loss, but suffered more severely at Blackland, losing about 20 men killed and wounded, besides a large number by disease at Corinth and Tupelo. It was sent to Mobile in the summer of 1862, and remained there until the following spring. Proceeding to Tullahoma, it was placed in Clayton's brigade and was in several small engagements, chiefly at Hoover's gap. In July, 1863, two additional companies were added and the Fifty-eighth Alabama was formed.

Consolidated with the Eighth Tennessee, under Col. Bushrod Jones, it was placed in Bate's brigade and took part in the battle of Chickamauga. On the first day of this great conflict it assisted in the capture of four pieces of artillery; and on the second day it was in the desperate charge which broke the enemy's line, losing in the battle 148 out of 254 men engaged. This regiment was one of the most distinguished at Chickamauga. It was saluted on the field by General Bate, its brigade commander. General Clayton commends the excellent order which marked its movements and relates how Captains Lee's and Crenshaw's companies accompanied him several miles in pursuit of the routed enemy.

It was united with the Thirty-second Alabama and placed in Clayton's brigade in November, 1863, taking part in the Chattanooga-Ringgold campaign. Out of 400 present at Missionary Ridge, it lost 250. The regiment wintered at Dalton and accompanied the army of Tennessee in the Dalton-Atlanta campaign, engaging in numerous battles and skirmishes, often with heavy loss. It fought at Resaca, New Hope and Kenesaw, and within ten days lost more than 100 in killed and wounded. Transferred to Holtzclaw's brigade, it moved with Hood into Tennessee; was severely engaged at Columbia, and took part in the terrible battles of Franklin and Nashville. It then went with the brigade to Mobile and was sent to assist General Gibson in his brilliant and heroic defense of Spanish Fort, March 31, 1865. It fought gallantly there and at Blakely, and finally was surrendered at Meridian.

Col. Bushrod Jones was a very able and gallant officer. He was frequently in command of a brigade, and is mentioned by General Gibson as one of the brigade commanders present at a council of war at Spanish Fort. His place at the head of the regiment was filled by Lieut.-Col. John W. Inzer, and for a short time, in the spring of 1865, by Major Kimbell. There were many casualties among the officers of this regiment. At Chickamauga, Capt. John Clow and Lieutenant Rader were killed, and Lieutenant-Colonel Inzer, Major Thornton, Adjutant Harris, Captains Crenshaw, Harrell, Avirett and Holland were wounded. Major Thornton was also wounded at Resaca and Atlanta; here Adjutant Hungerford and Captain Avirett were killed. Capt. Sidney P. Lister was killed at Missionary Ridge, and Capt. Sid Holland at Spanish Fort. Capts. W. E. Lee and George S. Markham were captured at Missionary Ridge.

EXTRACTS FROM OFFICIAL WAR RECORDS.

Ninth Battalion Alabama Infantry: Vol. X, Part 1— (383) April 6 and 7, 1862, at Shiloh. (394) Ordered to Corinth, April 3d.

Vol. XV—(1068) April, 1863, Col. Bushrod Jones; in Slaughter's brigade, department of the Gulf.

Vol. XXIII, Part 1—(611) June 24, 1863, at Garrison's Fork, mentioned by General Bate. (613, 614) Commended by General Bate, Middle Tennessee campaign, June 24 and 25, 1863, 5 wounded at Hoover's Gap.

Vol. XXIII, Part 2—(943, 959) Bate's brigade, Bragg's army, summer, 1863.

No. 42—(130) April, 1863, detached from Mobile and sent to General Bragg.

Captain Avirett's Company of Fifty-eighth Regiment: No. 42—(154) Mentioned in report of skirmish at Sandy Ridge, N. C., February 13, 1863. (508) Captain Avirett's company reported as 90 strong, holding pits on the Neuse, January 8, 1863.

No. 74—(841) Col. Bushrod Jones, in his report of operations, May 5th to 27th, Atlanta campaign, says: "May 13th Captain Avirett's company was detached as skirmishers under Maj. Harry Thornton." (844) Lieutenant Curry and Captain Avirett were wounded May 25th. (For other references, see notes on Fifty-eighth regiment.)

Fifty-eighth Alabama Infantry, formed from Ninth infantry battalion, consolidated with Thirty-second regiment after November, 1864. No. 50— (231) In Bate's brigade, Buckner's corps, Chickamauga campaign. Consolidated with Ninth Tennessee.

No. 51—(362) Gen. A. P. Stewart, in his report of battle of Chickamauga, says: "Clayton's brigade, aided by the Fifty-eighth Alabama, of Bate's brigade (Col. Bushrod Jones commanding), captured three pieces." (367) Loss at Chickamauga, 21 killed, 128 wounded, Lieut. W. H. Rader killed. (369) Commended in list of soldiers distinguished for gallantry. (384-386) Gen. William B. Bate speaks of capture of three pieces in which Colonel Jones participated. (388-391) Col. Bushrod Jones, in his report of the battle of Chickamauga (September 19th), says: "Lieutenant-Colonel Inzer behaved with conspicuous gallantry during the engagement, and rendered much valuable aid by words and example, in causing the men to charge with enthusiasm, and in reforming the regiment. Major Thornton's bearing was cool and gallant. He received a wound in the ankle early in the action which temporarily disabled him, preventing him from participating in the charge, but he found a loose artillery horse, mounted, and soon rejoined the regiment. Adjt. R. T. Harris, who had been wounded in several battles, received a severe flesh wound in the thigh early in the fight, while standing bravely at his post inciting and encouraging the men. I commend the conduct and bearing of both officers and men as deserving the highest praise. I saw none who failed to do his whole duty. Loss, 3 killed, 58 wounded, on first day. The bearing of the regiment in the second day's fight was even more gallant than on the first. Lieut. W. H. Rader, Company F, was the only officer killed. He fell, gallantly leading his men in the charge. Lieutenant-Colonel Inzer and Major Thornton, as on the first day, were eminently and conspicuously brave. Captain Harrell and Lieutenant Johnson, Captains Crenshaw and Holland, Lieutenants Clow, Ward, Perry, Rourk and Anderson, and Lieutenant Mills were severely wounded. Captain Avirett was wounded in the shoulder by a fragment of a shell before the charge, but he remained with his company and behaved with great coolness and gallantry." Commends Captain Lee, Lieut. J. F. McClellan, Lieutenant Goodwyn, Lieutenant Vandergrift and Lieutenant Hinton, who led their regiments bravely at all times and in the hottest fire. "Late in the evening the remnant of the regiment united in making a last charge . . . capturing a large number of prisoners. Regiment was saluted on the field by General Bate." (397) Mentioned in Lieutenant-Colonel Frayser's report. (402) General Clayton, speaking of pursuit of the enemy, says: "I take pleasure in mentioning that Captains Crenshaw and Lee, with their companies from the Fifty-eighth Alabama regiment of Bate's brigade, accompanied mine beyond the road. They are gallant officers." He speaks also of the excellent order in which the Fifty-eighth Alabama moved. (534) Roll of honor, battle of Chickamauga: Sergt. Joel B. Freeman (color-bearer), Company A; Sergt. S. C. Johnston, Company A; Private J. N. Ward, Company B; Sergt. J. L. Huddleston, Company C; Private J. H. Burgess (killed), Company D; Private Z. E. Lee, Company E; Private J. V. McGinnis, Company F; Private T. J. Mize, Company G; Private S. J. Harrell, Company H; Sergt. W. C. McClellen, Company I; Corp. J. R. Rogers, Company K.

No. 55—(661) Under Lieut.-Col. John W. Inzer, Clayton's brigade, Bragg's army, Chattanooga-Ringgold campaign. (745) With the Thirty-second Alabama; 8 killed, 34 wounded.

No. 56—(686) November 12, 1863, regiment transferred from Bate's brigade to Clayton's brigade, Stewart's division. (805) December 10th, with the Thirty-second Alabama, under Col. Bush Jones, in Clayton's brigade. (824) December, 14th Thirty-second and Fifty-eighth Alabama regiments, 325 strong, in Breckinridge's corps.

No. 57—(479) February 24 and 25, 1864, 3 killed, 31 wounded at Rocky Face mountain.

No. 73—(22) Mentioned at Resaca, Ga., May 15, 1864, in report of Atlanta campaign, by General Slocum (Union).

No. 74—(641, et seq.) Assignment as above, Atlanta campaign. July 10, 1864, in Holtzclaw's brigade, Clayton's division. (832-834) Commended by General Clayton in his report of operations, May 7th to 27th. Losses, 15 killed and 54 wounded, in Thirty-second and Fifty-eighth Alabama regiments, consolidated. (841-844) Col. Bushrod Jones says that on May 12th, one company of pickets was left under the command of Major Thornton. "I claim only for my regiment that, with a full knowledge of the superior forces massed in their front, they advanced with cool and deliberate gallantry, and that they endured all that brave men can be expected to do. ... I regret to state that Maj. Harry Thornton is among the wounded, but his wound, though disabling for several weeks perhaps, is not dangerous. He endeavored to remain with the regiment, but, after a trial of several days, he was compelled to go to the rear. ... May 25th, the losses were very heavy, equal to the average losses of a heavy battle. ... Lieut. J. G. Goldthwait was wounded in the wrist, and Capt. G. W. Cox had his left thigh broken; both behaved with distinguished gallantry. Lieutenant Mills was slightly wounded in the leg." At daylight, May 26th, the Fifty-eighth relieved the Eighteenth in the trenches (near New Hope church). May 15th, 15 killed, 54 wounded, out of 345 engaged. May 25th, 3 killed, 36 wounded, out of 225 engaged.

No. 78—(854) September 20, 1864, Maj. Harry I. Thornton, in Holtzclaw's brigade; Colonel Jones commanding brigade.

No. 79—(897) November 7, 1864, Thirty-second and Fifty-eighth consolidated, under Colonel Jones, 240 strong, with Gen. H. D. Clayton.

No. 93—(665) In Holtzclaw's brigade, army of Tennessee, Nashville campaign.

No. 103, No. 104—March 10, 1865, in Holtzclaw's brigade, district of the Gulf. April, called the Thirty-second. (1131) Consolidated regiment, under Major Kimbell, ordered to be ready to skirmish with the enemy near Magnolia, and, if pressed, fall back to Spanish Fort, March 20th.

THE FIFTY-NINTH ALABAMA INFANTRY.

The Fifty-ninth Alabama was formed from the Second and Fourth battalions of Hilliard's legion, at Charleston, Tenn., November 25, 1863, under the command of Col. Bolling Hall, Jr. It was in Gracie's brigade and took part in the East Tennessee campaign. It was at the investment of Knoxville, and the fights at Dandridge and Bean's Station. In April, 1864, it reached Richmond, and took part in the battles around that city; lost heavily at Drewry's, and was in the fight with Sheridan. It was in the trenches at Petersburg, and in conflicts in the vicinity, losing a number at Hatcher's Run and White Oak road. It was engaged at Appomattox and surrendered as part of Gordon's corps, Gen. Bushrod R. Johnson's division. Colonel Hall being wounded, and Lieut.-Col. John D. McLennan killed, at Drewry's, George W. Huguley succeeded to the command; Maj. Lewis H. Grumpier, who was distinguished for his gallantry in the battle of Chickamauga, was in command in April, 1865. Capt. H. H. Rutledge was killed at Drewry's, and Capt. Zach Daniel at Hatcher's Run; Adjt. Crenshaw Hall, Capts. S. E. Reaves and R. F. Manly were wounded at Drewry's; the latter was wounded and captured at Hatcher's Run; Capt. John E. Hall was wounded at Petersburg; Capts. J. C. Hendrix and J. W. Dillard died in the service, and Capt. J. Lang was twice wounded.

EXTRACTS FROM OFFICIAL WAR RECORDS.
Fifty-ninth Alabama infantry, formed from Second and Fourth battalions, Hilliard's legion, Col. Bolling Hall, Jr. No. 54—(534, 535) Mentioned in report of Gen. Bushrod Johnson, engagement at Bean's Station, December 14, 1863.

No. 58—(642) Gracie's brigade, Gen. Bushrod R. Johnson's troops, January 31, 1864.

No. 59—(722) March 31, 1862, in Gracie's brigade, Longstreet's department. (802) April 20, 1864, in Gracie's brigade, Gen. B. R. Johnson's corps.

No. 68—(207) In Gracie's brigade, Ransom's division. Forces in the Richmond and Petersburg lines, May 5 to 10, 1864.

No. 69—(862) May 31, 1864, in Gracie's brigade, Ransom's troops.

No. 81—(703) June 30, 1864, mentioned by Gen. Bushrod Johnson; about 250 strong.

No. 88—(1065) September 28, 1864, mentioned by Gen. John C. Babcock (Union). (1166) August, 1864, Lieut.-Col. George W. Huguley, in Gracie's brigade, Johnson's division. (1227) September 1, 1864, in Gracie's brigade with General Beauregard. (1311) September 30, 1864, in Gracie's brigade, Johnson's division.

No. 89—(1190) October 31, 1864, Gracie's brigade, B. R. Johnson's division. (1242) November 30, 1864, Gracie's brigade, B. R. Johnson's division. (1368) December 31, 1864, Gracie's brigade, B. R. Johnson's division.

No. 95—(233) March 25, 1865, mentioned in report of Colonel Weygant (Union), skirmish near Hatcher's Run. (268) March 25, 1865, mentioned in report of General Chamberlain (Union), skirmish near Hatcher's Run, says: "Advance was made with great vigor and boldness, though not in heavy force." (1274) Maj. Lewis H. Crumpler, in Moody's brigade, Johnson's division, Lee's army, April 9, 1865.

No. 96—(202) January 22, 1865, mentioned by General Parke (Union). (610) Mentioned by General Meade (Union). (1174) January 31, 1865, Lieut-Col. George W. Huguley, in Gracie's brigade, Lee's army. (1183) January 31, 1865, in Gracie's brigade, Lee's army. (1273) February 28, 1865, in Gracie's brigade, Lee's army.

No. 97—(219, 220) Mentioned by Colonel Weygant (Union), in report of fight near Watkins house, Petersburg, March 25, 1865.

THE SIXTIETH ALABAMA INFANTRY.

The Sixtieth Alabama was formed of four companies of the First, and six companies of the Third battalion, Hilliard's legion, under the command of Colonel Sanford, at Charleston, Tenn., November 25, 1863. It spent the winter in the campaign in East Tennessee and proceeded to Richmond in the spring. It lost heavily at Drewry's Bluff, where it was complimented on the field by General Gracie; was in the trenches at Petersburg and lost almost continually; suffered severely at White Oak road and Hatcher's Run. At Appomattox, it is said, the men were "huzzaing over a captured battery and a routed foe," when the news of the surrender was received. The regiment surrendered 165, rank and file. Col. John W. A. Sanford was wounded at Bean's Station. Lieut.-Col. Daniel S. Troy, who succeeded in command, was wounded at Drewry's, and was again wounded and captured at Hatcher's Run while gallantly bearing the colors of the Fifty-ninth Alabama in front of the charge of the two regiments. Major Hatch was killed, and Capts. S. A. Williams, John W. Smith and G. A. Tarbutton were wounded, at White Oak road; and Capt. David A. Clark died of wounds received at Appomattox.

EXTRACTS FROM OFFICIAL WAR RECORDS.

No. 54—(535, 536) Mentioned in report of Gen. Bushrod Johnson, engagement at Bean's Station, December 14, 1863.

No. 58—(642) Gracie's brigade, Gen. B. R. Johnson's troops, January 31, 1864.

No. 59—(722, 802) March and April, 1864, in Gracie's brigade, Bushrod R. Johnson's corps.

No. 68—(207) May 5 to 10, 1864, in Gracie's brigade, General Beauregard's forces near Richmond and Petersburg.

No. 69—(861) May 31, 1864, 342 present for duty. Gracie's brigade, Ransom's division. (902) June 22d, ordered to report to Gen. G. W. C. Lee, and placed at New Market hill.

No. 81—(670, 671) June 20, 1864, Gen. R. S. Ewell, Richmond, Va.; 342 men. (674) June 21st, ordered to hold New Market, Gen. G. W. C. Lee. (679) January 22d, ordered to report to Gen. Wade Hampton at Bottom's Bridge.

No. 82—(748) July 7, 1864, in Gracie's brigade, relieved by General Beauregard at New Market hill.

No. 88—(1065, 1066, 1213, 1227, 1311) Mentioned in Gracie's brigade, Johnson's division, commanded by Gen., G. T. Beauregard. (1238) September 8, 1864, ordered to report to General Hampton, by General Ewell.

No. 89—(198) October 13, 1864, regiment reported between Burnside mine and City Point railroad.—Letter of John C. Babcock (Union). (508) November 4th, mentioned as near Burnside mine. (893) December 9th, regiment reported as under marching orders. (1190, 1242, 1368) To December 31st, in Gracie's brigade, Bushrod R. Johnson's division.

No. 95—(233) March 26, 1865, mentioned by Lieutenant-Colonel Weygant (Union), operations of March 25, 1865, near Hatcher's Run; Lieutenant-Colonel Troy, leading brigade, wounded. (268) March 28th, mentioned by Gen. J. L. Chamberlain (Union) in report of same fight. (1274) April 9th, Moody's brigade, Johnson's division.

No. 96—(1174, 1183, 1273) In Gracie's brigade, Johnson's division, January and February, 1865.

No. 97—(219, 220) Letter from Lieut-Col. C. H. Weygant (Union) says: "In fight of March 25, 1865, Lieutenant-Colonel Troy, in command of Confederate force, was bearing the colors of the Fifty-ninth Alabama in front of the charge, when he was shot down and captured by a soldier of One Hundred and Twenty-fourth New York volunteers."

THE SIXTY-FIRST ALABAMA INFANTRY.

The Sixty-first regiment was organized at Pollard in September, 1863, and formed part of Clanton's brigade until the following January, when it was sent to Virginia and took the place of the Twenty-sixth in Battle's brigade. It was in Mobile in December, and in January, 1864, was sent to Orange Court House. It was under fire at the Wilderness with severe loss, and distinguished itself by the capture of a battery, and by a most desperate and successful attack upon General Jenkins and his New York zouaves. After fighting at Spottsylvania and Second Cold Harbor, it moved into Maryland with General Early. It lost heavily at Snicker's Gap, Winchester and Fisher's Hill; was in the trenches at Petersburg and engaged during the retreat to Appomattox, where it surrendered, 27 strong, under Capt. A. B. Fannin. It was commanded successively by Col. W. G. Swanson, Lieut.-Col. L. H. Hill,

Maj. W. E. Pinckard and Capt. Augustus B. Fannin, Jr. Lieutenant-Colonel Hill, Major Pinckard and Capt. W. H. Philpot were captured at Petersburg. Capt. A. B. Fannin, Jr., was wounded at Cold Harbor and Winchester. Capt. James W. Fannin was captured at Spottsylvania, and Capt. A. F. Zachary was wounded there. Capt. A. J. Slaughter was wounded at Snicker's Gap, Capt. A. D. McCaskill was killed at the Wilderness, and Capt. J. J. Joiner was killed at Hare's Hill.

EXTRACTS FROM OFFICIAL WAR RECORDS.

No. 42—(239, 240) Mentioned in Gen. J. H. Clanton's report of organization of his brigade; Col. W. G. Swanson commanding regiment, September 19, 1863. (275) Called also Fifty-fifth, in General Clanton's brigade, department of the Gulf, September 30th. (402, 511, 561) Called also Fifty-ninth, assignment as above, December, 1863, headquarters at Mobile, Ala. (549, 550) Report of Col. W. G. Swanson. (556) Commended in a communication of General Clanton.

No. 58 — (629, 726) General Polk says that special orders were issued, January 25, 1864, directing this regiment to proceed forthwith to northern Virginia.

No. 60—(1122) By special orders, No. 20, January 25, 1864, assigned to the army of Northern Virginia. (1176) By special orders, No. 36, assigned to Battle's brigade in place of O'Neal's regiment, February 12, 1864.

No. 67—(1083) Mentioned in Gen. C. A. Battle's communication relative to operations, May 8, 1864.

No. 78—(589) Mentioned in letter of General Clanton to General Polk, May 9, 1864.

No. 88—(1217) In Battle's brigade, Second corps, army of Northern Virginia, August 31, 1864; Lieut.-Col. Lewis H. Hill commanding regiment.

No. 89—(1194) Brigaded under General Battle in army of Northern Virginia, October 31, 1864; Maj. William E. Pinckard commanding regiment. (1246) November 30th, Col. William G. Swanson commanding. (1364) December 31st, Maj. William E. Pinckard commanding.

No. 90—(564) Battle's brigade, forces commanded by Lieut.-Gen. Jubal Early, battle of Cedar Creek, October 19, 1864; Maj. William E. Pinckard commanding regiment.

No. 95—(1270) Battle's brigade, Second corps, April, 1865; Capt. Augustus B. Fannin, Jr., commanding regiment.

No. 96—(1172, 118:) Battle's brigade, Second corps, army of Northern Virginia; Lieut.-Col. Lewis H. Hill commanding regiment.

RESERVE REGIMENTS AND BATTALIONS INFANTRY.

SIXTY-SECOND, SIXTY-THIRD AND SIXTY-FIFTH REGIMENTS.

There were about nine regiments and three battalions of reserves, composed for the most part of very young men, about two regiments being made up of old men, and they were organized principally for the defense of Mobile and the bay forts. Some of these were, in 1864, consolidated under the command of Col. Daniel Huger, of the First reserve regiment, and the new regiment was known as the Sixty-second Alabama. Others, under Col. Olin F. Rice, of the Second reserve regiment, were known as the Sixty-third. The First battalion, also called the Fourth reserve regiment, was consolidated with the Third and Fourth battalions under Lieut.-Col. E. M. Underhill, and called the Sixty-fifth Alabama; it was employed mainly in the defenses of Mobile, though a detachment was sent to Montgomery in April, 1865, and retired before Wilson's army to Girard, where it fought with severe loss and was captured. The Sixty-second and Sixty-third fought in General Thomas' brigade at Fort Gaines and Spanish Fort, losing a large number in killed and wounded. Relieved at Spanish Fort by Holtzclaw's brigade, they were sent to Blakely, where, after enduring the privations and perils of the siege of Blakely, they were captured, and were exchanged a few days before the final surrender of the department of the Gulf. Captain Johnson, of the Sixty-third, was killed, and Captain Ward, of the Sixty-second, wounded, at Spanish Fort. Capt. J. W. Pitts, who assisted in the defense of Talladega during Rousseau's raid, became major of the Sixty-second. This regiment, composed wholly of young men, was especially complimented by General Liddell for gallant conduct at Spanish Fort.

EXTRACTS FROM OFFICIAL WAR RECORDS.

First Reserve Regiment, Col. Daniel E. Huger: No. 74—(975) Major Walthall says: "Captain Pitts' company of boys on post duty at Talladega, July 13 to 15, 1864." (977) Major Walthall, in his report of operations, July 13th to 15th, says: "Captain Pitts' company required for duty at the bridge at Talladega, Rousseau's raid." No. 78— (814) September 3, 1864, under Col. Daniel E. Huger, in Liddell's brigade, Mobile. No. 79, No. 93, No. 94—In Thomas' command, Mobile, November and December, 1864. No. 101—(681) First and Second Reserves, home guards, in and about Mobile, January, 1865, 1,000 strong. No. 103—(831) February 16, 1865, at Mobile. Union report says: "A regiment of boys, about 600 strong, commanded by Colonel Withers (Huger)." (1045) March 10th, transferred from Taylor's command to Thomas'. (1046) March 10th, in Thomas' brigade, Mobile. No. 104 —(226) April 4, 1865, in Thomas' brigade.

Second Reserve Regiment, Col. Olin F. Rice: No. 78 —(814) September 3, 1864, Col. Olin F. Rice, in Liddell's brigade, district of the Gulf. No. 79—(876) November 1, 1864, Fuller's command, district of the Gulf. No. 94— (633) December 1, 1864, Fuller's command, department of Alabama, Mississippi and East Louisiana. No. 101— (681) First and Second. Alabama Reserves, home guards, 1,000 strong, January, 1865, at Mobile. No. 103—(264) April 8, 1865, Fort Blakely, Ala.; 15 killed, 42 wounded. (1045) March 10th, transferred from Taylor's command to Thomas'. (1046) Lieut.-Col. Junius A. Law, in Thomas' brigade, Mobile. No. 104—(226) April, 1865, in Thomas' brigade, Mobile.

Third Reserve Regiment, Col. William M. Brooks: No. 78—(814) September 3, 1864, Col. William M. Brooks, Thomas' brigade, district of Gulf. (887) September 30th, Thomas' brigade, department of Alabama, Mississippi and East Louisiana. No. 79—(901) Ordered to report to the commanding officer at Cahaba. (915) November 12, 1864, ordered to report to General Adams. No. 93— (1233) Six companies at Cahaba; Lieut.-Col. Samuel Jones. (1239) November 22d, ordered to Selma. (1244) November 24th, ordered to Pollard. No. 94—(634) December 1st, in Clanton's brigade. Six companies at Cahaba. No. 103—(968) February 17, 1865, Third Alabama Reserves ordered to report to General Adams at Selma, relieved at Mobile. (1045-1047) March 10th, Clanton's brigade, Mobile. No. 104—(364) Mentioned as at Montgomery, April 15, 1865.

First Reserve Battalion, Lieut.-Col. W. M. Stone (became Fourth Reserves): No. 78—(814, 887) September, 1864, Thomas' brigade, district of Mobile. No. 93— (1233) Called Fourth Alabama reserves, in Col. T. H. Taylor's command at Mobile, November 20, 1864. No. 94—(634) Same assignment as above, December 1, 1864. No. 103—(968) February 10, 1865, Fourth Reserves relieved at Mobile and ordered to report to General Adams at Montgomery. No. 104—(364) Mentioned as at Montgomery, April 15, 1865.

Third Reserve Battalion, Capt. F. S. Strickland: No. 78—(814) September 3, 1864, in Liddell's brigade, district of the Gulf, at Mobile. No. 79—(875) November 1st, in Baker's brigade, Liddell's division, Maury's army. No. 93—(1233) November 20th, detached from district of the Gulf with Fourth battalion, under Lieut.-Col. E. M. Underhill. No. 94—(633) December 1, 1864, with Fourth battalion, Baker's brigade.

Fourth Reserve Battalion: No. 79—(875) November 1, 1864, Baker's brigade, district of the Gulf, Mobile. No. 93—(1233) November 20th, Taylor's brigade, Mobile, with Third battalion, under Lieut.-Col. E. M. Underhill. No. 94—(633) December 1, 1864, same assignment, Baker's brigade.

First Junior Reserves Regiment: No. 103—(997) February 20, 1865, 330 for duty at Mobile.

Second Junior Reserves Regiment: No. 103—(997) February 20, 1865, 428 for duty at Mobile.

Third Senior Reserve Battalion: No. 103—(997) February 20, 1865, six companies at Pollard, one company Senior Reserves cavalry at Mobile; two companies Senior Reserves light artillery at Mobile. (998) Third Senior Reserves at Montevallo, February 20, 1865.

Fourth Senior Reserves: No. 103—(998) February 20, 1865, 150 for duty at Montgomery.

State Reserves. No. 78—(751) August 3, 1864, Colonel Patton's command reinforced by 388 Alabama State Reserve troops, Mobile, Ala. No. 86—(911) In Mobile on city defenses. Report of Maj. F. W. Marston, chief signal officer, December 22, 1864. No. 93—(1233) Under Lieut.-Col. Young L. Royston, at Selma, November 20, 1864. No. 104—(226) In Maury's command, Mobile, April, 1865.

HILLIARD'S LEGION.

Hilliard's Legion was organized at Montgomery, June, 1862, and consisted of five battalions; one of these, a mounted battalion, was early detached and became part of the Tenth Confederate cavalry. The Legion proceeded to Montgomery nearly 3,000 strong, under the command of Col. H. W. Hilliard, and was placed in McCown's brigade. It took part in the siege of Cumberland Gap, and spent the fall and winter in Kentucky and east Tennessee. In April, Col. J. Thorington took command of the Legion, and was succeeded in command of the First battalion by Lieut.-CoL J. Holt, the whole Legion serving in Gracie's brigade at Chickamauga. In this battle it earned a splendid reputation. The First and Second battalions suffered the heaviest loss, leaving more than half their number either dead or wounded on the field. Lieutenant-Colonel Holt was severely wounded, and the command of the First battalion fell upon Captain Huguley. Maj. Daniel S. Troy was in command after Chickamauga. Lieutenant-Colonel Hall and Captain Walden, successively in command of the Second battalion, were both wounded. This battalion was the first to plant its banner on the enemy's works. The colors were pierced by 83 bullets. The standard-bearer, Robert Y. Hiett, was made a lieutenant. The other battalions also fought nobly and suffered severely both in officers and men.

The Third was complimented on the field by General Pond. The legion continued fighting in Gracie's brigade in east Tennessee until, on November 25, 1863, it was dissolved. Parts of the First and Third were consolidated and formed the Sixtieth Alabama, under Col. J. W. A. Sanford; the Second and Fourth, under Col. Boiling Hall, Jr., became the Fifty-ninth Alabama. Three companies of the First battalion became the Twenty-third battalion, or Stallworth's sharpshooters. The history of the legion is continued in the records of these organizations.

EXTRACTS FROM OFFICIAL WAR RECORDS.
Vol. XVI, Part 1—(1010) September 22, 1862, at Cumberland Gap.
Vol. XVI, Part 2—(708) June 26, 1862, ordered to Chattanooga. (717) July 2d, mentioned by secretary of war. (720) July 4th, ordered to Atlanta, Ga. (726) July 11th, ordered to Chattanooga to report to Major-General McCown. (748) Mentioned by J. F. Belton, as ordered to report to General Stevenson, August 8th. (824) Reeves' (Fourth) battalion at Clinton, September 14th. (847, 873) September, at Cumberland Gap. (874) September 25th, cavalry ordered to Winchester. (975) Cavalry under Maj. M. M. Slaughter ordered to Flat Lick, October 22d. (984) October 31st, in McCown's division, Gen. E. Kirby Smith's force.

Vol. XX, Part 2—(412-414) November 20, 1862, headquarters Knoxville, Tenn., 1,095 present for duty; four battalions formed the Fifth brigade. (466) December 27th, First and Fourth battalions at Big Creek Gap; Second battalion at Cumberland Gap; Third battalion at Clinton.

Vol. XXIII, Part 2—(644, 645) February 20, 1863, with Gen. D. S. Donelson. First and Fourth battalions at Big Creek Gap; Second at Cumberland Gap; Third at Knoxville; Company A, First battalion, at Bristol. (711) March 9th, battalions as above. First battalion, Lieut.-Col. J. Thorington; Second, Lieut.-Col. Boiling Hall, Jr.; Third, Lieut.-Col. J. W. A. Sanford; Fourth, Maj. W. N. Reeves. Two companies of First at Clinton, one at Bristol. (792) April 25th, under Col. J. Thorington, in Gracie's brigade, headquarters Bean's Station, Tenn. (946) July 31, 1863, assignment as above. First battalion, Lieut.-Col. J. H. Holt; Second, Lieut.-Col. B. Hall, Jr.; Third, Lieut.-Col. J. W. A. Sanford; Fourth, Major McLennan; headquarters, Cumberland Gap. (949) August 3d, three battalions from Cumberland Gap ordered to Strawberry Plains to report to General Gracie.

No. 42—(556) General Clanton says that at Chickamauga, the colors of the Second battalion were pierced by eighty-two balls, and President Davis promoted Lieutenant-Colonel Hall to colonel, and the color-bearer to a lieutenancy. Says the Legion is in Gracie's brigade, May, 1864.

No. 51—(16) September 19 and 20, 1863, in Gracie's brigade, Bragg's army. (416) Gen. William Preston in his report of Chickamauga says: "The brigade advanced with splendid courage, but was met by a destructive fire of the enemy from the cover of their field-works on the hill. The Second Alabama battalion stormed the hill and entered the intrenchments. Here an obstinate and bloody combat ensued. Lieutenant-Colonel Hall was severely wounded while gallantly leading his command in the assault on the hill. The Second battalion, out of 239, lost 169 killed and wounded. In the action its colors were pierced in 83 places, and were afterward, by request, presented to his Excellency, the President, who promoted the brave standard-bearer, Robert Y. Hiett, for conspicuous courage. George W. Norris, of Captain Wise's company, of Hall's battalion, fell at the foot of the enemy's flagstaff and was buried where he so nobly died." Lieutenant-Colonel Holt, of the First battalion, was severely wounded. (418) General Preston commends the gallantry of

Lieutenant-Colonel Sanford, Major McLennan, Captain Walden and Surgeon Luckie. (421, 422) General Gracie's report: "The First battalion, Alabama Legion, sustained the heaviest loss. Of 239 carried into action, 169 were killed and wounded. Among the latter was Lieutenant-Colonel Holt, seriously, in the knee. Among the killed, Lieut. R. H. Bibb. . . . It was the Second battalion that first gained the hill and placed its colors on the enemy's works. Its colors bear marks of over eighty bullets. Its bearer, Robert Y. Hiett, though thrice wounded and the staff thrice shot away, carried his charge throughout the entire fight. He deserves not only mention, but promotion. Lieutenant-Colonel Hall behaved most gallantly, receiving a severe wound in the thigh. Capt. W. D. Walden, Company B, was wounded in the breast, arm and shoulder, inside the enemy's works. His case deserves special mention. Lieut.-Col. J. W. A. Sanford, commanding the Third battalion, Alabama Legion, nobly did his duty, sustaining heavy loss both in officers and men. Asst. Surgeon James B. Luckie, both in the field and at the hospital, was most attentive to the wounded, as, indeed, were all the medical officers of the command. Major McLennan, commanding the Fourth Alabama Legion, nobly did his duty, sustaining heavy loss both in officers and men." General Gracie also says: "To Lieutenant Gilmer, adjutant of the Alabama Legion, who, during the absence of its commander has acted as my assistant inspector-general, and to Messrs. George C. Jones and J. S. Harwell, both wounded, my thanks are due for services rendered at Chickamauga." (423) Col. Y. M. Moody, Forty-third Alabama, says: "This (Second) battalion assisted in holding enemy's works at Chickamauga. . . . On September 19th, the Third battalion, Alabama Legion, was left on top of a slight elevation, to support Jeffries' and Baxter's batteries. We remained at this point until the morning of the 20th, exposed during evening of the 19th to enemy's shells." (424, 425) Captain Huguley, of First battalion, says: "Colonel Holt was severely wounded early in the action, and the command devolved on me. We went into the engagement with 238, and had 24 killed and 144 wounded, 16 of whom were officers." (425, 426) Lieut. C. Hall says: "Lieutenant-Colonel Hall, while leading the command under the fiercest fire, was shot down at a time when by hard fighting we had almost reached the enemy's works. Captain Walden assumed command, and bravely led the still advancing line until shot down within the enemy's lines. Lieutenant Fisher, a brave officer of Company C, about this time was mortally wounded. The works were carried and the enemy driven before us in confusion. The battalion carried into action 230 aggregate; of these, 16 were killed, 75 wounded, many mortally." Commends bravery of Capt. L. H. Crumpler and Lieut. John H. Porter. (426, 427) Lieut.-Col. J. W. A. Sanford says: "We (Third battalion) carried into the fight on the 20th instant, 229 men. Of this number, 4 were killed and 42 wounded." He especially commends for courage and skill, Capt. John McCreless, Surgeon James B. Luckie, Corporal Hutto and Privates Hix, Turner and Tally of Company A; Sergeant Baygents and Privates Jackson, Brooks and Hall of Company B; Private Brown, Company C; Privates Hufham, Quillan and Jesse

L. Jackson of Company D; Sergeant Harris and Privates Harris, Lewis, Skinner and Williams of Company E; Privates Simmons, Patrick and Jackson of Company F. (427, 428) Major McLennan of Fourth battalion commends conduct of Privates McCain, Holly, King, Head, of Company A; Corporal French and Privates Anderson, Flournoy, Smith, of Company B; Sergeant Mahone, Sergeant Daniels and Privates Daniel, Hill, Rutledge, Bennett, of Company D; Sergeant Stuckey, Corporal Martin, Corporal Cumbie and Privates Phillips and Lancey, of Company E, for conspicuous gallantry on the field. Roll of honor, Chickamauga, First battalion: Adjt. John Massey, Private John H. Conner,* Company A; Private J. E. Wright, Company B; Private James M. Gibson, Company C; Private B. A. Davis,* Company D; Sergt. J. L. Cox,* Company E; Private A. J. Daw,* Company F. Second battalion: Capt. W. D. Walden, Company B; Private John H. Randall, Company A; First Sergt. Socrates Spigener, Company B; Private Benj. F. Temple,* Company C; Private William P. Jones, Company D; Private George W. Norris,* Company E; Corp. Jos. V. Castlebury,* Company F. Third battalion: Capt. John McCreless, Company E; Private Micajah Kirkland,* Company A; Private John Blankenship, Company C; Private Henry R. Lewis, Company C. Fourth battalion: Private Jackson Lee,* Company A; Corp. James E. French, Company B; Private B. F. Martin,* Company D; Private R. S. Turlington,* Company E.

No. 54—(452) November 30, 1863, Gracie's brigade, Gen. B. R. Johnson's forces. First battalion, Maj. D. S. Troy; Second, Capt. John H. Dillard; Third, Lieut.-Col. J. W. A. Sanford; Fourth, Maj. John D. McLennan.

No. 55—(659) In Gracie's brigade, Buckner's division; detached November 22d, for operations against Burnside in east Tennessee.

No. 56—(891) December 31, 1863, Gracie's brigade, Longstreet's corps. Parts of First and Third (Sixtieth Alabama), under Colonel Sanford; Second and Fourth (Fifty-ninth Alabama), under Colonel Hall.

No. 78—(589) May, 1864, General Clanton speaks of Legion as in Gracie's brigade. Same mention as above, No. 42, p. 556.

FIRST MOBILE REGIMENT INFANTRY.

The First Mobile regiment, called also the Mobile Guards, City battalion, and Local Defense corps, was organized for work in defense of Mobile and served in that city under command, successively, of Maj. W. S. Moreland, Col. A. W. Lampkin and Lieut.-Col. S. W. Cayce, until it was disbanded in the spring of 1865.

EXTRACTS FROM OFFICIAL WAR RECORDS.
No. 42—(511, 561) December, 1863, Maj. W. S. Moreland, Cantey's

* Killed in action.

brigade, Mobile. No, 58—(582) January 20, 1864, Col. A. W. Lampkin; assignment as above. No. 59—(861) April 30th, assignment as above. No. 78—(678) June 30th, Higgins' brigade, Mobile. (752) August 3d, assignment as above. No. 79—(876) November 1st, Lieut.-Col. S. W. Cayce, in Taylor's command, Mobile. No. 86—(911) December 22d, Mobile. No. 93—(1233) November 20th, called City battalion, in Taylor's command, Mobile. No. 94—(633) December 1st, in Taylor's command, Mobile. No. 101—(681) Mentioned as Brooks' Home Guards cavalry, in Maury's forces, Mobile, January, 1865. No. 103—(831) Union report says, about 300 men under Colonel Cayce, at Mobile, February 16, 1865. (931) Regiment disbanded by special orders from war department, January 25, 1865. (1046) Mention of City battalion and four companies of special service men, under Maj. William Hartwell, in Taylor's command, Maury's army, March 10, 1865.

FIFTH ALABAMA BATTALION OF INFANTRY.

The Fifth battalion was organized near Dumfries, Va., December, 1861, and was at first placed in Whiting's brigade, but was soon transferred to Archer's brigade, where it served the greater part of the war. It fought with heavy loss in the battles around Richmond, being engaged at Mechanicsville, Cold Harbor, Gaines' Mill, Frayser's Farm, Second Manassas, Fredericksburg and Chancellorsville. It went to Gettysburg 200 strong, and lost half its number. It was then placed on provost duty in Gen. A. P. Hill's corps, and remained in Virginia until it surrendered at Appomattox, 30 or 40 strong. Its first commander was Major Van de Graaff, but it was led at different times by Capts. S. D. Stewart, A. N. Porter, C. M. Hooper and Wade Ritter. Major Van de Graaf was wounded before Richmond, and at Fredericksburg. Capt. S. D. Stewart was wounded before Richmond and killed at Chancellorsville; Capt. A. N. Porter was wounded at Fredericksburg and Chancellorsville; Capt. Wade Ritter was wounded, and Capt. T. B. Bush was killed, at Second Manassas; Captain Burton was killed at Cold Harbor.

EXTRACTS FROM OFFICIAL WAR RECORDS.
    Vol. V—(529, 530) March 21, 1862, Mentioned by Gen. W. H. C. Whiting. (1030) January 14th, Wigfall's brigade, Gen. G. T. Beauregard's forces, near Dumfries.
    Vol. XI, Part 2—(276, 296, 309) Mentioned in reports of Seven Days' battles, by Union officers. (487) June to July, 1862, in Archer's brigade, Jackson's corps, engagements around Richmond. (504) June 26th to July 1st, 19 killed, 79 wounded, in fights before Richmond. (897, 898) Gen. J. J. Archer, in his report of Mechanicsville and Gaines' Mill, says: "The gallant and efficient Captain Van de Graaff, commanding the Fifth Alabama battalion, was killed, and the next captain in command, S. D. Stewart, wounded." (Van de Graaff was not killed, but severely wounded.)

Vol. XI, Part 3—(650) July 23, 1862, in Archer's brigade, Jackson's army; Captain Van de Graaff.

Vol. XII, Part 1—(434) April 20, 1862, at Fredericksburg, Va.

Vol. XII, Part 2—(180, 218) August 9, 1862, at Cedar Mountain, Va., 1 killed and 8 wounded. (549) September 1, 1862, Archer's brigade, Jackson's corps. (562) At Manassas, 2 killed and 17 wounded, report of Surgeon Guild. (700, 702) General Archer says: "Among the officers whose gallantry I especially noticed in the action were Lieut. Charles M. Hooper, Fifth Alabama."

Vol. XIX, Part 1— (807, 1002) Maryland campaign, September 14, 1862, at Harper's Ferry, Captain Hooper.

Vol. XXI—(542) July 23, 1862, Maj. A. S. Van de Graaff, in Archer's brigade, A. P. Hill's division. (554) Highly commended for action in battle of Fredericksburg, report of Gen. R. E. Lee. (560) At Fredericksburg, 3 killed, 18 wounded. (632) At Fredericksburg, in the pursuit of the retreating Federals, they charged with great gallantry and captured many prisoners; highly commended by Gen. T. J. Jackson. (646, 647) Gen. A. P. Hill says: "They gallantly aided in holding General Archer's line. . . . They gallantly chased the enemy across" the railroad and back to their reserves." (657, 658) General Archer: "They nobly discharged their duty under Maj. A. S. Van de Graaff, who was wounded, and afterward under Capt. S. D. Stewart, and drove back the enemy."

No. 39—(791) In Archer's brigade, battalion at Chancellorsville, lost 3 killed and 30 wounded. (926) Capt. S. D. Stewart, commanding battalion, was killed at Chancellorsville. (928) May 3, 1863, report of Capt. A. N. Porter of the Fifth Alabama (who was knocked senseless by the bursting of a shell), at Chancellorsville: "We were ordered to support Pegram's battery; after supporting this battery for about half an hour, we were ordered again to charge the fortifications, which we did successfully, compelling the enemy to retreat in haste. It was here the lamented Capt. S. D. Stewart fell. He had commanded the battalion during the engagement, and just as victory was about to perch upon its banner, he fell, a noble offering to his country's freedom. . . . The Fifth Alabama behaved heroically. . . . Lieutenant (William B.) Hutton, Company A, Fifth Alabama battalion, behaved gallantly till he received a mortal wound, from which he died the evening of the same day."

No. 44—(289) July 1 to 3, 1863, in Archer's brigade, A. P. Hill's corps. (333) At Gettysburg, 26 wounded. (647) Mentioned in Colonel Shepherd's report of Gettysburg campaign.

No. 48—To October 31, 1863, in Archer's brigade, Lee's army

No. 88—(1030) September 26, 1864, mentioned near Canal Basin, by Gen. John C. Babcock (Union). (1214) One hundred and fifty-one present for duty, Hill's corps, Lee's army, August 31st. (1219) Unattached. (1243) September 10th, 159 present.

No. 95—(1272) April, 1865, Capt. Wade Ritter, provost guard, Hill's corps, Lee's army.

No. 96—(1182) Capt. Wade Ritter, at headquarters, Gen. A. P. Hill's corps, January 31, 1865.

SEVENTEENTH BATTALION SHARPSHOOTERS.

Yancey's battalion of sharpshooters was organized in the summer of 1862; served with the army of Tennessee in the Stone's river campaign, and suffered severely in the battles of Murfreesboro and Chickamauga. It served in Deas' brigade from April, 1863, until July 31, 1864, when it was transferred to Johnston's brigade. After the battle of Chickamauga, it wintered with the brigade at Dalton and took part in the incessant fighting of the Dalton-Atlanta campaign. Captain Yancey, the first commander of the battalion, was succeeded in April, 1863, by Capt. James F. Nabers, who led the battalion until July, 1864, when Lieut. A. R. Andrews took his place

EXTRACTS FROM OFFICIAL WAR RECORDS.
Vol. XVI, Part 2—(764) August 18 and 20, 1862, Capt. B. C. Yancey, in Gen. Frank Gardner's brigade, General Polk's corps.
Vol. XVII, Part 2—(633) June 30, 1862, in Gardner's brigade, Bragg's army.
Vol. XX, Part 1—(658) Capt. B. C. Yancey, in Deas' brigade, army of Tennessee, Stone's river campaign. (677) Three killed, 15 wounded. (974) Roll of honor, battle of Murfreesboro: Privates John H. Rutherford, Company A, killed in action; Walter S. White, Company B.
Vol. XX, Part 2—(431) November 29, 1862, in Gardner's brigade, army of Tennessee.
Vol. XXIII, Part 2—(735) April 1, 1863, Capt. James F. Nabers, in Deas' brigade, army of Tennessee. (942, 958) To August 10, 1863, in Deas' brigade, Bragg's army.
No. 51—(15) September 19 and 20, 1863, in Deas' brigade, Bragg's army. (340) Captain Nabers' report, 1 killed, 9 wounded.
No. 56—(617, 805, 825) October to December, 1863, in Deas' brigade, army of Tennessee; December 14th, 59 strong.
No. 58—(589) January 20, 1864, in Deas' brigade, Johnston's army.
No. 59—(869) April 30, 1864, Deas' brigade, Johnston's army.
No. 74—(640-663) In Deas' brigade, Johnston's army, April 30th, Capt. J. F. Nabers; July 31st, Lieut. A. R. Andrews.

TWENTY-THIRD BATTALION SHARPSHOOTERS.

The Twenty-third battalion, Maj. Nicholas Stallworth, was formed of companies E, F and G, First battalion of Hilliard's legion, at Charleston, Tenn., November 25, 1863. Serving for several months in the East Tennessee campaign, it moved to Richmond in April. It lost heavily in skirmishes around Richmond and Petersburg, and suffered severely at Drewry's; a mere handful remained to surrender at Appomattox. Major Stallworth, as a captain in Hilliard's legion, was wounded at Chickamauga; Capt. W. E. Broughton was killed at Drewry's; Captain White was wounded, and Lieutenant Lampley succeeded in command.

EXTRACTS FROM OFFICIAL WAR RECORDS.
 No. 58—(642) Gracie's brigade, Gen. B. R. Johnson's troops, January 31, 1863.
 No. 59—(722, 802) Gracie's brigade, Bushrod R. Johnson's corps, April, 1864.
 No. 69—(862) Gracie's brigade, Ransom's troops, May 31, 1864, in department of Richmond. (902) Ordered to report to Gen. G. W. C. Lee, June 22d; placed at Market Hill.
 No. 88—(1166) Lieut. Samuel Salter, Gracie's brigade, Johnson's division, Beauregard's army. (1227) Gracie's brigade, Johnson's division, September, 1864.
 No. 89—(1190-1368) Gracie's brigade, Johnson's division, October to December, 1864.
 No. 95—(1274) Moody's brigade, Johnson's division, Lee's army, April 9, 1865.

FIRST CONFEDERATE BATTALION INFANTRY.

The First Confederate battalion was organized in the spring of 1862 from two companies of the Second Alabama, which was disbanding. It fought at Corinth, Baker's Creek, Vicksburg and Jackson; remained in Rust's brigade, army of Mobile, until April, 1863, when it was sent to Bragg's army and brigaded under Reynolds, and afterward, Adams. In March, 1864, it was transferred to the army of Northern Virginia and placed in Davis' brigade, where it served until the close of the war, fighting at the Wilderness, Cold Harbor, Petersburg, Weldon Railroad and Hatcher's Run. At the latter it was captured, April 2, 1865. It was commanded, successively, by Lieut.-Col. George Hoke Forney, Capt. J. M. Johnson, Lieut.-Col. Francis B. McClung and Capt. Anthony B. Bartlett. Colonel Forney was killed at the battle of the Wilderness; Capt. Mike Donahue was killed at Weldon Railroad; Capt. W. J. Scott was wounded at Second Cold Harbor.

EXTRACTS FROM OFFICIAL WAR RECORDS.
 Vol. X, Part 2—(396) Maj. L. W. O'Bannon commanding, mentioned in report of General Villepigue, April 6, 1862. (476) With Second Alabama, in Villepigue's troops, at Fort Pillow, April 30th. (608) Mentioned in troops in and around Grenada, Miss., June 12, 1862, 434 muskets.

Vol. XV—(1033) Maj. G. H. Forney, Rust's brigade, General Gardner's army, March 31, 1863.

No. 36—(252-256) General Pemberton's report of operations during siege of Vicksburg states that the battalion was sent to reinforce General Bowen, April 15, 1863. (663) Posted at Winkler's Bluff, April 30th; General Bowen's report of the battle of Port Gibson.

No. 38—(706-746) Assignment as above. Ordered to remain at Jackson and report to General Adams, April 15, 1863. (755, 756, 761, 773) Ordered to General Bowen, April 17, 1863. General Bowen says: "Just arriving," Grand Gulf, Miss., April 21, 1863. (936) Reynolds' brigade, Loring's division, May 30, 1863. (1040) Adams' brigade, Loring's division, July 30, 1863.

No. 42—(130) General Maury says battalion was detached from garrison of Mobile and sent to General Bragg, April, 1863.

No. 53, No. 56, No. 57, No. 58—In Adams' brigade, Loring's division, to January, 1864.

No. 59—(604, 659) Assignment as above, March, 1864. (672) Transferred to army of Northern Virginia, Gen. Joe Davis' brigade, March 24, 1864. (674) Ordered to report to General Lee for assignment to Gen. J. R. Davis' brigade, March 25, 1864. (676) Lieutenant-Colonel Forney ordered to rejoin his command at Cahaba, Ala., and proceed with it to the army of Northern Virginia, for assignment.

No. 60—(954) Col. George H. Sharpe (Union) says battalion has been added to Joe Davis' brigade, April 23, 1864.

No. 67—(noi) Private A. J. Sizemore, Company A, killed in battle of Bethesda Church; on roll of honor.

No. 69—(850) Company A, doing provost guard duty in Atlanta, ordered to join command in Lee's army, northern Virginia, May 30, 1864.

No. 80—(812) Roll of honor, battle of Weldon Railroad: Sergt. A. Hembree, Company A; Sergt. A. D. Stoude, Company B; Private John Dunnigan, Company D; Sergt. J. Maddon, Company F; Private John McNamara Company I. (813) Roll of honor, miscellaneous engagements: Corp. B. J. Hugan, Company B, Corinth, Port Hudson, Grand Gulf, Baker's Creek, Wilderness; Private John Kelly, Company C, Fort Pillow, Corinth, Grand Gulf, Port Hudson; Sergt. Adolph W. Leslie, Company E, Fort Pillow, Corinth, Port Hudson, Baker's Creek, Jackson, Wilderness, Spottsylvania Court House (killed in latter engagement); Private Patrick Finegan, Company F, Corinth, Port Hudson, Grand Gulf, Baker's Creek, Wilderness, Spottsylvania Court House, Bethesda Church; Private Mitchell Smith, Company I, Fort Pillow, Corinth, Port Hudson, Grand Gulf, Baker's Creek, Jackson, Wilderness, Spottsylvania Court House, Liberty Mills, Cold Harbor.

No. 88—(1218) Capt. J. M. Johnson, Davis' brigade, Heth's division, August 31, 1864. (1309) Lieut.-Col. Francis B. McClung, September 30, 1864.

No. 89—(1189, 1240, 1366) Assignment as above, December 31, 1864.

No. 95—(1272) Capt. Anthony B. Bartlett, assignment as above, the Appomattox campaign.

No. 96—(1173, 1182, 1271) Assignment as above, January and February, 1865; Maj. F. B. McClung commanding, January 31st.

No. 97—(124) Mentioned in General Humphrey's report of a fight near Watkins house, Petersburg, March 25, 1865.

MISCELLANEOUS BATTALIONS AND COMPANIES OF INFANTRY.

There were many small and independent commands organized, principally for the defense of Mobile. Captain Chisholm's company of State Guards, the Swanson Guards, and the Eufaula Minute Men, under Captain Hardy, served in Florida in the summer of 1863. Butts', Casey's, Harris' and Morrison's battalions, the Pelham Cadets, and Tuscaloosa Cadets, served at Mobile and in various parts of Alabama in 1864 and 1865.

Gracie's battalion, a detail from the Ninth, Tenth, and Eleventh regiments, served in April and May, 1862, in the Peninsular campaign, in Johnston's army; Moreland's sharpshooters at Rome, Ga., in 1864.

EXTRACTS FROM OFFICIAL WAR RECORDS.

Butts' Battalion, Home Guards: No. 101—(681) Battalion 300 strong, at Mobile, January, 1865.

Casey's Battalion, Home Guards: No. 101 — (681) Battalion 300 strong, at Mobile, January 18, 1865.

Gracie's Battalion: Details from Ninth, Tenth and Eleventh regiments: Vol. XI, Part 3—(480) April 30, 1862, 276 strong, in Kershaw's brigade, Peninsular campaign. (532) May 21st, in Johnston's army, Kershaw's brigade.

Harris' Battalion of Infantry, Capt. R. A. Harris: No. 78—(814, 887) September, 1864, Thomas' brigade, Mobile.

Morrison's Battalion of Infantry: No. 78—(799, 800) Capt. J. D. Morrison sent from Meridian to General Gardner at Mobile, with 180 officers and men, August 25, 1864. (814) September, 1864, in Thomas' brigade, Mobile.

Moreland Sharpshooters: No. 59—(872) April 30, 1864, in Cantey's brigade, Johnston's army, encamped at Rome, Ga. No. 74—(644) April 30, 1864, in Cantey's brigade, Johnston's army, encamped at Rome, Ga.

Tuscaloosa Cadets. No. 42—(556) May 9, 1864, mentioned by General Clanton as not liable to conscription when organized. No. 76—(954) August 10th, ordered to report to General Maury at Pollard, Ala. No. 78—(589). May 9th, mentioned by General Clanton. (734) July 29th, commended by Governor Watts, Montgomery, as well-drilled boys, under Col. L. C.

Garland, 220 or 230 strong, ordered to Blue mountain, (746) August 1st, ordered to report to Col. Henry Maury at Pollard. No. 101—(617, 681) Two hundred strong (all boys, about 16 years old), at Mobile, January 23, 1865. No. 103—(353) April 4, 1865, at Tuscaloosa, Croxton's raid. No. 104—(1177, 1178) March 30, 1865, commended by Colonel Garland, who protests against impressment of horses belonging to the corps. (1182) March 31st, at Tuscaloosa, Ala., mentioned by Gen. W. H. Jackson, in letter to Colonel Garland.

Captain Chisholm's company of State Guards: No. 47—(273) August 4, 1863, Captain Chisholm's company ordered by the governor to make arrests on the border of Florida.

Eufaula Minute Men, Capt. John Hardy: No. 47— (248) July 30, 1863, in Cobb's brigade, district of Middle Florida. (328) August 31, 1863, in Cobb's brigade, district of Middle Florida.

Pelham Cadets: No. 59—(861) Pelham Cadets, Capt. Price Williams, Jr., district of the Gulf, April 30, 1864. No. 77—(428) August 12, 1864, in garrison at Fort Gaines were 40 Pelham Cadets. No. 79—(676) November 1st, under Lieut. H. E. Witherspoon, Taylor's command. No. 86—(911) December 22, 1864, defenses of Mobile. No. 93—(1233) November 20, 1864, Taylor's command, Mobile. No. 94—(633) Same assignment, December 1, 1864. No. 96—(475) February 6, 1865, Pelham Cadets ordered out to disperse mob at Macon, report of General Grant. No. 101—(617) January 23d, 150 strong at Mobile. No. 103—(1046) March 10th, in Taylor's command, Mobile. No. 104—(226) In Maury's command, Mobile, April 4th. (261) April 7th, Admiral Thatcher says: "There are no troops in Mobile except the Pelham battalion of boys."

Swanson Guards: No. 42—(131, 157) August 1, 1863, in J. H. Clanton's brigade; Maj.-Gen. Dabney H. Maury commanding.

CHAPTER V.

THE ALABAMA CAVALRY COMMANDS — REGIMENTS, BATTALIONS AND DETACHED COMPANIES — REFERENCES TO THEIR SERVICES IN THE OFFICIAL RECORDS.

THE First Alabama cavalry was organized at Montgomery, November, 1861, under Col. J. H. Clanton. It was ordered to Tennessee, and was at Jackson, Tenn., March 6, 1862; ordered to Monterey March 31st, and opened the battle of Shiloh. Was with Generals Walker, Beall, Chalmers and Wheeler in the summer and fall of 1862; afterward served, successively, in the brigades of Generals Hagan, Russell, Morgan and Allen, of Wheeler's corps. It moved into Kentucky and was distinguished at Munfordville, Perryville, and the many cavalry battles fought by Wheeler in the Kentucky campaign. It also fought with him at Nashville, Stewart's Creek bridge, and various skirmishes preceding and incident to the battle of Murfreesboro. It was especially thanked by General Bragg for gallant conduct in that great battle. It was also part of the rear guard which protected the retreat from Tullahoma and Chattanooga, losing severely at Duck river; fought at Chickamauga, Clinton and Knoxville, and took a brilliant part in the Sequatchee raid, in which nearly 2,000 prisoners and a train of 1,000 provision wagons were captured.

The First Alabama cavalry took a very conspicuous part in the rout of Generals Stoneman, Garrard and McCook; and was also daily engaged in retarding Sherman's advance, and harassing the enemy's front and flank in the Dalton-Atlanta campaign. It was in fights at or near Middleton, Fosterville, Lafayette, Marietta, Noonday Creek and Big Shanty. Its colonel, James H. Clanton, was in the spring of 1863 commissioned a brigadier-general, and rendered very efficient service throughout the war until captured at Bluff Spring, Fla., in March, 1865. He was succeeded in the command by Col. William W. Allen, who was in turn promoted to the command of a brigade and afterward to a division, being commissioned major-general in March, 1865; he was wounded at Stewart's Creek, December, 1863. Lieutenant Ledyard, wounded at Murfreesboro, was promoted. Capt. David T. Blakey was wounded at Dandridge, and he became colonel on the promotion of Colonel Allen, and led the regiment in many brilliant actions. Lieut.-Col. Thomas Brown was killed at Woodsonville, Ky.; Adjt. Wesley Jones at Fiddler's Pond, Capt. George Speed at Noonday Creek, and Capt. Sydney E. Allen at Murfreesboro. This regiment was asked for by General Lee in the summer of 1863.

EXTRACTS FROM OFFICIAL WAR RECORDS

Vol. VII—(909-914) At Florence, Ala., February 26, 1862, 800 strong.

Vol. X, Part 1—(29) Near Tuscumbia, March 16, 1862. (90) General Sherman says: "First Alabama engaged and captured Federal pickets, April 4, 1862." This letter shows that Federals were surprised. (93) General Hardee says: "Enemy attacked Clanton's regiment near Mickey's April 4, 1862." (384, 532) Mentioned in reports of Bragg and Withers. (553) General Chalmers' report, Shiloh, says that Colonel Clanton's First regiment Alabama cavalry protected our flank from attack. "Colonel Clanton himself remained almost all the time with my brigade, and though constantly exposed to the most dangerous fire, exhibited the most fearless and exemplary courage, cheering on those who seemed included to falter or grow weary, and with a detachment of his cavalry supplying us with ammunition when our wagons could not reach us." (612) Mentioned by Capt. A. W. Avery, Shiloh. (853, 854) Highly commended in Col. Joseph Wheeler's report, Bridge Creek, May 28, 1862: "The conduct of the officers and men in this affair was commendable, subjected as they were to a heavy fire of both artillery and infantry, from a foe secreted by a density of undergrowth. They advanced steadily, not using their arms until they were ordered, when they fired with good effect.... The part of the line under the gallant Colonel Clanton was severely engaged about 10 to 11 o'clock on the morning of the 29th, in which several were wounded on both sides." Colonel Wheeler mentions the gallant and good conduct of Colonel Clanton, and Private James Kerns, who was wounded while gallantly rallying a line of Mississippi troops which had been driven from their position.

Vol. X, Part 2—(299) Mentioned at Jackson, Tenn., March 6, 1862, by Adjutant-General Garner, who says: "Colonel Clanton is gallant to rashness." (300) Mentioned by General Bragg, Jackson, Tenn., March 6th. (303) Mentioned by Gen. L. P. Walker in letter from Tuscumbia. (307) In General Walker's brigade, army of Mississippi Valley, General Ruggles' corps, March 9th. (376) Ordered to occupy position in front of Monterey, March 31st. (459) Total present, April 28th, 588, in General Beall's cavalry brigade. (534) May 21st, Clanton's cavalry ordered to report to General Hindman and General Trapier. (575) Clanton's cavalry assigned to duty with Chalmers' brigade, June 2d.

Vol. XVI, Part 1 — (893, 895, 897, 899) Gen. Joseph Wheeler's report: "On August 27, 1862, I moved across the Tennessee river at Chattanooga with a command consisting of parts of First Alabama regiments, etc. At Carthage, on September 7th, the First Alabama was detached from my command. ... At Horse Cave, near Cave City, on September 18th, was joined by first regiment. On September 21st, at a point about four miles from Green river, the First Alabama made a gallant resistance and handsome charge upon the enemy, in which Col. T. B. Brown was killed. ... The fighting on the north side of the river was done by the First Alabama, Third Georgia and

First Kentucky regiments, all of which acted well under great difficulties and disparity of numbers. . . . On the Perryville and Lebanon road, a charge, one of the most brilliant of the campaign, was made in column; detachments of the First and Third Alabama regiments cavalry with the gallant Cols. W. W. Allen and James Hagan, being in advance. ... In closing this report, I cannot speak in too great praise of the gallantry of the officers and men of the First and Third Alabama regiments, who were always ready to meet the enemy at any moment, performed all duties assigned them, and endured all hardships and privations without a murmur or complaint. The confidence I naturally placed in such noble officers and men caused me to call upon them, perhaps too frequently, for posts of danger and hardships, yet, never did they intimate that their details were more frequent than other commands, but with the greatest cheerfulness right bravely performed their double task thus imposed, simply because their commander placed in them unshaken and implicit trust and confidence. To the brave officers and men of these regiments and their gallant leaders, Colonels Allen and Hagan, I tender my warmest thanks."

Vol. XVI, Part 2 — (781) August 26, 1862, Colonel Allen's regiment assigned to Wheeler's brigade, left wing of army of Mississippi, and will report to General Hardee. (124) At Danville, July 8th. (804) Ordered to join General Polk in Tennessee, September 9th. (809) Mentioned by Adjutant-General Williamson, Tompkinsville, Ky., September 10th; ordered on picket duty on Scottsville road, (824) With Col. W. W. Allen, commanded by Gen. N. B. Forrest, assigned to the right wing, army of Mississippi, to report to General Polk, September 14th. (832) Assigned to temporary duty with left wing by order of General Bragg, Glasgow, Ky., September 15th. (843) Transferred to left wing to report to General Hardee, September 18th. (879) Held in readiness for immediate and rapid march, by order of General Wheeler, New Haven, Ky., September 26th. (891) Mentioned by Adjutant-General Poole, Bardstown, Ky., September

Vol. XVII, Part 1—(5-7) Mentioned in report of Colonel Lay; joined by a detachment of Colonel Clanton's regiment, June 15, 1862.

Vol. XVII, Part 2— (63-66) Mentioned by Col. P. H. Sheridan and General Rosecrans, 800 strong, July 2, 1862.

Vol. XX, Part 1 — (19) Murfreesboro, November 27, 1862, General Bragg desires General Wheeler to express to the First Alabama his appreciation of their gallant Conduct, which was not unexpected, and which was spoken of in Wheeler's report. (82) A detachment of cavalry of the First Alabama regiment attacked and captured all the cavalry outposts of the enemy and immediately returned to the Confederate lines.—Report of Gen. H. P. Van Cleve, U. S. army near Nashville, December 25th. (630) Mentioned in Federal report of skirmish at Stewart's Creek bridge, December 27th. (661) Colonel Allen commanding, in Wheeler's brigade, army of Tennessee, Stone's river campaign. (958-960) Mentioned in report of General Wheeler, chief of cavalry, as stationed at Stewart's creek, December 26th. Colonel Allen was wounded while fighting gallantly; Lieut. E. S. Ledyard also wounded in engagements incident to battle of Murfreesboro.

Vol. XXIII, Part 1—(135-137) Mentioned in skirmishes near Christiana, Tenn., March, 1863. (336, 340, 343, 346) Mentioned in Federal reports, near Murfreesboro, Middleton and Fosterville.

Vol. XXIII, Part 2—(677, 847) Mentioned by Colonel Prather and Gen. W. T. Martin. (943) In Hagan's brigade, Wheeler's corps, Bragg's army, July 31, 1863. (960) Commanded by Maj. A. H. Johnson, in Morgan's brigade, Wheeler's corps, August 10th.

No. 40—(738) Asked for by General Lee, April 20, 1863. (741) April 21st, Gen. S. Cooper says he thinks regiment will be sent to General Lee.

No. 42—(554) Governor Watts writes to General Polk that General Clanton "as the commander of the First Alabama, gained the most enviable fame as a gallant, dashing officer, before, after and at the battle of Shiloh." Senator R. W. Walker concurs as to character of General Clanton. (556) Mentioned by General Clanton in letter to General Polk, May 9, 1863.

No. 45—(886) Mentioned by General Lee, June 13, 1863.

No. 50—(232) In Hagan's brigade, Wheeler's corps, October 7, 1863.

No. 51—(19) Commanded by Lieut.-Col. D. T. Blakey, in Morgan's brigade, Wheeler's corps, Chickamauga campaign.

No. 52—(332) With General Wheeler, September 3, 1863, on the road to Trenton. (449) Gen. James S. Negley (Union) reports from Fowler's farm, September 8th, that this regiment is with General Wheeler, near Lafayette.

No. 53—(500) In Hagan's brigade, Wheeler's corps, August 15, 1863.

No. 54—(453) In Morgan's brigade, with General Longstreet, November, 1863.

No. 56—(619) In General Martin's division, Wheeler's corps, Bragg's army, October 31, 1863. (891) In Russell's brigade, Longstreet's army, December 31st.

No. 58—(634) Mentioned by General Longstreet, January 30, 1864. (642) Commanded by Col. W. W. Allen, in Russell's brigade, Longstreet's army, January 31st.

No. 59—(870) Commanded by Maj. A. H. Johnson, in Morgan's brigade, Wheeler's corps, April 30th.

No. 73—(819, 820, 822) Mentioned by Colonel Minty (Union), near Marietta, Ga., June 11, 1864; at Noonday Creek, June 21st.

No. 74—(642, et seq.) In Morgan's brigade, Wheeler's corps, April 30, 1864; in Allen's brigade, June to August. (962) Report of Col. D. T. Blakey, of the First Alabama cavalry, operations August 31, 1864.

No. 75—(436) Doing picket duty at Big Shanty, statement of A. B. Thornton, scout, June 8, 1864.

No. 78—(588) Letter from General Clanton to General Polk, May 9, 1864. (856) In Allen's brigade, Wheeler's corps, September 20th.

No. 99 — (352) Mentioned by General Kilpatrick (Union), Williston, S. C., February 8, 1865. (1071) Col. David T. Blakey, Hagan's brigade. Wheeler's corps, January 31st. (1275) Detachment under Capt. B. Kavanaugh ordered to move toward Jones' Ferry and thence toward Unionville, S. C., February 25th, by order of General Stewart.

THE SECOND ALABAMA CAVALRY.

The Second Alabama cavalry was organized at Montgomery in May, 1862; was in north Alabama for a short time and was then sent to Florida, where it was employed for a time; sent to Jackson, Miss., in April, 1863, and fought Grierson; was employed in Mississippi until October of that year, when it was sent to northern Alabama and Tennessee. It was in Chalmers' brigade continuously after August, 1863. In General Wheeler's cavalry corps, this regiment did arduous duty in the Dalton-Atlanta campaign, losing heavily in the battle of July 22d before Atlanta. It skirmished in Sherman's rear, fighting almost daily, and followed him to Greensboro, N. C.; it formed part of the escort of President Davis to Georgia, where it surrendered at Forsyth, 450 strong. It was commanded for a short time by Col. J. S. Prather, succeeded by Capt. R. G. Earle, who, after his promotion, was killed at Kingston, Ga. It was successively commanded by Lieut.-Cols. J. P. West and J. N. Carpenter, both of whom had risen from the rank of captain. Capt. Wm. L. Allen died in the service. Capt. J. W. Whisenant was wounded at Kenesaw, Capt. James A. Andrews at Nickajack, Capt. Wm. P. Ashley at Decatur, Ga.

EXTRACTS FROM OFFICIAL WAR RECORDS.
Vol. XVI, Part 1—(729) Mentioned in Colonel Milliken's (Union) report of skirmishes near Russellville, Ala., July, 1862, two companies of Second Alabama cavalry.

Vol. XVI, Part 2—(767) General Bragg's order, No. 121, Chattanooga, Tenn., August 21, 1862, says: "A portion of our cavalry, consisting of the companies of Captains Earle, Lewis and Roddey, led by Captain Roddey, has made another brilliant dash upon a superior force of the enemy, resulting in their utter discomfiture and the capture of 123 prisoners. The judgment and prudence of the previous dispositions exhibited high military skill. The vigor and boldness of the attack is a striking example of the spirit that now animates our cavalry and which is fast making them the terror of our invaders."

Vol. XXIII, Part 1—(136, 137) Mentioned by R. W. Johnson, March, 1863, and in Col. Fielder A. Jones' report; Col. J. S. Prather commanding.

No. 36—(535, 536) Mentioned in Col. C. R. Barteau's report, Grierson's raid from La Grange, Tenn., April 22, 1863. (560-580) Mentioned in Gen. Daniel Ruggles' report of May 13th. (690) Commended in General Ruggles' report of action at King's Creek, near Tupelo, Miss. (691) Col. J. Cunningham, in his report of action at King's creek, May 5th, says: "Two killed." (692) Mentioned by Maj. W. A. Hewlett, May 5th. (693) Mentioned in Col. C. R. Barteau's report of King's Creek, May 8th.

No. 37—(483) General Ruggles, in his report of fight at Rocky Crossing, Tallahatchee river, June 20, 1863, says: "Col. C. R. Barteau's Second Tennessee, Col. William Boyle's First Alabama, and R. H. Earle's Second Alabama regiments of cavalry vied with each other in pressing the enemy home."

No. 38—(291) Gen. G. M. Dodge, May 9, 1863, says: "The Second Alabama arrived at Okolona from Pensacola." (326) Mentioned as near Okolona, May 18th. (733) Maj. W. M. Inge's battalion ordered to report to Brigadier-General Chalmers, April 10th. (796) Col. C. R. Barteau, April 27th, says: "Ordered from Aberdeen to Buena Vista." (803) Gen. J. C. Pemberton says: "Just arrived at Jackson, Miss., April 29th. (835) Gen. S. B. Buckner, May 5th, says: "I sent the Second Alabama cavalry to General Pemberton to aid in covering northern Mississippi and Alabama." (917) The Second Alabama cavalry at Prairie Mound, Miss., May 24th. (973) Mentioned by General Ruggles, June 22d.

No. 53—(5) With General Ferguson at New Albany, Miss., October 1, 1863. (559) In Ferguson's brigade, August 27th, 949 strong. (576, 577) Mentioned in Gen. S. D. Lee's report of September 1st. (582) Mentioned by Gen. E. S. Ewell. (724) Ordered to move at once to the vicinity of Cherry creek and there await further orders from the major-general commanding, October 2d.

No. 54—(37, 38) Mentioned by Gen. S. W. Ferguson, October 31, 1863, as commanded by Colonel Earle near Courtland, Ala.

No. 56—(728) Under Col. R. G. Earle in Ferguson's brigade, Chalmers' division, November 20, 1863. (866) In Ferguson's brigade cavalry, in Mississippi, commanded by Gen. Stephen D. Lee, December 24th; Lieut.-Col. J. P. West commanding regiment.

No. 57—(333) Under Colonel Earle in Ferguson's brigade, Polk's army, February 20, 1864. (378) Mentioned by Gen. S. W. Ferguson.

No. 59—(605, 660, 864) In Ferguson's brigade, Jackson's division, General Polk's army, spring, 1864, No. 74—(646, 654, 660, 666) Under Lieut.-Col. John N. Carpenter, June 10, 1864; in Ferguson's brigade, army of Mississippi. July 31st, Ferguson's brigade, army of Tennessee.

No. 78—(857) September 20, 1864, in Ferguson's brigade, army of Tennessee.

No. 99—(1072) January 31, 1865, in Ferguson's brigade, Iverson's division, Wheeler's corps, department of South Carolina, Georgia and Florida; General Hardee commanding.

THE THIRD ALABAMA CAVALRY.

The Third Alabama cavalry was organized at Tupelo, June, 1862, and was formed of companies which had already seen hard service, some of them, as Murphy's battalion, at Shiloh. It was brigaded at various times under Generals Hagan, Morgan, Russell and Allen. It accompanied the army of Tennessee into Kentucky, where it was engaged in continual and arduous duty, protecting the flank and rear, watching communications, and raiding upon the enemy. It was engaged at Perryville, Murfreesboro, Shelbyville, Kingston and Knoxville. This regiment took a brilliant part in the famous Sequatchee raid. In the Dalton-Atlanta campaign it was continuously engaged in protecting Hood's movements and harassing Sherman's troops. It fought at Decatur, Ga., and assisted in the capture of Stoneman's column. It also took part in the fights about Macon, Aiken, Fayetteville, Bentonville, Raleigh and Chapel Hill, finally surrendering in North Carolina. Its first colonel, James Hagan, was several times wounded, and was promoted to the rank of brigadier-general. Captain Robins, who afterward became colonel, was wounded near Fayetteville. Capt. T. H. Mauldin commanded the regiment for a long time; finally resigned with the rank of lieutenant-colonel. Capt. J. D. Parish, who was wounded several times, also rose to the rank of lieutenant-colonel. Capt. William Cathy was killed at Perryville, Capt. Thomas Norris at Chapel Hill, and Capt. Thomas Lenoir at Resaca. Capt. Augustus Tomlinson died in the service.

EXTRACTS FROM OFFICIAL WAR RECORDS.
Vol. X, Part 1—(468, 469) General Bragg's report, Shiloh, says: "It would be a pleasing duty to record the deeds of many other noble soldiers, but as subordinate officers have done so in their reports, a repetition is unnecessary. I shall be pardoned for making an exception in the case of Capt. R. W. Smith, commanding a company of Alabama cavalry (Third regiment), which served as my personal escort during the action. For personal gallantry and intelligent execution of orders, frequently under the heaviest fire, his example has rarely been equaled. To him, his officers and his men, I feel a deep personal, as well as official, obligation." (531) Report of Capt. A. Tomlinson, Shiloh, says: "Entered the engagement with 57 men. Private McCurdy was shot in the right hand and Corp. W. D. King was wounded in the right arm." Report of Capt. J. Robins says: "Total number of men engaged, 73. My men behaved well, and were willing and ready to obey any order that was given them." These companies belonged to Third cavalry. (855) In Parish's company (Third cavalry), in affair on Monterey road, May 28th and 29th, one wounded; Col. Joseph Wheeler commanding.

Vol. XVI, Part 1—(894-897) Commended in Gen. Jos. Wheeler's report, Kentucky campaign. October 8, 1862, one of the most brilliant charges of the campaign was made in column: "Detachments of the First and Third Alabama cavalry, with the gallant Cols. W. W. Allen and James Hagan, being in advance, throwing the enemy's entire force of cavalry into confusion and putting it to flight. We pursued them at full charge for two miles, capturing many prisoners and horses in single combat, and driving the remaining under cover of their masses of infantry. The enemy also fled, terror-stricken, from a battery placed in advance of their general line and left it at our disposal." (899) Highly commended by General Wheeler. (See notes to First Alabama cavalry.)

Vol. XVI, Part 2—(787) In camp about five miles from Chattanooga. From communication of Gen. Sam Jones, Chattanooga, August 29, 1862. (790) Ordered to Sparta by letters from Lieut.-Col. G. G. Garner, August 29th and 30th. (843) Assigned to left wing of army of Mississippi, by command of General Bragg, September 18th. (844) Ordered by General Hardee to move forward, in direction of Cave City, and feel the enemy, September 18th. (879) Ordered by Col. Joseph Wheeler to be ready to march in one hour, New Haven, Ky., September 26th.

Vol. XVII, Part 2—(663) Mentioned in Gen. Sterling Price's communication, dated Tupelo, Miss., August 4, 1862, in which he states that Colonel Wheeler's command will arrive the following day, when Hagan's regiment will leave at once, en route for Chattanooga. (666) In communication to General Bragg, August 4th, Gen. Sterling Price asks that Hagan's and Wade's cavalry remain at Tupelo, Miss. He says: "I shall move forward immediately, and need more cavalry."

Vol. XX, Part 1—(16) Mentioned in Gen. J. W. Sill's (Union) report, November 26 and 27, 1862, of reconnaissance to La Vergne, Tenn., and skirmish. (642) Mentioned in Lieutenant-Colonel Murray's (Union) report of skirmishes at Franklin, December 26th and 27th, and Overall's creek, December 31st. (661) In Wheeler's brigade; Maj. F. Y. Gaines. (958) Mentioned in General Wheeler's report, December 26th. (961) Report of Capt. T. H. Mauldin, commanding, of skirmishes from December 26, 1862, to January 5, 1863, during which time the regiment lost in killed, wounded and missing, 25 men, including 3 lieutenants. (962) Capt. T. H. Mauldin recommends for promotion, for their gallantry in rallying the regiment and assisting in bringing it out in order from under a galling fire from the enemy's infantry and cavalry combined, on December 31st, Sergt-Maj. H. M. Cooper and Sergt. J. W. Norwood, of Company A.

Vol. XX, Part 2—(432) In army of Tennessee, in Polk's corps, about November 29, 1862, Company G, Capt. D. P. Forney, not brigaded; Withers' division. (448) Special orders: "Captain Forney's company, serving at Withers' division headquarters, will report at once to Brigadier-General Wheeler at La Vergne, by command of General Bragg, December 12th."

Vol. XXIII, Part 1—(140) Mentioned in report of Acting Asst. Adjt.-Gen. R. R. Gaines, March 6, 1863.

Vol. XXIII, Part 2— (456) Gen. A. McD. McCook's (Union) communication, headquarters Twentieth army corps, June 25, 1863, says: "Until the last ten days, a regiment of cavalry (Third Alabama) have been doing all the picket duty in this front." (943) In Hagan's brigade, Martin's division, Wheeler's corps, July 31st. (960) In Morgan's brigade, Martin's division, Wheeler's corps, August 10th.

No. 51—(19) Assignment as above, September 19 and 20, 1863. (71) Mentioned in extract of notes of Chickamauga campaign, Lieut. W. B. Richmond, September 9th. Mauldin with 75 men at Point Lookout; 3 killed, 10 wounded. Mouth of McLemore's cove covered by Mauldin's men.

No. 52—(332) Mentioned in Gen. Robert B. Mitchell's (Union) communication, dated September 3, 1863, Martin's division, Wheeler's cavalry. (449) Mentioned in Gen. J. S. Negley's communication, dated September 8, 1863, as near Lafayette.

No. 53—(500) In Hagan's brigade, Martin's division, Wheeler's corps, August 15, 1863.

No. 54—(453) Commanded by Lieut.-Col. T. H. Mauldin, Morgan's brigade, Martin's division, November 30, 1863. (546) Conspicuous for gallantry in engagement at Russellville, December 10th.—From Gen. W. T. Martin's report of the Knoxville, Tenn., campaign.

No. 56—(891) In Russell's brigade, Morgan's division, Martin's cavalry, Longstreet's force, December 31, 1863.

No. 58—(353) Mentioned, February 7, 1864, in Gen. George H. Thomas' (Union) report, dated Chattanooga, February 8, 1864.

No. 59—(870) In Morgan's brigade, Wheeler's corps, army of Tennessee, commanded by Gen. J. E. Johnston, April 30, 1864.

No. 73—(819-822) Mentioned by Colonel Minty, relative to movements in vicinity of Marietta, Ga., June, 1864.

No. 74—(650, et seq.) Assignments in Atlanta campaign. Col. James Hagan commanding, in Allen's brigade, Wheeler's corps, Johnston's army. (950) In General Wheeler's communication addressed to "Soldiers of the Cavalry Corps," dated June 18, 1864, he says: "The Third Alabama regiment, Colonel Mauldin, having been detached, dashed into Calhoun, defeated the enemy and destroyed a large, heavily-laden train of cars. A detachment also destroyed another large train a short distance north of the town."

No. 99—(1071) In Hagan's brigade, Allen's division, Wheeler's corps, department of South Carolina, Georgia and Florida, Gen. W. J. Hardee, January 31, 1865. (1314) Mentioned as having been sent over to Rocky river road, under Lieutenant-Colonel Robins, March 1st. (1418) Mentioned as having gone on the Smithfield road, March 17th.

Captain Lenoir's company, Alabama cavalry: Vol. XXIII, Part 2— (945) Mentioned, Atlanta, Ga., July 31, 1863, acting as escort, Polk's corps. (958) Lieut. W. J. Lee, escort in Bragg's army, August 10th. No. 51—(15) Capt. T. M. Lenoir, escort General Longstreet, Chickamauga campaign. Nos. 56, 58, 59, 74—(889) Mentioned as escort, Hindman's division, December, 1863, to June, 1864.

Col. S. J. Murphy's battalion, Alabama cavalry, composed of Alabama and Florida companies: No. 42—(130, 131) Total present, 223,

August 1, 1863, in Clanton's brigade, with General Maury. (157) Detachment, Mobile, August 10th, at Hall's mill and Pascagoula. No. 78—(814) Battalion Alabama cadets, under General Gardner, September 3, 1863.

RUSSELL'S FOURTH ALABAMA CAVALRY.

Russell's Fourth Alabama cavalry was organized at Murfreesboro, Tenn., in December, 1862, by the union of General Forrest's original battalion with six companies of the Fourth Alabama battalion and the Russell Rangers, or Fifteenth battalion Tennessee cavalry. It was in the attack on Fort Donelson and was attached, consecutively, to Russell's and Morgan's brigades, serving in the cavalry of the army of Tennessee. It was warmly engaged at Chickamauga, and bore a full share in the operations of Longstreet's campaign in east Tennessee. It took a brilliant part in the Sequatchie raid with four other Alabama regiments of cavalry; was in the Dalton-Atlanta campaign and assisted in the capture of Stoneman's column. When Hood moved into Tennessee, the Fourth was employed for some time in the Tennessee valley. After the battle of Nashville it was assigned to Forrest's corps, and surrendered with his troops at Gainesville. Col. A. A. Russell was twice wounded; he was early placed in command of a brigade, and the regiment was for a long time under command of Lieut.-Col. Jos. M. Hambrick, who was wounded at Calhoun, Ga.; Capt. Thomas W. Hampton was killed at Mossy Creek; Capt Oliver B. Gaston was captured, and died in prison; Capts. Henry F. Smith, W. C. Bacot, Flavlus J. Graham and David Davidson were wounded.

EXTRACTS FROM OFFICIAL WAR RECORDS.
Vol. XVII, Part 1—(593, 594, 595) Gen. N. B. Forrest, in his report of operations, December 18, 1862, says: "Col. A. A. Russell, Fourth Alabama cavalry, and Maj. N. W. Cox, Second battalion Tennessee cavalry, with their commands, were sent out on the left to destroy bridges and culverts on the railroads from Jackson to Corinth and Bolivar. . . . Colonel Russell and his command deserve especial notice for their gallantry in the fight at Lexington and Spring creek. Capt. F. B. Gurley, Fourth Alabama cavalry, with 12 men, charged a gun at Lexington supported by over 100 Federal cavalry. He captured the gun, losing his orderly-sergeant by the fire of the gun when within 15 feet of its muzzle." (598, 599) Col. George G. Dibrell says: "On the 18th December, the enemy attempted to destroy the bridge at Beech river, but were driven back by the Fourth Alabama.

Vol. XVII, Part 2—(462) Mentioned by Thomas A. Davies (Union), Columbus, Ky., December 23, 1862, as 450 strong.

Vol. XXIII, Part 1—(135) Mentioned by Gen. D. S. Stanley (Union), near Shelbyville, March 4, 1863. (379) Report of Gen. J. B. Turchin (Union) says: "200 of Russell's cavalry near Versailles, June 12th."

Vol. XXIII, Part 2,—(913) Gen. H. W. Walter, Chattanooga, July

15, 1863, says: "The Fourth regiment Alabama cavalry is especially detailed, and will report to Brigadier-General Pillow for duty." (943) In Russell's brigade, Martin's division, Bragg's army, July 31st.

No. 50—(232) Hagan's brigade, Wharton's division, Wheeler's corps, Chickamauga campaign.

No. 51—(19) Col. J. M. Hambrick commanding; in Russell's brigade, Martin's division, Wheeler's corps, army of Tennessee, September 19 and 20, 1863. (659) In skirmish near Larkinsville, Ala., September 25th. (688) Mentioned by Gen. George Crook (Union) in report of operations during October. (693) Mentioned in report of Col. Abram O. Miller, fights of October 3d, near McMinnville.

No. 52—(255) Mentioned by J. L. Abernathy (Union), in Trenton, August 31, 1863. (332) By Robert B. Mitchell (Union) as in Martin's division, on road to Trenton, September 3d. (449) By James S. Negley (Union) as near Lafayette, September 8th.

No. 53—(500) In Russell's brigade, Martin's division, Wheeler's corps, army of Tennessee, August 15, 1863. (545) Scouts ordered to rejoin their commands, August 24th. (632) Mentioned in General Hindman's general orders, September 10th.

No. 54—(445) Mentioned by Col. Wm. J. Palmer (Union), Flat Gap, December 23, 1863. (453) Gen. John T. Morgan's brigade, Martin's division; troops in east Tennessee, under General Longstreet, November 30th.

No. 56—(891) In Russell's brigade, Morgan's division, forces in east Tennessee, December 31, 1863.

No. 58—(642) Same assignment under General Longstreet, January 31, 1864.

No. 59—(283) Col. Jos. S. Gage (Union), Cottonville, Ala., says: "The Fourth regiment, Alabama cavalry, 900 men strong, arrived at Warrenton on the night of April 5, 1864, a part of Wheeler's command from Blue Hills." (870) In Morgan's brigade, Martin's division, army of Tennessee, Johnston commanding, April 30, 1864.

No. 73—(819) Mentioned by Colonel Minty (Union), near Marietta, Ga., June 12, 1864. (822) In front of enemy, Noonday Creek, Ga., June 21st.

No, 74—(642, et seq.) In Morgan's brigade, Martin's division, army of Tennessee, Atlanta campaign.

No. 75—(756) Mentioned by Gen. G. J. Pillow, June 2, 1864.

No. 78—(718) Gen. S. W. Melton says: "The four Alabama companies in McDonald's battalion are hereby transferred to Russell's Alabama regiment." (856) In Allen's brigade, Martin's division, army of Tennessee, General Hood commanding, September 20, 1864.

No. 93—(574, 609, 640) Mentioned by Federal officers: "Near Waterloo, Ala., January 4, 1865"; "Russell has 700 or 800 men," December 8, 1864. (775, 776) Report of Col. A. A. Russell of operations, October 26, 1864, to January 17, 1865, says: "After the evacuation of Decatur, my command pursued the retreating enemy from Huntsville to within fourteen miles of Stevenson (distance, forty-five miles), capturing about 450 negroes and 250 wagons, 1 train of cars and engine. My loss, 1 killed, 2 wounded." (1245) General Hood orders Russell's regiment to join Roddey's force and assist in the work of destroying the railroad from Decatur to Huntsville and thence to Stevenson, November 25, 1864.

No. 94—(521) Mentioned in report of Col. William Palmer (Union), January 5, 1865. (796) General Chalmers' orders, Fourth and Seventh consolidated, January 19th.

No. 103—(46) In skirmish near Gurley's Tank, February 16, 1865. (931) By order of Brigadier-General Chalmers, near Buena Vista, January 24th: "Captain Alexander, Fourth Alabama cavalry, will report with his command to Colonel Wheeler, commanding First Tennessee cavalry, at Columbus, or wherever he may be." (997) General Forrest ordered Colonel Russell to camp near Columbus. (1031) Ordered to Montevallo, March, 1865.

RODDEY'S FOURTH ALABAMA CAVALRY.

Roddey's Fourth Alabama was organized at Tuscumbia in October, 1862, and was sent to middle Tennessee, where it wintered, but early in the spring was sent into north Alabama. It met Dodge's advance below Tuscumbia, and was engaged in the pursuit of Streight. It was engaged most of the time in Roddey's brigade, repelling raids in north Alabama and making daring attacks. It was publicly commended in April, 1863, by General Bragg, for good discipline, etc. In the spring of 1864 it was transferred to the department of Alabama, Mississippi and East Louisiana, and fought with severe loss at Tishomingo in June, 1864. It repelled Wilson's raid, fighting all the way from Montevallo to Selma, where a large portion of the regiment was captured. Its first colonel, P. D. Roddey, was early in the war made a brigadier, and was succeeded in the command by Col. William A. Johnson, who led the regiment the greater part of the war; Lieutenant-Colonel Windes being for a short time in command. Colonel Johnson was wounded at Pulaski. Maj. Dick Johnson was killed near Moulton, Capt. James Williams at Courtland, and Capt. Thomas Williams near Huntsville. Capt. John C. Nelson was wounded and captured.

EXTRACTS FROM OFFICIAL WAR RECORDS.

Vol. XXIII, Part 2—(246) Gen. G. M. Dodge (Union) reports Colonel Roddey's regiment, 800 strong, at Tuscumbia landing, April 17, 1863. (708) Mentioned by Gen. John A. Wharton, March 18, 1863. Letter from Col. P. D. Roddey, Chapel Hill. (720, 721) Gen. J. A. Wharton, March 18th, says: "Part of regiment ordered to advance to College Grove." Letter from Colonel Roddey, Chapel Hill, March 22d. (728) General Bragg's order, March 28th, says: "Col. P. D. Roddey's regiment of Alabama cavalry is detached from Brigadier-General Martin's division, and will proceed to northern Alabama.

On his arrival at the Tennessee river, Colonel Roddey will relieve Brig.-Gen. S. A. M. Wood, in command of the district of Northern Alabama. (731) Letter from Colonel Roddey, Chapel Hill, March 31, 1863. (737) General orders, No. 69, headquarters army of Tennessee, April 2, 1863: "The general commanding is gratified at the inspection report of Colonels Roddey and Patterson's regiments of cavalry, made by Lieutenant-Colonel Grenfell, inspector of cavalry. The officers and men of these regiments were found to be zealous in the performance of their respective duties, the discipline was excellent, and the conduct of the men toward the citizens in the neighborhood of their camp was most praiseworthy. The arms were in good condition, and the clothing of the men neat and uniform. The general commanding tenders his thanks to Colonels Roddey and Patterson and the gallant officers and men of their commands for the interest manifested by them in perfecting their discipline and increasing their efficiency." (944) Col. W. A. Johnson, Roddey's brigade, Wheeler's corps, Bragg's army, July 31st.

No. 37—(674) Mentioned by Colonel Hatch (Union) in skirmishes on Forked Deer river, Tenn., July 13, 1863.

No. 38—(192) Roddey's regiment, 800 strong, with General Roddey at Tuscumbia, Ala., April, 1863. (614) In Roddey's brigade, Martin's division, Major-General Van Dorn's corps, February 2d.

No. 53—(501) In Roddey's brigade, Morgan's division, Wheeler's corps, army of Tennessee, August 15, 1863.

No. 54—(593, 594, 604) Mentioned in Federal reports.

No. 55—(664) In Roddey's brigade, detached, Wheeler's corps, Bragg's army, November 20, 1863.

No. 58—(237) W. A. Johnson's troops fight on Lamb's Ferry road, January, 1864. (339) Opposite Florence, February 6th. (590) In Roddey's brigade, Wharton's division, Wheeler's corps, army of Tennessee, Johnston commanding, January 20th.

No. 59—(389, 735) In north Alabama, April, 1864.

No. 74—(642) Roddey's brigade transferred to department Alabama, Mississippi and East Louisiana, April, 1864.

No. 77—(231) Nine wounded in battle of Tishomingo Creek, June 10, 1864. (544) General Forrest says: "Colonel Johnson and his brave troops on this occasion acted with conspicuous gallantry in marching up and assaulting the enemy's works." Report of Sulphur Springs Trestle, September 25th. (545, 547, 549) Colonel Johnson's troops mentioned in same report. "Colonel Johnson displayed every soldierly virtue. He was prompt in obeying orders. I regret to say that while gallantly leading his troops he was severely wounded."

No. 79—(278, 450) Between Fort Deposit and Guntersville, October, 1864.

No. 93—(641, 642) In north Alabama under Lieutenant-Colonel Windes, June 10, 1865. (1233) In Roddey's brigade, district of North Alabama, November 20, 1864.

No. 94—(634) Assignment as above; Maj.-Gen. D. H. Maury commanding department, December 1, 1864.

No. 103—(510, 1031) Ordered to Montevallo, March, 1865.

Williams' Battalion: No. 59—(429) In north Alabama, April 18, 1864. (735) Mentioned by R. W. Walker as near Moulton, March 26th. No. 77—(231) One killed, 5 wounded, at the battle of Tishomingo Creek, June 10, 1864. No. 99—(1150) Mentioned by Maj. John Devereux as having been originally in Hannon's command.

Julian's Battalion, Alabama Cavalry: Vol. XXIII, Part 2—(961) In Roddey's brigade, General Wheeler's corps, August 10, 1863. No. 53—(501) Same.

Newsom's company. Vol. XVI, Part 1—(828) Mentioned and commended by Brig.-Gen. T. C. Armstrong in report of skirmish near Courtland, July 25, 1862. No. 58—(614) In Bell's brigade, Forrest's cavalry, January 25, 1864.

THE FIFTH ALABAMA CAVALRY.

This regiment was organized at Tuscumbia in December, 1862, and was sent into middle Tennessee, where it began a brilliant career by skirmishes at Chapel Hill. After serving a short time in Martin's brigade, it was transferred to Roddey's, and served continuously during the war. It was in Florida for a short time during the fall of 1863, but much of its service was in northern Alabama and vicinity. It captured a wagon-train at Hamburg, 60 prisoners and a train at Hunt's Mill, and 130 prisoners at Madison Station. It blocked the railroad in Rosecrans' rear, fought General Long at Moulton, stampeded a regiment at Oak hill, and accompanied General Forrest on his Pulaski raid. It skirmished with Steedman as he marched into the Tennessee valley, and fought Wilson all the way from Montevallo to Selma, where it took part in the defense of the city. The greater part of the regiment surrendered at Selma, the remainder at Danville, Morgan county. Col. Josiah Patterson creditably commanded the regiment till the close of the war.

EXTRACTS FROM OFFICIAL WAR RECORDS.

Vol. XXIII, Part 1—(240) Mentioned by General Steedman (Union), April 15, 1863, as at Chapel Hill.

Vol. XXIII, Part 2—(362) Mentioned by Gen. J. M. Brannan, May 25, 1863, Chapel Hill. (708) Sent to College Grove to support party sent out by General Wharton, March 18, 1863. (737) General Bragg tenders his thanks to Colonel Roddey and Colonel Patterson, and the gallant officers and men of their commands, for the interest manifested by them in perfecting their discipline and increasing their efficiency. (841) Detached from General Martin's brigade to join General Roddey's, Tullahoma, May 18th. (944, 961) In Roddey's brigade, Wheeler's corps, August, 1863.

No. 41 — (746) Mentioned by Capt. M. M. Young (Union), Barrancas, Fla., September 9, 1863; members of regiment arrested at house of Spanish consul.

No. 42—(130) Total present, 372; sent to General Johnston, August 1, 1863.

Nos. 53, 55, 56—In Roddey's brigade, Wheeler's corps, August to December, 1863.

No. 57—(119) At Athens, Ala., January 26, 1864. (685) On Moulton road, April 24th. No. 58—(590) Roddey's brigade, Wheeler's corps, January 20th. No. 75—(756) Mentioned by General Pillow, Talladega, June 2d.

No. 58—(515) Mentioned in petition from Alabama members and senators for increase of Roddey's force on Tennessee river, January, 1864.

No. 59—(429) In north Alabama, April, 1864, mentioned by Col. Richard Rowett (Union). (609) Six companies Forrest's regiment, under Captain Warren, ordered to Marion county, Ala., to protect foundries, etc., March 10th. No. 77—(231) One killed, 3 wounded, in the battle of Tishomingo Creek, June 10, 1864.

No. 77—(362) Mentioned in report of Col. William T. C. Grower, skirmish at Pond Spring, Ala., July 26, 1864.

No. 78—(668) Report of Colonel Patterson, Pond Spring, Ala., June 27th.

No. 93—(1233) Commanded by Lieut.-Col. James M. Warren, in Roddey's brigade, with Gen. Richard Taylor, November 20th.

No. 94 — (634) In Roddey's brigade, with General Maury, December 1st.

No. 103—(455) Mentioned in report of Colonel Vail (Union), Bogler's creek, April 1st, and taking of Selma, April 2, 1865, as Patterson's regiment. (472) Mentioned in report of General Upton (Union), "Patterson's regiment passed through Elyton," about March 28th.

THE SIXTH ALABAMA CAVALRY.

The Sixth Alabama cavalry was organized early in 1863, and formed a part of Clanton's brigade. It served in Florida and was first engaged at Pollard. Ordered to north Alabama, it took part in the skirmishes near Decatur and in the Atlanta-Dalton campaign. It fought Rousseau at Ten Islands, where it lost heavily in killed and captured. Transferred to west Florida, it fought Steele at Bluff Springs, and also Wilson's column in south Alabama, laying down its arms at Gainesville.

EXTRACTS FROM OFFICIAL WAR RECORDS.

No. 42—(131-511) In Clanton's brigade, Western division, department of the Gulf, General Maury commanding, August 1, 1863. August

10th, Montgomery, Ala.; at Pollard, September 19th. (562) In Jenifer's brigade, army of Mobile, December 31, 1863.

No. 57—(333) Transferred to north Alabama, February, 1864.

No. 58—(550) Mentioned by Gen. D. H. Maury, January 12, 1864. (651) Ordered to report to General Clanton at Gadsden, from Meridian, Miss., February 1st.

No. 59—(214) At Tennessee river, near Decatur, April 1, 1864. (450) Near Danville, Ala., April 22d.

No. 73—(906) Lieutenant-Colonel Lary and Major McWhorter captured at Ten Islands, Coosa river, August 14, 1864.

No. 74—(646) In Armstrong's brigade, army of Mississippi, June 10, 1864. (653) Transferred to Clanton's brigade, June 30th. (677) In Jackson's division, army of Mississippi, June 10th.

No. 75—(756) Mentioned by Gen. G. J. Pillow, June 2, 1864.

No. 78—(691) Capt. George Goldthwaite, Blue Mountain, June 7, 1864, says: "Lieutenant-Colonel Lary commanding regiment"

No. 93—(1233) Commanded by Lieut.-Col. Charles H. Colvin, Clanton's brigade, department of Alabama, Mississippi and East Louisiana; Lieut.-Gen. Richard Taylor commanding, November 20, 1864.

No. 94—(634) In Clanton's brigade, district of Central Alabama, Brig.-Gen. D. W. Adams, December 1, 1864.

No. 103—(71) Mentioned by General Asboth (Union), Barrancas, February 26, 1865. (280, 281) Mentioned by General Steele (Union), operations near Blakely, Ala., March 11th to April 9th. (302, 308) Mentioned in report of operations near Escambia river, March 25th. (713, 834) February 25th, at Canoe Station, 700 strong, Colonel Colvin commanding. (1047) Commanded by Lieut.-Col. W. T. Lary, in Clanton's brigade, with General Maury, March 10th.

No. 104—(118) Mentioned as near Big Escambia bridge, March 27, 1865. (226) In Clanton's brigade.

THE SEVENTH ALABAMA CAVALRY.

The Seventh Cavalry was organized in July, 1863, as part of Clanton's brigade, and served for more than a year in Quarles', Clanton's, Page's, Patton's and Thomas' brigades, in the vicinity of Pensacola and the bay forts. In the fall of 1864, it reported to General Forrest at Corinth, and took part in the raid on Johnsonville and the fighting as Hood moved toward Nashville. It suffered severely at this time, especially in the night attack on Brentwood. The regiment, after recruiting, joined General Buford at Montevallo in March, 1865; confronted Wilson's corps from Benton to Girard, and took part in the last fighting of the war, surrendering at Gainesville, May 14, 1865. Col. Joseph Hodgson led the regiment throughout the war, though detachments were at various times commanded with brilliant success by Maj. Turner Clanton, Jr.,

Captain Ledyard, and others. Capt. Charles P. Storrs was wounded at Columbia; Adjt. William T. Charles was captured at one time, but escaped. Colonel Hodgson, after the close of the war, devoted himself to journalism, in which he became quite distinguished, and he was at one time State superintendent of education.

EXTRACTS FROM OFFICIAL WAR RECORDS.

No. 42—(239, 240) Mentioned in Gen. James H. Clanton's report of brigade organization, Pollard, Ala., September 19, 1863. (334) Gen. D. H. Maury, Mobile, October 17th, speaks very highly of Hodgson's regiment. (403) November 10, 1863, Quarles' brigade, department of the Gulf. (511, 561, 562) December, 1863, in Clanton's (Second) brigade; detachment in Higgins' (Third) brigade.

No. 58—(582) January 20, 1864, in Clanton's brigade.

No. 59—(861) April 30, 1864, four companies under Maj. Turner Clanton, Jr., in Page's brigade, district of the Gulf; detachment under Colonel Hodgson, Reynolds' brigade.

No. 65—(386-425) Mentioned in reports of General Asboth (Union), skirmish near Barrancas, April 4, 1864. Companies G, E and I of the Seventh at Camp Gonzales, July 22d. "Three companies left at Fifteen-mile Station," July 28th.

No. 66—(257) August 24, 1864, "Seventh cavalry at Pine Barren bridge."

No. 77—(873) Cadet company mentioned by General Chalmers, in referring to attack on Federal gunboats, October 30, 1864. (875) Specially commended in same letter for conduct opposite Johnsonville, November 4, 1864.

No. 78—(677, 678) June 30, 1864, effective total present, 451. (703) Two companies in Page's brigade at Bay forts, July 10th. (752) August 3, 1864, in Patton's brigade; two companies in Page's brigade. (814) September 3, 1864, Thomas' brigade, district of the Gulf, Gen. Franklin Gardner's forces. (874) Ordered, September 25th, to report to General Chalmers at Verona, Miss. (877) Colonel Hodgson ordered, September 26th, to stop his regiment at Egypt, and move it across to Panola. (879) September 27th, ordered to send four companies, under a field officer, to Corinth; bring rest to Panola. (885) Captain Ledyard, commanding, reports eight companies at Meridian, Miss., September 29th. (887) September 30th, Thomas' brigade, department of the Gulf, en route for Grenada, Miss.

No. 93—(760) Return of casualties for November, 1864, 2 killed, 28 wounded. (761) One killed, 12 wounded, December, 1864. (765) December 14, 1864, mentioned in report of General Chalmers as on Charlotte pike. (767) Commended in General Chalmers' report, especially in engagements of December 15th and 16th. Casualties from November 23 to December 6,

1864, 2 killed, 36 wounded. (1234) November 20, 1864, in Bell's brigade, Forrest's cavalry corps.

No. 94—(127) Information regarding movements of the Seventh near Bridgeport, December 7, 1864. (751) January 1, 1865, mentioned in orders. (796) Mentioned by General Chalmers in general orders, January 19, 1865.

No. 97—(786) Directed to Cherokee by command of Lieutenant-General Taylor, October 3, 1864.

No. 103—(997) Mentioned in General Forrest's orders, dated West Point, February 20, 1865. (1031) General Forrest says: "Have ordered Seventh to Montevallo," March 6th.

No. 104—(364) Mentioned in report of Captain Eaton (Union), Mobile, April 15, 1865.

THE EIGHTH ALABAMA CAVALRY.

The Eighth Cavalry was organized at Newbern, in April, 1864, by adding a company to Hatch's battalion which had already entered the service. It was ordered at once to Blue Mountain, and served under General Pillow. It took part in the fight at Ten Islands, August 14, 1864. In Armistead's brigade it lost heavily at Lafayette and Rome, Ga., and was transferred to west Florida, where it confronted Steele as he advanced on Pollard; was in several fights of minor importance, and finally surrendered at Gainesville. Col. Charles P. Ball was frequently in command of a cavalry brigade, and the regiment was led at times by Lieut.-Col. Lemuel D. Hatch and Maj. W. T. Poe. The regiment lost many gallant officers. Maj. R. H. Redwood and Capt. C. E. England were killed at Lafayette; Capt. G. S. Perrin was killed at Pine Barren creek; Capt. W. H. Lawrence was killed at Rome. At the battle of Lafayette, Ga., First Lieut. S. S. Johnson was killed. Captains Harrison and Rodes were captured, and Captain Harrison, Lieutenant McLemore, Sergeant White and Private Green were reported as conspicuous for gallantry.

EXTRACTS FROM OFFICIAL WAR RECORDS.

No. 59—(734, 735) Hatch's cavalry battalion, 150 strong, were ordered by General Polk, from Tuscaloosa, March 25, 1864, on a scouting expedition to the northern part of Alabama.

No. 73—(906) Mentioned in General Rousseau's report of fight at Ten Islands, August 14, 1864.

No. 74—(997) Gen. Gid. J. Pillow in his report of the engagement at Lafayette, Ga., June 24, 1864, says: "After Colonel Armistead was wounded, the command of his brigade devolved upon Colonel Ball, whose gallantry and skill in command were all that I could expect or wish.". Seven killed, 18 wounded at Lafayette, Ga., June 24, 1864. (998-999) Col. C. G. Armistead says: "To Col. C. P. Ball the command is greatly indebted for the good order and promptness with which it carried itself in the fight. By the death of Major Redwood, and the wounding of Lieutenant-Colonel Hatch, he was thrown entirely upon his own resources in maintaining the good order and efficiency of his command and the discipline of his troops." (1000-1002) Col. Charles P. Ball in his report says: "After a short but severe conflict, I succeeded in driving the enemy. I moved forward to the court house and gave the order to charge. This was nobly and gallantly done. The enemy opened a destructive fire from the court house, jail, and other buildings, which caused the line to fall back to cover, but it was soon rallied. In this charge the Ninth (Eighth) Alabama lost two gallant officers, Capt. C. E. England, Company E, and First Lieut. S. S. Johnston, commanding Company F, the former wounded, the latter killed, within twenty steps of the court house. Lieutenant-Colonel Hatch was wounded while gallantly leading his regiment. He, however, remained upon the field. Where all acted so gallantly it is hard to discriminate, but I cannot close without calling attention to Captain Harrison, Company H, Ninth (Eighth) Alabama, who was wounded and left in the hands of the enemy (where the fight was thickest, there he was); Lieutenant McLemore, Company D, Ninth (Eighth) Alabama, for conspicuous gallantry and good service; First Sergeant White, Company C, and Private Green, Company G, for their coolness and courage, being the only ones who followed to the court house. I regret having to mention the death of Maj. R. H. Redwood, Ninth (Eighth) Alabama."

No. 75 — (655) Mentioned by Major Douglas West, Demopolis, May 1, 1864. (691) Mentioned in Gen. S. D. Lee's army, 322 effective, May 10, 1864.

No. 78—(613) Ordered to Selma, May 21, 1864. (646) June 10th, under General Pillow. (791) Commanded by Lieut.-Col. L. D. Hatch, Armistead's brigade, district of Central and Northern Alabama, August 21st. (812) Present for duty 334, Talladega, Ala., September 1st, under Maj. W. T. Poe; Colonel Ball commanding cavalry force.

Nos. 93, 94—In Armistead's brigade, district of Central Alabama, to December, 1864.

No. 103—(281) Mentioned in report of Major-General Steele, April 12, 1865. (1047) Col. Charles P. Ball commanding, in Armistead's brigade, Maury's army, March 10th.

LIVINGSTON'S EIGHTH ALABAMA CAVALRY.

This regiment was organized at Gadsden, Ala., and ordered to Blue Mountain in July, 1864. It operated in the vicinity of the army of Tennessee around Dalton, and was with General Pillow for several months, when it was transferred to Clanton's brigade. It fought at Ten Islands, was sent to west Florida, and fought Steele's column at Bluff Spring with heavy loss. It then fought Wilson's corps as he advanced, and finally surrendered at Gainesville.

Capt. John Moore was killed at Ten Islands; Capt. J. F. Watson was killed near Pollard; Capt. T. J. Atkinson was wounded near Decatur and near Guntersville. This regiment was often called the Ninth, and is sometimes confused with Malone's Ninth, or Hatch's Eighth.

EXTRACTS FROM OFFICIAL WAR RECORDS.

No. 58—(651) General Clanton ordered to establish headquarters at Gadsden, Ala., and complete organization of the Eighth, February 1, 1864.

No. 75—(760) June 5, 1864, Col. Henry J. Livingston, with 200 to 250 men, ordered by General Pillow from Montevallo to Blue Mountain.

No. 78—(636) June 5, 1864, General Pillow ordered regiment, 200 to 250 strong, from Montevallo to Blue Mountain. (681) Ordered to Blue Mountain, July 1st. (791) In Clanton's brigade with General Adams, August 21st.

Nos. 93, 94—In Clanton's brigade with General Taylor, November and December, 1864.

No. 103—(302-308) Mentioned in front of the Union lines in operations March 25, April 9 and June 6, 1865, near Escambia river. (834) Six hundred strong, February 25th. (1047) Under Lieut.-Col. Thomas L. Faulkner, in Clanton's brigade with General Maury, March 10th.

No. 104—(118-226) Mentioned in Union reports, March and April, 1865.

THE NINTH ALABAMA CAVALRY.

The Ninth cavalry (also called Seventh) was formed near Tullahoma, May, 1863, by consolidating Malone's and Z. Thomason's battalions. It was in Wheeler's corps during the entire war.

It first served in Wharton's division until December, 1863, and was in many skirmishes. It was then brigaded under Morgan, Russell, Allen and Hagan, and was constantly engaged in skirmishing. It suffered severely at Shelbyville and in protecting Longstreet's corps. It was in the pursuit of Sherman during 1864 and 1865, and finally surrendered in North Carolina There were many casualties among its officers. Col. James C. Malone was wounded in Tennessee and at Noonday Creek. Lieut.-Col. Z. Thomason, Maj. Thomas H. Malone and Capt. S. S. Clayton were captured at Shelbyville. Adjt. William H. Binford died in the service. Capt. S. P. Dobbs was wounded at Shelbyville and in Georgia. Capt. James M. Robinson was wounded and captured; Capt. John B. Floyd was wounded at Noonday Creek; Capt. William E. Thompson was wounded in Tennessee and at Calhoun; Capt. Robert W. Figg was wounded at Dover; Capt. George Mason, who commanded the regiment in the summer of 1864, was wounded at Atlanta; Capt. James M. Stevenson was killed at Dover, Capt. William E. Wayland at Rome, and Capt. James E. Nance in South Carolina.

EXTRACTS FROM OFFICIAL WAR RECORDS.

Fourteenth Battalion cavalry, merged in Ninth cavalry regiment: Vol. XVII, Parts—(835) Two hundred and ten present for duty, January 14, 1863, headquarters Shelbyville, Wharton's cavalry brigade. Vol. XX, Part 1—(661) Lieut.-Col. James C. Malone, Wharton's brigade, Wheeler's corps, Stone's river campaign. (966) Mentioned by General Wharton, Stone's river campaign, in Colonel Cox's charge with First Confederate, etc. (969) Lieutenant-Colonel Malone highly commended by General Wharton. Vol. XXIII, Part 1—(66) Mentioned at engagement at Bradyville, Tenn., March 10, 1863, by Col. J. W. Paramore, Ohio cavalry. (160) Colonel Minty (Union) thinks Malone's battalion was in engagement at Milton, Tenn., March 20th.

Thomason's Battalion, also known as Nineteenth Battalion, merged into Ninth cavalry regiment: Vol. XXIII, Part 1—(277) Mentioned by Gen. W. T. Martin as skirmishing with the enemy, April 21, 1863, on Middleton road, near Hoover's gap. Vol. XXIII, Part 2—(730) Mentioned by General Wharton, Unionville, March 30, 1863.

Ninth Alabama Cavalry: Vol. XXIII, Part 1—(544) Mentioned in Gen. R. B. Mitchell's report of engagement of June 23, 1863, near Unionville, Tenn.

Vol. XXIII, Part 2—(943, 960) In Wharton's division, Wheeler's corps, Bragg's army, July 31, 1863.

No. 51—(19) Crews' brigade, Wheeler's corps, September 19 and 20, 1863.

No. 53—(500) Assignment as above, August, 1863. (554) By special orders, Gadsden, Ala., August 25th, Dr. B. F. Cross assigned to duty.

No. 54—(453) In Morgan's brigade, Martin's division, November 30, 1863. (548) Gen. W. T. Martin's report of engagement near Talbott's Station, December 29th, says: "I wheeled the Seventh Alabama to the right, and moved it into a cut of the railroad, securing a good position within 50 yards of the flank of the advancing infantry. The fire from the regiment and a countercharge by the Georgians soon drove the enemy into and through the woods, with heavy loss in killed and wounded." (778) Mentioned by Lieutenant-Colonel Roger (Union), as near Summerville, October 28th.

No. 56—(51) Mentioned as being in Lookout valley, November, 1863. (94) Mentioned as at Round Mountain. (619) October 31st, First brigade, Martin's division, Wheeler's corps. (623) Special orders, Missionary Ridge, November 1st, to report to Gen. Will T. Martin. (891) December 31, 1863, Russell's brigade, Morgan's division, Wheeler's cavalry corps.

No. 73 — (819, 822) Mentioned by Colonel Minty (Union), near Marietta, Ga., June 12, 1864, skirmish at McAfee's. At Noonday Creek, June 21st, regiment suffered severely.

No. 74—(642) April 30, 1864, Morgan's brigade, Martin's division, Wheeler's corps. (650, et seq.) June 30th, under Capt. George Mason, Allen's brigade, Wheeler's corps, Atlanta campaign.

No. 79 — (509) Capt. A. A. Smith (Union) reports attack on regiment, Clarksville, October 29, 1864.

No. 99—(352) Mentioned by General Kilpatrick, Williston, S. C., February 8, 1865, on road to Augusta. (1071) January 31st, under Capt. S. P. Dobbs, Hagan's brigade, Wheeler's cavalry.

THE TENTH ALABAMA CAVALRY.

The Tenth regiment of cavalry was organized in north Alabama in the winter of 1863-64, to form part of Roddey's command. It took part in the Pulaski raid and in numerous encounters, but its work was principally confined to outpost duty in the Tennessee valley. It was commanded by Col. Richard O. Pickett.

EXTRACTS FROM OFFICIAL WAR RECORDS.

No. 59—(93) Tenth regiment Alabama cavalry stationed at Mount Hope, Ala., March 19, 1864.

No. 78—(392) Pickett's regiment near Courtland, Ala., September 16th, General Granger's (Union) letter. (668) Mentioned by Col. Josiah Patterson, June 27th.

No. 93—(1233) In Roddey's brigade, district of North Alabama, Lieut.-Gen. Richard Taylor's army, November 20th.

No. 94—(634) December 1, 1864, in Roddey's brigade, district of North Alabama, General Maury's army.

THE ELEVENTH ALABAMA CAVALRY.

The Eleventh regiment of Alabama cavalry, commanded by Col. John R. B. Burtwell, comprised the Alabama companies of the regiment commanded by Col. Jeffrey E. Forrest (brother of General Forrest) added to some other companies. After Colonel Forrest's death, in February, 1864, the Tennessee companies in his regiment were detached and consolidated with other Tennessee companies, and the Alabama companies merged into Burtwell's regiment. As Forrest's, and afterward Wisdom's, regiment, it served with General Forrest in the attacks on Athens and Sulphur Trestle; fought with severe loss at Pulaski and in the Meridian expedition. Later it rendered effective service to Hood. During the last months of the war it was part of Roddey's force at Montevallo, in front of Wilson, and took part in the defense of Selma, laying down its arms at Decatur.

EXTRACTS FROM OFFICIAL WAR RECORDS.

J. E. Forrest's Regiment, Alabama cavalry: Four companies

transferred to Newsom's Eighteenth Tennessee. No. 52—(811) Mentioned at the main ford of Bear creek, by General Carr, Corinth, September 24, 1863.

No. 56—(179) Gone with Lee to north Mississippi, via Okolona, November 17, 1863. (645) Report of Gen. N. B. Forrest, Atlanta, Ga., November 7th. (646) Regiment ordered to west Tennessee, to General Forrest, November 7th. (751) General Forrest's letter to Colonel Ewell, Okolona, November 25th, 150 of regiment reported badly armed, etc.

No. 57—(352) Report of General Forrest, Meridian expedition. (355) One killed and 3 wounded in engagements, February 20 to 22, 1864. Col. J. E. Forrest killed, February 22d, near Okolona. (576) General Veatch (Union), Prospect, Tenn., April 11th, speaks of Wisdom's cavalry, D. M. Wisdom commanding Forrest's regiment. (621) Mentioned by General Chalmers in report of capture of Fort Pillow, April 12, 1864.

No. 59—(278) Wisdom's regiment at Williams' landing, five miles above Savannah, April 5, 1864. (460, 481) At Tuscumbia, April, 1864. (482) General Dodge, in west Tennessee, April 24th, says, Wisdom's is Forrest's old regiment. (594) Columbus, Miss., March 7th, assigned to Colonel Thompson's brigade, Forrest's cavalry. (609) Detachment ordered to Marion county, Ala., to protect foundries, by command of General Forrest, March 10th.

No. 78—(593) In Buford's division, with Gen. N. B. Forrest, May 10, 1864. (631) Buford's division, with Gen. S. D. Lee, June 1st. (647) Mentioned by General Forrest, Tupelo, Miss., June 26th, Tennessee companies consolidated with others, etc.

Eleventh Regiment, Alabama cavalry, also called Tenth, Col. John R. B. Burtwell: No. 93—(1233) November 20, 1864, Roddey's brigade, Taylor's army, district of North Alabama. No. 94—(634) December 1, 1864, Roddey's brigade.

THE TWELFTH ALABAMA CAVALRY.

The Twelfth regiment of Alabama cavalry was formed from a battalion recruited by Col. William H. Hundley and Major Bennett. It operated in east Tennessee and was consolidated with the First Alabama near Murfreesboro. It fought at Murfreesboro and Chickamauga. Four companies were added to it, and it was attached to Hagan's brigade. It saw hard and continuous fighting in the battles of the Dalton-Atlanta campaign. One company lost 20 men in killed and wounded while defending a bridge near Rome. At Atlanta it was complimented on the field by General Wheeler. It lost 25 or 30 men in a melee with Stoneman, and fought at Campbellsville, repulsing Brownlow's brigade, with a loss of 45 men. It fought at Averasboro, and disbanded the night before the surrender. Its first colonel was the gallant Warren S. Reese. He was succeeded by Marcellus Pointer, a brave and intrepid officer, who was badly wounded. Adjt. O. P. Casey and Captain Weaver were killed at Bentonville; Captain Musgrove was killed at Fayetteville, and Maj. A. J. Ingraham was disabled by a wound.

EXTRACTS FROM OFFICIAL WAR RECORDS.

Twelfth Battalion, Alabama cavalry, Col. Warren S. Reese: No. 74—(650-673) In Allen's brigade, Wheeler's corps, June to August, 1864, Atlanta campaign. No. 78 —(856) Assignment as above, September 20th.

Twelfth Regiment, Alabama cavalry: No. 92—(988) December 25, 1864, Col. Marcellus Pointer commanding, reported to Gen. R. H. Anderson, near Savannah, Ga. No. 99—(352) General Kilpatrick (Union) says Twelfth Alabama fought in battle, February 8, 1865, near Williston, S. C. (1071) In Hagan's brigade, Wheeler's corps, department of South Carolina, Georgia and Florida, January 31, 1865.

THE FIFTY-FIRST ALABAMA CAVALRY.

The Fifty-first Alabama cavalry regiment, known as Partisan Rangers, was recruited by Col. John T. Morgan, who had entered the war as a major of infantry, served for a time in Virginia, and returned home to raise a mounted regiment. It was sent to Alabama, served for a time in Tennessee, fought at Lavergne with General Forrest; was then attached to Wheeler's cavalry, and was brigaded under Morgan, Hagan and Allen. It took part in the Sequatchie raid, and was part of the force which captured 400 Federals at Maysville, and took part in the investment of Knoxville. It took a gallant part in the Stone's River and Chickamauga campaigns; was on Johnston's flank during the retreat to Dalton, fighting almost daily for three months, and lost heavily at Decatur and Jonesboro. It moved through Tennessee, and harassed General Sherman's forces very effectually in the Carolinas. About a week before the close of hostilities, it fought and captured a portion of the First Alabama United States regiment and finally surrendered at Raleigh, N. C.

Col. John T. Morgan was commissioned brigadier in November, 1863, and was for some time in command of a division and served with Generals Hood, Longstreet and Johnston. After the close of hostilities he returned to the profession of law, and in 1877 was sent to the United States Senate, of which body he has long been one of the most able and distinguished members. He was succeeded in command of the regiment by the gallant Lieut.-Col. J. D. Webb, who was mortally wounded near Decherd, Tenn., in July, 1863. Captain Battle was in command for a short time, and Capt. M. L. Kirkpatrick, who took command during the Chickamauga campaign, continued to lead the regiment until the close of the war.

EXTRACTS FROM OFFICIAL WAR RECORDS.

Vol. XVI, Part 1—(257) Mentioned by General Negley (Union) as in the neighborhood of Atlanta, fall of 1862.

Vol. XVI, Part 2—(717) Telegram of July 2, 1862, secretary of war to Governor Shorter, Montgomery, says: "I will order the Fifty-first Alabama regiment to Chattanooga." (792) Telegram from Governor Shorter, September 2d, to secretary of war, asks for the Fifty-first regiment cavalry to be sent to the southern part of the State. (795) Regiment sent to south Alabama as requested, September 4th. (802) Ordered by Gen. Sam Jones to proceed to Bridgeport and report to General Maxey, September 8th. (857) Gen. Sam Jones says, September 20th: "Protection no longer needed in Alabama. Regiment ordered toward Nashville to cooperate with Forrest." (862) Sent to Tullahoma, September 21, 1862. (890) Ordered up near Nashville to cooperate with the troops there, in harassing the enemy and cutting off foraging parties, September 29th. (916-918) Ordered to Lavergne by General Jones, October 6th. (929) Ordered to report to General Forrest, about October 9th.

Vol. XX, Part 1—(6) On the night of November, 1862, was placed by General Forrest to the right of the Murfreesboro pike with instructions to move forward on the Lebanon, Stone's river and Chicken pikes, and to drive in the Abolitionist pickets at daylight, which was done agreeably to orders, and in gallant style. (466) Mentioned in report of Gen. M. S. Hascall (Union) of skirmishes at Lavergne, etc., December. (648) Mentioned in report of Adjt. William S. Hall, battle of Murfreesboro. (661) In Gen. Joseph Wheeler's command; Stone's river campaign. (958) December 26, 1862, in General Wheeler's command, stationed at Stewart's creek, 10 miles northwest of Murfreesboro. (962-965) Lieut.-Col. J. D. Webb, in his report of Stone's river campaign, specially commends conduct of Capt. M. L. Kirkpatrick, Capt. L. W. Battle, Lieut. William M. Fitts, James W. Copilly, Ord.-Sergt. H. Clay Reynolds. He says the regiment bivouacked on Stone's river the night of December 27th "without rations." The gallant and brave Lieut. William M. Fitts was killed. December 29th, at Lavergne, charged a train of wagons, captured and burned 36 wagons, captured other wagons and teams and 50 prisoners. At Nolensville, captured 20 wagons and 50 prisoners. January 1st", captured wagons and prisoners. Lieut. J. J. Seawell was wounded and captured.

Vol. XXIII, Part 1—(28) Near Fosterville, February 1, 1863, report of Capt. L. W. Battle, Company B. (544) Mentioned in report of General Mitchell (Union), of fight near Uniontown, June 23d. (574) Mentioned in report of Maj. Charles B. Seidel (Union), fight near Decherd, Lieutenant-Colonel Webb mortally wounded, July 1st.

Vol. XXIII, Part 2—(943) Capt. M. L. Kirkpatrick, Hagan's brigade, Martin's division, Wheeler's cavalry, July 31, 1863. (960) August 10th, in Col. John T. Morgan's brigade, General Wheeler's corps.

No. 50—(232) October, 1863, in Colonel Hagan's brigade, Wheeler's cavalry corps. No. 51—(19) In Col. John T. Morgan's brigade, General Wheeler's corps, Chickamauga campaign.

No. 52—(332, 449, 485, 486) Union reports, on the road to Trenton, September 3, 1863; near Lafayette, September 8th; fight at Chickamauga creek, September 9th.

No. 54—(453) November 30, 1863, in Gen. John T. Morgan's brigade, Martin's division, Wheeler's cavalry.

No. 55, No. 56—Assignment as above, to December, 1863. December 31st, Russell's brigade, Morgan's division, Wheeler's cavalry.

No. 59—(870) April 30, 1864, in Morgan's brigade, General Wheeler's corps.

No. 73—(819-822) Mentioned by Colonel Minty (Union), in fight at McAfee's, June 11th, and near Noonday creek, Ga., June 21, 1864.

No. 74—(642) April 30, 1864, under Col. M. L. Kirkpatrick, in General Morgan's brigade, Wheeler's corps. (650-673) In General Allen's brigade, General Wheeler's corps, Atlanta campaign, June to August.

No. 78—(856) September 20, 1864, in Allen's brigade, Wheeler's corps.

No. 99—(352) Mentioned by Gen. J. Kilpatrick, Williston, S. C., February 8, 1865, on road to Augusta. (1071) January 31, 1865, Colonel Hagan's brigade, General Wheeler's corps.

THE FIFTY-THIRD ALABAMA CAVALRY.

The Fifty-third regiment of mounted infantry was organized in the fall of 1862, by the addition of several companies to Maj. T. F. Jenkins' battalion, which had already rendered gallant service at Shiloh. Major Jenkins and Captain Cox commanded mounted companies in the Seventh Alabama prior to April, 1862. The regiment was first placed in Roddey's brigade, and fought at Thompson's Station, Brentwood, Town Creek and in the pursuit of Streight. It was on picket duty at Dalton in April, 1864. When Roddey's brigade was transferred to General Polk's department, this regiment was detached and was brigaded under General Hannon, and afterward General Hagan, in General Wheeler's cavalry corps, and took part in the perilous fighting all the way from Dalton to Atlanta. It participated in the daring raid of 1864 in Sherman's rear, and captured 100 men and 1,500 beef cattle; it fought at Jonesboro and Resaca, and continued to harass the Federals in the Carolinas.

Its first colonel, M. W. Hannon, was early promoted to the command of a brigade. Lieut.-Col. J. F. Gaines, who succeeded in command, was wounded at Waynesboro. Major Jenkins and Capt. L. E. Locke were captured near Florence, and Capt. W. R. Davis near Rome.

EXTRACTS FROM OFFICIAL WAR RECORDS.

Jenkins' battalion, Alabama cavalry, called First Alabama battalion, merged into the Fifty-third Alabama cavalry: Vol. X, Part 1—(382) Mentioned, belonging to Polk's corps, April, 1862. (471) Mentioned by Gen. Daniel Ruggles, Shiloh, April 6 and 7, 1862. (527) Mentioned by Capt. William Ketchum. (529) Report of Maj. T. F. Jenkins, Shiloh. Number of men engaged on the 6th, 52; on the 7th, 47; 2 killed and 6 wounded. (530) Report of Capt. J. J. Cox of Prattville dragoons, Jenkins' battalion.

Fifty-third Alabama infantry, mounted, Partisan Rangers: Vol. XV—(903) Troops in the district of the Gulf, J. W. W. Mackall. Present for duty, 517; headquarters Mobile, December 20, 1862.

Vol. XXIII, Part 1—(119) Jenkins' squadron, 2 killed and 12 wounded, engagement at Thompson's Station, Tenn., March, 1863. (195) Colonel Dibrell's report of affair at Florence, March 25th, says: "Hannon's regiment was pouring volley after volley into the boats from the other side."

Vol. XXIII, Part 2—(944) Col. M. W. Hannon, Roddey's brigade, Wheeler's corps, July, 1863.

No. 55—(664) Assignment as above, November 20, 1863. No. 56—(619, 804, 888) Roddey's brigade, detached, Wheeler's corps, December, 1863.

No. 57 — (119) At Athens, Ala., January 26, 1864.

No. 59—(801) Mentioned April 20th, on picket duty in front of Dalton; not transferred with Roddey's brigade to Polk's department. (871) Lieut.-Col. J. F. Gaines, Hannon's brigade, Wheeler's corps, April 30th. (873) Company G, Capt. P. B. Mastin, Jr., escort to Walker's division.

No. 74—(642, et seq.) Hannon's brigade, Wheeler's corps, Atlanta campaign. (693) Ordered to Jonesboro to cooperate with General Armstrong in repelling raids coming in that direction, August 28, 1864. (946) Mentioned in report of Gen. Joseph Wheeler, battle of Resaca.

No. 78—(856) Hannon's brigade, Wheeler's corps, September 20, 1864.

No. 99—(980, 1072) Hagan's brigade, Wheeler's corps, January, 1865. (1148-1151) Mentioned by Maj. John G. Devereux, Augusta, Ga., February 10, 1865.

THE FIFTY-SIXTH ALABAMA CAVALRY.

The Fifty-sixth regiment of mounted infantry, known as Partisan Rangers, was organized in the summer of 1863, by the union of Hewlett's and Boyles' battalions of cavalry, both of which had done good service in the army of the Gulf as scouts and pickets, and had fought gallantly at King's Creek and other points in Mississippi. Attached to Ferguson's brigade, the regiment was sent to north Georgia and did arduous duty in the many battles of the Dalton-Atlanta campaign. After going with Hood into Tennessee, it turned and harassed Sherman on his march. It was in the trenches at Savannah and operated near Augusta, moved into the Carolinas and finally surrendered at Greensboro, 200 strong. Colonel Boyles was at one time in command of

Ferguson's brigade, and Lieut.-Col. William Martin took command of the regiment. Capt. Wm. McGill was killed near Decatur, and Capt. Thomas D. Hall was wounded near Kingston.

EXTRACTS FROM OFFICIAL WAR RECORDS.

Boyles' Mobile Dragoons: Vol. V—(868) Field return for March, 1862, 97 present for duty. Vol. XV—(850) October 31, 1862, in district of the Gulf, commanded by Maj.-Gen. J. H. Forney. No. 42—(39) June 8, 1863, in army of Mobile at Pascagoula.

Fifteenth battalion, Alabama cavalry, also called First battalion, merged into Fifty-sixth regiment, Partisan Rangers: No. 36—(689) Mentioned at Okolona, May 14, 1863, 350 strong, in report of General Ruggles, action at King's Creek, near Tupelo, Miss. No. 37—(483) Mentioned by Gen. Daniel Ruggles, in operations in northeastern Mississippi, as Colonel Boyles' First Alabama.

No. 38—(400) Mentioned by General Oglesby at Okolona, June 10, 1863. (837) General Ruggles, Okolona, May 5th, says: "Major Boyles' Alabama cavalry cannot be spared." (917) Mentioned at Okolona, May 24th (called the First). (973) Mentioned by General Ruggles, June 2 2d.

Thirteenth Battalion, merged into Fifty-sixth regiment, Partisan Rangers: Vol. XVII, Part 2—(815) Maj. W. A. Hewlett's Partisan Rangers. Gen. J. C. Pemberton's command, December, 1862. (818) Col. John Adams says, battalion stationed at Buttahatchie bridge, twelve miles north of Columbus, on the Aberdeen road, January 1, 1863. (846) Special orders, No. 3, January 19th, to picket and scout in advance on Aberdeen road.

No. 36—(690) Commended by General Ruggles in report of action at King's Creek, May 5, 1863. (691-693) Maj. W. A. Hewlett in his report of King's Creek, commends gallant and meritorious condtict of Capt. J. R. Shepherd and Lieuts. Samuel P. Morrow and H. H. Bibb.

No. 38—(611) In Ruggles' brigade, Pemberton's army, January 31, 1863. (639) One hundred men ordered to report to Major Mathews at Fayetteville, Ala., February 22d. (643) General Johnston orders Major Hewlett's battalion to report to General Ruggles for duty near Aberdeen; February 24th. (655) Ordered by General Ruggles to be armed, etc., March 6th. (699) Battalion has been disabled by camp diseases; to be pushed forward to Smithville, etc., Columbus, Miss., March 31st. (706) In Ruggles' brigade, April. (718) Ordered to be in readiness for marching orders, April 6th, at Buttahatchie bridge. (796) Ordered from Aberdeen to Buena Vista, April 27th. (917) Thirteenth Alabama battalion in the vicinity of Okolona, Miss., May 24th. (973) Mentioned by General Ruggles. United with Colonel Boyles' regiment and some Tennessee regiments, May 15th.

Fifty-sixth Alabama cavalry, Col. William Boyles: No. 53—(5) Mentioned by Union scout as at New Albany, Miss., October 1, 1863. (559) Mentioned in General Ferguson's report of troops, Okolona, Miss., August 27th. (576) Mentioned by Gen. S. D. Lee, with General Ferguson, Morton,

September 1st. (582) Mentioned, Morton, Miss., September 2d. (724) Ordered to move at once to vicinity of Cherry creek, by General Lee, October 2d.

Nos. 56, 57, 58, 59—In Ferguson's brigade, S. D. Lee's cavalry corps, November, 1863, to April, 1864.

No. 73—(756) Mentioned by Col. E. McCook (Union), Atlanta campaign.

No. 74—(646, et seq.) In Ferguson's brigade, Jackson's division, Gen. L. Polk's army, Atlanta campaign.

No. 75—(456) Mentioned by Colonel McCook (Union), June 11, 1864, as at Ackworth and Dallas.

No. 78—(857) Lieut.-Col. William Martin, Colonel Boyles commanding Ferguson's brigade, Wheeler's corps, September 20, 1864.

No. 94—(791) Company C transferred to Tenth Mississippi cavalry, special orders signed by Gen. John Withers, Richmond, Va., January 17, 1865.

No. 99—(1072) Ferguson's brigade, Wheeler's corps, January 31, 1865.

THE FIRST CONFEDERATE CAVALRY.

The First Confederate cavalry was one of General Wheeler's best regiments; several of the companies were men from Alabama, but the field officers were from other States. Captain Robertson's company was organized early in the war, and saw considerable service before it was consolidated with other companies. Captain Bradley's Company A was detached on escort duty all during the war, serving the greater part of the time in Forrest's division. The rest of the regiment was brigaded, successively, with General Wharton, General Russell, General Wade, General Humes, General Allen and General Anderson, in Wheeler's cavalry corps.

It was at Lavergne in November, 1862, and distinguished itself at Murfreesboro by its gallant charge and capture of the Seventy-fifth Illinois. It fought at Guy's Gap, Shelbyville, Trenton, Lafayette, Chickamauga, McAfee's, Noonday Creek, and in numberless skirmishes during the campaigns of the army of Tennessee. Capt. Charles H. Conner was in command continuously after the spring of 1863.

EXTRACTS FROM OFFICIAL WAR RECORDS.

First Confederate cavalry, Col. John T. Cox. Vol. VI— (835) Six companies ordered to Mobile, February 27, 1862, by General Bragg.

Vol. VII—(769) General Pillow reports Robertson's company of cavalry in Brownville, December 16, 1861. (910) Col. B. J. Lea reports Robertson's company scouting between Clifton and Savannah, February 26, 1862.

(918) Beauregard's confidential notes, March 4th, say that Robertson's cavalry is to remain at Henderson.

Vol. X, Part 2—(408) Col. W. H. Jackson asks for Robertson's cavalry to be sent to Trenton, Tenn., April 10, 1862.

Vol. XV—(19) General Van Dorn mentions cavalry escort under Lieutenant Bradley, Company A, in defenses of Vicksburg, 1862.

Vol. XVI, Part 1—(899) Commended in report of Gen. Joe Wheeler, Knoxville, October 30, 1862; Lieut.-Col. C. S. Robertson commanding.

Vol. XVII, Part 2—(835) Field returns, Wharton's cavalry, 156 effective, December 30, 1862.

Company A, Captain Bradley. Vol. XVII, Part 2— (661) Acting as cavalry escort, General Van Dorn's troops, July, 1862; 36 present. (814-847) Acting as cavalry escort for Colonel Jackson's corps, General Pemberton's troops, December, 1862; 29 present.

First Confederate regiment. Vol. XX,—(16) Reported as with Wheeler's cavalry at Lavergne, November 27, 1862. (329) Mentioned in Major Collins' (Union) report of advance on Murfreesboro. (661) Under Col. John T. Cox, Wharton's brigade, Wheeler's cavalry, December, 1862. (773) Hardee's report of battle of Murfreesboro says this regiment captured the Seventy-fifth Illinois regiment. Conduct highly commended. (966) General Wharton's report speaks of Cox's gallant charge and capture of prisoners. (969) Regiment again commended by General Wharton.

Vol. XX, Part 2—(446) Wharton's brigade, 136 effective total, two companies detached, December 10, 1862.

Vol. XXIII, Part 1—(537, 538) Mentioned in Union reports of Guy's Gap and Shelbyville, June, 1863.

Vol. XXIII, Part 2—(362) Gen. J. M. Brannan (Union) reports arrival of Cox's cavalry at Chapel Hill, May 25,

1863. (371) Mentioned as on picket duty near Shelbyville in letter to General Garfield, from Mrs. M. B. Lee, May 29th. (730) Mentioned in letter from General Wharton to General Wheeler, Unionville, March 30, 1863. (841) Attached to General Martin's brigade, May 18th. (943) Capt. C. H. Conner, Russell's brigade, Martin's division, Wheeler's corps, July. (944) Company A, Capt. John Bradley, escort in Armstrong's brigade, Forrest's division, July.

No. 38—(593) Company A at headquarters at Grenada, Miss., January 20, 1863.

No. 51 — (19) Russell's brigade, Martin's division, Wheeler's corps, Chickamauga campaign, September, 1863. No. 52—(332) Gen. R. B. Mitchell (Union) reports regiment on the road to Trenton, September 3, 1863, with Martin's division. (449) General Negley (Union) reports regiment near LaFayette, September 8, 1863.

No. 55—(663) Capt. C. H. Conner, in Wade's brigade, Kelly's division, Wheeler's cavalry corps, November, 1863. No. 56 — (619) First brigade, Kelly's division, Wheeler's cavalry corps, October 31, 1863. (640) Ordered to move on to Spring Place, November 6th.

No. 58 — (590) Hume's brigade, Kelly's division, "Wheeler's cavalry corps, January, 1864.

No. 73—(819, 822) Mentioned in Colonel Minty's (Union) reports of skirmish at McAfee's, June 11, 1864, and Noonday Creek, June 21st.

No. 94—(751) Mentioned in General Forrest's orders from Corinth, January 1, 1865.

THE THIRD CONFEDERATE CAVALRY.

The Third Confederate cavalry, which entered the service under Col. J. R. Howard, included seven Alabama companies. It served during the greater part of the war in Wheeler's cavalry, and fought throughout the campaigns in Kentucky and Tennessee in numberless raids and skirmishes. It fought at Murfreesboro, Triune, Hoover's Gap, Chickamauga, Bridgeport, Trenton, McAfee's, Noonday Creek. After the resignation of Colonel Howard, the regiment was commanded, successively, by Col. W. N. Estes and Col. P. H. Rice. It was constantly in demand for picket duty and scouting, and was distinguished for gallantry and endurance. Colonel Estes was killed near Chattanooga, and Colonel Rice was wounded in Georgia. Lieut.-Col. John McCaskill and Capt. Dan Clayton were wounded, and Adjt. N. Rothbock was killed, at Murfreesboro.

EXTRACTS FROM OFFICIAL WAR RECORDS.
Estes' Battalion, Alabama cavalry, Maj. W. N. Estes, merged into Third Confederate: Vol. X, Part 2—(573) In Leadbetter's brigade, Gen. E. Kirby Smith's army, May 31, 1862.

Third Confederate cavalry: Vol. XVI, Part 1—(889) General Maxey's report of fight near Graham's, August 30, 1862, mentions Captain Rice's company. (891) Highly commended by General Maxey. (1143) Report of Col. J. R. Howard of skirmishes near Mountain gap, October 14 to 16, 1862.

Vol. XVI, Part 2—(242) General McCook writes to General Buell that Howard's regiment is on road to Nashville, August 1, 1862. (267) "Howard has returned to Chattanooga," August 6th. (716) In Kirby Smith's forces, unattached. (743) Ordered to report to General Forrest, August 4th. (761) Ordered to remain near Chattanooga, August 17th, with General Maxey. (800) Ordered into Sequatchie valley, September 7th. (840) Gen. Sam Jones says he will send it, with Maxey's command, into Kentucky. (985) In Pegram's brigade, Heth's division, Gen. E. Kirby Smith's troops, October 31st.

Vol. XVII, Part 2—(835) Field return, with Wharton's brigade, 457 effective, December 30, 1862.

Vol. XX—(14) Report of Colonel Howard of skirmish near Tompkinsville, Ky., November 17, 1862; 4 killed, 3 wounded. (75) Mentioned in General Wharton's report, December 10th. (233) Mentioned in Union report of Stone's river, January 3, 1863. (661) Under Lieut. W. N. Estes, in Wharton's brigade, Wheeler's cavalry. (966) Mentioned in General Wharton's report of Murfreesboro.

Vol. XXIII, Part 1—(162) Mentioned in Wharton's report of fight at Triune, March 21, 1863. (430, 454, 458) Mentioned in reports of General Thomas, General Reynolds and Col. John T. Wilder (Union), of fight near Hoover's Gap. (578) Mentioned by Lieutenant-Colonel Lamborn (Union) as falling back to Tullahoma, June 27th.

Vol. XXIII, Part 2—(739) Wharton says: "Third will camp at Fairfield," April 4, 1863. (740) Col. Baxter Smith says regiment, under Col. W. N. Estes, was at Jacksonburg, April 5th. (915) General Anderson reports bridge over Sequatchie, near Jasper, burned by detachment under Capt. P. H. Rice, July 19th. (943, 960) Harrison's brigade, Wharton's division, Wheeler's corps, July.

No. 50—(232) Harrison's brigade, October 7, 1863. (468, 469) Captain Edmondson's company mentioned in Federal reports, at the Narrows, near Jasper, Tenn., August and September. (926) Mentioned in report of Eli Long, near Bridgeport, Ala., September 1st. (928) Report of Lieut.-Col. V. Cupp says, Estes, with 400 men, camped on road between Bridgeport and Trenton; speaks of skirmish, August 29th.

No. 51—(19) Harrison's brigade, Wharton's division, Wheeler's corps, Chickamauga campaign, September, 1863. (520) General Wheeler's report says Estes' regiment was picketing Tennessee river from Bridgeport to Guntersville, August 27th. No. 52—(232) Gen. J. M. Brannan (Union) reports a capture of some of Rice's cavalry; 4 killed near Battle creek, August 30, 1863. (257) General Wagner reports that regiment is patrolling river. (384) General Negley says Rice's cavalry, 300 strong, passed up valley, September 6th.

No. 53—(574) Mentioned in letter of Lieutenant-Colonel Mauldin, Trenton, Ga., August 31, 1863.

No. 56—(722) Col. H. B. Lyon reports Third, with 260 men, with him on way to Kingston, November 20, 1863. (807) Wade's brigade, Kelly's division, Wheeler's corps, December, 1863.

No. 58—(349) General Thomas (Union) says, scout reports four companies of Third Confederate cavalry in Cherokee county, February 7, 1864. (590) Hume's brigade, Kelly's division, Wheeler's cavalry corps, January 20th.

No. 73—(819, 822) Mentioned in Colonel Minty's report of skirmish at McAfee's, June 11th, and Noonday creek, June 21, 1864.

No. 74—(642) Col. P. H. Rice, Allen's brigade, Kelly's division, Wheeler's cavalry corps, April, 1864. (650) Lieut.-Col. John McCaskill, Anderson's brigade, Kelly's division, June. (652) Captain Billinglea's company, escort to Hindman's division. (658-673) Assignment as above, to August.

No. 75—(166) Mentioned in letter of Col. L. D. Watkins (Union), Wauhatchie, Tenn., May 13, 1864. No. 78—(856) Assignment as above, September 30th. No. 94—(127) Union scout reports regiment camping in Wills' valley, December 7, 1864, on their way to attack Whitesides.

No. 98—(1065) Hampton's cavalry corps, Johnston's army, April 9, 1865. No. 99—(1071) Col. P. H. Rice, Anderson's brigade, Allen's division, Wheeler's cavalry corps, Hardee's army, January 31, 1865.

THE EIGHTH CONFEDERATE CAVALRY.

The Eighth Confederate cavalry was organized after the battle of Shiloh, by the consolidation of Brewer's, Bell's and Baskerville's battalions, comprising six Alabama and four Mississippi companies. Brewer's, one of the first mounted bodies raised in the State, fought with distinction at Shiloh, and acted as rear guard for Polk's army. The Eighth moved with the army of Tennessee into Kentucky and fought with it before and after the battle of Murfreesboro; was in Wheeler's dash on Rosecrans' rear during the battle. It lost heavily at Shelbyville, where a portion of the regiment was captured, and suffered severely at Chickamauga and Dalton. It took part in the capture of Stoneman, and fought as infantry in the Dalton-Atlanta campaign. It was with Wheeler in his last raid into Tennessee, then moved into Virginia, except part of his regiment which was attached to Chalmers' brigade and skirmished in Alabama until the close of the war. The remainder fought Burbridge at Saltville, and pursued Sherman; fighting incessantly until it surrendered at Greensboro, 100 strong. Col. W. B. Wade was wounded in Tennessee. Lieut.-Col. J. S. Prather was wounded, and Major McCaa killed, at Murfreesboro; Maj. John Wright was wounded at Shelbyville; Captains Ferguson, Thompson and Lindsay and Adjutant Goodrich were captured. Capt. John McElderry was killed near Dalton, Capt. Joseph A. Mathews near Columbia; Capt. Henry Holmes was wounded at Boonsville and Jonesboro, and Capt. Francis Pinckard died in the service. Col. R. H. Brewer, of Brewer's battalion, was a graduate of West Point. He resigned, and was afterward killed in the valley of Virginia, in 1864.

EXTRACTS FROM OFFICIAL WAR RECORDS.

Brewer's Battalion, Alabama cavalry: Vol. VII—(854) At Paris, Tenn., January, 1862, in Stewart's brigade, Polk's army. (909) Mentioned by Gen. Daniel Ruggles, February 26th, Florence, Ala.

Vol. X, Part 1—(417) Mentioned in report of Colonel Russell, Shiloh, April 6 and 7, 1862. (461-463) Colonel Brewer in his reports of the battle of Shiloh says, command 200 strong; 2 killed and 10 wounded. He mentions Major Baskerville, to whom he is much indebted for coolness, etc. Acted as rear-guard to Polk's corps. (529) Mentioned in report of Captain Jenkins.

Vol. X, Part 2—(306) Unattached, General Polk's army, March 9, 1862. (375) Mentioned by Col. Preston Smith, March 31st, in skirmish near Adamsville. (382) Mentioned in General Hardee's division, April 1st, at Purdy. (385) Mentioned April 2d, scouting near Purdy. (415) Placed in position at Bethel, April 12th. (419) Mentioned in special orders, No. 12, April 14th. (435) General Maxey says: "Colonel Brewer's cavalry is destroying bridges at Purdy," April 23d. (456) Mentioned by General Maxey, Bethel, April 27th. (458) Ordered to protect the Mobile & Ohio railroad, by command of General Beauregard, April 28th. (459) Three hundred and forty-two present for duty, April 28th, General Beall's cavalry brigade. (493) Mentioned by Colonel Lindsay, Camp Foote, near Purdy, May 5th. (516) Mentioned by Adjutant-General Jordan, Corinth, May 12th. (519) Guarding the crossing, Memphis & Charleston railroad, May 13th. (582) Captain Falkner's company placed at intersection of roads from Iuka to Jacinto, June 4, 1862.

Vol. XVII, Part 2—(63) Attacked Colonel Sheridan, July 1, 1862; Asboth. (66) Mentioned by Colonel Sheridan, 200 strong, July 2d. (606) Tupelo, June 17th: "The general commanding takes pleasure in calling the attention of the armies of this department to the gallant conduct of Capt. B. B. McCaa and his command, of Brewer's cavalry regiment, on the morning of the 14th inst, when, by a bold and dashing charge, he put to flight a superior force of the enemy's cavalry. In this affair Private John Graham was especially distinguished, and will be rewarded with a badge of honor on some suitable occasion. This success should teach our cavalry forces what they can accomplish by bravery and daring, and should incite them to like deeds of valor." By command of General Beauregard, general orders, No. 74.

Capt. A. W. Bowie's company, Alabama cavalry: No. 75—(793) Mentioned near Rome, Ga., June 22, 1864, in letter from Maj. W. J. Walthall. No. 78—(686) Letter from Captain Bowie to Major Walthall, dated near Talladega, July 5th.

Eighth Confederate cavalry, Col. W. B. Wade. Vol. X—(868, 869) Reports of Capt. J. Falkner and Lieut. J. S. Prather, burning of Cypress creek bridge, May 30, 1862. (880) Report of Colonel Claiborne, Sixth Confederate cavalry, May 9th.

Vol. XVI, Part 1—(898, 899) General Wheeler mentions engagement on Perryville pike, October 11, 1862, in which regiment took part.

Vol. XVI, Part 2—(790) Mentioned by Gen. Sam Jones, Chattanooga, August 31, 1862. (912) Colonel Wharton mentions in communication to General Polk, October 5th. Says will be at Lebanon next day.

Vol. XVII, Part 1—(5-8) Reports of Col. J. F. Lay and Lieut.-Col. W. B. Wade of skirmish at Clear creek, near Baldwyn, June 15, 1862. (23) Mentioned in report of Col. Joseph Wheeler, expedition from Holly Springs to Bolivar, etc., July, 1862.

Vol. XVII, Part 2—(663) Regiment to leave Tupelo for Chattanooga, August 5, 1862. (666) General Price asks General Bragg to leave Wade's cavalry at Tupelo.

Vol. XX— (661) In Wheeler's brigade, Wheeler's cavalry, Stone's River campaign, January, 1863. (958) Report of Gen. Joseph Wheeler.

Vol. XXIII, Part 1—(27-29) Colonel Minty's report of skirmish near Rover, February 13, 1863. Capt. L. W. Battle's report of skirmish at Middleton, January 31st. (136, 137, 335, 343) Mentioned in Union reports of fighting at Middleton, May, 1863. (346) Mentioned in dispatch of General Martin to General Polk, May 22d. (534, 558) Mentioned in Union reports of Shelbyville, June 28th. Adjutant captured while endeavoring to protect the commanding officers.

Vol. XXIII, Part 2—(459) General Stanley reports regiment on way to Chapel Hill, June 25, 1863. (847) General Martin reports part of regiment captured at Fosterville, May 22d. (923) Lieutenant-Colonel Prather, with detachment of 230, near Decatur, July 21st. (943) Under Capt. J. H. Field, Hagan's brigade, Martin's division, Wheeler's corps, July. (960) Morgan's brigade, Martin's division, etc., August.

No. 51—(19) Under Lieut.-Col. John S. Prather, Morgan's brigade, Martin's division, Wheeler's corps, Chickamauga campaign. (520) General Wheeler's report of Chickamauga says that Wade's regiment was picketing from Guntersville to Decatur, August 27th.

No. 52—(449) General Negley (Union) reports regiment near Lafayette, September 8, 1863.

No. 53 — (371-374) Generals Hooker and Howard (Union) report regiment, 300 strong, at Trenton, October 14, 1863. (500) Under Capt. J. H. Field, in Hagan's brigade, Martin's division, August 15th. (589) Ordered to report to General Martin without delay. (708) Ordered to report to General Martin as soon as relieved by Ninth Kentucky cavalry, September 27th.

No. 54—(778) Lieut.-Col. J. C. Rodgers reports regiment near Summerville, October 28, 1863.

No. 56—(51) M. M. Phillips, scout, reports regiment in Lookout valley, November 5, 1863. (619) First brigade, Kelly's division, Wheeler's cavalry corps, October 31st. (640) General Martin reports Eighth Confederate as moving to Spring Place, November 6th. (807) Wade's brigade, Kelly's division, Wheeler's cavalry corps, December.

No. 58—(590) Humes' brigade, Kelly's division, January 20, 1864.
No. 59—(871) Lieut-Col. John S. Prather, Allen's brigade, Kelly's division, April 30th.

No. 73—(819, 822) Mentioned in Colonel Minty's report of skirmish at McAfee's, June 11th, and Noonday creek, June 21st. (823) Mentioned in Memphis Appeal, June 25th, in a report of fight at Latimar's mill, quoted by Colonel Minty.

No. 74—(642) Lieut.-Col. John S. Prather, Allen's brigade, Kelly's division, Wheeler's cavalry corps, April 30, 1864. (650) Anderson's brigade, June 30th. (658-673) Assignments as above. (944) Mentioned in General Wheeler's report of fight at Varnell's, May 9th. (950) Highly commended by General Wheeler in general orders, No. 6, for conduct at Varnell's; McElderry killed. (972, 973) Report of Lieut. John A. Vaughan commanding scouts, McCook's raid, July 27th to 31st.

No. 77—(496) Col. G. G. Dibrell's report of operations near Readyville, September, 1864, says Major Wright's cavalry were on picket duty there. No. 78—(856) Assignment as above, September 30th.

No. 92—(961) Mentioned by General Anderson as at Savannah, December 15, 1864.

No. 98—(1065) Hampton's cavalry corps, Johnston's army, April 9, 1865.

No. 99—(1071) Lieutenant-Colonel Prather, Anderson's brigade, Allen's division, Wheeler's cavalry corps, Hardee's army, January 31, 1865. (1283) Mentioned in letter of Col. G. G. Dibrell, on road from White Oak to Rocky mountain, February 26th.

No. 103—(433) Mentioned in Colonel Cooper's (Union) report of skirmish near Montgomery, April 13, 1865. (970) Ordered to Plymouth, February 13th. (993, 994) Attached to General Starke's brigade, February 18th. (1027) Part of regiment attached to Chalmers' brigade, March 3d. (1033) Ordered to report to General Armstrong, March 6th. (1051) A company ordered to Fulton to scout in the direction of Eastport, March 12th.

No. 104—(1122, 1127) Relieved from duty with Armstrong's brigade and ordered to rejoin Anderson's, March. 18, 1865.

THE TENTH CONFEDERATE CAVALRY.

The Tenth Confederate cavalry was organized at Murfreesboro from the battalion of Col. Charles T. Goode and Lieut.-Col. M. N. Slaughter's Seventeenth Alabama battalion of cavalry of Hilliard's legion, which had passed through the Kentucky campaign. In Pegram's brigade, it fought at Monticello, losing heavily; fought several battles in the Kentucky campaign, losing 160 men, and at Jimtown it lost 50 men. It fought at Chickamauga under General Forrest, and suffered severely. It was largely employed in picket and outpost duty. Brigaded, successively, under Generals Wade, Humes and Robinson, in Kelly's division, it fought with considerable loss at Resaca, New Hope, and all through the many battles of the Dalton-Atlanta campaign. It took part in Wheeler's last raid as far as Saltville; returned to the Carolinas, fought at Bentonville, and surrendered with Johnston's army, 300 strong. Colonel Goode, who was. wounded at Chickamauga, was promoted and retired. Col. W. J. Vason was wounded at Bentonville, Lieutenant-Colonel Slaughter at Cleveland, and Maj. J. B. Rudolph at New Hope. Adjt. James E. Mitchell was captured; Capt. J. J. Clements was wounded and captured at Jimtown; Captain Barnes was captured, and died in prison; Capt. T. A. Knight was wounded at Resaca.

EXTRACTS FROM OFFICIAL WAR RECORDS.

Vol. XXIII, Part 1—(830) Mentioned in General Hartsuff's (Union) report as in Confederate troops near Winchester, July 29, 1863. (839) At Big Creek Gap, July 25, 1863, report of Col. J. S. Scott commanding brigade. (840) Reported at Irvine, July 30th.

Vol. XXIII, Part 2—(568) Mentioned as near Mt. Vernon, Ky., July 29th. (644) At Kingston, Tenn., in Col. S. J. Smith's brigade, Donelson's forces, February 20, 1863. (711) At Kingston, March 19th. (793) Scott's brigade, Gen. W. G. M. Davis' forces, on outpost and special duty, April 25th. (946) Scott's brigade, Buckner's army, July 31st, brigade on duty in Kentucky.

No. 51—(20) Scott's brigade, Pegram's division, Forrest's corps, Chickamauga campaign, September, 1863.

No. 56—(619) First brigade, Kelly's division, Wheeler's cavalry corps, October 31, 1863. (639) Ordered to report by letter to General Kelly at Cleveland, Tenn., and continue picket duty, November 6th. (807) Wade's brigade, Kelly's division, Wheeler's cavalry corps, December.

No. 58—(590, 591) Humes' brigade, Kelly's division, January 20, 1864. Company A, Capt. John M. McKleroy, escort to Stewart's division.

No. 59— (871) Capt. T. G. Holt, Allen's brigade, Kelly's division, April 30, 1864.

No. 73—(819) Mentioned in Colonel Minty's (Union) report of skirmish at McAfee's, June 11th, and Noonday Creek, June 21, 1864.

No. 74—(642-644) Capt. T. G. Holt, Allen's brigade, Kelly's division, Wheeler's cavalry corps, April 30, 1864. (650) Capt. W. J. Vason, Anderson's brigade, Kelly's division, Wheeler's cavalry, June to August, 1864. No. 78— (856) Assignment as above, September 30th.

No. 92—(961) Mentioned by General Anderson as near Savannah, December 15, 1864.

No. 98—(1065) Hampton's cavalry corps, Johnston's army, April 9, 1865. (1122) Mentioned in General Wheeler's report, near Wilson's store, March 1st.

No. 99—(1071) Capt. W. J. Vason, Anderson's brigade, Allen's division, Wheeler's corps, Hardee's army, January 31, 1865. (1096) Mentioned in report of General Allen, February 4th. (1301) Mentioned in letter of Lieut.-Col. Jo Robins, March 1st.

THE FIFTEENTH CONFEDERATE CAVALRY.

The Fifteenth regiment of Confederate cavalry was organized early in 1864, at Mobile, and was composed of Alabama and Florida companies which had done coast duty for two or three years. It was placed under the command of Col. Henry Maury, and remained in the vicinity of Mobile and Pensacola the greater part of the year, except when it was sent in the fall to

Louisiana, and took part in a brilliant fight at Tunica. It served, successively, in Jenifer's, Reynolds', Patton's, McCulloch's, and Clanton's brigades, in Maury's army. The regiment was described at organization as "full, well mounted and well armed;" by December it had lost several hundred, and was reported as "poorly clad and scantily fed;" but in January, 1865, it was recruited from citizens of Mobile and vicinity, armed with miscellaneous weapons, and numbered 1,200 men. It was 800 strong in the city in February. The companies were almost always on detached duty, watching and checking the advance of the enemy and guarding the approaches to the city of Mobile. In April it was sent to establish a courier line to Demopolis. Before this could be done, the regiment took part in a disastrous fight at Claiborne. It blew up the magazine and evacuated Choctaw Bluff, April 14, 1865. The greater part of the men were disbanded, and the few who remained in arms were paroled at Demopolis. Col. Henry Maury was disabled by a wound just before the close of the war. He was detained in Mobile, and the regiment was led at Claiborne by Lieutenant-Colonel Myers. Capt. John H. Marshall was wounded and captured at Mississippi City.

EXTRACTS FROM OFFICIAL WAR RECORDS.

No. 58—(550) Mentioned in letter from Gen. D. H. Maury to General Polk, Mobile, January 12, 1864. (583) In Jenifer's brigade, General Maury's army, January 20th. (785) Maury's cavalry detached to different points in State and on coast, February 20th.

No. 59—(632, 633) Colonel Maury sent into Jones county to break up organized deserters who are destroying railroads, etc. Reports operations, March 12, 1864. (861) Reynolds' brigade, Maury's army, April 30, 1864.

No. 65—(399) General Asboth (Union) reports that Colonel Maury was attacked at Jackson bridge, Fla., and has returned to Fifteen Mile Station, May 25, 1864. (404, 405) Report of Capt. W. B. Amos, Company I, operations Yellow river, Fla., June 25th. (415) General Asboth reports Colonel Maury with 1,300 men on road to Pollard, July 23d. (418, 419) General Asboth says, Colonel Maury returned to Mobile, on July 24th, to protect city. (425) General Asboth reports three companies of Fifteenth at Pine Barren ridge, August 12th.

No. 66—(53, 56) General Asboth speaks of regiment as full, well mounted, well armed, under Colonel Maury and Lieutenant-Colonel Myers, near Pensacola, April, 1864. (89, 111, 165) Mentioned, further, by General Asboth. (257) General Asboth reports all of regiment ordered to Tensaw river, August 24th.

No. 78—(678) Col. Henry Maury, Patton's brigade, General Maury's army, June 30, 1864. (702) General Maury says regiment ordered to protect M. & O. railroad and Pascagoula, July 11th. (703) Five companies, 409 effective, ordered to Mobile, July. (751) Maury's regiment, 600 strong, has been sent to meet raid of enemy from Pensacola; army returns, August 3d. (814, 887) Liddell's brigade, Gardner's army, September, 1864.

No. 79—(875) Unattached in Maury's army, November 1, 1864.

No. 86—(425) Gen. J. Bailey (Union) says, six companies gone toward Milton, Fla., November 4, 1864; Colonel Maury's movements commented on. (675) Lieutenant Jackson (Union) reports regiment distributed as follows: "Three companies at Bluff Springs, three companies at Pollard, two companies at Milton, one company at Greenwood, one at Magnolia, with picket at Pine Barren ridge. Regiment numbers 700;" November 25th. (703) Same officer, November 28th, writes that on the 21st, five companies were at Greenwood, one company at Milton, three companies at Stockton, and Captain Bowen's company, 80 strong, doing picket duty at Pine Barrens. (911) Maj. F. W. Marston (Union) reports that Colonel Maury started about December 10th toward Pollard to meet reported advance of Federal forces; confronted and harassed General Davidson near Citronelle. Describes, them as "poorly clad and scantily fed."

No. 92—(419) Mentioned in report of Lieutenant-Colonel Spurling (Union) of fight at Pine Barren creek, November 17, 1864.

No. 93—(788) Mentioned in report of Gen. J. W. Davidson (Union) West Pascagoula, December 13, 1864. (1233) McCulloch's brigade, General Taylor's army,, November 20, 1864.

No. 94—(631) Mentioned in General Maury's orders, December 1, 1864. (633) In Liddell's division, Maury's army, December 1, 1864. (668) General Maury says regiment left Mobile, December 8, 1864; has ordered regiment to Leakesville, thence toward Bucatanna, etc.

No. 101—(601, 617) Capt. S. M. Eaton (Union) reports Maury's regiment "1,200 strong, composed of citizens of Mobile and vicinity, armed with miscellaneous weapons," on the Pascagoula road "facing and watching General Granger," January 21, 1865.

No. 103—(98, 137, 304, 305) Federal reports of attack on regiment at Claiborne, April 11, 1865. (636) Captain Eaton (Union) reports Maury's cavalry in and about city of Mobile, 1,000 strong, February 2d. (831) Statement of Perry Ryales, Mobile, February 16th, "Maury's cavalry, 800, doing provost-guard duty." (833, 834) Mentioned at Pollard and Mobile. (1047) In Maury's command, General Maury's army, March 10, 1865.

No. 104—(60) Report that regiment is sent to Blakely, March 22, 1865. (163) General Bailey (Union) reports, regiment close in his rear, March 31st. (226) Captain Eaton (Union) reports regiment in Clanton's brigade, April 4th. (364) Statement of Hugh McKeane, April 15th, reports 300 at Claiborne. Colonel Maury in city, wounded. (373) General Lucas (Union) mentions fight at Claiborne, April 11th; says detachment numbered 450. (450) General Asboth reports regiment collecting at Pollard under Captain Main, April 23d. (1172) Maury's command ordered to be kept ready to report movements of enemy, March 29th. (1216) Ordered to be ready to reinforce Wirt Adams, April 8th. (1226) Ordered to guard river above Choctaw, and establish courier line to Demopolis, April 11th. (1228) Has been ordered to cross from Claiborne, scout river and open communications with Demopolis,

April 12th. (1230-1232) Ordered to remain on west bank of Alabama river, April 12th. (1242) Couriers report defeat of Maury's command near Claiborne, April 15th. (1250) Capt. W. T. Smith confirms report of fight at Claiborne, says; Maury was not with command. Lieutenant-Colonel Myers was in command. Remnant of regiment near Greenville. Reported that Colonel Miles blew up magazine and evacuated Choctaw Bluff, April 14th.

THE FOURTH BATTALION, ALABAMA CAVALRY.

The Fourth Alabama battalion was made up of three companies from Alabama which went to Virginia in 1862. They were first assigned to the Jeff Davis legion, and afterward became part of the Phillips legion, Hampton's cavalry, in which organization they did some hard fighting. Their captains were Andrew P. Love, McKenzie and Roberts. Captain Love was captured at Dinwiddie.

EXTRACTS FROM OFFICIAL WAR RECORDS.
No. 82—(763) July 11, 1864, assigned, by special orders, No. 161, to the Jeff Davis legion of cavalry. (823) Field returns, July, 1864.
No. 88—(656) Transferred to Phillips' legion, September, 1864. (1219) August 10, 1864; Young's brigade, Butler's division, Hampton's cavalry corps. (1310) September, 1864, with Phillips' legion, assignment as above.

THE TWENTY-FOURTH BATTALION, ALABAMA CAVALRY.

The Twenty-fourth battalion of cavalry was organized late in the war; it was detached from Roddey's brigade when the latter was transferred to Polk's army in April, 1864, and remained with the army of Tennessee, serving with General Wheeler's cavalry. It was in Hannon's brigade until January, 1865, when it was transferred to Hagan's. Its record is the same as that of the Fifty-third Alabama. Maj. Robert B. Snodgrass, who commanded the battalion, was wounded three times.

EXTRACTS FROM OFFICIAL WAR RECORDS.
No. 59—(801) On picket in front of Dalton, April 20, 1864; not transferred to Polk's army with Roddey's brigade. (871) Maj. Robert B. Snodgrass, in Hannon's brigade, General Wheeler's corps, April 30th.
No. 74—(642, et seq.) In Hannon's brigade, General Wheeler's corps, Atlanta campaign. (956) Mentioned in General Wheeler's report of battle of Resaca.

No. 78—(856) Same assignment, September 20, 1864.

No. 99—(980) Mentioned in organization of corps commanded by General Wheeler, Charleston, S. C., January 2, 1865. Transferred to Hagan's brigade. (1072) Capt. R. P. Davis transferred to Hagan's brigade, Wheeler's corps, January 31st. (1148-1152) Mentioned by Maj. John Devereux, Augusta, Ga., February 10th.

THE TWENTY-FIFTH BATTALION, ALABAMA CAVALRY.

The Twenty-fifth battalion was sometimes called Mead's battalion. Capt. L. G. Mead commanded a company which operated very effectively in north Alabama and Tennessee in the summer and fall of 1862. He afterward raised a number of companies, and his men were spoken of as most reckless and daring. They were formed into battalions, the Alabama companies being consolidated into the Twenty-fifth battalion, in March, 1864, under the command of Maj. Miles E. Johnston, and serving in the neighborhood of the Tennessee river. They surrendered at Huntsville, May 11, 1865.

EXTRACTS FROM OFFICIAL WAR RECORDS.

Mead's company. Vol. XVI, Part 2—(758) August 15, 1862, ordered to operate in north Alabama and Tennessee, and report to nearest Confederate commander. (781) General Bragg's order, Chattanooga, Tenn., August 26, 1862. The following assignment of cavalry is announced: Crawford's, Mead's and Allen's regiment, commanded by Colonel Wheeler, to left wing of army of the Mississippi, and will report to Major-General Hardee.

Twenty-fifth Battalion, Maj. Miles E. Johnston. No. 103—(561, 562) Mentioned in report of Colonel Given, Huntsville, Ala., May 29, 1865, in report of surrender of Johnston's command. (563, 564, 566) Correspondence of Major Johnston, Huntsville, Ala., May, in regard to terms of surrender. (640) Mentioned by Gen. R. W. Johnson (Union), Pulaski, Tenn.; called Mead's battalion. (665) Mentioned by Col. W. J. Clift (Union), Fayetteville, Tenn., Mead's men "the most reckless and daring in the country." (1023) Special orders, No. 52, Richmond, Va., March 2, 1865. "The following companies Alabama cavalry raised within the enemy's lines by Capt. L. G. Mead, under authority of the war department, are hereby organized into a battalion, to be known as the Twenty-fifth battalion, Alabama cavalry: Capt. M. E. Johnston's, Capt. P. E. Cotton's, Capt. D. C. Nelson's, Capt. R. L. Welch's, Capt. W. M. Campbell's and Capt. John Cobb's."

BARBIERE'S RESERVE CAVALRY.

Barbiere's reserve cavalry consisted of six companies under the command of Maj. Joseph Barbiere, and served principally in central Alabama during the fall and winter of 1864-65.

EXTRACTS FROM OFFICIAL WAR RECORDS.
No. 93—(1233) In Armistead's brigade, central Alabama, General Taylor's army, November 20, 1864. No. 94—(634) In Armistead's brigade, central Alabama, General Maury's army, December 1, 1864. No. 103—(998) Barbiere's battalion cavalry, six companies, headquarters Wilsonville, February, 1865.

BEALL'S BATTALION, ALABAMA CAVALRY.

Beall's battalion of cavalry consisted of three companies of cavalry under the command of Maj. T. S. Beall, and served under General Beall, in Mississippi, in the spring of 1862.

EXTRACTS FROM OFFICIAL WAR RECORDS.
Vol. X, Part 2—(459) Present for duty, 42, April 28, 1862, General Beall's cavalry at Corinth, Miss.

GUNTER'S BATTALION, ALABAMA CAVALRY.

Gunter's battalion of cavalry was organized early in 1862, and was merged with Gibson's Eighteenth battalion of mounted infantry. It served with Forrest's cavalry, and engaged in numerous conflicts with the enemy along the Tennessee. In November it was dismounted; joined the army of Tennessee, was attached to Wood's brigade, and fought with heavy loss at Chickamauga. Maj. John T. Gibson, who succeeded Major Gunter in command, was killed at Chickamauga. The battalion afterward fought with Cleburne. It was attached to the Twenty-third Alabama without losing its organization.

EXTRACTS FROM OFFICIAL WAR RECORDS.
Vol. XVI, Part 2—(783) Mentioned by Gen. Sam Jones, Chattanooga, Tenn., August 27, 1862. (857) Moved to Tullahoma, September 20th. (890) Moved to Nashville, September 29th. (918) Sent to Lavergne, October 6th. (929) Ordered to report to General Forrest, Knoxville, October 9th.

HARDIE'S RESERVE CAVALRY.

Hardie's reserve cavalry consisted of six companies under command of Maj. Joseph Hardie, and served in Alabama and Georgia. Hardie's company is mentioned in reports of Rousseau's raid and at various points in Georgia. The battalion, 530 strong, was at Talladega in February, 1865, and was attached to General Maury's army.

EXTRACTS FROM OFFICIAL WAR RECORDS.
Hardie's Reserve Company: No. 74—(975) Mentioned "by Major Walthall in report of Rousseau's raid, July 14, 1864, about 20 men. No. 75—(793) Mentioned near Rome, Ga., June 22d. No. 78—(686) Mentioned by Captain Bowie, June 2 8th, at Cave Spring.

Hardie's Reserve Battalion: No. 93—(1233) In Armistead's brigade, central Alabama, November 20, 1864. No. 94—(634) In Armistead's brigade, central Alabama, December 1st. No. 103—(998) Hardie's battalion cavalry, six companies; 530 for duty; headquarters, Talladega, Ala

LEWIS' BATTALION, ALABAMA CAVALRY.

Lewis' battalion served in central Alabama and Georgia during the summer and fall of 1864, and until the close of the war. It consisted of five companies under Captains Harrell, Brooks, Morrison, Barnes and May. The gallant Major Lewis was killed while leading the battalion at Lafayette, Ga. He was succeeded in command by Maj. William V. Harrell.

EXTRACTS FROM OFFICIAL WAR RECORDS.
No. 74—(997) One killed, 5 wounded, at Lafayette, Ga., June 24, 1864. Maj. T. H. Lewis killed. (998, 999) Col. C. H. Armistead's report says: "Majors Lewis and Redwood have tested their devotion to our cause by sealing it with their blood." (1000, 1001) Colonel Ball's report of same. (1003) Capt. William V. Harrell's report says: "When nearly opposite the east end of the jail, the noble, gallant and chivalrous Major Lewis fell mortally wounded, while leading his men to the charge, addressing them in language of endearment and encouragement, stimulating them by word and example to the performance of deeds worthy of the world-wide reputation of the sons of the South for bravery and heroism. As the spirit of the lamented Lewis was about to bid adieu to its earthly tenement, his feeble voice was heard saying: 'Charge them, boys, charge them,' and right nobly did his gallant boys respond." (1004) One killed, 7 wounded at battle of Lafayette.

No. 78—(791) In Armistead's brigade, district of Central and Northern Alabama, commanded by Brig.-Gen. D. W. Adams, August 21, 1864. (812) Present for duty, 104, Talladega, Ala., September 1st.

No. 93—(1233) In Armistead's brigade, under Maj. William V. Harrell, central Alabama, November 20, 1864. No. 94—(634) In same brigade, December. No. 103— (1047) In same brigade, army of Mobile, March 10, 1865.

MORELAND'S BATTALION, ALABAMA CAVALRY.

Moreland's battalion was included in Roddey's brigade and was in north Alabama and Tennessee during the greater part of the winter and spring of 1863-64, serving for a time in Hannon's brigade. It fought at Tishomingo creek, June, 1864, and was attached to General Maury's army, serving in central and northern Alabama. It was paroled at Iuka, May 18, 1865.

EXTRACTS FROM OFFICIAL WAR RECORDS.
No. 52—(595) Mentioned by Gen. E. A. Carr (Union), Corinth, September 13, 1863. Left in valley on Roddey's departure. No. 54—(38) Mentioned by General Ferguson near Courtland, Ala., October 31, 1863. (603) Mentioned by Colonel Rowett (Union), Pulaski, Tenn., December 18th. Report of skirmish on Shoal creek, December 12th. No. 55—(664) Col. M. D. Moreland, Roddey's brigade, Wheeler's corps, detached, November 20, 1863.
No. 56—(92) Mentioned by Gen. J. D. Stevenson, Corinth, November 8, 1863. (619, 806, 888) In Roddey's brigade, Wheeler's corps, October to December, 1863. No. 58—(590) In Roddey's brigade, Wheeler's corps, January 20, 1864. No. 59—(429) Mentioned by Colonel Rowett, Bailey's Springs, April 18, 1864. (735) Mentioned, March 26th, as being near Moulton.
No. 77—(231) One killed, 5 wounded, at battle of Tishomingo Creek, June 10, 1864. (345) Reconnoissance near Tupelo, July 14th. No. 79—(817) Mentioned by General Forrest, October 12, 1864. No. 93—(1233) In Roddey's brigade, district of North Alabama, November 20th No. 94—(634) In Roddey's brigade, North Alabama, December 1st. No. 99—(1150) Mentioned by Maj. John G. Devereux, February 10, 1865, as having belonged to Hannon's original command. No. 104—(830) Paroled at Iuka, May 18, 1865.

STUART'S BATTALION, ALABAMA CAVALRY.

Stuart's battalion, commanded by Maj. James H. Stuart, served in north Alabama from the summer of 1864 until the close of the war, and was frequently engaged in scouting and skirmishing.

EXTRACTS FROM OFFICIAL WAR RECORDS.

No. 77—(362) Mentioned in report of Col. William T. C. Grower, expedition from Decatur to Courtland, and skirmish, July, 1864. No. 78—(668) In north Alabama, June, 1864, Col. Josiah Patterson's report. No. 93—(1233) In Roddey's brigade, district of North Alabama, November 20th. No. 94—(634) In Roddey's brigade, north Alabama, December 1st. No. 103—(48) Mentioned near Warrenton, February 17, 1865.

COMPANIES OF ALABAMA CAVALRY.

In addition to the regiments and battalions, there were a number of detached companies of Alabama cavalry, most of which served in the defense of Mobile and the Bay forts. Cottrill's, White's and Arrington's served at Pollard, Mobile and Fort Morgan in and after 1862; and Amos', Baldwin's, under Capt. T. C. Barlow, the Dorrence Rangers, under Capt. John W. Murrell, Goldsby's and Meador's companies served there later. Gordon's regiment is mentioned at Murfreesboro, and Houston's and Hubbard's at Fort Henry. Crocheron's Light Dragoons, under Capt. E. M. Holloway, served for a long time as escorts in the army of Tennessee.

EXTRACTS FROM OFFICIAL WAR RECORDS.

Captain Amos' Company. Vol. XV—(1068) Canty's brigade, Buckner's corps, April, 1863, at or near Pollard. No. 42—(39) June 8, 1863, in eastern division of department of the Gulf.

Baldwin's Rangers, Capt. T. C. Barlow. Vol. XV—(850) In army of Mobile, October 31, 1862. (1069) In Powell's brigade, General Buckner's corps, April, 1863, Perdido river. No. 42—(39, 131, 157) Powell's brigade, Mobile, to August, 1863, Camp Powell.

Cottrill's Scouts. Vol. VI—(499) Very highly commended in Col. W. L. Powell's report, January 20, 1862, of contest for possession of the schooner Andracita, formerly J. W. Wilder, near Fort Morgan.

Crocheron Light Dragoons, Capt. E. M. Holloway. Vol. XXIII, Part 2—(945, 958) Mentioned among escorts, Polk's army corps, Atlanta, July and August, 1863. Nos. 51) 59. 74—Same mention, September, 1863, to June, 1864.

Dorrence Rangers, Capt. John W. Murrell. Vol. XV— (850) Army of Mobile, October 31, 1862. (1069) Cumming's brigade, Buckner's corps, department of the Gulf, April, 1863, near Mobile. No. 42—(39) Department of the Gulf, June 8, 1863, at Pascagoula.

Captain Goldsby's Company Mounted Infantry. No. 65—(442) August 30, 1864, Brigadier-General Asboth, U. S. A., says of skirmish at Milton, Fla.: "Came upon Captain Goldsby with about 100 men." No. 78—(814) In Liddell's brigade, department of the Gulf, September 3, 1864. No.

104—(1261) Mentioned by Col. S. Jones, Demopolis, Ala., April 24, 1865; asks for couriers.

Capt. H. R. Gordon's Company. Vol. XX, Part 2— (432) Polk's corps, army of Tennessee, about November 39, 1862, near Murfreesboro.

Houston's and Hubbard's Companies. Vol. VII—(137-139, 140) At Fort Henry, February 5, 1862, General Tilghman's and Colonel Heiman's reports.

Captain Meador's Company. No. 103—(1045) Mentioned as reporting to General Clanton, March 10, 1865, department of the Gulf.

Mobile City Troop, Capt. E. T. Arrington. Vol. XV—(850) Army of Mobile, October 31, 1862. (1069) In Powell's brigade, April, 1863, Perdido river. No. 42—(39, 131, 157) In Powell's brigade, department of the Gulf, to August, 1863.

Captain White's Company. Vol. XV—(850) At Mobile, 1862.

CHAPTER VI.

BATTERIES COMPOSED OF ALABAMA TROOPS—THEIR ORGANIZATION AND OFFICERS—RECORDS FROM THE OFFICIAL REPORTS.

BURNETT'S BATTERY.

BURNETT'S battery was engaged in Samuel Jones' corps, in Mississippi, in the spring and summer of 1861.

EXTRACTS FROM OFFICIAL WAR RECORDS.
Vol. X, Part 1—(787) In Samuel Jones' corps, Tupelo, June 30, 1862.
Vol. XVII, Part 2—(632) Same assignment.

BURTWELL'S BATTERY.

Burtwell's battery was engaged, under its captain, J. R. R. Burtwell, in General Jackson's brigade, in Mississippi, in the spring of 1862.

EXTRACTS FROM OFFICIAL WAR RECORDS.
Vol. X, Part 2—(461, 549) In General Jackson's brigade, Corinth, April 28, 1862.
Vol. XVI, Part 2—(764) Same brigade, Tupelo, August 20, 1862.
Vol. XVII, Part 2—(633) Same brigade, Tupelo, June 30, 1862.

FIRST BATTALION OF ARTILLERY.

The First Alabama battalion of artillery was recruited at Mobile, Montgomery and Selma, and was organized in February, 1861, at Fort Morgan. It was made part of the army of Mobile in the spring of 1862, and was ordered to report at Chattanooga in July. It served, consecutively, with the brigades of Generals Shoup, Higgins and Page, and reached a very high plane of efficiency and discipline. It did gallant service at Forts Gaines, Powell and Morgan. No more heroic defense was ever made than that of this battalion at Fort Morgan. The detachment there engaged, fought until their guns were knocked out of position, losing 150 killed and wounded. The remainder was captured and the men sent to Elmira, N. Y., where one-half of them died of small-pox. The officers were sent to Fort Warren. The remnant of the battalion was transferred to Choctaw Bluff, March, 1865, and surrendered with the army of Mobile. Lieutenant-Colonel Forsyth was the first commander. He resigned, and was succeeded by Lieut. -Col. James T. Gee, who was captured at Fort Morgan. Maj. J. M. Gary and Capts. F. S. Ferguson, Lee Hammond, R. N. Campbell and J. W. Whiting were also captured there. Capts. Wm. B. Hughes and N. J. Smith were wounded and captured at Fort Morgan.

EXTRACTS FROM OFFICIAL WAR RECORDS.

Vol. VI—(819) Army of Mobile, February 1, 1862.

Vol. XVII, Part 2—(659) Forsyth ordered to report at Chattanooga, July 26, 1862.

No. 42—(39) In Slaughter's brigade, Maury's army, June 8, 1863. (131) In Powell's brigade, Maury's army, August 1st. (157) At Fort Morgan and Grant's Pass, August 10th. (275) In Shoup's brigade, September 30th, Maj. J. T. Gee. (402) In Shoup's brigade, November 10th. (511, 562) In Higgins' brigade, December.

No. 56—(630) Ordered to Meridian, November 4, 1863. (729) General Maury asks for battery, November 21st.

No. 58—(582) In Higgins' brigade, January 20, 1864.

No. 59—(861) Under Lieut.-Col. R. C. Forsyth, Page's brigade, April 30, 1864.

No. 77—(428) At Fort Gaines, August 3, 1864.

No. 78—(678, 752) Page's brigade, with General Maury, June to August, 1864.

No. 84—(230) Mentioned by Col. Albert Myer, July, 1864, 400 men at Fort Morgan.

No. 103—(1045) Transferred to Choctaw Bluff, March 10, 1865. (1047) Detachment under Lieut. P. Lee Hammond, in army of Mobile.

SECOND BATTALION OF ARTILLERY.

Battery A of this battalion, under the command of Capt. Stephen Charpentier, served in the defenses of Mobile until the spring of 1863, when it was attached to General Featherstone's brigade, and afterward did service in Mississippi, known as Charpentier's battery. Battery C served in General Hebert's brigade and lost heavily at the siege of Vicksburg, where its captain, T. K. Emanuel, was killed. The remnant of the battery continued to serve under the command of Capt. John D. Haynie in the army of Mobile until the surrender. Battery E seems to have served continuously under the command of Capt. J. B. Hutchisson, at or near Mobile.

EXTRACTS FROM OFFICIAL WAR RECORDS.

Battery A. No. 38—(936) Featherstone's brigade, May 30, 1863, Jackson, Miss. (1041) Same assignment, July 30th. (1050) Mentioned by Maj. L. Hoxton, near Morton, Miss., August 8th.

Battery C. No. 37—(326) Under Lieut. J. R. Sclater, in General Hebert's brigade, army of Vicksburg, July 4, 1863. (329) Capt. T. K. Emanuel killed at siege of Vicksburg. (369) Loss, 6 killed, 6 wounded, Vicksburg. (373) One wounded, June 25th. (378) Seven killed, 8 wounded, Vicksburg siege. No. 38—(1060) In Forney's division, August 29, 1863. No. 42—(131) In General Canty's brigade, Maury's army, August 1, 1863. (157) In Mobile, Ala., August 10th. No. 103—(1048) In Gladden's battery, army of Mobile, March 10, 1865.

Battery E. No. 42—(39) In Slaughter's brigade, Maury's army, June 8, 1863. No. 103—(1048) In Gladden's battery, army of Mobile, March 10, 1865.

Charpentier's Battery. No. 53—(515) Featherstone's brigade, Loring's division, army of Mississippi, August 20, 1863.

No. 56—(757). No. 57—(332). No. 58—(520, 584). No. 59—(604, 659) Assignment as above, to March, 1864. (863) Assignment as above, April 30th, but reported as in Myrick's battalion, Stevenson's division, April 24th. No. 74—(875) Mentioned in report of General Loring, near New Hope church, May 13, 1864. (994) Mentioned under Lieutenant Jenks, in report of Gen. G. J. Pillow, Oxford, Ala., June 30th. No. 75—(656) Mentioned in Loring's division, about May 1, 1864. No. 78—(791, 811, 887) With General Adams, central Alabama, August and September, 1864. No. 79—(865) With Maj. H. C. Semple, October, 1864. (872) Effective total, 64, at Mobile. (876) In Burnett's command, Maury's army, November 1st. No. 94—(633) With Major Semple, Maury's army, December 1, 1864. No. 101—(681) Mentioned, 70 strong, at Mobile, January 30, 1865. No. 103— (942) Called Jenks' battery, 76 present, with Maj. Henry C. Semple, army of Mobile, March 29, 1865. (1014) Started to Selma, February 25th. No. 104—(226) In Fuller's brigade, Wilcox county, Ala., April, 1865. (364) Jenks' battery, Montgomery, April, 1865.

ALABAMA STATE ARTILLERY BATTALION.

This battalion served at Mobile in Generals Fuller's and Higgins' brigades during the last few months of the war, and was sometimes called State Reserves. Battery C was commanded by Capt. John B. Todd, afterward by Lieut. R. H. Bush, and Battery D was commanded by Capt. Wm. M. Homer, formerly of Ketchum's battery.

EXTRACTS FROM OFFICIAL WAR RECORDS.

Battery C. No. 59—(861) Fuller's brigade, Maury's army, Mobile, April 30, 1864. No. 78—(632) Fuller's brigade, Gen. Stephen D. Lee's army, June 1st. (678) Higgins' brigade, June 30th. No. 79—(876) Fuller's command, Maury's army, November 1st. No. 93—(1235) In Maury's command, Gen.

Richard Taylor's army, November 20th. No. 94—(633) In Fuller's command, Maury's army, December 1st. No. 103—(1047) Called State Reserves, Lieut. R. H. Bush, Maury's army, March 10, 1865. No. 104—(207) Mentioned by Maj. A. M. Jackson, at Mobile, 55 present, April 3, 1865. (226) In Fuller's division, Wilcox county, April 4th.

Battery D. No. 59—(861) Fuller's brigade, Maury's army, Mobile, April 30, 1864. No. 78—(632) Fuller's brigade, Gen. S. D. Lee's army, June 1st. (678) With General Maury, June 30th. No. 79—(876) In Fuller's command, Maury's army, November 1st. No. 93—(1235) In Maury's command, Taylor's army, November 20th. No. 94—(633) In Fuller's command, Maury's army, December 1st. No. 103—(1047) Called State Reserves; Maury's army, March 10, 1865.

KETCHUM'S (GARRITY'S) BATTERY.

Ketchum's battery was organized at Mobile in May, 1861, and served for a short time at Pensacola. It was in Adams' brigade at Corinth, in March, 1861, and served in Gen. Preston Pond's brigade at Shiloh, where it lost seven men. Its captain was specially commended by the brigade commander at Shiloh, who says the safety of his whole command was due to Captain Ketchum. This battery was with Chalmers' brigade, Withers' reserve corps, in the summer of 1863, and was engaged at Munfordville, Perryville, Wildcat gap, and Murfreesboro, where it lost twenty-seven men, killed and wounded. It was ordered to Deas' brigade in July, 1863, and sent from Lookout Point to Gen. Patton Anderson, November, 1863. It fought at Chickamauga, Chattanooga and Missionary Ridge in Cheatham's corps, and sometimes with heavy loss. It was in Maury's artillery reserves in 1865, and fought at Spanish Fort, losing two men; finally surrendered at Meridian. Capt. Wm. H. Ketchum resigned and was succeeded in January, 1863, by Capt. James Garrity, who was wounded at Murfreesboro and Marietta. Lieut. Philip Bond, who commanded the battery in the summer of 1864, was killed at Jonesboro. Lieut. Maynard Hassell was killed near Atlanta.

EXTRACTS FROM OFFICIAL WAR RECORDS.,

Vol. X, Part 1—(13) Mentioned by General Gladden, March 12, 1862. (382) In Preston Pond's brigade, army of Mississippi, April 6th and 7th. (468) Mentioned in General Bragg's report of Shiloh. (471-474) Mentioned by General Ruggles. (516-519) Highly commended in Colonel Pond's report: "Captain Ketchum exhibited throughout the whole a degree of skill and courage which mark him as an artillery officer of the highest merit; in fact, the safety of my command is due to him." (523) Mentioned in Col. Marshall J. Smith's report. (525) Also in Colonel Looney's report. (527-531) Captain Ketchum's report. He commends in the highest terms,

Lieutenants Garrity, Bond and Carroll, and Corporal Ingalls, for gallantry, coolness and ability. (543) Mentioned in Colonel Marrast's report. (788) In General Chalmers' brigade, June 30th. (810) Commended in General Ruggles' report, Farmington, May 9th. (829, 830) Commended highly in Col. J. F. Pagan's report of same. (831) Mentioned in Captain Hoxton's report

Vol. X, Part 2—(307) In Col. D. W. Adams' brigade, March 9, 1862, Corinth. (388) Mentioned by General Ruggles, April 28th. (461) In Ruggles' brigade, April 28th. (500) Mentioned by R. H. S. Thompson, May 6th. (549) In Ruggles' division, May 26th.

Vol. XVI, Part 1—(975-979) Mentioned in General Chalmers' report, September 12 to 17, 1863, Munfordville, Ky. (982, 983) Seven wounded, Munfordville, report of Lieutenant Garrity. (985, 986) Mentioned in White's and Finley's reports of Munfordville.

Vol. XVI, Part 2—(764) In Chalmers' brigade, August 20, 1862. (817) At Glasgow, Ky., September 12th.

Vol. XVII, Part 2—(633) Withers' reserve corps, June 30, 1862.

Vol. XX, Part 2—(430, 431) Present, 115, November 29, 1862, reserve division, Polk's army.

Vol. XXIII, Part 2—(735, 843) In Withers' division; present, 101, May 19, 1863. (907) Ordered to report to General Deas, July 12th, from Chattanooga. (942, 958) In Deas' brigade, to August 10th.

No. 50—(229) In Hindman's division, Chattanooga, Tenn., October 7, 1863.

No. 51—(305) Mentioned in General Hindman's report of Chickamauga, September 20, 1863. (307) Five wounded, Chickamauga. (315) Mentioned by Patton Anderson. (329) Captain Garrity's report of Chickamauga. (351) Mentioned in Slaughter's report of Chickamauga.

No. 55—(675, 677) Ordered to report from Lookout Point to General Anderson, November 23, 1863. (725, 728) Mentioned in reports of Gen. John C. Brown and Capt. M. Van Den Corput, Lookout Mountain, November 24, 1863.

No. 56—(620, 808, 827, 886) In Hindman's division, 90 present, December 14, 1863.

No. 58—(589) In Hindman's division, January 20, 1864. (821) In Hood's corps, February 29th.

No. 59—(687) Organized, March 4, 1861; present for duty, March 29, 1864, 94. (698-700) Service of officers. Garrity made captain, January 1, 1863; engaged in the following battles: Shiloh, Farmington, Munfordville, Murfreesboro, Chickamauga, Missionary Ridge. (731) Effective, 95, Dalton, April 1, 1864.

No. 74—(643, et seq.) Hood's corps, Johnston's army, Atlanta campaign; July 10th, Lieut. Philip Bond commanding battery.

No. 79—(896) Mentioned by Col. R. F. Beckham, November 7, 1864.

No. 93—(668) Lee's corps, Hood's army, December 10, 1864. (692) Mentioned in report of Col. L. Hoxton.

No. 103—(1047) Artillery reserves, General Maury's army, March 10, 1865. No. 104—(226) Mentioned as in Fuller's division, April 4th.

JEFF DAVIS BATTERY.

The Jeff Davis battery, organized at Selma in May, 1861, was soon sent to Virginia, where it fought in Early's brigade at Manassas and at the battle of Seven Pines, losing 3 men at the latter place. In Hill's division, during the Seven Days' battles, it lost 3 killed and 14 wounded; at Cold Harbor, 3 killed and 10 wounded; at Gaines' Mill, 3 killed and 14 wounded. It also fought at Mechanicsville and many other points in Virginia, and was at South Mountain, Fredericksburg and Orange Court House. It took part in the terrible battle of Gettysburg. Serving, consecutively, in Long's and Page's brigades, it was in northern Virginia during the spring and summer of 1864, at Cedar Creek in October, 1864, and at Fort Clifton in March, 1865. It was almost continuously engaged. Its first captain was J. T. Montgomery, who was succeeded by J. W. Bondurant, and later it was commanded by W. J. Reese. The latter was in command during and after the battle of Gettysburg. These officers were all distinguished for their skill and gallantry.

EXTRACTS FROM OFFICIAL WAR RECORDS.

Vol. V—(1029) In Van Dorn's division, army of the Potomac, January 14, 1862.

Vol. XI, Part 1—(943) In battle Seven Pines, May 31, 1862. (961, 966) Mentioned by General Garland, who says, Bondurant delivered a telling fire with his six pieces. (967) One killed and two wounded at Seven Pines.

Vol. XI, Part 2—(485) In Hill's division, in Seven Days' fight about Richmond. (511) Mentioned by Captain Webb as in Garland's brigade. (623) Gen. D. H. Hill reports that Bondurant's battery drove Yankee artillery off the field, June 26, 1862. (624) Mentioned by Gen. D. H. Hill, June 27th. (626) General Hill says battery engaged at Mechanicsville and Cold Harbor; at the latter place had 3 killed and 10 wounded. (640, 645) Commended by General Garland at Gaines' Mill, June 27th, where they lost 3 killed and 14 wounded. (652) Maj. H. P. Jones says battery was actively engaged with battery of enemy, June 27th.

Vol. XI, Part 3—(482, 532) In Early's brigade, April 30, 1862, 80 present. (615) Called Hardaway's, army before Richmond; 110 present, June 23d. (650) In D. H. Hill's division, July 23d. (690) Mentioned by Pierson, chief of artillery.

Vol. XIX, Part 1—(809) In D. H. Hill's division, Novembers, 1862. (836) Two 3-inch and two 12-pound howitzers. (1020-1024) Mentioned, Hill's report of Maryland campaign, September 14 to 17, 1862. (1040) Mentioned by Col. D. K. McRae, South Mountain.

Vol. XIX, Part 2—(652) General Pendleton's report, October 2, 1862, Captain Bondurant (Jeff Davis artillery), an admirable battery that has rendered eminent service,, but he is its life; is now absent—sick.

Vol. XXI—(541, 1073) In D. H. Hill's division. (561) One killed and 3 wounded, battle of Fredericksburg.

No. 39—(1000) Mentioned by Col. T. M. Carter, May 2 and 3, 1864. (1044) Mentioned by Col. H. P. Jones, Orange Court House.

No. 40—(619) Proposed for army of Northern Virginia, Bondurant's battery, 4 guns, February, 1863. (626, 655, 729) Carter's battalion, Second corps. (637) Report of Lieut. E. P. Dandridge, February 20th, 83 present for duty.

No. 44—(287, 342) With O'Neal's brigade, Capt. W. J. Reese, Gettysburg, July 1st to 3d. (545, 603) Mentioned at battle of Gettysburg.

No. 48—(418) Mentioned as Reese's battery, in A. L. Long's report of fight at Bealeton, October 26, 1863, two men wounded. (423) Mentioned as Reese's battery by Col. Thomas Carter, commanding battalion, October 26th. (821) In General Long's division, army of Northern Virginia, October 31st.

Nos. 49, 60, 67, 88, 89—Army Northern Virginia; Young's brigade, December 31, 1863; Long's brigade, May, 1864; Page's battalion, February 28, 1865.

No. 90—(567) With Gen. J. A. Early, Cedar Creek, October 19, 1864.

No. 96—(1284) Present total, 87, Fort Clifton, March 6, 1865."

HARDAWAY'S BATTERY.

Hardaway's battery was recruited and armed by its first captain, Robert A. Hardaway; was sent to Virginia in 1861, and remained at Manassas until March, 1862. With the army of Northern Virginia, it saw continuous service during the war.

In the battle of Seven Pines, in the Seven Days' battles, and in all the great battles around Richmond, it gained the highest distinction. General Hill, the division commander, repeatedly commended this battery for gallant service, and speaks of Hardaway as the best practical artillerist he had seen in the service. Stonewall Jackson also commended its action at Fredericksburg. It lost heavily in the Seven Days' battles. It was also engaged and suffered severely at Chancellorsville, Gettysburg, Mine Run, the Wilderness, Spottsylvania and a great number of smaller engagements, finally surrendering at Appomattox. At the battle of Gettysburg it was called Hurt's battery, Captain Hardaway having been promoted to lieutenant-colonel and placed in command of a battalion, and succeeded by Captain Hurt, who was wounded in this battle. Capt. John W. Tullis was wounded and captured at Gettysburg. Lieut. George A. Ferrell was in command of the battery when it was surrendered at Appomattox.

EXTRACTS FROM OFFICIAL WAR RECORDS.

Vol. XI, Part 1—(946) In D. H. Hill's division, at Seven Pines.

Vol. XI, Part 2—(485) In D. H. Hill's division, Seven Days' battles, June 26 to July 1, 1862. (505) In Anderson's brigade; 12 wounded. (511) Mentioned, near Richmond, July 15th. (561) In battle of June 30th. (623) D. H. Hill's report, Hardaway's battery drove enemy's artillery from field. (624, 626) D. H. Hill reports battery distinguished at Mechanicsville and Cold Harbor. (630) One killed, 25 wounded, Seven Days' fights.

Vol. XI, Part 3—(615) One hundred and ten present before Richmond, June 28, 1862. (Called Hardaway's Jeff Davis.) (650) Gen. D. H. Hill's division, July 23d. (690) Two guns burst during Seven days' battles.

Vol. XIX, Part 1—(809, 836) In D. H. Hill's division, Maryland campaign. (838) Mentioned, Captain Barnwell's report. (1024) Mentioned, D. H. Hill's report of operations, July 23d to September 17th.

Vol. XIX, Part 2—(143) Commended, Gen. J. E. B. Stuart's report.

Vol. XXI—(36, 37) Highly commended in D. H. Hill's report of retreat of Yankee gunboats from Port Royal, Va., December 4, 1862. These gunboats, 4 in number, carried 21 guns, and had a complement of some 500 men. Hardaway opened upon them with his Whitworth gun, at a distance of 3 miles, and kept up his pitting until dark, when they fled down the river. This same gun of Hardaway's, at Upperville, drove entirely off the field a Yankee battery of artillery, a large force of cavalry and infantry, at a distance of 3 1/2 miles. Hill calls Hardaway "the best practical artillerist I have seen in service." (541) In D. H. Hill's division at Fredericksburg. (633) Commended by Stonewall Jackson, Fredericksburg. (642, 643) Commended in D. H. Hill's report, Fredericksburg; Hardaway shelled the gunboats. (1077) Mentioned by Gen. W. H. Taylor, December 24th.

No. 39—(793) In General Lee's army, May, 1863, as Hurt's battery. (879, 882) Mentioned by Maj. R. A. Hardaway, near Hamilton's Crossing, May 3d to 5th. (939) Mentioned by Gen. R. E. Rodes.

No. 40—(619, 626, 637, 656) Assignments in army of Northern Virginia. (729) In McIntosh's battalion, April 16, 1863.

No. 44—(290, 345) At Gettysburg, July 1st to 3d, in reserve artillery. (353) Mentioned in W. N. Pendleton's report. (674, 676) Mentioned in Maj. D. G. McIntosh's report.

No. 48—(437, 438) Lieutenant Crenshaw commanding; mentioned in D. G. McIntosh's report of engagement at Bristoe Station, October 14, 1863.

No. 60—(1269) Present for duty, 94 men, April 9, 1864, Camp Taylor.

No. 67—(1038) Mentioned in report of General Pendleton. No. 87—(858) Mentioned by same, operations of July 24, 1864.

No. 89—(1355) McIntosh's battalion, January 2, 1865, on or near James river.

No. 95— (1273) Lieut. Geo. A. Ferrell, Lee's army, Appomattox.

WATERS' BATTERY.

Waters' battery was organized in Mobile in 1861, and was there, 129 strong, early in 1862. It was in Corinth in the spring of 1862. In Manigault's brigade, Bragg's army, it went through the Kentucky campaign, and was engaged at Perryville, Munfordville, Murfreesboro, Chickamauga and Missionary Ridge. Here halt its force was captured, and the remnant was distributed in Cobb's Kentucky and Mayberry's Tennessee batteries. Its captain was David D. Waters.

EXTRACTS FROM OFFICIAL WAR RECORDS.

Vol. VI—(868) In Mobile, March, 1862, 129 present. Vol. X, Part 1—(789) In Manigault's brigade, Tupelo, June 30, 1862.

Vol. X, Part 2—(461, 549) In Trapier's brigade, Bragg's army, April to May, 1862.

Vol. XVI, Part 1—(983) Battle at Munfordville, September 16, 1862.

Vol. XVI, Part 2—(764) Capt. David D. Waters, in Manigault's brigade, August, 1862.

Vol. XX, Part 2—(430-432) Present, 106, at or near Murfreesboro, November 29, 1862, under Lieut. C. W. Watkins, in Manigault's brigade.

Vol. XXIII, Part 2—(735) Capt. D. D. Waters, in Manigault's brigade, April to August, 1863. (843) Present, 104, May 19th.

No. 51—(15) Lieut. C. W. Watkins, in Hindman's division, September 19 and 20, 1863. (307) Mentioned, at Chickamauga. (342) Mentioned in report of A. M. Manigault. (349) Mentioned in report of Colonel Reid. (356) Mentioned in report of Lieut. Geo. E. Turner.

No. 55—(659) Lieut. W. P. Hamilton, in Hindman's division, November 20, 1863.

No. 56—(620) In Cheatham's corps, with Bragg's army, October 31, 1863. (790) Ordered to report at Atlanta, December 6th. (832) Reported at Atlanta, to Colonel Wright, December 15th.

No. 59—(703) Some of this battery and fragments of others consolidated in Cobb's, January, 1864.

GAGE'S BATTERY.

Gage's battery was organized at Mobile in October, 1861, and remained under the command of Capt. Chas. P. Gage in the defenses of the city until the following spring. Sent north, it suffered severely at Shiloh, where its conduct was highly commended by Generals Withers and Chalmers. It then returned to Mobile, and was used in the defenses until the fall of the city. Lieuts. James Hill and James T. Hutchisson were promoted, and commanded the battery at different times.

EXTRACTS FROM OFFICIAL WAR RECORDS.

Vol. X, Part 1—(383) In General Chalmers' brigade, Shiloh. (532) General Withers in his report of Shiloh says: "With such batteries, however, as Robertson's, Girardey's and Gage's, there could be no failure." (549, 551, 552) Commended by Gen. James R. Chalmers; battery suffered severely and did manful service, July 6th. Vol. X, Part 2—(307) In Colonel Mouton's brigade, March 9, 1862.

WADDELL'S BATTERY.

Waddell's battery was organized in February, 1862, by taking six men from each company of the Sixth Alabama. It was placed in Tracy's brigade and sent to east Tennessee, and took part in the Kentucky campaign. It did gallant service at Baker's Creek, where it was badly cut up. In 1863 it went with Stevenson's division to Mississippi, and was in the siege of Vicksburg, where it was almost entirely lost; the remnant was divided into Emery's and Bellamy's batteries.

EXTRACTS FROM OFFICIAL WAR RECORDS.

Vol. XVI, Part 2—(984) In Tracy's brigade, October 31, 1862.

Vol. XX, Part 2—(413) In Tracy's brigade, November 20, 1862, east Tennessee.

No. 36—(318) Mentioned for gallant conduct at Baker's Creek. (640) Mentioned at Fort Gibson; four pieces captured.

No. 37—(63) Mentioned in Col. D. B. Hill's report of Champion's hill. (95, 96) Mentioned by General Stevenson at Baker's Creek, May 16, 1863. Stevenson says: "Captain Waddell fought one of the guns with his own hands." (99) Loss, 9 killed, 10 wounded, at Baker's Creek. (101) Mentioned by Gen. S. D. Lee, at Baker's Creek, (105) by Gen. A. Cumming, (110, 111) by Gen. F. M. Cockrell, who reports Waddell as a gallant, fearless officer. (326) In Gen. S. D. Lee's brigade, Vicksburg, July 4, 1863. (328) Loss, 9 killed, 30 wounded, at the siege. (350) Mentioned in Gen. Stephen D. Lee's report. (352) "Waddell was gallant and vigilant." (375) Mentioned by General Hebert.

No. 38—(612) In Tracy's brigade, January 31, 1863. (613) Ordered to Vicksburg. (703) In Stevenson's division, April 20th. (1059) Same assignment, August 29th.

No. 57—(484) Battalion Twenty, Alabama artillery, under Major Waddell, ordered to report to General Stevenson, near Dalton, February 25, 1864.

No. 59—(708) Waddell's battalion of artillery. Divided into Waddell's and Emery's batteries, 1863. Served in Kentucky campaign, and in Mississippi previous to siege of Vicksburg.

TWENTIETH BATTALION OF ARTILLERY.

After the surrender of Vicksburg, the remnant of Waddell's battery was reorganized into three batteries, under the command of Capt. Winslow D. Emery, Battery A; Capt. Richard H. Bellamy, Battery B, and Capt. T. J. Key, Battery C; and ordered, under the command of Major Waddell, to report to General Stevenson, near Dalton, February, 1864. It served in the army of Tennessee during the remainder of the war, generally in the reserve artillery, and was at Macon, Ga., in the fall of 1864. Captain Emery was wounded at Vicksburg.

EXTRACTS FROM OFFICIAL WAR RECORDS.

Battery A. No. 55—(662) Capt. Winslow D. Emery, in General Stevenson's division, November 20, 1863. No. 57—(484) Battalion under Major Waddell ordered to report to General Stevenson, near Dalton, February 25, 1864. No. 58—(821) In reserve artillery, army of Tennessee, February 29, 1864. No. 59—(687) Organized May, 1861; Johnston's army, 84 present, March 29, 1864. (708) Served in Kentucky campaign, and in Mississippi previous to siege of Vicksburg. (709) Hallonquist's report. (731) Sixty-two effective, April 1, 1864. (872) Reserve artillery, Johnston's army, April 30th. No. 74—(644-675) Reserve artillery, army of Tennessee, April to August, 1864. No. 78—(858) Hood's army, September 20, 1864, at Macon, Ga.

Battery B. No. 55—(662) Capt. Richard H. Bellamy, in General Stevenson's division, November 20, 1863. Nos. 57 and 58—As above. No. 59—(687) Organized, May, 1861. (708) Surrendered at Vicksburg with Emery's, as Waddell's battalion. (709) Bellamy's battery, total effective, 68, Hallonquist's report. (721) Effective, 65, April 1, 1864, Dalton, Ga. (872) Artillery reserve in Johnston's army, April 30th. No. 74—(644-675) In artillery reserve, army of Tennessee, April to August, 1864. (901) Commended by Gen. S. G. French, Kenesaw mountain, June 27th. (968) Mentioned by Maj. George Storrs, same battle. No. 78—(858) Hood's army, September 20, 1864, at Macon, Ga.

Battery C. No. 55—(662) Capt. T. J. Key, in General Stevenson's division, November 20, 1864. No. 57—(484) J. F. Waddell ordered to report to General Stevenson, near Dalton, February 25th.

GID NELSON BATTERY.

The Gid Nelson battery, also called Selden's and Lovelace's, was organized at Uniontown in the spring of 1862; was in Slaughter's, and afterward Cantey's, brigade, army of Mobile, during the summer of 1863. In January, 1864, it was at Jackson, Miss., commanded by Captain Selden. It was transferred to Walthall's division, army of Tennessee, and in June, 1864, was commanded by Lieut. Chas. W. Lovelace. It was in a fight near Kenesaw Mountain, June, 1864, and at Peachtree Creek in July. Here Lieutenant Lovelace was wounded, but remained at his guns until his ammunition was exhausted: Major Preston, chief of artillery, was killed while personally supervising this battery at Peachtree Creek. The battery was complimented on the field by General Reynolds. It fought with considerable loss at Jonesboro in August, and in October gained great distinction by the reduction of the blockhouse at Tilton, near Dalton, where 300 Union prisoners were taken. It fought at Nashville, losing heavily in guns and men; here Lieutenant Lovelace was captured. The battery was transferred to Mobile and commanded by Capt. W. M. Selden in March, 1865; it finally surrendered at Meridian. It was called, successively, by the names of its captains.

EXTRACTS FROM OFFICIAL WAR RECORDS.
No. 43—(39) In Slaughter's brigade, June 8, 1863. (131) In Cantey's brigade, battery commanded by Lieut. W. M. Selden, Mobile, August 1st. (157) In Cantey's brigade, Mobile, August 10th; one section, called Selden's, at Pollard,.

No. 58—(547, 548) Called Selden's, in department of Gulf; headquarters, Jackson, Miss., January 11, 1864. (582) Mentioned among troops in department of Gulf.

No. 74—(646) In Cantey's division, army of Mississippi, June 10, 1864. (653) Lieut. Charles W. Lovelace, Walthall's division, army of Tennessee, June and July, (667, 675) In Preston's battalion, Stewart's corps, siege or Atlanta. (873) Mentioned in report of Capt. Chas. Vanderford. (917) Mentioned in report of General Cockrell. (926) General Walthall, in his report .of the battle of Peachtree Creek, July 20th, says: "Selden's battery, under the immediate command of Lieutenant Lovelace, was gotten into an advantageous position, where it was so skillfully and rapidly served, that the flanking force was soon driven off in confusion." (938) Gen. D. H. Reynolds in his report of same fight, Peachtree Creek, says: "Major Preston promptly put Selden's battery (commanded by Lieutenant Lovelace) into position, and opened on the enemy with telling effect. The battery, under the immediate supervision of Major Preston and Lieutenant Lovelace, did noble service, and I regret to state that Major Preston was killed and Lieutenant Lovelace wounded; yet, although wounded, Lieutenant Lovelace kept his battery in position until it had fired its last round of ammunition." (967) Relieved by Barry's battery, 4

p. m., July 20th. (969) Report of Lieut. Chas. Lovelace on battle of Peachtree Creek. (979-981) Mentioned in journal of army of Tennessee.

No. 75—(771) Mentioned by Adjutant-General West, near Kenesaw mountain, June 12th.

No. 77—(812) Gen. A. P. Stewart says that Selden's battery reduced the blockhouse at Tilton, near Dalton, where 300 men were captured, October 13, 1864.

No. 78—(858) Stewart's corps, Hood's army, Nashville campaign.

No. 103—(1047) Commanded by Lieut. Wm. M. Selden at Mobile, March 10, 1865.

EUFAULA BATTERY.

The Eufaula battery was organized in February, 1862, under the command of Capt. John W. Clark; commenced a brilliant career in Stevenson's brigade, and served, successively, in Rains', Vance's and Bate's brigades. It fought with the army of Tennessee at Tazewell, Murfreesboro, Hoover's Gap, Chickamauga and Missionary Ridge. It opened and closed the battle of Chickamauga, where it lost six men. It also lost heavily at Missionary Ridge. It was commended for gallant service in the Atlanta campaign, and in 1865 it was transferred to Mobile, where it assisted in the defense of the city.

Capt. McDonald Oliver, who commanded the battery most gallantly during the greater part of the war, was killed near Atlanta. Lieutenant McKenzie and Lieut. W. W. Woods were also distinguished by their able command of this battery at different times.

EXTRACTS FROM OFFICIAL WAR RECORDS.

Vol. X, Part 2—(409) Mentioned by E. Kirby Smith, April 10, 1862. (573) In General Stevenson's brigade, with General Smith, May 31st.

Vol. XVI, Part 2—(698) At Knoxville, June 22, 1862. (715) Under Lieutenant McTyer, Stevenson's brigade, Gen. Kirby Smith, June 30th. (984) In Rains' brigade, Gen. Kirby Smith, October 31st.

Vol. XX, Part 2—(413) Under Capt. W. A. McTyer, in General Rains' brigade, east Tennessee, November 20, 1862. (492) January 10, 1863, present for duty, 138 men.

Vol. XXIII, Part 1—(603-606, 610) Mentioned in Gen. Bushrod R. Johnson's report, Hoover's Gap, and movements to vicinity of Chattanooga. (614) Mentioned and commended by Gen. Wm. B. Bate in his report of the battle of Hoover's Gap, June 24, 1863; two men killed.

Vol. XXIII, Part 2—(623-654) Return, 131 to 136 men, Shelbyville, Tenn., January to February, 1863. (655) In Vance's brigade, McCown's division, February 28th. (735) Bate's brigade, April 1st. (943) Bate's brigade, July.

No. 50—(231) In Bate's brigade, Stewart's division, Chattanooga, October 7, 1863.

No. 51—(16) Under Capt. McDonald Oliver, Stewart's division, at Chickamauga. (361-366) Mentioned in report of Gen. A. P. Stewart. (383-386) Mentioned in report of Gen. William Bate, who says: "I claim for this battery the honor of opening on Friday evening, and closing on Sunday evening, the battle of Chickamauga." (388) Two men killed, September 18th; 4 killed, September 19th, at Chickamauga. (394) Mentioned in report of Lieut. Joel Towers. (397) Mentioned in report of Lieut.-Col. R. Dudley Frayser. (399, 400) Report of Lieut. W. J. McKenzie. (535) Private John C. Carroll on roll of honor, battle of Chickamauga.

No. 55—(661) In Stewart's division, November 30, 1863.

No. 56—(620) Commanded by Lieut. Wm. J. McKenzie, Breckinridge's corps, army of Tennessee, October 31, 1863. (808-827, 887) Commanded by McDonald Oliver, Stewart's division, December.

No. 58—(590, 821) In Stewart's division, Hood's corps, army of Tennessee, February 29, 1864.

No. 59—(687) Under Oliver, 117 present, March 29, 1864. (700-702) Active service since May, 1862, in battles of Tazewell, Murfreesboro, Hoover's Gap, Chickamauga, Missionary Ridge; 5 killed. (731) Effective, 102 present for duty, April 1, 1864.

No. 74—(643, et seq.) In Hood's corps, during Atlanta campaign. (667) Under Lieutenant McKenzie, in Lee's corps, Hood's army, July 31st. (818) Conduct near New Hope church, May 25th, commended by Gen. A. P. Stewart.

No. 103—(1047) Under Lieut. Wm. W. Woods, Maury's army, Mobile, March 10, 1865.

SENGSTAK'S BATTERY.

Sengstak's battery, Capt. H. H. Sengstak, was organized at Mobile, December, 1861. It remained there, and at Columbus, Miss., until September, 1862. It served the greater part of the war in Maury's division, fought at Corinth, where it was specially commended by the division commander, and at the Hatchie. It wintered in northern Mississippi, and was in the siege of Vicksburg, where it lost heavily and was captured. When exchanged, the men were assigned to Barrett's battery, army of Tennessee. They were constantly engaged in the Dalton-Atlanta campaign in the battalion commanded by Major Waddell. It was transferred to the south, took part in the battle of Girard, where all its guns and most of the men were captured. Lieut. A. P. St. John was for a time in command; Lieut. Stanley H. Bell was wounded at Vicksburg.

EXTRACTS FROM OFFICIAL WAR RECORDS.

Vol. XVII, Part 1—(375) In General Maury's division, battle of Corinth, October, 1862. (383) Lost 1 killed. (385-388) Mentioned in General Price's report of battle. (394. 395) Commended in General Maury's report. No. 36—(467) Under Lieut. A. P. St. John, at Deer creek, March 25, 1863. No. 37—(327) In General Moore's brigade, July 4, 1:863, Vicksburg. (369) Four killed and 7 wounded, Vicksburg siege. (381) Mentioned by General Moore. No. 38—(613) In Maury's brigade, district of Louisiana, January 31, 1863. (704) In Maury's division, April 17th, Snyder's Bluff. (725) Mentioned by Col. E. W. Pettus, April 8th. (871, 872) Mentioned by Gen. J. H. Forney, Vicksburg, May 13th. (1060) In General Forney's division, Demopolis, March 14, 1864. No. 55—(663) Assigned to reserve artillery, November 19, 1863.

FOWLER'S (PHELAN'S) BATTERY.

Fowler's battery, Capt. W. H. Fowler, was organized in Tuscaloosa in January, 1862, and was composed of men who had served in Virginia as a company in the regiment recruited by R. E. Rodes. It was the first organization to re-enlist "for the war," and after serving at Mobile one year, joined the army at Tullahoma as part of Walthall's brigade. It fought at Chickamauga, where it suffered severely, and was highly commended for gallantry. It also lost heavily at Missionary Ridge; moved with Hood into Tennessee, and was engaged at Franklin and at Nashville, losing at the latter place, 8 killed and wounded.

It was then stationed at Mobile, where it remained till the close of the war, when it was surrendered with 130 men. It was commanded at times by Capt. John Phelan and Lieut. N. Venable, and at Mobile, in March, 1865, was in Gee's battalion. Captain Phelan, who had served since May, 1861, was wounded, and Lieut. Wm. Dailey was killed, at Resaca.

EXTRACTS FROM OFFICIAL WAR RECORDS.

Vol. XXIII, Part 2—(942, 959) In Walthall's brigade, Bragg's army, July and August, 1863.

No. 41—(497) Mentioned by R. B. Irwin (Union), at Mobile, April 15, 1863.

No. 50—(231) In Walthall's brigade, Chattanooga, October 7, 1863.

No. 51—(14) In Liddell's division, Chickamauga, September 19 and 20, 1863. (255-257) Mentioned by Captain Swett, chief of artillery. (271) Mentioned, Chickamauga. (272-274) Mentioned in General Walthall's report. (276) Officers and men commended by General Walthall for "coolness, daring and persistence throughout all the engagements." (286) Commended in Captain Fowler's report. (287) Loss, 6 killed", 17 wounded.

No. 56—(620) In Cheatham's corps, Bragg's army, October 31, 1863. (807) Commanded by Lieut. John Phelan, December 10th. (826) Total present, 126, December 14th. (884) In Cheatham's division, December 31st.

No. 59—(687) Organized May 1, 1861. (693-695) Lost 7 men at Chickamauga. Raised in Alabama, by Capt. R. E. Rodes, as infantry, served since April, 1862. Present, March, 1864, 116. (731) Effective, 95, April 1, 1864, army of Tennessee.

No. 74—(643, et seq.) In Hardee's corps, Johnston's army, Atlanta campaign, Capt. John Phelan commanding, April 30th.

No. 93—(669) In Cheatham's corps, Hood's army, December 10, 1864.

No. 103—(1047) In Gee's battalion, Mobile, March 10, 1865.

MONTGOMERY TRUE BLUES BATTERY.

The Montgomery True Blues battery, Capt. W. G. Andrews, was organized at Norfolk in January, 1863, and was composed of men from Montgomery, most of whom had served in a campaign in the Third Alabama infantry. They were sent to North Carolina and did garrison duty on the coast. They assisted in the capture of Plymouth, and blew up Fort Branch. When the Confederate line at Petersburg was broken, they tried to rejoin General Johnston's army and were disbanded at Ridgeway, April, 1865.

EXTRACTS FROM OFFICIAL WAR RECORDS.
Vol. XVIII—(190, 191) Under Lieut. Jas. E. Davis, at Kinston, March 8, 1863. No. 45—(947) Mentioned, Hill's army. (1068) In Saunders' battalion. No. 49—(692) In Saunders' battalion, Kinston, August 31, 1863. (851) Fifty-nine present, General Pickett's troops, November 27th. (906) In General Pickett's artillery, near Kinston, December 31st. No. 60—(1201) Effective total, 56, February, 1864, department of North Carolina. No. 69—(892) Johnston's division, Beauregard's army, June 10, 1864. No. 81—(648, 693) Mentioned in Beauregard's orders, June, 1863. No. 88—(1226) Under Capt. Edgar G. Lee, at Plymouth, N. C., September 1, 1864. No. 89—(1322) Called Lee's, in Moseley's battalion. No. 96—(1187) At Fort Branch, Bragg's army, January 31, 1865. No. 99— (1069, 1155) General Hoke's troops, February 10, 1865.

LUMSDEN'S BATTERY.

Lumsden's battery, Capt. C. L. Lumsden, was organized at Tuscaloosa, and reported at Mobile, November, 1861. After the battle of Shiloh, it relieved Gage's battery at Tupelo. It was in the battle of Corinth, in the Kentucky, Tennessee and North Georgia campaigns, and lost heavily in the battles of Farmington, Perryville, Murfreesboro and Kenesaw Mountain. From Dalton to Atlanta it lost 5 men, and at Nashville lost 28 men. As it was during the greater part of the war in the reserve artillery, it saw extremely hard service, being continually in demand. It was in the army of Mobile during the siege of Spanish Fort. At the end of the war it was transferred to Mississippi, where it surrendered.

Lieut. G. H. Hargrove was wounded at Nashville. Lieuts. A. C. Hargrove and John A. Caldwell were wounded at Spanish Fort.

EXTRACTS FROM OFFICIAL WAR RECORDS.

Vol. X, Part 2—(461, 549) In Chalmers' brigade, Corinth, April and May, 1862.

Vol. XVII, Part 2—(632) In General Walker's brigade, Tupelo, June 30, 1862.

Vol. XX, Part 2—(448) In reserve artillery, Murfreesboro, December 12, 1862.

Vol. XXIII, Part 2—(862) Mentioned by General Hardee, Beechwood, June 5, 1863. (944, 961) Artillery reserve, army of Tennessee, July and August, 1863.

No. 51—(292) Loss, 1 killed, 1 wounded, battle of Chickamauga, September 18 to 20, 1863. (459) Mentioned in B. R. Johnson's report. (493) Mentioned in Lieut. Wm. S. Everett's report.

No. 56—(620, 827, 888) In artillery reserve, army of Tennessee,, October to December, 1863, 109 present.

No. 58—(591, 821) In artillery reserve, army of Tennessee, 1864.

No. 59—(708) Service: At battle of Corinth, Miss., in Kentucky campaign; in campaign of Middle Tennessee and North Georgia. Lost men and horses at Farmington, May, 1862; at Perryville in October, 1862, and lost horses at Murfreesboro, December 31, 1862. (709) In reserve artillery, 117 present, March 12, 1864. (731) Ninety-four present, April 1st.

No. 74—(644, etseq.) In reserve artillery, Johnston's army, Atlanta campaign. (901) Commended by Gen. S. G. French, Kenesaw Mountain, June 27, 1864. (968) Mentioned by Maj. Geo. S. Storrs, same battle.

No. 78—(858) At Macon, Ga., July 31, 1864. No. 93— (668) Stewart's corps, Hood's army, December 10, 1864. (722) Mentioned in Gen. E. C. Walthall's report, December 1 St.

No. 103—(1047) At Mobile, in Maury's army, March 10, 1865. No. 104—(1195) Mentioned by General Gibson, Mobile, April 3d.

SEMPLE'S BATTERY.

Semple's battery was organized in Montgomery, March, 1862. It was ordered first to Mobile and afterward to the army of Tennessee, and was brigaded under Lowrey, Deshler, Woods, and in Cleburne's and Cheatham's corps. It was for a time in Hotchkiss battalion. It marched into Kentucky and fought at Perryville, Murfreesboro, Dug Gap, Chickamauga, Missionary Ridge, Ringgold, and lost heavily at Resaca, Atlanta and Jonesboro. It opened the battle of Franklin, and lost slightly there and at Nashville. It was then ordered to North Carolina, and surrendered at Augusta, Ga.

Capt. Henry C. Semple was early promoted, and was succeeded in command by Lieut. R. W. Goldthwaite, a very skillful officer. Capt. J. Pollard was killed at Murfreesboro; Lieut. E. G. McClellan was killed, and Lieut. Chas. Dowd was wounded, at Resaca.

EXTRACTS FROM OFFICIAL WAR RECORDS.

Vol. VI—(868) One hundred and nineteen present, army of Mobile, March 2, 1862.

Vol. XVI, Part 1—(1120) Commended in General Har-dee's report of Perryville, October 8, 1862.

Vol. XVI, Part 2—(1003) At Shelbyville, April 10, 1862.

Vol. XVII, Part 2—(659) Ordered from Mobile to Chattanooga, July 26, 1862.

Vol. XX, Part 2—(499) Mentioned in general orders, No. 7, Tullahoma, January 17, 1863.

Vol. XXIII, Part 1—(587) Mentioned by General Cleburne, at Liberty Gap, June 25, 1863. (598) Mentioned by J. H. Kelly as under command of Lieut. R. W. Goldthwaite at Liberty Gap.

Vol. XXIII, Part 2—(942) In Col. M. P. Lowrey's brigade (Wood's), July 31, 1863. (959) In Cleburne's division, August 10th.

No. 51—(13) In Deshler's brigade, Chickamauga, September, 1863. (139, 140-143) Mentioned by Gen. D. H. Hill. Speaking of action of September 11th: "Semple's magnificent battery was ordered up, and in a short time silenced the Yankee fire, with heavy loss, and the Yankee rout was complete." (145) Commended by General Cleburne. (154-156-158) Mentioned in report of Gen. P. R. Cleburne, who says Captain Semple rendered invaluable service and exhibited the highest gallantry, running his pieces within 60 yards of the enemy, and was ably sustained by Lieutenant Goldthwaite, of Semple's battery. He also commends Semple's "skill and judgment as acting chief of artillery." (162) Gen. S. A. M. Wood says in his report: "Semple's battery (attached to my brigade) was not under my control during this action. I, however, saw it placed in position by the chief of artillery, and its fire was of the greatest service in routing the enemy and silencing his batteries," Ten wounded. (167-196) Mentioned in reports of Chickamauga, by Col. Sam Adams, Col. E. B. Breedlove, Col. M. P. Lowrey, Lieut R. W. Goldthwaite, Gen. L. E. Polk, Col. R. Q. Mills, Capt. James P. Douglas. (536) Mentioned on roll of honor, battle of Chickamauga.

No. 55—(661) Commanded by Lieutenant Goldthwaite, November 20, 1863. (746-755) Mentioned in report of Gen. P. R. Cleburne. (757-760)

Report of Lieutenant Goldthwaite. (763-765) Mentioned in Col. D. C. Govan's and Col. John E. Murray's reports of battle of Ringgold, November 27th.

No. 56—(807, 885) In Cleburne's division, Hardee's army, December, 1863. (827) One hundred and twenty-one present.

No. 57—(483) Commended in report of T. R. Hotchkiss, near Dalton, February 25, 1864.

No. 58—(588) In Cleburne's division, January 20, 1864. (820) In Hardee's corps, army of Tennessee, February 29th.

No. 59—(687) Present 109, March 29, 1864. (693-695) Two killed at Perryyille, 4 at Murfreesboro, 2 at Chickamauga, 1 at Ringgold Gap. (731) Eighty-two present, April 1st. (871) In Hotchkiss' battalion, army of Tennessee, April 30th.

No. 42—(240) Mentioned by General Clanton, July 30, 1863.

No. 74—(643, et seq.) In Hardee's corps, Johnston's army, Atlanta campaign. (744, 745) Mentioned by General Granbury, August 31st and September 1st. (967) Mentioned in report of Capt. Thomas Key, 2 men wounded, July 22d.

No. 93—(669) In Cheatham's corps, Hood's army, December 10, 1864.

KOLB'S BATTERY.

Kolb's battery, Capt. R. F. Kolb, was originally organized at Eufaula as "Barbour's light artillery," April, 1862, 325 strong, under Maj. W. N. Reeves. It was attached to Hilliard's legion, with the exception of one company, which was equipped as artillery and commanded by Capt. R. F. Kolb. It served for some time in east Tennessee, and was at Big Creek gap and Bell's bridge in the spring and summer of 1863. It was with the army of Tennessee and took part in the battles of Knoxville, Chickamauga, Chattanooga, Missionary Ridge, the Dalton-Atlanta campaign", and subsequent movements in Tennessee. It surrendered at Augusta, Ga. During the war it lost about 70 killed and wounded, and 45 died of disease. Lieutenants Powers and Cherry commanded the battery at times.

EXTRACTS FROM OFFICIAL WAR RECORDS.

Vol. XVI, Part 2—(984) In Bradford's brigade, October 31, 1862, east Tennessee.

Vol. XX, Part 2—(414) In Colonel Bradford's brigade (Heth's division), November 20, 1862. (466) Mentioned in Heth's brigade, Big Creek gap, December 27th.

Vol. XXIII, Part 2—(644, 711, 792) In Palmer's brigade, Big Creek gap and Clinton, February to April, 1863. (946) In Frazer's brigade, July 31st, Bell's bridge. (948) Ordered to report at Knoxville, August 3d.

No. 51—(17) In Buckner's corps, Chickamauga, September, 1863. (449, 450) Mentioned in Major Williams' report, Chickamauga, 2 killed, 1 wounded.

No. 55—(660) In Buckner's division, November 20, 1863. (707, 708) General Wright, in report of Missionary Ridge, says: "Captain Kolb's guns were served with great coolness and signal gallantry, for which he is entitled to my thanks and the commendations of the country." (716) Report of Capt. R. F. Kolb.

No. 56—(620, 828, 888) Kolb's battery, present 102, December, 1863, in artillery reserve.

No. 57—(478) Mentioned in report of A. P. Stewart, February 24, 1864, army of Tennessee.

No. 58—(591, 617, 821) Mentioned in report of Gen. R. B. Johnson, January 26, 1864.

No. 59—(687, 708, 709) Organized, April, 1862. Present for duty, 115, March 29, 1864. Lost men and horses at Chickamauga. Total effective, 100, Hallonquist's report. (731) Effective, 96, April 1st. (872) Artillery reserve, Johnston's army, April 30th.

No. 74—(644, et seq.) In artillery reserve, Atlanta campaign. (667) Lieut. P. F. Powers, Lee's corps, July. (674) Lieut. Robt. Cherry, Lee's corps, August.

No. 77—(817) Mentioned in S. G. French's report of battle of Allatoona, October 4, 1864.

No. 78—(858) Hood's army, September 20, 1864, at Macon, Ga.

No. 93—(668) Stewart's corps, Hood's army, December 10, 1864.

TARRANT'S BATTERY.

Tarrant's battery was organized by General Clanton in June, 1863, and after remaining at Pollard several months, joined the army of Tennessee at Dalton. It took part in the battles of Resaca, Cassville, Lost Mountain, New Hope, Kenesaw, Peachtree Creek and Atlanta. The battery moved toward Tennessee, and was in the action at Decatur; it fought at Nashville, where it suffered severely, losing so many men and horses that the guns could not be removed. The remnant was sent to Blakely, where, after taking a heroic part in the defense, it finally surrendered. Capt. Edward Tarrant was captured at Blakely. Lieut. B. B. Hardwick was wounded at Kenesaw; he and Lieutenant Shepard were captured at Nashville.

EXTRACTS FROM OFFICIAL WAR RECORDS.

No. 42—(239, 240) Mentioned by General Clanton at Pollard, September 19, 1863. (402, 511) In Clanton's brigade, Mobile, November and December. No. 58— (547, 548, 582) In department of the Gulf, Clanton's brigade, January, 1864. No. 59—(861) In Reynolds' brigade, Mobile, April

30, 1864. No. 74—(646, et seq.) In Preston's battalion, Polk's corps, Atlanta campaign. (873) One killed, 4 wounded, report of Chas. Vanderford. No. 75—(668) Ordered to Dalton by General Maury, Mobile, Mays, 1864. (771) Under Major Preston, Cantey's brigade, near Kenesaw mountain, June 12th. No. 78— (589) Mentioned by General Clanton, Montgomery, May 9, 1864. (610) Mentioned in artillery returns of James L. Hoole, May 19th, as at Pollard. (858) In Trueheart's battalion, Stewart's corps, Hood's army, September 20th. No. 93—(668) Same assignment, Nashville campaign. No. 103—(1047) In Grayson's battalion, district of the Gulf, March 10, 1865.

CLANTON'S BATTERY.

Clanton's battery, Capt. N. H. Clanton, was organized in Montgomery county, in June, 1863, and was attached to General Clanton's brigade. It was for a time at Pollard and Mobile, was ordered to Gadsden, and served in northern and central Alabama and Georgia. Part of it was engaged near Rome, Ga. It was in the neighborhood of Columbus, Ga., at the close of the war.

EXTRACTS FROM OFFICIAL WAR RECORDS.
No. 42—(131, 157) In Gen. J. G. Clanton's brigade, August, 1863. (239) General Clanton's report, Pollard, Ala., September 19th. (275, 402, 511, 561) In Clanton's brigade, September to December. (556) Mentioned in letter from General Clanton. He says he organized this battery—his brother's.

No. 58—(547, 548) In department of the Gulf, January, 1864. (582) In Clanton's brigade, with General Maury, Mobile. (651) Ordered to report to General Clanton at Gadsden, February 1st.

No. 75—(657) Mentioned in General Polk's command about May 1, 1864.

No. 78—(791, 811, 887) In district of Central and Northern Alabama, General Adams, August and September, 1864.

No. 79—(865) With Maj. H. C. Semple, October 28, 1864. (872) Sixty-two present for duty in Adams' command, October 31st.

No. 94—(634) In central Alabama, Clanton's brigade, December 1, 1864.

No. 103—(494) Mentioned as near Columbus, Ga., April 16, 1865. (1002) At Mobile, ordered to report to Adams, February 21st.

WARD'S BATTERY.

Ward's battery, Capt. John J. Ward, was recruited in northern Alabama, and served with the army of Mississippi until the summer of 1864, when it was assigned to Storrs' battalion, army of Tennessee. It took part in the Dalton-Atlanta campaign, serving in many battles, being highly commended at Kenesaw Mountain for courage under severe fire. Captain Ward was mortally wounded near Nashville, July 27, 1864. He was succeeded in command by Capt. S. R. Cruse.

EXTRACTS FROM OFFICIAL WAR RECORDS.

No. 42—(39) In Slaughter's brigade, Mobile, June 8, 1863. (131, 157) In Cantey's brigade, Mobile, August. No. 58—(547, 548, 582) Department of the Gulf, January, 1864. No. 59—(861) In Fuller's brigade, Mobile, April, 1864. No. 74—(646, et seq.) Storrs' battalion, Polk's corps, Atlanta campaign. (873) Mentioned in report of Charles Vanderford, chief of ordnance. (901) Commended by Gen. S. G. French, Kenesaw Mountain, June 27th. (904) Captain Ward mortally wounded, near Atlanta, July 27th; Gen. S. G. French says: "Captain Ward was a fine soldier, and his loss was severely felt." (910, 911,968) Mentioned in General Young's and Major Storrs' reports of July 27th. No. 75—(668) Ordered to report to General Polk, May 5, 1864. (686) Ordered to Rome, Ga., May 9th. (771) Near Kenesaw mountain, June 12th. No. 76 —(989) Mentioned in Stewart's corps, August 25th. No. 78—(858) Stewart's corps, September 20th.

ROBERTSON'S (DENT'S) BATTERY.

Robertson's battery was organized early in the war as part of the army of Pensacola. It fought with Gladden's brigade at Shiloh, where its gallantry was the subject of universal commendation. Its conduct at Farmington and Bridge Creek was also highly commended. The battery lost heavily at Murfreesboro, Chickamauga and Missionary Ridge, fought continuously in the Atlanta campaign, and suffered severely at Franklin and Nashville. It was in Clanton's brigade, at Mobile, at the close of the war. It was commanded almost continuously by Captain Dent, and after the summer of 1863 was called by his name. It was composed only partially of men from Alabama.

EXTRACTS FROM OFFICIAL WAR RECORDS.

Vol. VI—(819) Army of Pensacola, February 1, 1862.

Vol. X, Part 1 —(383) General Gladden's brigade, Shiloh, April 6 and 7, 1862. (472) Mentioned in General Ruggles' report; (475) in Colonel Bankhead's report; (515) in Captain Hodgson's report. (532, 534) General Withers says: "With such batteries there could be no failure." (537) Commended in Col. D. W. Adams' report of Shiloh. (566) Mentioned in General Girardey's report. (788) In Gardner's brigade, Bragg's army, June 30th. (809, 810) Mentioned in General Ruggles' report of Farmington, May 9th, "distinguished for gallantry of captain and good conduct of men on the field." (813) Commended in General Anderson's report. (853, 854, 855)

Mentioned in Colonel Wheeler's report. Bridge Creek, May 28th and 29th. "This battery was skillfully and gallantly handled by Lieutenant Dent, of Robertson's battery, putting the enemy to flight." (924) Commended by Capt. David Provence.

Vol. X, Part 2—(307) Col. Joseph Wheeler's brigade, Corinth, March, 1862. (461, 549) Gardner's brigade, April and May.

Vol. XVI, Part 2—(764) In Gardner's brigade, August, 1862.

Vol. XVII, Part 2—(633) In Gardner's brigade, reserve corps, Bragg's army, June 30th.

No. 50—(229) In Hindman's division, Chattanooga, October 7, 1863. No. 52—(52) Mentioned in report of W. H. Lytle, August 16th.

No. 51—(15) In Hindman's division, battle of Chickamauga. (305-307) Commended by General Hindman. Loss, 3 killed, 13 wounded. (331) Commanded by Deas, Missionary Ridge, October 9th. (338, 343) Mentioned by Coltart and Manigault, Missionary Ridge. (460-463) Highly commended in affairs of September 20th, by Bushrod Johnson. (475, 476) Mentioned in Col. John S. Fulton's report, Chickamauga. (491) Highly commended by Lieut.-Col. R. B. Snowden. (501) Mentioned in Col. D. Coleman's report.

No. 55—(659) In Hindman's division, November 20, 1863. (741, 742) Mentioned in report of Gen. Wm. B. Bate.

No. 56—(620, 808, 827, 886) In Hindman's division, Breckinridge's corps, December, 1863.

No. 58—(589, 821) In Hood's corps, February 29, 1864.

No. 59—(687) Present for duty, 110, March 29, 1864. (698-700) Report of Maj. A. R. Courtney says Dent's battery, Capt. S. G. Dent, was present at Pensacola. Shiloh, 2 killed, 17 wounded; Farmington, 1 wounded; Murfreesboro, 2 killed, 23 wounded; Chickamauga, 3. killed, 19 wounded; Missionary Ridge, 7 killed, 21 wounded.

No. 74—(643, et seq.) Hood's corps, Johnston's army, April 30, 1864, during Atlanta campaign.

No. 93—(668) In Trueheart's battalion, Stewart's corps, Hood's army, December 10, 1864. (692) Mentioned by Colonel Hoxton as in Courtney's battalion, December 10th to 17th.

No. 103—(1047) In Clanton's brigade, Mobile, March 10, 1865.

CHAPTER VII.

BATTLES OF THE ARMIES IN VIRGINIA IN WHICH ALABAMA TROOPS WERE ENGAGED.

[In the following list of engagements the principal information intended to be given is the item "Alabama troops engaged," but the returns are so uncertain that it is not always possible to do this with accuracy. Such as is obtainable from the "Records" is given. "The abbreviations are k, killed; w, wounded; and m, missing, which also includes prisoners, and accounts for the large numbers frequently given under that head.—EDITOR.]

1861.

Blackburn's Ford, Va., July 18. Gen. Ewell, 1 brigade.—Federal, loss 19 k, 38 w, 26 m. Alabama troops, 5th Inf.

Bull Run, Va., July 21. Gen. G. T. Beauregard, 18,053; loss 387 k, 1582 w, 13 m.—Federal, Gen. I. McDowell, 18,572; loss 460 k, 1124 w, 1312 m. Alabama troops, 4th, 5th, 6th Inf.

Dranesville, Va., Dec. 20. Gen. Stuart, 1200; loss 43 k, 143 w, 8 m. —Federal, Gen. Geo. A. McCall, 3,100; loss 7 k, 61 w, 3 m. Alabama troops, 10th Inf.

1862.

Siege of Yorktown, Va., Apr. 5 to May 3. Gen. Jos. Johnston.— Federal, Gen. G. B. McClellan, 42,000. Alabama troops, 3d, 8th, 9th, 10th, 12th, 26th Inf.

Williamsburg, Va., May 5. Gen. James Longstreet, 13,816; loss 288 k, 975 w, 297 m.—Federal, Gen. G. B. McClellan, 42,000; loss 468 k, 1442 w, 373 m. Alabama troops, 4th, 5th, 6th, 8th, 9th, 10th, 12th, 13th, 14th, 26th Inf.

Lewisburg, W. Va., May 23. Gen. Heth; loss 38 k, 66 m.—Federal, Col. Crook, 2,000; loss 13 k, 53 w, 7 m. Alabama troops, 15th Inf.

Middletown, Newton, Front Royal and Winchester, Va., May 20 to June 10. Gen. T. J. Jackson, 16,000; loss 68 k, 329 w, 3 m.—Federal, Gen. N. P. Banks, 9,178; loss 62 k, 243 w, 1714 m. Alabama troops, 15th Inf.

Seven Pines (or Fair Oaks), Va,,, May 31. Gen. Longstreet, 8300; loss 980 k, 4749 w, 405 m.—Federal, Gen. McClellan, 14,000; loss 790 k, 3594 w, 647 m. Alabama troops, 3d, 4th, 5th, 6th, 8th, 9th, 10th, 11th, 12th, 13th, 14th, 26th Inf.; Jeff. Davis Batty.

Harrisonburg, Va., June 6. Gen. Jackson, 13,000; loss 17 k, 50 w, 3 m.— Federal, Gen. Fremont. Alabama troops, 15th Inf.

Cross Keys, Va., June 8. Gen. Jackson, 13,000; loss 56 k, 392 w, 47 m.— Federal, Gen. Fremont, 14,672; loss 14 k, 443 w, 127 m. Alabama troops, 15th Inf.

Port Republic, Va., June 9. Gen. Jackson, 13,000; loss 78 k, 533 w, 4 m.—

Federal, Gen. Shields, 2,500; loss 67 k, 393 w, 558 m. Alabama troops, 15th Inf.

Oak Grove, Va., June 25. Total loss 541.—Federal, Gen. Heintzelman; loss 67 k, 504 w, 55 m.

Mechanicsville, Va., June 26. Gens. Jackson and Longstreet, 10,000; total loss 1589.—Federal, Gen. Fitz John Porter, 5,000; loss 49 k, 207 w, 105 m. Alabama troops, 3d, 4th, 5th, 6th, 8th, 9th, 10th, 11th, 12th, 3th, 14th, 26th, 44th, 5th Battn. Inf.; Jeff. Davis and Hardaway's Battrs.

Gaines' Mill, Va., June 27. Gens. Longstreet and Jackson, 50,000; loss* 589 k, 2671 w, 24 m.—Federal, Gen. Fitz John Porter; loss 894 k, 3107 w, 2836 m. Alabama troops, same as at Mechanicsville.

Golding's Farm, etc., Va., June 28. Gen. Magruder. — Federal, Gen. Smith; loss 37 k, 227 w, 104 m. Alabama troops, 8th, 9th, 10th, 11th, 14th, 44th, 5th Battn. Inf.

Savage's Peach Orchard, Va., June 29. Gen. Magruder.—Federal, Gen. Sumner; loss 80 k, 412 w, 1098 m. Alabama troops, 8th, 9th, 10th, 11th, 14th, 44th, 5th Battn. Inf.

Frazer Farm, Glendale, White Oak, and Charles City Cross Rds., Va., June 30. Gen. Longstreet.—Federal, Gen. Hooker; loss 210 k, 1513 w, 1130 m. Alabama troops, 8th, 9th, 10th, 11th, 14th, 44th, 5th Battn. Inf.

Malvern Hill, July 1. Gen. R. E. Lee.—Federal, Gen. F. J. Porter; loss 397 k, 2092 w, 725 m. Alabama troops, same as at Mechanicsville.

Seven Days' Battles, Va., June 25 to July 1. Gen. R. E. Lee, 85,000; loss 3286 k, 15,909 w, 940 m.—Federal, Gen. McClellan, 105,445; loss 1734 k, 8062 w, 6053 m. Alabama troops, same as at Mechanicsville.

Cedar Mt., Va., Aug. 9. Gen. Jackson, 20,000; loss 241 k, 1120 w, 4 m.—Federal, Gen. Pope, 38,000; loss 314 k, 1445 w, 622 m. Alabama troops, 3d, 4th, 5th, 6th, 12th, 13th, 15th, 26th, 47th Inf.; Hardaway's and Jeff. Davis Battrs.

Second Bull Run, Aug. 16 to Sept 2. Gen. R. E. Lee, 49,000; loss** 1553 k, 7112 w, 109 m.—Federal, Gen. Pope, 70,000; loss 1747*** k, 8482 w, 4263 m. Alabama troops, 4th, 8th, 9th, 10th, 11th, 14th, 15th, 44th, 47th, 48th, 5th Battn. Inf.

Harper's Ferry, Va., Sept. 12 to 15. Gen. Jackson, 15,000.—Federal, Col. D. S. Miles; loss 14 k, 173 w, 12,520 m. Alabama troops, 3d, 5th, 6th, 8th, 9th, 10th, 11th, 12th, 13th, 14th, 15th, 26th, 44th, 47th, 48th, 15th Battn. Inf.; Hardaway's and Jeff. Davis Battrs.

Crampton's Gap, Md., Sept. 14. Gen. McLaws, 8,000; total loss 749. — Federal, Gen. Franklin; loss 113 k, 418 w, 2m. South Mt, Md., Sept. 14. Gen. Longstreet, 9,900; loss 494 k and w, 440 m.—Federal, Gen. Hooker,

---

* Loss does not Include Longstreet's and Hill's corps.
**Includes Bristoe, Groveton, Gainesville, Chantilly and Rappahannock.
***Includes Chantilly and Rappahannock.

17,268; loss 325 k, 1403 w, 85 m. Alabama troops, 8th, 9th, 10th, 11th, 14th, 44th Inf.

Antietam, Md., Sept. 17. Gen. R. E. Lee, 35,000; loss 1512 k, 7816 w, 1844 m.—Federal, Gen. McClellan, 60,000; loss 2108 k, 9549 w, 753 m. Alabama troops, 3d, 4th, 5th, 6th, 8th, 9th, 10th, 11th, 12th. 13th, 14th, 15th, 26th, 44th, 47th, 48th Inf.; 5th Battn. Inf.; Hardaway's and Jeff. Davis Battrs.

Maryland campaign, Sept. 12 to 20. Gen. R. E. Lee, 35,000; loss 1890 k, 9770 w, 2304 m.—Federal, Gen. McClellan, 87,000; loss 2661 k, 11704 w, 13491 m. Alabama troops, same as at Antietam.

Shepherdstown, Va., Sept. 19-20. Gen. R. E. Lee.—Federal, Gen. F. J. Porter, 2 brigades; loss 71 k, 161 w, 131 m. Alabama troops, same as at Antietam.

Fredericksburg, Dec. 13. Gen. R. E. Lee, 20,000; loss 608 k, 4116 w, 653 m.—Federal, Gen. Burnside, 116,683; loss 1284 k, 9600 w, 1769 m. Alabama troops, same as at Antietam.

1863.

Deserted House, Suffolk, Va., Jan. 30. Loss 8 k, 31 w.—Federal, Gen. M. Corcoran; loss 23 k, 108 w, 12 m.

Kelly's Ford, Va., Mar. 17.—Federal; loss 9 k, 35 w, 40 m.

Siege of Suffolk, Va., April 11 to 30. Gen. Longstreet, 20,000.—Federal Gen. John J. Peck, 24,000; loss 41 k, 223 w, 2 m.

Chancellorsville, Va., May 1 to 4. Gen. Jackson, 60,000; loss 1665 k, 9081 w, 2018 m.—Federal, Gen. J. Hooker, 130,000; loss 1606 k, 9762 w, 5919 m. Alabama troops, 3d, 5th, 6th, 8th, 9th. 10th, 11th, 12th, 13th, 14th, 26th, 5th Battn. Inf.; Jeff. Davis and Hurt's Battrs.

Winchester, Va., June 13 to 15. Gen. R. S. Ewell; loss 47 k, 219 w, 3 m. — Federal, Gen. Milroy; loss 95 Js, 348 w, 4000 m. Alabama troops, 3d, 5th, 6th, 12th, 26th Inf.; Jeff. Davis Batty.

Gettysburg, Pa., July 1 to 3. Gen. R. E. Lee, 70,000; loss 2592 k, 12,799 w, 5150 m.—Federal, Gen. Meade, 101,679; loss 3072 k, 14,497 w, 5434 m. Alabama troops, same as at Antietam.

Funkstown, Md., July 12. Gen. R. E. Lee; loss 26 k, 130 w, 60 m. —Federal, Gen. Meade; loss 14 k, 77 w, 6 m. Alabama troops, 3d, 5th, 6th, 8th, 9th, 10th, 11th, 12th, 13th, 14th. 26th Inf.

Falling Waters, Md., July 14. Gen. R. E. Lee.—Federal, Gen. Meade; loss 31 k, 58 w, 32 m. Alabama troops, 5th Battn.; 13th Regt. Inf.

Wapping Heights, Va., July 23. Gen. Longstreet.—Federal, Gen. French; loss 20 k, 83 w.

Brandy Station, Va., Aug. 1.—Federal, Gen. Buford; loss 21 k, 104 w, 20 m. Alabama troops, 12th Inf.

Bristoe Station, Va., Oct. 4. Gen. Heth, 2 divisions; loss 136 k, 797 w, 445 m.—Federal, Gen. Warren, 2 divisions; loss 50k, 335 w, 161 m. Alabama troops, 8th, 9th, 10th, 11th, 13th, 14th Inf.

Droop Mt., Va., Nov. 6.—Federal, loss 30 k, 88 w, 1 m.

Kelly's Ford, Va., Nov. 7. Loss 5 k, 59 w, 295 m.—Federal, Gen. French; loss 6 k, 36 w.

Mine Run campaign, Va., Nov. 26 to 30. Gens. A. P. Hill and R. S. Ewell; loss 98 k, 610 w, 104 m.—Federal, Gens. Warren and Sedgwick; loss 173 k, 1099 w, 381. Alabama troops, 3d, 5th, 6th, 12th, 26th, 8th, 9th, 10th, 11th, 13th, 14th Inf.; Hardaway's Batty.

Walker's Ford, W. Va., Dec. 2.—Federal, loss 9 k, 43 w, 12 m.

1864.

Morton's Ford, Va., Feb. 6.—Federal, loss 10 k, 208 w, 42 m.

Wilderness, Va., May 5 to 7. Gen. Lee, 61,000; total loss 11,400.— Federal, Gen. Grant, 118,000; loss 2246 k, 12,037 w, 3383 m. Alabama troops, 3d, 4th, 5th, 6th, 8th, 9th, 10th, 11th, 12th, 13th, 14th, 15th, 44th, 47th, 48th, 61st Inf.; Reeves' Batty.

Spottsylvania, Va., May 8 to 21. Gen. Lee, 9,000.—Federal, Gen. Grant; loss 2725 k, 13,416 w, 2258 m. Alabama troops, same as at Wilderness.

Arrowfield Church, Va., May 9-10.—Federal, Gen. Butler; loss 36 k, 188 w, 19 m.

Drewry's Bluff, Va., May 12 to 16. Gen. Beauregard, 25,000; total loss 2500.—Federal, Gen. Butler, 35,000; loss 390 k, 2380 w, 1390 m. Alabama troops, 41st, 43d, 59th, 60th, 23d Battn. Inf.

Ware Bottom Church, Va., May 18 to 20.—Federal, loss 103 k, 796 w, 49 m. Alabama troops, 41st, 43d, 59th, 60th, 23d Battn. Inf.

Bermuda Hundred, Va., May 16 to 30. Gen. Beauregard, 12,000.— Federal, Gen. Butler, 13,000; loss 18 k, 89 w, 21 m. Alabama troops, 41st, 43d, 59th, 60th, 23d Battn. Inf.

North Anna and Totopotomoy, Va., May 23 to 27. Gen. Lee; total loss 2000.—Federal, Gen. Grant; loss 223 k, 1460 w, 290 m. Alabama troops, 3d, 4th, 5th, 6th, 8th, 9th, 10th, 11th, 12th, 13th, 14th, 15th, 44th, 47th, 48th, 61st Inf.

Sheridan's raid, Va., May 25 to 30.—Federal, Gen. Sheridan; loss 110k, 450 w, 96 m. Alabama troops, 41st, 43d, 59th, 60th and Stallworth's 23d Battn. Inf.

Bermuda Hundred, Va., June 1 to 14.—Federal, loss 25 k, 134 w, 98 m. Alabama troops, 3d, 5th, 6th, 12th, 13th, 61st Inf.

Cold Harbor, Va., June 2, and Bethesda Church, Va., June 4. Gen. Lee 78,000; total loss 1700.—Federal, Gen. Grant, 103,875; loss 1844 k, 9077 w, 1816 m. Alabama troops, 3d, 4th, 5th, 6th, 8th, 9th, 10th, 11th, 12th, 13th, 14th, 15th, 44th, 47th, 48th, 61st Inf.; Hurt's Batty.

Petersburg assault, June 15 to 19. Gen. Beauregard, 20,000.—Federal, Gen. Hancock, 90,000; loss 1688 k, 8513 w, 1185 m. Alabama troops, 8th, 9th, 10th, 11th, 13th, 14th, 43d, 59th, 60th, and Stallworth's 23d Battn. Inf

Lynchburg, Va., June 17-18. Gen. Early; 10,000; total loss 200.— Federal, Gen. Hunter, 17,200; loss 103 k, 564 w, 271 m. Alabama troops, 3d, 5th, 6th, 12th, 61st Inf.

Weldon R. R., etc., Va., June 22.—Federal, loss 142 k, 654 w, 2166 m.

Petersburg Trenches, Va., June 20 to 30. Gen. Beauregard.—Federal, Gen. Hancock; loss 112 k, 506 w, 151 m.

Monocacy, Md., July 9. Gen. Early, 10,000; total loss 650.—Federal, Gen. Lew Wallace, 6,050; loss 123 k, 603 w, 568 m. Alabama troops, 3d, 5th, 6th, 12th, 61st Inf.; Jeff. Davis Batty.

Snicker's Ferry, Va., July 18. Gen. Early, 9,300.—Federal, Gen. Thoburn, 1 division; 65 k, 301 w, 56 m. Alabama troops, 3d, 5th, 6th, 12th, 61st Inf.; Jeff. Davis Batty.

Carter's Farm, Va., July 20. Gen. Ramseur, 1 division; total loss 400.— Federal, Gen. Averill, 2,350; loss 37 k, 175 w, 30 m. Alabama troops, 3d, 5th, 6th, 12th, 61st Inf.; Jeff. Davis Batty.

Winchester, or Kernstown, Va., July 24. Gen. Early, 7,800.—Federal, Gens. Crook and Averill; loss 134 k, 678 w, 391 m. Alabama troops, 3d, 5th, 6th, 12th, 61st Inf.; Jeff. Davis Batty.

New Market, Malvern Hill, Darbytown, Va., July 26 to 29. Gen. Beauregard; total loss 250.—Federal, Gen. Hancock, 1 corps and 2 divisions; loss 62 k, 34.0 w, 86 m.

Petersburg Mine, Va., July 30. Gen. R. E. Lee, 54,751; total loss* 677.— Federal, Gen. Grant, 77,321; loss 504 k, 1881 w, 1413 m. Alabama troops, 4th, 8th, 9th, 10th, 11th, 13th, 14th, 15th, 41st, 43d, 44th, 47th, 48th, 59th, 60th, 61st Inf.; 23d Battn.; Hurt's Batty.

Petersburg and Richmond, Va., July 1 to 31. Gen. R. E. Lee, 54,751; loss 54k, 751 w.—Federal, Gen. Grant, 77,321; loss 915 k, 3808 w, 1644 m. Alabama troops, same as at Petersburg Mine.

Deep Bottom, Va., Aug. 14 to 16. Total loss 1100.—Federal, loss 327 k, 1851 w, 721 m. Alabama troops, 15th Inf.

Weldon R. R.,Va., Aug. 18 to 20. Gen. A. P. Hill; loss 200 k; total loss 4000.—Federal, Gen. Warren; loss 251 k, 1148 w, 2879 m. Alabama troops, 8th, 9th, 10th, 11th, 13th, 14th Inf. * Elliott's S. C. brigade; others not reported,

Halltown, Va., Aug. 24. Gen. Early.—Federal, Gen. Sheridan; loss 9 k, 37 w, 16 m. Alabama troops, 3d, 5th, 6th, 12th, 61st Inf.; Jeff. Davis Batty.

Ream's Station, Va., Aug. 25. Gen. Hill; total loss 720.—Federal, Gen. Hancock; loss 140 k, 529 w, 2073 m. Alabama troops, 8th, 9th, 10th, 11th, 13th, 14th Inf.

Halltown, Va., Aug. 26. Gen. Early.—Federal, Gen. Torbert; loss 30 k, 141 w. Alabama troops, 3d, 5th, 6th, 12th, 61st Inf.; Jeff. Davis Batty.

Smithfield, Va., Aug. 29. Gen. Early.—Federal, Gen. Merritt, 1 division; loss 10 k, 90 w. Alabama troops, 3d, 5th, 6th, 12th, 61st Inf.; Jeff. Davis Batty.

Siege of Petersburg and Richmond, Va., Aug. 1 to 31. Gen. Lee, 34,677—

---

* Elliot's S. C. Brigade; Others not reported.

Federal, 58,923; loss 876 k, 4151 w, 5969 m. Alabama troops, Lee's army as above.

Berryville, Va., Sept. 3. Gen. Anderson.—Federal, Gen. Crook; loss 30 k, 182 w, 100 m. Alabama troops, 4th, 15th, 44th, 47th, 48th Inf.

Opequon, Or Winchester, Va., Sept. 19. Gen. Early, 15,000; loss* 226 k, 1567 w, 1818 m.— Federal, Gen. Sheridan, 45,000; loss 697 k, 3983 w, 338 m. Alabama troops, 3d, 5th, 6th, 12th, 61st Inf.; Jeff. Davis Batty.

Fisher's Hill, Va., Sept. 22. Gen. Early, 11,000; loss* 30 k, 210 w, 995 m.— Federal, Gen. Sheridan, 40,000; loss 52 k, 457 w, 19 m. Alabama troops, 3d, 5th, 6th, 12th, 61st Inf.; Jeff. Davis Batty.

Chaffin's Farm, Va., Sept. 28. Gen. Anderson.—Federal, Gens. Ames and Stannard; loss 383 k, 2299 w, 645 m. Alabama troops, 4th, 15th, 44th, 47th, 48th Inf.

Poplar Spring Church, Peebles' Farm, Pegram's, Va., Sept. 30. Gen. Anderson.—Federal, Gen. Meade; loss 189 k, 900 w, 1802 m. Alabama troops, 4th, 15th, 44th, 47th, 48th Inf.

Petersburg and Richmond, Va., Sept. 1 to 30. Gen. Lee, 35,088.— Federal, Gen. Grant, 70,000; loss 74 k, 304 w, 424 m. Alabama troops, Lee's army as above.

Darbytown Rd., Va., Oct. 7. Gen. Longstreet.—Federal, Gen. Kautz; loss 49 k, 253 w, 156 m. Alabama troops, 4th, 15th, 44th, 47th, 48th Inf.

Darbytown Rd., Va., Oct. 13.—Federal, Gen. Terry; loss 36 k, 358 w.

Cedar Cr., Va., Oct. 19. Gen. Early, 10,000; loss 320 k, 1540 w, 1050 m.— Federal, Gen. Sheridan, 37,000; loss 644 k, 3430 w, 1591 m. Alabama troops, 3d, 5th, 6th, 12th, 61st Inf.; Jeff. Davis Batty.

Boydtown Rd., or Hatcher's Run, Va., Oct. 27.—Federal, Gens. Warren and Hancock; loss 166 k, 1028 w, 564 m. Alabama troops, 41st, 59th, 60th Inf.; 1st Conf. Battn.

Darbytown Rd., or Fair Oaks, Va., Oct. 27. Total loss 451.—Federal, Gen. Hancock; loss 118 k, 787 w, 698 m.

Petersburg and Richmond, Va., Oct. 1 to 31. Gen. Lee, 47,307. —Federal, Gen. Grant, 85,046; loss 528 k, 2946 w, 2094 m. Alabama troops, Lee's army.

Petersburg and Richmond, Va., Nov. 1 to 30. Gen. Lee, 56,434.— Federal, Gen. Grant, 86,723; loss 57 k, 258 w, 108 m. Alabama troops, Lee's army.

Petersburg and Richmond, Va., Dec. 1 to 31. Gen. Lee, 66,533— Federal, Gen. Grant, 110,364; loss 66 k, 278 w, 269 m, Alabama troops, Lee's army.

Weldon R. R., Dec. 7 to 10.—Federal, Gen. Warren.

1865.

Siege of Petersburg, Va., Jan. 1 to 31. Gen. Lee.—Federal, Gen. Grant, 120,000; loss 51 k, 269 w, 81 m. Alabama troops, Lee's army.

* Cavalry not Included.

Siege of Petersburg, Va., Feb. 1 to 28. Gen. Lee, 54,000.—Federal, Gen. Grant, 120,000; loss 43 k, 257 w, 72 m. Alabama troops, Lee's army.

Dabney's Mills, Hatcher's Run, Va., Feb. 5 to 7. Gen. A. P. Hill. —Federal, Gens. Warren and Humphreys; loss 171 k, 1181 w, 187 m. Alabama troops, 8th, 9th, 10th, 11th, 13th, 14th Inf.

Fort Stedman, Va., Mar. 25. Gen. Gordon, 12,000; loss 120 k, 612 w, 1949 m.—Federal, Gen. Parke, 6th corps; loss 72 k, 450 w, 522 m. Alabama troops, 3d, 4th, 5th, 6th, 8th, 9th, 10th, 11th, 12th, 13th, 14th, 15th, 44th, 47th, 48th, 61st Inf.

Petersburg, Va., Mar. 25. Gen. Lee.—Federal, Gen. Grant; loss 103 k, 864 w, 209 m. Alabama troops, Lee's army.

Gravelly Run, Va., Mar. 29.—Federal, Gen. Ayres; loss 55 k, 306 w, 22 m.

White Oak Rd., Va., Mar. 31.—Federal, Gen. Warren; loss 177 k, 1134 w, 556m. Alabama troops, 41st, 59th, 60th Inf.; 1st Conf. Battn.

Petersburg, Va., Mar. 1 to 31. Gen. Lee, 46,000.—Federal, Gen. Grant; loss 58 k, 272 w, 98 m. Alabama troops, Lee's army.

Five Forks, Va., April 1. Gens. Pickett and F. H. Lee, 7,000.—Federal, Gens. Warren and Sheridan, 26,000; loss 124 k, 706 w, 54 m.

Petersburg, Va., April 2. Gen. Lee, 50,000.—Federal, Gen. Grant, 120,000; loss 124 k, 706 w, 54 m. Alabama troops, Lee's army.

Richmond, Va., April 3.—Federal, Gen. G. Weitzel.

Sailor's Cr., Va., April 6. Gens. Ewell and Anderson, 5,000.—Federal, Gens. Sheridan and H. G. Wright, 30,000; loss 166 k, 1014 w.

High Bridge, Va., April 6.—Federal, loss 10 k, 31 w, 1000 m.

Farmville, Va., April 7.—Federal; loss 58 k, 504 w, 9 m.

Appomattox, Va., April 9. Gen. Lee, 28,231; total loss 28,231.—Federal, Gen. Grant. Alabama troops, army of Virginia surrendered.

BATTLES OF THE WESTERN ARMY IN WHICH ALABAMA TROOPS WERE ENGAGED.

1861.

Santa Rosa, Fla., Oct. 9. Gen. R. H. Anderson, 1,000; loss 18 k, 39 w, 25 m.— Federal, Col. Harvey Brown, 500; loss 50 k, 20 m. Alabama troops, 1st and 7th Inf.

Wild Cat, Ky., Oct. 21. Gen. Zollicoffer; loss 11 k, 42 w.—Federal, loss 5 k, 21 w, 40 m. Alabama troops, 16th Inf.

Pensacola, Fort Pickens, Fla., Nov. 23. Gen. Bragg; loss 5 k, 23 w. —Federal, Lt. Slemmer, Capts. Ellison and McKean, the Niagara and Richmond 81st Art.; loss 5 k, 7 w. Alabama troops, 7th, 17th, 19th, 29th Inf.; 1st. Inf. as Art.

Sacramento, Ky., Dec. 28. Col. B. Forrest; loss 2 k, 3 w.—Federal, Gen. Geo. H. Thomas; loss 65 k, 17 w, 18 m.

1862.

Mill Springs, Ky., Jan. 19. Gen. Zollicoffer, 4,000; loss 125 k, 309 w, 95 m.—Federal, Gen. Geo. H. Thomas, 4,000; loss 39 k, 207 w, 15m. Alabama troops, 16th Inf.; Ketchum's Batty.

Roanoke Island, N. C., Feb. 8. Gen. Wise and Com. Lynch; loss 23 k, 58 w, 2527 m.—Federal, Gen. Burnside and Com. Goldsborough, 7,500, 24 gunboats; loss 37 k, 214 w, 13 m. Alabama troops, Montgomery True Blues Art.

Fort Donelson, Tenn., Feb. 14-16. Gen. Buckner, 17,000; loss 446 k, 1534 w, 13,829 m.—Federal, Gen. Grant and Com. Foote, 20,000, 6 gunboats; loss 500 k, 2108 w, 224 m. Alabama troops, Garvin's Battn.; 26th-50th, 27th Inf.

Near Shiloh, Tenn., April 4. Col. Clanton; loss 7 m.—Federal, loss 1 k, 1 m. Alabama troops, 1st Cav.

Shiloh, Tenn., April 6, 7. Gens. A. S. Johnson and Beauregard, 38,773; loss 1728 k, 8012 w, 959 m.—Federal, Gens. Grant and Buell, 70,863; loss 1754 k, 8408 w, 2885 m. Alabama troops, 16th, 17th, 18th, 19th, 21st, 22d, 25th, 26th-50th, 31st, 4th Batt. Inf.; Brewer's, Forrest's, Clanton's, Jenkins', Cav.; 1st, 3d, 53d Cav., Ketchum's, Gage's, Lumsden's Battrs.

New Madrid or Island No. 10, Tenn., March 16 to April 8. Gen. McCown, 15 regts.; loss 17 k, 13 w, 2000 m.—Federal, Gen. Pope and Com. Foote, 33 regiments, 17 boats; loss 17 k, 34 w, 3 m. Alabama troops, 1st, 54th Inf.

Huntsville, Ala., April 11. Total loss 200.—Federal, Gen. O. M. Mitchell, 8,000.

Farmington, Miss., May 9, 10. Gen. Ruggles.—Federal, loss 16 k, 148 w, 14 m. Alabama troops, 19th, 21st, 22d, 24th, 25th Inf.; Ketchum's Batty.

Rodgersville, Ala., May 13. Col. Adams.—Federal, Col. Starkweather, 1,000. Alabama troops, Adams' Cav.

Bridge Creek, Miss., May 28. Col. Jos. Wheeler, 1,000; loss 8k, 28 w, 7 m.—Federal, Gen. Stanley; loss 12 k, 70 w. Alabama troops, 25th, 19th, 26th, 1st Cav., Robertson's.

Tishimingo Cr., Miss., May 30. Col. Jos. Wheeler, 1,100, loss 1 w.— Federal, Gen. Granger, 5,000; loss 2 k, 10 w. Alabama troops, 19th, 22d Inf.; Dent's Batty.

Blackland, Miss., June 4. Alabama troops, 24th Inf.

Secessionville, S. C., June 16. Gen. N. G. Evans; loss 52 k, 144 w, 8 m.—Federal, Gen. Stevens, 6,600; loss 107 k, 487 w, 89 m.

Battle Creek, Tenn., June 21. Gen. Leadbetter.—Federal, Gen. Mitchell; loss 4 k, 3 w. Alabama troops, 46th Inf.; 3d Conf. Cav.

Murfreesboro, Tenn., July 13. Gen. Forrest, 2,000—Federal, Gen. T. T. Crittendon, 1 brigade; total loss, 1 brigade. Alabama troops, Forrest's Cav.; 1st, 51st Cav.; 3d Conf. Cav.

Middleburg, Bolivar Road, Forked Deer, and Jackson Road, Tenn., July. Jos. Wheeler; total loss 32.—Federal, total loss 120. Alabama troops, 8th Conf. Cav.

Baton Rouge, La., Aug. 5. Gen. J. C. Breckinridge, 2,600; loss 84 k, 315 w, 57m.—Federal, Gen. Thos. Williams, 2,500; loss 84 k, 266 w, 33 m. Alabama troops, 31st, 35th Inf.; 4th and Snodgrass' Battns.

Near New Market, Ala., Aug. 5.—Federal, Gen. R. L. McCook; loss 2 k, 1 w, 60 m. Alabama troops, Gurley's and Hambrick's Cos., Rangers.

Tazewell, Tenn., Aug. 6. Gen. C. L. Stevenson; loss 9 k, 40 w.— Federal, loss 3 k, 23 w, 50 m. Alabama troops, 30th, 31st, 46th Inf.; Eufaula Batty.

Bridgeport, Ala., Aug. 27. Gen. S. B. Maxey. Alabama troops, 32d Inf.

Altamont, Tenn., Aug. 30. Gen. Jos. Wheeler, 1 brigade; total loss 3.—Federal, Gen. McCook; total loss 35. Alabama troops, parts of 1st. 3d. Cav.

Stevenson, Ala., Aug. 31. Gen. S. B. Maxey. Alabama troops, 32d Inf.

Gallatin Road, Tenn., Sept. 6. Gen. Jos. Wheeler, 1 brigade.— Federal, Gen. McCook; total loss 20. Alabama troops, parts of 1st, 3d Cav.

Kentucky Line, Tenn., Sept. 8. Gen. Jos. Wheeler, 1 brigade.— Federal, Gen. McCook; total loss 40. Alabama troops, parts of 1st, 3d Cav.

Franklin Road, Tenn., Sept. 9. Gen. Jos. Wheeler, 1 brigade; total loss's.— Federal, Gen. McCook; total loss 70. Alabama troops, part of 1st Conf. Cav.

Scottsville Road, Tenn., Sept. 9. Gen. Jos. Wheeler, 1 brigade; total loss 9.— Federal, Gen. McCook; total loss 135.

Log Church, Tenn., Sept. 10. Gen. Jos. Wheeler, 1 brigade; total loss 5.— Federal, Gen. McCook; total loss 80.

Woodburn, Tenn., Sept. 11. Gen. Jos. Wheeler, 1 brigade.—Federal, Gen. McCook; total loss 30.

Smith's, Tenn., Sept. 11. Gen. Jos. Wheeler, 1 brigade; total loss 3. —Federal, Gen. McCook; total loss 18.

Mumfordsville, Ky., Sept, 14-17. Gen. Bragg, 16,000; loss 40 k, 211 w.— Federal, Col. Wilder, 4,200; loss 15 k, 57 w, 4076 m. Alabama troops, 22d, 28th, 33d Inf.; Waters' Batty.

Near Oakland, Ky., Sept. 16. Gen. Jos. Wheeler, 700; total loss 5. —Federal, total loss 14. Alabama troops, part of 1st Conf. Cav.

Bowling Green and Merry Oaks, Ky., Sept. 17. Gen. Jos. Wheeler, 700; total loss 6.—Federal, total loss 50. Alabama troops, part of 1st Conf. Cav.

Near Cave City, Ky., Sept. 18. Gen. Jos. Wheeler, 700; total loss 4. — Federal, total loss 23. Alabama troops, part of 1st Conf. Cav.

Horse Cave, Ky., Sept. 19. Gen. Jos. Wheeler, 700; total loss 15.— Federal, total loss 32. Alabama troops, parts of 1st, 3d Conf. Cav.

Bear Wallow, Ky., Sept 19. Gen. Jos. Wheeler, 700; total loss 7.— Federal, total loss 29. Alabama troops, parts of 1st, 3d Conf. Cav.

Iuka, Miss., Sept. 19. Gen. Price, 3,179; loss 86 k, 408 w, 199 m.— Federal, Gen. Rosecrans, 9,000; loss 141 k, 613 w, 36 m. Alabama troops, 37th Inf.

Mumfordsville, Ky., Sept. 20. Gen. Jos. Wheeler, 700; total loss 12. — Federal, Major Foster; total loss 40. Alabama troops, parts of 1st, 3d Conf. Cav.

Shepherdsville, Ky., Sept. 21. Gen. Jos. Wheeler, 700; total loss 25. —Federal, Col. Granger; total loss 75. Alabama troops, parts of 1st, 3d Cav.

Woodsonville, Ky., Sept. 21. Gen. Jos. Wheeler, 700; total loss 23. —Federal, total loss 75. Alabama troops, parts of 1st, 3d Cav.

Vinegar Hill, Ky., Sept. 22. Gen. Jos. Wheeler, 700; total loss 13. —Federal, total loss 70. Alabama troops, parts of 1st, 3d Cav.

New Lebanon Junc., Ky., Sept. 28. Gen. Jos. Wheeler, 700; total loss 3.— Federal, total loss 38. Alabama troops, part of 1st Cav.

Elizabethtown Rd., Ky., Sept. 29. Gen. Jos. Wheeler, 700; total loss 4.— Federal, total loss 30. Alabama troops, part of 1st Cav.

Louisville Pike, Ky., Oct. 1. Gen. Jos. Wheeler, 700; total loss 2.— Federal, total loss 20. Alabama troops, part of 1st Cav.

Shepherdsville Rd., Ky., Oct 2. Gen. Jos. Wheeler, 700; total loss 3. —Federal, total loss 35. Alabama troops, part of 1st Cav.

Near Bridge, Ky., Oct. 3. Gen. Jos. Wheeler, 700; total loss 6.— Federal, total loss 42. Alabama troops, part of 1st Cav.

Corinth, Miss., Oct. 3, 4. Gen. Van Dorn, 20,000; loss 505 k, 2150 w, 2183 m.—Federal, Gen. Rosecrans, 20,000; loss 355 k, 1841 w, 324m. Alabama troops, 1st, 31st, 35th, 37th, 42d, 49th Inf.; 4th Battn. Inf.; 1st Conf. Battn. Inf.

Bardstown Pike, Ky., Oct. 4. Gen. Jos. Wheeler; total loss 30.— Federal, total loss 170. Alabama troops, part of 1st Cav.

Perryville Pike, Ky., Oct 5. Gen. Jos. Wheeler; total loss 1.— Federal, total loss 32. Alabama troops, parts of 1st, 3d Cav.

Hatchie Bridge, Miss., Oct 5. Gen. Van Dorn.—Federal, Gen. Ord; loss 46 k, 493 w, 31 m. Alabama troops, 1st Conf. Battn.

Fair Grounds, Ky., Oct. 6. Gen. Jos. Wheeler; total loss 2.—Federal, total loss 15. Alabama troops, parts of 1st, 3d Cav.

Springfield, Ky., Oct. 6. Gen. Jos. Wheeler; total loss 5.—Federal, total loss 65. Alabama troops, parts of 1st, 3d Cav.

Burnt Cross Rds., Ky., Oct. 6. Gen. Jos. Wheeler total loss 2.— Federal, total loss 20. Alabama troops, parts of 1st, 3d Cav.

Beach Fork, Ky., Oct 6. Gen. Jos. Wheeler; total loss 8.—Federal, total loss 40. Alabama troops, parts of 1st, 3d Cav.

Grassy Mound, Ky., Oct 6. Gen. Jos. Wheeler; total loss 2.—Federal, total loss 30. Alabama troops, parts of 1st, 3d Cav.

Lavergne, Tenn., Oct. 7. Gen. S. R. Anderson, 2 regiments; loss 80 k and w, 175 m.—Federal, Gen. Palmer, 1 brigade; loss 5 k, 9 w, 4 m. Alabama troops, 32d Inf.

Brown Hill, Ky., Oct. 7. Gen. Jos. Wheeler; total loss 15.—Federal, total loss 200. Alabama troops, parts of 1st, 3d Cav.

Perryville Rd., Ky., Oct. 7. Gen. Jos. Wheeler; total loss 7.— Federal, total loss 80.

Perryville, Ky., Oct. 8. Gen. Bragg, 16,000; loss 510 k, 2635 w, 251 m.— Federal, Gen. Buell; loss 916 k, 2943 w, 480 m. Alabama troops, 16th,

22d, 27th, 33d, 45th, 18th Battn. Inf.; 1st, 3d Cav.; 1st Conf. Cav.; Waters', Lumsden's, Semple's Battrs.

Perryville, Ky., Oct. 8. Gen. Jos. Wheeler; total loss 174. Alabama troops, 16th, 22d, 27th, 33d, 45th, 18th Battn. Inf.; 1st, 3d Cav.; 1st Conf, Cav.; Waters', Lumsden's, Semple's Battrs.

Lawrenceburg, Ky., Oct. 9. Gen. E. K. Smith; loss 11 k.—Federal, loss 6 k, 8 w, 200 m.

Mackelville Pike, Ky., Oct. 9. Gen. Jos. Wheeler.—Federal, total loss 13. Alabama troops, 1st Cav.

Danville Rd., Ky., Oct. 9. Gen. Jos. Wheeler; total loss 9.—Federal, total loss 55. Alabama troops, parts of 1st, 3d Cav.

Danville Cross Rds., Ky., Oct. 10. Gen. Jos. Wheeler; total loss 13.— Federal, Col. Boyle, 1 regiment; total loss 74. Alabama troops, parts of 1st, 3d Cav., and 1st Conf. Cav.

Danville, Ky., Oct. 11. Gen. Jos. Wheeler; total loss 16.—Federal, total loss 80. Alabama troops, parts of 1st, 3d Cav., and 1st Conf. Cav.

Dick's Ford, Ky., Oct. 12. Gen. Jos. Wheeler; total loss 3.—Federal, total loss 27. Alabama troops, parts of 1st, 3d Cav.

Lancaster Rd., Ky., Oct. 13. Gen. Jos. Wheeler; total loss 10.— Federal, total loss 50. Alabama troops, parts of 1st, 3d Cav., and 1st Conf. Cav.

Lancaster, Ky., Oct. 14. Gen. Jos. Wheeler; total loss 30.—Federal, total loss 80. Alabama troops, parts of 1st, 3d Cav., and 1st Conf. Cav.

Crab Orchard Rd., Ky., Oct. 14. Gen. Jos. Wheeler; total loss.19. —Federal, total loss 75. Alabama troops, parts of 1st, 3d Cav., and 1st Conf. Cav.

Crab Orchard, Ky., Oct. 15. Gen. Jos. Wheeler; total loss 32.— Federal, total loss 140. Alabama troops, parts of 1st, 3d Cav., and 1st Conf. Cav.

Barren Mound, Ky., Oct. 15. Gen. Jos. Wheeler; total loss 7.— Federal, total loss 60. Alabama troops, parts of 1st, 3d Cav., and 1st Conf. Cav.

Mountain Gap, Ky., Oct. 16. Gen. Jos. Wheeler; total loss 7.—Federal, total loss 50. Alabama troops, parts of 1st, 3d Cav., and 1st Conf. Cav.

Mt. Vernon, Ky., Oct 16. Gen, Jos. Wheeler; total loss 8.—Federal, total loss 60. Alabama troops, parts of 1st, 3d Cav.

Valley Woods, Ky., Oct. 17. Gen. Jos. Wheeler; total loss 9.— Federal, total loss 72. Alabama troops, parts of 1st, 3d Cav.

Rocky Hill, Ky., Oct. 17.—Gen. Jos. Wheeler; total loss 11.—Federal, total loss 75. Alabama troops, parts of 1st, 3d Cav.

Cross Rds. to Big Hill, Ky., Oct. 18. Gen. Jos. Wheeler; total loss 13.— Federal, total loss 40. Alabama troops, parts of 1st, 3d Cav.

Little Rockcastle River, Ky., Oct. 18. Gen. Jos. Wheeler; total loss 6.— Federal, total loss 60. Alabama troops, parts of 1st, 3d Cav.

Mountain Side, Ky., Oct. 18. Gen. Jos. Wheeler; total loss 5.— Federal, total loss 35. Alabama troops, parts of 1st, 3d Cav.

Wild Cat, Ky., Oct. 19. Gen. Jos. Wheeler.—Federal, total loss 28. Alabama troops, parts of 1st, 3d Cav.

Near Wild Cat, Ky., Oct. 20. Gen. Jos. Wheeler; total loss 16.— Federal, total loss 39. Alabama troops parts of 1st, 3d Cav.

Pitman's Cross Rds., Ky., Oct. 21. Gen. Jos. Wheeler; total loss 1, — Federal, total loss 25. Alabama troops, parts of 1st, 3d Cav.

Pocotaligo, S. C., Oct. 22. Col. W. S. Walker; loss 21 k, 124 w, 18 m— Federal, Gen. Mitchell, 4,448; loss 43 k, 294 w, 3 m.

Nashville Pike, Tenn., Nov. 14. Gen. Jos. Wheeler; total loss 1.— Federal, total loss 20. Alabama troops, parts of 1st, 3d, 7th Cav.; 8th Conf. Cav.

Nashville, Tenn., Nov. 15. Gen. Jos. Wheeler; total loss 14.—Federal, total loss 40. Alabama troops, parts of 1st, 3d, 7th Cav.; 8th Conf. Cav.

Scrougesville and Lavergne, Tenn., Nov. 27., Gen. Jos. Wheeler; total loss 8.—Federal, Gen. Sill, 5 brigades; total loss 29. Alabama troops, parts of 1st, 3d, 51st Cav.; 8th Conf. Cav.

Kimbrough's, Tenn., Dec. 6. Gen. Jos. Wheeler; total loss 12.— Federal, total loss 90. Alabama troops, parts of 1st, 3d, 51st Cav.; 8th Conf. Cav.

Carter's Farm, Tenn., Dec. 9. Gen. Jos. Wheeler; total loss 15.— Federal, total loss 58. Alabama troops, 1st, 3d, 51st Cav.; 8th Conf. Cav,.

Lavergne, Tenn., Dec. 9. Gen. Jos. Wheeler.—Federal, loss 5 k, 48 w, 6 m. Alabama troops, 1st, 3d, 51st Cav.; 8th Conf. Cav.

Nolensville Pike, Tenn., Dec. 11. Gen. Jos. Wheeler; total loss 17, —Federal, total loss 3. Alabama troops, 1st, 3d, 51st Cav.; 8th Conf. Cav.

Little Bear Cr., Ala,, Dec. 12. Col. Roddey; loss 11 k, 30 w, 40 m.— Federal, Col. Sweeny; loss 1 k, 2 m. Alabama troops, Col. Roddey's Cav.

Lexington, Tenn., Dec. 18. Gen. Forrest; loss 7 k, 28 w.—Federal, loss 7 k, 10 w, 150 m. Alabama troops, Russell's 4th Cav.; Forrest's Cav.

Jackson, Tenn., Dec. 18. Gen. Forrest; loss 70 w, 3 m.—Federal, loss 30 w, 200 m. Alabama troops, Russell's 4th Cav.; Forrest's Cav.

Asylum Hill, Tenn., Dec. 21. Gen. Jos. Wheeler; total loss 3.— Federal, total loss 60. Alabama troops, parts of 1st, 3d Cav., 8th Conf. Cav.

Cox Hill, Tenn., Dec. 25. Gen. Jos. Wheeler; total loss 4.—Federal, total loss 36. Alabama troops, parts of 1st, 51st Cav.; 8th Conf. Cav.

Hillsboro Pike, Tenn., Dec. 25. Col. Malone. Alabama troops, Col. Malone's Battn.

Hurricane Cr., Tenn,, Dec. 26. Gen. Jos. Wheeler; total loss 11.— Federal, total loss 90. Alabama troops, parts of 1st, 51st Cav., and 8th Conf. Cav.

Lavergne, Tenn., Dec. 26. Gen. Jos. Wheeler; total loss 14.—Federal, total loss 120. Alabama troops, parts of 1st, 3d, 4th, 51st Cav., and 8th Conf. Cav.

Jefferson Pike, Tenn., Dec. 27. Gen. Jos. Wheeler; total loss 20.— Federal, total loss 60. Alabama troops, parts of 1st, 3d, 4th, 51st Cav., and 8th Conf. Cav.

Murfreesboro Pike, Tenn., Dec. 27. Gen. Jos. Wheeler; total loss 25.— Federal, total loss 130. Alabama troops, parts of 1st, 3d, 4th, 51st Cav., and 8th Conf. Cav.

Creek Bridge, Tenn., Dec. 27. Gen. Jos. Wheeler; total loss 12.— Federal, total loss 90. Alabama troops, parts of 1st, 3d, 4th, 51st Cav., and 1st, 3d, 8th Conf. Cav.

Stewart's Cr., Tenn., Dec. 28. Gen. Jos. Wheeler; total loss 6. —Federal, total loss 30. Alabama troops, parts of 1st, 3d, 4th, 51st Cav., and 1st, 3d, 8th Conf. Cav.

Stewart's Cr., Tenn., Dec. 29. Gen. Jos. Wheeler; total loss 28.— Federal, total loss 230. Alabama troops, parts of 1st, 3d, 4th, 51st Cav., and 1st, 3d, 8th Conf. Cav.

Murfreesboro Pike, Tenn., Dec. 29. Gen. Jos. Wheeler; total loss 5. — Federal, total loss 40. Alabama troops, parts of 1st, 3d, 4th, 51st Cav., and 1st, 3d, 8th Conf. Cav.

Overall's Cr., Tenn., Dec. 29. Gen. Jos. Wheeler; total loss 15.— Federal, total loss 110. Alabama troops, parts of 1st, 3d, 4th, 51st Cav., and 1st, 3d, 8th Conf. Cav.

Brick House, Tenn., Dec. 29. Gen. Jos. Wheeler; total loss 8.— Federal, total loss 80. Alabama troops, parts of 1st, 3d, 4th, 51st Cav., and 1st, 3d, 8th Conf. Cav.

Jefferson, Tenn., Dec. 30. Gen. Jos. Wheeler; total loss 10—Federal, Starkweather; loss 20 k, 40 w, 200 m. Alabama troops, parts of 1st, 3d, 4th, 51st Cav., and 8th Conf. Cav.

Near Burnett's, Tenn., Dec. 30. Gen. Jos. Wheeler.—Federal, total loss 20. Alabama troops, parts of 1st, 3d, 4th, 51st Cav., and 8th Conf. Cav.

Lavergne, Tenn., Dec. 30. Gen. Jos. Wheeler; total loss 15.—Federal total loss 1100. Alabama troops, parts of 1st, 3d, 4th, 51st Cav., and 8th Conf. Cav.

Rock Cr. Cross Rds., Tenn., Dec. 30. Gen. Jos. Wheeler; total loss 5.—Federal, total loss 90. Alabama troops, parts of 1st, 3d, 4th, 51st Cav., and 8th Conf. Cav.

Nolensville, Tenn., Dec. 30. Gen. Jos. Wheeler; total loss 12.— Federal, Col. M. B. Walker; total loss 400. Alabama troops, parts of 1st, 3d, 4th, 51st Cav., and 8th Conf. Cav.

Chickasaw Bluffs, Miss., Dec. 17, 1862, to Jan. 3, 1863. Gen. Pemberton, 25,000; loss 63 k, 134 w, 10 m.—Federal, Gen. Sherman, 33,000; loss 208 k, 1005 w, 563 m. Alabama troops, Ward's Batty.; 20th, 23d, 30th, 31st, 37th, 40th Inf.

Murfreesboro, Tenn., Dec. 31, 1862, to Jan. 2, 1863. Gen. B. Bragg, 37,712; loss 1294 k, 7945 w, 1027 m.—Federal, Gen. Rosecrans, 43,400; loss 1533 k, 7802 w, 3717 m. Alabama troops, 16th, 19th, 22d, 24th, 25th, 28th, 31st, 32d, 33d, 34th, 37th, 39th, 41st, 45th Inf.; Yancey's Battn.; Wheeler's Cav.; Garrity's, Waters', Ketchum's, Lumsden's, Robertson's, Semple's and Eufaula Battrs.

1863.

Rassell's, Tenn., Jan. 1. Gen. Jos. Wheeler; total loss 12.—Federal, total loss 70. Alabama troops, parts of 1st, 3d, 4th, 51st Cav., and 8th Conf. Cav.

Lavergne, Tenn., Jan. 1. Gen. Jos. Wheeler; total loss 40.—Federal, total loss 140. Alabama troops, parts of 1st, 3d, 4th, 51st Cav., and 8th Conf. Cav.

Near Murfreesboro, Tenn., Jan. 2. Gen. Jos. Wheeler; total loss 436.— Federal, total loss 3100. Alabama troops, parts of 1st, 3d, 4th, 7th, 51st Cav., and 1st, 3d, 8th Conf. Cav.

Cox's Hill, Tenn., Jan. 3. Gen. Jos. Wheeler; total loss 16.—Federal, total loss 80. Alabama troops, parts of 1st, 3d, 4th, 51st Cav., and 8th Conf. Cav.

Stone River, Tenn., Jan. 4. Gen. Jos. Wheeler; total loss 15.—Federal, total loss 20. Alabama troops, parts of 1st, 3d, 4th, 51st Cav., and 8th Conf. Cav.

Manchester Pike, Tenn., Jan. 5. Gen. Jos. Wheeler, total loss 24. —Federal, total loss 90. Alabama troops, parts of 1st, 3d, 4th, 51st Cav., and 8th Conf. Cav.

Mill Cr., Term., Jan. 8. Gen. Jos. Wheeler; total loss 1.—Federal, total loss 40. Alabama troops, parts of 1st, 3d, 4th, 51st Cav., and 8th Conf. Cav.

Off Texas, Hatteras, and Albemarle, Tenn., Jan. 11. Ad. Semmes.— Federal; loss 2 k, 3 w, 110 m.

Harding Pike, Tenn., Jan. 11. Gen. Jos. Wheeler; loss 1 w.—Federal, total loss 20. Alabama troops, parts of 1st, 3d, 4th, 51st Cav., and 8th Conf. Cav.

Harpeth Shoals, Tenn., Jan. 13. Gen. Jos. Wheeler; total loss 5.— Federal, total loss 650. Alabama troops, parts of 1st, 3d, 4th, 51st Cav., and 8th Conf. Cav.

Mill Cr., Tenn., Jan. 23. Gen. Jos. Wheeler; total loss 2.—Federal, total loss 85. Alabama troops, parts of 1st, 3d, 4th, 51st Cav., and 8th Conf. Cav.

Near Smyrna, Tenn., Jan. 26. Gen. Jos. Wheeler.—Federal, total loss 20. Alabama troops, parts of 1st, 3d, 4th, 51st Cav., and 8th Conf. Cav.

Iron Furnace, etc., Tenn., Feb. 3. Gen. Jos. Wheeler; total loss 168.—Federal, total loss 136.

Fort Donelson, Tenn., Feb. 3. Gen. Jos. Wheeler; total loss 260.— Federal; loss 16 k, 60 w, 50 m. Alabama troops, 4th, 7th Cav., 3d Conf., and Forrest's Cav.

Nolensville, Tenn., Feb. 15. Gen. Jos. Wheeler; total loss 10.— Federal, total loss 45. Alabama troops, 1st, 3d Conf., and 3d, 4th Cav.

Murfreesboro Pike, Tenn., Mar. 21. Gen. Jos. Wheeler; total loss 12.— Federal, total loss 50. Alabama troops, parts of 1st, 3d, 51st Cav., and 8th Conf. Cav.

Brentwood, Franklin, Tenn., Mar. 25. Gen. Forrest; loss 4 k, 4 w, 25 m.— Federal; loss 4 k, 19 w, 40 m. Alabama troops, Forrest's Cav., and 7th, 53d Cav.

Woodbury, Tenn., April 1. Gen Jos. Wheeler; total loss 15.—Federal, Gen. Granger; total loss 13. Alabama troops, 1st, 3d Cav.

Hadley's Bend and Hurricane Cr., Tenn., April 10. Gen. Jos. Wheeler; total loss 8.—Federal, Gen. Granger; total loss 320. Alabama troops, 1st, 3d, 4th, 51st Cav., and 1st, 3d, 8th Conf. Cav.

Bear Cr., Ala., April 17. Gen. Roddey; loss 6 k, 20 w.—Federal; loss 26 w, 16 m. Alabama troops, Roddey's Cav.

Cumberland R., Tenn., April 18. Gen. Jos. Wheeler; total loss 1.— Federal, Col. Minty; total loss 40. Alabama troops, parts of 1st and 3d Cav.

Tuscumbia, Ala., April 24. Gen. Roddey. Alabama troops, Roddey's Cav.

Streight's raid, Tuscumbia, Ala., to Rome, Ga,, April 27 to May 3. Gen. Forrest, 500.—Federal, Gen. Streight, 1,700; loss 12 k, 69 w, 1500 m. Alabama troops, 53d Cav.; Julian's Battn.

Town Cr., Ala., April 28. Gens. Forrest and Roddey; loss 1 k, 3w.—Federal, Gen. G. M. Dodge. Alabama troops, Forrest's and Roddey's Cav.

Day's Gap, Sand Mt. and Black Warrior Cr., Ala., April 30 to May 1. Gen. Forrest; loss 5 k, 50 w.—Federal, Gen. Straight: total loss 75. Alabama troops, sad Cav., and Julian's Battn.

Port Gibson, Miss., May 1. Gen. J. S. Bowen, 7,000; loss 1150 k and w, 500 m.—Federal, Gens. Grant and McClernand, 20,000; loss 130 k, 718 w, 5 m. Alabama troops, 20th, 23d, 30th, 31st, 37th, 46th Inf.; Wade's Batty.

Woodbury, Tenn., May 12. Gen. Jos. Wheeler; total loss 12—Federal; total loss 9. Alabama troops, parts of 1st Cav., and 3d Conf. Cav.

Jackson, Miss., May 14. Gen. Johnston, 9,000; total loss 845.—Federal, Gen. Grant; loss 42 k, 251 w, 7 m. Alabama troops, 32d, 41st, 54th, 55th Inf.; 2d Cav.; 1st Conf. Battn. Inf.; Nelson's and Waddell's Battrs.

Baker's Cr., Miss., May 16. Gen. Pemberton, 25,000; loss 2000 kand w, 1800 m.—Federal, Gen. Grant, 15,000; loss 426k, 1842 w, 189 m. Alabama troops, 20th, 23d, 27th, 30th, 31st, 35th, 37th, 40th, 42d, 46th, 54th, 55th Inf.

Big Black, Miss., May 17. Gen. Pemberton, 4,000; loss 600 k and w, 2500 m.—Federal, Gen. Grant; loss 39 k, 237 w, 3 m. Alabama troops, 236. Inf.

Siege of Vicksburg, Miss., May 18 to July 4. Gen. J. C. Pemberton, 30,581; loss 1260 k, 3572 w, 4227 m.—Federal, Gen. Grant and Adml. Porter, 75,000 and about 85 boats; loss 545 k, 3688 w, 303 m. Alabama troops, 20th, 23d, 27th, 30th, 31st, 35th, 37th, 40th, 42d, 46th, 54th, 55th Inf.; Emanuel's, Waddell's, Sengstak's, 20th Battn. Art.

Plain Stores, Port Hudson Plains, La., May 21. Gen. Beall; total loss 89.— Federal, Gen. Auger; loss 19 k, 81 w, 51 m. Alabama troops, 1st, 49th Inf.

Siege of Port Hudson, La., May 27 to July 9. Gen. F. Gardner, 7,000; loss 176 k, 447 w, 5500 m.—Federal, Adml. Farragut and Gen. Banks, navy and 14,000; loss 708 k, 3336 w, 319 m. Alabama troops, 1st, 27th, 31st, 49th, and 6th Battn. Inf.

Uniontown, Tenn., Tune 23. Gen. Jos. Wheeler; total loss 20.— Federal,

Gen. Stanley; total loss 170. Alabama troops, parts of 1st, 4th, 51st Cav., 1st Conf. Inf.

Hoover's Gap, Tenn., June 24. Gen. Bate, 1 brigade; loss 10 k, 50 w.— Federal, Col. J. E. Wilder, 1 brigade; loss 61 w. Alabama troops, 9th Battn., and Eufaula Batty.

Liberty Gap, Tenn., June 25. Gen. B. Johnson, 2 brigades.— Federal, Col. J. F. Miller; loss 40 w, 100 m. Alabama troops, 18th, 36th, 38th, and 9th Battn. Inf.

Guy's Gap, Tenn., June 27. Gen. Jos. Wheeler; total loss 41.—Federal, Gens. Granger and Stanley; total loss 40. Alabama troops, parts of 7th, 51st Cav.

Shelbyville Pike, Tenn., June 27. Gen. Jos. Wheeler; total loss 30.— Federal, Col. Minty; total loss 75. Alabama troops, parts of 1st, 3d, 4th, 5th Cav., and 1st, 8th Conf. Cav.

Shelbyville, Tenn., June 27. Gen. Jos. Wheeler; total loss 260.— Federal, Gens. Granger and Stanley; total loss 80. Alabama troops, parts of 1st, 3d, 4th, 5th Cav., and 1st, 8th Conf. Cav.

Tullahoma, Tenn., June 28. Gen. Jos. Wheeler; total loss 9.—Federal, Gen. Stanley; total loss 50. Alabama troops, parts of 1st, 3d Cav., and 8th Conf. Cav.

Manchester Rd., Tenn., June 29. Gen. Jos. Wheeler; total loss 5.— Federal, Gen. Stanley; total loss 80. Alabama troops, parts of 1st, 3d Cav., and 8th Conf. Cav.

Allisonia, Tenn., June 30. Gen. Jos. Wheeler; total loss 20.—Federal, Gen. Stanley; total loss 110. Alabama troops, parts of 1st, 3d Cav., and 8th Conf. Cav.

New Church, Tenn., July 1. Gen. Jos. Wheeler; total loss 25.—Federal, Gen. Stanley; total loss 120. Alabama troops, parts of 1st, 3d, 4th, 51st Cav., and 1st, 8th Conf. Cav.

Elk River, Tenn., July 2. Gen. Jos. Wheeler; total loss 30.—Federal, Gen. Stanley; total loss 150. Alabama troops, parts of 1st, 3d Cav.

Near Winchester, Tenn., July 3. Gen. Jos. Wheeler; total loss 3. —Federal, Gen. Stanley; total loss 40. Alabama troops, parts of 1st, 3d Cav.

University Pl., Tenn., July 4. Gen. Jos. Wheeler; total loss 11.— Federal, Gen. Stanley; total loss 100. Alabama troops, parts of 1st, 4th, 51st Cav.

Iuka, Miss., July 7 to 9. Col. Roddey.—Federal, loss 5 k, 3 w, 3 m. Alabama troops, Roddey's 4th Cav.

Near Corinth, July 7 to 9. Col. Roddey; loss 2 k.—Federal, total loss 21. Alabama troops, Roddey's 4th Cav.

Jackson, Miss., July 9 to 16. Gen. Jos. E. Johnston; loss 71 k, 504 w, 25 m.— Federal, Gen. Sherman; loss 100 k, 800 w, 100 m. Alabama troops, 32d, 40th, 41st Inf.; 1st Conf. Battn. Inf. 2d, 3d, 11th Cav.; Gid. Nelson's Batty.

Canton, Miss., July 18. Gen. W. H. Jackson; total loss 72.—Federal, loss 5 k, 20 w. Alabama troops, 32d, 40th, 41st Inf.; 1st Conf. Battn. Inf.; 2d, 3d, 11th Cav.; Gid. Nelson's Batty.

Caperton's Ferry, Ala., Aug. 29. Gen. Jos. Wheeler; total loss 6.— Federal, total loss 40. Alabama troops, parts of 3d Conf., and 51st Cav.

Wills' Valley, Ala., Aug. 31. Gen. Jos. Wheeler; total loss 3.—Federal, total loss 20. Alabama troops, parts of 3d Conf., and 51st Cav.

Wills' Cr., Ala., Sept. 1. Gen. Jos. Wheeler.—Federal, total loss 28. Alabama troops, parts of 3d Conf., and 51st Cav.

Davis Gap, Ala., Sept. 1. Gen. Jos. Wheeler; total loss 7.—Federal, total loss 40. Alabama troops, parts of 1st, 3d Cav., and 3d Conf. Cav.

Tap's Gap, Ala., Sept. 1. Gen. Jos. Wheeler; total loss 25.—Federal, total loss 150. Alabama troops, parts of 1st Cav., and 3d Conf. Cav.

McNeil's Gap, Ala., Sept. 1. Gen. Jos. Wheeler; total loss 9.—Federal, total loss 40. Alabama troops, parts of 1st Cav., and 3d Conf. Cav.

Alpine, Ga., Sept. 12. Gen. Jos. Wheeler; total loss 55.—Federal, total loss 200. Alabama troops, part of 3d Cav.

Near Summerville, Ga., Sept. 13. Gen. Jos. Wheeler; total loss 10. —Federal, total loss 15. Alabama troops, parts of 1st, 3d, 4th Cav., and 8th Conf. Cav.

Near LaFayette, Ga., Sept. 14. Gen. Jos. Wheeler; total loss 60.— Federal, total loss 11. Alabama troops, parts of 1st, 3d, 4th Cav., and 8th Conf. Cav.

Tryon Factory, Ga., Sept. 15. Gen. Jos. Wheeler; total loss 7.— Federal, total loss 55. Alabama troops, parts of 1st, 51st Cav., and 8th Conf. Cav.

Alabama Rd., Ga., Sept. 16. Gen. Jos. Wheeler; total loss 6.—Federal, total loss 35. Alabama troops, parts of 3d, 4th Cav., and 1st Conf. Cav.

McLemore's Cove, Ga., Sept. 17. Gen. Jos. Wheeler; total loss 60. —Federal, total loss 200. Alabama troops, parts of 1st, 3d, 8th Conf., and 1st, 3d, 51st Cav.

Owen's Ford, Ga., Sept. 18. Gen. Jos. Wheeler; total loss 20.— Federal, total loss 150. Alabama troops, parts of 1st, 8th Conf., and 1st, 3d, 51st Cav.

Chickamauga, Sept. 19, 20. Gen. Bragg, 66,000; loss 2389 k, 13,412 w, 2003 m.—Federal, Gen. Rosecrans, 69,000; loss 1656 k, 9749 w, 4774 m. Alabama troops, 4th, 15th, 16th, 18th, 19th, 22d, 24th, 25th, 28th, 32d, 33d, 34th, 36th, 38th, 39th, 41st, 43d, 44th, 45th, 47th, 48th, 50th, 58th Inf.; Hilliard's Legion; Garrity's, Fowler's, Dent's, Semple's and Kolb's Battrs.

Chickamauga, Sept 19. Gen. Jos. Wheeler; total loss 375.—Federal, total loss 3450. Alabama troops, parts of 1st, 3d, 8th Conf., and 1st, 3d, 4th, 5th, 7th, 51st, 53d Cav.

Chattanooga Valley and Stevenson's Gap, Tenn., Sept. 21. Gen. Jos. Wheeler; total loss 40.—Federal, total loss 1500. Alabama troops, parts of 1st, 3d, 51st Cav., and 8th Conf. Cav.

Chattanooga and Summertown, Tenn., Sept. 22. Gen. Jos. Wheeler; total loss 28.—Federal, total loss 95. Alabama troops, parts of 1st, 3d, 51st Cav., and 1st Conf. Cav.

Pt. Looko'ut, Tenn., Sept. 23. Gen. Jos. Wheeler; total loss 3.— Federal, total loss 30. Alabama troops, parts of 1st, 3d, 51st Cav., and 1st, 3d, 8th Conf. Cav.

Hiwassee, Tenn., Sept. 26. Gen. Jos. Wheeler; total loss 2.—Federal, total loss 66. Alabama troops, parts of 1st, 3d, 51st Cav., and 1st, 3d, 8th Conf. Cav.

Cotton Port Ford, Tenn., Sept. 30. Gen. Jos. Wheeler; total loss 20.—Federal, total loss 160. Alabama troops, parts of 1st, 4th Cav., and 3d, 8th Conf. Cav.

Mountain Gap, Tenn., Oct. 1. Gen. Jos. Wheeler: total loss 2.— Federal, total loss 30. Alabama troops, parts of 1st, 3d, 4th, 51st Cav., and 1st, 3d, 8th Conf. Cav.

Pitt's Cross Rds., Tenn., Oct. 2. Gen. Jos. Wheeler; total loss 4. —Federal, total loss 90. Alabama troops, parts of 1st, 3d, 4th, 51st Cav., and 1st, 3d, 8th Conf. Cav.

Anderson's Cross Rds., Tenn., Oct. 2. Gen. Jos. Wheeler; total loss 60.— Federal, total loss 1300. Alabama troops, parts of 1st, 3d, 4th, 51st Cav., and 1st, 8th Conf. Cav.

Valley Rd., Tenn., Oct. 2. Gen. Jos. Wheeler; total loss 46.—Federal, total loss 40. Alabama troops, parts of 1st, 3d, 4th, 51st Cav., and 1st, 8th Conf. Cav.

Near Dunlap, Tenn., Oct. 2. Gen. Jos. Wheeler; total loss 22.— Federal, total loss 35. Alabama troops, parts of 1st, 3d, 4th, 51st Cav., and 8th Conf. Cav.

Hill's Gap, Tenn., Oct. 3. Gen. Jos. Wheeler; total loss 20.—Federal, total loss 40. Alabama troops, parts of 1st, 3d, 4th, 51st Cav., and 8th Conf. Cav.

Thompson's Cool Sps., Tenn., Oct. 3. Gen. Jos. Wheeler; loss 6 k, 26 m.— Federal, total loss 40. Alabama troops, parts of 1st, 3d, 4th, 51st Cav., and 1st, 8th Conf. Cav.

McMinville, Tenn., Oct. 3. Gen. Jos. Wheeler; total loss 7 —Federal, total loss 587. Alabama troops, parts of 1st, 3d Cav., and 8th Conf. Cav.

McMinnville Rd., Tenn., Oct. 4. Gen. Jos. Wheeler; total loss 16.— Federal, total loss 30. Alabama troops, parts of 1st, 3d, 7th, 51st Cav., and 8th Conf. Cav.

Woodbury Rd., Tenn., Oct. 4. Gen. Jos. Wheeler; total loss 7.— Federal, total loss 20. Alabama troops, parts of 1st, 3d, 7th, 51st Cav., and 8th Conf. Cav.

Near Readyville, Tenn., Oct. 5. Gen. Jos. Wheeler; total loss 4. —Federal, total loss 30. Alabama troops, parts of 1st, 3d, 7th, 51st Cav., and 8th Conf. Cav.

Stone River Stockade, Oct. 5. Gen. Jos. Wheeler; total loss 4.— Federal, total loss 79. Alabama troops, parts of 1st, 3d Cav., and 1st, 8th Conf. Cav.

Christiana, Fosterville, War Trace, Tenn., Oct. 6. Gen. Jos. Wheeler; total loss 6.—Federal, total loss 110. Alabama troops, parts of 1st, 3d, 4th, 51st Cav., and 1st, 8th Conf. Cav.

Shelbyville, Tenn., Oct. 6. Gen. Jos. Wheeler; total loss 3.—Federal, total loss 35. Alabama troops, part of 7th Cav.

Farmington, Tenn., Oct. 7. Gen. Jos. Wheeler; total loss 86.—Federal, total loss 228. Alabama troops, parts of 1st, 3d, 51st Cav., and 1st, 8th Conf. Cav.

Sugar Cr., Tenn., Oct. 9. Gen. Jos. Wheeler; total loss 48.—Federal, total loss 25. Alabama troops, part of 3d Conf. Cav.

Elk River, Tenn., Oct. 9. Gen. Jos. Wheeler.—Federal, total loss 10. Alabama troops, part of 1st Cav.

Tennessee River, Tenn., Oct. 9. Gen. Jos. Wheeler; total loss 1.— Federal, total loss 15. Alabama troops, part of 1st Cav.

Tishomingo, Miss., and Cave Cr., Ala., Oct. 20 to 26. Gen. S. D. Lee; loss 10 k, 30 w,—Federal; loss 31 k, 81 w. Alabama troops, parts of 2d and 51st Cav.

Brown's Ferry and Wauhatchie, Tenn., Oct. 27. Gen. Longstreet; total loss 206.—Federal, loss 81 k, 360 w, 31 m. Alabama troops, 4th, 15th, 44th, 47th Inf.

Rockford, Tenn., Nov. 14. Gen. Jos. Wheeler.—Federal, total loss 300. Alabama troops, parts of 11st, 3d, 51st Cav.

Marysville, Tenn., Nov. 14. Gen. Jos. Wheeler; total loss 12.—Federal, total loss 250. Alabama troops, parts of 1st, 3d, 51st Cav.

Stock Cr., Tenn., Nov. 15. Gen. Jos. Wheeler; total loss 7.—Federal, total loss 50. Alabama troops, parts of 1st, 3d, 51st Cav.

Holston River near Knoxville, Tenn., Nov. 15. Gen. Jos. Wheeler; total loss 22.—Federal, total loss 400. Alabama troops, parts of 1st, 3d, 4th, 7th, 51st Cav., and 1st, 8th Conf. Cav.

Loudon Cr., Tenn., Nov. 15. Gen. Jos. Wheeler; loss 6k,to w.—Federal, loss 4 k, 12 w.

Knoxville Rd., Tenn., Nov. 16. Gen. Jos. Wheeler; total loss 27.— Federal, total loss 60. Alabama troops, parts of 1st, 3d, 4th, 7th, 51st Cav., and 1st, 8th Conf. Cav.

Campbell's Station, Tenn., Nov. 16. Gen. Jos. Wheeler; total loss 6.—Federal, total loss 35. Alabama troops, parts of 1st, 3d, 4th, 7th, 51st Cav., and 1st, 8th Conf. Cav.

Campbell's Station, Tenn., Nov. 16. Gen. Longstreet; total loss 300.—Federal, total loss 300. Alabama troops, 43d, 59th, 60th Inf.

Siege of Knoxville, Tenn., Nov. 17 to 23. Gen. Longstreet, 20,000; loss 182 k, 768 w, 192 m; also, Gen. Wheeler; total loss 190.—Federal, Gen. Burnside, 12,000; loss 92 k, 394 w, 207 m. Alabama troops, 15th, 31st, 47th, 48th, 59th, 60th, and Stallworth's Inf.; 1st 3d, 4th, 7th, 51st Cav.; 1st, 8th Conf. Cav.; Kolb's Batty.

Chattanooga, or Missionary Ridge, Nov. 23 to 25. Gen. Bragg; loss 361 k, 2180 w, 4146 m.—Federal, Gen. Grant, 60,000; loss 752 k, 4713 w, 350

m. Alabama troops, Ketchum's, Waters', Eufaula, Fowler's, Semple's, Kolb's, Robertson's Battrs.; parts of 3d, 8th, 10th, Conf. Cav.; 16th, 19th, 20th, 24th, 25th, 28th, 32d, 33d, 34th, 37th, 38th, 39th, 40th, 42d, 45th, 46th, 50th, 58th Inf.

Kingston, Tenn., Nov. 24. Gen. Jos. Wheeler; total loss 50.—Federal, total loss 50. Alabama troops, parts of 1st, 3d, 4th Cav., and 8th Conf. Cav.

Chickamauga Sta., Tenn., Nov. 25. Total loss 10.—Federal, total loss 60. Alabama troops, parts of 8th, 10th Conf. Cav.

Galesville Rd., Tenn., Nov. 26. Total loss 20.—Federal, total loss 75. Alabama troops, parts of 8th, 10th Conf. Cav.

Ringgold, Tenn., Nov. 27. Total loss 65.—Federal, total loss 150. Alabama troops, parts of 8th, 10th, and 3d Conf. Cav.

Fort Sanders, Nov. 29. Gen. Longstreet, 3 brigades; loss 80 k, 400 w, 300 m.—Federal, Gen. Burnside, 1,300; loss 20 k, 80 w. Alabama troops, 15th, 31st, 47th, 48th, 59th, 60th Inf.; Stallworth's Battn.; Kolb's Batty.

Cleveland Rd., Tenn., Nov. 30. Gen. Jos. Wheeler; total loss 6.— Federal, total loss 45. Alabama troops, parts of 3d, 8th, 10th Conf. Cav.

Morristown, Tenn., Dec. 10. Gen. Longstreet; loss 12 k, 20 w.— Federal, Gen. Garrard. Alabama troops, 15th, 59th, 60th, and Stallworth's Battn. Inf.

Bean's Sta,, Tenn., Dec. 14. Gen. Longstreet; total loss 290.— Federal, total loss 700. Alabama troops, 15th, 59th, 60th, and Stallworth's Battn. Inf.

Cleveland, Tenn., Dec. 22. Maj. White.—Federal; loss 1 k; total loss 6. Alabama troops, part of 1st Conf. Cav.

Charleston, Tenn., Dec. 28. Gen. Wheeler; total loss 57.—Federal, Col. Laibold; total loss 35. Alabama troops, parts of 3d, 8th, 10th Conf. Cav.

Cleveland, Tenn., Dec. 29. Gen. Wheeler; total loss 1.—Federal, total loss 28. Alabama troops, parts of 1st, 8th Conf Cav.

1864.

Near Chattanooga, Jan. 22. Gen. Jos. Wheeler.—Federal, total loss 21. Alabama troops, parts of 1st, 8th Conf. Cav.

Athens, Ala., Jan. 25. Col. Johnson; loss 30 w.—Federal; loss 20 w. Alabama troops, 4th Cav.

Florence, Ala., Jan. 26. Col. Roddey; loss 30 m.—Federal, Col. A. O. Miller; loss 10 w. Alabama troops, Roddey's Cav.

Fair Gardens, Tenn., Jan. 27. Gen. Martin; loss 65 k, 100 m.— Federal, total loss 100. Alabama troops, Martin's Cav.

Tunnel Hill, Ga., Jan. 28. Gen. Jos. Wheeler; loss 32 w.—Federal; loss 2 w. Alabama troops, Wheeler's Cav.

Tunnel Hill, Ga., Jan. 28. Gens. Stewart and Hindman. Alabama troops, Stewart's and Hindman's Inf.

Chickamauga Cr., Ga,, Jan. 30. Gen. Jos. Wheeler.—Federal, total loss 28. Alabama troops, parts of 1st, 3d, 10th Conf. Cav.

Sherman's expedition from Vicksburg to Meridian, Miss., Feb. 3 to Mar. 5. Gen. L. Polk; total loss 200.—Federal, Gen. Sherman, 20,000; loss 21 k, 68 w, 81 m. Alabama troops, 17th, 27th, 30th, 31st, 35th, 54th, 55th Inf.; 2d, 4th, 11th, 52d Cav.

Champion Hill, Baker's Cr., and Bolton Depot, Miss., Feb. 4. Gen. S. D. Lee; loss 10 k, 30 w.—Federal, loss 16 k, 40 w, 7 m. Alabama troops, 32d Inf.; 2d, 56th Cav.

Clinton and Jackson, Miss., Feb. 5. Gen. S. D. Lee; loss 10 k, 35 w.—Federal; loss 7 k, 30 w, 13 m. Alabama troops, 32d Inf.; 2d, 56th Cav.

Smith's raid, West Point, Miss., Feb. 21 to Mar. 8. Gen. Forrest, 2,500.—Federal, Gen. W. Sooy Smith, 7,000; loss 47 k, 152 w, 120 m. Alabama troops, Russell's 4th Cav.; 11th Cav.

Stone Church, Ga., Feb. 22. Gen. Jos. Wheeler; total loss 5.—Federal, total loss 40. Alabama troops, part of 10th Conf. Cav.

Tunnel Hill Rd., Ga., Feb. 23. Gen. Jos. Wheeler; total loss 9.— Federal, total loss 45. Alabama troops, parts of 1st, 3d Conf. Cav.

Tunnel Hill, Ga., Feb. 24. Gen. Jos. Wheeler; total loss 7.—Federal, total loss 36. Alabama troops, parts of 1st, 3d, 8th Conf. Cav.

Mill Cr., Ga., Feb. 24. Gen. Jos. Wheeler; total loss 16.—Federal, total loss 60. Alabama troops, parts of 1st, 3d, 8th Conf. Cav.

Buzzard's Roost, Ga., Feb. 25. Gen. Jos. Wheeler; total loss 20.— Federal, total loss 40. Alabama troops, parts of 1st, 3d, 8th Conf. Cav.

Rocky Face, Ga., Feb. 25. Gen. Jos. Wheeler; total loss 34.—Federal, total loss 212. Alabama troops, parts of 1st, 3d, 8th and 10th Conf. Cav.

Crow Valley, Ga., Feb. 25. Gen. Jos. Wheeler; total loss 10.— Federal, total loss 55. Alabama troops, parts of 1st, 3d, 10th Conf. Cav.

Varnell Station, Ga., Feb. 26. Gen. Jos. Wheeler; total loss 4.— Federal, total loss 38. Alabama troops, parts of 1st, 3d, 10th Conf. Cav.

Rocky Face, Ga., Feb. 27. Gen. Jos. Wheeler; total loss 14.—Federal, total loss 15. Alabama troops, parts of 1st, 8th Conf. Cav.

Ringgold Pass, Ga., Feb. 27. Gen. Jos. Wheeler; total loss 6.— Federal, total loss 16. Alabama troops, parts of 1st, 8th Conf. Cav.

McLean's Hill, Ga., Feb. 27. Gen. Jos. Wheeler; total loss 2.—Federal, total loss 17. Alabama troops, parts of 1st, 8th Conf. Cav.

Leet's Mill, Ga., Mar. 6. Gen. Jos. Wheeler; total loss 4.—Federal, total loss 38. Alabama troops, parts of 3d, 8th Conf. Cav.

Gunter's Landing, Ala., Mar. 8. Capt. H. F. Smith, 65; loss 1 k, 4 w.—Federal, 70; loss 1 k, 3 w, 66 m. Alabama troops, Capts. Henry's, May's, Smith's Cos.

Ringgold Rd., Ga., Mar. 31. Gen. Jos. Wheeler; total loss 3.— Federal, total loss 27. Alabama troops, parts of 1st, 10th Conf. Cav.

Pensacola, Fla., April 2. Maj. Randolph; loss 10 w, 11 m.—Federal; loss 3 w. Alabama troops, 7th Cav.

Ducktown Rd., Ga., April 3. Gen. Jos. Wheeler; total loss 1— Federal, total loss 29. Alabama troops, part of 8th Conf. Cav.

Plains Store, La., April 7. Gen. Wirt Adams; loss 2 m.—Federal; loss 1 k, 4 w, 3 m. Alabama troops, Adams' Cav.

Fort Pillow, Tenn., April 12. Gen. Forrest, 2 brigades; loss 14 k, 86 w.—Federal, Major L. F. Booth, 557; loss 163 k and w, 237 m. Alabama troops, Russell's 4th Cav.; 7th, 11th Cav.

Taylor's Ridge, Ga., April 14. Gen. Jos. Wheeler; total loss 1.— Federal, total loss 16. Alabama troops, part of 8th Conf. Cav.

Nickajack Trace, Ga., April 23. Gen. Jos. Wheeler.—Federal, loss 5 k, 9 w, 22 m. Alabama troops, Wheeler's scouts.

Ringgold Bridge, Ga., April 29. Gen. Jos. Wheeler; total loss 2.— Federal, total loss 19. Alabama troops, parts of 1st, 3d Conf. Cav.

Stone Church, Ga., May 1. Gen. Jos. Wheeler; total loss 4.—Federal, total loss 32. Alabama troops, parts of 1st, 3d. and 8th Conf. Cav.

Lee's Cross Rds., Ga., May 2. Gen. Jos. Wheeler; total loss 4.— Federal, total loss 32. Alabama troops, parts of 8th, 10th Conf. Cav.

Chickamauga Cr., Ga., May 3. Gen. Jos. Wheeler; total loss 7.— Federal, total loss 65. Alabama troops, parts of 1st, 8th, 10th Conf. Cav.

Red Clay, Ga., May 3. Gen. Jos. Wheeler; total loss 1.—Federal, total loss 15. Alabama troops, parts of 1st, 8th, 10th Conf. Cav.

Varnell Rd., Ga., May 4. Gen. Jos. Wheeler; total loss 5.—Federal, total loss 80. Alabama troops, parts of 1st, 3d, 8th Conf. and 53d Cav.

Near Tunnel Hill, Ga,, May 5. Gen. Jos. Wheeler; total loss 14.— Federal, total loss 120. Alabama troops, parts of 1st, 3d, 8th, 10th Conf. Cav.

Tunnel Hill, Ga., May 6. Gen. Jos. Wheeler; total loss 19.—Federal, total loss 55. Alabama troops, parts of 1st, 3d, 8th, 10th Conf. Cav.

Tunnel Hill, Ga., May 7. Gen. Jos. Wheeler; total loss 22.—Federal, total loss 80. Alabama troops, parts of 1st, 3d, 8th, 10th Conf. Cav.

Ridge, Ga., May 7. Gen. Jos. Wheeler; total loss 13—Federal, total loss 55. Alabama troops, parts of 1st, 3d, 8th, 10th Conf. Cav.

Dug Gap, Ga., May 8. Gen. Jos. Wheeler; total loss 30.—Federal, total loss 450. Alabama troops, parts of 1st, 3d, 8th, 10th Conf. Cav.

Cleveland Rd., Ga., May 8. Gen. Jos. Wheeler; total loss 2.— Federal, total loss 26. Alabama troops, parts of 1st, 8th Conf., and 53d Cav., and Snodgrass' Battn.

Buzzard Roost Gap, Ga., May 8. Gen. Pettus. — Federal, Gen. Howard, 4th corps. Alabama troops, 20th, 23d., 30th, 31st, 46th Inf.

Rocky Face Ridge, Tunnel Hill, Mill Cr. Gap, Buzzard Roost, Snake Cr., and near Dalton, May 9. Gen. Johnston, 43,000; total loss 600.—Federal, Gen. Sherman, 98,797; loss 200 k, 637 w Alabama troops, 16th, 20th, 30th, 36th, 37th, 40th Inf.

Resaca, Ga., May 9. Gen. Canty. Alabama troops, Canty's brigade.

Railroad, Ga., May 9. Gen. Wheeler; total loss 3.—Federal, total loss 22. Alabama troops, parts of 1st, 3d, 8th Conf., and 53d, and Snodgrass' Battn, Inf.

Near Varnell's, Ga., May 9. Gen. Wheeler; total loss 36.—Federal, Gen.

La Grange; loss 100 m; total loss 260. Alabama troops, parts of 1st, 8th Conf., 53d, and Snodgrass' Battn. Inf.

Mill Cr. Gap, Ga., May 10. Gen. Bates.

Cleveland Rd., Ga., May 11. Gen. Jos. Wheeler; total loss 7.— Federal, Gen. Stoneman; total loss 40. Alabama troops, parts of 3d, 8th Conf. and 53d.

Dalton, Ga., May 11. Gen. Jos. Wheeler; total loss 81.—Federal, Gen. Sherman, total loss 255. Alabama troops, parts of 1st, 3d, 8th, 10th Conf.

Rocky Face, Ga., May 12. Gen. Jos. Wheeler; total loss 12.—Federal, total loss 90. Alabama troops, parts of 1st, 3d, 8th, 10th Conf.

Resaca, etc., Ga., May 13 to 16. Gen. Johnston, about 55,000; total loss 2800.— Federal, Gen. McPherson, 103,000; loss 600 k, 2147 w. Alabama troops, 16th, 18th, 19th, 23d, 29th, 30th, 36th, 37th, 38th, 40th, 45th, 55th, 58th Inf.; Semple's and Tarrant's Battrs.

Dalton, Ga., May 13. Gen. Jos. Wheeler; total loss 7.—Federal, total loss 35. Alabama troops, parts of 1st, 8th, 10th Conf.

Ridge, Ga., May 13. Gen. Jos. Wheeler; total loss 9.—Federal, total loss 60. Alabama troops, parts of 1st, 8th, 10th Conf.

Tilton, Ga., May 13. Gen. Jos. Wheeler; total loss 23.—Federal, total loss 145. Alabama troops, parts of 1st, 3d, 8th, 10th Conf., and 53d Cav.

Oostanaula, Ga., May 14. Gen. Jos. Wheeler; total loss 14.—Federal, total loss 70. Alabama troops, parts of 1st, 3d, 8th, 10th Conf., and 53d Cav.

Resaca, Ga., May 14. Gen. Jos. Wheeler; total loss 135.—Federal, total loss 490. Alabama troops, parts of 1st, 3d, 8th, 10th Conf., and 1st, 3d, 4th, 7th, 51st, 53d Cav., and 24th Battn. Inf.

Spring Pl. Rd., Ga., May 14. Gen. Jos. Wheeler; total loss 3. —Federal, total loss 4. Alabama troops, parts of 1st, 3d, 4th, 7th, 51st Cav.

Calhoun, Ga., May 15. Gen. Jos. Wheeler; total loss 28.—Federal, total loss 120. Alabama troops, parts of 1st, 3d, 4th, 7th, 51st Cav.

Calhoun Rd., Ga., May 16. Gen. Jos. Wheeler; total loss 22.—Federal, total loss 90. Alabama troops, parts of 1st, 3d, 8th Conf. Cav.

Six engagements at Adamsville, Ga., May 17. Gen. Jos. Wheeler; total loss 120.—Federal, total loss 480. Alabama troops, 1st, 3d, 8th, 10th Conf., and 1st, 3d, 4th, 7th, 51st, 53d Cav.

Madison Station, Ala., May 17. Col. Patterson, 500; total loss 7.— Federal, 400; loss 80 m. Alabama troops, 5th Cav., and Stewart's Battn.

Near Cassville, Ga., May 18. Gen. Jos. Wheeler; total loss 32.— Federal, total loss 120. Alabama troops, parts of 1st, 8th, 10th Conf.

Kingston Rd., Ga., May 19. Gen. Jos. Wheeler; total loss 21.— Federal, total loss 160. Alabama troops, parts of 1st, 3d, 4th, 7th, 51st Cav.

Cassville, Ga., May 19 to 22. Gen. Johnston.—Federal, Gen. Sherman. Alabama troops, Gen. Johnston's army as above.

Etowah River, Ga., May 20. Gen. Jos. Wheeler; total loss 26.— Federal, total loss 220. Alabama troops, parts of 1st, 3d, 8th Conf.

Cassville, Ga., May 24. Gen. Jos. Wheeler; total loss 19.—Federal, total loss 420. Alabama troops, parts of 1st, 3d, 8th and 10th Conf.

Dallas and New Hope Ch., May 25 to June 4. Gen. Johnston; total loss 3000.—Federal, Gen. Sherman; total loss 2400. Alabama troops, 1st, 18th, 23d, 25th, 29th, 30th, 36th, 37th, 38th, 40th, 45th, 54th, 58th Inf.; 56th Cav.; Tarrant's Batty.

New Hope Ch., May 26. Gen. Jos. Wheeler; total loss 32.—Federal, total loss 190. Alabama troops, parts of 1st, 3d, 4th, 7th, 51st Cav.

Decatur, Ala., May 26. Loss 15 m.—Federal, total loss 30.

Pickett's Mill, Ga., May 27. Gen. Jos. Wheeler; total loss 356.— Federal, Gen. Howard; total loss 3600. Alabama troops, parts of 1st, 3d, 8th, 10th Conf., and 1st, 3d Cav., and Lowrey's brigade.

Allatoona Rd., Ga., May 28. Gen. Jos. Wheeler; total loss 18.— Federal, total loss 155. Alabama troops, parts of 1st, 3d, 8th, 10th Conf., and 1st, 3d, 4th, 7th, 51st Cav.

Burnt Hickory, Ga., May29. Gen. Jos. Wheeler; total loss 13.— Federal, total loss 60. Alabama troops, parts of 1st, 3d, 8th Conf., and 1st, 3d, 4th, 7th, 51st Cav.

Moulton, Ala., May 28 and 29. Gen. Roddey; loss 15 k; total loss 30. — Federal, Col. Long; loss 4 k, 14 w. Alabama troops, 45th Inf.; Roddey's Cav.

Atlanta, Ga., May 30. Gen. Jos. Wheeler; total loss 16.—Federal, total loss 170. Alabama troops, parts of 1st, 3d, 4th, 7th, 51st, 53d Cav.

Marietta, Ga., May 31. Gen. Jos. Wheeler; total loss 23.—Federal, total loss 200. Alabama troops, parts of 1st, 3d, 4th, 7th, 51st, 53d Cav.

Atlanta Works, June 1 to 3. Gen. Jos. Wheeler; total loss 72.—Federal, total loss 680. Alabama troops, parts of 1st, 3d, 4th, 7th, 51st, 53d Cav.

Davis Cross Rds., June 4. Gen. Jos. Wheeler; total loss 9.—Federal, total loss 70. Alabama troops, 24th Battn.

Atlanta Works, June 6 to 8. Gen. Jos. Wheeler; total loss 31.— Federal, total loss 145. Alabama troops, parts of 1st, 2d, 8th Conf., and 1st, 3d, 4th, 7th, 51st Cav.

Ackworth Rd., June 7. Gen. Jos. Wheeler; total loss 36.—Federal, total loss 140. Alabama troops, parts of 1st, 8th Conf., and 1st, 3d Cav.

Entrenchments, June 9. Gen. Jos. Wheeler; total loss 24.—Federal, total loss 200. Alabama troops, parts of 1st, 3d, 4th, 7th, 51st Cav.

Near Atlanta, June 9, Gen. Jos. Wheeler; total loss 10.—Federal, Gen. McCook; total loss 25. Alabama troops, parts of 1st, 3d, 4th, 7th, 51st Cav., and 1st, 8th, 10th Conf. Cav.

Price's Cross Rds., Miss., June 10. Gen. Forrest, 3,500; loss 131 k, 475 w.—Federal, Gen. Sturgis, about 5,000; loss 223 k, 394 w, 1623 m. Alabama troops, 11th Cav.

Kenesaw Mt, including Pine Mount, Pine Knob, Gulp's, McAfee's, Golgotha, Lattimer and Powder Springs, June 9 to 30. Gen. Johnston, 60,000; total loss 4600.—Federal, Gen. Sherman, 112,819; loss 1370 k, 6500 w, 800 m. Alabama troops, army of Tennessee (as at New Hope).

Bell's Ferry Rd., Ga., June 11. Gen. Jos. Wheeler; total loss 29.— Federal, total loss 150. Alabama troops, parts of 1st, 3d, 4th Cav.

Marshy Cr., Ga., June 12. Gen. Jos. Wheeler, total loss 31.—Federal, total loss 120. Alabama troops, parts of 1st, 8th, 10th Conf., and 53d Cav.

Canton Rd., Ga., June 13. Gen. Jos. Wheeler; total loss 30.—Federal, total loss 160. Alabama troops, parts of 1st, 8th, 10th Conf.

Open Field, Ga., June 14. Gen. Jos. Wheeler; total loss 44.— Federal, total loss 175. Alabama troops, parts of 1st, 4th, 51st Cav.

Noonday Cr., Ga., June 15. Gen. Jos. Wheeler; total loss 31.—Federal, total loss 200. Alabama troops, parts of 1st, 4th, 51st Cav., and 1st, 8th Conf. Cav.

Artillery fight, Ga., June 16. Gen. Jos. Wheeler; total loss 13.— Federal, total loss 80. Alabama troops, parts of 1st, 8th, 10th Conf. Cav.

Green Meadows, Ga., June 17. Gen. Jos. Wheeler; total loss 15.— Federal, total loss 70. Alabama troops, part of 10th Conf. Cav.

Bell's Ferry Rd., Ga., June 18. Gen. Jos. Wheeler total loss 29— Federal, total loss 110. Alabama troops, parts of 1st, 51st, 53d Cav.

McAfee's, Ga., June 19. Gen. Jos. Wheeler; total loss 41.—Federal, total loss 270. Alabama troops, parts of 1st, 8th, 10th Conf., and 1st, 3d, 4th, 7th, 51st Cav.

Canton Rd., Ga., June 20. Gen. Jos. Wheeler; total loss 65.—Federal, total loss 350. Alabama troops, parts of 1st, 8th, 10th Conf., and 1st, 3d, 53d Cav.

Noonday Cr., Ga., June 21. Gen. Jos. Wheeler; total loss 22.—Federal, total loss 80. Alabama troops, parts of 8th, 10th Conf.

Canton Rd., Ga., June 22. Gen. Jos. Wheeler: total loss 40.—Federal, total loss 150. Alabama troops, parts of 1st, 3d Cav.

Near McAfee's, Ga., June 23. Gen. Jos. Wheeler; total loss 61.— Federal, total loss .130. Alabama troops, parts of 1st, 8th, 10th Conf. Cav.

Rice's Farm, Ga., June 24. Gen. Jos. Wheeler: total loss 32.— Federal, total loss 125. Alabama troops, parts of 1st, 4th, 7th Cav.

Breastworks, Ga., June 26. Gen. Jos. Wheeler; total loss 40.—Federal, total loss 150. Alabama troops, parts of 1st, 8th, 10th Conf., and 1st, 3d, 4th 7th, 51st, 53d Cav.

Works near Rice's, Ga., June 27. Gen. Jos. Wheeler; total loss 59. —Federal, total loss 450. Alabama troops, parts of 1st, 8th, 10th Conf., and 1st, 3d, 4th, 7th, 51st, 53d Cav.

Marietta Rd., Ga., June 28. Gen. Jos. Wheeler; total loss 37.—Federal, total loss 130. Alabama troops, parts of 1st, 3d, 4th, 7th, 51st, 53d Cav.

Rosswell Rd., June 29. Gen. Jos. Wheeler; total loss 30.—Federal, total loss 70. Alabama troops, parts of 1st, 8th, 10th Conf., and 3d, 4th, 51st Cav.

Near Marietta, Ga., June 30. Gen. Jos. Wheeler; total loss 42.— Federal, total loss 140. Alabama troops, parts of 1st, 3d, 4th, 7th Cav.

Cannonade, Ga., July 1. Gen. Jos. Wheeler; total loss 28.—Federal, total loss 75. Alabama troops, parts of 1st, 3d, 4th, 7th Cav., and 1st, 8th, 10th Conf. Cav.

Near Mil. School, Ga., July 3. Gen. Jos. Wheeler; total loss 65.— Federal, total loss 300. Alabama troops, parts of 1st, 3d, 4th, 7th, 51st, 53d Cav., and 1st, 8th, 10th Conf. Cav.

Boggy Cr., July 4. Gen. Jos. Wheeler; total loss 40.—Federal, total loss 100. Alabama troops, parts of 1st, 3d, 51st Cav., and 1st, 8th, 10th, Conf. Cav.

Pace's Ferry Rd., Ga., July 5. Gen. Jos. Wheeler; total loss 67.— Federal, total loss 300. Alabama troops, parts of 51st, 53d Cav.; 24th Battn.

On Chattahoochie, Ga., July 6. Gen. Jos. Wheeler; total loss 27.— Federal, total loss 50. Alabama troops, parts of 1st, 8th, 10th Conf.

Artillery enfilading line, Ga., July 7. Gen. Jos. Wheeler, total loss 18.—Federal, total loss 80. Alabama troops, parts of 1st, 3d, 7th Cav.

Isham's Ford, etc., Ga., July 8. Gen. Jos. Wheeler; total loss 9.— Federal, total loss 70. Alabama troops, parts of 1st, 8th, 10th Conf.

Near Isham's Ford, Ga., July 9. Gen. Jos. Wheeler; total loss 31. —Federal, total loss 120. Alabama troops, parts of 7th, 51st, 53d Cav.; 24th Battn.

Decatur Rd., Ga., July 11. Gen. Jos. Wheeler; total loss 40.—Federal, total loss 110. Alabama troops, parts of 1st, 8th, 10th Conf.

On Chattahoochie, Ga., July 12. Total loss 44.—Federal, total loss 150. Alabama troops, parts of 1st, 3d, 4th, 7th, 51st, 53d Cav.; 1st, 3d, 8th, 10th Conf. Cav.

Atlanta Rd., Ga., July 13. Total loss 39.—Federal, total loss 170. Alabama troops, parts of 1st, 3d, 4th, 7th, 51st, 53d Cav.; 1st, 3d, 8th, 10th Conf. Cav.

Near Rosswell's, Ga., July 14. Total loss 20.—Federal, total loss 80. Alabama troops, parts of 1st, 3d, 4th, 7th, 51st, 53d Cav., and 1st, 3d, 8th, 10th Conf. Cav.

Stone Mt. Rd., Ga., July 15. Total loss 25.—Federal, total loss 90. Alabama troops, parts of 1st, 3d, 4th, 7th, 51st, 53d Cav., and 1st, 3d, 8th, 10th Conf.

Decatur Rd., Ga., July 16 to 19. Total loss 37.—Federal, total loss 135. Alabama troops, parts of 1st, 3d, 4th, 7th, 51st, 53d Cav., and 1st, 3d, 8th, 10th Conf. Cav.

Buckhead, etc., Ga., July 17. Total loss 49.—Federal, total loss 220. Alabama troops, parts of 1st, 3d, 4th, 7th, 51st, 53d Cav., and 1st, 3d, 8th, 10th Conf. Cav.

Near Decatur, Ga., July 18. Total loss 20.—Federal, total loss 80. Alabama troops, parts of 1st, 3d, 4th, 7th, 51st, 53d Cav., and 1st, 3d, 8th, 10th Conf. Cav.

R. R. Crossing, Ga., July 18. Total loss 10.—Federal, total loss 90. Alabama troops, parts of 1st, 3d, 4th, 7th, 51st, 53d Cav., and 1st, 3d, 8th, 10th Conf. Cav.

Decatur, Ga., July 19 to 22. Total loss 134.—Federal, total loss 610. Alabama troops, parts of 1st, 3d, 4th, 7th, 51st, 53d Cav., and 1st, 3d, 8th, 10th Conf. Cav.

Georgia R. R., Ga., July 19. Total loss 13.—Federal, total loss 70. Alabama troops, parts of 1st, 3d, 4th, 7th, 51st, 53d Cav., and 1st, 3d, 8th, 10th Conf. Cav.

Peachtree Cr., Ga., July 19-20. Total loss 50.—Federal, total loss 246. Alabama troops, parts of 1st, 3d, 4th, 7th, 51st, 53d Cav., and 1st, 3d, 8th, 10th Conf. Cav.

Near Atlanta, Ga., July 20. Gen. Jos. Wheeler; total loss 23.—Federal, total loss 180. Alabama troops, parts of 1st, 3d, 4th, 7th, 51st, 53d Cav., and 1st, 3d, 8th, 10th Conf. Cav.

Mill Rd., Ga., July 22. Gen. Jos. Wheeler; total loss 14.—Federal, total loss 130. Alabama troops, parts of 1st, 3d, 4th, 7th, 51st, 53d Cav., and 1st, 3d, 8th, 10th Conf. Cav.

Georgia R. R., Ga., July 23. Gen. Jos. Wheeler; total loss 6.—Federal, total loss 50. Alabama troops, parts of 1st, 3d, 4th, 7th, 51st, 53d Cav., and 1st, 3d, 8th, 10th Conf. Cav.

On Hardee's right, July 25. Gen. Jos. Wheeler; total loss 9.—Federal, total loss 40. Alabama troops, parts of 1st, 3d, 4th, 7th, 51st, 53d Cav., and 1st, 3d, 8th, 10th Conf. Cav.

Swamps, Ga., July 26. Gen. Jos. Wheeler; total loss 11.—Federal, total loss 56. Alabama troops, parts of 1st, 3d, 4th, 7th, 51st, 53d Cav., and 1st, 3d, 8th, 10th Conf. Cav.

Chattahoochie R., Ga., July 6 to 10. Gen. Johnston; total loss 600.— Federal, Gen. Sherman; loss 80 k, 450 w, 200 m. Alabama troops, army of Tennessee (as at New Hope).

Rousseau's raid, Ala., July 11-12. Loss 8 k, 60 w.—Federal, Gen. Rousseau; loss 3 k, 30 w.

Tupelo, Miss., July 13 to 15. Gens. Forrest and S. D. Lee, 12,000; loss 153 k, 794 w, 49 m.—Federal, Gen. A. J. Smith, 14,000; loss 82 k, 568 w. Alabama troops, 4th, 5th, 10th, 11th, 53d Cav.

Chewa Sta., M. & W. P. R. R., July 18. Total loss 40. Alabama troops, 400 reserves.

Peachtree Cr., July 20. Gen. Hood, 45,000; loss 1113 k, 2500 w, 1180 m.—Federal, Gen. Sherman; loss 300 k, 1400 w. Alabama troops, 1st, 16th, 17th, 18th, 19th, 20th, 22d, 23d., 26th, 27th, 29th, 30th, 33d, 34th, 35th, 37th, 38th, 39th, 40th, 45th, 49th, 50th, 54th, 55th, 57th Inf.; Yancey's Battn.; Semple's, Tarrant's, Gid. Nelson's Battrs.; Wheeler's Cav.

Atlanta, Ga., Hood's 1st sortie, July 22. Gen. Hood, 40,000; loss 2482 k, 4000 w, 2017 m.—Federal, Gen. Sherman; loss 500 k, 2141 w, 1000 m. Alabama troops, 1st, 16th, 17th, 18th, 19th, 20th, 22d, 23d, 26th, 27th, 29th, 30th, 33d, 34th, 35th, 37th, 38th, 39th, 40th, 45th, 49th, 50th, 54th, 55th, 57th Inf.; Yancey's Battn.; Semple's, Tarrant's, Gid. Nelson's Battrs.; Wheeler's Cav.

Ezra Chapel, 2d sortie, July 28. Gen. Hood.—Federal, Gen. Sherman; loss

100 k, 600 w. Alabama troops, 1st, 16th, 17th, 18th, 19th, 20th, 22d, 23d, 26th, 27th, 29th, 30th, 33d., 34th, 35th, 37th, 38th, 39th, 40th, 45th, 49th, 50th, 54th, 55th, 57th Inf.; Yancey's Battn.; Semple's, Tarrant's, Gid. Nelson's Battrs.: Wheeler's Cav.

Wheeler's pursuit of Stoneman, etc., at Snapfinger Cr., Shoal Cr., Lithonia, Jonesboro, Flint River, Clear River, Fayetteville Rd., Woody Hill, Newnan, Sunshine Cr., near Corinth, near Franklin, near Jug Tavern, Ga., July 27 to 31. Gen. Jos. Wheeler, 4,500; total loss 300.—Federal, Gens. Stoneman and Garrard, 4,500. Alabama troops, parts of 1st, 3d, 4th, 7th, 51st, 53d Cav.; 1st, 8th, 10th Conf. Cav.

Atlanta, Ga., Aug. 2. Gen. Jos. Wheeler; total loss 7.—Federal, total loss 65. Alabama troops, Wheeler's Cav.

Buckhead Rd., Ga., Aug. 3. Gen. Jos. Wheeler; total loss 9.—Federal, total loss 55. Alabama troops, Wheeler's Cav.

Decatur Rd., Ga., Aug. 4. Gen. Jos. Wheeler; total loss 10.—Federal, total loss 70. Alabama troops, Wheeler's Cav.

Mill Rd., Ga., Aug. 5. Gen. Jos. Wheeler; total loss 13.—Federal, total loss 80. Alabama troops, Wheeler's Cav.

Mobile Bay, Aug. 5. Adml. Buchanan and Gen. R. L. Page, 3 ships and 1,500; loss 12k, 20 w, *280 m.—Federal, Adml. Farragut and Gen. Granger, 14 ships and 1 army corps; loss 200 k, 170 w, 4 m. Alabama forces, ram Tennessee; gunboats Morgan, Gaines, Selma; 1st Battn. of Art.; Capt. Cothran's Co., 21st Inf. Fort Gaines, Aug. 8. Col. Anderson, 600; loss*— m.—Federal, Adml. Farragut. Alabama troops, part of 21st Inf.; 1st Battn. Art.; Pelham's cadets and reserves.

Wheeler's raid in Sherman's rear through Ga., Tenn., N. Ala., Aug. 10 to Sept. 9. Gen. Jos. Wheeler; total loss 125.—Federal, Gens. Rousseau and Kilpatrick; total loss 1900. Alabama troops in different engagements, parts of 1st, 3d, 8th, 10th Conf.; 1st, 3d, 4th, 7th, 51st, 53d Cav.; 24th Battn. Cav.

Ten Islands, Ga., Aug. 14. Gen. Clanton.—Federal, Gen. Rousseau. Alabama troops, 6th, 8th Cav.

Fort Morgan, Aug. 23. Gen. R. L. Page, 400; loss* 1 k, 2 w, 396 m.—Federal, Adml. Farragut and Gen. Granger, 14 ships and 5,500; loss 7 w. Alabama troops, parts of 21st Inf., and 1st Art.

Jonesboro, Ga., Aug. 31 and Sept. 1. Gen. S. D. Lee; total loss 2000.—Federal, loss 1149 w. Alabama troops, Lee's corps and Hardee's corps.

Athens, Ala., Sept. 23. Gen. Forrest, 4,500; loss 5 k, 26 w.—Federal, Col. Campbell; loss 1400 m, total loss 1900. Alabama troops, 4th, 5th, 11th, 53d Cav.

Sulphur Branch Trestle, Sept. 25. Gen. Forrest—Federal, loss 200 k, 30 w, 820 m. Alabama troops, 11th Cav., Forrest's Cav.

*Prisoners at Forts Gaines, Powell and Morgan, estimated, 1464.

Pulaski, Tenn., Sept 27. Gen. Forrest; total loss 25. Alabama troops, 11th Cav., Forrest's Cav.

Blockhouse, Tenn., Oct. 1. Gen. Forrest—Federal, total loss 65. Alabama troops, 11th Cav., Forrest's Cav.

Sweetwater, Ga., Oct. 1 to 3. Gen. Jos. Wheeler.—Federal, Gen. Kilpatrick. Alabama troops, parts of 1st, 3d, 7th, 51st Cav.

Near Dalton, Ga., Oct. 2. Gen. Jos. Wheeler; total loss 2.—Federal, total loss 35. Alabama troops, parts of 1st, 3d, 7th, 51st Cav.

Snake Cr. Gap, Ga., Oct. 15. Gen. Jos. Wheeler; total loss 15.— Federal, total loss 90. Alabama troops, parts of 1st, 3d., 7th, 51st Cav.

Maddox Gap, Ga., Oct. 16. Gen. Jos. Wheeler; total loss 13.— Federal, total loss 32. Alabama troops, parts of 1st, 3d, 7th, 51st Cav.

La Fayette, Ga., Oct. 17. Gen. Jos. Wheeler; total loss 8.—Federal, total loss 46. Alabama troops, parts of 1st, 3d, 7th, 51st Cav.

Cane Cr., Ga., Oct. 17. Gen. Jos. Wheeler; total loss 10.—Federal, total loss 27. Alabama troops, parts of the 1st, 3d, 7th, 51st Cav.

Grave Level Church, Oct. 18. Gen. Jos. Wheeler; total loss 14.— Federal, total loss 30. Alabama troops, same as at Cane Creek.

Tryon Factory, Ga., Oct. 18. Gen. Jos. Wheeler, total loss 6.—Federal, total loss 27. Alabama troops, same as at Cane Creek.

Summerville Rd., Ga., Oct. 18. Gen. Jos. Wheeler; .total loss 15.— Federal, total loss 45. Alabama troops, same as at Cane Creek.

Chattooga R., Ga., Oct. 19. Gen. Jos. Wheeler; total loss 12.— Federal, total loss 38. Alabama troops, same as at Cane Creek.

Eaglesville, Ala., Oct. 19. Gen. Jos. Wheeler; total loss 15.—Federal, total loss 30. Alabama troops, same as at Cane Creek.

Blue Pond Rd., Ala., Oct. 20. Gen. Jos. Wheeler; total loss 10.— Federal, total loss 22. Alabama troops, same as at Cane Creek.

Little River, Ala., Oct 21. Gen. Jos. Wheeler.

Round Mt. Ironworks, Ala., Oct. 22. Gen. Jos. Wheeler; total loss 20.— Federal, total loss 60. Alabama troops, same as at Cane Creek.

Turkeytown Rd., Ala., Oct. 23. Gen. Jos. Wheeler; total loss 7.— Federal, total loss 25. Alabama troops, same as at Cane Creek.

Turkeytown, Ala., Oct. 24. Gen. Jos. Wheeler; total loss 25.—Federal, total loss 70. Alabama troops, same as at Cane Creek.

Near Gadsden, Ala., Oct. 25. Gen. Jos. Wheeler; total loss 30.— Federal, total loss 100. Alabama troops, same as at Cane Creek.

Near Goshen, Ala., Oct. 26. Gen. Jos. Wheeler; total loss 7.—Federal, total loss 40. Alabama troops, same as at Cane Creek.

Big Shanty and Ackworth, Ga., Oct. 2. Gens. Stewart and Loring.— Federal, loss 420 m. Alabama troops, 1st, 55th, 57th, 26th, 27th, 29th Inf.; 56th Cav.; Lumsden's, Selden's, Tarrant's Battrs.

Allatoona, Ga., Oct. 5. Gen. French.—Federal, Gen. Corse, 1,944; loss 142 k, 353 w, 213 m.

Eastport, Miss., Oct. 10. Col. D. C. Kelly.—Federal, total loss 250. Alabama troops, 7th Cav.

Dalton, Ga., Oct. 13. Gen. Hood.—Federal, Col. Johnson; total loss 400. Alabama troops, army of Tennessee.

Decatur, Ala., Oct. 26 to 29. Total loss 125.—Federal, total loss 155. Alabama troops, 4th, 53d Cav.

Fort Heiman, Tenn., Oct. 28 to 30.—Federal, U. S. gunboats; total loss 22. Alabama troops, Chalmers' and Buford's Divs.; Forrest's Cav.

Florence, Ala., Oct. 30. Gen. Ed. Johnson.

Jonesboro, Ga., Nov. 15. Gen. Jos. Wheeler; total loss 5.—Federal, total loss 40. Alabama troops, parts of 2d, 53d, 56th Cav.; 24th Battn. Cav.; Inge's, Perrin's and Miller's regiments.

Lovejoy Sta., Ga., Nov. 16. Gen. Jos. Wheeler; total loss 38.— Federal, total loss 30. Alabama troops, parts of 2d, 53d, 56th Cav.; 24th Battn. Cav.; Inge's, Perrin's and Miller's regiments.

Bear Cr., Ga., Nov. 16. Gen. Jos. Wheeler; total loss 8.—Federal, total loss 50. Alabama troops, parts of 2d, 53d, 56th Cav.; 24th Battn. Cav.; Inge's, Perrin's and Miller's regiments.

Towaliga, Ga., Nov. 17. Gen. Jos. Wheeler; total loss 5.—Federal, total loss 40. Alabama troops, parts of 2d, 53d, 56th Cav.; 24th Battn. Cav.; Inge's, Perrin's and Miller's regiments.

Run's Cr., Ga., Nov. 18. Gen. Jos. Wheeler; total loss 4.—Federal, total loss 24. Alabama troops, parts of 2d, 53d, 56th Cav.; 24th Battn. Cav.; Inge's, Perrin's and Miller's regiments.

Ulcofaw, Ga., Nov. 19. Gen. Jos. Wheeler; total loss 2.—Federal, total loss 39. Alabama troops, parts of 2d, 53d, 56th Cav.; 24th Battn. Cav.; Inge's, Perrin's and Miller's regiments.

Near Macon, Ga., Nov. 20. Gen. Jos. Wheeler; total loss 5.—Federal, total loss 42. Alabama troops, parts of 2d, 53d, 56th Cav.; 24th Battn. Cav.; Inge's, Perrin's and Miller's regiments.

Walnut Cr., Ga., Nov. 20. Gen. Jos. Wheeler; total loss 3.—Federal, total loss 45. Alabama troops, parts of 2d, 53d., 56th Cav.; 24th Battn. Cav.; Inge's, Perrin's and Miller's regiments.

Griswaldville, Ga., Nov. 21. Gen. Jos. Wheeler; total loss 6.—Federal, total loss 36. Alabama troops, parts of 2d, 53d, 56th Cav.; 24th Battn. Cav.; Inge's, Perrin's and Miller's regiments.

Myrack's Mill, Ga., Nov. 22. Gen. Jos. Wheeler; total loss 35.— Federal, total loss 130. Alabama troops, parts of 2d, 53d, 56th Cav.; 24th Battn. Cav.; Inge's, Perrin's and Miller's regiments.

Ball's Ferry, Ga., Nov. 24. Gen. Jos. Wheeler; total loss 2.—Federal, total loss 20. Alabama troops, parts of 2d, 53d, 56th Cav.; 24th Battn. Cav.; Inge's, Perrin's and Miller's regiments.

Oconee, Ga., Nov. 25. Gen. Jos. Wheeler; total loss 7.—Federal, total loss go. Alabama troops, parts of 2d, 53d, 56th Cav.; 24th Battn. Cav.; Inge's, Perrin's and Miller's regiments.

Sandersville, Ga., Nov. 25. Gen. Jos. Wheeler; total loss 12.—Federal, total loss 70. Alabama troops, parts of 2d, 53d, 56th Cav.; 24th Battn. Cav.; Inge's, Perrin's and Miller's regiments.

Ogechee, Ga., Nov. 26. Gen. Jos. Wheeler; total loss 2.—Federal, total loss 48. Alabama troops, parts of 2d, 53d, 56th Cav.; 24th Battn. Cav.; Inge's, Perrin's and Miller's regiments.

Sylvan Grove, Ga., Nov. 27. Gen. Jos. Wheeler; total loss 9.— Federal, total loss 70. Alabama troops, parts of 2d, 53d, 56th Cav.; 24th Battn. Cav.; Inge's, Perrin's and Miller's regiments.

Swampy Cr., Ga., Nov. 27. Gen. Jos. Wheeler; total loss 6.—Federal, total loss 20. Alabama troops, parts of 2d, 53d, 56th Cav.; 24th Battn. Cav.; Inge's, Perrin's and Miller's regiments.

River Cr., Ga., Nov. 27. Gen. Jos. Wheeler; total loss 3.—Federal, total loss 25. Alabama troops, parts of 2d, 53d, 56th Cav.; 24th Battn. Cav.; Inge's, Perrin's and Miller's regiments.

Hill, Ga., Nov. 27. Gen. Jos. Wheeler; total loss 4.—Federal, total loss 20. Alabama troops, parts of 2d, 53d, 56th Cav.; 24th Battn. Cav.; Inge's, Perrin's and Miller's regiments.

Whitehead's, Ga., Nov. 27. Gen. Jos. Wheeler; total loss 4.—Federal, total loss 25. Alabama troops, parts of 2d, 53d, 56th Cav.; 24th Battn. Cav.; Inge's, Perrin's and Miller's regiments.

Waynesboro, Ga., Nov. 27. Gen. Jos. Wheeler; total loss 15.— Federal, total loss 30. Alabama troops, parts of 2d, 53d, 56th Cav.; 24th Battn. Cav.; Inge's, Perrin's and Miller's regiments.

Near Waynesboro, Ga., Nov. 28. Gen. Jos. Wheeler; total loss 3. —Federal, total loss 40. Alabama troops, parts of 2d, 53d, 56th Cav.; 24th Battn. Cav.; Inge's, Perrin's and Miller's regiments.

Carter's, Ga., Nov. 28. Gen. Jos. Wheeler; total loss 10.—Federal, total loss 42. Alabama troops, parts of 1st, 2d, 3d, 7th, 51st, 56th Cav.; Inge's, Perrin's and Miller's regiments.

Cross Rds., Ga., Nov. 28. Gen. Jos. Wheeler; total loss 12.—Federal, total loss 70. Alabama troops, parts of the 1st, 2d, 3d, 7th, 51st, 56th Cav., and Inge's, Perrin's and Miller's regiments.

Buckhead Church, Ga., Nov. 28. Gen. Jos. Wheeler; total loss 25. —Federal, total loss 150. Alabama troops, parts of the 1st, 2d, 3d, 7th, 51st, 56th Cav., and Inge's, Perrin's and Miller's regiments.

Buckhead Cr., Ga., Nov. 28. Gen. Jos. Wheeler; total loss 24.— Federal, total loss 120. Alabama troops, parts of the 1st, 2d, 3d, 7th, 51st, 56th Cav., and Inge's, Perrin's and Miller's regiments.

Reynolds' Farm, Ga., Nov. 28. Gen. Jos. Wheeler; total loss 74.— Federal, total loss 250. Alabama troops, parts of the 1st, 2d, 3d, 7th, 51st, 56th Cav., and Inge's, Perrin's and Miller's regiments.

Near Louisville, Ga., Nov. 29. Gen. Jos. Wheeler; total loss 3.— Federal, total loss 20. Alabama troops, parts of the 1st, 2d, 3d, 7th, 51st, 56th Cav., and Inge's, Perrin's and Miller's regiments.

Louisville Rd., Ga., Nov. 30. Gen. Jos. Wheeler; total loss 3.— Federal, total loss 35. Alabama troops, parts of the 1st, 2d, 3d, 7th, 51st, 56th Cav., and Inge's, Perrin's and Miller's regiments.

Shady Grove, Ga., Dec. 1. Gen. Jos. Wheeler; total loss 5.—Federal, total loss 28. Alabama troops, parts of the 1st, 2d, 3d, 7th, 51st, 56th Cav., and Inge's, Perrin's and Miller's regiments.

Rock Cr. Church, Ga., Dec. 2. Gen. Jos. Wheeler; total loss 9.— Federal, total loss 40. Alabama troops, parts of the 1st, 2d, 3d, 7th, 51st, 56th Cav., and Inge's, Perrin's and Miller's regiments.

Thomas Sta., Ga., Dec. 3. Gen. Jos.Wheeler.—Federal, total loss 30. Alabama troops, parts of the 1st, 2d, 3d, 7th, 51st, 56th Cav., and Inge's, Perrin's and Miller's regiments.

Waynesboro, Ga., Dec. 4. Gen. Jos. Wheeler; total loss 90.—Federal, total loss 170. Alabama troops, parts of the 1st, 2d, 3d, 7th, 51st, 56th Cav., and Inge's, Perrin's and Miller's regiments.

Stateboro, Ga., Dec. 5. Gen. Jos. Wheeler; total loss 2.—Federal, total loss 32. Alabama troops, parts of the 1st, 2d, 3d, 7th, 51st, 56th Cav., and Inge's, Perrin's and Miller's regiments.

Near Jacksboro, Ga., Dec. 6. Gen. Jos. Wheeler.—Federal, total loss 10. Alabama troops, parts of the 1st, 2d, 3d, 7th, 51st, 56th Cav., and Inge's, Perrin's and Miller's regiments.

Black Cr., Ga., Dec. 7. Gen. Jos. Wheeler; total loss 1.—Federal, total loss 15. Alabama troops, parts of the 1st, 2d, 3d, 7th, 51st, 56th Cav., and Inge's, Perrin's and Miller's regiments.

Savannah River, Dec. 7. Gen. Jos. Wheeler; total loss 11.—Federal, total loss 80. Alabama troops, parts of the 1st, 2d, 3d, 7th, 51st, 56th Cav., and Inge's, Perrin's and Miller's regiments.

Swamp, Ga., Dec. 7. Gen. Jos. Wheeler; total loss 12.—Federal, total loss 90. Alabama troops, parts of the 1st, 2d, 3d, 7th,,51st, 56th Cav., and Inge's, Perrin's and Miller's regiments.

Gravestein's, Ga., Dec. 8. Gen. Jos. Wheeler; total loss 3.—Federal, total loss 75. Alabama troops, parts of the 1st, 2d, 3d, 7th, 51st, 56th Cav., and Inge's, Perrin's and Miller's regiments.

Ebenezer Church, Ga., Dec. 8. Gen. Jos. Wheeler.—Federal, total loss 80. Alabama troops, parts of the 1st, 2d, 3d, 7th, 51st, 56th Cav., and Inge's, Perrin's and Miller's regiments.

Engagement of rear guard, Dec. 9. Gen. Jos. Wheeler; total loss 4. —Federal, total loss 35. Alabama troops, parts of the 1st, 2d, 3d, 7th, 51st, 56th Cav., and Inge's, Perrin's and Miller's regiments.

Middleground Rd., Ga., Dec. 10. Gen. Jos. Wheeler.—Federal, total loss 25. Alabama troops, parts of the 1st, 2d, 3d, 7th, 51st, 56th Cav., and Inge's, Perrin's and Miller's regiments.

Near Springfield, Dec. 10. Gen. Jos. Wheeler; total loss 2.—Federal, total loss 30. Alabama troops, parts of the 1st, 2d, 3d, 7th, 51st, 56th Cav., and Inge's, Perrin's and Miller's regiments.

Siege of Savannah, Ga. Gen. Jos. Wheeler; total loss 128.—Federal, total loss 280. Alabama troops, parts of the 1st, 2d, 3d, 7th, 51st, 56th Cav., and Inge's, Perrin's and Miller's regiments.

Lawrenceburg, Tenn., Nov. 22. Gen. Forrest, 10,000; total loss 50. —Federal, total loss 50. Alabama troops, 6th, 12th Cav.

Mt. Pleasant, Nov. 23. Gen. Forrest; loss 5 k, 30 w.—Federal, Gen. Stanley; loss 20 k, 100 w, 60 m. Alabama troops, Chalmers' division and Forrest's escort.

Campbellville and Lynnville, Tenn., Nov. 24. Alabama troops, 6th, 12th Cav.

Columbia, Tenn., Nov. 29. Gen. Pettus. Alabama troops, 20th, 23d, 30th, 31st, 46th Inf.

Spring Hill, Tenn., Nov. 29. Gen. Hood, 40,000; loss 1750 k.—Federal, Gen. Schofield, 28,000.

Franklin, Tenn., Nov. 30. Gen. Hood, 40,000; loss 1750 k, 3800 w, 702 m.—Federal, 28,000; loss 189 k, 1033 w, 1104 m. Confederate troops, Cheatham's and Stewart's corps, and Gen. Ed. Johnson's division, army of Tennessee.

Skirmishing before Nashville, Tenn., Dec. 1 to 14. Gen. Hood, 30,000.—Federal, Gen. Thomas, 55,000; loss 16 k, 100 w. Confederate troops, Cheatham's and Stewart's corps, and Gen. Ed. Johnson's division, army of Tennessee.

Murfreesboro, Tenn., Dec. 5 to 8. Gen. Forrest; total loss 197.— Federal, Gen. Rousseau; total loss 175. Confederate troops, Forrest's Cav.

Nashville, Tenn., Dec. 15-16. Gen. Hood, 23,053; total loss 15000.— Federal, Gen. Thomas, 70,000; loss 400 k, 1740 w. Alabama troops, 1st, 16th, 18th, 19th, 20th, 22d, 24th, 25th, 26th, 27th, 28th, 29th, 30th, 31st, 32d, 33d., 34th, 35th, 36th, 38th, 39th, 45th, 46th, 49th, 50th, 57th, 58th Inf.; 7th Cav.; Dent's, McKenzie's, Kolb's, Selden's, Tarrant's, Lumsden's, Phelan's, Goldthwaite's Battrs.

Hollow Tree Gap, Tenn., Dec. 17. Gen. Hood; total loss 413. Alabama troops, 18th, 19th, 22d, 25th, 32d, 36th, 38th, 39th, 50th, 58th Inf., and McKenzie's Batty.

Franklin, Tenn., Dec. 17. Gen. Hood; total loss 1800. Alabama troops, army of Tennessee, as at Nashville.

Pine Barren Cr., Fla., Dec. 17 to 19. Gen. Maury.—Federal, loss 7 k, 32 w, 10 m. Alabama troops, 15th Conf. Cav.

Anthony's Hill, Tenn., Dec. 25. Gen. Hood; loss 15 k, 40 w.—Federal, Gen. Thomas; total loss 200. Alabama troops, 7th Cav.; Kolb's, Lumsden's Battrs.

Sugar Cr., Tenn., Dec. 26. Gen. Hood.—Federal, Gen. Thomas; loss 400 k and w, 100 m. Alabama troops, 7th Cav.; Kolb's, Lumsden's Battrs.

Pond Spring, Ala., Dec. 29. Loss 1 k, 2 w, 45 m.—Federal, loss 1 k,

1865.

Scottsboro, Ala., Jan. 8. Loss 1 k, 5 w, 5 m.

Savannah Rd., S. C., Jan. 19. Gen. Jos. Wheeler; total loss 12.— Federal, total loss 35. Alabama troops, parts of the 1st, 3d, 51st Cav., and 3d, 10th Conf. Cav.

Pocotaligo Rd., S. C., Jan. 20. Gen. Jos. Wheeler; total loss 18.— Federal, total loss 45. Alabama troops, parts of the 1st, 3d, 51st Cav., and 3d, 10th Conf. Cav.

Combahee Rd., S. C., Jan. 22. Gen. Jos. Wheeler; total loss 11— Federal, total loss 30. Alabama troops, parts of the 1st, 3d, 51st Cav., and 3d, 10th Conf. Cav.

Robertsville Rd., S. C., Jan. 27. Gen. Jos. Wheeler; total loss 19. —Federal, total loss 40. Alabama troops, parts of the 1st, 3d, 51st Cav., and 3d, 10th Conf. Cav.

Robertsville, S. C., Jan. 27. Gen. Jos. Wheeler, total loss 12.— Federal, total loss 60. Alabama troops, parts of the 1st, 3d, 51st Cav., and 3d, 10th Conf, Cav.

Near McBride's Bridge, Feb. 1. Gen. Jos. Wheeler; total loss 17 — Federal, total loss 50. Alabama troops, parts of the 1st, 3d, 51st Cav., and 3d, 10th Conf. Cav.

Hickory Hill, S. C., Feb. 1. Gen. Jos. Wheeler; total loss 19.—Federal, total loss 40. Alabama troops, parts of the 1st, 3d, 51st Cav., and 3d, 10th Conf. Cav.

Loper's Cross Rds., S. C., Feb. 2. Gen. Jos. Wheeler; total loss 48. —Federal, total loss 120. Alabama troops, parts of the 1st, 3d, 51st Cav., and 3d, 10th Conf. Cav.

Lawtonville Rd., S. C., Feb. 2. Gen. Jos. Wheeler; total loss 17.— Federal, total loss 50. Alabama troops, parts of the 1st, 3d, 51st Cav., and 3d, 10th Conf. Cav.

Lawtonville, S. C., Feb. 2. Gen. Jos. Wheeler; total loss 20.—Federal, total loss 80. Alabama troops, parts of the 1st, 3d, 51st Cav., and 3d, 10th Conf. Cav.

Whippy Swamp, S. C., Feb. 2. Gen. Jos. Wheeler; total loss 10.— Federal, total loss 50. Alabama troops, parts of the 1st, 3d, 51st Cav., and 3d, 10th Conf. Cav.

Hayward's, S. C., Feb. 3. Gen. Jos. Wheeler; total loss 9.—Federal, total loss 28. Alabama troops, parts of the 1st, 3d, 51st Cav., and 3d, 10th Conf. Cav.

Duck Cr. Rd., S. C., Feb. 3. Gen. Jos. Wheeler; total loss 17.— Federal, total loss 80. Alabama troops, parts of the 1st, 3d, 51st Cav., and 3d, 10th Conf. Cav.

Rivers' and Braxton's Bridges, S. C., Feb. 3. Gen. Jos. Wheeler; total loss 45.—Federal, total loss 148. Alabama troops, parts of the 1st, 3d, 51st Cav., and 3d, 10th Conf. Cav.

Springtown, S. C., Feb. 6. Gen. Jos. Wheeler; total loss 14.—Federal, total loss 50. Alabama troops, parts of the 1st, 3d, 51st Cav., and 3d, 10th Conf. Cav.

Salkahatchie Rd., S. C., Feb. 6. Gen. Jos. Wheeler; total loss 15.— Federal, total loss 70. Alabama troops, parts of the 1st, 3d, 51st Cav., and 3d, 10th Conf. Cav.

Graham's Turnout, S. C., Feb. 6. Gen. Jos. Wheeler; total loss 4. —Federal, total loss 38. Alabama troops, parts of the 1st, 3d, 51st Cav., and 3d, 10th Conf. Cav.

Blackwell's, S. C., Feb. 7. Gen. Jos. Wheeler; total loss 19.—Federal, total loss 50. Alabama troops, parts of the 1st, 3d, 51st Cav., and 3d, 10th Conf. Cav.

Binnaker's Bridge Rd., S. C., Feb. 9. Gen. Jos. Wheeler; total loss 11.—Federal, total loss go. Alabama troops, parts of the 1st, 3d, 51st Cav., and 3d, 10th Conf. Cav.

Orangeburg Rd., S. C., Feb. 10. Gen. Jos. Wheeler; total loss 10.— Federal, total loss 35. Alabama troops, parts of the 1st, 3d, 51st Cav., and 3d, 10th Conf. Cav.

Aiken, S. C., Feb. 11. Gen. Jos. Wheeler; total loss 50.—Federal, total loss 300. Alabama troops, parts of the 1st, 3d, 51st Cav., and 3d, 10th Conf. Cav.

Black Cr., defending Columbia, S. C., Feb. 14. Gen. Jos. Wheeler; total loss 19.—Federal, total loss 170. Alabama troops, parts of the 1st, 3d, 51st Cav., and 3d, 10th Conf. Cav.

Columbia Rd., S. C., Feb. 15. Gen. Jos. Wheeler; total loss 31.— Federal, total loss 80. Alabama troops, parts of the 1st, 3d, 51st Cav., and 3d, 10th Conf. Cav.

Congaree Cr., S. C., Feb. 15. Gen. Jos. Wheeler; total loss 33.— Federal, total loss 75. Alabama troops, parts of the 1st, 3d, 51st Cav., and 3d, 10th Conf. Cav.

Saluda River, S. C., Feb. 16. Gen. Jos. Wheeler; total loss 12.— Federal, total loss 48. Alabama troops, parts of the 1st, 3d, 51st Cav., and 3d, 10th Conf. Cav.

Broad River, S. C., Feb. 17. Gen. Jos. Wheeler; total loss 17.—Federal, total loss 60. Alabama troops, parts of the 1st, 3d, 51st Cav., and 3d, 10th Conf. Cav.

Winnsboro, S. C., Feb. 17. Gen. Jos. Wheeler; total loss 9.— Federal, total loss 45. Alabama troops, parts of the 1st, 3d, 51st Cav., and 3d, 10th Conf. Cav.

Winnsboro, S. C., Feb. 17. Gen. Jos. Wheeler; total loss 6.— Federal, total loss 30. Alabama troops, parts of the 1st, 3d, 51st Cav., and 3d, 10th Conf. Cav.

Sack of Columbia, S. C., Feb. 16 and 17. Gens. Hampton and Wheeler.—Federal, Gen. Logan; loss 20 w. Alabama troops, parts of 1st, 3d, 51st Cav., and 3d, 8th, 10th Conf. Cav.; Jeff. Davis Legion,

Wadesboro, S. C., Feb. 19. Gen. Jos. Wheeler; total loss 13.—Federal, total loss no. Alabama troops, parts of 1st, 3d, 51st Cav., 3d, 10th Conf. Cav.

Near Youngsville, S. C., Feb. 20. Gen. Jos. Wheeler; total loss 10. —Federal, total loss 95. Alabama troops, parts of 1st, 3d, 51st Cav., and 3d, 10th Conf Cav.

Chesterville, S. C., Feb. 21. Gen. Jos. Wheeler; total loss 14.— Federal, total loss 125. Alabama troops, parts of 1st, 3d, 51st Cav., and 3d, 10th Conf. Cav.

Lansford, S. C., Feb. 24. Gen. Jos. Wheeler; total loss 16.—Federal, total loss 60. Alabama troops, parts of 1st, 3d, 51st Cav., and 3d, 10th Conf. Cav.

Cane Cr., S. C., Feb. 26. Gen. Jos. Wheeler; total loss 40.—Federal, total loss 220. Alabama troops, parts of 1st, 3d, 51st Cav., and 3d, 10th Conf. Cav.

Near Wilson's store, S. C., Mar. 1. Gen. Jos. Wheeler; total loss 19.—Federal, total loss 80. Alabama troops, parts of 1st, 3d, 51st Cav., and 3d, 10th Conf. Cav.

Lexington, S. C., Mar. 2. Gen. Jos. Wheeler; total loss 16.—Federal, total loss 120. Alabama troops, parts of 1st, 3d, 51st Cav., and 3d, 10th Conf. Cav.

Near Monroe, S. C., Mar. 3. Gen. Jos. Wheeler; total loss 11.— Federal, total loss 80. Alabama troops, parts of 1st, 3d, 51st Cav., and 3d, 10th Conf. Cav.

Cross Rds., S. C., Mar. 3. Gen. Jos. Wheeler; total loss 12.—Federal, total loss 65. Alabama troops, parts of 1st, 3d, 51st Cav., and 3d, 10th Conf. Cav.

Hornsboro, S. C., Mar. 4. Gen. Jos. Wheeler; total loss 22.—Federal, total loss 90. Alabama troops, parts of 1st, 3d, 51st Cav., and 3d, 10th Conf. Cav.

Near Wadesboro, S. C., Mar. 5. Gen. Jos. Wheeler; total loss 19.— Federal, total loss 60. Alabama troops, parts of 1st, 3d, 51st Cav., and 3d, 10th Conf. Cav.

Near Rockingham, S. C., Mar. 7. Gen. Jos. Wheeler; total loss 12. —Federal, total loss 35. Alabama troops, parts of 1st, 3d, 51st Cav., and 3d, 10th Conf. Cav.

Near Rockingham, S. C., Mar. 9. Gen. Jos. Wheeler; total loss 7. —Federal, total loss 56. Alabama troops, parts of 1st, 3d, 51st Cav., and 3d, 10th Conf. Cav.

Near Jacksonville, S. C., Mar. 10. Gen. Jos. Wheeler; total loss 65. —Federal, total loss 480. Alabama troops, parts of 1st, 3d, 51st Cav., and 3d, 10th Conf. Cav.

Fayetteville, S. C., Mar. 11. Gen. Jos. Wheeler; total loss 13.— Federal, total loss 45. Alabama troops, parts of 1st, 3d, 51st Cav., and 3d, 10th Conf. Cav.

Near Neuse, S. C., Mar. 12. Gen. Jos. Wheeler; total loss 6.—Federal, total loss 30. Alabama troops, parts of 1st, 3d, 51st Cav., and 3d, 10th Conf. Cav.

River Rd., S. C., Mar. 13. Gen. Jos. Wheeler; total loss 17.—Fed-eral, total loss 25. Alabama troops, parts of 1st, 3d, 51st Cav., and 3d, 10th Conf. Cav.

Silver Run, S. C., Mar. 13. Gen. Jos. Wheeler; total loss 14.—Federal, total loss 60. Alabama troops, parts of 1st, 3d, 51st Cav., and 3d, 10th Conf. Cav.

Pine Woods, S. C., Mar. 14. Gen. Jos. Wheeler; total loss.12.— Federal, total loss 50. Alabama troops, parts of 1st, 3d, 51st Cav., and 3d, 10th Conf. Cav.

Smith's Hill, S. C., Mar. 14. Gen. Jos. Wheeler; total loss 14.— Federal, total loss 20. Alabama troops, parts of 1st, 3d, 51st Cav., and 3d, 10th Conf. Cav.

Black River, S. C., Mar. 15. Gen. Jos. Wheeler; total loss 5.—Federal, total loss 42. Alabama troops, parts of 1st, 3d, 51st Cav., and 3d, 10th Conf. Cav.

Near Black River, S. C., Mar. 15. Gen. Jos. Wheeler; total loss 14. —Federal, total loss 69. Alabama troops, parts of 1st, 3d, 51st Cav., and 3d, 10th Conf. Cav.

Averasboro, N. C., Mar. 16. Gen. Hardee, 3 divisions; loss 108 k, 540 w, 217 m.—Federal, Gen. Slocum, 3 divisions; loss 77 k, 477 w. Alabama troops, parts of 1st, 3d, 51st Cav., and 3d, 10th Conf. Cav.; Jeff. Davis Legion.

Near Averasboro, N. C., Mar. 16. Gen. Jos. Wheeler; total loss 111.—Federal, Gen. Kilpatrick; total loss 270. Alabama troops, parts of 1st, 3d, 51st Cav., and 3d, 10th Conf. Cav.

Near Mingo Cr., N. C., Mar. 17. Gen. Jos. Wheeler; total loss 16. —Federal, total loss 30. Alabama troops, parts of 1st, 3d, 51st Cav., and 3d, 10th Conf. Cav.

Boyd's Sta., Ala., Mar. 18.—Federal, loss 5 k. 1 m.

Bentonville, N. C., Mar. 19 to 21. Gen. Jos. Wheeler; total loss 157.—Federal, total loss 395. Alabama troops, parts of 1st, 3d, 51st Cav., and 3d, 10th Conf. Cav.

Mill Cr., N. C., Mar. 22. Gen. Jos. Wheeler; total loss 20.—Federal, total loss 48. Alabama troops, parts of 1st, 3d, 51st Cav., and 3d, 10th Conf. Cav.

Black Cr., N. C., Mar. 22. Gen. Jos. Wheeler; total loss 10.—Federal, total loss 38. Alabama troops, parts of 1st, 3d, 51st Cav., and 3d, 10th Conf. Cav.

Goldsboro Rd., Nahunta Swamp, Little River, N. C., Mar. 22. Gen., Jos. Wheeler; total loss 28.—Federal, total loss 236. Alabama troops, parts of 1st, 3d, 51st Cav., and 3d., 10th Conf. Cav.

Kinston, N. C., Mar. 19.—Federal, Gen. Schofield. Alabama troops, 34th Inf.

Bentonville, N. C., Mar. 19 to 21. Gen. Johnston, 10,000; loss 239 k, 1694 w, 673 m.—Federal, Gen. Sherman, 60,000; loss 191 k, 1168 w, 287 m. Alabama troops, 1st, 16th-45th, 17th, 19th, 20th, 22d-(25th, 39th, 50th), 23d,

24th, 28th, 34th, 27th-(35th, 49th, 55th, 57th), 29th, 30th, 37th-(42d, 54th) Inf.

Pine Barren Cr., Ala., Mar. 25. Gen. Maury; loss 275 m.—Federal, Gen. Steele; loss 2 k, 10 w. Alabama troops, 15th Conf., and 8th Cav. reserves.

Spanish Fort, Ala., Mar. 26 to April 8. Gen. Gibson; loss 93 k, 395 w, 250 m.—Federal, Gen. Canby, 32,000; loss 100 k, 695 w. Alabama troops, 18th, 21st, 32d, 36th, 37th, 38th, 58th Inf.; Ketchum's, Lumsden's Battrs.

Wilson's raid, Ala. and Ga., Mar. 22 to April 24. Gen. Forrest; loss 1200 k and w, 6820 m.—Federal, Gen. Wilson, 12,500; loss 99 k, 598 w, 28 m. Alabama troops, 4th, 5th, 7th, 8th, 11th Cav., and State reserves.

Montevallo, etc., Ala., Mar. 31. Gen. Adams; total loss 100.—Federal, Gen. Upton, 1 division; loss 12 k, 30 m. Alabama troops, 4th, 5th, 7th, 8th Cav.

Trion, Ala., April 1. Gen. Jackson.—Federal, Gen. Croxton, 1 brigade; loss 3 k, 10 w, 20 m. Alabama troops, 5th Cav.

Mt. Pleasant, Ala., April 1. Gen. Forrest, 1,500; total loss 63.— Federal, Gen. Wilson; loss 5 w.

Centreville, Ala., April 1. Gen. Jackson; total loss 15.—Federal, Gen. Croxton. Alabama troops, 4th, 5th, 7th, 8th Cav.

Bogler's Cr., Ala., April 6. Gen. Forrest, 7,000; loss 1500 m.—Federal, Gen. Wilson; loss 30 k, 60 w. Alabama troops, 5th Cav.

Selma, Ala., April 2. Gen. Forrest, 7,000; loss 1500 m.—Federal, Gen. Wilson, 9,000; loss 42 k, 270 w, 7 m. Alabama troops, 4th, 5th, 7th, 11th Cav.

Scottsville, Ala., April 2. Gen. Jackson; loss 3 k, 10 w.—Federal, Gen. Wilson; loss 1 k, 8 w, 6 m. Alabama troops, 5th Cav.

Northport, Ala., April 3. Loss 60 m.—Federal, Gen. Wilson.

Tuscaloosa, Ala., April 4. Col. Garland; loss 150 m,—Federal, Gen. Wilson. Alabama troops, corps of cadets.

Sipsey Swamp, Ala., April 6. Gen. Wirt Adams.—Federal, Gen. Wilson; loss 4 k, 24 w, 30 m. Alabama troops, Adams' Cav. and reserves.

Fort Blakely, Ala., April 9. Gen. Liddell; loss 500 k and w, 2400 m.—Federal, Gen. Canby, 31,000; loss* 189 k, 1201 w, 27 m. Alabama troops, Thomas' boy reserves, 6th Cav., Tarrant's Batty., 15th Conf. Cav.

Montgomery, Ala., April 12-13. Loss 50 m.—Federal, Gen. Wilson. Alabama troops, several companies of militia.

Near Raleigh, Hillsboro Rd., Morrisville, Chapel Hill Rd., Creek near Chapel Hill, N. C., April 12 to 15. Gen. Jos. Wheeler; total loss 68.—Federal, total loss 290. Alabama troops, parts of 1st, 3d, 51st Cav., 3d, 10th Conf. Cav.

Fort Tyler, Ala., April 16. Gen. R. C. Tyler, 265; loss 19 k, 28 w, 218 m.—Federal, Gen. Wilson; loss 7 k, 29 w. Alabama troops, boys and convalescents.

Columbus, Ga., April 16. 3,000; loss 1200 m.—Federal, Gen. Wilson; loss 6 k, 24 w.

* Losses of Mobile campaign.

Macon, Ga., April 20. Loss 2193 surrendered.

Mumford's Sta., Ala., April 23. Loss 150 surrendered.

Greensboro, N. C., April 26. Gen. Johnston; loss 29,924 surrendered. Confederate troops, army of Tennessee.,

Meridian, Miss., May 4. Gen. Taylor; loss 10,000 surrendered. Confederate troops, army of Mobile.

Irwinsville, Ga., May 10. President Davis and escort; total loss 21. —Federal, Col. Pritchard; loss 2 k, 4 w.

INDEX

Abercrombie, Robert H. 36, 76, 115, 139, 140
Aberdeen, MS 205
Abernathy, J. L. 188
Abernathy, John E. 100, 102
Abernathy, Samuel 106, 114
Abney, Joel P. 151, 152
Ackia, MS
    Battle of 4
Ackworth, GA 206, 275
Ackworth Road, GA 270
Adairsville, GA
    Battle of 73
Adams, _____ (Private, 34th Infantry) 117
Adams, Daniel Weisiger 29, 110, 112, 166, 193, 220, 228, 245, 284
Adams, John 174, 205, 254
Adams, John C. 120
Adams, John Quincy 13
Adams, Samuel 113, 114, 115, 140, 241
Adams, William Wirt 29, 76, 197, 216, 226, 227, 244, 268, 284
Adamsville, GA 269
Adrian, John D. 137
Aiken, James 66, 68
Aiken, SC 281
    Battle of 184
Alabama, CSS 31
Alabama Indians 3
Alabama River 4, 25, 217
Alabama Road, GA 263
Alabama Units
    Artillery
        1st Battalion 224, 274
        2nd Battalion, Battery A 225
        2nd Battalion, Battery C 225, 226
        2nd Battalion, Battery E 225, 226

        20th Battalion 234, 261
        Alabama State Artillery Battalion 226, 259
        Alabama State Artillery Battalion, Battery C 226
        Albertus' Battery 30
        Barbour's Light Artillery 242
        Barrett's Battery 237
        Baxter's Battery 169
        Bellamy's Battery 233, 234
        Burnett's Battery 224
        Burtwell's Battery 224
        Clanton's Battery 244
        Dent's Battery 254, 263, 279
        Emanuel's Battery 261
        Emery's Battery 233, 234
        Eufaula Battery 236, 255, 259, 262, 266
        Fowler's Battery 263, 266
        Gage's Battery 232, 254
        Garrity's Battery 263
        Gee's Battalion 239
        Gid Nelson Battery 235, 262, 273, 274
        Gladden's Battery 226
        Goldthwaite's Battery 279
        Hardaway's Battery 230, 231, 248, 249, 250
        Hurt's Battery 230, 231, 249, 250, 251
        Jeff. Davis Battery 229, 230, 248, 249, 251, 252
        Jeffries' Battery 169
        Ketchum's Battery 226, 227, 254, 259, 266, 284
        Kolb's Battery 242, 243, 263, 265, 266, 279
        Lovelace's Battery 235
        Lumsden's Battery 239, 254, 257, 259, 275, 279, 284
        McKenzie's Battery 279

Montgomery True Blues Battery 239, 254
Nelson's Battery 261, 273
Phelan's Battery 279
Reeve's Battery 250
Robertson's Battery 245, 246, 254, 259, 266
Saunders' Battalion 239
Selden's Battery 235, 275, 279
Semple's Battery 240, 257, 259, 263, 266, 269, 273, 274
Sengstak's Battery 237, 261
Tarrant's Battery 243, 269, 270, 273, 274, 275, 279, 284
Waddell's Battery 233, 234, 261
Wade's Battery 261
Ward's Battery 244, 259
Waters' Battery 104, 232, 257, 259, 266

Cavalry
  1st Alabama Battalion 203, 205
  1st Regiment 178, 179, 180, 181, 183, 184, 185, 200, 254, 255, 256, 257, 258, 259, 260, 261, 262, 263, 264, 265, 266, 269, 270, 271, 272, 273, 274, 275, 277, 280, 281, 282, 283
  2nd Battalion (Martin's) 266
  2nd Regiment 182, 183, 261, 262, 267, 276, 277, 278, 279
  3rd Regiment 180, 184, 185, 186, 254, 255, 256, 257, 258, 259, 260, 261, 262, 263, 264, 265, 266, 269, 270, 271, 272, 273, 274, 275, 277, 280, 281, 282, 283, 284
  4th Battalion 217
  4th Regiment 52, 188, 258, 259, 260, 261, 262, 263, 264, 265, 266, 267, 268, 269, 270, 271, 272, 273, 274, 276, 284
  4th Regiment (Roddey's) 189, 258, 261, 262, 266, 270
  4th Regiment (Russell's) 187, 255, 267, 268
  5th Regiment 262, 263, 269, 273, 274, 284
  6th Regiment 192, 274, 279, 284
  7th Regiment 189, 193, 194, 195, 198, 203, 258, 260, 262, 263, 264, 265, 267, 268, 269, 270, 271, 272, 273, 274, 275, 276, 277, 279, 284
  8th Regiment 195, 196, 266, 274, 284
  8th Regiment (Livingston's) 196
  9th Regiment 197
  9th Regiment (Malone's) 197, 198
  10th Regiment 199, 266, 273
  11th Regiment 199, 200, 262, 267, 268, 270, 273, 274, 284
  12th Battalion 201
  12th Regiment 200, 201, 279
  13th Battalion 205
  14th Battalion 198, 258
  15th Battalion 205
  17th Battalion 213
  18th Battalion Mounted Infantry 219
  19th Battalion 198
  24th Battalion 217, 272, 274, 276, 277, 278, 279
  24th Battalion (Snodgrass' Battalion) 268
  25th Battalion 218
  51st Regiment 254, 258, 259, 260, 261, 262, 263, 264, 265, 269, 270, 271, 272, 273, 274, 275, 277, 280, 281, 282, 283, 284
  51st Regiment, Partisan Rangers 201, 202, 270
  52nd Regiment 267
  53rd Regiment 52, 203, 217, 254, 260, 261, 263, 268, 269, 271, 272, 273, 274, 276, 277, 278, 279
  56th Regiment 204, 205, 267, 270, 275, 276, 277, 278, 279
  Adams' Cavalry 254, 268
  Alabama Cadets Battalion 187
  Amos' Company 222
  Arrington's Company 222
  Baldwin's Company 222
  Baldwin's Rangers 222
  Baskerville's Battalion 210
  Beall's Battalion 219
  Bell's Battalion 210
  Boyles' Mobile Dragoons 205
  Brewer's Battalion 210, 254
  Brooks' Home Guards Cavalry 171

Clanton's Regiment 254
Cottrill's Company 222
Cottrill's Scouts 222
Crocheron's Light Dragoons 222
Dorrence Rangers 222
Forrest's Regiment 254, 258, 260, 274
Goldsby's Company Mounted Infantry 222
Gordon's Regiment 222
Gunter's Battalion 219
Hardie's Reserve 220
Hatch's Cavalry Battalion (aka 8th Cav.) 195
Hewlett's Battalion 204
Houston's Regiment 222, 223
Hubbard's Regiment 222, 223
Jenkins' Battalion 203, 254
Julian's Battalion 191, 261
Lewis' Battalion 220
McDonald's Battalion 188
Meador's Company 222, 223
Mead's Battalion 218
Mobile City Troop 223
Moreland's Battalion 221
Murphy's Battalion 184
Newsom's Company 191
Prattville Dragoons 204
Stuart's Battalion 221, 269
Thomason's Battalion 198
Wheeler's Scouts 268, 273, 274
White's Company 222, 223
William's Battalion 191
Hilliard's Legion 161, 162, 167, 168, 169, 173, 242, 263
Infantry
  1st Alabama, Mississippi, and Tennessee Regiment 152
  1st Battalion 95, 130
  1st Mobile Regiment 170
  1st Regiment 33, 34, 35, 36, 76, 78, 107, 115, 139, 253, 254, 256, 261, 270, 273, 274, 275, 279, 283, 284
  2nd Battalion 130, 168
  2nd Regiment 36, 132, 174
  3rd Battalion 130
  3rd Regiment 8, 24, 37, 38, 48, 51, 99, 239, 248, 249, 251, 252, 253, 284
  4th Battalion 105, 130, 154, 155, 254, 256
  4th Battalion (Snodgrass') 269
  4th Regiment 40, 42, 136, 138, 145, 248, 249, 250, 251, 252, 253, 263, 265, 276, 7, 143, 144
  5th Battalion 171, 172, 248
  5th Regiment 37, 43, 44, 45, 46, 47, 96, 97, 99, 248, 249, 250, 251, 252, 253
  6th Battalion 148, 155, 261
  6th Regiment 37, 48, 49, 50, 51, 99, 233, 248, 249, 250, 251, 252, 253, 38
  7th Regiment 52, 253
  8th Regiment 53, 54, 55, 67, 103, 248, 249, 250, 251, 253
  9th Battalion 157, 158, 262
  9th Regiment 56, 57, 58, 60, 62, 176, 248, 249, 250, 251, 253
  10th Regiment 59, 60, 61, 176, 248, 249, 250, 251, 253
  11th Regiment 61, 62, 176, 248, 249, 250, 251, 253, 7
  12th Regiment 38, 63, 64, 65, 67, 83, 141, 248, 249, 250, 252, 253
  13th Regiment 66, 248, 249, 250, 251, 253
  14th Regiment 68, 248, 249, 250, 251, 253
  15th Battlion 248
  15th Regiment 70, 71, 72, 73, 136, 138, 143, 144, 145, 146, 248, 249, 250, 251, 252, 253, 263, 265, 266
  16th Battalion 155
  16th Regiment 36, 73, 74, 76, 115, 139, 140, 141, 253, 254, 256, 257, 259, 263, 266, 268, 269, 273, 274, 279, 283
  17th Regiment 36, 77, 78, 107, 139, 253, 254, 267, 273, 274, 283
  18th Battalion 113, 115, 257
  18th Regiment 78, 79, 81, 120, 160, 254, 262, 263, 269, 270, 273, 274, 279, 284
  19th Regiment 7, 81, 126, 128, 149, 253, 254, 259, 263, 266, 269, 273, 274, 279, 283
  20th Regiment 83, 84, 85, 107, 108,

142, 259, 261, 266, 268, 273, 274, 279, 283
21st Regiment 86, 254, 274, 284
22nd Regiment 87, 88, 89, 90, 95, 96, 126, 149, 151, 153, 254, 255, 257, 259, 263, 273, 274, 279, 283
23rd Battalion 167, 250, 251, 283
23rd Regiment 90, 91, 107, 111, 135, 141, 142, 219, 259, 261, 268, 269, 270, 273, 274, 279
24th Battalion 269
24th Regiment 92, 93, 94, 102, 104, 105, 116, 117, 254, 259, 263, 266, 279, 284
25th Regiment 87, 89, 90, 95, 126, 149, 151, 152, 153, 254, 259, 263, 266, 270, 279, 283
26th Regiment 38, 45, 46, 52, 65, 96, 97, 98, 99, 126, 127, 141, 149, 150, 163, 248, 249, 254, 273, 274, 275, 279
26th-50th Regiment 254
27th Regiment 100, 102, 118, 119, 147, 148, 149, 154, 155, 156, 157, 254, 257, 261, 267, 273, 274, 275, 279, 284
28th Regiment 93, 94, 103, 104, 116, 117, 255, 259, 263, 266, 279, 284
29th Regiment 36, 78, 105, 106, 107, 139, 141, 253, 269, 270, 273, 274, 275, 279, 284
30th Regiment 91, 107, 108, 141, 142, 255, 259, 261, 267, 268, 269, 270, 273, 274, 279, 284
31st Regiment 107, 109, 141, 142, 147, 148, 155, 254, 255, 256, 259, 261, 265, 266, 267, 268, 279
32nd Regiment 110, 111, 112, 120, 157, 158, 160, 255, 259, 261, 262, 263, 266, 267, 279, 284
33rd Regiment 36, 76, 113, 115, 139, 140, 141, 255, 257, 259, 263, 266, 273, 274, 279
34th Regiment 93, 94, 102, 104, 105, 116, 259, 263, 266, 273, 274, 279, 283, 284
35th Regiment 100, 102, 118, 119, 134, 147, 149, 154, 155, 156, 157, 256, 261, 267, 273, 279, 284

36th Regiment 120, 121, 262, 263, 268, 269, 270, 279, 284
37th Regiment 121, 123, 127, 129, 132, 133, 152, 255, 256, 259, 261, 266, 268, 269, 270, 273, 274, 284
38th Regiment 120, 124, 125, 262, 263, 266, 269, 270, 273, 274, 279, 284
39th Regiment 87, 90, 95, 96, 126, 127, 149, 150, 151, 152, 153, 259, 263, 266, 273, 274, 279, 283
40th Regiment 123, 124, 127, 128, 129, 133, 259, 261, 262, 266, 268, 269, 270, 273, 274
41st Regiment 129, 130, 135, 250, 251, 252, 253, 259, 261, 262, 263
42nd Regiment 122, 123, 124, 127, 132, 133, 256, 261, 266, 284
43rd Regiment 130, 134, 135, 169, 250, 251, 263, 265
44th Regiment 42, 136, 138, 143, 144, 145, 248, 249, 250, 251, 252, 253, 263, 265
45th Regiment 36, 76, 115, 139, 140, 257, 259, 263, 266, 269, 270, 273, 274, 279, 283
46th Regiment 91, 107, 128, 141, 142, 144, 254, 255, 261, 266, 268, 279
47th Regiment 136, 138, 143, 145, 146, 248, 249, 250, 251, 252, 253, 263, 265, 266
48th Regiment 136, 138, 143, 144, 145, 146, 248, 249, 250, 251, 252, 253, 263, 265, 266
49th Regiment 100, 102, 118, 120, 147, 148, 154, 155, 156, 157, 256, 261, 273, 274, 279, 284
50th Regiment 52, 87, 90, 96, 126, 149, 150, 151, 152, 153, 263, 266, 273, 274, 279, 283, 95
54th Regiment 119, 122, 123, 124, 133, 134, 151, 152, 153, 156, 254, 261, 267, 270, 273, 274, 284
55th Regiment 100, 102, 119, 120, 147, 153, 154, 155, 156,

157, 164, 261, 267, 269, 273, 274, 275, 284
57th Regiment 100, 102, 120, 147, 154, 156, 273, 274, 275, 279, 284
58th Regiment 110, 112, 120, 157, 158, 159, 160, 263, 266, 269, 270, 279, 284
59th Regiment 130, 135, 161, 162, 163, 164, 167, 170, 250, 251, 252, 253, 265, 266
60th Regiment 130, 135, 162, 167, 170, 250, 251, 252, 253, 265, 266
61st Regiment 163, 250, 251, 252, 253
62nd Regiment 165
63rd Regiment 165
64th Regiment 165
65th Regiment 165
Butts' Battalion 176
Casey's Battalion 176
Chisholm's Company of State Guards 176, 177
Eufaula Minute Men 176, 177
Garvin's Battalion 254
Gracie's Battalion 176
Hale's Thirty-first Regiment 147
Harris' Battalion 176
Inge's Regiment 276, 278. *See also* Alabama Units: Infantry: 18th Regiment
Inge's Regiment 278, 279
Limestone Rebels 150
Miller's Regiment 276, 278, 279
Mobile Guards 170
Morrison's Battalion 176
Norwood's Battalion 153
Pelham Cadets 176, 177, 274, 284
Perrin's Regiment 276, 278, 279. *See also* Alabama Units: Infantry: 8th Regiment
Snodgrass' Battalion 153. *See also* Alabama Units: Infantry: 4th Battalion (Snodgrass')
Swanson Guards 176, 177
Tuscaloosa Cadets 176
Jeff Davis Legion 217, 281, 283

Reserves
  1st Battalion 165, 166
  1st Junior Reserves 166
  1st Regiment 165
  2nd Junior Reserves 166
  2nd Regiment 165
  3rd Battalion 165, 166
  3rd Regiment 166
  3rd Senior Reserves 167
  4th Battalion 165, 166
  4th Regiment 165, 166
  4th Senior Reserves 167
  8th Cavalry Reserve 284
  Barbiere's Reserve Cavalry 219
  Hardie's Reserve 220
  Senior Reserves Light Artillery 167
  State Reserves 167, 284
  Thomas' Boy Reserves 284
Sharpshooters
  17th Battalion (Yancey's Battalion) 173, 259, 273, 274
  23rd Battalion (Stallworth's) 173. *See also* Alabama Units: Sharpshooters: Stallworth's Sharpshooters
  Moreland's Sharpshooter Battalion 176
  Stallworth's Sharpshooters 130, 135, 167, 265, 266
  Stone's Alabama Battalion Sharpshooters 128, 129
Aldridge, Enoch 145
Aldridge, Jesse G. 145
Alexander, _____ (Captain, 4th Cav., (Russell's) 189
Alexander, D. W. 75
Alexander, G. L. 153, 154
Allatoona, GA 275
  Battle of 243
Allatoona Road, GA 270
Allen, E. J. 36, 45, 49, 54
Allen, Frank 88
Allen, John 106
Allen, Sydney E. 178
Allen, William L. 182, 197
Allen, William Wirt 178, 180, 181, 182, 184, 186, 188, 198, 201, 203, 206, 209, 212, 214, 218
Allison, J. H. 70
Allisonia, TN 262

Alpine, GA 263
Altamont, TN 255
Amerine, J. P. W. 156
Ames, Adelbert 252
Amorine, P. W. 122
Amos, W. B. 215
Anderson, Hezekiah 159
Anderson, _____ (Private, Hilliard's Legion) 170
Anderson, _____ (Colonel) 27
Anderson, Bartlett 88
Anderson, Charles D. 83, 86
Anderson, David M. 107, 108
Anderson, George B. 231
Anderson, James Patton 52, 83, 92, 104, 139, 140, 150, 227, 228, 245
Anderson, Richard Heron 33, 55, 58, 61, 63, 69, 136, 137, 201, 252, 253
Anderson, Robert Houston 206, 209, 212, 214, 253
Anderson, Samuel Read 256
Anderson, W. H. 82
Anderson's Cross Roads, TN 264
Andersonville, GA 99
Andracita (schooner) 222
Andrews, A. R. 173
Andrews, James A. 182
Andrews, W. G. 239
Anthony's Hill, TN 279
Antietam, MD. *See also* Sharpsburg, MD Battle of 53, 65, 249
Apalachee Artillery Battery 78
Appomattox Court House, VA 36, 40, 48, 52, 56, 62, 63, 68, 73, 130, 135, 137, 139, 143, 145, 147, 161, 162, 163, 171, 174, 176, 230, 232, 253
Archer, James Jay 67, 68, 171, 172
Arkansas Units
  Infantry
    8th Regiment 30
Arlington, James 47
Armistead, Charles G. 195, 219, 220
Armistead, E. H. 88, 90
Armistead, Frank Crawford 193
Armistead, H. 40, 41
Armistead, Herbery E. 87
Armistead, R. B. 87, 88
Armistead, Robert D. 87
Armstrong, Frank Crawford 204, 207, 213

Armstrong, T. C. (Frank C.) 191
Army in the Tennessee 107
Army of Mississippi 35, 78, 86, 88, 95, 99, 101, 102, 106, 140, 149, 154, 179, 180, 193, 226, 227, 235, 244
Army of Mobile 36, 77, 79, 82, 84, 86, 88, 92, 95, 120, 124, 128, 174, 193, 205, 221, 222, 223, 224, 225, 226, 235, 240, 285
Army of Northern Virginia 38, 39, 42, 43, 48, 49, 50, 55, 56, 58, 61, 63, 65, 67, 69, 71, 73, 96, 98, 99, 137, 143, 144, 145, 146, 164, 175, 230, 231, 253
Army of Pensacola 77, 245
Army of Tennessee 35, 72, 76, 77, 78, 81, 82, 85, 89, 90, 91, 92, 93, 95, 96, 100, 104, 105, 106, 108, 110, 112, 114, 115, 122, 123, 124, 125, 126, 128, 130, 131, 133, 140, 141, 142, 143, 144, 150, 152, 156, 157, 160, 173, 180, 183, 185, 186, 187, 188, 190, 196, 206, 217, 219, 222, 234, 235, 236, 237, 239, 240, 242, 243, 270, 273, 276, 279, 285
Army of the Mississippi 53, 74, 75, 79, 82, 103, 111, 114, 116, 129, 148, 218
Army of the Peninsula 54
Army of the Potomac 229
Army of the Potomac (CSA) 40, 56
Army of the Shenandoah 40
Army of the West 119, 132
Army of Vicksburg 84, 85, 91, 108, 109, 123, 128, 133, 142, 226
Arnold, George W. 150, 151
Arnold, W. R. 156
Arrington, _____ 109
Arrington, E. T. 223
Arrington, S. L. 109
Arrington, Thomas M. 109, 110
Arrowfield Church, VA
  Battle of 250
Ashboth, Alexander S. 35, 36, 193, 194, 215, 216, 222
Ashe, R. Y. 62
Ashe, Thomas P. 111
Ashford, A. E. 118, 119

292

Ashford, Fred A. 74
Ashford, Frederic A. 75, 140
Ashford, Frederick A. 74, 76
Ashley, William P. 182
Asylum Hill, TN 258
Athens, AL 27, 192, 199, 204, 266, 274
Atkinson, T. J. 197
Atlanta, GA 35, 83, 103, 120, 124, 126, 149, 168, 175, 200, 201, 203, 222, 232, 240, 270, 273, 274
    Battle of 77, 78, 87, 90, 105, 107, 113, 114, 116, 120, 122, 123, 126, 139, 149, 158, 197, 227, 235
    Campaign for 31, 33, 73, 77, 78, 81, 87, 90, 97, 103, 109, 110, 113, 115, 118, 121, 122, 124, 125, 126, 127, 133, 139, 141, 147, 152, 154, 155, 156, 157, 158, 160, 173, 178, 182, 184, 186, 187, 188, 192, 198, 200, 201, 203, 204, 206, 210, 213, 217, 228, 236, 237, 239, 240, 242, 243, 245, 246
Atlanta Road, GA 272
Aubrey, George 105
Auburn, AL 68, 78, 121, 145
Auger, Christopher C. 261
Augusta, GA 124, 204, 218, 242
Austin, John E. 81, 112
Autossee, Al
    Battle of 6
Averasboro, NC 283
    Battle of 33, 200
Averett, A. E. 73
Averill, William W. 251
Avery, A. W. 179
Avirett, John A. Jr. 158, 159
Ayres, Jack 83
Ayres, Romeyn 253

Babcock, John C. 43, 161, 163, 172
Bacot, W. C. 187
Bagley, J. N. 109
Bailey, J. E. 65
Bailey, Joseph 216
Bailey's Springs, AL 221
Baine, David W. 68, 69

Baker, Alpheus 122, 123, 127, 129, 133, 152, 153, 166
Baker, B. H. 49
Baker, E. O. 51
Baker's Creek, MS 267
Baker's Creek, MS 261
    Battle of 83, 90, 100, 107, 108, 109, 118, 119, 122, 141, 142, 151, 154, 174, 175, 233
Baldwin, D. P. 7
Baldwyn, MS 211
Ball, Charles P. 195, 196, 220
Ballard, A. M. 47
Ball's Ferry, GA 276
Baltimore, MD 12
Bane, John P. 146
Bankhead, Smith P. 245
Banks, James 121
Banks, Nathaniel P. 27, 248, 261
Banks, Willis 126
Bankston, M. L. 68
Barber, Y. M. 135
Barbiere, Joseph 219
Barbour, John G. 94
Bardstown, KY 180
Bardstown Pike, KY 256
Barlow, Francis C. 37
Barlow, T. C. 222
Barnes, _____ (Captain, 10th Conf. Cav.) 213
Barnes, Dixon 71
Barnes, John 136
Barnes, W. P. 220
Barnett, G. B. 73
Barnwell, John G. 231
Barr, _____ (Captain) 26
Barren Mound, KY 257
Barry, J. N. 82
Barry, Robert L. 235
Barteau, Clark R. 183
Bartlett, Anthony B. 174, 176
Barton, Seth Maxwell 84, 107, 109
Barton Station, AL 25
Baskerville, Charles 210
Bate, William Brimage 121, 157, 158, 159, 236, 246, 262, 269
Baton Rouge, LA 5, 118, 255
    Battle of 147, 148, 153, 154
    Engagement at 118

Battle Creek, AL
　Engagement at 111, 209
Battle Creek, TN 254
Battle, Cullen A. 37, 38, 39, 48, 51, 65,
　99, 163
Battle, Lee W. 201, 202, 212
Bay Shore, AL 78
Baygents, James F. 169
Beach Fork, KY 256
Bealeton, VA
　Battle of 230
Beall, T. S. 219
Beall, William Nelson Rector 34, 101,
　147, 148, 155, 178, 179, 211, 219,
　261
Bean, J. F. 73
Bean's Station, TN 70, 266
　Battle of 132, 134, 135, 136, 161, 162,
　168
Bear Creek, AL 261
Bear Creek, GA 276
Bear Creek, MS 200
Beason, W. B. 147
Beauregard, P. G. T. 33, 36, 40, 44, 45,
　49, 56, 60, 62, 64, 86, 105, 132,
　135, 136, 148, 161, 162, 171, 174,
　207, 211, 239, 248, 250, 251, 254
Beck, Franklin K. 90, 91
Becker, W. P. 138
Beckham, R. F. 228
Bee, Barnard E. 40
Beech Grove, KY 74
Beech River 187
Beechwood, TN 240
Beeson, W. B. 102, 149
Belknap, William W. 140
Bell, _____ (Lieutenat, 36th Infantry)
　121
Bell, Alexander R. 115
Bell, H. M. 130
Bell, Joel 125
Bell, John (Presidential Candidate) 12, 13
Bell, John T. 68, 69
Bell, John W. 112
Bell, Stanley H. 237
Bell, Stephen E. 62
Bell, Thomas H. 48, 49
Bell, Tyree Harris 191, 195, 242
Bellamy, Richard H. 234
Bell's Ferry Road, GA 271

Belmont, MO
　Battle of 31
Belton, Joseph F. 109, 168
Benjamin, J. R. 77
Bennett, _____ (Private, Hilliard's
　Legion) 170
Bennett, A. D. 200
Benning, Henry L. 42, 72
Bentley, David E. 74, 75
Benton, AL 193
Benton, Matthew 51
Bentonville, NC
　Battle of 33, 81, 83, 87, 90, 92, 95,
　106, 107, 109, 116, 122, 126, 128,
　141, 152, 156, 184, 201, 213, 283
Bermuda Hundred, VA
　Battle of 137, 145, 250
Berry, W. T. 71
Berryville, VA 252
Best, Robert 133
Bethel, MS 211
Bethel, TN 211
Bethesda Church, VA
　Battle of 175, 250
Bethune, William C. 156
Betts, William H. 66
Bibb, Joseph B. 90, 91, 92, 108, 110,
　141, 142
Bibb, R. H. 169
Bickerstaff, J. B. 116
Bickerstaff, James H. 117
Bienville, Jean Baptiste Lemoyne 3
Big Black River, MS
　Battle of 90, 91, 101, 261
Big Creek Gap, TN 168, 214, 242
Big Escambia Bridge, FL 193
Big Hill, KY 257
Big Shanty, GA 129, 181, 275
　Battle of 178
Billinglea, _____ 209
Binford, William H. 197
Binnaker's Bridge Road, SC 281
Black Creek, GA 278
Black Creek, NC 283
Black Creek, SC 281
Black, J. R. 89
Black, Pickens W. 59
Black River, SC 283
Black Warrior Creek, AL 261
Black Warrior River 3, 29

Blackford, Eugene 44, 46, 47, 99
Blackland, MS 254
Blackland, TN 92
   Battle of 157
Blackwell, SC 281
Blakely, AL 216. *See also* Fort
   Blakely, AL
Blakey, David T. 178, 181, 182
Blankenship, John 170
Blockhouse, TN 275
Blount County, AL 25
Blue, _____ (Major) 6
Blue Hills, AL 188
Blue Mountain, AL 177, 193, 195,
   196, 197
Blue Pond Road, AL 275
Bluff Springs, FL 178, 192, 196, 216
Bodie, Capers W. 133
Boggess, W. H. 109, 147, 148
Boggy Creek, GA 272
Bogler's Creek, AL 192, 284
Boiling, Allen 55
Boiling, John, Jr. 78
Bolivar, MS 211
Bolivar Road, TN 254
Bolivar, TN 187
Bolton Depot, MS 267
Bond, Philip 227, 228
Bondurant, J. W. 229, 230
Bone, Johnson 117
Bonham, M. F. 37
Boonesboro, MD
   Battle of 37, 40, 41, 43, 44, 46, 48,
     50, 64, 65, 66, 96, 97, 98
Boonsville, GA
   Battle of 210
Booth, L. F. 268
Boston, MA 15
Boswell, William H. 93
Boteler's Ford, VA
   Battle of 72
Bottom's Bridge, VA 163
Bounds, Jopseph H. 98
Bowen, _____ 75
Bowen, _____ (Capt., 15th Conf.
   Cav.) 216
Bowen, John Stevens 91, 175, 261
Bowie, A. W. 211, 220
Bowie, M. L. 51
Bowles, P. D. 42, 43, 144

Bowling Green, KY 52, 255
Boyce, William 75
Boyd, _____ (Private, 33rd Infantry)
   114
Boyd's Station, NC 283
Boydtown Road, VA 252
Boyle, _____ 257
Boyle, William 183
Boyles, William 204, 205, 206
Bozeman, D. A. 137
Bradford, A. H. 242
Bradford, Paul 59, 107
Bradley, John 206, 207
Bradyville, TN
   Battle of 198
Bragg, Braxton 7, 9, 25, 33, 34, 36, 52,
   70, 72, 75, 77, 78, 79, 80, 82, 83,
   84, 85, 86, 88, 91, 92, 94, 95, 102,
   106, 108, 110, 112, 114, 116, 120,
   124, 125, 127, 128, 130, 131, 140,
   142, 144, 145, 146, 150, 158, 160,
   168, 173, 174, 175, 178, 179, 180,
   181, 182, 184, 185, 186, 188, 189,
   190, 191, 198, 206, 211, 218, 227,
   232, 238, 239, 245, 253, 255, 256,
   259, 263, 265
Brainard, H. C. 70, 71
Brandy Station, VA
   Battle of 64, 249
Brannan, John M. 191, 207, 209
Brannon, T. J. 127
Brantley, William Felix 90, 96, 124, 151
Branyon, W. L. 97, 99
Bratton, William M. 62
Braxton's Bridge, SC 280
Brazleton, William W. 62
Breckinridge, John C. 12, 13, 105, 110,
   111, 112, 118, 125, 130, 131, 142,
   147, 148, 153, 154, 160, 237, 246,
   255
Breedlove, Ephriam B. 76, 115, 139,
   140, 241
Brentwood, TN 193, 260
   Battle of 203
Brewer, George E. 141, 142
Brewer, R. H. 210
Brewster, Wilson L. 61
Brewton, Caleb W. 61
Brick House, TN 259
Bridge Creek, MS 254

Bridge Creek, TN
   Battle of 82, 94, 149, 150, 179, 245, 246
Bridge, KY 256
Bridgeport, AL 195, 202, 209, 255
   Engagement at 110, 111, 208
Bridges, W. L. 150
Brindley, Thomas M. 87
Bristoe Campaign 38, 51
Bristoe Station, VA
   Battle of 66, 67, 231, 249
Bristol, TN 168
Broad River 281
Bronson, Thomas M. 129
Brooke, John R. 37
Brooks, _____ (Private, Hilliard's Legion) 169
Brooks, Henry 220
Brooks' Station, VA 69
Brooks, William M. 166
Broughton, L. P. 66
Broughton, W. E. 174
Brown, _____ (Private, Hilliard's Legion) 169
Brown, Bayless C. 40
Brown, Berry G. 106
Brown, C. F. 55
Brown, George P. 59
Brown, Harvey 253
Brown Hill, KY 256
Brown, James A. 68
Brown, John 9
   Raid on Harpers Ferry 9, 24
Brown, John C. 64, 108, 228
Brown, Monroe 88
Brown, Thomas 178, 179
Brown, W. S. 65
Browning, J. R. 116
Brownlow, James P. 200
Brown's Ferry, AL 25
Brown's Ferry, TN 265
   Battle of 70
Brownville, TN 206
Bruce, _____ (Private, 43rd Inf) 136
Bruce, Newton 136
Bruce, W. S. 147
Bruckner, J. T. 151
Bruckner, John C. 150
Brundridge, J. W. 58
Bryan, David F. 97, 98

Bryan, Goode 7
Bucatanna, AL 216
Buchanan, Franklin 274
Buchanan, James 16
Buck, William A. 92
Buckhead Church, GA 277
Buckhead Creek, GA 277
Buckhead, GA 272
Buckner, Simon Bolivar 43, 73, 77, 79, 120, 125, 132, 136, 138, 144, 158, 170, 183, 214, 222, 243, 254
Buell, Don Carlos 25, 208, 254, 256
Buena Vista, AL 189
Buena Vista, MS 205
Buffalo, NY 14
Buford, _____ (Major) 43
Buford, Abraham 101, 119, 147, 148, 151, 152, 153, 155, 193, 200, 276
Buford, John 249
Buford, W. W. 125
Bulger, Michael J. 143, 144
Bull Run, VA 45
   Second Battle of 30
Bullen, _____ (Lieutenant, 36th Infantry) 121
Bullock, Edwin C. 79
Bumpers, Nathaniel J. 93
Burbridge, Stephen 210
Burch, John 116, 117
Burgess' Farm, VA
   Battle of 62
Burgess, J. H. 159
Burk, F. M. 146
Burkett, Evander 127
Burnett, F. M. 47
Burnett, Thomas J. 77, 78
Burnett's, TN 259
Burnside, Ambrose E. 40, 60, 163, 170, 249, 254, 265, 266
Burnside Mine 163
Burnt Cross Roads, KY 256
Burnt Hickory, GA 270
Burr, Aaron 5
Burr, John G. 7
Burr, William H. 107
Burt, Mason W. 51
Burton, V. B. 171
Burtwell, John R. B. 199, 200, 224
Bush, C. G. 55
Bush, R. H. 226, 227

Bush, R. T. 54
Bush, Richard R. 115
Bush, T. B. 171
Bushnell, _____ 89
Bussey, Charles E. 124, 126
Butler, B. 98
Butler, Benjamin F. 43, 250
Butler, Bennet 7
Butler, W. L. 103, 104, 105
Buttahatchie Bridge, MS 205
Butterfield, F. 90
Button, Silas P. 115
Buzzard's Roost, GA 268
    Battle of 73
Buzzard's Roost, GA 267
Byrd, J. M. 154

Cabots, 1
Cadell, Joseph C. 62
Cahaba, AL 147, 149, 166, 175
Cain, S. V. 88
Caldwell, John A. 240
Caldwell, John H. 59, 60
Calhoun County, AL 29
Calhoun, GA 186, 187, 197, 269
Calhoun, John C. 9
Calhoun Road, GA 269
Camp Defiance, AL 6
Camp Foote, TN 211
Camp Gonzales, FL 194
Camp Powell, AL 222
Campbell, _____ 27
Campbell, James M. 143, 144
Campbell, R. N. 225
Campbell, W. M. 218
Campbell, Wallace 274
Campbell's Station, TN 265
Campbellsville, TN 200, 279
Canal Basin, VA 172
Canby, Edward R. S. 27, 28, 284
Cane Creek, GA 275
Cane Creek, SC 282
Caney, John 54
Cannon, D. C. 73
Canoe Station, FL 193
Cantey, James 35, 71, 72, 78, 86, 99,
    105, 106, 170, 176, 222, 226,
    235, 244, 268

Canton, MS 100, 262
Canton Road, GA 271
Canton, TN 152
Caperton's Ferry, AL 263
Capon Springs, WV 15
Carlton, Joseph L. 117
Carmen, E. A. 110
Carpenter, J. M. 80
Carpenter, John N. 182, 183
Carpenter, Nathan M. 121
Carr, Eugene A. 200, 221
Carroll, Henry F. 228
Carroll, John C. 237
Carroll, W. H. 52, 74
Carson, C. F. 75
Carson, John R. 139
Carter, _____ (Private, 24th Infantry)
    93
Carter, Arthur B. 154
Carter, GA 277
Carter, J. F. 66
Carter, John C. 94, 103, 105, 116, 117
Carter, Thomas H. 230
Carter's Farm, TN 258
Carter's Farm, VA 251
Carthage, KY 179
Cartier, 1
Casey, O. P. 200
Casey, Silas 64
Cassville, GA 269
    Battle of 73, 77, 78, 81, 243
Castello, James 55
Castlebury, Joseph V. 170
Castleman's Ferry, VA
    Battle of 43
Cathy, William 184
Cave City, KY 179, 185, 255
Cave Creek, AL 265
Cave Spring, AL 220
Cayce, Stewart W. 86, 170, 171
Cedar Creek, VA
    Battle of 48, 52, 66, 229, 230, 252
Cedar Hill, VA
    Battle of 36
Cedar Mountain, VA 248
Cedar Run, VA
    Battle of 71, 143, 145
Centreville, AL 284
Centreville, VA 44, 56
Chadick, William D. 150

Chaffin's Bluff, VA
  Battle of 137
Chaffin's Farm, VA
  Battle of 252
Chalmers, James R. 82, 150, 178, 179,
  182, 183, 189, 194, 200, 210, 213,
  227, 228, 233, 240, 276, 279
Chamberlain, Bartlett S. 93
Chamberlain, John C. 86
Chamberlain, Joshua Lawrence 72, 136,
  162, 163
Chambers County, AL 29
Chambersburg, PA 99
Champion's Hill, MS 267
  Battle of 83, 84, 91, 109, 233
Chancellorsville, VA
  Battle of 37, 38, 43, 44, 46, 47, 48, 50,
  51, 53, 55, 56, 58, 59, 61, 63, 64,
  65, 66, 67, 68, 69, 97, 98, 171, 172,
  230, 249
Chandler, J. L. 112
Chantilly, VA
  Battle of 70, 72, 143
Chapel Hill, NC 189, 284
  Engagement at 184
Chapel Hill Road, NC 284
Chapel Hill, TN 189, 191, 207, 212
Chapman, Stephen P. 93
Chappell, P. W. 65
Charles City Road, VA 137, 248
Charles, William T. 194
Charleston Harbor 86
Charleston, SC 218
Charleston, TN 161, 162, 173, 266
Charlotte Pike, TN 194
Charlotteville, VA 138
Charlton, Richard 76
Charpentier, Stephen 225
Chase, Salmon P. 18, 19
Chattahoochie River 272, 273
Chattanooga, GA 113
Chattanooga, TN 26, 52, 73, 81, 107,
  108, 109, 111, 119, 129, 130, 134,
  135, 138, 141, 168, 178, 179, 182,
  185, 186, 187, 202, 208, 211, 218,
  219, 224, 225, 228, 236, 238, 246,
  263, 265, 266
  Battle of 227, 242
Chattanooga Valley, TN 263

Chattanooga-Ringgold Campaign 76,
  80, 157, 160
Chattooga Road, GA 275
Cheatham, Benjamin Franklin 31, 85,
  123, 127, 129, 134, 227, 232,
  239, 240, 242, 279
Cherbourg, France 31
Cherokee, AL 195
Cherokee County, AL 25, 209
Cherokees 5, 6
Cherry Creek, MS 183, 206
Cherry, Robert 242
Cherry, Robert H. 75, 76
Chester, John W. 37
Chesterville, SC 282
Chewa Station, GA 273
Chicago, IL 12, 72
Chickamauga Creek, GA 266, 268
Chickamauga, GA 263
  Battle of 30, 31, 40, 42, 70, 73, 74,
  76, 78, 79, 81, 82, 87, 89, 92, 93,
  94, 95, 102, 104, 105, 110, 112,
  113, 114, 115, 116, 120, 121, 124,
  125, 126, 127, 130, 131, 134,
  135, 136, 137, 138, 139, 140,
  143, 145, 149, 150, 157, 158,
  159, 161, 167, 168, 169, 170,
  173, 174, 178, 181, 186, 187,
  188, 200, 201, 202, 206, 207,
  208, 209, 210, 212, 213, 214,
  219, 227, 228, 232, 236, 237,
  238, 240, 241, 242, 245, 246
Chickamauga Station, TN 266
Chickasaw (Indian Village) 3
Chickasaw Bayou, MS
  Battle of 91, 109, 122
Chickasaw Bluffs, MS 91, 259
  Battle of 142
Chickasaws 4, 5
Chicken Pikes, TN 202
Childress, _____ (Lieut., 49th Inf.)
  148
Chilton, R. H. 42
Choctaw, AL 216
Choctaw Bluff, AL 2, 86, 120, 215,
  217, 224, 225
Choctaws 4
Christian, J. F. 47
Christiana, TN 181, 264
Citronelle, AL 216

298

City Point Railroad 163
Claiborne, AL 215, 216
Claiborne, F. L. 5, 6
Claiborne, Thomas 211
Clanton, James Holt 156, 163, 164,
  166, 168, 170, 176, 177, 178,
  179, 180, 181, 182, 187, 192,
  194, 196, 197, 215, 216, 223,
  242, 243, 244, 245, 246, 254, 274
Clanton, N. H. 244
Clanton, Turner Jr. 193
Clark, _____ (Lieutenant) 28
Clark, Christopher 47
Clark, David A. 162
Clark, Edmund 55
Clark, John 34
Clark, John W. 236
Clark, Whitfield 126, 127
Clarke County, AL 2, 3
Clarke, John D. 66
Clarksville, TN 199
Clay, C. C. 26
Clay, Hugh L. 7
Claysville, AL 26
Clayton, Dan 208
Clayton, Henry D. 33, 79, 80, 81, 110,
  112, 113, 120, 121, 123, 124, 125,
  126, 127, 149, 150, 157, 159, 160
Clayton, Joseph C. 126
Clayton, S. S. 197
Clear Creek, MS 211
Clear River 274
Cleburne, Patrick R. 75, 76, 114, 140,
  219, 240, 241
Clemens, James 112
Clemens, Jeremiah 7
Clements, J. J. 213
Clements, James F. 139
Clements, L. M. 130
Clements, Newton N. 149, 150
Cleveland, Grover 53
Cleveland, John G. 120, 121
Cleveland Road, GA 268, 269
Cleveland Road, TN 266
Cleveland, TN 213, 214, 266
Clift, W. J. 218
Clifton, J. M. 153, 154
Clifton, TN 206
Clifton, William C. 126, 127
Clinton, MS 101, 267

Clinton, TN 135, 168, 242
  Battle of 178
Cloud, T. N. 116
Clow, John 158, 159
Clower, Eli 143, 145
Cobb, Fred H. 117
Cobb, Howell 177
Cobb, John 218
Cobb, M. A. 91
Cochran, Samuel L. 54
Cocke, T. 136
Cockrell, Francis Marion 233, 235
Coffee, John R. 5, 7, 8
Coffey, Aaron 88
Cohen, A. B. 62
Coker, J. F. 95
Coker, L. 150
Cold Harbor, VA
  First Battle of (Gaines' Mill) 30, 40,
    44, 48, 229, 231
  Second Battle of (1864) 36, 43, 44,
    53, 56, 59, 62, 66, 70, 137, 145,
    163, 171, 174, 175, 250
Coleman, Augustus A. 128
Coleman, David 246
Coleman, Henry D. 59
Coleman, T. K. 40
Coleman, William G. 7
College Grove, TN 189
Collins, Joseph P. 207
Collins, T. R. 73
Colquitt, Alfred Holt 38, 51, 67
Colquitt, John N. 116
Coltart, John G. 52, 127, 149, 150, 151,
  246
Columbia, GA 210
Columbia Road, SC 281
Columbia, SC 281
Columbia, TN 279
  Battle of 92, 94, 109, 111, 141, 157,
    194
Columbus, Christopher 1
Columbus, GA 244, 284
  Battle of 29
Columbus, KY 187
Columbus, MS 3, 121, 127, 128, 132,
  200, 205, 237
Columbus, TN 189, 205
Colvin, Charles H. 193
Combahee Road, SC 280

Commercial (Ohio Newspaper) 19
Confederate Provisional Congress 7
Confederate States Units
  Cavalry
    1st Regiment 198, 206, 255, 256, 257, 259, 260, 261, 262, 263, 264, 265, 267, 268, 269, 270, 271, 272, 273, 274
    2nd Regiment 270
    3rd Regiment 208, 209, 254, 255, 256, 259, 260, 261, 263, 264, 265, 266, 267, 268, 269, 270, 273, 274, 280, 281, 282, 283
    6th Regiment 211
    8th Regiment 210, 211, 254, 258, 259, 260, 261, 262, 263, 264, 265, 266, 267, 268, 269, 270, 271, 272, 273, 274, 281
    10th Regiment 213, 266, 267, 268, 269, 270, 271, 272, 273, 274, 280, 281, 282, 283, 284
    15th Regiment 214, 215, 279, 284
  Infantry
    1st Battalion 174, 252, 253, 256, 261, 262
    1st Regiment 262
    4th Regiment 152
    15th Regiment 111
Congaree Creek, SC 281
Connecticut Units
  Cavalry
    10th Regiment 167
  Infantry
    15th Regiment 149
Conner, Charles H. 206, 207
Conner, David 31
Conner, John H. 170
Conoly, J. K. 146
Conoly, John F. 106, 153, 154
Constitutional Union Party 12
Cook, R. M. 66
Cook, Walter 59
Cooper, Edward F. 92, 93
Cooper, H. M. 185
Cooper, Samuel 99, 181
Cooper, W. E. 114
Cooper, W. H. 73
Cooper, Wickliffe 213
Coosa, AL 2
Coosa River 5, 193

Copilly, James W. 202
Corcoran, Michael 249
Corinth, GA 274
Corinth, MS 25, 26, 78, 79, 81, 85, 87, 88, 92, 102, 113, 118, 119, 133, 147, 148, 149, 157, 158, 187, 193, 194, 208, 211, 219, 221, 224, 227, 228, 232, 237, 240, 246, 256, 262
  Battle of 33, 48, 122, 133, 148, 153, 155, 157, 174, 175, 238, 239, 240
  Siege of 132
Corse, Montgomery Dent 62, 275
Cortez 3
Costa, AL 2
Costello, D. P. 95
Costello, Pierre 95
Cothran, John F. 274
Cotrel, J. H. 150
Cotton, J. K. P. 142
Cotton, P. E. 218
Cotton Port Ford, TN 264
Cottonville, AL 188
Courtland, AL 7, 73, 183, 189, 191, 199, 221, 222
Courtney, A. R. 246
Covington, B. R. 116
Cowan, J. H. 154
Cowan, Jon H. 47
Cowen, Robert W. 59
Cox, _____ (Captain, 53rd Cav.) 203
Cox, G. W. 111, 113, 160
Cox, H. M. 68
Cox, H. W. 65
Cox, Henry W. 64
Cox Hill, TN 258
Cox, J. J. 204
Cox, J. L. 170
Cox, Jesse J. 52
Cox, John T. 198, 206
Cox, Nicholas 187
Cox, Samuel A. 145
Cox's Hill, TN 260
Crab Orchard, KY 257
Crab Orchard Road, KY 257
Craig, _____ (Lieutenant, 34th Infantry) 117

Craig, _____ (Sergeant, 28th infantry) 104
Craig, William 104, 105
Crampton's Gap, MD
 Battle of 248
The Crater
 Battle of 62
Crater, The, Petersburg, VA
 Battle of 53
Crawford, James 86
Crawford, Martin J. 218
Creek Bridge, TN 259
Creeks 5, 6
Cregnies, _____ (Lieutenant) 34
Crenshaw, _____ (Lieut., Hurt's Artillery Batter 231
Crenshaw, Edward 157, 158, 159
Crevillan (Crivillan), Andrew 93, 94
Crews, Charles C. 198
Critcher, John M. 59
Crittenden, George B. 74
Crittenden, Robert 114, 115
Crittendon (Crittenden), Thomas T. 254
Crockett, M. A. 117
Crook, George 188, 248, 251
Cross, B. F. 198
Cross, James R. 142
Cross Keys, VA
 Battle of 70, 71, 249
Cross Roads, GA 277
Cross Roads, SC 282
Crossland, Edward 29, 118
Crow Valley, GA 267
 Battle of 120
Crowe, James M. 56, 59
Croxton, John T. 29, 177, 284
Croxton's Raid 177
Crump, W. N. 148
Crumpler, Lewis H. 162, 169
Cuba 4
Culpeper, VA 43
Culver, Isaac F. 49, 51
Culver, J. F. 51
Cumberland Gap, TN 74, 103, 107, 109, 134, 135, 167, 168
Cumberland River 261
Cumbie, William M. 170
Cumming, Alfred 55, 79, 120, 124, 125, 222, 233

Cunningham, Arthur S. 59
Cunningham, Charles J. L. 156
Cunningham, Hugh 7
Cunningham, James D. 59, 60, 183
Cupp, Valentine 209
Curry, Joseph T. 158
Curry, John, 55
Curry, W. B. 104
Curtis, _____ (Captain) 7
Cusac, Peter 94
Cushing 12
Cypress Creek Bridge, AL 211

Dabney's Mills, VA 253
Dade, B. Frank 87
Dailey, William 238
Dallas, GA 206, 270
Dalton, GA 40, 77, 78, 83, 97, 99, 100, 103, 110, 113, 116, 120, 122, 123, 124, 126, 127, 133, 134, 141, 147, 149, 151, 157, 173, 196, 201, 203, 204, 210, 217, 234, 235, 236, 240, 242, 243, 244, 268, 269, 275, 276
 Battle of 73, 78, 81, 92, 142, 210, 228, 276
Dam No. 1. *See* Lee's Mill, VA: Battle of
Dandridge, E. P. 230
Dandridge, TN
 Battle of 137, 161, 178
Daniel, _____ (Sergeant, Hilliard's Legion) 170
Daniel, D. C. 154
Daniel, Junius 38
Daniel, T. C. 137
Daniel, W. L. 71
Daniel, Zach 161
Daniels, _____ (Private, Hilliard's Legion) 170
Dansby, John 127
Danville, AL 191, 193
Danville Cross Roads, KY 257
Danville, KY 257
Danville Road, KY 257
Darby, J. B. 80, 81
Darbytown Road, VA
 Battle of 73, 143, 145, 251, 252
 Battle of (Oct. 13, 1864) 252
D'Artaguette 4

Darwin, C. A. 64
Dauphin Island, AL 3, 27, 28
Davidson, David 187
Davidson, I. W. 85
Davidson, John W. 216
Davies, Thomas A. 187
Davis, B. A. 170
Davis, C. 75
Davis Cross Roads, GA 270
Davis, Edmund 112
Davis Gap, AL 263
Davis, J.T. 64
Davis, James E. 239
Davis, Jefferson 41, 59, 168, 182, 285
Davis, John O. 122
Davis, John W. 83, 85
Davis, Joseph Robert 175
Davis, Newton N. 92, 93, 94
Davis, Nicholas 7
Davis, Nick 82
Davis, T. W. W. 103
Davis, W. G. M. 214
Davis, W. R. 203
Daw, A. J. 170
Dawson, Reginald H. 66
Day's Gap, AL 261
Dayton, Patrick 125
de Narvaez, Pamfilo 1
De Soto, Diego 2
De Soto, Hernando 1, 2, 3
De Vaudreuil 4
DeArman, J. N. 145
Deas, Z. C. 72, 82, 86, 87, 88, 89, 90, 95, 126, 149, 150, 151, 173, 227, 228, 246
Deaton, John H. 54, 56
Decatur, AL 119, 189, 192, 193, 197, 199, 212, 222, 270, 276
  Battle of 139, 205
Decatur, GA 182, 272
  Battle of 184, 201, 243
Decatur Road, GA 272, 274
  Battle of 81
Decherd, TN
  Battle of 201, 202
Declaration of American Independence 18
Dedman, James M. 83, 84, 85
Deep Bottom, VA
  Battle of 70, 251

Deer Creek, MS
  Engagement at 128, 238
Deloach, Melbourn 93
Democraic Convention of 1860
  in Baltimore 12
  in Richmond, VA 12
Democratic Convention of 1860 9, 10
  Cincinnati Platform 10
  in Charleston, SC 12
Demopolis, AL 4, 85, 101, 122, 133, 141, 142, 156, 196, 215, 216, 223, 238
Denman, A. W. 137
Dennett, William B. 92, 93
Dent, S. H. 245, 246
Derby, A. J. 121
Derby, Charles A. 137
Derrill, Jack 107
Deserted House, VA 249
Desha, _____ (Captain) 7
Deshler, James 240
Detroit, MI 5
Devereux, John G. 191, 204, 218, 221
d'Iberville, Pierre L. 3
Dibrell, George G. 187, 204, 213
Dickey, James B. 155
Dickinson, A. J. 50
Dick's Ford, KY 257
Dickson, Barton 76
Dickson, John S. 118
Digby, W. H. 51
Dillard, J. W. 161
Dillard, John H. 170
Dinwiddie Court House, VA 217
Dixon, George E. 86
Dixon, John A. 102
Dobbs, S. P. 197, 199
Dodge, Greenville M. 25, 76, 101, 183, 189, 200, 261
Dodson, William E. 114, 115
Dog River 3
Donahue, Mike 174
Dondero, Louis 65
Donelson, Daniel Smith 168, 214
Donnell, Robert 87
Donoho, W. E. 54
Douglas, James P. 241
Douglas, Stephen A. 11, 12, 13
Dove, James H. 112
Dover, GA 197

Dowdell, James F. 122
Dowdle, James H. 98
Downman, _____ (Captain) 7
Drake, Joseph 97
Dranesville, VA
  Battle of 59, 60, 248
Dred Scott Decision 9, 10
Drewry's Bluff, VA 130, 132, 135, 161, 162, 174, 250
Droop Mountain, WV
  Battle of 249
Duck Creek Road, SC 280
Duck River, AL 107
Duck River, TN
  Battle of 178
Ducktown Road, GA 267
Duff, Michael, 55
Dug Gap, GA 268
Duggan, Martin 93
Duke, William H. 54
Dumas, Reuben 112
Dumfries, VA 171
Duncan, Johnson Kelly 93
Dunklin, James H. 114
Dunklin, William T. 137
Dunlap, TN 264
Dunlap, William H. C. 93
Dunn, Columbus 38
Dunnigan, John 175
Durham, S. A. 50
Durritt, T. J. 79
Dutch Gap, VA 130
Dwight, William 34, 148

Eady, Thomas H. 65
Eaglesville, AL 275
Eagleville, TN 112
Earle, Richard Gordon 7, 8, 182
Earle, Thomas W. 84
Early, Jubal A. 39, 46, 52, 66, 71, 163, 229, 250, 251, 252
  Raid on Washington 36
Easton, Thomas S. 111
Eastport, AL 213
Eastport, MS 275
Eaton, S. M. 195, 216
Ebenezer Church, GA 278
Eccanachaca, AL
  Battle of 6

Echols, James W. 116
Ector, Matthew Duncan 128
Eddins, Benjamin T. N. 132
Edmondson, T. P. 209
Edwards, _____ (Capt., 48th Inf.) 146
Edwards Depot, MS 101, 152, 155. *See also* Baker's Creek, MS: Battle of
Edwards, J. K. 73
Edwards, Jeptha 147, 148
Egypt, MS 194
Eilands, J. N. 89
Elizabethtown Road, KY 256
Elk River, TN 262, 265
Ellerbee, C. H. 128, 129
Elliott, J. T. 136
Elliott, James K. 85, 107, 108
Elliott's, Stephen, Jr. 251
Ellis, Reuben 145
Ellison, _____ (Captain) 253
Ellison, George H. 38
Ellison, Samuel 95
Elmira, NY 224
Elmore, _____ (Captain) 7
Elyton, AL 192
Emanuel, T. K. 225, 226
Emery, Winslow D. 234
Emrich, John P. 53, 56
Emuckfa, AL
  Battle of 6
Enfield Rifles 111
England, C. E. 195, 196
Enholm, George B. 93
Enriquez, Don Carlos 2
Enterprise, MS 119
Escambia River 193, 197
Espy, T. F. 127
Estes, John 119
Estes, W. N. 208, 209
Estissays, J. W. 101
Ethridge, William R. 136
Etowah County, AL 25
Etowah River, GA 269
Eubank, William 93
Eubanks, T. J. 145, 146
Eufaula, AL 242
Eutaw, AL 29
Evans, C. E. 122
Evans, James W. 51, 154
Evans, Nathan George "Shanks" 254
Evansport, VA 69

Everett, Edward 12
Everett, William S. 240
Ewell, Benjamin S. 200
Ewell, R. S. (Richard Stoddert) 38, 45, 47, 49, 51, 63, 64, 67, 71, 163, 183, 248, 249, 250, 253
Ewing, R. L. 146
Ezell, T. C. 125
Ezra Church, GA
   Battle of 81, 94, 103, 105, 117, 273

Fair Gardens, TN 266
Fair Grounds, KY 256
Fair Oaks Station, VA 37
Fair Oaks, VA
   Battle of 37, 53, 248. *See also* Seven Pines, VA: Battle of
Fairfax Court House, VA 44
Fairfield, AL 209
Faison, Alexander M. 156
Faith, W. C. 62
Falkner, Jefferson M. 211
Falling Waters, MD
   Battle of 249
Fannin, Agustus B. 163
Farley, _____ (Captain) 57
Farmington, MS 254
Farmington, TN 228, 265
   Battle of 82, 85, 88, 92, 94, 157, 228, 240, 245, 246
Farmville, VA 253
   Battle of 48, 145
Farragut, David Glasgow 27, 261, 274
Farris, D. C. 41
Farris, Robert C. 77
Faught, J. J. 88
Fauk, C. J. 73
Faulkner, Thomas L. 197
Fayette County, AL 96
Fayetteville, AL 205
Fayetteville, NC
   Battle of 184, 201
Fayetteville Road, GA 274
Fayetteville, SC 282
Fayetteville, TN 218
Feagin, Isaac B. 71, 72
Featherstone, Winfield Scott 127, 128, 225, 226

Felton, Thaddeus 118
Fergus, W. C. 132, 133
Ferguson, A. C. 117
Ferguson, A. C. 117
Ferguson, F. S. 225
Ferguson, N. R. E. 44
Ferguson, Samuel W. 128
Ferguson, Samuel Wragg 128, 183, 204, 205, 221
Ferguson, W. A. 210
Ferrell, George A. 231, 232
Ferris, C. C. 40
Field, Charles William 43, 73, 138, 144, 146
Field, J. H. 212
Fielder, S. K. 80
Fielder, Sherman K. 79, 80
Fields, George 62
Fifteen-mile Station, FL 194, 215
Figg, Robert W. 197
Figures, H. S. 145
Finegan, Patrick 175
Finley, James L. 228
First Alabama Volunteers (Mexican War) 7
Fisher, William T. 169
Fisher's Hill, VA 163, 252
Fishing Creek, KY
   Battle of 73
Fitts, William M. 202
Five Forks, VA
   Battle of 253
Flat Gap, TN 188
Flat Lick, TN 168
Fletcher, Richard T. 62, 63
Flevin, James H. 153
Flewellen, James 126
Flint River 274
Florence, AL 5, 101, 179, 190, 204, 210, 266, 276
Florence, SC 203
Flournoy, _____ (Private, Hilliard's Legion) 170
Flournoy, Augustus S. 48, 50
Flowers, Abner 127
Floyd, John 6
Floyd, John B. 197
Folk, E. 68
Foote, Andrew Hull 254

Ford, _____ (Captain, 28th Infantry) 104
Forked Deer River 190
Forked Deer, TN 254
Forney, D. P. 185
Forney, George Hoke 174, 175
Forney, John H. 59, 61, 63, 77, 86, 120, 123, 128, 133, 205, 226, 238
Forney, William H. 8, 56, 59, 60, 61, 68, 79, 106, 125
Forrest, Jeffrey E. 199
Forrest, Nathan Bedford 25, 26, 27, 29, 94, 110, 111, 180, 187, 191, 192, 193, 195, 199, 200, 201, 202, 206, 208, 213, 214, 219, 221, 253, 254, 258, 260, 261, 267, 268, 270, 273, 274, 275, 276, 279, 284
Forsyth, Charles 38
Forsyth, GA 182
Fort Barrancas, FL 6, 8, 28, 35, 36, 192, 193, 194
Fort Blakely, AL 28, 165, 193, 243, 284
  Siege of 28, 158, 165
Fort Bowyer, AL 6
Fort Branch, NC 239
Fort Clifton, VA 229
Fort Deposit, AL 190
Fort Donelson, TN 101, 187, 254, 260
  Capture of 30, 96, 97, 100
Fort Filippe 4
Fort Gaines, AL 24, 27, 28, 85, 86, 165, 177, 224, 274
Fort Gibson, MS 233
Fort Harrison, VA
  Battle of 70, 73, 145
Fort Heiman, TN 100, 276
Fort Henry, TN 97, 100, 101, 222, 223
Fort Louis (de la Louisiana) 3
Fort McRee, FL 8
Fort Mims, AL 3, 5
Fort Mitchell, AL 70
Fort Morgan, AL 6, 24, 27, 30, 36, 86, 92, 134, 222, 224, 225, 274
Fort Pemberton, MS
  Battle of 151
Fort Pickens, FL 253
Fort Pillow, TN 33, 36, 86, 174, 175, 200, 268

Fort Powell, AL 87, 224
Fort Sanders, TN 266
Fort Stedman, VA 253
Fort Stoddard 5
Fort Tombecbee 4
Fort Toulouse 4
Fort Tyler, AL 24, 29, 284
Fort Warren, MA 224
Foster, _____ 255
Foster, _____ (Private, 33rd Infantry) 114
Foster, George W. 132, 133
Foster, J. A. 106
Foster, R. S. 43
Foster, Thomas J. 26, 99
Fosterville, GA
  Battle of 178
Fosterville, TN 181, 202, 212, 264
Fowler, John 97, 98, 99
Fowler, W. H. 238
Fowler, W. P. 93
Fowler's Farm, TN 181
Fox, Matthew 48, 49
France 1
Francis, John C. 107, 108
Frank, Thomas 34
Franklin, GA 274
Franklin, N. S. 47
Franklin, R. L. 47
Franklin Road, TN 255
Franklin, TN 185, 260
  Battle of 30, 33, 36, 74, 76, 77, 79, 81, 87, 90, 92, 94, 97, 100, 102, 103, 105, 111, 116, 118, 139, 140, 147, 149, 154, 156, 158, 238, 245, 279
Franklin, William B. 248
Frayser, R. Dudley 159, 237
Frayser's Farm, VA
  Battle of 53, 54, 56, 57, 59, 60, 61, 62, 68, 69, 96, 171, 248
Frazer, John Wesley 103, 242
Frazier, J. W. 53
Fredericksburg, VA 69, 230
  Battle of 30, 36, 37, 40, 42, 46, 48, 50, 55, 59, 61, 63, 64, 65, 66, 67, 70, 72, 96, 98, 137, 143, 144, 146, 171, 172, 229, 230, 231, 249
Freeman, George C. 139, 140
Freeman, Joel B. 159
Freeman's Ford, VA 41

Fremont, John C. 71, 249
French, _____ (Corporal, Hilliard's Legion) 170
French, James E. 170
French, Samuel Gibbs 69, 128, 234, 240, 243, 245
French, William H. 249, 250
Front Royal, VA
   Battle of 70, 248
Fry, Birkett D. 66, 67, 68
Fugitive Save Law 14
Fuller, Charles A. 133, 166, 226, 229
Fulmer, _____ (Private, 24th Infantry) 93
Fulton, AL 213
Fulton, John S. 246
Funkstown, MD
   Battle of 249
Fussell's Mill, VA
   Battle of 70, 145

Gaddes, Robert 55
Gadsden, AL 193, 196, 197, 198, 244, 275
Gaffney, D. E. 139
Gage, Charles P. 232
Gage, Joseph S. 188
Gaines, A.L. 88
Gaines, Abner C. 87
Gaines, CSS 27, 274
Gaines, Edmund Pendleton 5
Gaines, F. Y. 185
Gaines, John F. 203
Gaines' Mill, VA 171
   Battle of 40, 41, 44, 45, 46, 48, 50, 53, 54, 56, 57, 59, 60, 62, 67, 70, 96, 97, 171, 229. *See also* Cold Harbor, VA: Second Battle of (1864)
Gaines, R. R. 185
Gainesville, AL 187, 192, 193, 196
Gaither, J. R. 105
Galesville Road, TN 266
Gallatin Road, TN 255
Gamble, J. C. 51
Gammell, George W. 143, 144
Ganavan, James 54
Gardner, Franklin 34, 82, 89, 95, 101, 118, 126, 148, 149, 150, 155, 173, 175, 176, 187, 194, 215, 245, 261

Gardner, John R. 147
Garfield, James A. 207
Garland, L. C. 177
Garland, R. W. 74, 75
Garland, Samuel 229
Garner, George G. 179, 185
Garner, Thomas 76
Garrard, Kenner 178, 266, 274
Garrard, W. W. 109
Garrison, D. H. 64
Garrison, J. D. 54
Garrison's Fork, TN 158
Garrity, James 227, 228
Garrott, Isham W. 83, 84, 91, 107, 109, 142
Garvin, John S. 46, 47, 96, 97, 98, 150
Gary, George W. 137, 138
Gary, J. M. 225
Gaston, Oliver B. 187
Gates, John C. 70, 72
Gates, William C. 144
Gayle, Bristow B. 64, 97
Geddes, Robert 54
Gee, James T. 225, 238
George, J. W. 125
Georgia Campaign 81, 94, 100. *See also* Atlanta, GA: Campaign for
Georgia Military School 272
Georgia Railroad 273
Georgia Units
   Artillery
      Girardey's Battery 233
   Cavalry
      3rd Regiment 179
      Phillips Legion 217
Gettysburg Campaign 61, 138, 172
Gettysburg, PA
   Battle of 36, 38, 39, 40, 42, 43, 44, 47, 51, 53, 55, 56, 58, 59, 61, 63, 64, 65, 66, 67, 68, 70, 72, 97, 98, 137, 138, 143, 144, 145, 146, 171, 229, 230, 231, 249
Gibbs, _____ 7
Gibraltar, Spain 31
Gibson, James M. 170
Gibson, John H. 113, 115, 155, 219
Gibson, John H. (T.) 219
Gibson, Randell Lee 28, 87, 112, 158, 284
Gibson, W. C. 95

Gilbert, J. E. 150, 151
Gilbreath, Montgomery 147, 148
Gilchrist, J. M. (N.) 44, 47
Gilchrist, James C. 139
Gilder, Preston S. 128, 129
Gillis, Dougle W. 56, 57
Gilmer, J. N. 169
Gilmore, Quincy A. 135
Ginnery, William 94
Girard, AL 165, 193
   Battle of 237
Girardey, Victor Jean Baptiste 245
Given, William 218
Gladden, Adley Hogan 86, 88, 95, 149, 150, 227, 245
Gladden, W. H. 121
Glasgow, KY 180, 228
Glendale, VA
   Battle of 54, 57, 62, 248
Glenn, H. V. 73
Glover, H. W. 70
Goff, J. M. 46
Golding's Farm, VA
   Battle of 248
Goldsboro Road, NC 283
Goldsborough, Louis Malesherbes 254
Goldthwait, J. G. 113, 115, 160
Goldthwaite, George 193
Goldthwaite, R. W. 140
Golgotha, GA 270
Goliad Massacre 7
Golightly, R. C. 145, 146
Gonzalez, _____ (Captain) 29
Goode, Burton 47
Goode, Charles T. 213
Goodgame, John C. 64, 65, 66, 98
Goodrich, L. L. 210
Goodson, Joab 137
Goodwin, Edwin 118, 119
Goodwin, William S. 139
Goodwyn, Albert T. 159
Goolsby, C. D. 105
Gordon, Jesse A.P. 135
Gordon, A. M. 50, 51
Gordon, Augustus M. 48, 50
Gordon, H. R. 223
Gordon, James A. 135
Gordon, John B. 37, 45, 46, 49, 64, 97, 130, 161, 253
Gordon, P. 135

Gordon, R. H. 62
Gordon, W. H. P. 121
Gordonsville, VA 72
Goring, J. A. 133
Goshen, AL 275
Gould, J. McKee 84
Govan, Daniel C. 242
Gracie, Archibald, Jr. 62, 130, 132, 134, 135, 136, 161, 162, 163, 167, 168, 169, 170, 174
Gracie's Salient, VA 132
Graham, Flavius J. 187
Graham, James H. 103, 104
Graham, John 211
Graham's Turnout, SC 281
Granbury, Hiram Bronson 242
Grand Gulf, MS 175
   Battle of 175
Granger, _____ (Col. USA) 256
Granger, Gordon 27, 91, 199, 216, 254, 261, 262, 274
Grant, Ulysses S. 177, 250, 251, 252, 253, 254, 261
Grant's Pass, AL 85, 225
Grassy Mound, KY 256
Grave Level Church, GA 275
Gravelly Run, VA 253
Gravelly Springs, AL 28
Gravestein, GA 278
Gray, G. H. 134
Grayson, John Breckinridge 244
Great Britain 5
Greeley, Horace 15, 16, 18, 20
Green, (Private, 8th Cav.) 196
Green, _____ (Private, 8th Cav.) 195
Green, James R. 93
Green, Martin Edwin 91
Green Meadows, GA 271
Green River 179
Greene, A. C. 81
Greene, Alexander A. 122, 123
Greene County, AL 3
Greene, Joel G. 122
Greene, Moses B. 122
Greene, R. M. 51
Greene, William N. 137
Greensboro, NC 31, 95, 97, 100, 103, 106, 107, 149, 154, 182, 204, 210, 285
Greenville, AL 217

Greenwood, FL 216
Greenwood, J. T. 69
Greer, C. P. 116
Gregg, John 29, 30
Gregg, Maxcy 71
Gregor, Robert M. 74
Grenada, MS 34, 174, 194, 207
Grenfell, G. St. Leger 190
Grice, E. 73
Grierson, Benjamin 182
Grierson's Raid 182
Griffin, John W. 54
Griffitts, P. L. 82
Grimes, Bryan 48
Grimmett, William 143, 144
Griswaldville, GA 276
Groveton, VA 41
Grower, William T. C. 192, 222
Grumpier, Lewis H. 161
Guerry, P. V. 70, 71
Guild, Lafayette 41, 172
Gulley, E. S. 83
Gully, Ezekiel 128
Gulp's, GA 270
Gunter, William T. 219
Gunter's Landing, AL 26, 267
Guntersville, AL 26, 190, 197, 209, 212
Gurley, Frank B. 187, 255
Gurley's Tank, AL 189
Guy's Gap, TN 262
   Action at 206, 207
Gwin (Gwynne), Andrew D. 150
Gwin, J. H. 80

Hadley's Bend, TN 261
Hagan, James 178, 180, 181, 182, 184, 185, 186, 188, 197, 199, 200, 201, 202, 203, 212, 217, 218
Hagood, R. H. 82
Hailey, J. C. 106
Hale, H. W. 51
Hale, S. F. 62
Hale, Smith D. 147
Hale, Stephen H. 62
Haley, John W. 133
Hall, _____ (Private, Hilliard's Legion) 169
Hall, Bolling, Jr. 161, 167, 168, 169, 170

Hall, C. 169
Hall, C. K. 127
Hall, Crenshaw 161
Hall, J. A. 93
Hall, J. B. 93
Hall, J. M. 38
Hall, James A. 93
Hall, John E. 161
Hall, John R. 121
Hall, Joseph 93
Hall, Josephus M. 44, 46, 47, 48, 51, 65, 98
Hall, Thomas D. 205
Hall, W. A. 54
Hall, W. T. 39
Hall, William 140
Hall, William S. 202
Hallonquist, James H. 234, 243
Hall's Mill, MS 187
Halltown, VA 251
Hambrick, Joseph M. 187, 188, 255
Hamburg, AL 191
Hamilton, Thomas 94
Hamilton, W. P. 232
Hamilton's Crossing, VA 231
Hamlin, Hannibal 25
Hammett, B. F. 115
Hammond, J. Henry 79, 80
Hammond, P. Lee 225
Hampton, Thomas W. 187
Hampton, VA 36
Hampton, Wade 163, 210, 213, 214, 217, 281
Hancock, J. B. 50
Hancock, Winfield S. 69, 250, 251, 252
Handley, James M. 141, 142
Hanley, _____ 93
Hanna, John 118
Hanna, John M. 106
Hannon, _____ (Captain) 54
Hannon, Moses Wright 191, 203, 204, 217, 221
Hanover Court House, VA
   Battle of 70
Hanover Junction, VA
   Battle of 137, 145
Hansell, _____ (Captain) 26
Hanson, Roger Weightman 129, 131
Hardaway, J. T. 130, 131

Hardaway, Robert A. 229, 230
Hardcastle, Aaron B. 75
Hardee, William Joseph 30, 31, 52, 74,
　79, 92, 108, 110, 112, 114, 123,
　128, 129, 131, 140, 179, 180,
　183, 185, 186, 207, 210, 211,
　213, 214, 218, 239, 240, 242,
　273, 274, 283
Harder, William W. 136
Hardie, Joseph 220
Harding Pike, TN 260
Hardwick, B. B. 243
Hardwick, William M. 145, 146
Hardy, H. H. 38
Hardy, John 176, 177
Hare's Hill, VA
　Battle of 164
Hargrove, A. C. 240
Hargrove, G. H. 240
Hargroves, Lemuel 126
Harper, _____ (John or Joseph) 80
Harper, L. J. T. (M. J. T.) 61
Harper, M. J. T. 59
Harper, M. L. 73
Harper, Micajah 95
Harper's Ferry, WV 40, 53, 172, 248
　Capture of 56, 59, 61, 137, 143
Harpeth Shoals, TN 260
Harrell, C. L. 158, 159
Harrell, S. J. 159
Harrell, William V. 220
Harris, Robert T. 158
Harris, _____ (Private, Hilliard's
　Legion) 170
Harris, _____ (Sergeant, Hilliard's
　Legion) 170
Harris, John G. 83
Harris, John W. 74, 75
Harris, Lemuel 62
Harris, N. H. 51
Harris, O. M. 55
Harris, R. A. 176
Harris, R. T. 159
Harris, W. C. 136
Harris, William 115
Harrison, James 195, 196
Harrison, Thomas 209
Harrisonburg, VA 249
　Battle of 247
Hart, B. R. 88

Hart, Benjamin R. 87, 90
Hart, R. D. 135
Hartford, USS 27
Hartsuff, George L. 214
Hartwell, William 171
Harwell, J. S. 169
Hascall, Milo S. 202
Hassell, Maynard 227
Hatch, _____ (Major, 59th Inf.) 162
Hatch, Edward 190
Hatch, Lemuel D. 195, 196
Hatch, T. A. 121
Hatcher's Run, VA
　Battle of 130, 132, 136, 161, 162, 163,
　174, 252
Hatchie Bridge, MS 256
　Battle of 133
Hatchie River 237
Hatten, W. E. 115
Hatteras, USS 31, 260
Havana, Cuba 4
Hawes, James Morrison 148
Hawkins, A. 130, 132
Hawkins, W. M. 103
Hawthorn, Alexander Travis 114
Hayes, Archer 59
Haynes, Z. 55
Haynie, John D. 225
Hays, James L. 148
Hayward, SC 280
Hazard, John B. 92, 93
Hazel River 59
Hazel River, VA
　Battle of 70, 71
Hazlewood, Marion F. 95
Head, _____ (Private, Hilliard's
　Legion) 170
Healey, Robert J. 81, 82
Hearin, W. J. 124
Hebert, Loius 123, 225, 226, 233
Heiman, Adolphus 97, 101, 223
Heintzelman, Samuel P. 248
Helm, Benjamin Hardin 130, 131
Helvenston, Alexander H. 74, 75
Hembree, A. 175
Henderson, TN 207
Hendrix, J. C. 161
Henegan, Charles S. 120
Henry, Hugh W. 90
Henry, Samuel 56, 57, 60

Herbert, Hilary A. 53, 55
Herbert, J. 55
Herndon, Thomas H. 120
Hester, James T. 90, 92, 141
Heth, Henry 67, 68, 135, 175, 208, 242, 248, 249
Hewitt, G. W. 103
Hewlett, W. A. 183, 205
Hexauer, Win 45
Hiawassee River 130
Hickory Hill, SC 280
Hiett, Robert Y. 167, 168
Higgins, Edward 86, 171, 194, 224, 225, 226
Higgins, J. J. 77
Higgins, William L. 120
High Bridge, VA
    Battle of 253
High, Joseph B. 81, 82
High Point, NC 116
Higley, John H. 123, 124, 128, 129, 134
Higley, William H. 93
Hill, _____ (Private, 43rd Inf) 136
Hill, _____ (Private, Hilliard's Legion) 170
Hill, A. P. 57, 58, 97, 171, 172, 250, 251, 253
Hill, B. A. 70
Hill, Benjamin Jefferson 79, 142, 149, 151
Hill, D. B. 233
Hill, D. H. (Daniel Harvey) 37, 45, 46, 50, 64, 65, 67, 112, 114, 120, 229, 230, 231, 239, 241
Hill, E. Y. 56, 57
Hill, GA 277
Hill, James 233
Hill, L. H. 163
Hill, R. H. 70, 71
Hill, R. J. 88
Hill, W. F. 73
Hill, William 76
Hillabee, AL 6
Hilliard, H. W. 167, 213
Hill's Gap, TN 264
Hill's Point, VA 137
Hillsboro Pike, TN 258
Hillsboro Road, NC 284

Hindman, Thomas C. 72, 82, 105, 127, 151, 179, 186, 188, 209, 228, 232, 246, 266
Hines, D. V. 69
Hinton, A. S. 159
Hippler, Charles, Jr. 54
Hiwassee, TN 264
Hix, Mason 169
Hobbs, Thomas H. 56, 57
Hobson, E. Lafayette 44, 45, 46, 47, 48
Hodge, George B. 102
Hodges, William 75
Hodgson, Joseph 193
Hodgson, W. Irving 245
Hodo, D. C. 82
Hoistein, W. H. 116
Hoke, Robert Frederick 72, 239
Holcombe, Edward P. 77, 78
Holcombe, Thomas H. 62
Holland, Gill G. 158, 159
Holland, Sid 158
Hollinsworth (Hollingsworth), William P. 82
Hollow Tree Gap, TN 279
Holloway, E. M. 222
Holly Springs, MS 211
Holly, W. F. 170
Holly, W. W. 125
Hollywood, AL 113
Holmes, F. H. 69
Holmes, Henry 210
Holmes, Theophilus Hunter 69
Holston River, TN 265
Holt, John H. 167, 168, 169
Holt, T. G. 214
Holtzclaw, James Thadeus 28, 79, 80, 81, 113, 120, 121, 124, 125, 126, 157, 160, 165
Home, E. W. 105
Homer, William M. 226
Hood, John Bell 41, 42, 72, 73, 76, 78, 81, 90, 92, 94, 97, 100, 102, 105, 109, 110, 111, 113, 118, 121, 123, 124, 125, 127, 128, 129, 137, 138, 141, 143, 144, 146, 147, 149, 151, 154, 155, 156, 157, 184, 187, 188, 189, 199, 201,

204, 228, 234, 236, 237, 238,
   239, 240, 242, 243, 244, 246,
   273, 276, 279
Hooker, George W. 49
Hooker, Joseph 43, 66, 212, 248, 249
Hoole, James L. 244
Hooper, Charles M. 171
Hoover's Gap, TN 124, 157, 158,
   198, 208, 209, 236, 262
Hopkins, Francis M. 104
Horn, Daniel H. 114
Horne, Elijah W. 94
Hornsboro, SC 282
Horse Cave, KY 179, 255
Horse Shoe Bend, AL
   Battle of 6
Hotchkiss, T. R. 242
Housatonic, USS 86
House, J. T. 142
Houston, Hugh L. 81, 82
Houston, W. A. 117
Houston, William W. 108
Howard, H. M. 54
Howard, J. N. 55
Howard, James R. 130, 208
Howard, Oliver O. 212, 268, 270
Howard, W. 80
Howell, J. C. 154
Hoxton, Llewellyn 225, 228, 229, 246
Hubbard, George C. 119
Huddleston, J. L. 159
Hudgins, B. A. 130
Hudgins, L. D. 130
Hudson, M. G. 93
Hufham, _____ (Private, Hilliard's
   Legion) 169
Hugan, B. J. 175
Huger Battery, AL 27
Huger, Benjamin 37, 137
Huger, Daniel E. 95, 165
Huggins, John T. 38
Hugh, M. 54
Hughes, Adolphus A. 100, 145, 146
Hughes, T. M. 135
Hughes, W. L. 109
Hughes, William B. 225
Hughston, T. F. 80
Huguley, George W. 161, 167, 169
Hulls, Alfred C. 112

Humes, William Young Conn 206, 208,
   209, 212, 213, 214
Humphrey, Benjamin Grubb 176
Humphreys, Andrew A. 43, 253
Humphries, W. S. 75
Hundley, Daniel R. 109
Hundley, William H. 200
Hungerford, Walter H. 158
Hunley, Peter F. 79, 81, 121
Hunt, Thomas H. 130, 131
Hunt, W. C. 48
Hunt, William 118
Hunt, William H. 97
Hunter, C. H. 65
Hunt's Mill, AL 191
Huntsville, AL 7, 24, 68, 81, 150, 188,
   189, 218, 254
Huntsville, TN 135
Hurlbut, Stephen A. 106
Hurricane Creek, TN 258, 261
Hurt, William B. 230
Hurtel, C. P. 93
Husbands, J. L. 89
Hutchinson, A. H. 121
Hutchisson, J. B. 225
Hutchisson, James T. 233
Hutto, J. C. 150
Hutto, Joseph 169
Hutton, William B. 172

Illinois Units
   Infantry
      75th Regiment 206, 207
Indiana Units
   Infantry
      17th Regiment 53
Ingalls, Osborne M. 228
Inge, Richard F. 79, 80
Inge, W. M. 183
Ingersol, Andrew J. 86
Ingraham, A. J. 201
Inman, Alexander 88
Inzer, John W. 158, 159, 160
Irby, Thomas E. 7, 53, 54
Irish, Milton 7
Iron Furnace, TN 260
Irvine, TN 214
Irwin, L. F. 125

Irwin, R. B. 238
Irwinsville, GA 285
Isbell, W. A. 100, 101
Isham's Ford, GA 272
Island No. 10, MO 33, 34, 151, 254
Island of Massacre (Dauphin Island), AL 3
Iuka, MS 121, 211, 221, 255, 262
 Battle of 122
Iverson, Alfred 38, 51, 65, 183
Ives, John 93
Ives, Samuel S. 100, 101, 102, 118, 119, 147, 149

J. W. Wilder (schooner) 222
Jacinto, MS 211
Jacksboro, GA 278
Jackson, _____ (Capt., 45th Inf.) 139
Jackson, _____ (Private, Hilliard's Legion) 169, 170
Jackson, A. 73
Jackson, A. M. 81, 87, 216, 227
Jackson, AL 26
Jackson, Andrew 5, 6
Jackson Bridge, FL 215
Jackson, J. T. 121
Jackson, James 100, 101, 139, 143, 144, 146
Jackson, Jesse L. 170
Jackson, John 73
Jackson, John A. 124
Jackson, John King 77, 79, 82, 86, 92, 93, 101, 111, 193, 206
Jackson, Joseph 54
Jackson, Lewis E. 74, 75
Jackson, MS 101, 119, 128, 130, 131, 151, 154, 155, 175, 182, 183, 225, 235, 261, 262, 267
 Battle of 100, 110, 112, 118, 174, 175
Jackson Road, TN 254
Jackson, Thomas "Stonewall" J. 9, 37, 40, 41, 44, 45, 46, 50, 54, 57, 64, 67, 70, 71, 72, 96, 97, 143, 145, 146, 171, 230, 248, 249
Jackson, TN 36, 86, 178, 179, 187, 258
Jackson, Warren A. 95
Jackson, William Hicks 29, 177, 207, 224, 262, 284

Jacksonburg, AL 209
Jacksonville, SC 282
Jamaica 31
James, Gilliam 46
James, John 62
James River 43, 138, 144, 147, 232
James River Fleet 31
Jamestown, TN 74
Jamestown, VA 1
Jansen, Augustus 53, 54
Jasper, TN 209
Jefferson Pike, TN 258
Jefferson, Thomas 18
Jefferson, TN 259
Jemison, R., Jr. 26
Jenifer, Walter H. 193, 215
Jenkins, David T. 163
Jenkins, Micah 69
Jenkins, T. F. 210
Jenkins, T. G. 52
Jenkins, Thomas F. 203, 204
Jenks, John J. 226
Jennings, James 55
Jennison, George A. 92, 93, 94
Jewett, John F. 86
Jewett, O. S. 124
Jimtown, KY 213
Jimtown, TN 213
Johnson, _____ (Capt., 63rd Inf.) 165
Johnson, A. H. 181
Johnson, B. B. 36
Johnson, Bradley 45, 64
Johnson, Bushrod R. 97, 101, 104, 132, 136, 161, 162, 163, 170, 174, 236, 240, 243, 246, 262
Johnson, Calloway 125
Johnson, Dick 189
Johnson, Edward 127, 276, 279
Johnson, G. W. 44
Johnson, J. M. 174, 175
Johnson, J. S. 218
Johnson, James H. 122
Johnson, John G. 143
Johnson, Joseph (47th Inf) 143
Johnson, Lewis 276
Johnson, Lewis W. 61, 159
Johnson, Richard W. 182, 218
Johnson, S. S. 195
Johnson, W. C. 136

Johnson, W. M. 117
Johnson, W. W. 73
Johnson, William A. 189, 190, 266
Johnson's Island, Ohio 92
Johnsonville, TN 193, 194
Johnston, Albert Sidney 9, 52, 254
Johnston, B. 148
Johnston, Charles G. 86
Johnston, George D. 89, 90, 95
Johnston, George Doherty 151
Johnston, J.F. 80
Johnston, Joseph E. 9, 31, 36, 40, 41,
    50, 55, 57, 59, 60, 69, 73, 76, 78,
    81, 83, 85, 90, 92, 96, 97, 98,
    100, 101, 102, 105, 106, 107,
    115, 119, 120, 123, 124, 125, 129,
    139, 147, 148, 149, 151, 152,
    153, 154, 155, 157, 173, 176,
    186, 188, 192, 201, 205, 210,
    213, 218, 228, 234, 239, 240,
    242, 243, 246, 248, 261, 262,
    268, 269, 270, 273, 276, 283, 285
Johnston, Joseph T. 137
Johnston, Lewis W. 59
Johnston, M. E. 218
Johnston, Miles E. 218
Johnston, S. C. 159
Johnston, S. S. 196
Joiner, J. J. 164
Joiner, Vincent H. 112
Jolly, John J. 134, 135, 136
Jones, Allen T. 44
Jones' Bluff, AL 4
Jones, Bushrod 81, 110, 112, 121, 125,
    157, 158, 159, 160, 174
Jones County, AL 215
Jones, E. P. 47
Jones, Egbert J. 7, 40
Jones' Ferry, SC 182
Jones, Fielder A. 182
Jones, Frank 127
Jones, G. P. 51
Jones, G. W. W. 75, 76
Jones, George C. 169
Jones, H. L. 51
Jones, H. P. 229, 230
Jones, J. 80
Jones, J. H. 154
Jones, J. P. 34
Jones, J. T. 77

Jones, John A. 137, 138, 139
Jones, John H. 113
Jones, R. A. 115
Jones, R. M. 7
Jones, R. S. 73
Jones, Robert T. 64, 83
Jones, S. 223
Jones, Sam 33, 77, 111, 154, 166, 185,
    202, 208, 211, 219, 224
Jones, Thomas M. 106
Jones, Wesley 178
Jones, William P. 170
Jonesboro, GA 274, 276
    Battle of 73, 77, 78, 81, 83, 87, 90, 92,
    107, 109, 116, 120, 126, 139, 141,
    201, 203, 204, 210, 227, 235
Jordan, C. S. 105
Jordan, Charles H. 103, 104
Jordan, Thomas 211
Joseph, _____ (Lieut., 48th Inf.) 146
Judge, Thomas J. 68
Jug Tavern, GA 274
Justice, Joseph H. 79, 80

Kane, Michael 55
Kautz, August V. 252
Kavanaugh, B. 182
Kearsarge, USS 31
Keeling, R. H. 64
Keenum, Willis 98
Keeton, James N. 63
Keigwin, James 109
Keith, J. J. 111, 112
Kellar, James 5
Kelly, D. C. 275
Kelly, D. W. 120
Kelly, John 175
Kelly, John Herbert 29, 30, 207, 209,
    212, 214
Kelly, T. A. 55
Kelly's Ford, VA
    Battle of 30, 97, 249, 250
Kendrick, J. C. 122
Kendrick, Jopel C. 122
Kendrick, W. B. 134
Kenesaw, GA
    Battle of 33, 77, 81, 114, 157, 182,
    243

Kenesaw Mountain, GA
  Battle of 73, 83, 234, 236, 240, 245, 270
Kennedy, _____ 45
Kennedy, A. 72
Kennedy, Joshua 53, 54
Kent, James 137
Kentucky Campaign 81, 90, 92, 113, 184, 213, 232, 233, 234
Kentucky Line, TN 255
Kentucky Units
  Artillery
    Cobb's Battery 232
  Cavalry
    1st Regiment 180
    9th Regiment 212
  Infantry
    2nd Regiment 131
    4th Regiment 131
    6th Regiment 131
Kerns, James 179
Kernstown, VA
  Battle of 43
Kershaw, Joseph Brevard 176
Ketchum, Charles T. 124, 125
Ketchum, William H. 7, 204, 227
Key, T. J. 234
Key, Thomas 242
Kidd, A. J. 79, 80
Kidd, Reuben V. 40
Kilpatrick, Judson 182, 199, 201, 274, 275, 283
Kimball, T. A. 75
Kimbell, John C. 111, 112, 113, 158, 160
Kimbell, Thomas J. 92, 94
Kimbrough, George R. 82, 83
Kimbrough, TN 258
King, _____ (Private, Hilliard's Legion) 170
King, D. R. 145
King, J. Horace 56, 57, 58, 59
King, W. D. 184
King, William R. 8
King, William T. 137
King's Creek, MS
  Action at 183
  Battle of 204, 205
Kingston, GA 182
  Battle of 8, 205
Kingston Road, GA 269

Kingston, TN 209, 214, 266
  Battle of 184
Kinston, NC 239, 283
  Battle of (March 1865) 83, 87, 95, 105, 107, 109, 116, 141, 149
Kirk, James 60
Kirkland, John. A. 47
Kirkland, Micajah 170
Kirkpatrick, M. L. 201, 202
Knight, T. A. 213
Knighton, Joseph H. 129
Knox, Allen B. 133
Knox, David 105
Knox, J. C. 121
Knox, Samuel L. 33, 34, 35, 36
Knoxville Road, TN 265
Knoxville, TN 52, 74, 84, 91, 108, 109, 135, 168, 186, 219, 236, 265
  Battle of 70, 137, 143, 145, 178, 184, 242
  Siege of 134, 161, 201, 265
Kolb, R. F. 242
Kyle, Osceola 141

La Fayette, GA 275
La Grange, AL 118
La Grange, Oscar Hugh 269
La Grange, TN 182
La Salle 3
Lafayette, GA 220, 263
  Battle of 178, 195, 220
Lafayette, TN 186, 188, 212
  Battle of 206
Lagrange, Oscar H. 29
Lake Erie 15
Lamar, L. Q. C. 57
Lambert, R. A. 80
Lambert, William 117
Lambeth, C. H. 68
Lamborn, Charles P. 209
Lamb's Ferry Road, AL 190
Lampkin, Alexander W. 170
Lampley, Harris D. 139, 140, 174
Lancaster, KY 257
Lancaster Road, KY 257

Lancey, _____ (Private, Hilliard's
    Legion) 170
Lane, _____ 53
Lane, R. H. 156, 157
Lane, W. H. 54
Lanford, John B., 136
Lang, J. 161
Lanier, Thomas C. 132, 133, 134
Lankford, A. R. 80, 125, 126
Lankford, N. 93
Lansford, SC 282
Larey, P. H. 50
Larkin, J. R. 125
Larkinsville, AL 188
Larry, W. R. 89
Lary, Washington T. 193
Latham, Hugh 106
Latham, James A. 128
Latimar's Mill, GA
    Action at 212
Lattimer, GA 270
Lauderdale County, AL 28
Lavergne, TN 110, 111, 185, 202, 206,
    207, 219, 256, 258, 259, 260
    Battle of 201
Law, Evander McIvor 41, 42, 43, 72,
    73, 136, 137, 138, 143, 144, 145,
    146, 147
Law, Junius A. 166
Lawless, William 65
Lawrence, _____ (Major) 6
Lawrence, W. H. 195
Lawrenceburg, KY 257
Lawrenceburg, TN 279
Lawtonville, SC 280
Lay, John F. 180, 211
Lea, Benjamin J. 206
Leach, J. M. 122
Leadbetter, Danville 52, 134, 135, 141,
    208, 254
Leadbetter, G. C. 147
Leakesville, AL 216
Leary, Patrick 55
Leary, William 87, 89, 90
Lebanon, TN 202, 211
LeBaron, William M. 92
Ledyard, _____ (Capt., 7th Cav.)
    194
Ledyard, E. D. 194
Ledyard, E. T. 178, 181

Lee, Wayne E. 157
Lee, Daniel 125
Lee, Edgar G. 239
Lee, Fitzhugh 132, 253
Lee, George W. 54
Lee, George Washington Custis 163, 174
Lee, Jackson 170
Lee, M. B., Mrs. 207
Lee, Moses 145, 146
Lee, Robert E. 9, 29, 30, 37, 38, 40, 41,
    43, 44, 46, 56, 58, 61, 63, 66, 96, 99,
    132, 136, 139, 144, 146, 162, 172,
    175, 178, 181, 231, 232, 248, 249,
    250, 251, 252, 253
Lee, S. D. 35, 81, 83, 84, 85, 90, 91, 92,
    96, 103, 105, 108, 109, 110, 117,
    124, 127, 141, 142, 151, 183, 196,
    200, 205, 226, 229, 233, 237, 243,
    265, 267, 273, 274
Lee, W. E. 158, 159
Lee, W. J. 186
Lee, William 40, 59, 60
Lee, Z. E. 159
Lee's Cross Roads, GA 268
Lee's Mill, VA
    Battle of 71
Leet's Mill, GA 267
Leftwich, W. W. 40
Leland, John D. 132
Lenderman, N. B. 130, 131
Lenoir, _____ (Captain) 186
Lenoir, T. M. 186
Leonard, John O. 89
Leslie, Adolph W. 175
Letcher, John 19
Lewis, _____ (Captain, 2nd Cav.) 182
Lewis, _____ (Private, Hilliard's
    Legion) 170
Lewis, H. L. D. 87
Lewis, Henry R. 170
Lewis, Joseph C. 121
Lewis, Joseph H. 131, 132
Lewis, Joshua 76
Lewis, P. H. L. 115
Lewis, T. H. 220
Lewis, Thomas N. 220
Lewisburg, WV
    Battle of 248
Lexington, SC 282
Lexington, TN 187, 258

Liberty Gap, TN 262
Liberty Mills, VA
   Battle of 175
Liddell, St. John R. 114, 124, 153, 165, 166, 215, 216, 222, 238, 284
Light, P. M. 150
Lightfoot, J. B. 38
Lightfoot, James N. 49, 51, 65
Lightfoot, Thomas 48, 50
Ligon, _____ (Captain) 7
Limestone County, AL 27
Lincoln, Abraham 12, 13, 19, 20, 23
   Assassination of 29
Lindsay, A. J. 211
Lindsay, Lewis E. 40
Lindsay, Thomas D. 210
Lindsey, Henry C. 144
Lister, Sidney P. 158
Lithonia, GA 274
Little Bear Creek, AL 25, 258
Little, Benjamin B. 87
Little, Lewis Henry 122
Little River, AL 275
Little River, NC 283
Little Rockcastle River, KY 257
Livingston, Henry J. 197
Lloyd, Lee 73
Loachapoka, AL 116, 141, 143
Locke, L. E. 203
Locke, M. B. 34
Lockwill, J. H. 98
Log Church, TN 255
Logan, John A. 281
Logan, W. H. 105
Logan's Cross Roads, KY
   Battle of 74
Lollar, Hugh G. 103, 105
Lomax, Tennent 7, 8, 24, 36
Long, Armistead Lindsay 229, 230
Long, Eli 29, 191, 209, 270
Long, W. H. 117
Longmire, John J. 90
Longstreet, James 41, 42, 54, 55, 57, 60, 62, 69, 72, 73, 116, 132, 136, 137, 138, 143, 144, 145, 146, 150, 161, 170, 181, 186, 187, 197, 201, 248, 249, 252, 265, 266
Lookout Creek, TN 42, 137, 144, 146
Lookout Mountain, TN 138, 228
   Battle of 85, 90, 91, 103, 108, 113, 121, 122, 123, 127, 133, 134
Lookout Point, TN 227, 228
Lookout Valley, TN 42, 72, 145, 198, 212
Loomis, John Q. 88, 94, 95
Looney, Robert F. 227
Loper's Cross Roads, SC 280
Loring, William Wing 100, 101, 102, 106, 118, 119, 147, 149, 151, 152, 155, 175, 226, 275
Lost Mountain, GA
   Battle of 243
Lott, E. B. 121
Lott, Washington 120
Loudon Creek, TN 265
Loughlin, _____ (Sergeant, 49th Inf.) 148
Loughry, P. 53, 54
Louisiana Units
   Infantry
      1st Regiment 88
Louisville, GA 277
Louisville Pike, KY 256
Louisville Road, GA 278
Love, _____ (Private, 24th Infantry) 93
Love, Andrew P. 88, 217
Lovejoy's Station, GA 77, 78, 276
   Battle of 81
Lovelace, Charles W. 235
Lowell, J. B. 106, 155
Lowrey, Mark Perrin 76, 106, 115, 139, 140, 240, 241, 270
Lowther, Alexander 71, 73
Lucas, Thomas J. 216
Luckie, James B. 169
Lumsden, C. L. 239
Lynch, John 54
Lynch, William Francis 254
Lynchburg, VA 30, 61
   Battle of 250
Lynnville, TN 279
Lyon, Hylan B. 209
Lythgoe, Augustus J. 103

M. & W. P. Railroad 273
Mackall, J. W. W. 204
Mackelville Pike, KY 257

Macon, GA 177, 234, 240, 243, 276, 285
  Battle of 184
Macon, J. M. 127
Madding, Isaac C. 76
Maddon, J. 175
Maddox Gap, GA 275
Madigan, D. 51
Madison Station, AL 26, 191, 269
Madrid Bend, MO 34
Magnolia, AL 160
Magnolia, FL 216
Magruder, John Bankhead 54, 55, 57, 62, 69, 98, 248
Mahone, _____ (Sergeant, Hilliard's Legion) 170
Mahone, William 56, 59, 61, 63, 68
Main, _____ (Capt., 15th Conf. Cav.) 216
Majors, A. 64
Malone, James C. 197, 198, 258
Malone, Jim 150
Malone, Thomas H. 197
Malvern Hill, VA 251
  Battle of 36, 37, 40, 41, 44, 46, 48, 67, 68, 70, 96, 97, 248
Manassas Gap, VA
  Skirmish at 38
Manassas Junction, VA 48, 64
Manassas, VA 41, 53, 69, 230
  Battle of 7
  First Battle of 40, 49, 229, 248
  Second Battle of 40, 41, 44, 55, 56, 59, 61, 69, 70, 71, 72, 137, 143, 144, 145, 171, 172, 248
Manchester Pike, TN 260
Manchester Road 262
Manchester, TN 131
Manigault, Arthur M. 93, 94, 102, 103, 105, 116, 117, 232, 246
Manly, Basil 21
Manly, R. F. 161
Manston, _____ (Lieutenant) 43
Marengo County, AL 3
Marietta, GA 181, 186, 188, 198, 227, 270, 271
  Battle of 81, 83, 178
Marietta Road, GA 271
Marion County, AL 96, 200
Market Hill, VA 174

Markham, George S. 158
Marks, Samuel B. 66
Marrast, John C. 87, 88, 89, 228
Marsh, _____ (Colonel) 44
Marsh, E. 128, 129
Marshall County, AL 26
Marshall, John H. 215
Marshy Creek, GA 271
Marston, F. W. 167, 216
Martin, _____ Corporal, Hilliard's Legion) 170
Martin, B. F. 170
Martin, B. J. 73
Martin, G. B. 40
Martin, H. F. 47
Martin, James B. 59, 60
Martin, John D. 122
Martin, Samuel M. 127
Martin, William 205, 206
Martin, William Thompson 181, 186, 188, 189, 191, 198, 202, 207, 212, 266
Maryland Campaign 37, 41, 46, 50, 55, 57, 61, 63, 65, 66, 67, 69, 72, 98, 137, 146, 172, 230, 231, 249
Maryland Heights, MD 58
Maryland Units (U. S.)
  Infantry
    3rd Regiment 66
Marysville, TN 265
Mason, George 197, 198
Massachusetts Units
  Infantry
    1st Regiment 40
Massey, John 170
Massingale, B. D. 84
Mastin, G. B. 41
Mastin, P. B., Jr. 204
Matamora 4
Matapony, VA
  Battle of 68
Mathews, H. M. 205
Mathews, Joseph A. 210
Mathews, L. S. 115
Mathieson, G. W. 90, 91, 108, 109, 110
Matthews, C. H. 126
Maubila, AL 2
Maubilians 2
Mauldin, Tyirie Harris 184, 185, 186, 209

Maury, Dabney Herndon 28, 34, 35, 78, 79, 86, 106, 111, 113, 120, 124, 128, 132, 133, 152, 153, 156, 166, 167, 171, 175, 176, 177, 187, 191, 192, 194, 196, 197, 199, 208, 215, 216, 217, 219, 220, 221, 225, 226, 229, 237, 240, 244, 284
Maury, Harry 36, 111, 112, 177
Maury, Henry 214, 215
Maury, Randell Lee 240
Maxey, E. N. 136
Maxey, Samuel Bell 111, 202, 211, 255
May, John L. 8
May, Joseph J. 74
May, M. G. 58
May, R. W. 65
May, William 220
Mayes, James E. 68, 69
Mayes, William M. 76
Maynard, C. M. 53, 54
Mayo, R. M. 68
Mays, P. H. 55
Mayse, John L. 125
Maysville, TN 201
McAdory, _____ 79, 80
McAdory, W. R. 103
McAfee's, GA 208, 214, 270, 271
  Skirmish at 198, 203, 206, 209, 212
McAlexander, Edward 100, 102, 120, 154, 155, 156, 157
McAlpin, A. 125
McAlpine, Blanton 7
McBride's Bridge, SC 280
McCaa, B. B. 210, 211
McCain, _____ (Private, Hilliard's Legion) 170
McCall, George A. 248
McCane, Thomas A. 78
McCarty, John B. 48, 50
McCarty, W. A. 80
McCaskill, _____ (Capt., 46th Inf) 141
McCaskill, A. D. 164
McCaskill, John 208, 209
McCassells, J. 64
McClellan, George B. 40, 41, 60, 69, 248, 249
McClellan, J. F. 159
McClellan, William B. 94, 95
McClelland, John B. 150
McClellen, W. C. 159

McClernand, John A. 261
McClung, Francis B. 174, 175
McConnell, W. K. 108
McCook, Alexander McD. 29, 185, 208, 213
McCook, Edward M. 270
McCook, Edwin M. 178, 206
McCook, Robert L. 255
McCord, R. A. 68
McCord, Robert H. 130
McCown, John Porter 34, 167, 168, 236, 254
McCoy, Franklin J. 86
McCoy, Henry 116
McCoy, Robert 136
McCracken, William G. 93
McCrary, Robert A. 53, 55
McCreless, John 169, 170
McCulloch, Robert 215, 216
McCurdy, _____ (Private, 3rd Cav) 184
McCurdy, L. L. 55
McDonald, J. W. 123
McDowell, Irvin 248
McElderry, John S. 210, 212
McEntee, J. 59
McFarland, _____ (Lieut., 46th Inf.) 141
McGaughey, John H. 74, 75, 76
McGee, James 7
McGhee, William S. 107
McGill, William 205
McGinnis, George F. 142
McGinnis, J. V. 159
McGrath, _____ (Lieutenant) 54
McGraw, W. H. 54
McGregor, William 30
McIntosh, D. G. 231
McKean, _____ (Captain) 253
McKeane, Hugh 216
McKee, J. D. 114
McKenzie, Bethune B. 217
McKenzie, W. R. D. 82
McKenzie, William J. 236, 237
McKenzie, William R. 81
McKewn, Hugh 54
McKinney, George W. 150
McKinstry, Alexander 111
McKleroy, John M. 214
McLain, J. T. 150

McLaughlin, John D. 53, 54
McLaws, Lafayette 54, 67, 71, 248
McLean's Hill, GA 267
McLemore, Ulyses Thaddeus 195, 196
McLemore, Owen K. 40, 41, 68
McLemore's Cove, GA 263
McLemore's Cove, TN 186
McLennan, John D. 161, 168, 169, 170
McLeod, William A. 103
McInnis, A. D. 43
McIntosh, A. 70, 71
McMahon, F. S. 76
McMath, James H. 62
McMicken, John 76
McMillan, H. C. 88
McMillan, J. P. 134
McMillan, William W. 78
McMinnville Road, TN 264
McMinnville, TN 188, 264
McMullen, J. P. 153
McMurray, Francis 90
McNamara, John 175
McNeill, William D. 133, 134
McNeil's Gap, AL 263
McPherson, James B. 269
McPrince, Thomas 87
McRae, Charles M. 35
McRae, Duncan K. 230
McSpadden, Samuel K. 72, 81, 82
McTyer, William A. 236
McVey, J. J. 89
McWhorter, Eliphalet A. 193
Mead, Lemuel G. 218
Meade, George Gordon 162, 249, 252
Meadow, William W. 94
Meadows, James D. 34
Meadows, W. W. 122
Mechanicsville, VA
  Battle of 48, 53, 66, 68, 96, 171, 229, 231, 248
Meek, James T. 121
Meigs, Montgomery C. 69
Melton, Benjamin F. K. 39
Melton, S. W. 188
Memphis & Charleston Railroad 211
Memphis Appeal 212
Memphis, TN 33
Menefee, Albert 143

Menefee, W. C. 127
Meness, John A. 136
Meridian, MS 28, 35, 81, 101, 111, 120, 124, 158, 176, 193, 194, 199, 200, 225, 235, 267, 285
Merritt, Wesley 43, 251
Merry Oaks, KY 255
Metts, J. G. 116
Mexican War 7, 8, 24, 48
Mexico 1, 3, 8
Micars, R. A. 80
Michailoffsky, C. I. 88, 89
Michie, _____ (Thomas) 62
Michie, T. J. 62
Michigan Units
  Cavalry
    2nd Regiment 29
Mickey's, TN 179
Mickle, John M. 79, 80
Middleburg, TN 254
Middleground Road, GA 278
Middleton, GA
  Battle of 178
Middleton Road, TN 198
Middleton, TN 181, 212
Middletown, VA
  Battle of 248
Miles, D. S. 44, 248
Miles, William R. 217
Mill Creek, GA 267
Mill Creek Gap, GA 268, 269
Mill Creek, NC 283
Mill Creek, TN 260
Mill Road, GA 273, 274
Mill Spring, KY
  Battle of 73, 74
Mill Springs, KY 254
Miller, _____ 276, 278, 279
Miller, A. J. 127
Miller, Abram O. 188, 266
Miller, J. F. 262
Milligan, Augustus L. 156
Milliken, Minor 182
Mills, Rogers Q. 241
Mills, Thomas S. 69
Mills, Ulee W. 106
Mills, W. B. 70, 71
Mills, William P. 159, 160
Milner, J. B. 54
Milroy, Robert H. 249

319

Milton, FL 216, 222
Mims, William J. 135, 136
Mine Run Campaign 250
Mine Run, VA 38, 48, 51
   Battle of 97, 230
Mingo Creek, NC 283
Mink, William 93
Minor, H. A. 57
Minter, John A. 124, 152
Minton, P. A. 89
Minty, Robert H. G. 181, 186, 188, 198, 203, 208, 209, 212, 214, 261, 262
Missionary Ridge, TN 265
   Battle of 31, 73, 81, 83, 85, 90, 91, 92, 94, 103, 108, 110, 111, 112, 113, 115, 116, 117, 120, 121, 122, 123, 124, 126, 127, 133, 134, 139, 141, 149, 157, 158, 198, 227, 228, 232, 236, 237, 238, 242, 245, 246
Mississippi City, MS 215
Mississippi River 3
Mississippi Units
   Cavalry
      10th Regiment 206
   Infantry
      7th Regiment 132
      Jeff Davis Legion 217
Mitchel, Ormsby M. 24
Mitchell, F. E. 150
Mitchell, James B. 117
Mitchell, James E. 213
Mitchell, Julius C. B. 66, 116
Mitchell, Ormsby M. 258
Mitchell, Robert B. 65, 186, 188, 198, 202, 207, 254
Mitchell, T. C. 134
Mize, T. J. 159
Mizell, _____ 114
Mobile & Ohio Railroad 78, 211, 215
Mobile, AL 4, 6, 7, 27, 28, 31, 34, 77, 78, 79, 81, 83, 84, 85, 86, 87, 90, 92, 94, 105, 120, 123, 124, 127, 128, 134, 152, 153, 156, 157, 158, 163, 164, 165, 166, 167, 170, 175, 176, 177, 187, 195, 204, 206, 214, 215, 216, 222, 223, 224, 225, 226, 232, 235, 236, 237, 238, 239, 240, 243, 244, 245, 246, 285
Mobile Bay 3, 27

Mobile Bay, AL
   Battle of 274
Mock, W. R. 115
Monocacy, MD
   Battle of 251
Monroe, SC 282
Monterey Road, TN
   Engagement on 184
Monterey, TN 178, 179
Montevallo, AL 189, 191, 193, 195, 197, 199, 284
Montezuma 3
Montgomery, AL 4, 7, 9, 21, 24, 29, 48, 59, 66, 77, 83, 87, 90, 99, 105, 124, 152, 165, 166, 167, 176, 178, 182, 193, 202, 213, 224, 239, 240, 244, 284
Montgomery, J. T. 229
Monticello, KY 74
   Action at 213
Moody, George 93, 94, 162
Moody, Y. M. 135, 136, 163, 169
Moore, _____ (Captain) 26
Moore, A. M. 114, 115
Moore, Andrew Barry 21, 24
Moore, H. H. 51
Moore, J. B. 80
Moore, J. C. 129
Moore, James M. 125
Moore, John 197
Moore, John C. 82, 86
Moore, John Creed 122, 123, 127, 128, 129, 133, 238
Moore, R. J. 88
Moore, Samuel H. 38
Moore, Sydenham 7, 62
Moorer, D. W. 51
Mordecai, Waller 87, 89
Moreland, M. D. 221
Moreland, William S. 170
Morgan County, AL 25, 191
Morgan, CSS 27, 274
Morgan, John Hunt 178, 181, 184, 186, 187, 197, 198, 201, 212
Morgan, John Tyler 44, 188, 201, 202
Morris, Benjamin 106
Morrison, J. D. 176
Morrison, John D. 220
Morristown, TN 135, 266
Morrisville, NC 284

320

Morse, Allen 74
Morton, MS 205, 225
Morton's Ford, VA
   Battle of 250
Moseley, E. F. 239
Mosley, E. B. 47
Mossy Creek, GA 187
Mote, James A. 95
Moulton, AL 119, 189, 191, 192, 221, 270
   Engagement at 101
Mount Hope, AL 119, 199
Mount Pleasant, AL 284
Mount Pleasant, TN 279
Mount Vernon, AL 24
Mountain Gap, KY 257
Mountain Gap, TN 208, 264
Mountain Side, KY 257
Mouton, Alfred 233
Moxley, William M. 79
Mt. Vernon, AL 120
Mt. Vernon, KY 214, 257
Mulligan, A. L. 156
Mumford's Station, AL 285
Munfordville, KY
   Battle of 87, 103, 178, 227, 228, 232, 255
   Siege of 53, 102, 113
Munsel, Joseph 98
Murfee, J. T. 130
Murfreesboro Pike, TN 202, 258, 259, 260
Murfreesboro, TN 181, 187, 200, 207, 213, 222, 223, 240, 254, 259, 260, 279
   Battle of 30, 73, 74, 75, 81, 82, 87, 89, 92, 93, 94, 95, 102, 104, 110, 111, 112, 113, 114, 116, 126, 130, 131, 139, 148, 149, 150, 154, 173, 178, 180, 184, 202, 206, 207, 208, 209, 210, 227, 228, 232, 236, 237, 240, 242, 245, 246
Murphey, Topley 104
Murphy, R. 55
Murphy, Samuel J. 186
Murphy, V. S. 78
Murphy, Virgil S. 77
Murphy, W. C. 56, 57, 58
Murray, A. 40
Murray, Alfred R. 124

Murray, Eli Houston 185
Murray, John E. 242
Murrell, John W. 222
Muscogees 3
Muscoso 2
Musgrove, _____ (Capt., 12th Cav.) 201
Musgrove, F. A. 103
Musgrove, William H. 106
Myer, Albert 225
Myers, Albert J. 87
Myers, T. H. 215
Myers, T. J. 215
Myrack's Mill, GA 276
Myrick, R. L. 88

Nabbers, J. E. 82
Nabers, James F. 173
Nahunta Swamp, NC 283
Nail, Duke 53
Nance, James E. 197
Nansemond River 137
Napoleon 1
Narrows, TN 209
Narvaez 2
Nash, Jesse G. 101, 130, 132
Nashville Pike, TN 258
Nashville, TN 90, 121, 142, 147, 155, 157, 160, 180, 193, 202, 208, 219, 240, 244, 258, 279
   Battle of 33, 74, 77, 79, 81, 83, 87, 92, 94, 97, 100, 103, 105, 107, 109, 111, 116, 118, 120, 126, 139, 141, 147, 154, 156, 158, 178, 187, 235, 238, 243, 245
Natchez, MS 3
Neal, _____ (Asst. Surgeon) 35
Negley, James S. 181, 186, 188, 201, 207, 209, 212
Neil, Francis 93
Neilson, John H. 137
Nelson, A. B. 93
Nelson, B. T. 89
Nelson, D. C. 218
Nelson, John C. 189
Nesmith, S. Perry 48, 49
Nettles, _____ 93
Neuse, SC 282
New Albany, MS 183, 205

New, A'Mbrose 93
New Bern, AL 157
New Church, TN 262
New France 1
New Haven, KY 180, 185
New Hope Church, GA 270
New Hope, GA 226, 273
   Battle of 33, 78, 90, 94, 105, 107, 120, 121, 122, 123, 124, 125, 126, 127, 133, 139, 152, 157, 160, 213, 243
New Jersey Units
   Infantry
      33rd Regiment 102
New Lebanon Junc, KY 256
New Madrid, TN 254
New Market, AL 255
New Market Hill, VA 163, 251
New Market, VA 163
New Orleans, LA 4, 6
New Road, VA 137
New York Herald 19
New York, NY 18, 19
New York Times 19
New York Tribune 16, 17, 18
New York Units
   Infantry
      124th Regiment 163
New Yrok Units
   Infantry
      42nd Regiment 37
Newbern, AL 195
Newnan, GA 29, 274
Newsom, John F. 200
Newton, VA
   Battle of 248
Niagara, USS 253
Nichols, _____ (Colonel) 6
Nickajack, GA
   Battle of 182
Nickajack Trace, GA 268
Ninth Regulars (Mexican War) 7
Nix, J. 109, 110
Nodine, Richard H. 134
Nolensville Pike, TN 258
Nolensville, TN 202, 259, 260
Noonday Creek, GA 271
   Battle of 178, 181, 188, 197, 198, 203, 206, 208, 209, 212, 214
Norfolk, VA 239
Norman, John C. 114

Norris, George W. 168, 170
Norris, Thomas 184
North Anna, VA
   Battle of 250
Northcott, J. R. 88
Northport, AL 29, 284
Northrup, Julius A. 93
Norwood, J. W. 185
Norwood, John W. 154
Nott, H. J. 88
Nott, James Deas 87, 88, 89
Numney, S. J. 116
Nunnally, Peter 154

Oak Hill, AL 191
Oakland, KY 255
Oates, William C. 71, 145
O'Bannon, L. W. 174
O'Brien, William J. 92, 93
Oconee, GA 276
Oden, Henry 107
O'Donohoe, John 47
Ogechee, GA 277
Oglesby, John D. 76
Oglesby, Richard J. 205
O'Hara, C. W. 80
O'Hara, Theodore 64
Okolona, MS 183, 200, 205
Oliver, James M. 143
Oliver, John C. 112
Oliver, McDonald 236, 237
Oliver, Starke H. 92, 93, 94, 103
Oliver, W. G. 116, 117
O'Neal, Edward A. 37, 38, 45, 46, 47, 51, 56, 65, 77, 78, 96, 97, 98, 99, 106, 230
Oostanaula, GA 269
Open Field, GA 271
Opequon, VA
   Battle of 252
Orange Court House, VA 58, 163, 230
   Battle of 229
Orangeburg Road, SC 281
Orchard Knob, TN 91
Ord, Edward O. C. 60, 256
Orear, E. 106
Orizaba, Mexico 7, 8
Ortiz, Jean 2
Otey, C. C. 49

Oven, AL 120
Overall's Creek, TN 185, 259
Owen Bluff, AL 86
Owen's Ford, GA 263
Owens, John 34
Owens, William A. 38
Ox Hill, VA
   Battle of 71
Oxford, AL 226

Pace's Ferry Road, GA 272
Padgett, J. J. 122
Pagan, J. F. 228
Page, Richard Lucian 27, 28, 86,
   193, 194, 224, 225, 229, 274
Pakenham, _____ (Brit. Gen.) 6
Palmer, John M. 256
Palmer, Joseph B. 111, 112, 242
Palmer, Solomon 82, 83
Palmer, William J. 188, 189
Panola, AL 194
Paramore, J. W. 198
Parham, R. T. B. 93
Parhan, _____ (Captain) 29
Paris, TN 210
Parish, J. D. 184
Parish, J. W. 84
Park, Frank 70
Parke, J. G. 66
Parke, John G. 162, 253
Parker, G. 86
Parker, W. C. Y. 62
Parsons, Jesse 98
Pascagoula, MS 187, 205, 215, 216, 222
Patrick, _____ (Private, Hilliard's Legion) 170
Patten, J. B. 118
Patterson, Archibald A. 95
Patterson, Josiah 26, 190, 191, 192, 199, 222, 269
Patterson, Thomas H. 107, 108
Patterson, William 107
Patton, Isaac W. 193, 194, 215
Patton, John I. 167
Patton, William A. 74, 75
Payne, F. A. 147

Payne's Farm, VA
   Battle of 47
   Engagement at 38
Peachtree Creek, GA 273
   Battle of 33, 73, 77, 78, 81, 100, 102, 105, 106, 126, 154, 155, 156, 235, 243
Peacock, _____ 107
Peacock, J. B. 95
Pearl River 100
Pearson, _____ (Colonel) 6
Peck, John J. 249
Peebles' Farm, VA
   Battle of 252
Peeden, James 75
Pegram, John 172, 208, 213, 214
Pegram's, VA
   Battle of 252
Pegues, C. J. 47
Pegues, Christopher C. 44, 45
Pelham, John 30
Pemberton, John C. 34, 84, 91, 101, 108, 109, 125, 128, 133, 148, 151, 152, 155, 175, 183, 205, 207, 261
Pendergrass, Jonh J. 67
Pendleton, A. S. 47
Pendleton, William Nelson 230, 231
Peninsular Campaign 64, 176
Penley, J. L. 88
Pennington, C. 122
Pennsylvania Units
   Infantry
      53rd Regiment 37
      81st Regiment 37
Pensacola Bay 3, 28
Pensacola, FL 3, 4, 6, 8, 33, 40, 43, 52, 77, 81, 88, 91, 105, 106, 113, 153, 154, 183, 193, 215, 227, 245, 246, 253, 267
   Bombardment of (Nov.22-23, 1861) 33
Peppenhorst, Henry H. 136
Perdido River 222, 223
Perkins, John B. 124
Perrin, Abner Monroe 56, 58, 61
Perrin, G. S. 195
Perry, _____ (Capt., 45th Inf.) 139
Perry, John T. 159
Perry, William Flank 42, 73, 137, 138, 143, 145, 147

Perryville and Lebanon Road, TN 180
Perryville, KY 257
  Battle of 30, 31, 87, 100, 103, 113, 114, 139, 178, 184, 227, 232, 240, 242, 256
Perryville Pike, KY 211, 256
Perryville Road, KY 256
Peteet, W. Young 129
Petersburg Campaign 40, 44, 48, 56, 130, 137, 138, 145
Petersburg Mine, VA
  Battle of 251
Petersburg, VA 36, 53, 56, 59, 62, 63, 64, 66, 68, 70, 130, 132, 135, 136, 161, 162, 163, 174, 176, 239, 251, 252, 253
  Assault (June 1864) 250
  Siege of 251
Pettus, Edmund Winston 83, 84, 85, 91, 107, 108, 109, 110, 141, 142, 238, 279
Petty, E. O. 127
Pevey, J. D. 115
Phelan, John 238, 239
Phelan, Thomas 53, 54
Phelan, Watkins 37, 39
Philips, J. R. 54
Phillips, _____ (Private, Hilliard's Legion) 170
Phillips, M. M. 212
Phillips, Wendell 13
Philpot, W. H. 164
Pickens, Andrew P. 7
Pickens County, AL 3
Pickens, Samuel B. 38, 64, 65, 98
Pickering, Alfred S. 83, 84
Pickett, A. H. 38
Pickett, George E. 54, 239, 253
Pickett, Richard O. 199
Pickett's Mill, GA 270
  Battle of 73, 78
Pierce, Junius J. 92
Pierson, S. F. 229
Pillow, Gidion J. 7, 101, 188, 192, 193, 195, 196, 197, 206, 226
Pinckard, Francis 210
Pinckard, Lucius 68, 69
Pinckard, W. E. 164
Pine Barren Creek, FL 279
  Battle of 195

Pine Barren, FL 194
Pine Barren Ridge (Bridge), FL 215, 216
Pine Knob, GA 270
Pine Mount, GA 270
Pine Woods, SC 283
Pinkerton, Allen 45
Pitman's Cross Roads, KY 258
Pitt's Cross Roads, TN 264
Pitts, J. M. 151
Pitts, J. W. 165
Pitts, S. H. 117
Pitts, W. N. 151
Plains Store, LA 261, 268
Plant, Joseph 125
Platt, _____ (Captain) 7
Platt, J. E. 125
Plymouth, NC 239
Pocotaligo Road, SC 280
Pocotaligo, SC 258
Poe, W. T. 195, 196
Point Lookout, TN 264
  Engagement at 186
Pointer, Marcellus 200, 201
Polk, Leonidas 34, 35, 78, 82, 89, 92, 95, 101, 104, 111, 112, 119, 126, 129, 140, 149, 150, 152, 155, 164, 173, 180, 181, 182, 183, 185, 186, 195, 203, 204, 206, 210, 211, 212, 215, 217, 222, 223, 228, 241, 244, 245, 267
Pollard, AL 35, 105, 106, 156, 163, 166, 167, 176, 192, 193, 194, 195, 197, 215, 216, 222, 235, 243, 244
Pollard, Samuel J. 80
Ponce de Leon, John 1
Pond, Preston 167, 227
Pond Spring, AL 279
  Skirmish at 192
Poole, D. H. 180
Pope, John 248, 254
Poplar Spring Church, VA 252
Port Gibson, MS 82, 83, 84, 90, 91, 107, 109, 122, 261
  Battle of 141, 142, 175
Port Hudson, LA 33, 34, 100, 101, 118, 147, 148, 153, 155, 261
  Battle of 175
Port Hudson Plains, LA 261

324

Port Republic, VA
   Battle of 71, 249
Port Royal, VA 231
Porter, A. N. 171, 172
Porter, B. L. 82
Porter, David Dixon 261
Porter, Fitz John 248, 249
Porter, John H. 169
Porter, Mitchell T. 83, 85
Portis, John W. 133
Portugal 2
Posey, A. 93
Posey, Ben Lane 124, 125
Potomac River 96
Powder Springs, GA 270
Powell, A. 73
Powell, James W. 141, 142
Powell, Joseph 153
Powell, Samuel 140
Powell, W. L. 222, 225
Powell, William H. 54, 86
Powers, James P. 84
Powers, P. F. 242
Powers, W. H. 38
Poyner, John H. 127
Prairie Mound, MS 183
Prather, John S. 181, 182, 210, 211, 212, 213
Pratt, R. H. 84
Prentiss, Benjamin M. 77, 78, 79
Preston, John Smith 112, 118, 134, 135
Preston, William 168
Preston, William C. 235, 244
Prewitt, D. M. 121
Price, Alfred C. 40, 41
Price, H. I. 51
Price, Sterling 101, 122, 185, 211, 238, 255
Price's Cross Roads, GA 270
Pride, G. 75
Priest, E. 127
Prince, J. H. 62
Prince, O. H. 135
Pritchard, _____ (Colonel, USA) 285
Pritchett, O. W. 135
Proskaner, Adolph 64, 65
Prospect, TN 200
Provence, David 246

Pruett, John 34
Pryor, Roger A. 54, 55, 69
Pulaski Raid 199
Pulaski, TN 191, 199, 218, 221
Purdy, TN 211

Quarles, William Andrew 35, 36, 78, 107, 193, 194
Quattlebaum, W. H. 73
Quillan, _____ (Private, Hilliard's Legion) 169

Rader, W. H. 158, 159
Ragland, James M. 93
Ragland, Thomas 77, 78
Ragsdale, C. P. 55
Raiford, Phillip H. 7
Railroad, GA 268
Rains, G. J. 67, 98
Rains, James Edwards 236
Raleigh, NC 201, 284
   Engagement at 184
Raleigh, Walter 1
Ralls, John P. 26
Ramseur, S. D. 38, 39, 48, 52, 251
Ramsey, _____ (Lieutenant) 44
Ramsey, M. S. 45
Randall, John H. 170
Randolph, _____ (Maj.) 267
Ransom, Matthew Whittaker 161
Ransom, Robert 132, 136, 163, 174
Ransom, Walter 38
Rappahannock River 41, 137, 143
Rappahannock River, VA
   Battle of 71
Ray, Archibald D. 151
Rayburn, John Y. 56
Readyville, TN 213, 264
Reagan, Richard C. 59
Ream's Station, VA
   Battle of 251
Reaves, S. E. 161
Red Clay, GA 268
Red River Campaign 27
Redden, R. D. 97, 98
Redwood, R. H. 195, 196, 220
Reed, George 44

Reeder, William C. 97
Reek, G. M. 98
Reese, _____ (Captain, 28th Infantry) 104
Reese, Carlos 104
Reese, W. J. 229, 230
Reese, Warren S. 200
Reeves, W. N. 168, 242
Reichard, Augustus 139, 140
Reid, John C. 93, 103, 116, 232
Renfro, William T. 44, 46, 47
Renfroe, _____ 87, 89
Rentz, John W. 66
Republican Convention of 1860 12
Republican Party 10
Resaca, GA 268, 269
   Battle of 73, 77, 78, 81, 90, 103, 105, 107, 110, 113, 120, 121, 122, 123, 124, 125, 126, 127, 133, 134, 139, 152, 154, 157, 158, 160, 184, 203, 204, 213, 217, 238, 243
Reynolds, Arthur E. 174
Reynolds, D. H. 35, 84, 194, 215, 235, 243
Reynolds' Farm, GA 277
Reynolds, H. Clay 202
Reynolds, James 55
Reynolds, Joseph J. 209
Reynolds, S. W. 116
Rhett, Thomas 40
Rhoades, Isaac N. 95
Rhodes, W. J. 109
Rice, Horace 74
Rice, Olin F. 165, 166
Rice, P. H. 208, 209
Rice's Farm, GA 271
Richards, T. B. 124
Richardson, N. D. 150
Richardson, William 150
Richey, _____ (Sergeant, 42nd Inf) 134
Richey, Clark 132
Richmond Campaign 43, 73
Richmond, USS 253
Richmond, VA 5, 12, 29, 30, 31, 36, 40, 41, 45, 50, 54, 56, 60, 63, 66, 67, 69, 70, 71, 77, 96, 97, 99, 132, 135, 136, 137, 143, 161, 162, 171, 174, 218, 229, 230, 231, 251, 252, 253
Richmond, W. B. 186

Riddle, Patrick P. 137
Riddle, T. G. 117
Ridge, GA 268, 269
Ridgeway, J. C. J. 63
Ridgeway, VA 239
Ridley, George 115
Riggs, Thomas 141
Riley, _____ (Private, 33rd Infantry) 114
Riley, T. M. 47, 98
Riley, Thomas M. 48
Ringgold Bridge, GA 268
Ringgold, GA
   Battle of 73, 113, 141, 242
Ringgold Gap, GA
   Battle of 115, 139, 140
Ringgold Pass, GA 267
Ringgold Road, GA 267
Ringgold, TN 266
Riser, Thomas M. 80
Ritter, Wade 171, 172
River Creek, GA 277
River Road, SC 283
Rivers' Bridge, SC 280
Rivers, John D. 147
Rix, Henry J. 117
Roanoke Island, NC 254
Robbins, W. F. 146
Roberds, A. C. 109
Roberts, _____ (Captain, 39th Inf) 126
Roberts, A. C. 84, 90, 91
Roberts, G. A. 217
Roberts, L. P. 150
Roberts, M. 151
Roberts, Samuel M. 93
Robertson, Charles S. 206, 207
Robertson, H. J. 47
Robertson, James W. 118
Robertson, S. M. 122
Robertsville Road, SC 280
Robertsville, SC 280
Robins, Josiah 184, 186, 214
Robinson, Cornelius, Jr. 39
Robinson, G. T. L. 55
Robinson, James 5
Robinson, James M. 197
Rock Creek Cross Roads, TN 259
Rock Creek, GA 278
Rockford, TN 265

Rockingham, SC 282
Rocky Crossing, MS
   Battle of 183
Rocky Face, GA 267, 269
Rocky Face Ridge, GA 268
   Battle of 73, 80, 83, 91, 107, 112, 120, 121, 122, 123, 124, 125, 126, 127, 129, 152, 160
Rocky Hill, KY 257
Rocky Mount, NC 213
Roddey, _____ (Captain, 2nd Cav.) 182
Roddey, Philip Dale 25, 26, 27, 29, 77, 100, 110, 189, 190, 191, 199, 200, 203, 204, 217, 221, 258, 261, 270
Roden, C. 80
Rodes, C. E. 195
Rodes, Robert Emmett 37, 38, 43, 44, 45, 46, 48, 49, 50, 52, 63, 64, 96, 97, 98, 231, 238, 239
Rodgers, James C. 212
Rodgersville, AL 254
Rodriguez, _____ (Portuguese) 2
Roebuck, Robert W. 74, 75
Roger, James C. 198
Rogers, J. R. 159
Rogers, John 64
Rogers, T.W. 86
Rolling Fork, MS
   Engagement at 128
Rome, GA 2, 25, 106, 176, 200, 203, 211, 220, 244, 245, 261
   Battle of 195
Roper, Charles W. 95
Rosecrans, William S. 87, 180, 191, 210, 255, 256, 259, 263
Ross, P. D. 66
Rosswell, GA 272
Rosswell Road, GA 271
Rothbock, N. 208
Round Mountain Ironworks, AL 275
Round Mountain, TN 198
Rourk, _____(Lieut., 58th Inf.) 159
Rouse, C. D. 38
Rouse, Napoleon B. 87, 96
Rousseau, Lovell H. 27, 165, 192, 195, 220, 273, 274, 279
Rousseau's Raid 273
Rover, TN 212

Rowett, Richard 192, 221
Royston, Young L. 53, 54, 55, 167
Rucker, E. W. 34
Rudolph, John B. 213
Ruffin, Sheppard 79, 80
Ruggles, Daniel 34, 118, 179, 183, 204, 205, 210, 227, 245, 254
Run's Creek, GA 276
Rushing, J. T. 73
Russell, Alfred A. 52, 111, 178, 181, 184, 186, 187, 188, 189, 197, 198, 203, 206, 207
Russell, Benjamin H. 74, 75
Russell, Robert Milton 210
Russellville, AL 182
Russellville, TN 74, 186
Rust, Albert 118, 148, 153, 155, 174, 175
Rutherford, F. A. 90
Rutherford, John H. 173
Rutland, H. W. 75
Rutledge, _____ (Private, Hilliard's Legion) 170
Rutledge, H. H. 161
Ryales, Perry 216
Ryan, James 55
Ryan, John 77
Ryan, R. B. 101
Ryan, T. S. 55

Sacramento, KY 253
Sailor's Creek, VA
   Battle of 253
Salem Church, VA
   Battle of 53, 58
Salem, VA
   Battle of 56, 59, 61, 68
Salkahatchie Road, SC 281
Salmon, Henry 117
Salter, Samuel 174
Salter, Thomas 75
Saltville, VA
   Battle of 210, 213
Saluda River 281
Sand Mountain, AL 261
Sanders, John C. C. 56, 59, 61, 62, 63, 68
Sandersville, GA 277
Sands, R. M. 38

Sandy Ridge, NC
  Skirmish at 158
Sanford, James H. 143
Sanford, John H. 34
Sanford, John W. 162, 167, 168, 169, 170
Santa Rosa Island, FL 27, 253
  Battle of 33
Sapps, B. F. 106
Sargeant, Harvey G. 75
Satcher, H. F. 73
Satterwhite, _____ (Private, 43rd Inf) 136
Saunders, William H. 62
Savage, James H. 82
Savage, Thomas J. 86
Savage's Peach Orchard, VA
  Battle of 248
Savannah, GA 201, 204
  Siege of 279
Savannah River 278
Savannah Road, SC 280
Savannah, TN 200, 206, 213, 214
Sawyer, Benjamin F. 92, 94
Scales, William W. 136
Schofield, H. B. 95
Schofield, John M. 279, 283
Schwartz, G. 54
Sclater, J. R. 226
Scott, _____ (Private, 24th Infantry) 93
Scott, A. W. 93
Scott, David 136
Scott, Dred 9
Scott, John S. 214
Scott, Thomas Moore 102, 119, 147, 149, 154, 155, 156
Scott, W. J. 174
Scott, Winfield 7
Scottsboro, AL 280
Scottsville, AL 284
Scottsville Road, KY 180
Scottsville Road, TN 255
Screws, Benjamin H. 36, 78, 107
Scrougesville, TN 258
Scruggs, L. H. 41, 43
Seabrook, J. P. 125
Searcy, C. J. 122
Searcy, J. R. 55
Seawel, J. J. 202
Seay, Thomas 114

Secessionville, SC 254
Sedgwick, John 250
Seibels, John J. 7, 8, 48, 49
Seidel, Charles B. 202
Selden, Joseph 235
Selden, William M. 236
Sellers, A. 111
Sellers, Samuel 68
Sellers, William 89
Selma, AL 29, 101, 102, 136, 147, 152, 166, 167, 189, 191, 192, 196, 199, 224, 226, 284
Selma, CSS 27, 274
Seminole War 6
Seminoles 5
Semmes, Paul Jones 67
Semmes, Raphael 31, 260
Semple, H. C. 226, 241, 244
Sengstak, H. H. 237
Sequatchie Raid 30, 178, 184, 187, 201
Sequatchie Valley 208
Sessions, C. L. 115
Seven Days' Battles 37, 64, 67, 71, 171, 230, 231, 248
Seven Pines, VA
  Battle of 8, 36, 39, 40, 41, 43, 44, 45, 48, 49, 50, 53, 54, 56, 57, 59, 60, 61, 62, 64, 66, 68, 83, 96, 97, 98, 229, 231, 248. *See also* Fair Oaks, VA: Battle of
Sevigny 4
Seymour, Truman 50
Shaaff, F. Key 73
Shackelford, Thaddeus H. 152
Shackleford, _____ (Captain) 7
Shady Grove, GA 278
Shannon, _____ (Captain in 1787) 5
Sharpe, George H. 175
Sharpsburg, MD
  Battle of 30, 37, 40, 41, 43, 44, 46, 48, 50, 53, 55, 56, 59, 61, 64, 65, 66, 67, 68, 70, 72, 96, 98, 137, 143, 144, 145, 146, 249
Sheffield, J. L. 42, 72, 138, 144, 145, 146
Shehorn, James 116
Shelby Springs, AL 102
Shelbyville Pike, TN 262

Shelbyville, TN 187, 198, 207, 236, 262, 265
   Battle of 184, 197, 206, 210, 212
Shelley, Charles Miller 36, 44, 45, 76, 78, 84, 100, 102, 107, 115, 120, 139, 141, 157
Shelley, J. D. 7
Shelley, James E. 59, 60, 61
Shelton, John R. 135, 136
Shelton, T. H. 121
Shepard, F. B. 67
Shepard, Seth 243
Shepherd, J. R. 205
Shepherd, Samuel G. 172
Shepherdstown, VA
   Battle of 30, 249
Shepherdsville, KY 255
Shepherdsville Road, KY 256
Sheridan, Philip H. 161, 180, 211, 251, 252, 253
Sheridan's Raid 250
Sherman, William D. 273
Sherman, William T. 77, 129, 178, 179, 182, 184, 201, 203, 204, 210, 259, 262, 267, 268, 269, 270, 273, 274, 283
Shields, James 7, 248
Shields, John G. 54
Shiloh, TN
   Battle of 30, 31, 52, 73, 74, 75, 77, 78, 79, 81, 82, 85, 86, 87, 88, 94, 95, 113, 147, 148, 149, 150, 153, 154, 157, 158, 178, 179, 181, 184, 203, 204, 210, 227, 228, 232, 239, 245, 246, 254
Shoal Creek, GA 274
Shoal Creek, TN
   Skirmish at 221
Short, Edwin W. 93
Short, William E. 104
Shorter, Eli S. 79
Shorter, John Gill 202
Shortridge, Eli 54
Shoup, Francis Ashbury 224, 225
Sickles, Daniel E. 54, 57
Sill, Joshua W. 149, 185, 258
Silver Run, SC 283
Simmons, _____ (Private, Hilliard's Legion) 170
Simonton, John M. 155

Sims, A. D. 125
Sims, William S. 114
Sipsey Swamp, AL 284
Sizemore, A. J. 175
Skinner, Jonathan J. 170
Skinner, S. J. 88
Slaton, William F. 122
Slaughter, A. J. 164
Slaughter, J. E. 77, 79, 124, 128, 156, 158, 225, 226, 228, 235
Slaughter, John N. 105, 116, 117, 120
Slaughter, M. M. 168, 213
Slaughter, Miles M. 213
Slaughter, Thomas G. 95
Slay, Hiram 111, 112
Slemmer, Adam 253
Slocum, Henry W. 47, 160, 283
Small, Isham B. 145
Smith, Richard Inge 121
Smith, _____ (private 24th Infantry) 93
Smith, _____ (Private, Hilliard's Legion) 170
Smith, A. A. 199
Smith, A. J. 107, 273
Smith, Ashbel 133
Smith, B. F. 98
Smith, Baxter 209
Smith, Drewry H. 127
Smith, E. T. 7
Smith, Edmund Kirby 71, 83, 84, 91, 107, 109, 134, 135, 141, 168, 208, 236, 257
Smith, G. W. 117
Smith, Gaines C. 56, 58
Smith, Gustavus A. 140
Smith, Gustavus W. 41, 60, 62
Smith, H. D. 75
Smith, H. F. 26, 267
Smith, Henry F. 187
Smith, Horace M. 152
Smith, Isaac R. 114
Smith, J. 54
Smith, J. D. 126
Smith, J. Maury 116
Smith, J. N. 87, 89
Smith, Jacob 105
Smith, James R. 105
Smith, John D. 66
Smith, John F. 61

Smith, John T. 66, 67
Smith, John W. 162
Smith, M. 80
Smith, Marshall J. 227
Smith, Martin L. 128
Smith, Melancthon 31
Smith, Mitchell 175
Smith, N. J. 225
Smith, Nat M. 68, 69
Smith, P. H. 95
Smith, Patrick H. 95
Smith, Preston 211
Smith, R. Inge 45
Smith, R. W. 184
Smith, Robert H. 120
Smith, Sidney B. 97, 99
Smith, Thomas 139
Smith, U. S. 41, 42
Smith, W. B. 92
Smith, W. G. 89
Smith, W. R. 26
Smith, W. T. 217
Smith, Warren 57
Smith, William D. 93
Smith, William F. 61, 248
Smith, William R. 97
Smith, William Sooy 267
Smith, William T. 59
Smithfield, NC 77, 90, 92, 100, 107, 114, 115, 129, 147, 151
Smithfield, VA 251
Smith's Hill, SC 283
Smith's Raid 267
Smith's, TN 255
Smithville, AL 119
Smithville, MS 205
Smyrna, TN 260
Snake Creek, GA 268
Snake Creek Gap, GA 275
Snapfinger Creek, GA 274
Snead, C. H. 68, 69
Snicker's Ferry, VA
   Battle of 251
Snicker's Gap, VA
   Battle of 64, 163
Snodgrass, John 102, 153, 154, 155
Snodgrass, Robert B. 217
Snowden, Robert B. 246
Snyder's Bluff, MS
   Battle of 238

Somers, USS 31
South Carolina Secession Convention 18
South Mountain, MD
   Battle of 50, 65, 68, 98, 229, 230
Spain 1, 2, 4
Spanish Fort, AL 27, 28, 85, 113, 120, 122, 124, 133, 158, 160, 165, 227, 284
   Siege of 28, 79, 111, 158, 165, 240
Sparta, MS 185
Speed, George 178
Spencer, G. E. 72
Spigener, Socrates 170
Spinks, John F. 141
Spottsylvania Court House, VA
   Battle of 36, 40, 43, 44, 48, 53, 59, 62, 64, 68, 70, 137, 143, 145, 163, 175, 230, 250
Spring Creek, TN 187
Spring Hill, TN 279
   Battle of 139
Spring Place Road, GA 269
Spring Place, TN 208, 212
Springfield, GA 278
Springfield, KY 256
Springtown, SC 280
Sprowl, J. 55
Spurling, Andrew B. 216
St. Augustine, FL 1
St. John, A. P. 237
St. John, C. B. 146
St. Lawrence River 1
Stackpoole, John T. 87, 90
Staggers, David R. 66, 67
Stallworth, Nicholas 173
Stalworth, _____ 114
Stanford, T. Q. 126
Stanley, David S. 187, 212, 254, 262, 279
Stannard, George J. 252
Stansel, Martin L. 130, 131, 132
Starke, Peter Burwell 213
Starkweather, John C. 254, 259
Stateboro, GA 278
Steedman, Isaiah G. W. 33, 34, 35, 191
Steele, _____ (Captain) 26
Steele, A. N. 62
Steele, Frederick 28, 192, 193, 195, 196, 284

330

Steele, William 127, 128
Stephens, John L. 135
Stephens, Leonidas 141
Stephenson, _____ (Sergeant, 43rd Inf) 136
Stevens, Isaac I. 254
Stevens, John 90
Stevenson, AL 111, 189, 255
Stevenson, Carter Littlepage 83, 84, 91, 107, 108, 109, 110, 141, 142, 168, 221, 226, 233, 234, 236, 255
Stevenson, James M. 197
Stevenson, TN
  Capture of 110
Stevenson's Gap, TN 263
Stewart (Stuart), James H. 26
Stewart, _____ (Sergeant, 33rd Infantry) 114
Stewart, Alexander Peter 35, 36, 76, 81, 102, 107, 112, 115, 120, 121, 123, 125, 139, 154, 157, 159, 160, 182, 210, 214, 235, 236, 237, 240, 243, 244, 245, 246, 266, 275, 279
Stewart, Charles S. 86
Stewart, David 80
Stewart, F. 86
Stewart, Frederick K. 86
Stewart, George W. 80
Stewart, J. B. 150
Stewart, Martin L. 63
Stewart, S. D. 171, 172
Stewart, Samuel D. 118
Stewart's Creek Bridge, TN
  Battle of 178, 180
Stewart's Creek, TN 202, 259
Stinnet, E. H. 151
Stock Creek, TN 265
Stockton, AL 216
Stokes, W. P. 47
Stone Church, GA 267, 268
Stone, H. Clay 80
Stone Mountain Road, GA 272
Stone River Stockade, TN 264
Stone River, TN 260
Stone, Thomas O. 128, 129
Stone, W. M. 166
Stoneman, George 178, 184, 187, 200, 210, 269, 274
Stone's River 202, 209

Stone's River Campaign 82, 89, 104, 131, 173, 180, 198, 201, 212
Storrs, Charles P. 194, 234
Storrs, George S. 240, 245
Stoude, A. D. 175
Stout, John 95
Stover, Joshua 143, 146
Strawberry Plains, TN 168
Strawbridge, James 79
Street, Thomas A. 148
Streight, Abel 25, 189, 203, 261
Streight's Raid 261
Stribling's Artillery Battery 137
Strickland, F. S. 166
Strickland, James R. 55
Stringer, Orville A. 79, 80
Strudwick, O. L. 63
Stuart, James H. 221
Stuart, JEB 30, 57, 60, 231, 248
Stubbs, J. G. 34
Stuckey, _____ (Sergeant, Hilliard's Legion) 170
Stuckey, E. S. 98
Sturgis, Samuel D. 270
Suffolk, VA 37, 143
  Battle of 70, 137, 249
  Siege of 146
Sugar Creek, TN 265, 279
Sullivan, J. 40
Sulphur Branch Trestle, AL 274
Sulphur Springs Trestle, MS 27, 190
Sulphur Trestle, AL 199
Summers, John 47
Summers, L. F. 53
Summers, Leonard F. 54
Summertown, TN 263
Summerville, GA 263
Summerville Road, GA 275
Summerville, TN 198, 212
Sumner, Edwin V. 248
Sumner, R. F. 105
Sumner, W. D. 88, 89
Sumter, CSS 31
Sunflower River 122
Sunshine Creek, GA 274
Swamp, GA 278
Swampy Creek, GA 277
Swanson, W. G. 163, 164
Sweat, E.H. 93
Sweeny, Thomas William 25, 258

Sweetwater, GA 275
Swett, Charles 238
Swicegood, Adam 47
Sylvan Grove, GA 277
Sylvester, J. A. 135
Syracuse, NY 14

Tait, Felix 90
Talbird, Henry 130
Talbot, A. J. 127
Talbott's Station, TN 198
Taliaferro, Alexander G. 143, 145
Taliaferro, William Booth 143, 145, 146
Talladega, AL 107, 108, 165, 192, 196, 211, 220
Tallahatchee, AL 5
Tallahatchee River 183
Tallen, J. B. 54
Tally, (Private, Hilliard's Legion) 169
Tally, J. M. J. 93
Tally, Jefferson M. J. 93
Tampa Bay 1, 2
Taney, Roger B. 10
Tap's Gap, AL 263
Tarbutton, G. A. 162
Tarrant, Edward 243
Tarrant, Ira 130, 132
Tate, J. F. 78
Tattnall, J. R. F. 106
Tatum, _____ 93
Tayloe, George E. 62, 63
Taylor, George W. 68
Taylor, M. J. 47, 98
Taylor, Richard 124, 192, 193, 197, 199, 200, 216, 219, 227, 285
Taylor, T. S. 100, 101
Taylor, Thomas 97, 98
Taylor, Thomas Hart 87, 91, 141, 142, 165, 166, 171, 177
Taylor, W. H. 69, 231
Taylor, William 60
Taylor's Ridge, GA 268
Tazewell, TN 255
   Battle of 107, 109, 141, 236, 237
Teague, John M. 137
Tecumseh 5
Tecumseh, USS 27
Tedder, James M. 88
Temple, Benjamin F. 170

Ten Islands, AL 192, 193, 195, 196
Ten Islands, GA 274
Tennessee Campaign 103
Tennessee, CSS 27, 274
Tennessee River 25, 26, 101, 190, 192, 193, 209, 218, 219, 265
Tennessee Units
   Artillery
      Barry's Battery 235
      Mayberry's Tennessee 232
   Cavalry
      1st Regiment 189
      2nd Battalion 187
      2nd Regiment 183
      15th Battalion 187
      18th Regiment 200
   Infantry
      8th Regiment 157
      9th Regiment 158
      27th Regiment 75
      40th Regiment 152
Tensaw River 215
Terrell, Lee R. 143
Terrell, Mickleberry P. 68
Terry, Alfred H. 252
Texas Independence 7
Texas Units
   Infantry
      4th Regiment 146
      7th Regiment 30
Thatcher, H. K. 177
Thirteenth Regiment of Regulars (Mexican War) 7
Thoburn, Joseph 251
Thomas, Allen 109
Thomas, Bryan Morel 28, 79, 87, 165, 166, 176, 193, 194
Thomas, George H. 74, 186, 209, 253, 254, 279
Thomas, J. Whitt 48
Thomas Station, GA 278
Thomason, B. A. 150
Thomason, Zach 7, 197
Thompson, Albert P. 118, 200
Thompson, J. M. 154
Thompson, J. W. 118
Thompson, John 154, 210
Thompson, R. H. Smith 228
Thompson, Wells 121
Thompson, William E. 197

332

Thompson's Cool Springs, TN 264
Thompson's Hill,. *See* Port Gibson, MS
Thompson's Station, TN
  Battle of 203, 204
Thorington, Jack 167, 168
Thornton, A. B. 181
Thornton, E. Q. 127
Thornton, Ed. 81
Thornton, H. I. 126
Thornton, Harry J. 111, 113, 158, 159, 160
Thornton, L. H. 47
Tilghman, Lloyd 97, 101, 151, 152, 223
Tillinghast, J. W. 121
Tilton, GA 235, 236, 269
Tilton, William S. 51
Tims, George W. 76
Tingle, W. D. 67
Tinsley, W. J. (J. W.) 117
Tishomingo, MS 265
  Battle of 189, 190, 191, 192, 221
Todd, John B. 226
Tomlinson, Augustus 184
Tompkinsville, KY 180, 208
Torbert, _____ (Capt., 45th Inf.) 139
Totopotomoy, VA
  Battle of 250
Toulmin, Harry T. 83, 87, 89, 90, 95, 96, 149, 151, 152, 153
Towaliga, GA 276
Towers, Joel 237
Town Creek, AL 261
Town Creek, TN
  Battle of 203
Trabue, Robert P. 131, 147, 148, 153, 154
Tracy Battery, AL 27
Tracy, Edward D. 64, 81, 82, 84, 91, 107, 108, 109, 110, 141, 142, 233
Trapier, James Heyward 102, 103, 179, 232
Travis, E. F. 88
Treaty of Paris, 1763 1
Trenton, GA 203, 209
Trenton, TN 181, 188, 207, 209, 212
  Battle of 206, 208
Treutlen, John F. 71
Trimble, Isaac R. 70, 71, 72

Trimmer, William 72
Trimmier, Theodore G. 130, 132
Trion, AL 284
Triune, TN
  Battle of 73, 208, 209
Troy, AL 156
Troy, Daniel S. 162, 163, 167, 170
Trueheart, Daniel 244, 246
Truss, James D. 59
Tryon Factory, GA 263, 275
Tubb, Daniel F. 136
Tucker, Davis 55
Tucker, E. 64
Tullahoma, TN 73, 81, 111, 120, 130, 131, 139, 149, 157, 178, 191, 197, 202, 209, 219, 238, 262
Tullis, John W. 231
Tunica Bayou, LA
  Battle of 215
Tunnel Hill, GA 266, 267, 268
  Battle of 73
Tunnel Hill Road, GA 267
Tupelo, MS 78, 79, 114, 116, 121, 139, 157, 183, 184, 185, 200, 205, 211, 221, 224, 232, 239, 240, 273
Turchin, John Basil 24, 27, 187
Turkeytown, AL 25, 275
Turkeytown Road, AL 275
Turlington, R. S. 170
Turner, _____ (Private, Hilliard's Legion) 169
Turner, Henry B. 106
Turpin, John H. 103
Tuscaloosa, AL 29, 129, 130, 177, 195, 238, 239, 284
Tuscaloosa County, AL 96
Tuscumbia, AL 5, 25, 74, 96, 100, 179, 189, 190, 191, 200, 261
Tuscumbia Landing, AL 189
Tuskaloosa 2
Tutwiler, Julia S. 30
Tyler, Dan 58
Tyler, R. C. (Robert Charles) 29, 284

Ulcofaw, GA 276
Underhill, E. M. 165, 166
Union Mills Ford, VA 49
Uniontown, AL 235

Uniontown, TN 261
   Battle of 202
Unionville, SC 182
Unionville, TN 198, 207
United States Military Academy at West Point 7, 24, 31, 103, 210
United States Naval Academy 31
United States Units
   Artillery
      81st Battery 253
   Infantry
      1st Regiment 201
University Plain (Depot), TN 262
Upperville, VA 231
Upton, Emory 29, 192, 284
Usleton, John A. 150

Vail, Jacob G. 192
Valley Road, TN 264
Valley Woods, KY 257
Van Cleve, H. P. 180
Van de Graaff, A. S. 171
Van Den Corput, Max 228
Van Dorn, Earl 34, 64, 118, 119, 133, 147, 148, 154, 190, 207, 229, 256
Vance, Robert Frank 236
Vanderford, Charles 235, 244, 245
Vandergrift, A. B. 159
Vann, _____ (Private, 25th Infantry) 95
Vansandt, George W. 112
Varnell, GA
   Action at 212
Varnell Road, GA 268
Varnell Station, GA 267
Varnell's, GA 268
Vason, William 213, 214
Vaughan, E. B. 149
Vaughan, John A. 213
Veatch, James C. 200
Venable, N. 238
Venable, Nathan J. 81
Vera Cruz, Mexico 7, 31
Verona, MS 194
Versailles, TN 187
Vicksburg, MS 34, 91, 107, 110, 118, 119, 122, 127, 128, 130, 133, 142, 147, 148, 151, 152, 153, 207, 233, 234, 267
   Siege of 83, 84, 90, 91, 107, 109, 123, 133, 141, 142, 154, 174, 175, 225, 226, 233, 234, 237, 261
Villepigue, John Bordenave 34, 174
Vinegar Hill, KY 256
Vines, Hosea 105
Virginia Units
   Artillery
      Pegram's Battery 172
   Infantry
      10th Regiment 146
      23rd Regiment 145

Waddell, James F. 233, 234, 237
Wade, _____ 185
Wade, William B. 206, 207, 209, 210, 211, 212, 213, 214
Wadesboro, SC 281, 282
Wagner, George D. 209
Wakefield, Hezekiah B. 35
Walden, W. D. 167, 169, 170
Walker, C. F. 54
Walker, Clifton 82
Walker County, AL 96
Walker, Henry Harrison 68
Walker, J. M. 121
Walker, James A. 72
Walker, John M. 120
Walker, L. P. 40, 68, 77, 82, 178, 179
Walker, Lucius M. 151, 152
Walker, M. B. 259
Walker, N. B. 89
Walker, Richard W. 181, 191
Walker, William H. T. 128, 204, 240
Walker, William Stephen 258
Walker's Ford, WV
   Battle of 250
Wall, J. H. 87, 89
Wallace, J. Y. 68
Wallace, Lew 251
Wallow, KY 255
Walnut Creek, GA 276
Walter, H. W. 187
Walters, L. 98
Walters, Walter 93

Walthall, Edward Cary 35, 36, 100,
    107, 139, 140, 165, 235, 238, 240
Walthall, W. J. 211
Walthall, W. T. 220
Wapping Heights, VA
    Battle of 249
War Trace, TN 264
Ward, _____ (Capt., 63rd Inf.) 165
Ward, Alfred G. 47
Ward, J. N. 159
Ward, John J. 244
Ward, Reedy 150
Ward, Rudy 151
Ward, S. A. 159
Ware Bottom Church, VA
    Battle of 250
Warren, _____ (Captain) 26
Warren, D. O. 75
Warren, E. T. H. 144, 146
Warren, Gouverneur K. 51, 52, 66,
    249, 250, 251, 252, 253
Warren, James M. 192
Warren, Thomas J. 192
Warrenton, AL 188, 222
Wartburg, TN 74
Wartrace, TN 114
Washington, CD 44
Washington, DC 16, 17, 27, 31, 36
Washington, George 14
Waterloo, AL 188
Waters, David D. 104, 232
Watkins, C. W. 232
Watkins House, VA 162, 176
Watkins, L. D. 210
Watkins, William H. 135
Watson, Edgar 48
Watson, Hugh M. 7
Watson, J. F. 197
Watson, J. N. 75
Watts, Thomas H. 77, 176, 181
Watts, William A. 76
Wauhatchie, TN 210, 265
    Battle of 70
Waul, Thomas N. 84, 108
Wayland, W. L. 57
Wayland, William E. 197
Wayne's Hill, TN 131
Waynesboro, GA 277, 278
    Battle of 203
Weams, _____ (Captain) 70

Weatherford 3
Weaver, J. J. 200
Webb, J. D. 201, 202
Webb, James E. 229
Webster, Daniel 14, 15
Weedon, John 87, 88, 89, 102, 147, 148,
    149
Weems, Walker H. 49
Weitzel, Godfrey 253
Welch, George W. 125
Welch, R. G. 116, 117
Welch, R. L. 218
Weldon Railroad
    Battle of 53, 174, 175, 251
Wellington, _____ (34th Regiment)
    117
Wells, G. C. 94
Welsh, W. R. 124
Wemyss, James A. 120, 121, 125
West, Douglas 196
West, John P. 182, 183
West Pascagoula, MS 216
West Point, AL 29
West Point, MS 267
West Point, VA 45
West, William 88
Wethered, Marcus Lafayette 45
Wetumpka, AL 4
Weygant, Charles H. 162, 163
Whaley, George 59
Whaley, J. G. 116
Wharton, Gabriel Colvin 188
Wharton, John A. 189, 190, 191, 197,
    198, 206, 207, 208, 211
Wheelan, J. P. 54
Wheeler, Joseph 30, 78, 81, 88, 95, 103,
    150, 178, 179, 180, 181, 182, 183,
    184, 185, 186, 188, 189, 190, 191,
    197, 198, 199, 200, 201, 202, 204,
    206, 207, 209, 211, 212, 213, 214,
    217, 218, 221, 246, 254, 255, 256,
    257, 258, 259, 260, 261, 262, 263,
    264, 265, 266, 267, 268, 269, 270,
    271, 272, 273, 274, 275, 276, 278,
    279, 280, 281, 282, 283, 284
Wheeler, Nathaniel F. 112
Wheeler's Raid 274
Whippy Swamp, SC 280
Whisenant, J. W. 182
White, _____ 266

White, George S. 195, 196
White, Hiram L. 80
White, James 6
White, Moses 75
White Oak, NC 213
White Oak Road, VA
   Battle of 130, 132, 161, 162, 253
White Oak, VA
   Battle of 248
White, Peter 75
White Plains, VA
   Battle of 145
White, T. H. 228
White, W. J. 127
White, Walter S. 173
Whitehead, GA 277
Whitesides, TN 210
Whitfield, J. P. 34
Whiting, J. W. 225
Whiting, William Henry Chase 40, 41, 171
Whitney, Isaac M. 90
Whitney, J. M. 88
Wigfall, Louis Trezevant 171
Wiggins, W. S. 121
Wigginton, J. W. 145, 147
Wilcox, A. J. 47
Wilcox, Albert J. 44, 47
Wilcox, Cadmus M. 53, 54, 55, 56, 57, 60, 62, 63, 69, 98
Wilcox County, AL 226, 227
Wilcox, O. B. 44
Wild Cat, KY 253, 257, 258
Wildcat Gap, TN 227
Wilder, John T. 53, 209, 255, 262
Wilderness, VA
   Battle of 36, 40, 43, 44, 48, 53, 56, 62, 64, 66, 68, 70, 137, 138, 143, 145, 163, 164, 174, 175, 230, 250
Wiley, J. Horatio 156, 157
Wiley, L. D. 44, 45
Wiley, Samuel S. 93
Wilkerson, Simeon C. 80
Willett, Elbert D. 128, 129
Williams, _____ (Private, Hilliard's Legion) 170
Williams, Frank 54
Williams, J. W. 80
Williams, James 189
Williams, James M. 86

Williams, Jere H. J. 56, 57, 58
Williams' Landing, TN 200
Williams, Price 177
Williams, Richard 35
Williams, Robert 75
Williams, S. A. 162
Williams, Samuel C. 243
Williams, Thomas 189, 255
Williamsburg Road, VA
   Battle of 145
Williamsburg, VA 30
   Battle of 53, 54, 56, 57, 58, 59, 60, 63, 68, 69, 96, 248
Williamson, G. F. 125
Williamson, George 180
Williamson, J. F. 80
Williamson, James S. 68, 69
Willingham, James J. 48, 49
Williston, SC 182, 199, 201, 203
Wills' Creek, AL 263
Wills, George D. 40
Wills, Robert K. 133
Wills' Valley, AL 263
Wills' Valley, TN 210
Wilson, _____ (Private, 24th Infantry) 93
Wilson, A. B. 75
Wilson, Brice 74, 75
Wilson, Francis H. 125
Wilson, J. W. 56
Wilson, James 127
Wilson, James H. 28, 165, 189, 191, 192, 193, 196, 199, 284
Wilson, John F. 103
Wilson, W. J. 105
Wilson's Raid 284
Wilson's Store, SC 214, 282
Wilsonville, AL 219
Winchester, TN 168, 214, 262
Winchester, VA 30, 163
   Battle of 36, 43, 248
   Battle of (July 24, 1864) 44, 48, 49, 64, 251
   Battle of (June 13-15, 1863) 249
   Battle of (May 25, 1862) 70, 71
   Battle of (Sept. 1864) 252
Winder, Charles Sidney 64, 99
Windes, F. M. 189, 190
Wingfield, J. H. 34
Winkler's Bluff, MS 175

Winn, Walter E. 62
Winnsboro, SC 281
Winston County, AL 96
Winston, John A. 53, 54, 55, 67, 103
Winter, John A. 122
Wisdom, Dew Moore 199, 200
Wise, John F. 168, 254
Withers, John 206
Withers, Jones M. 7, 33, 36, 79, 82, 84, 86, 88, 89, 91, 92, 93, 95, 101, 103, 116, 123, 126, 140, 149, 150, 152, 165, 179, 185, 227, 228, 233, 245
Witherspoon, H. E. 177
Wood, Alfred C. 68
Wood, Elias 104
Wood, H. C. 143, 146
Wood, P. G. 103
Wood, R. K. 97, 98
Wood, Sterling A. M. 40, 52, 74, 75, 76, 114, 139, 140, 190, 219, 240, 241
Wood, William 93, 100
Wood, William B. 74, 75
Woodburn, TN 255
Woodbury Road, TN 264
Woodbury, TN 261
Woodell, Benjamin 39
Woodruff, Lewis T. 80, 120, 121
Woods, Michael L. 141
Woods, William W. 236, 237
Woodsonville, KY 256
  Battle of 178
Woodward, John J. 57, 59, 60
Woody Hill, GA 274
Wooten, H. N. 65

Wright, _____ (Sergeant, 34th Infantry) 117
Wright, Ambrose Ransom 136, 137
Wright, Horatio G. 253
Wright, J. E. 170
Wright, John 210
Wright, John T. 213
Wright, L. P. 105
Wright, M. H. 232
Wright, Marcus 130, 131, 243
Wright, R. G. 100
Wright, W. A. 120
Wright, W. H. 124
Wylie, Samuel S. 93

Yadkin River Bridge, NC 126, 128
Yalabusha River 155
Yancey, B. C. 173
Yazoo City, MS 133
Yellow River, FL 215
Yorktown, VA 36, 41, 53, 54, 60, 62, 63, 67, 97
  Siege of 56, 59, 69, 96, 248
Young, A. 93
Young, Andrew 93, 94
Young, Garrett 152, 153
Young, J. P. 80
Young, M. M. 192
Young, Pierce Manning Butler 217, 230
Young, William H. 245
Youngsville, SC 282

Zachary, A. F. 164
Zollicoffer, Felix Kirk 71, 73, 74, 253, 254

LaVergne, TN USA
15 December 2010
208925LV00001B/136/A